THE CAMBRIDGE HANDBOOK OF TWIN PEAKS FINANCIAL REGULATION

First proposed in 1994, the Twin Peaks model of financial system regulation employs two specialist peak regulators: one charged with the maintenance of financial system stability and the other with market conduct and consumer protection. This volume, with contributions from more than thirty scholars and senior regulators, provides an in-depth analysis of the similarities and differences in the Twin Peaks regimes that have been adopted around the world. Chapters examine the strengths and weaknesses of the model, provide lessons from Australia (the first to adopt the model) and offer a comparative look at the potential suitability of the model in leading non-Twin Peaks jurisdictions. A key resource for central bankers, public policy analysts, lawyers, economists, politicians, academics and students, this work provides readers with a comprehensive understanding of the Twin Peaks model and a roadmap for countries considering its adoption.

ANDREW GODWIN is Associate Professor and Director of Studies for Banking and Finance at Melbourne Law School, the University of Melbourne, Australia. His teaching and research interests include finance and insolvency law, transactional law, financial regulation (particularly disclosure and regulatory systems), property law and the regulation of the legal profession. He has worked closely with governments, financial regulators and international organisations on financial regulation reforms.

ANDREW SCHMULOW is Senior Lecturer in Law at the School of Law, University of Wollongong, Australia. He also holds visiting positions at universities in South Africa and South Korea. He advised South Africa's National Treasury on the drafting of the Conduct of Financial Institutions Act, and the World Bank on designing an indicator framework to measure consumer financial well-being.

T0381560

The Cambridge Handbook of Twin Peaks Financial Regulation

Edited by

ANDREW GODWIN

Melbourne Law School

ANDREW SCHMULOW

University of Wollongong School of Law

Shaftesbury Road, Cambridge CB2 8EA, United Kingdom

One Liberty Plaza, 20th Floor, New York, NY 10006, USA

477 Williamstown Road, Port Melbourne, VIC 3207, Australia

314–321, 3rd Floor, Plot 3, Splendor Forum, Jasola District Centre, New Delhi – 110025, India

103 Penang Road, #05–06/07, Visioncrest Commercial, Singapore 238467

Cambridge University Press is part of Cambridge University Press & Assessment,
a department of the University of Cambridge.

We share the University's mission to contribute to society through the pursuit of
education, learning and research at the highest international levels of excellence.

www.cambridge.org
Information on this title: www.cambridge.org/9781009295680

DOI: 10.1017/9781316890592

First published 2021
First paperback edition 2023

A catalogue record for this publication is available from the British Library

Library of Congress Cataloging-in-Publication data
NAMES: Godwin, Andrew, editor. | Schmulow, Andrew, 1970– editor.
TITLE: The Cambridge handbook of Twin Peaks financial regulation / edited by Andrew Godwin, Melbourne Law
School; Andrew Schmulow, University of Western Australia School of Law.
DESCRIPTION: Cambridge, United Kingdom ; New York, NY : Cambridge University Press, 2021. | Series: Cambridge
law handbooks | Includes bibliographical references.
IDENTIFIERS: LCCN 2020042870 (print) | LCCN 2020042871 (ebook) | ISBN 9781107186422 (hardback) |
ISBN 9781316890592 (epub)
SUBJECTS: LCSH: International finance–Law and legislation. | Financial institutions, International–Law and legislation. |
Banks and banking, International–Law and legislation.
CLASSIFICATION: LCC K4444 .C36 2021 (print) | LCC K4444 (ebook) | DDC 343/.03–dc23
LC record available at https://lccn.loc.gov/2020042870
LC ebook record available at https://lccn.loc.gov/2020042871

ISBN   978-1-107-18642-2   Hardback
ISBN   978-1-009-29568-0   Paperback

Contents

Figures

Tables

Contributors

Douglas W. Arner is the Kerry Holdings Professor in Law at the University of Hong Kong (HKU). At HKU, he is Director of the Asian Institute of International Financial Law and Faculty Director of the LLM in Corporate and Financial Law, LLM in Compliance and Regulation, and the new LITE (Law, Innovation, Technology, Entrepreneurship) Lab. He is a senior visiting fellow of Melbourne Law School, University of Melbourne, and a member of the Advisory Board of the Centre for Finance, Technology and Entrepreneurship. Arner coordinates Introduction to FinTech, the largest FinTech online course on edX. He has published 18 books and more than 150 articles, chapters and reports.

Janos Barberis is a FinTech Foundation lecturer; Head of Entrepreneurship at the Centre for Financial Technology and Entrepreneurship, London; and founder of SuperCharger. He is a research fellow at the Asian Institute of International Financial Law and a PhD candidate at the Faculty of Law, the University of Hong Kong.

Jeff Carmichael AO is Australasian Practice Leader for Promontory. He is a recognised expert in regulatory structure, design and effectiveness. He was formerly chairman of the Australian Prudential Regulation Authority. Before that he held senior positions with the Reserve Bank of Australia and was Professor of Finance at Bond University. He has served on a number of government inquiries and government and private sector boards. Carmichael has a PhD in Economics from Princeton University. He was awarded an AO in 1995 for services to finance, education and the community.

Jessica Cheung is a trainee solicitor at Lau, Horton & Wise LLP (Hong Kong). She is also a graduate of the University of Warwick (LLB), Peking University (LLM) and the City University of Hong Kong (PCLL).

Helen Dervan is a senior lecturer in law at Auckland University of Technology, where she teaches banking and financial services law and law of trusts. She has published nationally and internationally in both fields, and her current research focuses on prudential regulation. She practised in the City of London in banking and international finance litigation before commencing her academic career. Dervan holds a BCL from the University of Oxford, and is a recipient of the Rex Mason Prize for excellence in legal writing.

Femke de Vries is, by special appointment, Professor of Supervision at the University of Groningen, and Managing Partner at &samhoud, a strategic consultancy firm. She worked in financial supervision for fifteen years, including as Divisional Director and Secretary-General at the Dutch Central Bank, as a board member of the Netherlands Authority for Financial Markets (the Dutch securities commission and conduct regulator). After the global financial crisis she became a member of the Financial Stability Board's (FSB) working group on the effectiveness of supervision.

Evan Gibson is a postdoctoral research fellow with the Asian Institute of International Financial Law at the University of Hong Kong. He specialises in researching and publishing on economic and financial law, and financial regulation. Previously, Dr Gibson held the position of Research Fellow at the University of New South Wales.

Andrew Godwin is Associate Professor and Director of Studies for Banking and Finance at Melbourne Law School, the University of Melbourne, Australia. His teaching and research interests include finance and insolvency law, transactional law, financial regulation (particularly disclosure and regulatory systems), property law and the regulation of the legal profession. He has worked closely with governments, financial regulators and international organisations on financial regulation reforms.

Li Guo is a professor of law at Peking University (PKU) Law School, and the chief editor of Peking University Law Journal in English. He has also taught and researched at Cornell, Duke, Freiburg, Sydney, Vanderbilt and Case Western Reserve universities, and is the recipient of the Humboldt Foundation Fellowship. His scholarly interests cover financial laws, social development and comparative studies. Guo serves as an expert committee member of the China Securities Regulatory Commission, the Shanghai Stock Exchange, the Asset Management Association of China, among others. He is a graduate of PKU, Southern Methodist University and Harvard Law School.

Roy Havemann is Chief Director for Financial Markets and Stability at the National Treasury of South Africa. He is responsible for legislative and regulatory design, focusing on prudential, financial stability and capital markets issues. Havemann first joined the National Treasury in 2002 in the economic forecasting unit. Shortly after the start of the 2008 financial crisis, he joined the tax and financial sector policy division to lead South Africa's post-crisis regulatory reform programme. This included the introduction of a Twin Peaks system. He has an MSc in Economics from the London School of Economics and a PhD from Stellenbosch University. He was previously in the strategic finance team at Deloitte.

Robin Hui Huang is Professor in the Faculty of Law, Chinese University of Hong Kong; Adjunct Professor of Law at the University of New South Wales (UNSW); Li Ka Shing Visiting Professor in the McGill Law School; and Honorary Professor at East China University of Political Science and Law. He received two bachelor degrees, in mechanical engineering and in law, a master's degree in law from Tsinghua University in Beijing, China and a PhD from the Faculty of Law, UNSW. He is a leading expert in the field of corporate law, securities regulation, financial law, commercial dispute resolution and foreign investment, with a particular focus on Chinese and comparative law issues.

Youkyung Huh is a director of Consumers Korea, an organisation focused on creating safer and fairer markets for consumers. She is a member of the Korean Bar Association, serving as legal counsel at the Korean Financial Supervisory Service (FSS) and in private practice. She sits on the FSS Insurance Policy Review Committee and the Korean Copyright Commission. Huh is a doctoral candidate at the University of Virginia Law School, investigating financial regulatory structures with a focus on consumer protection. She earned LLM degrees from Georgetown University Law School (2014) and Harvard Law School (2013) and a master's degree from Seoul National University (2012).

Simon Jensen is a consultant at Buddle Findlay, one of New Zealand's pre-eminent financial services firms, having retired as a partner in 2019. Prior to joining Buddle Findlay, Jensen was general counsel at Westpac New Zealand Limited, one of New Zealand's four major banks. He is a specialist in prudential regulation, payment systems, banker–customer relationships and corporate governance. He is an editor of one of New Zealand's leading banking law texts, Tyree's Banking Law in New Zealand, wrote the 'Directors and the Law' section of the Institute of Directors training materials and was a winner of the 2018 Honourable Rex Mason Prize for a published article, for an article he co-authored with Helen Dervan entitled 'Prudential Regulation in 21st Century New Zealand: The Case for Deposit Insurance'.

Hongjoo Jung has been teaching at Sungkyunkwan University since 1991. He was the founding president of Korean Academy of Financial Consumers (KAFC) from 2010 to 2012 and the founding chairperson of the International Academy of Financial Consumers (IAFICO) from 2015 to 2019. Jung received his doctoral degree in applied economics and managerial science at the Wharton School, USA; an MS at the Stern School, NYU; and a BA at Seoul National University. He is a global citizen who enjoys international travels and sabbaticals.

Steve Kourabas is a lecturer in, and deputy director of, the Centre for Commercial Law and Regulatory Studies, Monash University Law School. Kourabas's areas of specialisation include financial regulation, international economic law and corporate governance. He has a special interest in technological innovation in finance and corporate law, and teaches predominantly in this area. Before joining Monash, he worked as an in-house counsel in government and within corporations. He received master's and doctoral degrees from Duke Law School.

Karel Lannoo is CEO of the Centre for European Policy Studies (CEPS), the leading European think tank based in Brussels. He has published widely on European and international policy, with a special focus on financial markets regulation. His latest book, The Great Financial Plumbing: From Northern Rock to Banking Union (2015), covered the EU's financial crisis response.

Donato Masciandaro is Full Professor of Economics at Bocconi University, Milan, where he holds the Chair in Economics in Financial Regulation. He is the Director of the Baffi Carefin Centre on Banking, Finance and Regulation. He is a member of the Management Board and Honorary Treasurer of the SUERF (Société Universitaire Européenne de Recherches Financières). He is associate editor of the Journal of Financial Stability and an editorial board member of the Italian Economic Journal. He served as a visiting scholar at the IMF Institute, and was a consultant at the World Bank, the Inter-American Development Bank and the United Nations.

Patrick McConnell has been a senior manager in, and a consultant to, large international financial institutions, corporations and governments on multiple continents for over thirty-five years. His expertise is in information technology, governance and risk management. He holds a doctoral degree in business administration with a thesis on finance and technology, and is a fellow of the British Computer Society (FBCS). He has been published widely in risk journals and has written a number of books and book chapters, including on trading room technology and on strategic and operational risk management.

Gail Pearson is Professor of Business Law at the University of Sydney. She writes on financial services and commercial and consumer law, and has various roles internationally and domestically in consumer affairs, including on the Australian Securities and Investments Commission (ASIC)'s Consumer Affairs Panel and as immediate past president of the International Association of Consumer Law. She has also undertaken research in India and ASEAN.

Ruth Plato-Shinar is Full Professor of Banking Law and Financial Regulation at the Netanya Academic College, Israel, where she also serves as Director of the Centre for Banking Law and Financial Regulation. The opinions expressed in her books and numerous articles have become binding precedents from Israel's Supreme Court. She is the Advisory Committee Chairperson of the Commissioner of Financial Service Providers; the Advisory Board Deputy Chairperson of the Commissioner of Capital Markets, Insurance and Savings; a member of the Advisory Committee to the Governor of the Bank of Israel; and a member of the License Committee of the Supervisor of Banks.

Ian Ramsay is the Harold Ford Professor of Commercial Law and also Redmond Barry Distinguished Professor at Melbourne Law School, University of Melbourne, where he is Director of the Centre for Corporate Law. Ramsay has published extensively on corporate law, financial regulation and corporate governance issues both internationally and in Australia. He has wide experience as an expert consultant to government reviews and as a member of government advisory committees, including his appointment as chair of the independent panel appointed by the government to review the Australian financial system's external dispute resolution and complaints framework.

Davide Romelli is an assistant professor of economics at Trinity College Dublin, Ireland. He is also a research affiliate of IM-TCD (International Macro-TCD) and SUERF – The European Money and Finance Forum, and a fellow of the BAFFI-CAREFIN centre, Bocconi University. His research focuses on international finance and macroeconomics, central banking and financial supervision. Romelli holds a PhD in Economics from ESSEC Business School and THEMA-University of Cergy-Pontoise, awarded jointly.

Andrew Schmulow is Senior Lecturer in Law at the School of Law, University of Wollongong, Australia. He also holds visiting positions at universities in South Africa and South Korea. He advised South Africa's National Treasury on the drafting of the Conduct of Financial Institutions Act, and the World Bank on designing an indicator framework to measure consumer financial well-being. He has previously provided advice to the governments of South Korea and New Zealand, and in 2018 was invited by the Australian Banking Royal Commission to provide insights into combating regulatory capture. That advice was reflected in Recommendation 6.14 of the Royal Commission's Final Report, and subsequently in the Financial Regulator Assessment Authority Bill, currently before Australia's Federal Parliament.

Dirk Schoenmaker is a professor of banking and finance at the Rotterdam School of Management, Erasmus University and Director of the Erasmus Platform for Sustainable Value Creation. He is also a fellow at the think tank Bruegel. His research covers the fields of sustainable finance, central banking, financial supervision and European banking. Before joining RSM, he worked at the Dutch Ministry of Finance and the Bank of England.

Schoenmaker is (co-)author of Principles of Sustainable Finance, Financial Markets and Institutions: A European Perspective and Governance of International Banking: The Financial Trilemma.

Heidi Mandanis Schooner is Professor of Law at Columbus School of Law, the Catholic University of America. Her research focuses on the regulation of financial institutions. She has served as a consultant to the International Monetary Fund and to various federal and state agencies. Before entering academia in 1992, Schooner was in-house counsel for a regional bank holding company. She also practised in the General Counsel's Office of the Securities and Exchange Commission.

Olaf Sleijpen is Executive Director for Monetary Affairs and Financial Stability at De Nederlandsche Bank and alternate member of the governing council of the ECB. He has been a professor at the Maastricht School of Business and Economics since 2007. Before joining the governing board of DNB in 2020, Sleijpen held different positions as Director of Supervision within the DNB. Between 2004 and 2011 he worked with the largest pension fund and pension provider in the Netherlands. From 2001 to 2004, he was adviser to ECB President Wim Duisenberg, after holding various other positions within DNB.

Michael W. Taylor has had a varied career as an academic, journalist and public official, working at various times for the Bank of England, the International Monetary Fund, the Hong Kong Monetary Authority and the Central Bank of Bahrain. He has published widely on financial regulation, including a textbook entitled Global Bank Regulation (with Heidi Schooner, 2009), as well as producing the founding statement for the Twin Peaks model, for the London think tank the Centre for the Study of Financial Innovation, in 1995.

Corlia van Heerden holds the ABSA Chair in Banking Law in Africa and is a professor in the Mercantile Law Department in the Faculty of Law, University of Pretoria. Her main interests are banking regulation (with a particular focus on models of regulation, central banking, SIFI regulation, bank resolution and deposit guarantees), credit law and consumer protection law. She also has a keen interest in and has lectured in insolvency law, competition law and law of civil procedure.

Marco van Hengel is Senior Financial Stability Expert at De Nederlandsche Bank. He specialises in financial sector reform, supervisory governance and European supervision. He has written several articles about trends in regulation and supervision, financial architecture and the Twin Peaks model. Van Hengel has been a member of various working groups and international review teams for the Financial Stability Board and Bank of International Settlements, and coordinated several external national and international evaluations of DNB policies. Before joining DNB in 2010, he was Senior Economist and Financial Specialist at the Dutch Ministry of Finance.

Gerda van Niekerk has a BCom LLB LLD from the University of Pretoria. She practised as an attorney for twenty-five years. Currently she is a senior lecturer at the University of Limpopo in the Mercantile Law Department. Her fields of interest are financial regulation, financial economic law, business law, central banks, financial stability and banking law.

Nicolas Véron co-founded Bruegel in Brussels in 2002–05, joined the Peterson Institute for International Economics in Washington DC in 2009 and is currently employed on equal terms by both organisations as a senior fellow. His research is primarily on financial systems and financial services policies. He is also an independent board member of the global derivatives trade repository arm of DTCC, a financial infrastructure company that operates on a non-profit basis. In September 2012, Bloomberg Markets included Véron in its yearly global '50 Most Influential' list with reference to his early advocacy for a European banking union.

Foreword

Howell E. Jackson[*]

Scholarship on financial regulation tends to focus on legal standards for safeguarding the solvency of financial institutions or protecting the public from misconduct in financial transactions. When it comes to regulatory design, the most commonly studied topic is the development of regulatory networks that have emerged in recent decades to create an international financial architecture. Much less attention has been focused on the evolution of the organisational structure of supervisory agencies at the national level, even though that is where the lion's share of regulation is done. Work of this sort is immensely challenging, as it is inherently comparative and requires expertise and experience across a host of jurisdictions. In this volume, Andrew Godwin and Andrew Schmulow fill that gap by offering the first comprehensive examination of one of the most significant organisational innovations in financial regulation of the past quarter-century: the emergence of the Twin Peaks regulatory structure.

During the final decades of the twentieth century, as the boundaries between the traditional financial sectors of banking, securities and insurance began to merge and financial firms increasingly operated in multiple sectors, policymakers were led to explore new regulatory structures that also move beyond traditional sectoral boundaries. While some jurisdictions, such as Japan and several northern European countries, took the fairly straightforward step of combining sectoral agencies like banking departments and securities commissions into a single consolidated body, others chose the more innovative Twin Peaks approach, which deconstructs sectoral agencies and reassembles the resources into a pair of industry-wide bodies: one focused on market conduct requirements that protect customers and market structures, and a second targeted at the prudential regulations that ensure the safety and soundness of financial firms. In addition to breaking down entrenched supervisory silos, Twin Peaks reforms allow for both regulatory specialisation and the reduction of persistent conflicts between consumer protection mandates – which tend to reduce firm profitability – and solvency concerns – which lead supervisors to favour strong firm earnings.

While the theory underlying Twin Peaks oversight is elegant and compelling, the actual manner in which the Twin Peaks regimes have been implemented has varied considerably across jurisdictions and now, after more than two decades of experience, the time is ripe to investigate how the Twin Peaks model works in practice, and where the challenges lie. Originally the brainchild of former Bank of England official and volume contributor Michael Taylor, Twin Peaks had its first and most fulsome implementation with the Australian Securities

[*] James S. Reid, Jr, Professor of Law, Harvard University

and Investments Commission (ASIC) and the Australian Prudential Regulation Authority (APRA). As this volume so nicely documents, the model has been taken up in an increasing number of jurisdictions over the years, from the Netherlands to New Zealand, eventually even finding its way back to Albion shores in the post-financial crisis reforms of the past decade. Interestingly, the Twin Peaks approach has now also been adopted in South Africa, perhaps heralding a trend towards Twin Peaks structures in the developing world. While the United States remains, as always, an outlier, Professor Schooner's chapter documents the extent to which one can even see glimmers of Twin Peaks arrangements in America's Byzantine regulatory structure.

The Cambridge Handbook of Twin Peaks Financial Regulation does an admirable job of reconstructing the history of the Twin Peaks revolution, with contributions from those who were present at the founding, as well as expert commentators on all of the major jurisdictions that have adopted the Twin Peaks regime, along with several others from jurisdictions likely headed in that direction in the near future. With this volume, the readers will find a richly documented education of the paths that Twin Peaks reforms have followed, as well as the most promising steps forward. One of the virtues of this collection is that it includes chapters exploring the implications and potential value of Twin Peaks reforms for countries such as Israel or China that maintain more traditional regulatory structures. The influence of Twin Peaks reforms extends well beyond the model's formal adoptions. The collection also illustrates, with admirable clarity, the principal difficulties of implementing an effective system of Twin Peaks oversight.

A recurring theme in the volume is the importance of coordination across Twin Peaks regimes, which necessarily involves overlapping supervision of many firms by both the market conduct authority and the prudential regulatory authority. Complete separation of regulatory objectives is impractical and so the principal operating units in a Twin Peaks regime need to find ways to work in harmony. In certain respects, this problem of coordination is similar to the one that national authorities face in cross-border supervision, and the various mechanisms documented in the volume employ a number of familiar instruments, including memoranda of understanding and documentation of shared principles. While the need for coordination may strike some readers as a weakness of the Twin Peaks approach, one must recognise that similar, if not more confounding, issues of coordination are faced in sectoral models of regulation, where financial conglomerates are also subject to overlapping jurisdictions. Even within consolidated regulatory bodies, coordination must be imposed across operational divisions, so the question is not whether supervisory coordination is required, but rather whether the coordination is more easily and efficiently accomplished through Twin Peaks models, as opposed to organisational alternatives.

A second question about Twins Peaks regimes, touched upon in multiple chapters, is whether financial regulation can really be divided into just two peaks or whether, in fact, macroprudential regulation focusing on systemic risk represents a third peak, and perhaps financial crime/anti-money laundering constitutes at least another foothill. Throughout the volume this tension plays out most clearly in discussions of the appropriate relationship between the central bank/monetary authority and the prudential regulatory authority. As the chapters explore, a variety of approaches are possible, including embedding the prudential authority within the central bank (as is done in the United Kingdom) or imposing structural distance (as is true in Australia). Weaknesses in prudential restraints, as well as widespread market misconduct of the sort preceding the Global Financial Crisis, can pose systemic risks, thus arguing in favour of a tight connection between central bank officials and Twin Peaks agencies. On the other hand, regulatory focus is one of the key virtues of Twin Peaks reforms and blurring the lines between monetary authorities and supervisory agencies can muddle matters. Moreover, especially in times of economic stress, there are advantages in separation, as conflicts can emerge with macroprudential concerns focused on avoiding pro-cyclical policies, and the prudential authority's responsibilities for ensuring the solvency of individual firms. There is no consensus on this issue, but proper integration of Twin Peaks agencies with the third peak of macroprudential oversight is an important design consideration.

Beyond the question of how closely Twin Peaks agencies should be anchored to monetary authorities, there is a separate design issue of how far out into the real economy the regulatory perimeters of regulatory agencies should extend. While sectoral agencies are naturally bound to specific institutional structures, like banks or insurance companies or securities firms, Twin Peaks supervisors are grounded in regulatory objectives: firm solvency and market misconduct. As several chapters explore, one of the advantages of Twin Peaks systems is that they are better suited to reach beyond traditional sectors to areas such as finance companies (New Zealand) or Fintech innovations (Hong Kong). With the rise of big tech and the ever-rising importance of various flavours of shadow banking, the comparative advantages of Twin Peaks structures should continue to grow. Objectives-based supervision may just be a better fit for the twenty-first-century economy.

For scholars, students, policymakers and practitioners, *The Handbook* provides both an invaluable history and a stimulating window into what the future might hold.

Acknowledgements

This book has been as much a journey for us as it has been a destination and there are many people to whom we owe irredeemable debts of gratitude. First, our sincere thanks go to Michael Taylor for his pioneering inspiration and generous suggestions as to who might be able to join us on our trek. We are also grateful to our research colleagues who have supported us throughout the process of researching Twin Peaks: Timothy Howse, Malcolm Anderson, Chenjie Ma, Amy Feng, Tom Monotti, Timothy Tabalujan and James Occleshaw. We are indebted to our employer institutions – the University of Melbourne and the University of Wollongong – for their support and for providing us with the time and funds to pursue this research project. We are also indebted to the University of Pretoria and, in particular, Corlia van Heerden and her colleagues in the Department of Mercantile Law for inviting us to the Twin Peaks Colloquium in 2017 and for providing us with access and insights into South Africa's transition towards Twin Peaks, and to colleagues in the South African National Treasury, and in particular Roy Havemann, for inviting us to participate in the design and implementation of the Twin Peaks model in South Africa.

We are immensely grateful to Matt Gallaway and the team at Cambridge University Press for their invitation to us to publish such a book and for their patience and support in what has been a much longer trek than we had originally anticipated.

Last, but certainly not least, we are grateful to the contributors and to other fellow travellers who have encouraged us along the journey towards Twin Peaks, including Eddy Wymeersch, Howell Jackson, Emilios Avgouleas, Parker Hood, Yuan Kang and Kevin Davis.

Introduction

The Genealogy and Topography of Twin Peaks

Andrew Godwin and Andrew Schmulow

1.1 THE GENEALOGY OF TWIN PEAKS

The Cambridge Dictionary defines 'genealogy' as 'the study of the history of the past and present members of a family or families'.[1] The word itself traces its roots back to the Greek word *genea*, meaning 'race' or 'generation'. Genealogy therefore focuses attention on the origin or genesis of a family at a fixed point in time and also on the evolution or development of a family over time.

The same dictionary defines 'topography' as 'the physical appearance of the natural features of an area of land, especially the shape of its surface'. The earth's surface – or terrain – is multifaceted and consists of different features, including mountain ranges, peaks and fault lines.

Over the past two decades, an increasing number of jurisdictions have moved towards a model – or family – of financial regulation that is known as Twin Peaks. This model was pioneered in Australia following recommendations by the Wallis Inquiry, which was established in 1996 to review the financial system.[2] The model separates financial regulation into two broad functions: market conduct regulation (which includes consumer protection) and prudential regulation. Each of these functions is vested in a separate 'peak' regulator. The Twin Peaks model has subsequently been adopted by the Netherlands, Belgium, New Zealand, the United Kingdom and South Africa. The model has also been considered in the United States.[3]

There are at least two models with which the Twin Peaks model is generally compared. The first, the 'institutional model', focuses on the form of the regulated institution (e.g., a bank, an insurer or a securities firm), and establishes a separate specialist regulator for that institution. Under this approach, the relevant regulator supervises all activities undertaken by the institution, irrespective of the market or sector in which the activities take place; and the institution is normally regulated by one regulator alone. The institutional approach is often referred to as an

---

[1] https://dictionary.cambridge.org/dictionary/english/genealogy.

[2] For the recommendations of the Wallis Inquiry, see Financial System Inquiry (1996) Final Report, https://treasury.gov .au/publication/p1996-fsi-fr. The Twin Peaks model was first examined in Michael Taylor, '"Twin Peaks": A Regulatory Structure for the New Century', Centre for the Study of Financial Innovation, London, 1995. See also Michael W. Taylor, 'The Road from Twin Peaks – And the Way Back' (2000) 16 *Connecticut Insurance Law Journal* 61. Since 1998, when the Twin Peaks model was adopted in Australia, almost 80 per cent of OECD countries have changed their regulatory architecture. Marco van Hengel, Paul Hilbers and Dirk Schoenmaker, 'Experiences with the Dutch Twin Peaks Model: Lessons for Europe' in A. Joanne Kellermann, Jacob de Haan and Femke de Vries (eds) *Financial Supervision in the 21st Century* (Springer, 2013), 188. Much of the text in this part is drawn from Andrew Godwin, 'Introduction to Special Issue – The Twin Peaks Model of Financial Regulation and Reform in South Africa' (2017) 11 (4) *Law and Financial Markets Review* 151–3.

[3] See Department of Treasury, Blueprint for a Modernized Financial Regulatory Structure (2008), 13–14, 142–3.

offshoot of the broader sectoral or 'operational' approach, under which institutions are regulated by reference to the sector in which they operate or the business in which they engage. For example, where a financial institution offers banking products and life insurance, it might be regulated by both the banking and insurance regulators.[4] The sectoral or operational model, like the institutional model, becomes increasingly difficult to operate as the complexity of financial products, and of financial institutions, increases – a reality that has become more significant with the rise of financial conglomerates and institutions that operate on a cross-sector basis. The sectoral model can create coordination challenges and regulatory overlap between the relevant regulators, as multiple regulators may end up supervising the same activity. As early as 1996, Michael Taylor presciently argued that 'a regulatory system which presupposes a clear separation between banking, securities and insurance is no longer the best way to regulate a financial system in which these distinctions are increasingly irrelevant'.[5]

The second model – the 'unified', 'super-regulator' or 'integrated' model – attempts to address the problems experienced by the institutional and sectoral approaches by creating a single regulator to supervise both the conduct of market participants and the prudential soundness of financial institutions. This model was championed by the United Kingdom prior to its move to Twin Peaks. One of the perceived problems with this model, however, is that '[p]rudential and conduct of business … regulation require[s] fundamentally different approaches and cultures and there may be doubt about whether a single regulator would, in practice, be able to effectively encompass these to the necessary degree'.[6] Another issue with the unified approach is that a single regulator 'might not have a clear focus on the different objectives and rationales of regulation and supervision, and might not make the necessary differentiations between different types of institution and business'.[7]

The Twin Peaks model is considered to have certain advantages over the other two models outlined above. First, the two peak regulators are more likely to have 'dedicated objectives and clear mandates to which they are exclusively committed'.[8] Secondly, there is less danger that one aspect of regulation – such as market conduct regulation – will come to dominate the regulatory landscape.[9] Instead, under the Twin Peaks model, regulatory culture, which encompasses the attitudes, policies and practices adopted by regulators in fulfilling their objectives, can be fostered depending on the function of the regulator and the culture that it needs, to perform its role effectively. This avoids the issue of having multiple 'cultures' under the one roof, as might be the case with a unified regulator, where different cultures arise because of different

---

[4] Some commentators refer to the sectoral or operational model as a functional approach, under which each type of business is 'overseen by a separate, "functional" regulator'. See Group of Thirty, *The Structure of Financial Supervision – Approaches and Challenges in a Global Marketplace* (6 October 2008). For a thorough analysis of the various models, see D. Llewellyn, 'Institutional Structure of Financial Regulation and Supervision: The Basic Rules' (Paper presented at a World Bank seminar Aligning Supervisory Structures with Country Needs, Washington, DC, 6 and 7 June 2006); E. Wymeersch, 'The Structure of Financial Supervision in Europe: About Single Financial Supervisors, Twin Peaks and Multiple Financial Supervisors' (2007) 8(2) *European Business Organization Review* 237; J. Kremers and D. Schoenmaker, 'Twin Peaks: Experiences in the Netherlands' (LSE Financial Markets Group Paper Series Paper 196, December 2010); E. Pan 'Structural Reform of Financial Regulation' (2011) 19 *Transnational Law and Contemporary Problems* 796; Andrew D. Schmulow, 'The Four Methods of Financial System Regulation: An International Comparative Survey' (2015) 26(3) *Journal of Banking and Finance Law and Practice* 169.

[5] M. Taylor, Peak Practice: How to Reform the UK's Regulator System. London, Centre for Study of Financial Innovation' (1996), as cited in Llewellyn (n 4) 19.

[6] See Llewellyn, (n 4) 26.

[7] Ibid 23.

[8] Ibid 27.

[9] As occurred in the United Kingdom prior to the Global Financial Crisis.

regulatory objectives.[10] Thirdly, the model may be better adapted towards keeping pace with the growing complexity of financial markets and the continuing rise of financial conglomerates.[11] Further, the Twin Peaks model may avoid the inherent conflict of interest that arises within a unified regulator. As was noted by the UK Joint Committee on the draft Financial Services Bill (JCFSB) in 2010:

> [T]he evidence of the recent financial crisis suggests that mixing functions can contribute to a lack of focus on rising macro-prudential risk and difficulties in moving to a 'war footing' when that risk becomes substantial. In addition, the incentives are different. For example, consumer protection can be well served by keeping a bank open, while stability is well served by closing it.[12]

There are also perceived disadvantages of the Twin Peaks model. First, it may create regulatory overlap with dual-regulated entities. The model means that it is 'inevitable that two separate regulators would have two separate rule books and two separate systems'.[13] In the United Kingdom, it was noted in 2013 that 'approximately 2,000 firms [would] be subject to dual regulation'.[14] If not carefully managed, this could place a 'considerable burden'[15] on regulated entities and lead to poor information-sharing and coordination.

Secondly, there is a general risk that cooperation and coordination between the regulators will not be sufficient and that potentially serious consequences will ensue. While these risks can be managed through robust coordination and liaison channels, it nevertheless remains a key concern for jurisdictions that have adopted the model.[16] Clear mandates and effective coordination between the regulators are key to making the model work.[17]

Finally, and depending on how the Twin Peaks model is implemented, there may be a conflict of interest within the central bank. This can arise if the central bank is responsible for both prudential regulation and monetary policy, as is the case in New Zealand. Llewellyn has suggested that 'a central bank with responsibility for preventing systemic risk is more likely to loosen monetary policy on occasions of difficulty'.[18] At the same time, this aspect may also be viewed as creating a synergy 'arising from [the central bank's] knowledge of monetary policy and financial market developments'.[19]

Today, and in the aftermath of the lessons learned during the Global Financial Crisis (GFC), Twin Peaks has come to be widely regarded as the optimal approach to regulating the financial

---

[10] It has also been noted that conduct regulators tend to be staffed by lawyers, who take a more prescriptive and ex post view of enforcement, and prudential regulators tend to be staffed by economists, who take more of a guidance role and a more ex ante view.

[11] One of the core innovations of Twin Peaks is the conglomerate view it takes to oversight.

[12] House of Commons, Treasury Committee, *Financial Regulation: A Preliminary Consideration of the Government's Proposals*, Seventh Report of Session 2010–11 (Vol 1), [83].

[13] Ibid.

[14] Financial Stability Board, Peer Review of the United Kingdom (Report, 2013), 7–8.

[15] Joint Committee on the Draft Financial Services Bill (JCFSB), *Report, Together with Formal Minutes and Appendices*, HL Paper 236, HC 1447, [285].

[16] See New Zealand Treasury, Financial Sector Regulatory Agencies – Regulatory Impact Statement (2010), https://treasury.govt.nz/publications/risa/regulatory-impact-statement-financial-sector-regulatory-agencies.

[17] For further discussion of this issue, see Andrew Godwin and Ian Ramsay, 'Twin Peaks – The Legal and Regulatory Anatomy of Australia's System of Financial Regulation' (2015) 26 *Journal of Banking and Finance Law and Practice* 240; Andrew Godwin, Timothy Howse and Ian Ramsay, 'A Jurisdictional Comparison of the Twin Peaks Model of Financial Regulation' (2016) 18(2) *Journal of Banking Regulation* 103.

[18] Llewellyn (n 6) 29.

[19] Van Hengel, Hilbers and Schoenmaker (n 2) 186.

system.[20] Of the four models in use,[21] Twin Peaks is alone in recognising that good market conduct and consumer protection have equal importance with prudential regulation.[22]

The separation of conduct oversight and prudential regulation defines Twin Peaks, and represents its greatest strength as compared to other regulatory models. This conclusion is supported by two central lessons derived from the GFC: the subprime industry in the United States was an instance of market misconduct and consumer abuse writ large. In the analysis of that event, and supported by the findings of the US Senate Inquiry, we now understand more fully that conduct issues can also represent a catalyst for a financial crisis.[23] From the findings produced in the United Kingdom, and in particular the Turner Review of the culpability of the FSA, and the collapse of Northern Rock, HBOS and RBS, we now also better understand that conduct and prudential regulation are inherently a 'pushmepullme',[24] and as such cannot be enforced by the same agency.[25] 'When prudential and consumer protection regulation are combined in a single agency, at least one of them is likely to be done badly.'[26]

To address this deficiency, the best solution would appear to be to separate conduct and prudential regulation and create them as equals. It is this solution that Twin Peaks offers that has been driving its adoption internationally. Because Australia adopted Twin Peaks first,[27] Australia's experience with the model is longer and more comprehensive, and so has served as a template for subsequent adopters and for those countries contemplating adoption in the future.

1.2 THE TOPOGRAPHY OF TWIN PEAKS

1.2.1 *Design Choices*

Previous research has suggested that at least four questions are fundamental to the topography or design of the Twin Peaks model:[28] (1) Where should the prudential regulator be housed? (2) How should the functions and objectives of the Twin Peaks regulators be defined? (3) How should the relationship between each regulator and the government be structured? (4) How

---

[20] Financial Markets Authority (FMA), 'Presentation by Sean Hughes to the New Zealand Capital Markets Forum', News, Speeches, 2011; John Manley, 'Dutch Regulator Says "Twin Peaks" Supervision Best' (Financial Regulatory Forum, Reuters, United States ed, 2009); Erika Botha and Daniel Makina, 'Financial Regulation and Supervision: Theory and Practice in South Africa' (2011) 10(11) *International Business & Economics Research Journal* 35.

[21] Schmulow (n 4).

[22] Joseph J. Norton, 'Global Financial Sector Reform: The Single Financial Regulator Model Based on the United Kingdom FSA Experience – A Critical Reevaluation' (2005) 39(1) *International Lawyer* 45; Treasury Committee House of Commons, 'Financial Regulation: A Preliminary Consideration of the Government's Proposals', series edited by Commons Select Committees, in *Seventh Report of Session 2010–11* (Vol I: Report, together with formal minutes, No HC 430–I, Vol 1, House of Commons, Parliament of the United Kingdom, 27 January 2011), 32.

[23] The Financial Crisis Inquiry Commission, *The Financial Crisis Inquiry Report* (Final Report of the National Commission on the Causes of the Financial and Economic Crisis in the United States, January 2011), xviii, 113, 125–6, 160, 227–30, www.govinfo.gov/content/pkg/GPO-FCIC/pdf/GPO-FCIC.pdf.

[24] A Llama-like creature with two heads, one at each end of its body; a creation from the *Doctor Dolittle* series of children's books.

[25] See n 23 at 159, 171, 307–8; Adair Turner, *The Turner Review: A Regulatory Response to the Global Banking Crisis* (March 2009), 92, www.actuaries.org/CTTEES_TFRISKCRISIS/Documents/turner_review.pdf; FSA, *The Failure of the Royal Bank of Scotland* (Financial Services Authority Board Report, December 2011), § 28 at 27, www.fca.org.uk/publication/corporate/fsa-rbs.pdf.

[26] Michael W. Taylor, '"Twin Peaks" Revisited . . . A Second Chance for Regulatory Reform' (Centre for the Study of Financial Innovation, No 89, September 2009).

[27] Recommendation 1: Wallis Inquiry, 31 March 1997, 31, and Recommendation 31 (n 2) at 42.

[28] For a detailed discussion of these questions, see Godwin, Howse and Ramsay (n 17), from which much of the analysis in this chapter is drawn.

should coordination between the regulators be achieved? Each of these questions is discussed below.

1.2.1.1 Where Should the Prudential Regulator Be Housed?

The first question is where the prudential regulator should be housed. Three options are relevant in this regard: (1) the prudential regulator is an entirely distinct entity that sits outside of the central bank; (2) the prudential regulator is a subsidiary of the central bank; and (3) the prudential regulator exists as a department within the central bank.

Australia stands alone in adopting the first option. Prior to 2016, the United Kingdom operated a model in which its Prudential Regulation Authority (PRA) was a subsidiary of the Bank of England (BoE). Legislation passed in 2016[29] ended the PRA's status as a subsidiary and constituted the BoE as the PRA, the functions of which are now exercised by the BoE acting through the Prudential Regulation Committee. The purpose of this reform was to 'maximise the synergies of having monetary policy, macro-prudential policy and micro-prudential policy under the aegis of one institution'.[30] In addition to the United Kingdom, following the 2016 reforms, the Netherlands, Belgium and New Zealand have adopted the third option. South Africa has also adopted the third option, although its prudential regulator exists within the central bank as a separate juristic person.[31]

1.2.1.2 How Should the Functions and Objectives of the Twin Peaks Regulators Be Defined?

The second question is how the functions and objectives of the Twin Peaks regulators should be defined. Adequately demarcating the responsibilities of the market conduct regulator and prudential regulator is critical to the success of a Twin Peaks model.[32] The necessity of regulators having clear responsibilities and objectives is reflected in the Basel 'Core Principles for Effective Banking Supervision'[33] ('Basel Core Principles') and the 'Insurance Core Principles'.[34]

The Twin Peaks jurisdictions are broadly consistent in relation to the functions and objectives of the market conduct regulators. There are, however, some differences in terms of whether the objectives are prioritised – often reflected in whether there is a 'main objective' or a 'strategic objective' – and whether the market conduct regulator is required to have regard to competition. For example, the legislation governing the UK Financial Conduct Authority (FCA) provides for two types of high-level objectives: a 'strategic' objective of ensuring that 'the relevant markets function well'[35] and the 'operational' objective of consumer protection, integrity and competition.[36] In addition, the FCA has a 'competition objective' as one of its operational objectives.[37] The market conduct regulator in Australia, the Australian Securities and Investments Commission, was also recently given a competition mandate.[38]

---

[29] *The Bank of England and Financial Services Act 2016.*
[30] HM Treasury Bank of England Bill: Technical Consultation (2015), 3.
[31] See Chapter 9.
[32] See the discussion in Godwin, Howse and Ramsay (n 17).
[33] Basel Committee on Banking Supervision, Core Principles for Effective Banking Supervision (2012), 21.
[34] International Association of Insurance Supervisors, Insurance Core Principles (2011), 1. See also IOSCO, Objectives and Principles of Securities Regulation (2010), Principle 1: 'The responsibilities of the Regulator should be clear and objectively stated.'
[35] *Financial Services Act 2012* (FS Act), Part 2 amendments to the FSM Act, s 1B(2).
[36] FS Act, Part 2 amendments to the FSM Act, s 1B(3).
[37] FS Act, Part 2 amendments to the FSM Act, s 1E.
[38] See Chapter 5.

The variations in the functions and objectives of the prudential regulators are greater than in the case of the market conduct regulators, although there is overlap in terms of references to prudential supervision and financial stability. The legislation in both Australia and the United Kingdom provides that the prudential regulator must have regard to competition.[39]

The United Kingdom appears to be unique because the BoE, acting as the PRA, has the power to prevent the FCA from acting in limited circumstances. This is effectively a veto power, and will be used where 'an action to be taken by the FCA . . . is likely to threaten the stability of the UK financial system'.[40]

1.2.1.3 How Should the Relationship between Each Regulator and the Government Be Structured?

The third question concerns the structure of the relationship between each regulator and the government. This is a question that is relevant to all regulatory models, and goes to the issue of operational independence. One supplementary question that is directly relevant to the Twin Peaks model, however, is whether the government can determine which regulator is the lead regulator. This is relevant because a key challenge for Twin Peaks jurisdictions is how they manage 'dual-regulated entities'; namely, entities that are regulated by both the market conduct regulator and prudential regulator. The UK Treasury has the power to establish the 'boundaries' between the two regulators:

[Section] 3G Power to establish boundary between FCA and PRA responsibilities

(1) The Treasury may by order specify matters that, in relation to the exercise by either regulator of its functions relating to PRA-authorised persons, are to be, or are to be primarily, the responsibility of one regulator rather than the other.

(2) The order may –
   (a) provide that one regulator is or is not to have regard to specified matters when exercising specified functions;
   (b) require one regulator to consult the other.[41]

Where this power is exercised, a draft order must be laid before Parliament unless it is a matter of urgency.[42]

The ability to determine who is the 'lead supervisor' or 'primary regulator' has been said to '[create] problems in terms of coordinating supervisory action, information flows and, ultimately, crisis intervention'.[43] When the PRA's veto power in relation to the FCA is taken into account, it is clear that the United Kingdom has deliberately built features into its twin peaks model to ensure that only one regulator will act where necessary. This provides an interesting point of difference with Australia. While both Australian regulators are subject to a general ministerial directions power, this falls short of the minister being able to determine which regulator is to take primary responsibility for a matter.[44] It remains to be seen to what extent

---

[39] Subsection 8(2) of the APRA Act; FS Act, Part 2 amendments to the FSM Act, s 2H.
[40] Explanatory Note, FS Act, para 10. The provision is set out in FS Act, Part 2 amendments to the FSM Act, s 3I. In 2011 the IMF raised concerns about this veto power, and stated that 'without appropriate safeguards, this arrangement [had] the potential to limit FCA independence and also to cause uncertainty in decision making'. International Monetary Fund, United Kingdom: IOSCO Objectives and Principles of Securities Regulation: Detailed Assessment of Implementation. Report No 11/232, July 2011, 23.
[41] FS Act, Part 2 amendments to the FSM Act.
[42] FS Act, Part 2 amendments to the FSM Act, s 3H.
[43] Wymeersch (n 4) 262.
[44] See APRA Act, s 12 and ASIC Act, s 12.

the 'power to establish boundaries' in the UK undermines the independence of the regulators, and whether it evinces a lack of faith in the ability of the regulators to coordinate matters effectively between themselves.

1.2.1.4 How Should Coordination between the Regulators Be Achieved?

The fourth question is how coordination between the regulators should be achieved. Coordination is often seen as an element of broader cooperation, which includes information-sharing and consultation.[45]

Coordination between the regulators in a Twin Peaks jurisdiction is critical to the model's success. As has been noted with respect to the United Kingdom, the model is 'unlikely to function effectively if the different parts ... operate in a silo manner'.[46] The chief difficulty is recognising what is necessary for effective coordination, and how this is best achieved. Some jurisdictions establish a formalised regime for coordination. For example, the United Kingdom imposes a prescriptive statutory duty on the regulators to cooperate in discharging their functions.[47] This is expressed as a duty of the market conduct regulator – the FCA – and the PRA to ensure the coordinated exercise of their functions.[48] The FCA and PRA must coordinate by obtaining information from each other in matters of 'common regulatory interest'.[49] This only applies to the extent that it is compatible with the advancement of each regulator's objectives, and the burden of compliance is not unduly disproportionate to the benefit.[50] For the purposes of the FCA, 'objectives' means 'operational objectives'.[51] The Memorandum of Understanding between the FCA, BoE and PRA echoes this duty by stating that 'the FCA, the Bank and the PRA, will share information related to markets and markets infrastructure where materially relevant to another of them both at their own initiative and upon each other's request, where legally permissible'.[52] A separate duty to cooperate exists between the Treasury, the BoE and the PRA to coordinate the discharge of their functions 'so far as they ... relate to the stability of the UK financial system ... and affect the public interest'.[53] By contrast, other jurisdictions such as Australia see 'coordination among the agencies [being] ... a largely informal arrangement'.[54]

A widely used mechanism to help facilitate coordination between the regulators is the preparation of Memoranda of Understanding. These typically detail the arrangements between the regulators regarding areas such as the exchange of information, coordination, sharing of fees and dispute resolution. For example, in the United Kingdom the PRA and FCA are under a duty

---

[45] NBB Report 2013 – Preamble, Economics and financial developments, Prudential Regulation and Supervision, 227–8.

[46] Financial Stability Board, Peer Review of the United Kingdom (Report, 2013), 7–8.

[47] See also the Netherlands, where both the AFM and DNB are under general statutory duties to cooperate. One translation of the general duty reads 'the supervisor shall collaborate closely with a view to laying down generally binding regulations and policy rules, in order to ensure that these are equivalent wherever possible insofar as they relate to matters that are both subject to prudential supervision and supervision of conduct.' AFS Act, s 1:46(1).

[48] *Financial Services Act 2012* (FS Act), Part 2 amendments to the *Financial Services and Markets Act 2000* (FSM Act), s 3D.

[49] FS Act, Part 2 amendments to the FSM Act, s 3D(1)(b).

[50] FS Act, Part 2 amendments to the FSM Act, s 3D(2)(a), (b).

[51] Ibid s 3D(4). The operation of this provision was explained in the Explanatory Note to the *Financial Services Act 2012*: Explanatory Note, FS Act, para 168.

[52] Memorandum of Understanding between the Financial Conduct Authority and the Bank of England, including the Prudential Regulation Authority (March 2015) para 8.

[53] FS Act, s 64.

[54] International Monetary Fund, Australia: Financial System Stability Assessment (IMF Country Report No 12/308, November 2012), 28. See the discussion in Chapter 5.

to 'prepare and maintain a memorandum which describes in general terms . . . the role of each regulator in relation to the exercise of functions conferred by or under this Act'.[55] This Memorandum of Understanding (MoU) must be reviewed at least once a year, given to the Treasury, and tabled before Parliament.[56] This provision is prescriptive about the types of information that must be contained in the MoU vis-à-vis coordination between the regulators. Another MoU is required to be prepared and maintained between the Treasury, BoE and PRA with respect to crisis management.[57] This is designed to set out 'who is in charge of what and when between HM Treasury and the Bank (including the PRA) in a financial crisis'.[58] The approach in the United Kingdom can be contrasted with the approach to financial crisis management in Australia, where the relevant MoU provides that each member of the Council of Financial Regulators is responsible for any decisions that fall directly within its remit.[59] As a result, the framework of coordination essentially involves collective responsibility for managing a financial crisis on the part of the financial regulators, the central bank and the government.

A common element of Twin Peak jurisdictions is the existence of a 'coordinating body'. This body may be a creature of statute or it may be an informal forum for representatives of the regulators to meet. The membership of the body (and whether it includes representatives of government) varies from jurisdiction to jurisdiction.

1.2.2 *Surveying Twin Peak Terrains*

The outline of the different topography and design choices given above indicates that there are many variations in designing a Twin Peaks model. There is no 'one size fits all' model and there is no rulebook about how a jurisdiction should approach the task. Looking at the design choices, and considering why they were made, leads to a couple of observations.

First, there are different approaches in terms of the role and functions of the central bank, particularly in relation to prudential supervision. Australia, for example, stands alone in housing its prudential regulator completely outside of its central bank. In the United Kingdom, the BoE acts as the prudential regulator through the Prudential Regulation Committee. The Netherlands and Belgium rely on their central bank, which has diminished responsibility for monetary policy as a result of their membership of the EU, while the central bank in New Zealand has complete responsibility for monetary policy and prudential regulation. As noted above, the prudential regulator in South Africa operates as a separate juristic person within the central bank. Two key observations emerge from these choices. The first is that achieving synergies is considered by some jurisdictions to be important. The second is that there appears to be a trend towards giving the central bank more power, not less.

The notion of achieving synergies is captured by the view that the central bank – with its highly specialised set of skills, processes and experience – is best situated to undertake the task of prudential supervision. There is great sway in the argument that the central bank would be the most obvious choice, particularly given the interconnected nature of monetary policy and

---

[55] FS Act, Part 2 amendments to the FSM Act, s 3E(1)(a).
[56] FS Act, Part 2 amendments to the FSM Act, s 3E(4),(5) & (6).
[57] FS Act, s 65.
[58] Bank of England, Memoranda of Understanding on financial crisis management (2015) para 4, www.bankofengland .co.uk/-/media/boe/files/memoranda-of-understanding/mou%20between%20the%20bank%20including%20the%20pra %20and%20hm%20treasury%20re%20financial%20crisis%20management.
[59] Memorandum of Understanding on Financial Distress Management between the Members of the Council of Financial Regulators, para 5.2.

prudential regulation. The counter-argument is that this in itself creates potential conflict because the differences between prudential supervision and monetary policy are important and at times contradictory. Moreover. there is evidence indicating that each entity performs either a macro- or microprudential role; the prudential regulator usually the latter. It is clear from the experience in the Netherlands, Belgium, New Zealand, the United Kingdom and South Africa that synergies are considered desirable. On the other hand, the Australian experience has so far demonstrated that it is possible to conduct prudential supervision outside of the central bank.

The trend towards giving the central bank more power is important because it contradicts global patterns prior to the Global Financial Crisis, whereby a central bank conducting prudential supervision was more representative of a developing country than a developed one.

In 2010 the European Central Bank, after conducting a survey of various EU jurisdictions, made reference to this apparent trend. It noted:

> [T]he survey confirms the departure from the sectoral model and highlights a clear tendency towards further enhancing the role of central banks in supervisory activities. The latter development is underpinned by the experience during the financial crisis, which highlighted the information-related synergies between the central banking and the prudential supervisory function. This rationale may explain another important finding of the survey, namely that the involvement of the central bank in financial supervision seems to be increasingly strengthened through the adoption of the 'twin peaks' model.[60]

It follows that a trend may be underway towards giving the central bank more power.

Secondly, there are significant differences in terms of how Twin Peaks jurisdictions achieve regulatory coordination. This is often expressed as a divide between the 'soft law' and 'hard law' approach to regulation. Hard law is seen as giving rise to legally enforceable obligations – such as duties to cooperate arising under statute, or obligations to prepare an MoU. Conversely, soft law relies on persuasive instruments that are themselves not legally binding, such as MoUs, mission statements and informal coordinating bodies.[61]

The IMF, speaking with respect to Belgium's structured product regulation, has discussed the benefits of each approach:

> A 'soft law' approach ... provides a way for regulators to respond in a significantly more timely way to market change and innovation than may be possible under 'hard law' regulation. A move to 'hard law' on the other hand, provides industry with certainty, reduces opportunities for inconsistent application and interpretation and allows for other regulatory approaches (including rules about product governance) to be applied.[62]

A survey of the terrain in Twin Peaks jurisdictions reveals that there are many different ways of approaching the critical task of regulatory coordination. While coordination is central to the functioning of a Twin Peaks model, this does not mean that it must be enshrined in statute. Each jurisdiction strikes its own unique balance of formal and informal means for achieving effective coordination between the market conduct and prudential regulators.

---

[60] European Central Bank, 'Recent Developments in Supervisory Structures in the EU Member States (2007–2010)' (2010), 5.

[61] For a fuller discussion of hard law and soft law, see generally Godwin and Ramsay (n 17).

[62] International Monetary Fund (IMF) Financial Sector Assessment Program Update – Technical Note – Securities Markets Regulation and Supervision (Report, 2013), 7–8.

For example, Australia, New Zealand and the Netherlands fall at the 'soft law' end of the spectrum and are largely informal. Belgium, as noted by the IMF, contains a mixture of 'formal and . . . informal' procedures for coordination.[63] The United Kingdom, arguably, reflects a 'hard law' approach to cooperation. It establishes its coordinating body under statute, imposes multiple and overlapping duties to cooperate, creates a procedure for the government to define the lead regulator and sets out a detailed process to enable the prudential regulator to veto the market conduct regulator. A similar approach has been adopted in South Africa.

It is likely that there are disadvantages to both the soft and hard law approach: the soft law approach might be regarded as less transparent and create uncertainty for the regulated community due to a lack of guidance, whereas the hard law approach may create a 'tick-the-box' mentality when it comes to complying with the legislation and discourage cooperation through other means. Ultimately, whether an approach is successful will likely depend more on the culture of the regulators than on the specific mechanism through which they cooperate.

The DNB remarked in 2010 that the 'twin peaks supervisory model . . . that was introduced in the Netherlands in 2004 is increasingly being adopted by other countries'. Given the relatively new nature of the model, it may be difficult to identify the strength of this long-term trend. However, as the actions of Australia, the United Kingdom, Belgium, New Zealand, the Netherlands and South Africa show, there is growing support in favour of the Twin Peaks model. It is telling that no jurisdiction has yet abandoned Twin Peaks in favour of another model. It is likely to remain relevant for some time to come.

1.3 OUTLINE OF CHAPTERS

The chapters in this book present a range of perspectives from academics, regulators and policymakers. Amongst other things, the chapters highlight the extent to which Twin Peaks is as much a journey or trek as it is a destination. There are many themes that the chapters explore. These include the perceived benefits of the Twin Peaks model arising out of its flexibility and adaptability, the importance of the transitional stage for those jurisdictions that adopt the model and the reality that there is no unique or single version of Twin Peaks – each jurisdiction that contemplates a move towards Twin Peaks needs to consider its own circumstances (including regulatory culture) in determining whether the model is appropriate and, if so, how the model should be adapted for its own purposes.

Part I, entitled 'Surveying the Terrain', contains three chapters. The first two chapters, those by Michael Taylor and Jeff Carmichael, examine the origins of the Twin Peaks model and its evolution and development in the United Kingdom and Australia, respectively.

As the author of the seminal research that provided a navigational compass for the Twin Peaks model, Michael Taylor is a fitting person to launch the trek. Chapter 2 examines the three periods or episodes of Twin Peaks to date and traces the evolution of the model in the United Kingdom from an academic concept 'to its post-Global Financial Crisis rehabilitation as an institutional arrangement that is capable of addressing some of the most obvious shortcomings in regulatory structures revealed by the crisis'. As a prelude to the discussion about mainland China in subsequent chapters, Taylor notes that '[t]he decision by the Chinese government in March 2018 to merge the banking and insurance regulators, while keeping the securities regulator as a separate agency, represents a further step towards the adoption of a Twin Peaks structure in a major economy'.

---

[63] Ibid.

Chapter 3 is written by one of Australia's Twin Peaks pioneers, Jeff Carmichael, who met with Taylor as Australia was considering a move towards Twin Peaks during its Financial System Inquiry in 1996, and subsequently became the inaugural chairman of the Australian Prudential Regulation Authority (APRA). His chapter reviews the evolution of the Twin Peaks model in Australia, including the challenges in designing an appropriate legislative framework, dealing with regulatory boundaries and managing the institutional transition to Twin Peaks. Voicing the hope that the commitment to regulatory cooperation will continue, Carmichael suggests that if that commitment were lost at some point in the future, it would not be surprising if there were calls to embed APRA within the Reserve Bank of Australia and to impose a hierarchy in which systemic stability sits above the Twin Peaks of prudence and conduct.

This question of where the prudential regulator should be housed – a question that goes to the heart of architectural design – is considered by Donato Masciandaro and Davide Romelli in Chapter 4. Their chapter explores the principles that might be used to evaluate the central bank's involvement as prudential supervisor in a Twin Peaks setting. Adopting a political economy and econometric analysis, Masciandaro and Romelli suggest that two drivers are relevant in answering this question: the necessity to address and fix the consequences of a systemic crisis (the crisis driver) and the opportunity to implement a supervisory change when the proportion of peer countries undertaking reforms is higher (the bandwagon driver). Interestingly, they note that Australia is an outlier in this regard.

Part II of the book, entitled 'The Trek towards Twin Peaks', contains chapters that explore how various jurisdictions have adopted and adapted the Twin Peaks model. Chapter 5 by Andrew Godwin, Ian Ramsay and Andrew Schmulow explores the challenges that Australia has faced during the course of its Twin Peaks trek. Consistent with Taylor's comments about the flexibility and adaptability of the model, the authors note the extent to which the model in Australia has adapted to changing circumstances and challenges, and been tested, debated and adjusted. Further, echoing comments by Masciandaro and Romelli, the authors observe that Australia continues to be an outlier among Twin Peaks jurisdictions in at least two significant areas: the structure of the prudential regulator as a statutory body that is separate from the Reserve Bank of Australia, and the relatively informal, 'soft law' approach to regulatory coordination that has been adopted to date. The experience in Australia therefore serves as a useful point of comparison with other Twin Peaks jurisdictions.

An examination of New Zealand follows in Chapter 6, in which Helen Dervan and Simon Jensen argue that the adoption of the Twin Peaks model has improved New Zealand's financial regulatory system. However, significant regulatory vulnerabilities remain in areas such as the decision-making structure for prudential regulation, and the structure of prudential regulation in New Zealand generally. The chapter notes that New Zealand is still transitioning towards Twin Peaks, and highlights the importance of regulatory coordination and cooperation, particularly given the integration between Australia and New Zealand, and the unique interdependence that this creates.

Chapter 7 offers combined regulatory and academic perspectives on the experience of the Twin Peaks model in the Netherlands. In this chapter, Marco van Hengel, Olaf Sleijpen and Femke de Vries note the challenges associated with transitioning to the Twin Peaks model in the Netherlands, particularly in terms of the relationship between the regulators, and achieving effective coordination between them. The chapter suggests that, to a large extent, the model has delivered on its main objectives in the Netherlands, although developments internationally and in the European Union demonstrate a shift towards a more sectoral approach – a theme that is explored further in Chapters 16 and 17.

A regulator's perspective is also offered in Chapter 8, in which Roy Havemann outlines the Twin Peaks system as it has been adapted to South Africa, which is the first emerging market to adopt the model. Noting that Twin Peaks in South Africa might best described as 'a mountain, two peaks and some molehills', Havemann explores the benefits of Twin Peaks in terms of deepening capital markets and increasing living standards, and suggests that a key question is what the role of the Twin Peaks authorities should be in transformation.

The experience of South Africa is analysed further in Chapter 9 by Corlia van Heerden and Gerda van Niekerk, who examine the role of the South African Reserve Bank (SARB) as central bank in the South African Twin Peaks model, and compare this with its role prior to the adoption of Twin Peaks. The authors note the extent to which the adoption of the model has clarified the role of the SARB, its objectives, functions and powers. Although recognising that housing the prudential regulator as a separate juristic entity within the central bank is an optimal arrangement for a resource-constrained emerging market such as South Africa, the authors identify potential conflicts between financial stability and prudential regulation.

Part III of the book, entitled 'Different Topographies', contains chapters that explore the topography in various jurisdictions that have not adopted the Twin Peaks model and consider whether it would be appropriate to adopt the model in the relevant jurisdiction, and, if so, how it might be adapted for this purpose.

A broad range of perspective are offered. In line with one of the key themes of the book – namely, that each jurisdiction needs to consider its own circumstances (including regulatory culture) – there are different views as to the relevance and appropriateness of Twin Peaks, whether in the medium term or the long term. Chapter 10 by Ruth Plato-Shinar provides an insightful contrast to the view that Twin Peaks is universally appropriate or suitable for every jurisdiction. After noting various indicators in favour of a consolidated approach, Plato-Shinar recommends that Israel's sectoral approach be maintained for the present, although she suggests that Israel can learn from the experiences of Twin Peaks countries in areas such as inter-agency cooperation. The analysis raises interesting questions about the degree to which the size and make-up of a financial market is relevant in terms of the suitability of Twin Peaks to that market.

Douglas Arner, Evan Gibson and Janos Barberis follow with an examination of the Special Administrative Region of Hong Kong. By contrast with the chapter by Plato-Shinar, Chapter 11 highlights the weaknesses of Hong Kong's current sectoral model and the benefits that might arise from adopting the Twin Peaks model, particularly in the context of technological development in the capital markets and the impact of financial technology (FinTech). In particular, the authors argue that coordination between regulators in Hong Kong and Mainland China, which requires the utilisation of regulatory technology (RegTech), would be facilitated by a move towards a Twin Peaks regulatory architecture.

By contrast with the sectoral approach in Israel and Hong Kong, Chapter 12 by Youkyung Huh and Hongjoo Jung explores the weaknesses of the integrated approach in South Korea, including the so-called revolving door phenomenon. Their comprehensive analysis highlights the relevance of the political economy to regulatory design and the fact that attempts to reform the overall architecture of a financial supervisory system will inevitably have an impact upon many stakeholders, including the regulators themselves. Huh and Jung argue that by comparison with the integrated model, the Twin Peaks model provides advantages in terms of regulatory specialisation and allows independent cross-checking between the regulatory goals of prudential regulation and market conduct regulation, without compromising one another.

On the other side of the Yellow Sea, Mainland China presents as a jurisdiction in which significant regulatory reforms are ongoing, and a debate has been underway for some time as to whether the Twin Peaks model should be adopted. In Chapter 13, Li Guo and Jessica Cheung advocate a move towards the Twin Peaks model in China, arguing that the inspiration for Twin Peaks 'is obvious as a result of the rise of systemic risks in China's interconnected market and the growing concern for consumer protection'. Their proposed reforms would see the establishment of a consumer protection authority that is separate from prudential regulation. They note that although recent reforms appear to have reinforced the current sectoral framework, the establishment of a Financial Stability and Development Committee is, to some extent, consistent with proposals to switch to a Twin Peaks model when the economy becomes further integrated.

The relevance of transition and choosing the right time for a move to a Twin Peaks model in Mainland China is a theme that is picked up by Robin Hui Huang in Chapter 14. Huang also advocates that China adopt the Twin Peaks model in the long term. However, the appropriate time for this 'will depend ultimately on the extent to which the recent reinforcement of the current sector-based regulatory structure can effectively cope with the challenges of new developments and innovations in the marketplace'. Huang's chapter highlights the extent to which fundamental reform requires political appetite and is often crisis-driven.

No book that attempts to examine international developments in financial regulation would be complete without a chapter on the United States. In Chapter 15, Heidi Mandanis Schooner outlines the US financial regulatory structure, which is a hybrid system that embodies some of the principles of the Twin Peaks model, and then examines the financial stability architecture in the United States following the Global Financial Crisis and recent developments. Following an examination of technological developments such as FinTech and distributed ledger technology, Schooner suggests that 'a Twin Peaks architecture is better suited to technological innovations that defy institutional and activity norms as its design is based on regulatory functions or goals instead of on activities or entities'.

In the final two chapters in Part III, the book travels across the Atlantic to examine the position in the European Union. In Chapter 16, Dirk Schoenmaker and Nicolas Véron explore how the EU might move towards a Twin Peaks model and argue that new challenges in the European financial sector make the sectoral structure increasingly out-of-date. To deal with these challenges, the EU should commit to a Twin Peaks model as a long-term aspirational goal. One of the key reasons for such a goal, they suggest, is the need for the EU27 to upgrade the supervision of its capital markets after Brexit.

Striking a slightly more cautious note in this regard, Karel Lannoo in Chapter 17 examines the recent review of the European Supervisory Authorities (ESA) and the extent to which the ESA have moved towards strengthening sectoral supervision. Notably, however, Lannoo aligns with the view of Schoenmaker and Véron in suggesting that the most important task for the EU is to set itself a guiding vision, namely, a 'vision of what the EU wants to achieve in a particular financial sector and adapt the desirable European supervisory structure to that'.

Part IV of the book, entitled 'Seismic Activity and Fault Lines', contains three chapters that explore various challenges and tensions under the Twin Peaks model. In Chapter 18, Gail Pearson examines the overlap between prudential regulation and conduct regulation in the area of consumer protection and ongoing detriment to consumers in Australia, despite significant steps to protect their interests. Pearson also highlights the increasing attention being paid by the regulators to risk culture and conduct risk, and selects home lending as a case study to examine developments in this regard. The chapter highlights challenges occasioned by line-blurring within the Twin Peaks model and the central role that consumer protection performs.

The theme of culture is taken up in Chapter 19 by Patrick McConnell, who explores the need for regulators to supervise the culture of firms, particularly 'macroculture' and how culture influences conduct and misconduct by individual staff within regulated firms. The chapter proposes a novel approach under which Twin Peaks regulators can supervise culture and 'patrol' the boundaries between different cultural models. McConnell's chapter highlights the increasing expectations on regulators to supervise culture within the regulated community, and the ways in which this might be undertaken effectively within the Twin Peaks model.

The final chapter, by Andrew Godwin, Steve Kourabas and Ian Ramsay, considers the post-GFC shift towards macroprudential regulation and its systemic financial stability goal, and examines steps to reconcile the Twin Peaks model of regulation with the increased significance attributed to maintaining systemic financial stability. The chapter notes that although the Twin Peaks model appears to be conducive to systemic financial stability concerns, systemic financial stability and macroprudential regulation did not feature prominently in the design of the prototype Twin Peaks model, as adopted in Australia. The authors then explore the different approaches to macroprudential regulation in the United Kingdom and Australia and conclude by noting that the true test will be whether each approach proves resilient in the face of systemic financial stress.

In its return to Australia – the first jurisdiction to adopt the Twin Peaks model – the book completes its global trek to Twin Peaks and its exploration of the Twin Peaks topography, including its peaks, surrounding mountains and foothills. It is our hope, to borrow T. S. Eliot's immortal words, that 'the end of all our exploring will be to arrive where we started and know the place for the first time'.[64]

---

[64] T. S. Eliot, 'Little Gidding' in *Four Quartets*.

PART I

Surveying the Terrain

The Three Episodes of Twin Peaks

Michael W. Taylor

2.1 INTRODUCTION

The Twin Peaks – or an 'objectives-based' – structure of financial regulation envisages two, and only two, regulatory agencies responsible for prudential and business conduct regulation, respectively. Initially proposed a little over twenty years ago, the history and practice of the Twin Peaks model falls into three discrete periods or episodes. This chapter explores each of these episodes, tracing the evolution of the model from an academic concept, which was criticised by many regulators and market practitioners for its impracticality, to its rehabilitation following the Global Financial Crisis as an institutional arrangement that is capable of addressing some of the most obvious shortcomings in regulatory structures revealed by the crisis.

The first episode of Twin Peaks saw the model developed and promoted in the United Kingdom during the mid-1990s.[1] It originated in response to a financial regulatory system that had become excessively complex and which was widely recognised as falling behind the rapid evolution of the financial sector following structural deregulation in the 1980s. The concept initially attracted interest from the UK Labour Party (then in opposition but soon to form a government in 1997) and from some regulatory practitioners in the United Kingdom. However, the Bank of England was implacably opposed to the concept and strongly defended its role in banking supervision, which the Twin Peaks structure threatened to remove. The first episode concluded with the Twin Peaks model receiving its first endorsement by an official body, the Australian Financial System Inquiry (the Wallis Committee) in 1996.

The second episode involved the implementation of a Twin Peaks structure in both Australia and the Netherlands, but not in the United Kingdom. The Wallis Committee recommendations were adopted by the Australian government, resulting in the formation of two regulatory agencies, the Australian Prudential Regulatory Authority (APRA) and the Australian Securities and Investments Commission (ASIC). The Reserve Bank of Australia retained its role as payments system regulator but had no ongoing regulatory responsibilities. By contrast, in the Netherlands, a Twin Peaks structure was adopted in which the prudential regulator was in effect a department of the central bank, De Nederlandsche Bank. However, neither of these pioneering approaches to Twin Peaks found favour in the United Kingdom.

---

[1] M. Taylor, *'Twin Peaks': A Regulatory Structure for the New Century* (Centre for the Study of Financial Innovation, 1995).

Following the British Labour Party's landslide election victory in 1997 it abandoned its interest in Twin Peaks and instead embraced the concept of a single financial regulatory agency for all banking, securities, investment management and insurance activities with respect to both prudential and business conduct matters. This agency – eventually to be named the Financial Services Authority (FSA) – became a model that was widely emulated and for a time appeared to represent the future of financial sector regulation. The UK approach was lauded by the International Monetary Fund (IMF) in its Article IV reports on the British economy and was promoted in other member countries through the IMF's technical assistance work. During this second episode, Twin Peaks seemed to be something of a curiosity, confined to a few mid-sized economies which had for idiosyncratic reasons stopped short of the complete integration of all regulatory functions in a single agency. In those few countries that had adopted a Twin Peaks system, there remained political pressure towards full integration in a single agency.

The third episode began with the Global Financial Crisis and the subsequent re-evaluation of the single regulator model. In particular, the crisis exposed the limitations of a single regulatory agency both in the run-up to the crisis – when the United Kingdom's FSA stood accused of having prioritised business conduct regulation over prudential regulation – and in subsequent crisis management. In addition, the crisis resulted in greater emphasis being placed on macro-prudential regulation which required close coordination with the central bank, both with respect to the assessment of systemic risk and in terms of the interaction between macropru-dential measures and monetary policy. It resulted in the dismantling of the most high-profile of the single regulators – the UK Financial Services Authority – and the creation of a Twin Peaks model in the United Kingdom, the country for which it had originally been designed.[2]

This chapter provides a brief overview of each of these episodes, with the focus on the first of them. The rationale and background to the Twin Peaks concept is explained, along with the factors that contributed to the debate on regulatory structure in the United Kingdom in the mid-1990s. The subsequent episodes are more extensively covered in other contributions to this volume and therefore their coverage in this chapter is correspondingly schematic. In conclusion, the factors that led to the rise and fall of the rival single-regulator model will be briefly reviewed.

2.2 EPISODE ONE: THE ORIGINS OF TWIN PEAKS

The context in which the Twin Peaks concept was developed was provided by three factors that came into alignment in mid-1990s Britain. They were (1) rapid industry change; (2) an ongoing debate on regulatory reform; and (3) the politics of regulatory reform.

2.2.1 *Industry Change*

The traditional regulatory system, at least in the Anglo-Saxon world, was constructed around the existence of clear lines of demarcation between the activities engaged in by banks, insurance companies and securities firms. For much of the post-war period these demarcation lines remained clear and strictly enforced. In the United States they were the product of Depression-era structural regulation, such as the *Banking Act 1933* (the 'Glass–Steagall Act'),

---

[2] M. Taylor, 'Regulatory Reform in the U.K.' (2013) 18 *North Carolina Banking Institute* 227, http://scholarship.law.unc .edu/ncbi/vol18/iss1/19.

or of the post-war *Bank Holding Company Act 1956*.[3] Countries that were influenced by the US regulatory approach, such as Japan, also adopted rigid structural separation between banking and securities trading. In the United Kingdom, and other countries that were influenced by the British approach, the separation between what were, in effect, different sectors of the financial industry was not the product of law, but of custom and practice enforced by the 'moral suasion' of the Bank of England or privately ordered rules such as those of the London Stock Exchange.[4]

By the early 1990s the rigid separation between different segments of the financial system had begun to break down.[5] For most of the preceding decade governments in both the United States and Britain had pursued a deregulatory push with the aim of revitalising economic growth, including through a more dynamic financial sector which would improve the efficiency with which capital was allocated. In consequence, they had begun to dismantle the structural regulations that had kept the financial sector clearly segmented for at least a generation. As a result of these deregulatory measures, banks, securities firms and insurance companies started to become more closely integrated. A key development was the emergence of financial conglomerate groups in which at least two of the three main financial industry segments were combined. Although such groups had been a long-standing feature of continental European financial systems (known as Allfinanz in Germany and Bancassurance in France), for the Anglo-Saxon countries financial conglomerates represented a significant new departure. Britain was somewhat ahead of the United States in witnessing the formation of these groups, given that the chief structural barriers were removed as part of the London Stock Exchange's 'Big Bang' reforms in 1986. Although these reforms were adopted in part in anticipation of a major regulatory overhaul in the United States, legislation was delayed for over a decade until the passage of the *Gramm–Leach–Bliley Act* in 1999. The impact of European Union legislation, which was constructed on the assumption that it would apply to diversified financial groups, was also important in shaping the emerging structure of the British financial sector.

Alongside the formation of financial conglomerate groups, the relaxation of structural regulations also permitted the formation of new types of financial instruments and markets. Derivative contracts provided one such example. The emergence of new financial markets and products arguably changed the nature of systemic risk, with a wider variety of types of financial intermediary now having the potential to cause disruption to the financial system. Securities firms or insurance companies had become major derivatives dealers; the consequences of their failure to honour their contracts would be every bit as much of a threat to the stability of the financial system as would the failure of a major bank. Moreover, these new markets also had consequences in terms of consumer protection since many new products did not fit neatly into the traditional categories of deposits, tradable securities and insurance contracts around which consumer protection legislation was designed. The integration of derivatives into deposit contracts, for example by offering a rate of return linked to the performance of a specific stock index rather than an interest rate, created difficult issues for consumer protection regulation.

These two trends – the formation of financial conglomerates and the emergence of new financial products and markets – became known in shorthand as the 'blurring of boundaries' between the different segments of the financial system. With the gradual erosion of the once

---

[3] H. Schooner and M. Taylor, 'United Kingdom and United States Responses to the Regulatory Challenges of Modern Financial Markets' (2003) 38 *Texas International Law Journal* 317, 327–9.

[4] Ibid.

[5] Tripartite Group of Bank, Securities and Insurance Regulators, 'The Supervision of Financial Conglomerates' (1995), www.bis.org/publ/bcbs20.pdf. Subsequently the Tripartite Group was renamed the Joint Forum.

bright lines which had separated banking, securities and insurance, the question then arose as to how the regulatory system should respond.

As already noted, this question came to prominence in Britain ahead of the rest of the world. This reflected the fact that Britain had been in advance of the United States when it came to dismantling structural regulation, in part due to the fact that such regulation had been predominantly informal rather than based on statute. While traditions of Allfinanz or Bancassurance elsewhere in the European Union meant that there was nothing fundamentally new about financial conglomerates in those countries, for Britain the emergence of these groups did present a major departure from past practice. As a result, the regulatory consequences of structural deregulation entered into British policy debates in advance of most other major economies.

2.2.2 *The British Debate on Regulation*

Although British academics had begun to debate issues relating to regulatory structure in the early and mid-1990s, their focus at the time was not on broad questions of institutional design but on two narrower, arguably parochial, issues – the role of the Bank of England in banking supervision and how to reform the United Kingdom's recently introduced, but apparently ineffective, system of business conduct regulation. These two debates on regulatory reform preoccupied different groups of academics and ran along parallel tracks. The case for combining, or separating, monetary policy and banking supervision was largely the preserve of economists. Addressing business conduct regulation was largely the focus of legal scholars. There was little overlap between the two groups and only in relatively rare cases did an economist consider the broader institutional implications (the work of Charles Goodhart stands out clearly in this regard).[6] Most UK legal scholars lacked a background in economics, especially since the US law and economics movement had not gained much of a foothold in British law schools at the time. In consequence, there was little overlap between what were effectively two separate policy debates, and there was a lack of either a rigorous analytical framework or of comparative studies of regulatory arrangements elsewhere in the world that could be used to assess the advantages and disadvantages of different institutional arrangements.

The question of the Bank of England's role in banking supervision rose to prominence in the early 1990s as the movement to grant the central bank monetary policy independence gathered force. Central bank independence became an important focus for British policy debates as successive monetary policy frameworks failed to match the superior inflation performance of countries with politically independent central banks, such as Germany. However, if the Bank of England were to gain independence from government in setting interest rates, this raised the question whether it should continue as the agency responsible for banking supervision.[7]

This aspect of the debate was concerned with potential conflicts between the Bank's role as a monetary policy authority and its regulatory role. The Bank had only recently seen its role evolve from its traditional, informal exercise of authority over the British banks (and other financial institutions with which it maintained a close dealing relationship, such as the Discount Houses) to one that had been formally enshrined in statute, first as a consequence of Britain's accession

---

[6] See C. A. E. Goodhart et al, *Financial Regulation: Why, How, and Where Now?* (Bank of England, 1997); and C. A. E. Goodhart, 'The Organisational Structure of Banking Supervision' (FSI Occasional Papers No 1, Financial Stability Institute, 1 November 2000), 1–46, www.bis.org/fsi/fsipapers01.pdf.

[7] See M. Taylor, 'Central Bank Independence: The Policy Background' in M. Blair (ed) *Blackstone's Guide to the Bank of England Act 1998* (Oxford University Press, 1998).

to the then European Economic Community (the *Banking Act 1979*) and then shortly afterwards by the *Banking Act 1987*. Several academic studies had argued that a central bank with supervisory responsibilities tended to err on the side of monetary laxity, perhaps to help support the institutions it supervised.[8] At the same time, it was recognised that an independent Bank of England would exercise considerable authority: the issue was whether also exercising the functions of a bank regulator would represent a step too far in the concentration of power. At the heart of this debate was whether the United Kingdom should adopt a model of an independent central bank that was also a bank regulator (the US Federal Reserve model) or of an independent central bank which had no direct supervisory responsibilities (the German Bundesbank model).

Although the Bank's senior management may have regarded relinquishing its bank supervisory responsibilities as a price worth paying to achieve monetary policy independence, its official position was to favour an arrangement closer to that of the US Federal Reserve. The Bank argued that there were close synergies between its monetary policy and banking supervision functions.[9] Notwithstanding the structural shifts that had occurred in the preceding decade, the Bank continued to argue that banks remained 'special' institutions, uniquely the source of systemic risk, with which the central bank needed to keep a close relationship given its role as the lender-of-last-resort. Nonetheless, the debate around independence did have the effect of putting the Bank of England's supervisory role under scrutiny at a time when it was already coming under criticism for its undistinguished track record as a regulatory agency (see Section 2.2.3).

The second dimension to the British debate around regulatory structure concerned the 'alphabet soup' of regulatory agencies that had been created by the *Financial Services Act 1986*. This Act introduced statute-based regulation of the securities and investments industries for the first time in Britain, with a particular focus on sales practices. However, in deference to the City of London's traditions, the advent of statute-based regulation had incorporated a large element of 'self-regulation' administered through a series of 'self-regulating organisations' (SROs). Structured around the City's past practices, rather than the direction of travel of the rapidly evolving financial system, the SROs distinguished, for example, between futures traders and dealers in securities, and between life insurance products that were sold by the insurers' own salesforces and those which were sold by independent financial advisers. The SROs were overseen by the Securities and Investments Board (SIB), a non-governmental agency exercising powers delegated to it by a government minister. To complicate matters further, the SIB created its own rulebook to which those of the SROs were expected to conform. The result was a regulatory system of considerable complexity which failed to meet the City's expectations of continuing self-regulation while falling short in its primary responsibility of protecting the consumer. Reform seemed essential, and a number of academic proposals to address the shortcomings of the existing system were forthcoming.

The radicalism of the Twin Peaks concept was that it treated these two debates not as separate but as interrelated and proposed a common solution to both in the form of an objectives-based regulatory system. The Bank of England would lose its role as a bank supervisor, but to an agency that was responsible for the prudential supervision of all systemically significant financial

---

[8] C. A. E. Goodhart and D. Schoenmaker, 'Institutional Separation between Supervisory and Monetary Agencies' (1992) 51(9/12) *Giornale degli Economisti e Annali di Economia* 353–439, 0017-0097, www.jstor.org/stable/23247860.

[9] E. A. J. George, Governor, Bank of England, The Bank of England – Objectives and Activities (Capital Market Research Institute, Frankfurt, Germany, 5 December 1994).

intermediaries rather than to a banking commission. The SROs and SIB would be replaced by a single, statutory business conduct regulator.

2.2.3 *The Politics of Regulatory Reform*

While the debate on regulatory reform rumbled on among academics and members of the policy community, there was little immediate political will to embark on a major change in the regulatory system. In the mid-1990s the British Conservative government under John Major had a narrow parliamentary majority and was absorbed by European issues (in particular the ratification of the Maastricht Treaty which laid the foundations for the European Monetary Union) and managing the fallout from a severe economic recession. These conditions ensured that there was neither the political will nor the capacity to consider a major reform to the regulatory system which had, itself, been the creation of successive Conservative governments during the previous decade.

The lack of political priority assigned to regulatory reform was buttressed by resistance to change both from senior British officials and from the regulated industry. Nowhere was this more true than the senior executives of the Bank of England. The Bank's role as the statutory regulatory authority for British banks was by no means assured. The Labour government which had enacted the 1979 *Banking Act* had considered creating a specialist banking commission separate from the central bank,[10] and the Bank's subsequent performance as a bank regulator saw it harshly criticised on at least three separate occasions within a roughly ten-year period: first, due to the failure of Johnson Matthey Bankers in 1984 (which resulted in the *Banking Act 1987*); then after the failure of the Bank of Credit and Commerce International (BCCI) in 1991;[11] and finally with the collapse of the venerable investment bank Barings Brothers in 1995.[12] The widely perceived shortcomings of the Bank of England's regulation during its early years as a statutory agency created a defensive attitude on the part of its senior management to any proposals that might result in a significant overhaul of the regulatory system.

The Bank's resistance to reform was strengthened by another consideration, namely that the United Kingdom's regulatory system was still in its infancy. Statute-based regulation had arrived comparatively late in the United Kingdom, with the banking and securities industries remaining largely free of governmental regulation until into the late 1970s and mid-1980s, respectively. Although the regulated industry remained hostile, by and large, to the statute-based regulatory framework, at the same time it had made a heavy investment in complying with the new regime. In consequence, any proposal that would result in the infant regulatory system being torn up at the roots had the potential to increase the large sunk costs that the industry already had been forced to absorb. This also made many leading figures in the financial industry question the need for further regulatory change.

Political inertia only started to be overcome in the mid-1990s when the likelihood increased that a general election, which was required to be held before May 1997, would bring about a change of government. Under the dynamic leadership of its youthful leader, Tony Blair, the Labour Party began to appear as a government-in-waiting for the first time in a decade and a half. In opposition, Labour began to show increased interest in the cause of regulatory reform,

[10] M. Moran, *The Politics of Banking: The Strange Case of Competition and Credit Control* (Macmillan, 2nd ed, 1986), 120.

[11] HM Stationary Office, 'Inquiry into the Supervision of the Bank of Credit & Commerce International' (1992).

[12] HM Stationary Office, 'Report of the Board of Banking Supervision Inquiry into the Circumstances of the Collapse of Barings' (1995).

although its willingness to consider reform was due to considerations of political tactics, in particular the stick it offered with which to beat the incumbent government, rather than abstract considerations of an evolving financial services sector. One regulatory issue that played strongly with Labour politicians was what became known as the 'pensions mis-selling scandal', the bulk of which related to transactions that had taken place in the 1980s but which did not become public until 1993. Pensions mis-selling had particular salience for Labour politicians since one of the worst affected groups had been public sector workers who had been persuaded to transfer out of their occupational (defined benefit) pension schemes into defined contribution private schemes, even though it was likely that their retirement benefits would be worse as a result.[13] In the Labour Party's account – which was partially supported by investigations by regulatory agencies – this episode pointed to a regulatory failure as the mis-selling had occurred as the result of high-pressure sales tactics by commission-hungry salespeople.[14]

While pensions mis-selling convinced Labour politicians of the need for reform at the retail, business conduct end of the market, the sequence of regulatory lapses that bedevilled the Bank of England also provided a convenient stick with which to beat both the Bank and the Conservative government, which had been largely responsible for creating Britain's system of financial regulation. In consequence of these two lines of criticism – wholesale and retail – the Labour Party was more open to proposals for radical reform of the system of regulation.

Such, then, was the situation in Britain when the Twin Peaks proposal was first made in a paper published by a London-based think tank, the Centre for the Study of Financial Innovation (CSFI), in December 1995. An earlier paper published by the CSFI in 1993 had made the case for more limited reform in the shape of an independent banking commission outside the central bank. The nominal author had been Andrew Hilton, the CSFI's founder, although it was widely known that the actual author had been a senior industry figure who wished to maintain anonymity to avoid antagonising the Bank of England. The subsequent CSFI paper, of which the present writer was the author, was entitled *Twin Peaks: A Regulatory Structure for the New Century*. It appeared some two years after the CSFI first mooted a banking commission and was much more radical in its proposals. This was partly an indication of how rapidly the debate in the United Kingdom had moved in the intervening period.

However, Twin Peaks did not win universal support. Although a few senior regulators endorsed the proposal,[15] many others were critical, most notably senior officials of the Bank of England.[16] The financial services industry also was lukewarm in its response to these ideas, reflecting the lack of appetite for further changes in a financial regulatory system that had only recently been adopted and fully implemented. The shortcomings of the existing system, especially in terms of its excessive complexity and scope for regulatory duplication and overlap, were widely acknowledged; but there was little sense of urgency or appetite to deal with these problems. Thus, by the middle of 1996 the Twin Peaks concept appeared to have been comprehensively buried: dismissed as 'excessively radical' and 'costly', it was seen as predominately an exercise in academic 'neatness and tidiness' with little chance of actually being adopted in practice. Despite a follow-up paper, *Peak Practice*, also published by the CSFI, which aimed to show how a Twin Peaks model might be created in practice by a process of evolution, the

---

[13] See, eg, 318, Parl Deb, HC (6th ser) (1998), 716, 718.

[14] M. Taylor, 'Central Bank Independence: The Policy Background' in M. Blair (ed) *Blackstone's Guide to the Financial Services & Markets Act of 2000* (Oxford University Press, 2000).

[15] See J. Treanor, 'Regulators Back Taylor's Twin Peaks Theory', *The Independent*, 29 October 1996, www.independent .co.uk/news/business/regulators-back-taylors-twin-peaks-theory-1360780.html.

[16] H. Davies, 'Financial Regulation: Why, How and By Whom' (1997) 37 *Bank of England Quarterly Bulletin* 107, 111.

concept was widely dismissed as impractical. Having at first described the CSFI's Twin Peaks paper as 'a Gower report for the 21st century', the Labour Party's spokesman on the City of London soon abandoned his initial interest in the idea.[17] Instead, the Labour Party treated the Twin Peaks debate as a useful outrider for its own more modest regulatory reform proposals, allowing it to present them as a moderate set of measures in contrast to the 'revolutionaries' advocating Twin Peaks. Going into the 1997 general election, Labour's only manifesto commitment to regulatory reform was to replace the business conduct system administered by the SIB and SROs with a statutory securities commission.[18] On other aspects of regulatory reform the Labour Party was silent.

Twin Peaks was saved from being consigned to the dustbin of impractical academic concepts by the Australian Financial System Inquiry (also known as the Wallis Committee, chaired by businessman Stan Wallis). The author met two members of the inquiry (Professors Ian Harper and Jeffrey Carmichael) during their fact-finding trip to the United Kingdom in mid-1996. They had studied the Twin Peaks paper and showed considerable interest in the potential that such a structure might have to address one of the main themes that the Wallis Committee had identified: how to design an institutional structure of regulation that would not only be effective given the current state of Australia's financial sector, but would also be robust in the face of the changes that the Committee expected to occur over the following decade. A Twin Peaks structure commended itself to the Inquiry for its adaptability to changes that it anticipated would occur as a consequence of some of its other recommendations to remove most of the remaining structural regulation in Australia's financial system. These changes were anticipated to increase overlap between the different segments of the financial industry, with increased competition between banks and non-banks, leading to a 'blurring of boundaries' in Australia's financial system similar to what the British system had been experiencing.

Twin Peaks was included as an option in the Wallis Committee's Discussion Paper published in November 1996, and then was put forward as a recommendation in its final report published in March 1997. The Australian Treasurer at the time, Peter Costello, endorsed the recommendations with respect to a Twin Peaks regulatory structure and announced that legislation would be forthcoming to adopt the Twin Peaks model in Australia, which became the first country to embrace this form of regulatory structure.

2.3 EPISODE TWO: FROM CONCEPT TO IMPLEMENTATION

Following the Australian government's endorsement of a Twin Peaks structure, legislation was introduced into parliament to give effect to the Wallis Inquiry's recommendations. The *Australian Prudential Regulation Authority Act*, with a commencement date of 1 July 1998, established the Australian Prudential Regulatory Authority (APRA) as the regulator of deposit-taking institutions, including banks, building societies and credit unions, as well as of insurance companies and large superannuation (retirement pension) funds. APRA was established as an independent agency outside the Reserve Bank of Australia (RBA), the Australian central bank. APRA's primary statutory responsibility would be as a prudential regulator that would focus on the safety and soundness of the entities it supervised. APRA was also to be responsible for dealing with institutions that were unable to meet their obligations through its administration of the

---

[17] M. O'Brien, 'Labour's Proposals for Regulation into the 21st Century' (1997) 5 *Journal of Financial Regulation and Compliance* 115, 115–17.

[18] Labour Party, 'Labour's Business Manifesto' (1997).

financial claim schemes provided for in the *Banking Act 1959* and the *Insurance Act 1973*. APRA was required to do all of this in close cooperation with the RBA, which would be available to provide liquidity support if necessary.

The Australian Securities and Investments Commission (ASIC) was established shortly after APRA as an independent statutory body. It was set up under and administers the *Australian Securities and Investments Commission Act 2001* (ASIC Act), while most of its regulatory responsibilities derive from the *Corporations Act 2001* (Corporations Act). ASIC was established as the business conduct regulator responsible for market integrity and consumer protection across the financial system in Australia. It regulates companies, financial markets, financial services organisations and market professionals. It is not a prudential supervisor. It issues guidelines, preferred practices, regulatory guidelines and codes of conduct. It also has enforcement powers.

Finally, in Australia's Twin Peaks structure the RBA retained responsibility for interest rates, financial stability and payment systems. It has oversight responsibilities for the latter that include ensuring that licensed clearance and settlement facilities for securities and derivatives conduct their affairs in a manner consistent with financial stability. To facilitate cooperation between APRA, ASIC and the RBA, Australia established the Council of Financial Regulators (CFR), It was to be chaired by the RBA Governor and attended also by a representative of the Treasury, the purpose of which was to oversee inter-agency cooperation and coordination.

However, at the time that Australia was legislating its Twin Peaks structure into existence, the UK government was striking out in a radically different direction. The May 1997 general election resulted in a Labour government with a large majority. One of its first acts was to grant monetary policy independence to the Bank of England, although the initial announcement contained no indication of whether this move had implications for the Bank's regulatory role. Only after the passage of several days did the government announce that the Bank would lose its statutory responsibility for banking supervision, and the SIB would become the nucleus of a new agency (NewRO) with responsibility for banking, securities and investment regulation. However, the boundaries of the new agency's remit were left unclear even in this follow-up statement, with no mention of the future fate of such obvious candidates for inclusion as the regulation of building societies (mutual credit institutions) and insurance companies. Only after the passage of several more days did it become clear that NewRO would subsume the responsibilities of no fewer than nine existing regulatory agencies.

I have written elsewhere about the policy process that resulted in the new government's decision to create a single regulatory agency without prior consultation. As I have argued, there is a strong case for concluding that the decision was driven by the exigencies of the legislative timetable rather than as the result of careful assessment of the relative merits of different models, although it would be surprising had Treasury officials not given some consideration to these issues and not prepared a set of proposals for consideration by the new ministers. However, once the decision was taken a process was set in train that inevitably led to the consolidation of all regulatory functions – prudential and business conduct – over all the segments of the financial industry. In the course of time, NewRO became the Financial Services Authority.

Buttressed by the size of its parliamentary majority, and representing a fresh approach after almost two decades of Conservative rule, the new government enjoyed a long honeymoon period with high approval ratings. The Conservative Party, unfamiliar with opposition after its long years in power and debilitated by its heavy election loss, appeared unsure whether or how it should attack the planned changes to the regulatory system. For a time, the Conservatives used the line of attack that the FSA would be a 'leviathan' that represented an excessive concentration of power.[19] But their criticisms failed to gain much traction and the financial services industry, keen to cultivate a good relationship with the new government, for the most part did not join in. The result was that the decision to create the FSA passed off without much overt challenge. In a little over one year, opinion in Britain had shifted from dismissing Twin Peaks as excessively radical to uncritically embracing a regulatory structure that was much more radical still.

The rationale for the creation of the FSA was constructed retrospectively.[20] A large part of the justification for the creation of a single regulator drew on arguments that had been put forward in favour of a Twin Peaks structure: the emergence of financial conglomerates and the "blurring of boundaries" between different segments of the financial sector.[21] However, as Twin Peaks represented the main rival to a single integrated regulator, and could no longer be simply dismissed as excessively radical, it was incumbent on the FSA's proponents to explain why their solution was superior. The main pillar of their case was that prudential and conduct of business regulation involved many of the same judgements and that both involved the review of issues like the adequacy of internal systems and controls.[22] Rather than having two separate sets of regulatory personnel reviewing the same issues, asking the same question, and diverting management time, it was better to have one integrated regulatory team under a single management structure. In effect, a Twin Peaks approach was criticised for wanting to perpetuate the duplication and overlap of regulatory authority and activity, which had been one of the industry's main complaints about the existing system. A single regulator would deliver regulation more efficiently and effectively than a Twin Peaks structure, leading to both higher standards of regulation and a lower regulatory burden. For a government keen to promote its market-friendly credentials, these claims were warmly received by the financial industry and its representatives.

The UK government also won support for the single regulator model from the IMF at the conclusion of its 1998 annual Article IV consultation on the economy. In the mission's concluding statement, the IMF staff observed:

> As regards other policies, the Government has reformed financial sector regulation by establishing the Financial Services Authority (FSA), an initiative that should prompt improvements. In the United Kingdom, where financial regulation has been spread thus far among nine separate bodies, the shift to a single regulator will clarify regulation and improve supervision of increasingly integrated multi-sector financial institutions. Unified supervision of complex financial groups will also strengthen the FSA's ability to regulate the City's large, internationally integrated financial market. Consumer protection, a major mandate of the FSA, should also be strengthened and become more uniform.[23]

The IMF did point to a risk regarding the separation of banking supervision from the lender-of-last-resort function and urged a combination of 'formal structures and working level relationships' to ensure the Bank and the FSA were well coordinated. However, this strong endorsement from the IMF – echoing the government's own case for a single regulator – provided important support to a project that had been announced with little of the advance preparation normally associated with an institutional change of this magnitude.

---

[19] See, eg, M. McElwee and A. Tyrie, *Leviathan at Large: The New Regulator for the Financial Markets* (Centre for Policy Studies, 2000), 1–2.
[20] C. Briault, 'The Rationale for a Single National Financial Services Regulator' (FSA, Occasional Paper No 2, 1999), 6.
[21] HM Stationary Office, 'Financial Services and Markets Bill: A Consultation Document, Pt. 1' (2008).
[22] H. Davies and D. Green, *Global Financial Regulation: The Essential Guide* (Polity Press, 2008), 192. See also Briault (n 20) at 20.
[23] www.imf.org/en/news/articles/2015/09/28/04/52/mcs122198.

The positive reviews of the FSA continued almost up until the Global Financial Crisis. An examination of the FSA's operations by the National Audit Office (NAO), published in 2007, concluded that 'the FSA is highly regarded within the financial services industry in the UK and internationally' and that its 'risk-based approach is increasingly seen as a model to be followed by other regulators'.[24] The FSA had contributed to London's thriving position as an international financial centre, and other jurisdictions also felt that the single regulator model provided the City of London with an important source of competitive advantage. A 2007 report by McKinsey & Company on New York's future as a financial centre, commissioned by then New York Mayor Michael Bloomberg and Senator Charles Schumer, favourably contrasted the United Kingdom's principles-based regulation with that of the United States. The report concluded:

> An increasingly heavy regulatory burden and a complex, cumbersome regulatory structure with overlaps at the state and national levels is causing an increasing number of businesses to conduct more and more transactions outside the country. For many executives, London has a better regulatory model: it is easier to conduct business there, there is a more open dialogue with practitioners, and the market benefits from high-level, principles-based standards set by a single regulator for all financial markets.[25]

There was certainly little sign in this report of a regulatory model that was badly failing or of the tensions to come.

In the ten years following its adoption in the United Kingdom, the 'FSA model', as it came to be known, was widely emulated elsewhere in the world. A range of countries followed the United Kingdom in embracing the single-regulator model, including Austria, Belgium, Colombia, Germany, Ireland, Japan, Korea and Latvia.[26] Indonesia also announced plans to create a unified regulatory agency outside the central bank as part of its IMF programme, although actual implementation did not occur for a further ten years.

Against this background, the adoption of the Twin Peaks model in the Netherlands appeared positively quixotic. In 2002 the Dutch government bucked the international trend towards establishing a single unified regulatory agency by adopting a Twin Peaks model of supervision.[27] This differed from the Australian approach in that the Netherlands central bank (DNB) was assigned the role of the prudential supervisor of all financial institutions rather than an independent agency as had been the case with APRA. However, the role of ASIC was mirrored by the Authority for Financial Markets (AFM), which was responsible for conduct-of-business supervision. Although announced in 2002, the full transition to the Twin Peaks structure was only completed in 2007, with the introduction of the *Act for Financial Supervision* (AFS). With some irony, the Dutch Twin Peaks model was only formally completed a matter of months before the Global Financial Crisis, which would upend assumptions about the alleged superiority of the single-regulator model.

---

[24] National Audit Office, *The Financial Services Authority – A Review under Section 12 of the Financial Services and Markets Act 2000* (April 2007), 5.

[25] McKinsey & Company, *Sustaining New York's and the US' Global Financial Services Leadership* (January 2007), 80.

[26] See Appendix 1 of Marc Quintyn, Silvia Ramirez and Michael W. Taylor, 'The Fear of Freedom: Politicians and the Independence and Accountability of Financial Sector Supervisors' (series edited by International Monetary Fund, in IMF Working Paper, No WP/07/25, Monetary and Capital Markets Department, International Monetary Fund, Washington, DC, February 2007), 1–50, www.imf.org/external/pubs/ft/wp/2007/wp0725.pdf).

[27] Kingdom of the Netherlands, 'Netherlands: Publication of Financial Sector Assessment Program Documentation: Technical Note on Financial Sector Supervision: The Twin Peaks Model' (IMF Country Report No 11/208, July 2011).

2.4 EPISODE 3: TWIN PEAKS AFTER THE GLOBAL FINANCIAL CRISIS

The Global Financial Crisis brought to prominence three aspects of regulation that challenged the alleged superiority of the single-regulator model over a Twin Peaks structure.

The first concerned crisis management arrangements – in effect, how regulatory institutions cooperate and coordinate across their different mandates during periods of financial instability, including bank failures. Crisis management involves many issues, but ultimately resolves to questions of the liquidity and solvency of financial institutions. A bank facing liquidity difficulties is likely to need emergency liquidity assistance (ELA) from the central bank. For the central bank to lend in this situation it will generally need access to supervisory data to reduce the likelihood that it is lending to an insolvent financial institution and to identify good-quality assets that can be used to collateralise the ELA. Where a financial institution is clearly insolvent, the authorities need to determine whether to liquidate the institution (imposing losses on creditors, including potentially depositors) or to provide fresh equity. Generally, the main source of an equity injection would be the finance ministry (Treasury), although in some jurisdictions the deposit insurance scheme may also have the mandate to provide an equity injection as part of a 'lower cost' resolution. In this case also, access to supervisory data to assess an institution's viability and capital needs is essential. So is coordination with the central bank, which is likely to be an important creditor due to earlier ELA lending, and which might be required to provide additional liquidity support as part of a resolution package.

For at least two decades prior to the formation of the FSA, the United Kingdom had not experienced any episodes of serious financial distress. This may have bred a degree of complacency about the need for adequate crisis management preparedness and planning, and it also meant that when the FSA was established such matters were treated as an afterthought. Although a Tripartite Memorandum of Understanding (MoU) was drawn up between the Treasury, the Bank of England and the FSA to govern crisis management,[28] the arrangements envisaged were rarely tested in practice and the Joint Crisis Management Committee established by the MoU rarely met.[29] The institutional distance that had grown between the Bank and the FSA – a risk alluded to in the IMF's warnings a decade earlier – undermined the timeliness of information-sharing, and the effectiveness of a coordinated response across the two agencies. The arrangements also assumed that the Treasury would be the glue that held this system together, thus potentially involving it in the minutiae of crisis management decision-making – including in the central bank's ELA decisions – a role that it was ill-equipped to perform and that hampered the ability to reach quick decisions in an environment where time was of the essence. In consequence, when the financial crisis struck, the United Kingdom was ill-prepared to deal with the fallout, and reliance on the Tripartite Memorandum of Understanding resulted in a situation in which, as a Committee of the House of Lords put it with some exasperation, 'no one was in charge' of managing the crisis.[30] The creation of a single regulator, especially given its separateness from the central bank, and the failure to develop and test mechanisms to ensure institutional cooperation, were widely viewed as having contributed to this state of affairs.[31]

A second issue brought to prominence by the financial crisis was the importance of *macroprudential* regulation. Although the first identified use of the term 'macroprudential' was in the

---

[28] G. Brown et al, *Memorandum of Understanding between HM Treasury, the Bank of England and the Financial Services Authority* (2009).
[29] House of Commons Treasury Committee, 'The Run on the Rocks' (2007–8), HC 5-1, at 107.
[30] 737 Parl Deb, HL (7th ser) (2012) 13 (UK).
[31] J. Sassoon, 'Britain Deserves Better Financial Regulation', *Financial Times*, 8 March 2009.

late 1970s in internal documents of the Basel Committee, the term had not entered into public discourse by the time of the mid-1990s debate on Twin Peaks in the United Kingdom. Even among the regulatory community, most discussion of prudential regulation was still conceptualised in terms of ensuring the safety and soundness of individual financial institutions. The current meaning of macroprudential regulation as regulation focused on ensuring the stability of the financial system as a whole through guarding against correlated failures by financial institutions only entered into public discourse following the Asian Financial Crises of 1997–98. It was brought to prominence in a speech given in 2000 by the then General Manager of the Bank for International Settlements, Andrew Crockett.[32]

Interest in macroprudential regulation spiked after the Global Financial Crisis, which many leading commentators attributed to the build-up of financial imbalances whose sudden unwinding turned out to have severe macroeconomic consequences. Reflecting on the experience of the crisis, the then Chairman of the FSA, Lord Adair Turner, commented: 'we need a new set of macro-prudential policy tools which will enable the authorities more directly to influence the supply of credit [...]. These tools are needed because credit/asset price cycles can be key drivers of macroeconomic volatility and potential financial instability'.[33]

However, developing a new toolkit was one thing. Who should be entitled to use it was another. The disparate range of policy tools that were encompassed by the 'macroprudential' rubric ranged from those that were clearly within the scope of bank supervisors – countercyclical capital requirements for banks and loan-to-value ratios on mortgage lending – to those which were clearly not, such as taxes on real estate purchases that would be varied according to the state of the economic cycle. As Crockett had observed a decade earlier, 'addressing financial stability is a multifaceted task. It involves a number of authorities with different perspectives and responsibilities. Indeed, some of the policy levers lie in the hands of authorities whose main task is not to address financial stability at all, even though their tools and decisions can have a significant impact on the process.'[34]

A consensus emerged that the majority of these tools should be handled by the central bank owing to their overlap with its monetary policy function. Tools like countercyclical capital buffers provided an extra dimension to taming the credit cycle, which the central bank had traditionally sought to do through its control over short-term interest rates.[35] However, if the central bank was to be the custodian of the new toolbox, this raised a further question about its relationship with the bank supervisory agency, especially if the latter was an independent agency. There was no question that the new macroprudential tools and traditional safety and soundness regulation (now renamed as 'microprudential') overlapped to a considerable extent. This raised an important institutional question about how to ensure there was coordination between the two.[36]

In addition to these two major consequences of the Global Financial Crisis, a final point emerged in the post-mortems specifically concerning the FSA's performance as a regulator in the years immediately prior to the crisis. In contrast to the plaudits the FSA had won from the

---

[32] Andrew Crockett, 'Marrying the Micro- and Macro-Prudential Dimensions of Financial Stability' (Basel, 21 September 2000), www.bis.org/review/rr000921b.pdf.

[33] 'What Do Banks Do, What Should They Do, and What Public Policies Are Needed to Ensure Best Results for the Real Economy?' (Speech at Cass Business School, London, 17 March 2010).

[34] Crockett (n 32).

[35] See Bank of England, 'Instruments of Macroprudential Policy' (2011), www.bankofengland.co.uk/paper/2011/instruments-of-macroprudential-policy f.

[36] See in particular E. Nier, L. I. Jácome, J. Oskinski and P. Madrid, 'Institutional Models for Macroprudential Policy' (IMF Staff Discussion Notes 11/18, International Monetary Fund, 2011).

NAO and the Bloomberg–Schumer report, in the cold light of day following the crisis it became apparent that the FSA had prioritised business-conduct regulation over prudential regulation. In consequence, it had missed several important warning signals of the build-up of financial risks and of excessive risk-taking at individual financial institutions, such as Northern Rock and the Royal Bank of Scotland. Hence, in contrast to the claims of the FSA's supporters that there were substantial synergies between prudential and conduct-of-business regulation, the limits of these synergies had been starkly revealed by the crisis. While some of the relevant supervisory judgements did overlap, especially on such matters as internal controls and the probity of management, the FSA's focus on conduct-of-business matters had led to the relative neglect of prudential regulation. Moreover, as the House of Lords Select Committee on Economic Affairs observed,

> There is also a cultural difference between conduct-of-business and prudential supervision. Conduct-of-business supervision is often performed by lawyers. Prudential supervision is largely an economic activity, particularly at the macro level. It seems likely that either a lawyerly or an economic approach would dominate in a supervisory body that performed both prudential and conduct-of-business supervision, and that this dominance would reduce the effectiveness of the dominated half of the organisation.[37]

The Committee went on to observe that the function that received the greatest emphasis would be that having the greatest political saliency: this means that in normal times, when bank failures are rare, consumer protection regulation is likely to be the main focus of agency attention. This appeared to have been the case with the FSA's pre-crisis allocation of resources, recognition of which helped to undermine the case for a single financial regulator.[38]

These three issues – crisis management, macroprudential regulation and ensuring adequate prioritisation of microprudential regulation even in periods of relative stability – added up to a powerful challenge to the single-regulator model. In consequence, the Twin Peaks structure of regulation received fresh impetus, albeit with the important modification that the prudential 'peak' was now increasingly identified with an autonomous unit within the central bank rather than a stand-alone agency.[39] Thus, when the UK government dismantled the FSA and created a Prudential Regulatory Authority and a Financial Conduct Authority from its remains, the former was housed in the Bank of England. In this sense the Dutch model of Twin Peaks seemed to have greater international transferability than the Australian one. The perceived superiority of the Dutch model of Twin Peaks was due to the close coordination that it permitted in both crisis management and macroprudential regulation, given the prudential regulator's status as a unit within the central bank. These considerations also raised the question as to whether Australia should follow suit, although the Murray Inquiry, the successor to the Wallis Inquiry, which reported in 2014, ultimately concluded that there was no case for changing Australia's 'relatively informal and decentralised' approach to financial stability.

2.5 CONCLUSION

In the course of its relatively short life, the Twin Peaks concept has experienced three distinct episodes. In the first, it was a primarily academic concept, addressed mainly to parochial concerns relating to the United Kingdom's regulatory system, but drawing on trends and

---

[37] Select Committee on Economic Affairs, Banking Supervision and Regulation, 2008–09, HL 101-1, at 33.
[38] Ibid.
[39] M. Jacomb, *Re-Empower the Bank of England* (Centre for Policy Studies, 2009), 2–4.

developments in the financial sector that were of universal significance. In the second episode, Twin Peaks was largely side-lined by the fashionable single-regulator structure, which achieved international prominence as a result of UK regulatory reform that was more radical than even the Twin Peaks proposal had envisaged. To the extent that Twin Peaks was not completely eclipsed during this episode was mainly due to its adoption in Australia and the Netherlands, two countries that had seemingly bucked the trend towards fully integrated regulatory agencies. In the most recent episode, the Global Financial Crisis exposed the shortcomings of the single-regulator model and revived interest in Twin Peaks as offering an institutional solution to several major issues that the crisis had posed for the institutional structure of regulation. The decision by the Chinese government in March 2018 to merge the banking and insurance regulators, while keeping the securities regulator as a separate agency, represents a further step towards the adoption of a Twin Peaks structure in a major economy.[40]

It is doubtful that the third episode of Twin Peaks will be the last. The demands on institutional structures of regulation continue to evolve, as does the industry that regulatory agencies are charged with overseeing. It would be foolhardy to assert that the superiority of a Twin Peaks structure will always be apparent, and that at some future point there will not be further pressure for change. Nonetheless, one of the virtues of a Twin Peaks structure is that its inherent flexibility provides the ability for regulation to adapt as the underlying conditions of the financial system change. The third episode of Twin Peaks may have a longer run than the first two.

---

[40] www.bloomberg.com/news/articles/2018-03-13/china-announces-plan-to-merge-banking-insurance-regulators.

3

Reflections on Twenty Years of Regulation under Twin Peaks

Jeffrey Carmichael

3.1 INTRODUCTION

The 'Twin Peaks' model of financial regulation refers to an architecture in which separate agencies take most, if not all, responsibility respectively for prudential and conduct regulation within a country.[1] The distinctive characteristic of Twin Peaks is that it allocates regulatory responsibilities by type of regulation rather than the traditional approach of allocating by institutional groupings.

Twin Peaks emerged as an architecture of interest during the late 1990s, a period in which many countries reorganised their regulatory responsibilities, primarily with a view to amalgamating agencies. The motivation for amalgamation was driven in some countries by a desire to better supervise financial conglomerates; in others, it was driven by a desire to make more efficient use of scarce regulatory resources. While the most common form of regulatory amalgamation in the 1990s and early 2000s was a unified agency, which took responsibility for both prudential and conduct regulation for all financial institutions, the Twin Peaks model was established in both Australia (in 1998) and the Netherlands (in 2002). More recently, it was introduced in the United Kingdom (2012) and in South Africa (2017).

On cursory inspection of the evidence, the Twin Peaks architecture has performed creditably, without any suggestion that it offers a fail-safe approach to financial regulation. With two decades having passed since it was first introduced, it is timely to reflect on its strengths and weaknesses. Importantly, the Global Financial Crisis of 2008 (GFC) generated much introspection about the effectiveness of financial regulation, some of which has implications for regulatory architecture.

This chapter reviews the philosophy that underpinned the introduction of Twin Peaks in Australia in 1998, the lessons that have been learned from the Australian experience and from the Global Financial Crisis, and the way in which those experiences might have shaped the recommendations of the Australian Financial System Inquiry (which recommended Twin Peaks) were it being undertaken today rather than two decades ago.

---

[1] The term 'Twin Peaks' is usually attributed to Michael Taylor – *Peak Practice: How to Reform the UK's Regulatory System* (Centre for Study of Financial Innovation, October 1996) – and the first country to implement this architecture was Australia, in 1998, following the 'Wallis Inquiry' – see Financial System Inquiry (Final Report, 1996), https://treasury.gov.au/publication/p1996-fsi-fr).

3.2 THE TWIN PEAKS PHILOSOPHY AS APPLIED IN AUSTRALIA CIRCA 1998

In June 1996, the Australian government formed a Committee of Inquiry to provide a stocktake of the results arising from the widespread deregulation of the Australian financial system since the early 1980s, consider the forces driving further change and make recommendations on the nature of the regulatory arrangements needed to ensure an efficient, responsive, competitive and flexible financial system.

The Financial System Inquiry, or 'Wallis Inquiry' as it became known, delivered its Final Report in March 1997.[2] The cornerstone of the 115 recommendations in the Final Report was a proposal to take a completely new approach to Australia's regulatory architecture by establishing the stand-alone Australian Prudential Regulation Authority (APRA) to regulate and supervise Australian financial institutions for safety and soundness (prudence), and to expand the remit of the then Australian Securities Commission (ASC) to regulate conduct of business by Australian financial institutions; the expanded ASC was rebadged as the Australian Securities and Investment Commission (ASIC).[3] APRA was established and ASIC expanded on 1 July 1998.

In its report, the Wallis Committee set out a comprehensive view of the role of financial regulation, as well as its view of the fundamental difference between prudential and conduct regulation. In summary, the committee argued that

- The case for any form of financial regulation should be grounded in market failure. Importantly, the cost of regulatory intervention (both direct costs, in terms of agency budgets, and indirect costs, in terms of costs borne by industry, including any impact on innovation and competition) should be lower than the cost to society of correcting a market failure.
- In the case of prudential regulation, market failure was argued to be the informational asymmetry between buyers and sellers of certain financial products. Noting that financial products are essentially conditional promises (i.e., promises to make certain payments under certain conditions), the committee noted that asymmetry is exacerbated, and therefore the case for regulatory intervention is increased, in cases where a promise is difficult to keep, where a promise is difficult for the customer to understand and where the failure of an institution to deliver on its promises could cause social damage. With these considerations in mind, the committee argued that banking, insurance and pension products were strong candidates for prudential supervision.[4] Importantly, the committee argued that, in balancing the costs and benefits of correcting market failure, not all financial promises in the Australian financial system warranted prudential regulation.
- The case for conduct regulation was seen to be much broader. Market failure associated with misconduct arises from the fact that financial products and services are more exposed to potential misrepresentation and fraud than most non-financial products and services. The additional risks associated with financial products and services arise from the complexity of the products and services, and from the fact that the gap between what is promised and what is delivered is often not revealed until the passage of considerable

---

[2] See *Australian Financial System Inquiry Final Report* (n 2).

[3] This chapter will often use the terms 'regulation' and 'supervision' interchangeably. Where a distinction is warranted, the chapter will follow the widely acknowledged World Bank convention of using 'regulation' to refer to the laws, rules and standards that shape financial sector behaviour and 'supervision' to refer to the oversight (for example, through off-site analysis and on-site inspections) of those laws, rules and standards.

[4] The pension industry in Australia is referred to as the superannuation industry. To avoid confusion, the term 'pension' will generally be used in this chapter.

time. Conduct regulation extends to ensuring that the way in which financial products and services are marketed and traded (including through organised exchanges) is fair and efficient.

While the justifications for prudential and conduct regulation arise from distinctly different market failures, the case for assigning them to separate regulatory agencies required further justification. The Wallis Committee provided five reasons for its proposed separation.

First, the regulatory objectives for prudence and conduct may conflict. For example, there may be situations in which maintaining safety and soundness is better achieved by dealing with a troubled institution on an orderly and confidential basis, so as to avoid panic or market disruption, whereas preserving the integrity of a market demands that prudential problems be disclosed, so that investors and creditors can make fully informed decisions. While allocating the objectives to separate agencies does not remove the need to resolve such conflicts, it ensures that they are not resolved internally within a single agency that may not give sufficient priority to one or the other objective.

Second, the regulatory focuses of conduct and prudence are quite different. While conduct regulators focus on how institutions interact with their clients and other stakeholders (disclosures, fairness, suitability of products and so on), prudential regulators focus on the way in which institutions are run (ensuring that they are safe and sound, and generally are able to meet their promises). This distinction has generated the common analogy that conduct regulators are like police (investigating and prosecuting those who break the rules), whereas prudential regulators are more like doctors (concerned about preventing problems in the first place and maintaining the long-term health of their patients).[5] It has also generated the view that conduct regulators are primarily 'regulators' while prudential regulators are primarily 'supervisors'.[6]

Third, the range of institutions that each of these two (conduct regulators and prudential regulators) regulates is quite different. Whereas prudential regulation tends to be focused on balance sheet quality and risk management of a narrow group of institutions such as banks, insurance companies and similar institutions that provide socially sensitive financial products, conduct regulation typically applies to every institution that provides a financial service. Put differently, the Wallis Committee saw financial products (and therefore financial product providers) as the main province of prudential regulators, whereas the main province of conduct regulators was financial services (and therefore financial service providers), although the committee acknowledged that conduct regulators also had a (possibly minor) role to play in regulating financial products.

Fourth, the regulatory cultures appropriate to the two are quite different. Whereas conduct regulators typically have an extremely high ratio of lawyers on their staff (reflecting their police-like role), prudential regulators are typically staffed by economists, accountants, actuaries and other finance specialists (reflecting their doctor-like role). These different professional backgrounds in a single regulator can lead to cultural clashes, or result in the dominance of one culture to the detriment of the other.

Finally, the tools used by the two types of regulator tend to be quite different. Prudential regulators focus on prevention by setting requirements for capital adequacy; good governance; fitness and propriety; and risk management. These are designed to minimise the probability of institutional failure. Conduct regulators, in seeking to limit the scope for misrepresentation and

---

[5] This distinction, which is widely quoted, is usually attributed to Sir Howard Davies, inaugural chair of the UK Financial Services Authority.

[6] Using the World Bank distinction between the two concepts as noted in n 3.

fraud, focus primarily on enforcing disclosure of relevant, accurate information to strengthen market efficiency and fairness. In addition to regulating disclosures, conduct regulators may set rules for conducting business with integrity, skill and due care; managing conflicts of interest; suitability of products and services; eliminating inappropriate sales techniques; ensuring privacy and confidentiality; protecting customers against fraud; and preventing market manipulation. Collectively, these conduct rules are designed to encourage fairness and efficiency of markets and of transactions between providers of financial products and services and their customers.

While all these considerations contributed to the Wallis Committee's recommendation to establish Twin Peaks, the primary driver behind the recommendation was the first – that is to say, singleness of focus. One of the most difficult challenges faced by any regulator is the requirement to balance potentially competing objectives. This conflict is a feature of the institutional model of regulation where, for example, a banking regulator is typically required to regulate for both prudence and conduct.[7] The Wallis Committee proposed that each regulator should have a single objective, with the tools, resources and accountability for meeting its objective.

It is important to note that the Wallis Committee extended this logic beyond prudential and conduct regulation. In applying the logic of regulating to counteract market failure, the committee identified four main sources of market failure: imprudence; misconduct; anticompetitive behaviour; and systemic instability. The Wallis Committee recommendations effectively established a 'Quadruple Peaks' model for Australia with[8]

- APRA responsible for prudential regulation;
- ASIC responsible for conduct regulation;
- the Australian Competition and Consumer Commission (ACCC) responsible for competition regulation; and
- the Reserve Bank of Australia (RBA) responsible for systemic stability regulation.

Whereas APRA and ASIC were limited in scope to providers of financial products and services, ACCC has a competition remit that extends to non-financial products and services.

3.3 IMPLEMENTING TWIN PEAKS IN AUSTRALIA: LESSONS FROM THE PAST TWO DECADES

The Wallis Committee's recommendation to establish Twin Peaks required a major reorganisation of the existing regulatory architecture in Australia. In total, nine existing agencies were combined to form APRA. At APRA's core were the banking regulators previously located in the RBA, and the insurance and pension regulators previously located in the Insurance and Superannuation Commission (ISC). The additional agencies were largely state-based regulators that had been established in the early 1990s to regulate and supervise credit unions and building societies (and subsequently friendly societies); these state-based agencies had been welded into a federal structure under the Australian Financial Institutions Commission, which was a creation of the state treasurers.

---

[7] There is a reasonable case to be made that combining prudential and conduct roles in many banking regulatory agencies around the world, and their clear emphasis on prudence, was instrumental in the almost complete neglect of misconduct by banks prior to the end of the 1900s.

[8] While the full Australian regulatory architecture is more accurately described as a quadruple peaks model, to avoid confusion it will be referred to throughout this chapter as Twin Peaks, as it contains the two fundamental pillars (prudential and conduct) that characterise Twin Peaks.

Twin Peaks also required a major shift in the approaches of APRA and ASIC to their respective areas of responsibility. Central to the new approach was a desire to harmonise the regulatory requirements applying to different institutions that offered essentially the same financial products or services. Thus, for example, deposit-takers were expected to meet essentially the same prudential requirements, regardless of whether they did so under the corporate form of a bank, a credit union or a building society. Similarly, firms offering financial advice to retail investors were expected to meet essentially the same regulatory requirements, regardless of whether they did so under the corporate form of a bank, an insurance company, a pension fund or an independent advisory company.

The lessons from this period are divided into five topics: the high points; the low points; the importance of the legal framework; regulatory boundaries; and institutional transition.

3.3.1 *High Points*

The prudential high point of the first two decades under Twin Peaks was unquestionably the way in which the Australian financial system weathered the 2008 GFC. While there were arguably many contributing factors, including the abundance of local mortgage-backed lending opportunities (which reduced the incentive for Australian banks to seek higher-yielding investments abroad) and the introduction by the Australian government of a comprehensive deposit guarantee (which mitigated the pressure for wholesale deposit funds to flow out of Australia following the GFC), the strength of the Australian prudential framework provided a strong foundation for Australian banks to withstand the global fallout that followed the failure of Lehman Brothers. Two key policy initiatives played a role in that strength.

First, whereas some countries had actively competed for international business by lowering prudential standards within the tolerances allowed by the Basel Committee, APRA had remained conservative in setting capital requirements. Studies at the time suggested that Australian banks were required to hold up to double the regulatory capital of banks in other countries with similar balance sheet structures.[9] Recognition of the fact, post-2008, that 'country discretions' under the Basel Accord permitted such wide variations, while still essentially being classed as compliant with the accord, played a significant role in the approach of the Basel Committee to recasting the post-GFC international capital requirements with a much tighter range of country discretions.

Second, prior to 2008, APRA had actively sought to close the gaps in regulation between banks and insurers. Those same regulatory gaps had allowed insurers, such as AIG in the United States, to take on risks that were too costly for banks in terms of the regulatory capital charges that applied at the time. APRA believed that, to the extent banks and insurers were members of the same financial conglomerate, taking advantage of such regulatory arbitrages would weaken the entire group.

Both initiatives can be attributed at least partly to the introduction of Twin Peaks. The first reflected APRA's single objective – prudential soundness. Free from the conflicts that can be

---

[9] These studies were conducted by individual banks and industry and are not publicly available. While there may have been a 'self-serving' bias in the studies, the basis of their argument was fundamentally sound. There is no dispute that APRA was among the toughest, if not the toughest, of the major financial system regulators in terms of its use of discretions permitted by the Basel Committee. For example, at the time of the GFC, APRA had imposed materially more restrictive rules than other major jurisdictions with respect to the treatment and definition of Residual Tier 1 capital instruments, the capital treatment of value of in-force business of insurance subsidiaries of banks and the deduction of net tangible assets of non-consolidated, non-banking subsidiaries.

raised by additional objectives such as competition, growth of the financial sector and good conduct, APRA was able to implement prudential standards that it regarded as appropriate to its single objective. The second, harmonisation of regulatory standards across industry sectors, was an explicit objective of the Australian regulatory system following the introduction of Twin Peaks. The need for harmonisation, and the importance of eliminating regulatory arbitrage between regulatory regimes, was a particular focus of the Wallis Report and reflects the philosophy of regulating by type of risk rather than type of institution.

In terms of conduct regulation, the high point was the introduction of the Australian Financial Services Licence (AFSL). The AFSL is a single-licence regime under which any entity wishing to provide a financial service in Australia must have a licence from ASIC to do so. While an applicant may elect to apply for different categories of licence within the AFSL, the principle remains that any entity providing a financial service in Australia without an AFSL is unlicensed and therefore in breach of the law. Australia was the first country to introduce such a universal licensing regime and it has proved to be one of the most powerful tools available to a conduct regulator.

The strengths of the universal licensing regime include that it

- identifies all providers of financial services to the regulator;[10]
- similarly identifies legitimate providers to customers (who can request to see the provider's licence before transacting); and
- establishes a franchise value for such providers (a value which can be taken away if the provider engages in misconduct or breaches the regulator's rules).

The role of licensing under Twin Peaks is not widely understood. It has sometimes been implemented as a dual-licensing requirement and sometimes as a single licence with 'two keys'. As applied in Australia, the approach is dual licensing. For any prudentially regulated institution to operate in the Australian market it must first obtain both a prudential licence from APRA and an AFSL from ASIC. The prudential licence is effectively a licence to operate as a product provider (for example, a licence to operate as a deposit taker or a life insurer). The conduct licence appropriate to the particular product provider is the AFSL that enables the institution to service (for example, market and distribute) the particular products(s) that APRA is licensing it to provide. To operate within the law, the institution (if subject to prudential regulation) requires both licences.

While this may appear to create a conflict for prudentially regulated institutions, in that the two regulators' licensing requirements could conflict, in Australia ASIC has made clear that, where the requirements overlap, it accepts APRA's approval in satisfying the relevant ASIC requirements.[11] This avoids unnecessary duplication, conflict and cost.

3.3.2 *Low Points*

The prudential low point for APRA was the loss of the HIH Insurance group in early 2001. While HIH was the largest insurance failure in Australia's history, it accounted for less than 0.05 per

---

[10] The converse situation was experienced by APRA, which, prior to changes to the *Superannuation Industry (Supervision) Act* in 2004, did not have the legal power to license trustees of pension funds, despite having regulatory responsibilities for several thousand such funds. Prior to receiving this licensing power, APRA was not even aware of the existence of some of the funds for which it had regulatory responsibilities.

[11] See, for example, the guidance on risk management systems and resources in ASIC's *Regulatory Guide 104: Licensing: Meeting the General Requirements* (2015).

cent of the industry assets supervised by APRA and less than 0.05 per cent of the number of institutions supervised by APRA. It was nevertheless a major failure by Australian historical standards, and a 'moment of truth' for APRA in several ways.[12]

The Report of the Royal Commission, headed by Justice Owen, that followed HIH's failure made clear that APRA 'did not cause or contribute to the collapse of HIH. Nor could it have taken steps to prevent the failure of the company'. Justice Owen nevertheless made clear that, in his opinion, 'APRA did not give sufficient consideration to the consequences of reform and full integration' and 'APRA's regulation of the HIH group was inadequate and not of the standard to be expected of a regulator in APRA's position'.[13]

HIH was a turning point for APRA. Following its digestion of the volumes of information produced for the Royal Commission, as well as an extensive internal review, APRA emerged a much stronger regulator.[14] Ironically, the loss of HIH, while damaging to APRA's reputation at the time, laid the groundwork for the stronger prudential platform that helped the Australian financial system weather the GFC seven years later.

Two particular lessons that emerged from the failure of HIH were linked to the establishment of Twin Peaks: the first was the level of management distraction that can occur during a period of institutional change; the second was the potential loss of critical skills and institutional memory during change. While neither of these is unique to Twin Peaks, the extent of change involved with a move to Twin Peaks is likely to amplify both. These two lessons are discussed further in Section 3.3.5 on institutional transition.

In contrast with APRA's experience, the low points of conduct regulation over the past two decades are less clear-cut. Arguably, the low points have been the repeated breaches of conduct rules by the major Australian banks, the criticism aimed at ASIC by Parliamentary Committees and, more recently, a Royal Commission over these breaches. These Parliamentary and Royal Commission hearings have served to highlight ASIC's limitations in terms of powers and resources.

In response to concerns about ASIC's effectiveness, in 2015 the Australian government established an expert panel to review ASIC's capabilities. While the panel found that many of ASIC's regulatory capabilities are in line with global best practice, it recognised that ASIC needed additional support if it is to deliver on its mandate.[15] Key areas in which the panel found ASIC to be below international best practice were:

- its governance model and leadership processes;
- its information technology, data infrastructure and management information systems; and
- its approach to stakeholder management.

The panel noted that there was a material expectations gap between what ASIC could reasonably deliver and what its external stakeholders expected. The panel observed that ASIC needed to become less reactive and more strategic in its approach to regulation. Importantly, the panel

---

[12] Much has been written about the failure of HIH and there is little to be gained from repeating the details here. See, for example, HIH Royal Commission, *The Failure of HIH Insurance* (Commonwealth of Australia, 2003), and Mark Westfield, *HIH: The Inside Story of Australia's Biggest Corporate Collapse* (John Wiley & Sons Australia, 2003).

[13] See Report of the Royal Commission into HIH Insurance (No 32, 13 May 2003), ss 24.1.12 and 24.1.13.

[14] The internal review was conducted by John Palmer, previously Superintendent of Financial Institutions in Canada. His report (J. Palmer, *Review of the Role Played by the Australian Prudential Regulation Authority and the Insurance and Superannuation Commission in the Collapse of the HIH Group of Companies* (2001)) was included in the documents published by the Royal Commission into HIH Insurance (n 13).

[15] The ASIC Capability Review Panel, *Fit for the Future: A Capability Review of the Australian Securities and Investments Commission*, A Report to Government (Australian Government Printer, 2015).

found that ASIC's public sector culture was a constraining factor in terms of innovation and strategic thinking. External constraints, including the need for stronger enforcement powers and a perceived funding shortage, were also identified.

The panel made thirty-four recommendations to strengthen ASIC's capabilities going forward. These were in addition to recommendations made by the 2014 Financial System Inquiry to strengthen ASIC's capabilities.[16] In response, the government committed to progressing the recommendations relating to its role, including committing additional funds to strengthen ASIC's surveillance, data analytics and enforcement capabilities. Central to the reforms are the introduction of an industry-funded approach to ASIC's budgetary needs, which was adopted in 2017. This has brought ASIC's resourcing into line with APRA's industry-funded model.[17]

3.3.3 *The Importance of the Legal Framework*

The way in which APRA was established highlighted a weakness that took several years to be fully recognised. The *APRA Act 1998* was a minimalist piece of legislation that did little more than establish APRA as a regulatory agency. Notwithstanding some vague general powers in the Act, APRA continued to draw its regulatory and supervisory powers from the underlying industry sector laws.

Given that one of the primary motivations for creating APRA was to establish regulatory neutrality by harmonising the regulatory approach to different institutions offering essentially the same financial products, this reliance on existing sectoral laws was a material handicap.

The law covering the general insurance industry provides possibly the starkest example of the limitations of this approach. Within months of establishing APRA, it became clear that the *Insurance Act 1973* was outdated and incapable of supporting APRA's objective of harmonising its regulatory approach. The Act provided APRA with no basis for applying a risk-based prudential framework. Instead, it provided a legalistic approach to assessing solvency, and very limited powers of intervention. During the course of 2000, APRA began seeking revisions to the Act to bring it more into line with the legal framework for regulating deposit-taking institutions such as banks. APRA gained little political support for the reforms, and even less from the industry. It was not until after HIH failed and the Royal Commission highlighted weaknesses in the *Insurance Act* that the momentum for change shifted, and the necessary reforms were implemented.

A second weakness in the legal framework under which APRA operated was the wide range of differences and inconsistencies in the sectoral laws. Under some laws, APRA had the power to issue prudential standards; under others it did not. Under some laws, APRA could issue prudential instruments without the need for parliamentary approval; under others it could not. In no case could APRA issue a common standard covering the prudentially regulated industry as a whole. These differences hampered APRA's ability to harmonise its approach to regulation and supervision.

Many, but not all, of these weaknesses have since been rectified through revisions to the sectoral laws. On reflection, it would have been much simpler to have consolidated at least the regulatory components of each of the sectoral laws (for example, objectives, powers,

---

[16] See *Financial System Inquiry: Final Report* (Australian Government Printer, 2014).

[17] Despite the Wallis Committee's recommendation to introduce industry funding as a way of removing regulation (for both APRA and ASIC) from political budgetary pressures, it has been disappointing to see APRA forced to accept funding cuts linked to the government's budget, even though such cuts have no impact on the government's budget position.

instruments) into the *APRA Act*. The South African *Financial Sector Regulation Act 2017* takes this latter approach and should provide the two Twin Peaks agencies with a much stronger legal foundation for harmonising their approaches to regulating and supervising both prudence and conduct across different industry sectors in South Africa.

For example, the *Financial Sector Regulation Act* has the following features:

- Chapter 7 of the Act establishes the range of regulatory instruments that may be issued by the Prudential Authority (PA) and the Financial Sector Conduct Authority (FSCA). Part 1 of the chapter establishes a common process for making regulatory instruments, including a mandatory public consultation process and the requirement to submit proposed instruments to parliament before they become effective. Part 2 establishes the range of matters and financial institutions for which the PA and FSCA may issue standards. For example, under section 105(3) the PA may, without limitation, issue prudential standards on the following:[18]

  (a) financial soundness requirements, including requirements in relation to capital adequacy, minimum liquidity and minimum asset quality;

  (b) matters on which a regulatory instrument may be made by the PA in terms of a specific financial sector law (for example, the Insurance Act);

  (c) matters that may in terms of any other provision of the Act be regulated by prudential standards, including matters related to the preservation of systemic stability, if so directed by the South African Reserve Bank; and

  (d) any other matter that is appropriate and necessary for achieving any of the PA's aims.

Similarly, under section 106, the FSCA may, without limitation, issue conduct standards on the following:

(a) efficiency and integrity requirements for financial markets;

(b) measures to combat abusive practices;

(c) requirements for the fair treatment of financial customers, including in relation to

  i the design and suitability of financial products and financial services;

  ii the promotion, marketing and distribution of, and advice in relation to, those products and services;

  iii the resolution of complaints and disputes concerning those products and services, including redress;

  iv the disclosure of information to financial customers; and

  v principles, guiding processes and procedures for the refusal, withdrawal or closure of a financial product or a financial service by a financial institution in respect of one or more financial customers, including

    - disclosures to be made to the financial customer; and

    - reporting of any refusal, withdrawal or closure to a financial sector regulator;

(d) any other matter that is appropriate and necessary for achieving any of the FSCA's aims.

- Chapter 9 of the Act provides the PA and FSCA with common powers to gather information from regulated institutions (and in some cases more broadly), to carry out on-site inspections and to conduct investigations of suspected wrongdoing.

---

[18] The examples below are summaries of the relevant sections of the Act and do not cover the full range of powers and constraints imposed. For a comprehensive understanding of the relevant sections, see South Africa's *Financial Sector Regulation Act 2017*.

- Chapter 10 of the Act provides the PA and FSCA with broad-ranging enforcement powers, including the power to issue directives, remove persons from key positions, enter into enforceable undertakings, debar certain individuals and impose administrative penalties.

The key feature of these provisions in the South African Act is that they have broad application. While the powers vary between the two Twin Peaks agencies, each has the capacity to apply its powers to all institutions within its regulatory mandate. This approach is strengthened by section 9 of the Act, which makes it clear that, in the event of an inconsistency between the Act and the underlying sectoral laws, the provisions in the Act prevail.

ASIC has similarly struggled for effectiveness under inadequate laws. In ASIC's case, the primary law under which it operates is the *Australian Corporations Act 2001*. The ASIC Review Panel and the 2014 Financial Sector Inquiry noted that the Act is excessively complex and lacking in certain critical enforcement powers. In its response to the panel's report, the Australian government committed to implement the recommendations to

- provide ASIC with a product intervention power to enable ASIC to respond to market problems in a flexible, timely, effective and targeted way;
- introduce product distribution obligations for industry to foster a more customer-focused culture;
- review ASIC's enforcement regime, including penalties, to ensure that it effectively deters misconduct; and
- strengthen consumer protections in the ePayments Code, which regulates consumer electronic payments and includes a number of consumer protections, to ensure that it keeps pace with emerging technologies.

3.3.4 *Regulatory Boundaries*

While the boundaries between prudential and conduct regulation may have appeared conceptually clear to the Wallis Committee, in practice they are far from clear. For example, both APRA and ASIC set requirements on disclosure of information; both agencies impose requirements on governance arrangements; and both agencies impose similar, although not identical, requirements with respect to financial strength and risk management, as part of the licensing requirements for financial institutions. In addition, there are many other less significant ways in which the requirements of the two agencies overlap.

Wherever there are boundary overlaps, there is potential for conflict between regulators and for industry confusion. Establishing the boundaries between prudential and conduct regulation requires both an understanding of the different objectives of the agencies and a high level of inter-agency cooperation (and a measure of common sense).

The key to resolving boundary issues under Twin Peaks is recognising that there are certain situations in which one or the other regulator has clear authority. For example, in the early days of Twin Peaks in Australia, a situation arose in which APRA directed a regulated institution to raise additional capital. Historical practice in such situations, at least in Australia, would have been for the institution to raise the capital without revealing to the market that the regulator was requiring the capital raising to address prudential concerns. ASIC, however, observed that APRA's direction to raise capital was relevant information for the market in pricing the capital raising. Under Twin Peaks, it was clear that ASIC's position should prevail, since market disclosure was ASIC's regulatory responsibility under its conduct mandate.

The idea of a clear hierarchy of responsibility for certain decisions was central to the thinking of the Wallis Committee in proposing Twin Peaks. In the committee's view of the world, if a decision were needed on a matter of conduct, ASIC should prevail; if the matter were primarily prudential, APRA should prevail; if the matter were primarily about competition, the ACCC should prevail; and if the matter were primarily about systemic stability, the RBA should prevail.

In some situations, however, the hierarchy of responsibility can be less clear-cut. For example, to be granted an AFSL from ASIC, the applicant must demonstrate minimum levels of financial soundness, risk management and other skills. If the same institution is simultaneously applying for a licence from APRA, for example to operate as a bank, it must meet very different standards with respect to these same requirements. As noted earlier, rather than duplicate and create potential conflict, ASIC has issued guidance that makes it clear that meeting APRA's licensing standards on certain matters (such as financial soundness and risk management skills) automatic-ally satisfies ASIC's requirements on the same matters. In issuing that guidance, ASIC recog-nised that APRA's requirements for a prudential licence are almost certain to be more onerous than its own requirements for an AFSL.

The extent of the overlap and the need for cooperation in Australia has increased with the introduction of the Bank Executive Accountability Regime (BEAR), which is similar in many respects to the United Kingdom's Senior Manager Regime. The announcement of APRA's BEAR regime evoked an inevitable response from industry about the potential for overlap between APRA and ASIC. The key element is that APRA registers accountable persons (APs). The definition of APs includes a prescriptive list (including certain board members and senior officers), plus individuals who have significant influence over conduct and behaviour, and whose actions could pose risks to the business and its customers. All APs need to be registered with APRA prior to appointment. APRA's expectations of APs are quite extensive (including ensuring that activities for which they are responsible are effectively controlled and comply with regulatory requirements and standards, and that any delegations are appropriate and discharged effectively). BEAR also gives APRA broad powers to direct banks to review and adjust remuner-ation policies and practices. Importantly, BEAR provides APRA with strong enforcement powers, including civil penalties and the right to disqualify APs. While BEAR has been interpreted by some as a simple extension of APRA's existing fit and proper regime, it has been interpreted by others as a shift to a more regulatory (as opposed to supervisory) model, with an ASIC-like focus on enforcement and penalties.

The overlap between prudential and conduct regulation in Australia has been further extended by the introduction of product design and distribution obligations on the part of product issuers and distributors and the conferral of product intervention powers on ASIC.[19]

The Wallis Committee assumed that there would be a high level of cooperation between the regulatory agencies and that common sense would prevail in resolving overlaps. In general, this has been the case in Australia, but cooperation and common sense should never be taken for granted. Humans are inherently territorial, and history is replete with situations in which self-interest has dominated common sense, with less than ideal consequences.[20]

---

[19] See further in Chapter 5

[20] In Australia, the Council of Financial Regulators provides a regular forum for sharing information and coordinating actions among the major financial regulatory agencies, and the Commonwealth Treasury. The council proved to be very effective during the crisis of 2008. Importantly, formal coordination mechanisms in the form of committees and joint activities are integrated at a number of levels throughout the agencies.

3.3.5 *Institutional Transition*

While the move to Twin Peaks in Australia was no different in many respects from the numerous regulatory reorganisations that have taken place across the globe, it highlighted the risks that can be associated with institutional transition. In Australia, the creation of APRA involved the amalgamation of nine separate agencies. Only the creation of the FSA in the United Kingdom, at around the same time, had involved such a major disruption to staff and established regulatory relations. Two particular lessons stood out from APRA's experience.

First, institutional transition is distracting for staff. While the priority for any regulatory agency must always be on meeting its statutory mandate, organisational and managerial issues inevitably distract from the agency's day-to-day activities. In times of institutional transition, these distractions are heightened, especially where multiple predecessor agencies are being combined. In such cases, the focus of senior staff is likely to be materially distracted by issues such as deciding the organisational structure of the new agency, determining the speed at which to move to the new structure, assessing the skill base of the combined predecessor agencies, defining the target culture of the new agency, and so on.

The challenges raised by such transitional issues for APRA were highlighted by Justice Owen in his Report on the HIH Inquiry. In that report he made the following observations:[21]

- The shift of ISC resources to Sydney created a 'significant logistical distraction to senior management'.
- 'At the same time as there were shortages in skills and staff in the front-line supervisory positions, APRA's senior executives had little time to involve themselves in these tasks. Executive management devoted considerable time to building infrastructure for APRA; effecting the transfer of legislative functions, personnel, and financial resources to APRA from the former entities; developing new and integrated supervision arrangements and policies; liaising with industry to explain APRA; managing the relocation of staff and assets from Canberra to Sydney; consulting with staff and unions in respect of the transition issues; and liaising with the APRA board. This restricted the extent to which senior and more experienced judgment could be brought to bear on difficult problems encountered in supervising institutions such as HIH.'

Second, institutional transition is likely to lead to the loss of key staff and institutional memory. In APRA's case, the absorption of the former ISC, which was located in Canberra, into APRA, which was located in Sydney, inevitably resulted in a loss of experienced staff due to their unwillingness to change location.[22] The loss of institutional knowledge and experience could have been damaging to the effectiveness of the new agency, until such time as these could be rebuilt. Again, this challenge was highlighted by Justice Owen, who made the following observations in his HIH Final Report:

- 'APRA conceded the move to full integration and the relocation to Sydney had the consequence that its personnel charged with the responsibility of supervising HIH during

---

[21] The quotes in this section are all from s 24.16 of the HIH Royal Commission Report (n 13).

[22] At the same time that many senior staff were accepting redundancies following the creation of APRA, the agency experienced ongoing problems in attracting and keeping professional people in its supervisory divisions (particularly staff with general insurance experience). Overall, the rate of staff turnover was quite high in the first years of APRA's existence. Whereas in July 1999, 89 per cent of APRA staff were from its predecessor organisations, the figure was 55 per cent some nineteen months later. Some 288 former ISC staff left the organisation in the first two and a half years of APRA's existence. See the HIH Royal Commission Report (n 13).

the critical period from the beginning of 2000 until 15 March 2001 had little knowledge or experience of general insurance, or of the HIH group and the history of ISC supervision of HIH and FAI.'

- 'At the same time that APRA was managing fundamental change, fewer people and resources were made available to it compared to its various Commonwealth and state predecessors.'

While the risks and challenges posed by institutional transition are real, they should not be used as reasons for avoiding architectural change if the case for change is otherwise sound. The lessons from the establishment of APRA are that the risks need to be managed. The following guidelines draw on APRA's experiences:

1 While there is never an ideal time for institutional change, implementing change at a time when the risk level in the industry is relatively benign is likely to minimise the risk of regulatory issues being overlooked due to distraction from business-as-usual activities.
2 It may help reduce the risks associated with distraction if additional resources, dedicated to and experienced with institutional change, can be made available to assist with the establishment of the new agency.
3 It may be helpful to put in place mechanisms to minimise the loss of institutional memory and critical skills. This could include offering retention bonuses and other retention incentives for key staff. It should also include in-depth recording of the regulatory history of individual institutions, as well as the historical regulatory approach to the relevant industry sectors. More generally, the potential for losing staff increases directly with the level of uncertainty associated with change. Uncertainty, in turn, increases directly with the length of time it takes to effect change (including passing legislation) and with lack of communication. It is essential to manage uncertainty through regular communication and reassurance to staff members about their futures in the new agency.

3.4 LESSONS FROM THE GFC

The GFC was a watershed in financial regulation, in that it brought into question the effectiveness of the entire global approach to regulating financial products and services. This is not the place to conduct a comprehensive review of the lessons from the GFC. Rather, this section will focus on the lessons most relevant to regulatory architecture.

It is useful at this point to recall the view of prudential and conduct regulation as posited by the Wallis Committee (see Table 3.1).

TABLE 3.1. *Wallis Committee: distinctions between prudential and conduct regulation.*

Prudential regulation	Conduct regulation
• Inward looking (focused on the health of the regulated institution)	• Outward looking (focused on the regulated institution's treatment of its customers and stakeholders)
• Proactive and preventative (doctors)	• Reactive and enforcement-oriented (police-like)
• Primarily supervisory	• Primarily regulatory (with a heavy focus on disclosure)
• Narrow in focus (covering only a small number of institutional groups)	• Broad in focus (covering all financial product and service providers)
• Focused primarily on financial products	• Focused primarily on financial services
• Finance and audit culture	• Legal culture

While these distinctions are something of a caricature, they were arguably a reasonable representation of global regulatory thinking at the time Australia implemented Twin Peaks. The GFC brought some of these distinctions into question, without necessarily undermining the Twin Peak architecture which, in the case of Australia at least, was seen as a factor that helped Australia survive the GFC with minimal damage.

The following sub-sections address the main challenges arising from the GFC to the Wallis Committee's 1997 view of the regulatory landscape.

3.4.1 *Conduct Regulation Requires More than Just Disclosure*

The Wallis Committee saw high-quality disclosure as the backbone of good conduct regulation. Many of the recommendations of the Wallis Report revolved around the nature and extent of disclosure. The emphasis on disclosure was consistent with the committee's view that conduct regulation should not be inherently supervisory. It reflected the committee's belief that provision of financial services essentially involves matters between 'consenting adults' and thus, provided the necessary information is disclosed, there is no case for overly intrusive regulatory intervention.

The GFC challenged this notion. While inadequate disclosure was a characteristic of most sub-prime mortgage securities and their variants in the period leading up to the GFC, the reality is that many of the securities offered in this period were fundamentally unsuitable for most purposes. That many of these securities were sold to retail and small-business customers highlighted the possibility that a much broader range of financial products (that is to say, beyond conventional banking, insurance and pension products) required regulatory oversight. Importantly, the type of regulatory oversight required went far beyond disclosure.

Following the GFC, the focus of conduct regulation shifted beyond disclosure, to include product suitability and treating customers fairly.[23] Importantly, this period saw a change in the way conduct regulators viewed financial products. Prior to the GFC, most conduct regulators saw their responsibility with respect to financial products as limited to the quality of product disclosure at the point of sale. Following the GFC, conduct regulators expanded their role with respect to financial products to include the entire product life cycle.

The GFC also shifted the focus of conduct regulators away from regulating organised markets towards retail provision of financial products and services.

While this evolution brought conduct regulators further into the grey area between prudential and conduct regulators, it did not fundamentally challenge the Twin Peaks architecture.

3.4.2 *Conduct Regulation Should Be More Proactive than We Thought*

As noted above, prior to the GFC conduct regulation was regarded as primarily reactive, focused on enforcing breaches of the rules, rather than being preventative.

Reflections on the GFC found conduct regulators to have been deficient in not detecting the toxic nature of many financial products being marketed in large quantities during the early 2000s. Consistent with the shift in focus from product disclosure to product suitability, following the GFC, conduct regulators worldwide have attempted to become more preventative by

---

[23] The 'treating customers fairly' regime in the United Kingdom predated the GFC. However, following the GFC, interest in this approach quickly spread to other countries.

increasing their supervisory activities, with thematic reviews and a greater use of on-site inspec-tions (as distinct from investigations, which typically only follow suspicion of wrongdoing).

It goes without saying that a preventative approach to conduct regulation requires a much greater use of supervisory activities to detect potential problems before they become breaches, or at least before they become endemic. In the Australian context, ASIC has found itself in the invidious position of being under pressure from parliament and the media to be increasingly proactive at the same time that its resources are being reduced. That situation is only now being remedied by the commitment of additional resources. Some of those additional resources are being targeted at making greater use of technology to help close the gap between conduct regulatory capacity and community expectations. So-called RegTech (that is to say, the use of technology, including cognitive tools to assist both industry and regulators to address regulatory compliance) has the potential to completely transform the way conduct regulators (and pruden-tial regulators to a lesser extent) conduct their oversight in coming years. That transformation is, nevertheless, likely to be half a decade or more away.

While this shift of conduct regulators into the supervisory area has further exacerbated the grey area between prudential and conduct regulators, again it does not fundamentally challenge the Twin Peaks architecture; it has led to changes in regulatory methodology rather than in regulatory objectives.

3.4.3 *Prudential Regulation Should Be Broader than We Thought*

At the time Twin Peaks was implemented in Australia, the Wallis Committee argued that, on cost–benefit grounds, prudential regulation should be limited to institutions that offered deposit products, insurance products and pension products. The GFC introduced two additional categories of institutions as candidates for prudential oversight: financial market infrastructures (FMIs), such as exchanges and clearing houses, and shadow banks.

The importance of prudential oversight of FMIs was highlighted during the GFC by the global exposure of the international financial system to exchange-traded financial products, including derivative products. More importantly, the GFC highlighted the even greater expos-ure of the international financial system to derivative products, traded over-the-counter (OTC). Whereas systemic exposure to exchange-traded derivatives was mitigated in large part by the practice of posting margins to cover mark-to-market losses on positions, managing the bilateral risks associated with OTC derivative positions was left largely to individual counterparties. The material use of OTC derivatives in the packaging and repackaging of sub-prime securities in the period leading up to the GFC added significantly to systemic risks at the time, as well as to the complexity of assessing the flow-on risks of allowing institutions to fail.

Subsequent to the GFC there has been a global push by the G20 countries to force settlement of OTC derivative products, where possible, onto organised markets.[24] In some respects this has simply shifted risk from global banks to the FMIs that operate organised markets. While these FMIs have well-established mechanisms to deal with market disruption, they are far from failsafe mechanisms.[25] Risk concentration in these previously unregulated financial institutions high-lighted the need to extend prudential oversight to include them. While this is still an evolving

---

[24] Where OTC derivatives have not been suitable for clearing and settling within an organised market structure, the Basel Committee has introduced alternative counterparty credit requirements to mitigate the risks of unchecked exposures.

[25] These mechanisms typically include some form of 'socialising' the losses by sharing them among member institutions.

area, many countries now extend their prudential frameworks to include organised exchanges, clearing houses and other FMIs.

Shadow banking refers to unregulated financial institutions that provide bank-like products. The concept of shadow banking predates the GFC by many years and was seen as a possible response to regulation, with the shadow institutions arbitraging the regulatory framework by organising themselves in legal forms that escaped the regulatory net. The GFC highlighted the risks posed by this sector. In the United States, in particular, non-bank lenders were central to the growth of the mortgage industry and non-bank institutions were central to the packaging of mortgage-backed securities.

Following the GFC, the concept of shadow banking has been broadened to include not just banking products but also other types of financial products. The motivation for being classified as part of the shadow sector remained, however, very much grounded in evading regulation, either fully or in part, by arbitraging outdated definitions of regulated institutions based on institutional types.

The shadow banking sector is estimated to currently represent assets of around 23 per cent of the total asset base of the whole financial sector. In March 2017, the Basel Committee on Banking Supervision published a draft framework for regulating the shadow banking sector. The focus of the framework is to mitigate the systemic risks arising from the interaction of this sector with the regulated sector. The application of regulations to this sector globally is still, however, a work in progress.

A particular area of concern among regulators is the role being played by technology (commonly known as FinTech) in the provision of financial services by unregulated entities. At the more established end of the spectrum, telecommunications companies and supermarkets have made inroads into payments, and the distribution of credit and insurance products. More recently, the emergence of cryptocurrencies and their underlying blockchain platforms have provided an alternative to long-established regulated payments, clearing and settlement systems. Peer-to-peer lending and crowd-funding systems have made inroads into providing credit and capital to small and medium-sized businesses. These disruptive technologies offer the prospect of considerably lower transactions costs for distributing financial products and services. At the same time, they have challenged regulators in terms of both how to assess the risks involved and how to regulate providers that often transcend not only traditional product and service definitions but also national boundaries.

One of the strengths of the Twins Peaks architecture, at least as implemented in Australia, is that it focuses less on defining regulated institutions based on institutional types and more on the products and services offered. Thus, for example, APRA licenses deposit-taking, rather than banks. While the coverage of Twin Peaks requires constant monitoring, the ability of shadow institutions to escape regulation by selecting a particular corporate form has been materially diminished. However, given that APRA regulates deposit-taking, but not credit provision, Australia has not been insulated against the growth of shadow banking in credit.[26]

Regulation in Australia is also no less challenged by FinTech disruption than is regulation in other countries. It will be interesting to reflect in another decade on whether Twin Peaks provides a superior architecture for addressing disruptive technologies. In part that may be determined by the willingness of the Twin Peaks regulators to use the flexibility, given to them under their framework.

---

[26] A report into global trends in shadow banking by the Financial Services Board in May 2017 noted that lending by other financial institutions in Australia was growing at around 10 per cent per annum.

3.4.4 *Systemic Stability Is More Complex than We Thought*

As noted earlier, the Wallis Committee viewed Australia's financial regulatory architecture as having four regulatory peaks. While the creation of the prudential and conduct peaks was the centrepiece of the new architecture, the recognition of a systemic stability peak was just as important, even though the committee did not recommend any material change to the architecture at the time to address systemic stability. The potential flaw was not in failing to identify the need for a systemic stability peak, but in underestimating its importance.

The GFC changed fundamentally the way in which regulators worldwide viewed the sources of systemic instability. Importantly, whereas the Wallis Committee viewed safety and soundness of individual financial institutions as a building block for systemic stability, post-GFC thinking has focused on the potential for systemic instability to arise, even when individual financial institutions appear to be otherwise sound. This externality arises from the interconnectedness of financial institutions, the opacity of the interconnections and the role that financial institutions can play in supporting financial bubbles.[27]

A part of the post-GFC focus on systemic stability was popularisation of the term 'macroprudential' policy (to distinguish it from conventional 'microprudential' policy, which is aimed at the safety and soundness of individual institutions).[28] Underlying macroprudential policy is the idea that conventional microprudential tools may be adjusted to address emerging systemic risks (for example, by restricting credit to certain sectors). Since the renewed interest in macroprudential policy has not introduced any additional regulatory tools, the relevant tools will simply be referred to in this chapter as 'prudential' tools (capital adequacy, leverage ratios, risk management requirements and so on).

Not only has the macroprudential focus not provided any new tools, it is debatable whether the idea of adjusting microprudential settings to help meet macroprudential objectives involves any fundamentally new insights. In the Australian context, APRA has argued that macroprudential supervision is 'something that the prudential regulator already undertakes'.[29] APRA has also pointed to historical periods prior to the GFC in which prudential policy was used to address systemic concerns. While the debate about the semantics of the term 'macroprudential' may be light-hearted, beneath it lies a more serious debate about how the use of prudential tools for systemic purposes should be governed.

On the matter of governance, the world appears to fall into three main camps:[30]

- The first, into which the Australian Twin Peaks regulators fall, regards both the decision to use prudential tools to address systemic issues and the implementation of those tools as a matter strictly for the prudential regulator. While APRA is not opposed to using its prudential toolkit in this way, in the event the RBA (or Treasury) believes more aggressive settings are warranted it is up to them to convince APRA to adjust them. The Australian regulators emphasise that this clear delineation of responsibility works because there is a history of full cooperation between the regulators of the different peaks.

---

[27] Interconnectedness extends beyond domestic financial systems and, indeed, beyond the banking system.

[28] An entertaining history of the term 'macroprudential' can be found in P. Clement, 'The Term "Macroprudential": Origins and Evolution' (March 2010) BIS *Quarterly Review* 59.

[29] C. Littrell, 'Macro Prudence and Macro-prudential Supervision' (speech to 3rd Annual Risk Day Conference, Macquarie University Centre for Financial Risk, Sydney, 2013).

[30] See Chapter 24.

- The second, into which the UK and South African regulators fall, regards the decision to use prudential tools to address systemic issues as belonging to a separate systemic regulator or decision-making body. However, once the decision has been made, the execution of the policy is the province of the prudential regulator. This approach imposes a hierarchy on regulatory objectives in which systemic stability is seen as a higher order than safety and soundness of individual institutions.[31] This approach, arguably, implies less confidence on the part of lawmakers that the regulatory peaks will cooperate. Interestingly, in both the United Kingdom and South Africa the prudential regulator resides within the central bank, unlike Australia, where the agencies are separate.[32]
- The third, into which a number of countries fall, considers that not only the decision to use prudential tools but also the implementation of those tools should reside with the central bank rather than the prudential agency. In some cases, this has resulted in central banks retaining an on-site supervisory capacity, despite responsibility for prudential regulation having been transferred to a separate prudential agency.

While the dynamics between macroprudential and microprudential policy will take more time to resolve fully, the third approach identified above is clearly contrary to the philosophy underlying Twin Peaks. Whether the governance of regulatory tools for macro and micro purposes should reside in the central bank or rely on cooperation between the agencies with responsibility for systemic and prudential regulation may well be decided by reference to whether the agencies are separated or the latter is embedded in the former. Where the prudential regulatory authority is embedded in the central bank there is an implicit hierarchy of Peaks. In such cases, it makes some sense to impose the same hierarchy on the governance of prudential tools for systemic purposes.

3.5 REFLECTING ON THE LESSONS

The Wallis Committee's recommendation to implement a Twin Peaks regulatory architecture some twenty years ago was seen at the time as both bold and risky. Many opponents of the proposed sweeping changes argued that the existing system was not broken and did not need fixing. Despite the resistance, the government at the time moved swiftly to implement the new architecture, and it has stayed largely intact since. The interesting question after twenty years of experience with Twin Peaks, including living through the most dramatic and disruptive international financial crisis for three-quarters of a century, is whether the Wallis Committee, if sitting today, would recommend differently.

Without canvassing each member of the committee, the answer to this question must be treated as speculative at best. However, an objective assessment of experience suggests that the fundamental Twin Peaks philosophy would likely still remain, as would the core features of the recommended architecture.

The lessons from experience are nonetheless relevant to any country considering such a reform, and would undoubtedly shape many of the supporting recommendations if they were being made today:

---

[31] For example, s 30 of the South African *Financial Sector Regulation Act 2017* gives the South African Reserve Bank clear power to direct the Prudential Authority to issue prudential standards or directives on specified matters for systemically important financial institutions.

[32] See Chapter 4.

- There is little doubt that the committee would recognise the regulatory world as more complex than it believed it to be twenty years ago. In particular, the assumed clear boundaries between prudential and conduct regulation have proved to be anything but clear. While this has required a high level of cooperation between the Peaks to resolve areas of overlap, that cooperation has been more than evident in Australia. It is also clear with hindsight that both prudential and conduct regulation today are both broader and more challenging than the committee believed it to be twenty years ago. As noted above, these 'realities' may have changed the demands on regulators and regulatory resources, but they have not damaged the integrity of the Twin Peaks architecture. If anything, experience has added strength to the case for the primary pillar of the Twin Peaks recommendation, namely, singleness of focus.
- There is also little doubt that the complexities of institutional change and legal restructuring are more challenging than they were perceived to be by the committee twenty years ago. While these considerations would undoubtedly lead to some supporting recommendations relating to implementation, again they would be unlikely to impact on the underlying architectural recommendation.

The one question on which the committee would almost certainly spend much more time than it did twenty years ago is whether, in light of the upgraded importance of, and focus on, financial stability following the GFC, the prudential authority should be located within the central bank. The potential outcome from such deliberations is far from clear-cut. While the Australian regulatory system has arguably flourished under an architecture in which the prudential, conduct and systemic regulators are separate and equal, it has done so largely because of a commitment by all the regulators to cooperation. If that commitment is lost at some point in the future, it would not be surprising if there were calls to embed APRA within the RBA and to impose a hierarchy in which systemic stability sits above the Twin Peaks of prudence and conduct. Hopefully, such a day will not arise.

In conclusion, it is important to note that no regulatory architecture is perfect and no architecture is likely to be optimal under all circumstances; architecture is not an end in itself. A good architecture does not guarantee good regulation; more than anything else good regulation requires good-quality regulators. A strong architecture is one that supports good regulators by establishing clarity of objectives, minimising conflicts, empowering the regulators to act and doing as much as possible to facilitate a common approach to risk across the financial sector. While the Twin Peaks architecture provides such support, it is a necessary, but not sufficient, condition for good regulation.

4

Twin Peaks and Central Banks

Economics, Political Economy and Comparative Analysis

Donato Masciandaro and Davide Romelli

4.1 INTRODUCTION

The Global Financial Crisis (GFC) highlighted the importance of establishing prudential architectures to address problems of financial stability. Among the different supervisory regimes, the Twin Peaks model (TPM) has attracted an increasing degree of attention.[1]

One of the fundamental issues in implementing the Twin Peaks regime is deciding where the prudential supervisor should be housed, given that so far three options have been explored: namely, the prudential supervisor could be outside the central bank, or be a subsidiary of the central bank, or be completely inside the central bank.[2] In other words, from the point of view of economics, the key question is to determine central bank involvement in the Twin Peaks model; the more the central bank is involved, the more it is likely to become – de jure or de facto – the lead supervisor.

Such involvement deserves particular attention. In general, central banks can be part of the prudential settings, but their role is far from being homogeneous across countries, reflecting the fact that, according to economic theory, there are pros and cons in extending central bank influence to prudential supervision. The issue is then genuinely both theoretical and institutional, and it is even more relevant in studying the Twin Peaks model.

The aim of this chapter is twofold: first, it offers a systematic review of the economics and politics of central bank involvement as prudential supervisor in a Twin Peaks regime, framing it in the overall discussion concerning the evolution of the central bank role after the GFC. The analysis will highlight that the traditional economic debate on the pros and cons of central bank involvement in supervision remains inconclusive.

Consequently, it will be shown that it is more fruitful to focus attention on the political cost and benefit analysis, given that it is the politicians in charge who decide, from time to time and country by country, the shape of the supervisory regime. The direction of such an influence should not be taken for granted.

Secondly, the chapter discusses the results that have already been obtained in exploring the drivers that can explain the recent reforms in central bank involvement in supervision and focuses attention on the central bank position in those countries that have already adopted the Twin Peaks model. The goal is to better understand how the central bank role in the monetary

---

[1] A. Godwin, T. Howse and I. Ramsay, 'A Jurisdictional Comparison of the Twin Peaks Model of Financial Regulation' (2016) *Journal of Banking Regulation*, doi:10.1057/s41261-016-0005-0.
[2] Ibid.

policy area has been associated with central bank involvement to date as prudential supervisor in a Twin Peaks regime.

The remainder of the chapter is structured as follows. Section 4.2 reviews the economics of central bank involvement in supervision, highlighting the arguments in favour of (*insourcing view*) and against (*outsourcing view*) a deeper role of the central bank as prudential supervisor when a Twin Peaks regime is established. It concludes that the optimal degree of central bank involvement will depend – from time to time and country by country – on the preferences of the national policymakers in charge. Therefore, in Section 4.3 a political economy analysis is implemented, using a simple theoretical framework that sheds light on how the insourcing view and the outsourcing view can shape the preferences of politicians, and explains the central bank's involvement as prudential supervisor in a Twin Peaks regime, including the possibility of supervisory setting inertia, i.e. the existence of frictions and lags in explaining the supervisory reforms. Taking stock of the theoretical insights – as well as recent empirical results on such issues – Section 4.4 discusses central bank involvement in supervision in five existing Twin Peaks regimes: Australia, Belgium, Netherlands, New Zealand and the United Kingdom. Section 4.5 concludes.

4.2 CENTRAL BANKING AND THE TWIN PEAKS MODEL: ECONOMICS

After the GFC, the analysis of central bank involvement as prudential supervisor in the Twin Peaks model needed to be framed as part of an overall discussion concerning the evolution of the responsibilities of central banks alongside their core role of monetary policy. In many cases, the central banks have mandates to pursue financial stability, gaining new powers and tools.

The enlargement of the central bank perimeter, however, has not been homogeneous. The expansion of goals and tools has varied across countries. At least two reasons can explain this lack of uniformity. On the one hand – as will be shown below – no theoretical consensus has been reached as to the optimal approach. On the other hand – as will be discussed in Section 4.4 – the enlargement of central bank responsibilities has happened mainly as a necessary and immediate response to the GFC. In such cases, the political urgency to implement certain policy decisions is likely to override the opportunity to find the best central bank architecture.

Without a theoretical benchmark and with the necessity of facing conventional and unconventional trade-offs between monetary and financial stability, the heterogeneous expansion of the central bank's powers reflects the difficulties in designing new interactions with different players – including politicians and other regulatory agencies – that may conflict with the core monetary policy function (in the mainstream context shaping the monetary regime, at least up to the GFC, the lender-of-last-resort function combines with the monetary role exclusively in both temporary and extraordinary times).

A discussion of such conflicts becomes relevant when the Twin Peaks model is analysed. As is well known,[3] the TPM supervises the banking and financial markets in accordance with two regulatory functions: on the one hand, market conduct and consumer protection; on the other hand, financial stability via prudential supervision. In designing the TPM, one of the crucial issues is deciding where and how the prudential supervisor should be housed.[4] Here the discussion concerning the central bank's involvement in supervision becomes relevant.

---

[3] Ibid.
[4] Ibid.

How should we approach evaluation of the central bank's role when the decision concerns the degree of its involvement in prudential supervision (hereafter 'supervision')? Drawing on recent insights from economics and political economy, the crucial question is how the location of a new policy function inside the central bank can change its effectiveness in pursuing its main function, namely the monetary policy function.

In other words, the housing of a given responsibility or function inside the central bank has to be evaluated on the basis of an overall cost and benefit analysis. This section applies that perspective in discussing the central bank's involvement in supervision in a TPM regime.

Financial liberalisation has caused monetary policy and supervision to be considered as stand-alone policy fields, in the sense that each has been assigned distinct objectives. Historically, the functions of monetary policy and lender-of-last-resort have been assigned to the central bank. Financial supervision – to the extent that there was such a function – was housed either in the central bank or in a separate institution, with some countries adopting a hybrid situation.

The separation of these policy fields led very quickly to the critical question of whether their combination in one institution could lead to conflicts of interest. This section discusses the economics of the role of central bank involvement in prudential (or micro) supervision (CBIS). The aim is to show that the most relevant contributions of this huge literature provide inconclusive recommendations.[5]

Theoretically, the central bank's involvement in pursuing banking goals can be evaluated from two different perspectives: macro-supervision and micro-supervision.

Nowadays, the central bank is generally considered to be the sole monetary authority, that is, the agent designated by society to manage liquidity in order to pursue monetary policy goals. By being sources of liquidity and lenders-of-last-resort (LLR),[6] central banks are naturally involved in preventing and managing systemic banking crises[7]

[5] For further details see D. Masciandaro and M. Quintyn, 'The Governance of Financial Supervision: Recent Developments' (2015) 29 *Journal of Economic Surveys* 1–25. See also J. E. Colliard, 'Optimal Supervisory Architecture and Financial Integration in a Banking Union' (Working Paper Series, European Central Bank, No 1786, 2015); T. M. Eisenbach, D. O. Lucca and R. M. Towsend, 'The Economics of Bank Supervision' (NBER Working Paper, No 22201, National Bureau of Economic Research, 2016).

[6] On the LLR after the GFC see D. Domanski, R. Moessner and W. Nelson, *Central Banks as Lender of Last Resort: Experiences during the 2007–2010 Crisis and Lessons for the Future* (Finance and Economics Discussion Series, Federal Reserve Board, No 110, 2014); P. Tucker, *The Lender of Last Resort and Modern Central Banking: Principles and Reconstruction* (Bank of International Settlements, 2014), 10–42; C. W. Calomiris, M. Flandreau and L. Laeven, 'Political Foundations of the Lender of Last Resort: A Global Historical Narrative' (CEPR Discussion Paper Series, No 909, 2016); M. Dobler, S. Gray, D. Murphy and B. Radzewick-Bak, 'The Lender of Last Resort Function after the Global Financial Crisis' (IMF Working Papers, No 16, 2016); and R. S. Grossman, 'Banking Crises' (CESifo Working Paper Series, No 5900, 2016).

[7] C. Goodhart and D. Schoenmaker, 'Institutional Separation between Supervisory and Monetary Agencies' in C. Goodhart (ed) *The Central Bank and the Financial System* (MIT Press, 1995); C. Goodhart and D. Schoenmaker, 'Should the Functions of Monetary Policy and Banking Supervision Be Separated?' (1995) 47 *Oxford Economic Papers* 539–60; D. Masciandaro, 'Divide et Impera: Financial Supervision Unification and Central Bank Fragmentation Effect' (2007) 23(2) *European Journal of Political Economy* 285–315; D. Lacoue-Labarthe, 'L'Évolution de la Supervision Bancaire et de la Réglementation Prudentielle' (2003) 73 *Revue d'Economie Financière* 39–63; J. C. Rochet, 'Macroeconomic Shocks and Banking Supervision' (2004) 1(1) *Journal of Financial Stability* 93–110; E. W. Nier, 'Financial Stability Frameworks and the Role of Central Banks: Lessons from the Crisis' (IMF Working Paper 09/70, 2009); A. Blinder, 'How Central Should the Central Bank Be' (2010) 48(1) *Journal of Economic Literature* 123–33; C. Goodhart, 'The Changing Role of Central Banks' (BIS Working Papers, No 326, 2010); M. Brunnermeier, A. Crockett, C. Goodhart, M. Hellwig, A. Persaud and H. Shin, 'The Fundamental Principles of Financial Regulation' (2009) *Geneva Reports on the World Economy*, No 11; C. Borio, 'Monetary and Prudential Policies at the Crossroads: New Challenges in the New Century' (BIS Working Papers, No 216, 2007); C. Borio, 'Central Banking Post-Crisis: What Compass for Uncharted Waters?' (BIS Working Papers, No 353, 2011); E. W. Nier, L. Jácome, J. Osiński and P. Madrid, 'Institutional Models for Macroprudential Policy' (IMF Staff Discussion Notes 11/18, 2011);

(macro-supervision)[8] – in advanced, emerging[9] or developing economies – in close coordination with those government agencies that are entrusted with responsibility for financial stability.[10]

But should central banks also be in charge of pursuing financial stability through prudential oversight of individual banks, i.e. micro-supervision? The question is a long-standing one. It was where the actual discussion started, long before the formal distinction was recognised between macro-supervision and micro-supervision.

On the one hand, micro-supervision is a task that historically was not always assigned to central banks.[11] Furthermore, the last two decades – known as the Age of Great Moderation[12] – were characterised by a decrease in CBIS.[13] On the other hand, in previous decades several central banks had been actively and deeply involved in pursuing tight structural control,[14] which was considered part and parcel of the overall responsibility of the central bank for the management of liquidity.

Going beyond the historical cyclical patterns and focusing on the economics of the relationship between monetary and supervision policies, it is possible to disentangle the pros (*integration view*) and cons (*separation view*) of having monetary and supervisory functions under one roof.[15] The two positions can be labelled using two other expressions: the integration perspective can be referred to as the *insourcing view*, given that the two functions – i.e. monetary and banking policies – are allocated inside the central bank, while the separation perspective can be

E. W. Nier, J. Osiński, L. Jácome and P. Madrid, 'Towards Effective Macroprudential Policy Frameworks: An Assessment of Stylized Institutional Models' (IMF Working Paper 11/250, 2011); B. Bernanke, 'The Effect of the Great Recession on Central Bank Doctrine and Practice', Board of Governors of the Federal Reserve System, 2011 (mimeo); A. Lamfalussy, 'The Future of Central Banking under Post-Crisis Mandates' (BIS Papers, No 55, 2010); C. Bean, 'Central Banking Then and Now', Sir Leslie Melville Lecture, Australian National University, Canberra, 2011 (mimeo).

[8] Gersbach claims that macroprudential supervision should be put outside the realm of central bank responsibilities in order to avoid time inconsistency in pursuing the monetary policy goals: see H. Gersbach, 'A Framework for Two Macro Policy Instruments: Money and Banking Combined' (CEPR Policy Insight, No 58, 2011).

[9] M. Kawai and P. J. Morgan, 'Central Banking for Financial Stability in Asia' (ADBI Working Paper Series, Asian Development Bank Institute, No 377, 2012).

[10] F. De Graeve, T. Kick and M. Koetter, 'Monetary Policy and Financial (In)stability: An Integrated Micro–Macro Approach' (2008) 4(3) *Journal of Financial Stability* 205–31; S. Gerlach, A. Giovannini, C. Tille and J. Vinals, 'Are the Golden Days of Banking Over? The Crisis and the Challenges' (2009) *Geneva Reports on the World Economy*, No 10; P. Angelini, S. Neri and F. Panetta, 'Monetary and Macroprudential Policies' (Working Paper Series, No 1449, European Central Bank, 2012). For a survey see S. Oosterloo and J. de Haan, 'Central Banks and Financial Stability: A Survey' (2004) 1(2) *Journal of Financial Stability* 257–73.

[11] S. Ugolini, 'What Do We Really Know about the Long Term Evolution of Central Banking?' (Norges Bank Working Paper Series, No 15, 2011).

[12] See among others Bean(n 7).

[13] D. Masciandaro and M. Quintyn, 'Reforming Financial Supervision and the Role of the Central Banks: A Review of Global Trends, Causes and Effects (1998–2008)', *CEPR Policy Insight* (Centre for Economic Policy Research, No 30, 2009); B. Eichengreen and N. Dincer, 'Who Should Supervise? The Structure of Bank Supervision and the Performance of the Financial System' (NBER Working Paper, No 17401, National Bureau of Economic Research, 2011).

[14] A. Cagliarini, C. Kent and G. Stevens, 'Fifty Years of Monetary Policy: What Have We Learned?' in C. Kent and M. Robson (eds) 50th Anniversary Symposium, Conference Volume (Reserve Bank of Australia, 2010); Goodhart (n 7); M. Bordo, 'Long Term Perspectives on Central Banking' in A. Berg et al (eds) *What Is a Useful Central Bank?* (Norges Banks Occasional Papers, No 42, 2011); G. Toniolo, 'What Is a Useful Central Bank? Lessons from Interwar Years' in A. Berg et al (eds) *What Is a Useful Central Bank?* (Norges Banks Occasional Papers, No 42, 2011).

[15] The integration vs separation approach was introduced in D. Masciandaro, 'Back to the Future? Central Banks as Prudential Supervisors in the Aftermath of the Crisis' (2012) 12(2) *European Company and Financial Law Review* 112–30. See also M. F. Hellwig, 'Financial Stability, Monetary Policy, Banking Supervision, and Central Banking' (MPI Collective Goods Preprint, No 2014/9, 2016).

TABLE 4.1. *Central bank as prudential supervisor in the Twin Peaks model: two views.*

Benefits identified by the insourcing view	Risks identified by the outsourcing view
Information gains	Moral hazard risks
Human capital gains	Uncertainty risks
	Reputational risks
	Capture risks
	Bureaucratic overpower risks

symmetrically labelled as the *outsourcing view*, given that the central bank is mainly focused on monetary policy responsibilities (Table 4.1).

The justification for the central bank's involvement in supervision or CBIS (*insourcing view*) is usually supported by arguments pertaining to the informational advantages and economies of scale that derive from bringing all functions under the umbrella of the authority in charge of managing liquidity.[16] One additional argument is that the human capital employed by central banks is presumably better equipped to manage supervisory issues.[17] Having access to all information would help central banks, which possess higher skills, to act as more effective supervisors. In other words, setting up a supervisory authority different from the central bank is not considered efficient and CBIS brings potential gains to both activities. Putting it in another way, the insourcing view stresses the information and human capital (I&HC) gains that a central bank's involvement in supervision can produce; such gains can be considered relevant in promoting the role of the central banker as prudential supervisor in a TPM regime.

At the same time, the economic literature acknowledges that central banks that are involved in supervision can produce greater policy failure costs (*outsourcing view*). In other words, limited central bank involvement is better. It is important to highlight that the risk of policy failure is endogenous with respect to the distribution of power: it exists only if the supervisor is the central bank acting as liquidity manager. The risk of policy failure can be variously motivated, shedding light on the various sources of the risk of policy failure.

First, if the supervisor can discretionally manage liquidity, the risk of moral hazard (and therefore forbearance) in banks that are supervised can increase: regulated firms know that their supervisor can bail them out[18] (*moral hazard risk*). If the supervisor were different from the liquidity manager, this source of moral hazard would not exist. The public bailout can be implemented using other procedures – such as state capital injections – but all other things being equal, the public bailout is less likely to occur if the central bank is not the supervisor.

Secondly, discretionary action by the central bank can increase uncertainty in supervised markets, as the recent on-again/off-again rescues of financial firms in the United States have

[16] See, among others, Bernanke (n 7); R. J. Herring and J. Carmassi, 'The Structure of Cross-Sector Financial Supervision' (2008) 17(1) *Financial Markets, Institutions and Instruments* 51–76; J. Klomp and J. De Haan, 'Central Bank Independence and Financial Stability' (2009) 5 *Journal of Financial Stability* 321–38; O. Blanchard, G. Dell'Ariccia and P. Mauro, 'Rethinking Macroeconomic Policy' (IMF Staff Position Note, SPN/10/03, 2010); Blinder (n 7); Lamfalussy (n 7); L. Papademos, 'Central Bank Mandates and Governance Arrangements' (BIS Papers, No 55, 2010).

[17] M. Apinis, M. Bodzioch, E. Csongradi, T. Filipova, Z. Foit, J. Kotkas, M. Porzycki and M. Vetrak, 'The Role of National Central Banks in Banking Supervision' in *Selected Central and Eastern European Countries* (Legal Working Paper Series, No 11, European Central Bank, 2010); T. Ito, 'Monetary Policy and Financial Stability: Is Inflation Targeting Passé?' (ADB Economics Working Paper Series, No 206, Asian Development Bank, Manila, 2010); Lamfalussy (n 7).

[18] Masciandaro (n 7); Lamfalussy (n 7).

demonstrated[19] (*uncertainty risk*). If the supervisor is also the liquidity manager, greater moral hazard and greater uncertainty are likely to emerge.

Thirdly, it has been said that monetary policy responsibilities can negatively affect the central bank's behaviour as supervisor,[20] given the existence of reputational risk,[21] as well as potential conflicts of interest between monetary policy and supervision management[22] (*reputational risk*).

Fourthly, the central bank can use its powers in liquidity management to please its banking constituency rather than to pursue social welfare. In this respect, the central bank can become the most dangerous case of a supervisor being captured by those being supervised, i.e. the banks,[23] given that the banking industry may be more inclined to capture supervisors that are powerful,[24] because a captured authority with additional powers yields more possibilities that benefit the banking constituency (*capture risk*).

Finally, combining banking supervision and monetary policy in the hands of the central bank can create an overly powerful bureaucracy, with the related risk of misconduct, thus raising fears of 'democratic deficit'[25] (*bureaucratic overpower risk*).

Summing up, the effectiveness of supervisory policies can be hampered if the central bank acts as supervisor, being more likely to create five different sources of risk: moral hazard, uncertainty, reputation, capture and bureaucratic (MURCB) risks. The same conclusion can be reached if we consider the integration/separation dilemma from the point of view of monetary policy.[26] Putting it differently, the outsourcing view highlights the MURCB costs that

---

[19] J. Taylor, 'Macroeconomic Lessons from the Great Deviation', 25th NBER Macro Annual Meeting, 2010 (mimeo).

[20] V. P. Ioannidou, 'Does Monetary Policy Affect the Central Bank's Role in Bank Supervision?' (2005) 14 *Journal of Financial Intermediation* 58–85.

[21] Papademos (n 16).

[22] C. Goodhart and D. Schoenmaker, 'Institutional Separation between Supervisory and Monetary Agencies' in C. Goodhart (ed) *The Central Bank and the Financial System* (MIT Press, 1995); Goodhart (n 7); Blinder (n 7); Gerlach et al (n 10); D. Masciandaro and M. Quintyn, 'Who and How: Measuring the Financial Supervision Architectures and the Role of the Central Banks' (2011) 32 *Financial Supervision Herfindahl Hirschman Index, Journal of Financial Transformation* 9–14.

[23] J. R. Barth, D. E. M. Nolle, T. Phumiwasana and G. Yago, 'A Cross Country Analysis of the Bank Supervisory Framework and Bank Performance' (2004) 12(2) *Financial Markets, Institutions & Instruments* 67–120; S. Djankov, R. La Porta, F. Lopez-de Silanes and A. Shleifer, 'The Regulation of Entry' (2002) 117(1) *Quarterly Journal of Economics* 1–37; M. Quintyn and M. Taylor, 'Regulatory and Supervisory Independence and Financial Stability' (2003) 49(2) *CESifo, Economic Studies* 259–94; P. C. Boyer and J. Ponce, 'Central Banks and Banking Supervision Reform' in S. Eijffinger and D. Masciandaro (eds) *The Handbook of Central Banking: Financial Regulation and Supervision after the Crisis* (Edward Elgar, 2011); P. C. Boyer and J. Ponce, 'Regulatory Capture and Banking Supervision Reform' (2011) 8 *Journal of Financial Stability* 206–17.

[24] Boyer and Ponce, 'Central Banks and Banking Supervision Reform' (n 23); Boyer and Ponce, 'Regulatory Capture and Banking Supervision Reform' (n 23).

[25] T. Padoa Schioppa, 'Financial Supervision: Inside or Outside the Central Banks?' in J. Kremers, D. Schoenmaker and P. Wierts (eds) *Financial Supervision in Europe* (Edward Elgar, 2003), 160–75; Masciandaro (n 7); Blinder (n 7); Y. Oritani, 'Public Governance of Central Banks: An Approach from New Institutional Economics' (BIS Working Papers, No 299, Bank for International Settlements, 2010); Goodhart (n 7); Eichengreen and Dincer (n 13).

[26] For comprehensive reviews of the literature, that consider the question also from the monetary policy effectiveness point of view, see: Goodhart and Schoenmaker (n 22); Goodhart (n 7); M. Arnone and A. Gambini, 'Architecture of Supervisory Authorities and Banking Supervision' in D. Masciandaro and M. Quintyn (eds) *Designing Financial Supervision Institutions: Independence, Accountability and Governance* (Edward Elgar, 2007), 262–308; Masciandaro (n 7); and B. Hussain, 'Integrated Financial Supervision and Its Implications for Banking Sector Stability', Stern School of Business, New York University, 2009 (mimeo). On this issue, as well as on the related consequences on central bank governance, see also: Arnone and Gambini, 'Architecture of Supervisory Authorities and Banking Supervision' (above); A. Crockett, 'Central Bank Governance under New Mandates' (BIS Papers, No 55, 2010); Papademos (n 16); L. Svensson, 'Inflation Targeting after the Financial Crisis, Challenges to Central Banking', Reserve Bank of India Conference, 2010 (mimeo); B. Aydin and E. Volkan, 'Incorporating Financial Stability in Inflation Targeting Frameworks' (IMF Working Paper 11/224, 2011); and M. Woodford, 'Inflation Targeting and Financial Stability' (NBER Working Paper Series, No 17967, National Bureau of Economic Research, 2012). For the

a central bank involvement in supervision can produce; such costs can be considered crucial in avoiding the role of the central bank as supervisor in a TPM regime.

This overview demonstrates that the debate between the insourcing and the outsourcing views remains inconclusive. There simply is no optimal solution to the CBIS debate. This conclusion is confirmed by the empirical work undertaken in this respect, although it should be said that econometric analyses of the topic are rare and of recent times.

The integration view finds empirical support in a study[27] that used the degree of compliance with Basel Core Principles to investigate the possible relationship between the compliance capacity of each country and the way these countries have organised the role of the central bank in the supervisory process. By contrast, the separation view finds support in a subsequent analysis showing that the performance of financial markets is better when supervision is delegated to an agency that is different from the central bank.[28] However, the results also offers some evidence in favour of supervisory consolidation being established within the central bank. Similarly, another analysis found that countries with deeper financial markets and those undergoing rapid financial deepening can better foster financial stability – i.e. reduce the likelihood of banking crises such as the crisis during the period 2007–12 – by having banking supervision in the central bank.[29] Yet other research has claimed that placing supervision inside or outside the central bank does not have a significant impact on the quality of supervision.[30]

A new dimension was added to the CBIS discussion when the overall architecture of supervision came under discussion, as noted in the previous section. While unified (or integrated) supervisors were recommended in some cases because of efficiency and effectiveness gains, the question as to whether the unified supervisor should be housed in the central bank remained open. The insourcing view argued that this would allow the central bank to better prevent systemic crises from arising, because the central bank would also be informed about imbalances arising in the non-bank segments of the financial sector. The outsourcing view claimed that if all supervision was placed in the hands of the central bank, the latter would then also be responsible for supervising institutions it traditionally never dealt with, as lender-of-last-resort or as monetary policy agent. So, the argument went, extending the supervisory reach of the central bank to cover these other financial institutions would put pressure on extending its lender-of-last-resort safety net as well, hence creating additional opportunities for moral hazard and reputational risk.

At the end of the day, the brief review of the literature shows that the various arguments lead to conflicting predictions in terms of what the optimal involvement of the central bank in supervision should be.

Such insights can be useful in discussing the central bank involvement in a TPM regime. No consensus has been reached on what the best degree of CBIS should be in principle, since

---

specific relationship between central bank involvement in supervision and the (internal and external) monetary regimes, see L. Dalla Pellegrina, D. Masciandaro and R. V. Pansini, 'New Advantages of Tying One's Hand: Banking Supervision, Monetary Policy and Central Bank Independence' in S. Eijffinger and D. Masciandaro (eds) *The Handbook of Central Banking, Financial Regulation and Supervision after the Crisis* (Edward Elgar, 2011), 279–315; and L. Dalla Pellegrina, D. Masciandaro and R. V. Pansini, 'Do Exchange Rate Regimes Affect the Role of Central Banks as Banking Supervisors?' (2012) 33(1) *European Journal of Law and Economics*.

[27] Arnone and Gambini (n 26).

[28] Eichengreen and Dincer (n 13).

[29] M. Melecky and A. Podpiera, 'Institutional Structures of Financial Sector Supervision, Their Drivers and Historical Benchmarks' (2013) 9 *Journal of Financial Stability* 428–44.

[30] M. Čihák and R. Podpiera, 'Experience with Integrated Supervisors: Governance and Quality of Supervision' in D. Masciandaro and M. Quintyn (eds) *Designing Financial Supervision Institutions: Independence, Accountability and Governance* (Edward Elgar, 2007), 309–41.

it is impossible to conclude that the integration view is superior to the separation view, or vice versa.

The natural conclusion is that the heterogeneous patterns of CBIS that in general are observed in reality – including the existing TPM regimes[31] – cannot be explained by the existence of a superior setting for delegating powers to central banks. Rather, the differing arguments supporting the insourcing view or the outsourcing view appear to be given variable weight by the policymakers who design and implement central bank involvement in supervision, depending on the circumstances that they face. Therefore, the attention of research has naturally shifted towards analysis of the incentives that shape the behaviour of policymakers in determining the rules governing the role of central banks as supervisor.[32]

4.3 CENTRAL BANKING AND THE TWIN PEAKS MODEL: POLITICAL ECONOMY

If we assume that the policymaker has already chosen the TPM setting, what are the drivers that shape the question of where supervision should be housed? Here we shed light on the relevance of the political preferences in determining the central bank's involvement in supervision using an optimisation framework, which seems an efficient way to take into account the abundant, consolidated and still growing literature on the topic. In doing so a political economy approach is adopted, arguing that the policymakers' actual choices relating to the central bank's role are conditional on the economic and institutional environment existing at a given time, which in turn determines the political weight attached to the pros and cons of the CBIS.

The framework is based on three hypotheses. First, gains and losses of a given central bank setting are variables computed by the incumbent policymakers, who maintain or reform the supervisory regime following their own preferences. Secondly, policymakers are predominantly politicians. As such, they are held accountable at elections for how far they have managed to please voters. All politicians are career-oriented agents, motivated by the goal of pleasing voters in order to win elections. The main difference among various types of politicians concerns which kinds of voters they wish to please in the first place. Therefore, CBIS is likely to change over time depending on political preferences, which are not automatically coincident with the social ones. Thirdly, a final step deserves particular attention: thus far, it has been assumed that cognitive or behavioural biases do not affect the relevant players. But what are the effects if cognitive or behavioural biases influence the preferences of the political actors, citizens and/or politicians? Such a perspective characterises behavioural political economy (BPE).[33] Here we study how the presence of loss-aversion among the incumbent national politicians can shape their decisions.

Consider an economy where we suppose that the citizens would like a TPM setting under which the central bank's involvement in supervision is the optimal one; that is, where the potential pros and cons in having the central banker as prudential supervisor are taken into account in a complete and systematic way.

---

[31] Godwin, Howse and Ramsay (n 1).

[32] D. Masciandaro, 'Politicians and Financial Supervision outside the Central Bank: Why Do They Do it?' (2009) 5(2) *Journal of Financial Stability* 124–47.

[33] J. Schnellenbach and C. Schubert, 'Behavioral Political Economy: A Survey' (2015) 40 *European Journal of Political Economy* 395–417.

In a democracy, citizens assign to the elected policymakers the task of designing the optimal level of CBIS – the setting that guarantees the overall TPM effectiveness. For the sake of simplicity, suppose that the elected policymakers represent both legislative and executive powers; in other words, the interests of the majority of the Parliament and of the government in charge are perfectly aligned.

The incumbent policymakers are authorised by society to determine and implement the optimal level of CBIS. Our policymaker is a politician. Let $V(t_i, \pi)$ be the utility function of the politician i:[34]

$$V(t_i, \pi) = B(t_i, \pi) - C(t_i, \pi) \tag{4.1}$$

where $B(t_i, \pi)$ and $C(t_i, \pi)$ are respectively the expected benefits and costs and π is the optimal level of CBIS. On top of that, each politician weighs benefits and costs through their personal beliefs. The individual heterogeneous preferences are summarised in parameter t, which represent the individual type and captures their degree of conservativeness, i.e. attitude to involving the central bank in supervisory functions.

Let us recall that the central bank involvement in supervision implies both expected benefits – I&HC gains – and expected costs – MURCB losses – that can be different both from time to time and country by country. Therefore, it is the politician in charge – in a given country and at a given moment – that individually attaches weighting to the pros and cons and determines the actual CBIS.

The specification of the utility function of the politician is sufficiently general to include as special cases the two different types of politician that are usually analysed in the recent economic literature: the so-called helping-hand politician and the grabbing-hand politician. The politician type depends on which players the incumbent policymakers would like to please: it is possible to assume that the policymakers wish to please the citizens (*helping-hand view*); alternatively, it can be assumed that the policymakers' aim is to please specific constituencies, i.e. the relevant lobbies (*grabbing-hand view*).[35]

Assume that in a standard way for each politician, the comparative I&HC benefits in determining the CBIS are increasing and concave at the CBIS level. In other words, the efficiency gains in involving the central banker as supervisor increase with the level of involvement but at a decreasing rate:

$$\frac{\partial B(t, \pi)}{\partial \pi} > 0, \quad \frac{\partial B^2(t, \pi)}{\partial \pi} < 0 \tag{4.2}$$

The first expression summarises the assumption that the benefits B are positively correlated with the level of CBIS π, while the second expression recalls that such benefits are at the same time decreasing. For example, regarding the informational gains that derive from bringing the supervisory functions under the central bank umbrella, assume that such gains increase with central bank involvement, but at a decreasing rate. This can also be depicted as follows:

---

[34] Such a utility function has been used in discussing monetary policy issues in Favaretto and Masciandaro and introduced in the economic policy analysis in Alesina and Passarelli: see F. Favaretto and D. Masciandaro, 'Doves, Hawks and Pigeons: Behavioural Monetary Policy and Interest Rate Inertia' (2016) 27 *Journal of Financial Stability* 50–58; A. Alesina and F. Passarelli, 'Loss Aversion in Politics' (NBER Working Paper Series, No 21077, 2015).
[35] For more details on such a perspective, see Masciandaro (n 32).

At the same time, in a symmetric and standard way, we can assume that the comparative MURCB costs in determining the CBIS are increasing and concave at the CBIS level. In other words, the effectiveness risks also increase with the role of the central bank as prudential supervisor at an increasing rate:

$$\frac{\partial C(t, \pi)}{\partial \pi} > 0 \frac{\partial C^2(t, \pi)}{\partial \pi} \geq 0 \qquad (4.3)$$

The first expression summarises the assumption that the costs C are positively correlated with the level of CBIS π, while the second expression recalls that such costs are at the same time increasing. For example, regarding the different sources of risks deriving from having the central bank act as supervisor, we can assume that such risks increase with the central bank involvement, and at an increasing rate. This can also be depicted as follows:

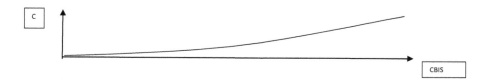

It is worth noting that the different assumption in terms of gains – which are positive but decreasing – and costs – which are negative and increasing – is the simplest way to capture the trade-off that politicians have to address and fix in order to identify from time to time the optimal degree of central bank involvement. With other assumptions, the identification of optimal CBIS is trivial; for example, if the gains should be positive and increasing and the costs negative but decreasing, the optimal central bank involvement in supervision should be easily and perfectly consistent with the insourcing view, i.e. the supervisory powers should be completely inside the central bank.

Finally, we can assume that the politicians are heterogeneous with respect to their preferences. In other words, they can attach weightings in different ways to both the expected gains and the expected costs of the CBIS.

The preference heterogeneity with the degree of conservativeness can be summarised: they can be indexed such that more conservative politicians – those politicians that dislike central bank involvement in supervision, or in other words are more likely to share the outsourcing view – bear higher marginal costs and/or enjoy lower marginal benefits from increasing the CBIS level:

$$\frac{\partial B_\pi(t_i, \pi)}{\partial t_i} \leq 0; \quad \frac{\partial C_\pi(t, i\pi)}{\partial t_i} \geq 0 \qquad (4.4)$$

The first expression summarises the assumption that the more conservative is the politician – i.e. a higher t level – the less they appreciate the benefits B in having a central bank involved in supervisory affairs and, consistently, the second expression says that a conservative politician – i.e. a higher t level – weights significantly the costs C of central bank involvement in supervision.

Given the assumptions in equations 4.1 – 4.3, we can be sure that the politician will choose a central bank involvement in supervision that is different from zero in order to capture the fact that the central bank can always be involved in addressing and fixing financial stability issues, at least in extraordinary times and/or temporarily, for example by acting as lender-of-last-resort:

$$\frac{\partial B(t_i, 0)}{\partial \pi} > \frac{\partial C(t_i, 0)}{\partial \pi} \tag{4.5}$$

Each politician, whatever their degree of conservativeness – i.e. whatever their t level – acknowledges that the benefits B in involving the central banker – i.e. defining the level π – are greater than the costs C. The politicians disagree, however, on the optimal level of CBIS, being heterogeneous in terms of conservativeness.

Therefore, what should be the optimal level of central bank involvement or CBIS? Each politician will find such a level where the marginal benefits of CBIS match the corresponding marginal costs:

$$\frac{\partial B_\pi(t_i, \pi)}{\partial \pi} = \frac{\partial C_\pi(t_i, \pi)}{\partial \pi} \tag{4.6}$$

The crucial effect of the political behaviour is that – depending on the type of the politician in charge – the optimal CBIS will depend from time to time and country by country on the degree of conservativeness of such a politician:

$$\frac{\partial \pi^*}{\partial t_i} < 0 \tag{4.7}$$

The expression summarises the fact that in equilibrium, the optimal degree of the CBIS π^* is inversely associated with the conservativeness of the incumbent politician; the more sympathetic is the politician with the outsourcing view, the lower will be the central bank involvement in supervision. The optimal degree of CBIS will be dependent on the personal degree of conservativeness.

In other words, the more the incumbent politician dislikes the expected costs of having a central banker acting as supervisor, the less will be the central bank's involvement at the CBIS level in the TPM regime. Figure 4.1 graphically depicts the relationship between the CBIS level and the politician type in terms of conservativeness: given the TPM setting, the more

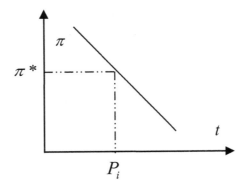

FIGURE 4.1. Conservativeness and CBIS level.

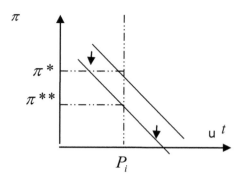

FIGURE 4.2. Expected political risks and the CBIS level.

conservative the incumbent politician, the less involvement the central bank will have as prudential supervisor. If the politician in charge is the policymaker P_i, in building up the TPM regime their choices regarding the level of central bank involvement in prudential supervision will be equal to $\pi*$ (Figure 4.1).

Where $\pi*$ is the optimal CBIS level; P_i is the incumbent politician; π is the CBIS level and t is their degree of conservativeness.

As demonstrated, the optimal CBIS will depend on the preferences of the policymakers. It is worth noting that any shock that modifies the drivers that influence both the expected benefits and costs in having the central banker as prudential supervisor will change the optimal CBIS level, given the individual conservativeness. Such a simple and general framework can be applied in analysing the temporal and/or geographical evolution of the CBIS level. In order to offer a concrete application, we can recall that before the GFC, the outsourcing view was the dominant one:[36] those banks with full responsibility for monetary policy – the Federal Reserve, the European Central Bank, the Bank of England, the Bank of Japan – did not have full responsibility for supervisory policy. The worldwide rise of specialisation in monetary policy led to reforms that gave central banks a clear mandate, focusing on price stability and greater political and economic independence. This does not mean that these banks were not concerned with financial stability – actually the opposite was true, as could later be observed during the GFC – but they usually tended to address it from a macroprudential perspective and as a function of their primary mission: monetary policy. On top of that, among central banks that did not have full responsibility for monetary policy, such as those belonging to the European Monetary Union, several central banks were more involved in supervision. Among these it is worth noting the two cases of the Netherlands and Belgium, both of which adopted a TPM setting. The explanation is simple: when the central banker is no longer the unique manager of liquidity – as is the case with the central banks of the Eurozone members – the expected downsides of involving them in supervision become weaker and the insourcing view can gain momentum.

Now if we interpret the outsourcing trend as the general outcome of an increasing sensibility of the national policymakers with respect to the MURCB costs, we can mimic such a trend as an increase in the expected risks (losses) due to the central bank's involvement in supervision that decreases the optimal CBIS level from $\pi*$ to $\pi**$ (Figure 4.2), while the interpretation of the outliers – i.e. the countries that increased the CBIS – goes in the other direction.

---

[36] Masciandaro and Quintyn (n 13).

In other words, when in general and on average all the politicians become more sympathetic to the outsourcing view, the relationship between the central bank involvement π and the degree of conservativeness t – i.e. the line in the graphic – shifts downward and for every incumbent politician P_i, the optimal central bank involvement $\pi*$ will be lower – i.e. it becomes equal to $\pi**$.

Mirroring this, we can recall that after the GFC there was a sort of Great Reversal: the insourcing view gained momentum:[37] in particular, in advanced, European and EU economies, central bank involvement in supervision has increased, indicating that politicians attached greater weight to the expected I&HC benefits that a higher CBIS level could produce.

Summing up, the optimal CBIS in a TPM regime is a state-dependent equilibrium, and the crucial driver is the policymaker who decides to maintain or to reform a given supervisory regime, taking into account their perceptions of the expected gains and losses.

Finally, it must be acknowledged that the incumbent policymaker is likely to be influenced by the existing status quo. In other words, we have to consider the possibility that frictions and lags can characterise the evolution of a supervisory regime.

How do we capture the role of the status quo? We can assume that the degree of prudence of the policymaker matters, i.e. how they individually discount gains and losses in changing a given supervisory setting. We can capture the role of prudence – or if you wish of relevant risk-aversion – by assuming that politicians dislike the political losses proportionally more than the political gains.

In other words, with loss-aversion, and for every supervisory setting, losses loom larger than gains, and both are evaluated with respect to a given status quo. Here we adopt a prospect theory approach – which so far 'remains the most important theoretical contribution to behavioural economics'[38] – and assume loss-aversion, i.e. politicians perceive any outcome as expected gains and losses relative to a reference point, which represents their endowment.[39] Let $z > 0$ be the parameter that captures the loss aversion of the politicians and let π^{SQ} be the status quo for the CBIS level. Given equation 4.5, the status quo CBIS level is ever positive – so we can analyse in general how a given supervisory architecture can change if a shock occurs. With loss-aversion, an increasing CBIS level – $\pi > \pi^{SQ}$ – entails more benefits than costs, but higher expected costs yield psychological losses, which amount to the following:

$$z\big(C(t_i, \pi) - C(t_i, \pi^{SQ})\big) \tag{4.8}$$

When the incumbent politician is loss-adverse, given their conservativeness t, any change from the existing level of central bank involvement in supervision π^{SQ} to a higher level π implies a risk, which means a cost z.

On the other hand, reducing the CBIS level – $\pi < \pi^{SQ}$ – overall entails fewer benefits than costs, with psychological losses in terms of benefits amounting to the following:

$$z\big(B(t_i, \pi^{SQ}) - B(t_i, \pi)\big) \tag{4.9}$$

[37] Ibid.

[38] R. H. Thaler, 'From Cashews to Nudges: The Evolution of Behavioural Economics' (2018) 108(6) *American Economic Review* 1265–87.

[39] D. Kahneman and A. Tversky, 'Prospect Theory: An Analysis of Decision Under Risk' (1979) 47 *Econometrica* 263–91; N. C. Barberis, 'Thirty Years of Prospect Theory in Economics: A Review and Assessment' (NBER Working Paper Series, n. 18621, 2012); N. C. Barberis, 'Richard Thales and the Rise of Behavioral Economics' (2018) 120(3) *The Scandinavian Journal of Economics* 661–84.

The opposite is also true: when the incumbent politician is loss-adverse, given their conservative-ness t, any change from the existing level of central bank involvement in supervision π^{SQ} to a lower level π implies a risk, which means a cost z.

Therefore, if the incumbent politician is loss-averse, they dislike any change in the insti-tutional setting, i.e. they will try to maintain the existing level of central bank involvement in supervision, avoiding designing and/or implementing any supervisory reform. In such cases there is a status quo bias, which can be labelled supervisory regime inertia.

In conclusion, if the politicians are loss-averse, a change in the CBIS is less likely to occur. Such framework can explain why in establishing a new supervisory setting – for example, a new TPM regime – inertia in changing the central bank position can occur.

4.4 CENTRAL BANKING AND THE TWIN PEAKS REGIMES: COMPARATIVE ANALYSIS

The previous two sections reached the general conclusion that the patterns of CBIS that are observed in reality – including the TPM cases – cannot be explained by the existence of a superior setting for delegating powers to central banks: the differing arguments supporting the insourcing view or the outsourcing view are likely to be a set of variables to which different weightings are attached by the policymakers in charge who design and implement the supervis-ory regime, depending on the circumstances that they face from time to time and country by country.

Therefore, the question becomes genuinely empirical: what explains the reforms in the central bank involvement in prudential supervision? This section elaborates on the general results that have already been obtained and then focuses on Twin Peaks regimes.

In a recent econometric analysis,[40] a new empirical approach has been proposed to investigate the likely triggers of reforms in the architecture of financial sector supervision. To that end, a new dataset has been created containing information on the authorities responsible for financial sector supervision (banking, insurance and financial markets) in a large sample of 105 countries over the period 1996–2013.

Using this data, a new index of *Central Bank Involvement in Supervision* (CBIS Index) was born and was then applied in order to identify the full set of reforms implemented in supervisory architecture in our sample of countries. This new index updates and extends previous attempts to measure central bank involvement in financial supervision in several ways.

First, previous indexes have considered separately the issue of unified versus sectoral supervi-sion[41] and whether this supervision should be assigned to a central bank.[42] A bridge between these two approaches has been created by investigating why and how countries adopt *unified* financial sector supervision *inside* the central bank. Secondly, the analysis has been focused on the involvement of central banks in the supervision of the *entire* financial sector, i.e. banking, insurance and securities markets. It is a matter of fact that, given the creation of international financial conglomerates, the concept of supervision cannot be focused exclusively on banking supervision. The interplay between banks, insurance companies and financial markets poses

---

[40] D. Masciandaro and D. Romelli, 'Central Banks as Supervisors: Do Crises Matter?' (2018) 52 *European Journal of Political Economy* 120–40.

[41] Melecky and Podpiera (n 29).

[42] D. Masciandaro, 'E Pluribus Unum? Authorities Design in Financial Supervision: Trends and Determinants' (2006) 17(1) *Open Economies Review* 73–102; and Masciandaro (n 32).

new challenges for the institutional settings of financial supervisors.[43] Finally, with the availability of a large panel of countries and time span, the first full set of reforms in the institutional design of financial sector supervision has been constructed in order to understand what drives countries to modify their supervisory architecture over time. Two main drivers of reforms have been highlighted.

First, episodes of systemic banking crisis significantly increase the probability that a country reforms its supervisory structure (*crisis driver*). This result is specific to financial sector turmoil and does not hold with other types of crisis, such as currency crises or economic recessions.

Using and extending the meaning of the theoretical framework described in the previous section, we can interpret the relationship between supervisory reforms and a crisis arising out of a systemic banking crisis as a relevant trigger that changes the political benefits that supervisory architecture reform, including the central bank's role, can produce. Does the crisis driver matter in explaining the features of the actual TPM regimes?

In Australia, the TPM regime was established in 1998 and prudential supervision is housed in a separate statutory body outside the Reserve Bank of Australia, which remains responsible for monetary policy and financial stability;[44] i.e. at the corresponding CBIS level π^*_A is close to zero. The original supervisory setting was modified, however, after a financial (insurance) crash in 2001. Here, the crisis driver appears to be relevant.

In the Netherlands,[45] the TPM regime was established in 2001 and prudential supervision has been housed inside the Dutch Central Bank since 2004. In this case, the corresponding CBIS level π^*_{NE} is relatively high. It is worth noting that the Dutch Central Bank is among those central banks that do not have full responsibility for monetary policy, given that the Netherlands is a member of the European Monetary Union. As noted in the previous paragraph, the Netherlands can be a paradigmatic example of a country where national politicians, in circumstances where the central bank is no longer the unique manager of liquidity, consider the expected downside risks of involving it in supervision to be lower, and share the insourcing view.

In New Zealand, the TPM regime was definitively established in 2011 and prudential supervision was housed inside the Prudential Supervisory Department of the Reserve Bank of New Zealand.[46] In the case of New Zealand, it can be claimed that the corresponding CBIS level π^*_{NZ} is relatively high. The crisis driver seems to matter also in the New Zealand case: the GFC, as well as numerous financial failures, are considered to have been the main triggers of the TPM establishment.

In 2011, the Belgian government also established a TPM regime and the prudential supervision was housed inside the National Bank of Belgium.[47] The Belgian CBIS level π^*_B can be evaluated as relatively high. As in the Dutch case, the National Bank of Belgium is among those central banks that do not have full responsibility for monetary policy, being one more example of the effect of European Monetary Union membership, i.e. to reinforce the insourcing view. The crisis driver seems to be present and relevant also in the Belgian experience, given the collapse of two of the country's bigger banks during the GFC.

---

[43] P. De Grauwe, 2008, 'There Is More to Central Banking than Inflation Targeting', *The First Global Financial Crisis of the 21st Century* (London: CEPR-VoxEU Publication, July 2008), 159; Masciandaro and Quintyn (n 22).

[44] Godwin, Howse and Ramsay (n 1).

[45] Ibid.

[46] Ibid.

[47] Ibid.

TABLE 4.2. *Twin Peaks country models: CBIS level and regime drivers.*

Country	CBIS level	Crisis driver	Bandwagon driver	Inertia effect
Australia	Low	No	No	No
Belgium	High	Yes	Yes	No
The Netherlands	High	No	Yes	No
New Zealand	High	Yes	Yes	No
United Kingdom	High	Yes	Yes	Yes

In the United Kingdom, the TPM regime was effectively established in 2013 and the prudential supervisor was created as a subsidiary of the Bank of England;[48] the corresponding CBIS level π^*_{UK} can be considered in the middle between the lowest level π^*_A and the higher levels, as π^*_B or π^*_{NE} or π^*_{NZ}. After three years – in 2016 – the status of the UK prudential supervisor as a subsidiary ended and its function was deeply incorporated within the Bank of England, increasing the CBIS level π^*_{UK}. The lagged increase in the central bank role can be interpreted as a case of supervisory reform inertia due to the existing risks of maximising the insource process – i.e. the complete merger between monetary policy and prudential policy. The crisis driver mattered also in the UK case: the GFC forced the government to step in to reform the supervisory setting.

Furthermore, a second and equally important effect seems to matter, the so-called *bandwagon driver*. Countries are more likely to change their supervisory architecture when the proportion of countries undertaking reforms around the world or on the same continent is higher. The novel result has been tested by employing spatial econometric techniques to construct groups of peer countries based on geographical distance and trade relationships.[49] We show that countries whose financial architecture is farthest from the average of the peer group are more likely to reform. These findings bring new insights to a growing literature on the importance of an international convergence in institutional design.[50]

Also, in this case the theoretical framework offers a possible explanation: the bandwagon effect can reduce the political risks – i.e. the opportunity costs – in changing the supervisory regime and/or the role of the central bank, increasing the likelihood of reform. Again, does the bandwagon driver matter in explaining the features of the actual TPM regimes?

In the Netherlands, the supervisory reform appeared to be influenced by the fact that at around the same time, France and Germany considered the opportunity to explore the possibility of supervisory reforms.[51] In New Zealand and in Belgium it is likely that the political decision to implement the TPM regime was strengthened by the experience of neighbouring countries, Australia and Netherlands respectively.[52] Australia can also be considered to be the reference point for the United Kingdom's establishment of a TPM regime.[53]

Summing up (Table 4.2), the heterogeneity of the CBIS level, as well as the existence of both the crisis driver and the bandwagon driver in specific country cases, appears to be confirmed

---

[48] Ibid.

[49] See also P. Elhorst, E. Zandberg and J. de Haan, 'The Impact of Interaction Effects among Neighbouring Countries on Financial Liberalization and Reform: A Dynamic Spatial Panel Data Approach' (2013) 8(3) *Spatial Economic Analysis* 293–313; C. Bodea and R. Hicks, 'International Finance and Central Bank Independence: Institutional Diffusion and the Flow and Cost of Capital' (2015) 77(1) *Journal of Politics* 268–84.

[50] A. Abiad and A. Mody, 'Financial Reform: What Shakes It? What Shapes It?' (2005) 95(1) *American Economic Review* 66–88; T. Persson and G. Tabellini, 'Democratic Capital: The Nexus of Political and Economic Change' (2009) 1(2) *American Economic Journal: Macroeconomics* 88–126.

[51] Godwin, Howse and Ramsay (n 1).

[52] Ibid.

[53] Ibid.

when the actual TPM experiences are considered. The inertia effect appears to be present in the UK case, while Australia is the true outlier, i.e. without either the crisis driver or the bandwagon driver.

4.5 CONCLUSION

This chapter has discussed both the economics and the political economy principles that can be used to evaluate the central bank's involvement as prudential supervisor in a Twin Peaks setting. It reached the general conclusion that the specific role of the central bank that is observed in actual Twin Peaks regimes cannot be explained by the existence of a superior setting for delegating powers to central banks: the differing arguments supporting the insourcing view – in favour of having the prudential supervisor housed in the central bank – or the outsourcing view – against such a proposition – are likely to be a set of variables that are individually weighted by the policymakers in charge who design and implement the supervisory regime, depending on the circumstances they face from time to time and country by country.

Therefore, the research questions become genuinely empirical: Is central bank involvement in supervision a heterogeneous variable? Are there relevant drivers that can explain the supervisory reform pattern? This chapter elaborated on the general results that have already been obtained in the literature and then speculated specifically on existing Twin Peaks regimes.

Analysing the establishment of the Twin Peaks regime in Australia, Belgium, the Netherlands, New Zealand and the United Kingdom, the heterogeneity of the central bank involvement as prudential supervisor can be confirmed, and that on average two drivers appear to be relevant in motivating the incumbent policymakers in reforming their supervisory settings: the necessity to address and fix the consequences of a systemic crisis (*crisis driver*) and the opportunity to implement a supervisory change when the proportion of peer countries undertaking reforms is higher (*bandwagon driver*). In this respect, the true outlier appears to be the Australian case, where the relevance of the two drivers is completely absent. Finally, the inertia effect – i.e. lagged TPM reform due to the risks in implementing it – appears to be evident only in the UK case.

PART II

The Trek towards Twin Peaks

5

Twin Peaks in Australia

The Never-Ending Trek?

Andrew Godwin, Ian Ramsay and Andrew Schmulow

5.1 INTRODUCTION

The Oxford Dictionary defines a trek as 'a long arduous journey, especially one made on foot'.[1] As it is applied to the Twin Peaks financial regulatory model, the analogy with a 'trek' is somewhat apposite. For most jurisdictions that have adopted the model, the journey has been in response to discontent with their previous model. For some jurisdictions, the further journey towards adjusting the model to accommodate changing circumstances and challenges, and achieving the right settings, is continuing and has been a long and relatively arduous one. This has certainly been the case in Australia.[2]

The Twin Peaks model was pioneered in Australia following recommendations by the Wallis Inquiry, which was established in 1996 to review the financial system.[3] The model separates financial regulation into two broad functions: market conduct regulation (which includes consumer protection) and prudential regulation. Each of these functions is vested in a separate regulator. In Australia, market conduct regulation is vested in the Australian Securities and Investments Commission (ASIC) and prudential regulation is vested in the Australian Prudential Regulation Authority (APRA). The central bank, the Reserve Bank of Australia (RBA), remains responsible for monetary policy and financial stability, including ensuring a safe and reliable payments system.[4]

---

[1] Oxford Dictionary, https://en.oxforddictionaries.com/definition/trek.

[2] See n 112, for current reforms to Australia's regulatory model, some twenty-four years into its operation.

[3] For the recommendations of the Wallis Inquiry, see http://fsi.treasury.gov.au/content/downloads/FinalReport/overview .pdf. The Twin Peaks model was first examined in Michael Taylor, '"Twin Peaks": A Regulatory Structure for the New Century' (Centre for the Study of Financial Innovation, London, 1995). See also Michael W. Taylor, 'The Road from Twin Peaks – And the Way Back' (2000) 16 *Connecticut Insurance Law Journal* 61; Michael W. Taylor, 'Regulatory Reform after the Financial Crisis: Twin Peaks Revisited' chapter 1 in Robin Hui Huang and Dirk Schoenmaker (eds) *Institutional Structure of Financial Regulation: Theories and International Experiences*, Routledge Research in Finance and Banking Lawn (Routledge, 1st ed, 2014), 1–280; Michael W. Taylor, 'Welcome to Twin Peaks', *Central Banking Journal* (17 August 2010), www.centralbanking.com/central-banking-journal/feature/2042899/welcome-twin-peaks; Richard K. Abrams and Michael W. Taylor, 'Issues in the Unification of Financial Sector Supervision' (IMF Working Paper, No WP/00/213, December 2000), www.imf.org/external/pubs/ft/wp/2000/wp00213.pdf; Michael W. Taylor, 'Regulatory Reform after the Financial Crisis: Twin Peaks Revisited' in Robin Hui Huang and Dirk Schoenmaker (eds) *Institutional Structure of Financial Regulation: Theories and International Experiences* (Routledge, 2014); Michael W. Taylor, 'Peak Practice: How to Reform the UK's Regulatory System' (Centre for the Study of Financial Innovation, No 23, October 1996); Michael W. Taylor, '"Twin Peaks" Revisited... A Second Chance for Regulatory Reform' (Centre for the Study of Financial Innovation, No 89, September 2009); Michael W. Taylor, 'The Search for a New Regulatory Paradigm' (1998) 49(3) *Mercer Law Review* , 793.

[4] As applied to Australia, the term is somewhat of a misnomer. When Taylor's proposal was adopted by Australia's 1998 Financial System Inquiry (Stan Wallis, Bill Beerworth, Professor Jeffrey Carmichael, Professor Ian Harper and Linda Nicholls, Financial System Inquiry, 31 March 1997, 1-771, 26) it was clearly articulated as a triple-peak system

This chapter explores the legal and regulatory framework in Australia, the challenges that have arisen in areas such as coordination and functional separation between the Twin Peaks regulators, and the outcomes from numerous reviews in which the model has been subject to scrutiny.

Section 5.2 explores the evolution of the Twin Peaks model[5] in Australia and certain challenges that have arisen in governance, information-sharing and coordination, and in funding arrangements. Section 5.3 surveys the terrain in Australia by outlining the recommendations from a review of the financial system in 2014, the Financial System Inquiry (FSI), and subsequent recommendations and reforms, including those proposed by or arising out of the Royal Commission into Misconduct in the Banking, Superannuation and Financial Services Industry in 2019 (the 'Financial Services Royal Commission'). Section 5.4 concludes.

5.2 EVOLUTION

Many of the factors motivating the adoption of the Twin Peaks model in Australia were articulated by the Wallis Inquiry, which was established in 1996 to review the financial system.[6] Three factors were identified in particular: innovation in product design and distribution, which had 'blurred the boundaries between financial instruments and institutions'; increasing competition from new competitors in the financial market; and 'conglomeration, which was occurring within financial services institutions'.[7] These three factors appear to be common to all jurisdictions that have adopted the model.[8]

('three agencies' to use the terminology of the FSI Report). The Reserve Bank of Australia (RBA) would be given a macroprudential role. That said, the core of the model as adopted by Australia was the creation of two additional peaks over and above the central bank, one exclusively focused on prudential regulation, the other focused on conduct issues. Since then the term Twin Peaks has been used to describe separate prudential and conduct agencies, such as that in Australia, and notwithstanding the role played by the central bank.

[5] Much has been written about the Twin Peaks model of financial regulation by comparison with other models. Even countries like the USA, which have for a long time argued that the complexity of the financial system made it difficult to streamline the financial regulatory system, have flirted with the idea of adopting a Twin Peaks model. See Henry M. Paulson Jr., Robert K. Steel, David G. Nason, Kelly Ayers, Heather Etner, John Foley III, Gerry Hughes, Timothy Hunt, Kristen Jaconi, Charles Klingman, C. Christopher Ledoux, Peter Nickoloff, Jeremiah Norton, Philip Quinn, Heidilynne Schultheiss, Michael Scott, Jeffrey Stoltzfoos, Mario Ugoletti and Roy Woodall, 'The Department of the Treasury Blueprint for a Modernized Financial Regulatory Structure' (United States Government Department of the Treasury, Washington, DC, March 2008), 1–218, www.treasury.gov/press-center/press-releases/Documents/Blueprint .pdf. For a thorough analysis of the various models, see D. Llewellyn, 'Institutional Structure of Financial Regulation and Supervision: The Basic Rules' (Paper presented at a World Bank seminar Aligning Supervisory Structures with Country Needs, Washington, DC, 6 and 7 June 2006); E. Wymeersch, 'The Structure of Financial Supervision in Europe: About Single Financial Supervisors, Twin Peaks and Multiple Financial Supervisors' (2007) 8(2) *European Business Organization Review* 237; J. Kremers and D. Schoenmaker, 'Twin Peaks: Experiences in the Netherlands' (LSE Financial Markets Group Paper Series Paper 196, December 2010); E. Pan, 'Structural Reform of Financial Regulation' (2011) 19 *Transnational Law and Contemporary Problems* 796; Andrew D. Schmulow, 'The Four Methods of Financial System Regulation: An International Comparative Survey' (2015) 26(3) *Journal of Banking and Finance Law and Practice* 169.

[6] For the recommendations of the Wallis Inquiry, see https://treasury.gov.au/sites/default/files/2019-03/01-fsi-fr-Prelim.pdf (the 'Wallis Report'). For a detailed analysis of the Wallis Inquiry in relation to the Twin Peaks model that was adopted in Australia, see A. Godwin and I. Ramsay, 'Twin Peaks – The Legal and Regulatory Anatomy of Australia's System of Financial Regulation' (2015) 26 *Journal of Banking and Finance Law and Practice* 240. Much of the analysis in this chapter is drawn from this article.

[7] Wallis Report (n 6) 'Overview', 14.

[8] For a comparative analysis of jurisdictions that have adopted the Twin Peaks model, see A. Godwin, T. Howse and I. Ramsay, 'A Jurisdictional Comparison of the Twin Peaks Model of Financial Regulation' (2016) 18(2) *Journal of Banking Regulation* 103, 106–9.

The Wallis Inquiry made two critical recommendations for the purpose of this analysis. First, it recommended that a single agency be established for the regulation of companies, market conduct and consumer protection.[9] Noting that conduct and disclosure regulation in Australia had previously 'been provided through a variety of agencies, with arrangements governed by the institutional form of the service provider', the Wallis Inquiry considered that 'such arrangements [were] inconsistent with the emerging structure of markets' and 'resulted in inefficiencies, inconsistencies and regulatory gaps and [were] not conducive to effective competition in financial markets'.[10] Accordingly, a separate market conduct regulator was established, which is now known as the Australian Securities and Investments Commission (ASIC).[11]

Secondly, the Wallis Inquiry recommended that a single prudential regulator be established to carry out prudential regulation in the financial system.[12] It considered that '[c]ombining prudential regulation in a single regulator [would] better accommodate the emergence of wide-ranging financial conglomerates and enable a more flexible approach over time to changes in the focus of prudential regulation'. This was quite prescient, particularly in view of the increasing focus on financial stability and macroprudential regulation.[13] Further, '[s]uch an entity [would] be better placed to reduce the intensity of regulation, and so lower its cost, in the likely event that new technologies or other developments facilitate a reduction in systemic risks'.[14]

In a move that was to diverge from the subsequent practice in other Twin Peaks jurisdictions, the Wallis Inquiry recommended that the prudential regulator 'should be separate from, but cooperate closely with, the Reserve Bank of Australia' (RBA)[15] and that 'strong mechanisms should be established to ensure appropriate coordination and cooperation between the two agencies'.[16] The Australian Prudential Regulation Authority (APRA) is established as a body corporate[17] and operates entirely outside of the RBA.

The advantages and disadvantages of locating the prudential regulator outside the central bank have been debated extensively in the literature.[18] In the case of Australia, the Wallis Report identified several reasons for a separate prudential regulator, including that separation would

---

[9] Wallis Report (n 6) Recommendation 1. Prior to Wallis consumer protection was, in general, vested in the Australian Competition and Consumer Commission (ACCC). However, the protection of consumers of financial services was removed from the ACCC, and vested in ASIC, on 1 July 1998. See further s 12A, *Australian Securities and Investments Commission Act* (Cth), No 51 of 2001 (Australia); Australian Securities and Investments Commission, Annual Report 1998/99, Australian Securities and Investments Commission, 18 October 1999.

[10] Ibid 17. According to the Wallis Report (n 6) at 17–18, '[r]egulation for the integrity of market conduct, consumer protection and the regulation of companies have significant synergies. These functions should therefore be combined'.

[11] See *Australian Securities and Investments Commission Act 2001* (Cth).

[12] Wallis Report, 'Overview' (n 6) Recommendation 31. This involved transferring all prudentially regulated financial corporations from state jurisdiction to Commonwealth jurisdiction in a move away from the state-based regulation as is still much the case in the United States.

[13] See Chapter 21 for a discussion about macroprudential regulation.

[14] Wallis Report, 'Overview' (n 6) 21.

[15] The RBA, Australia's central bank, is responsible for monetary policy and financial stability, including ensuring a safe and reliable payments system. It also acts as lender of last resort (Glenn Stevens, 'Liquidity and the Lender of Last Resort' in *Speeches*, published by Reserve Bank of Australia, 15 April 2008).

[16] Wallis Report, 'Overview' (n 6) Recommendation 32. Coordination and cooperation were to be achieved by making provision for 'full information exchange between the RBA and [APRA]' and for 'RBA participation in [APRA] inspection teams'. Further, '[a] bilateral operational coordination committee, chaired by an RBA deputy governor, should be established to coordinate information exchange, reporting arrangements on financial system developments, and other ongoing operational cooperation between the RBA and [APRA], including cooperation in establishing clear procedures for the management of regulated entities which experience financial difficulties': Wallis Report, 'Overview' (n 6) 11–12.

[17] *Australian Prudential Regulation Authority Act 1998* (Cth) (APRA Act) s 13.

[18] For an outline of the arguments on each side, see Godwin, Howse and Ramsay (n 8) 109–11; Schmulow (n 5) 164, 169.

allow the RBA and APRA to focus clearly on their primary objectives and would clarify lines of accountability.[19] By contrast, those who are in favour of housing the prudential regulator within the central bank point to the importance of a close relationship between monetary and prudential policymakers and the benefits of maximising the synergies of monetary policy, microprudential policy and macroprudential policy.[20] For example, the purpose of the reform in the United Kingdom, under which the functions of prudential regulation are now exercised by the Bank of England (BoE, acting through the Prudential Regulation Committee), was expressed to be to 'maximise the synergies of having monetary policy, macro-prudential policy and micro-prudential policy under the aegis of one institution'.[21]

The position in Australia can also be contrasted with the position in New Zealand, where the 'Prudential Supervision Department' operates under the auspices of the Reserve Bank of New Zealand (RBNZ).[22] It can also be contrasted with the position in Belgium and the Netherlands, where the central bank is responsible for prudential supervision, and South Africa, where the Prudential Authority operates as a separate juristic person within the central bank.[23]

The discussion below examines challenges that have arisen in three areas: (1) governance; (2) information-sharing and coordination; and (3) funding arrangements. These are areas in which there has been significant reform over the years and are therefore useful in setting the scene for a survey of the broader terrain in Section 5.3.

5.2.1 *Governance*

The Wallis Report recommended that the regulatory agencies should have boards of directors 'responsible for their operational and administrative policies, the fulfilment of their respective legislative mandates and their performance', with a majority of independent directors and substantial cross-representation.[24] Accordingly, APRA was originally governed by a board consisting of a majority of independent members and an independent chair. In addition, there was cross-representation with both the RBA and ASIC represented on the APRA Board.[25]

The governance of APRA changed in 2003 following the recommendations of the HIH Royal Commission, which was established to examine issues arising out of the collapse in 2001 of the

---

[19] Wallis Report, 'Overview' (n 6) 17. In addition, separation would clarify that there was no implied or automatic guarantee of any financial institution or its promises in the event of insolvency. See Godwin, Howse and Ramsay (n 8) 110.

[20] For a discussion about 'the potential of synergy arising from knowledge of monetary policy and financial market developments within supervisory practice', see M. van Hengel, P. Hilbers and D. Schoenmaker, 'Experiences with the Dutch Twin-Peaks Model: Lessons for Europe' in J. A. Kellermann, J. de Haan and F. de Vries (eds) *Financial Supervision in the 21st Century* (Springer, 2013), 232. The benefit of combining functions needs to be weighed against the risk of a conflict of interest emerging within the central bank. For example, it has been suggested that 'a central bank with responsibility for preventing systemic risk is more likely to loosen monetary policy on occasions of difficulty': Llewellyn (n 5) 29; Schmulow (n 5) 170.

[21] HM Treasury, Bank of England Bill: Technical Consultation (2015), 3.

[22] T. Fiennes and C. O'Connor-Close 'The Evolution of Prudential Supervision in New Zealand' (2012) 75 *Reserve Bank of New Zealand: Bulletin* 5.

[23] For further information about South Africa, see van Heerden and van Niekerk in Chapter 9.

[24] See Wallis Report, 'Overview' (n 6) Recommendation 108. This arrangement subsequently changed following the reforms introduced as a result of the HIH Report.

[25] The former s 19 of the APRA Act provided that the Board would consist of the following members: '(a) a Chair; (b) the CEO; (c) 2 members, each of whom is either the Governor or the Deputy Governor of the Reserve Bank or an officer of the Reserve Bank Service; and (d) 1 member who is also an ASIC member or an ASIC staff member: and (e) 4 other members'.

general insurer, HIH Insurance Limited and reported in 2003.[26] In place of the non-executive board structure, control was vested in a small, full-time executive, comprising a chief executive and two or three commissioners appointed by the government. According to the HIH Report, this 'would make APRA more efficient and better able to discharge the responsibilities it has'.[27]

In addition, the HIH Report queried the benefits of cross-representation, including the risk that it would impede regulatory coordination, and recommended that 'the direct involvement of representatives of the Australian Securities and Investments Commission and the Reserve Bank of Australia in the governance of the Australian Prudential Regulation Authority be discontinued'.[28] By contrast, the Prudential Regulation Committee in the United Kingdom, through which the Bank of England exercises the functions of the prudential regulator, adopts the cross-representation model, with a committee comprising 'the Governor of the Bank of England; Deputy Governors for Financial Stability, Markets and Banking, and Prudential Regulation; the Chief Executive of the Financial Conduct Authority; a member appointed by the Governor with the approval of the Chancellor; and six other external members appointed by the Chancellor'.[29]

5.2.2 *Information-Sharing and Coordination*

Coordination, as reflected in Principle 3 of the Basel Core Principles,[30] is particularly important for the Twin Peaks model to operate effectively, because a market participant may be regulated by both regulators. Effective coordination requires consultation, information-sharing (within an appropriate confidentiality framework) and cooperation in areas such as supervision and enforcement action.

In Australia, the Wallis Inquiry recognised the importance of information-sharing and coordination between the regulators, and recommended that the Council of Financial Regulators coordinate a broad range of activities 'with the aims of facilitating the cooperation of its three members (the RBA, [APRA] and [ASIC]) across the full range of regulatory functions, and the attainment of regulatory objectives with the minimum of agency and compliance costs'.[31]

Following the HIH collapse, various deficiencies in coordination were identified by the HIH Report, which recommended that the exchange of information between APRA and ASIC be reinforced, and that it 'be undertaken in a systematic way (through both formal and informal means) and based on clear protocols'.[32] Accordingly, a new provision was inserted in the APRA Act to confirm that 'APRA should, in performing and exercising its functions and powers, have

---

[26] For a summary of the HIH Royal Commission and the HIH Report, see https://parlinfo.aph.gov.au/parlInfo/search/display/display.w3p;query=Id:%22library/prspub/XZ896%22.

[27] Ibid lxi. See Recommendation 18, https://webarchive.nla.gov.au/awa/20030426200550/http://www.hihroyalcom.gov.au/finalreport/Front%20Matter,%20critical%20assessment%20and%20summary.HTML.

[28] Ibid 210, Recommendation 20. According to the HIH Report, the evidence suggested that 'staff may have assumed that necessary exchange of information would be occurring at board level obviating the need for communication at a working level'. Instead, the HIH Report suggested that coordination 'should be developed through regular formal and informal mechanisms involving agency staff at various levels' and that 'the Council of Financial Regulators, which has representation from the Treasury as well as the agencies, would ... be a more appropriate forum for the strategic consideration of issues affecting the financial services sector'. HIH Report (n 26) 209.

[29] See www.bankofengland.co.uk/about/people/prudential-regulation-committee.

[30] Basel Committee on Banking Supervision, 'Core Principles for Effective Banking Supervision' (September 2012): 'Principle 3 – Cooperation and collaboration: Laws, regulations or other arrangements provide a framework for cooperation and collaboration with relevant domestic authorities and foreign supervisors. These arrangements reflect the need to protect confidential information.'

[31] See Wallis Report, 'Overview' (n 6) Recommendation 112.

[32] HIH Report (n 26) 223–4.

regard to the desirability of APRA cooperating with other financial sector supervisory agencies, and with other agencies specified in regulations for the purposes of this subsection'.[33] In addition, the HIH Report stated that the exchange of information and coordination between the two agencies 'should not be discretionary but built into the operating procedures of the agencies'.[34] This was the first occasion on which information-sharing between ASIC and APRA was found lacking, and on which reforms were effected to address this deficiency, but not the last. A related recommendation was that 'APRA take steps to ensure that it effectively exchanges with relevant foreign regulators information and intelligence on the operations of Australian insurers with international operations'.[35]

Similar concerns to those outlined in the HIH Report were voiced some ten years later with the collapse of Trio Capital in Australia. Trio Capital was a superannuation fund trustee, and licensed responsible entity for seventeen managed investment schemes which included investments in several overseas vehicles, amongst them hedge funds. Trio went into voluntary administration on 19 December 2009 and was placed into liquidation on 22 June 2010. ASIC launched criminal and administrative actions against Trio Capital, its directors and other parties on the ground of alleged misappropriation of investor funds.[36]

Unlike HIH, which involved a general insurer, the collapse of Trio Capital involved a superannuation fund trustee and several managed investment schemes. HIH revealed deficiencies in terms of APRA's response to information and the lack of coordination between APRA and ASIC. There was also a lack of clarity as to the functions and responsibilities of each regulator. By comparison, Trio Capital's failure highlighted deficiencies in terms of poor information-sharing between the two regulators, and the need to encourage proactive information-sharing between the regulators; namely, effective information-sharing that is unsolicited.

In its report on the collapse of Trio Capital,[37] the Parliamentary Joint Committee on Corporations and Financial Services found that '[c]ommunication between ASIC and APRA was lacking'[38] and that when ASIC commenced its surveillance of the hedge funds, it did not seem to be aware of the failure of Trio Capital to provide information to APRA.[39] Noting that 'the Memorandum of Understanding between ASIC and APRA contains sections on mutual assistance and coordination, information sharing and unsolicited assistance', the report encouraged the regulators 'to continuing sharing information, even where a request for the information [had] not been received'.[40] This was, in effect, the second occasion on which information-sharing between ASIC and APRA was found lacking.

The experience from the HIH and Trio Capital collapses highlights the critical importance of information-sharing between APRA and ASIC, particularly at the operational levels of each regulator. It also highlights the importance of ensuring that each regulator responds in a timely and effective manner to problems experienced by regulated entities and coordinates the

---

[33] Section 10A of the APRA Act.

[34] HIH Report (n 26) 223.

[35] Ibid lxxi, Recommendation 40. There are now several memoranda of understanding in place between APRA and foreign regulators.

[36] Australian Securities and Investments Commission, Submission, Financial System Inquiry, April 2014, 191. For an analysis of the Trio Capital collapse in the context of the increasing regulatory overlap between ASIC and APRA, see A. Godwin, A. S. Kourabas and I. Ramsay, 'Twin Peaks and Financial Regulation: The Challenges of Increasing Regulatory Overlap and Expanding Responsibilities' (2016) 49(3) *The International Lawyer* 273.

[37] Commonwealth, Parliamentary Joint Committee on Corporations and Financial Services, 'Inquiry into the Collapse of Trio Capital' (Report, May 2012).

[38] Ibid xix–xx.

[39] Ibid 77.

[40] Ibid 84.

performance of functions and responsibilities between both regulators (although this has not always been achieved in practice).

Camacho and Glicksman have noted that '[c]oordination can be formal or informal. It can be long or short-term, and frequent or occasional. Coordination can be voluntary and cooperative, or mandated by legislative or executive action'.[41] Adopting this categorisation, regulatory coordination in Australia is primarily informal, long-term, frequent, voluntary and cooperative in nature. In addition, coordination is based on soft law memoranda of understanding (MoUs) between the regulatory bodies and between each regulatory body and the RBA, and on the published statements and policy documents issued by the regulatory bodies. The soft law approach in Australia is reflected in the fact that, to date, neither the creation of the Council of Financial Regulations nor the form or content of the regulatory MoUs is prescribed by statute.

The soft law approach was reinforced by the Interim Report of the Australian Financial System Inquiry (the FSI) of 2014, which drew on the submission of the RBA in stating that '[l]egislation cannot be relied on to promote a culture of cooperation, trust and mutual support between domestic regulatory agencies. These have been highlighted as essential elements of an effective financial stability framework, especially during a crisis'.[42] Of greater importance to the regulators in Australia, the RBA suggested, is cultivating a culture of coordination, under which the focus is on regulatory performance rather than regulatory structure.[43]

There are four aspects to the policy framework (although not necessarily its implementation) supporting coordination that are critical to the approach in Australia, all of which are inter-related: (i) proactive information-sharing between the regulators; (ii) consultation and mutual assistance between the regulators; (iii) practical measures to encourage and facilitate coordination; and (iv) an effective coordination body.[44]

Proactive information-sharing is intended to be underpinned by the confidentiality provisions in the relevant legislation, which allow confidential information to be shared between the regulators to assist them to perform their functions or exercise their powers.[45] It is further supported by provisions in the MoUs that relate to information-sharing.

Consultation and mutual assistance between the regulators is intended to be facilitated by regular meetings, consultations, proactive dialogue and liaison between the regulators (although the value and relevance of the coordination in these fora is questionable, as will be discussed in Section 5.2.2). In its 2013–14 Annual Report, for example, APRA asserted that regulatory liaison meetings 'focus on policy issues or operational supervision matters' and enforcement liaison meetings 'discuss broad enforcement-related issues, coordinate specific actions related to jointly regulated institutions and discuss cases identified by one agency that may have relevance to the

---

[41] A. Camacho and R. Glicksman, 'Functional Government in 3-D: A Framework for Evaluating Allocations of Government Authority' (2014) 51 *Harvard Journal on Legislation* 19, 56.

[42] Financial System Inquiry, *Interim Report* (July 2014), 3–119. Details of the FSI and its Final Report are available at https://treasury.gov.au/publication/c2014-fsi-final-report. See further in Section 5.3 for an overview of the Financial System Inquiry and its recommendations.

[43] See the comments of Malcom Edey, 'Macroprudential Supervision and the Role of Central Banks' (Regional Policy Forum on Financial Stability and Macroprudential Supervision Hosted by the Financial Stability Institute and the China Banking Regulatory Commission, 28 September 2012): 'Key aspects [of coordination] include an effective flow of information across staff in the market operations and macroeconomic departments of a central bank and those working in the areas of financial stability and bank supervision. Regular meetings among these groups to focus on risks and vulnerabilities and to highlight warning signs can be very valuable. A culture of coordination among these areas is very important in a crisis because, in many instances, a stress situation is first evident in liquidity strains visible to the central bank, and the first responses may be calls on central bank liquidity.'

[44] See Godwin and Ramsay (n 6) 260–4.

[45] See, for example, s 56 of the APRA Act.

other'.[46] Laudable as those sentiments appear, however, their implementation continues to be questioned. The practical measures designed to encourage and facilitate coordination between the regulators include informal communications and secondments.[47]

The fourth aspect to the policy framework supporting coordination in Australia – one that is critical to the effective operation of the Twin Peaks model – is a coordinating body for the relevant regulatory agencies, namely, the Council of Financial Regulators (CFR). It has been noted that the CFR 'operates as a high-level forum for co-operation and collaboration among its members'.[48] The CFR has no statutory basis in Australia and 'has no legal functions or powers separate from those of its individual member agencies'.[49] As outlined in the RBA's submission to the FSI, its membership comprises APRA, ASIC, the RBA and the Treasury; meetings are chaired by the Reserve Bank Governor and are 'typically held four times per year but can occur more frequently if required'. The RBA has asserted that, '[m]uch of the input into CFR meetings is undertaken by interagency working groups, which has the additional benefit of promoting productive working relationships and an appreciation of cross-agency issues at the staff level' (although whether such arrangements go far enough must now be questioned in light of the findings of the Financial Services Royal Commission[50]). Asserting that the CFR had worked well since its establishment, the RBA submitted to the FSI that the 'experience since its establishment, and especially during the crisis, [had] highlighted the benefits of the existing non-statutory basis of the CFR'.[51] In light of the need for change identified by the Financial Services Royal Commission, and the further reforms underway as a result of those findings,[52] it is open to question whether the informal, soft law approach followed in Australia is proving sufficiently robust.

In Australia, these arrangements are currently underpinned by a Memorandum of Understanding (2019 MoU) between APRA and ASIC, signed on 28 November 2019, which replaced a previous MoU signed on 18 May 2010 (2010 MoU). As compared with the 2010 MoU, which referred to a 'framework of cooperation', the 2019 MoU broadens the concept of cooperation by referring to a 'framework for engagement, including coordination, cooperation and information sharing, between APRA and ASIC'.[53] It also places greater emphasis on the proactive provision of information and documents between the agencies,[54] and recognises different types of engagement, which may involve action on the part of the agencies to:

---

[46] Australian Prudential Regulation Authority, 'Annual Report 2013–14' (Report, 2014) Ch 4.

[47] Australian Securities and Investments Commission, 'Speech to Australian Prudential Regulation Authority leadership team' (30 June 2011), http://web.archive.org/web/20140212234835/http://www.asic.gov.au/asic/pdflib.nsf/LookupByFileName/Speech-to-APRA-leadership-team-1.pdf/$file/Speech-to-APRA-leadership-team-1.pdf, 5–7. These practical measures were also reflected in the APRA 2013–14 Annual Report. APRA, 'Annual Report' (n 46) Ch 4.

[48] The Council of Financial Regulators, 'Memorandum of Understanding on Financial Distress Management between the Members of the Council of Financial Regulators' (18 September 2008).

[49] The Council of Financial Regulators, 'About the CFR' (11 May 2015), www.cfr.gov.au/about.html.

[50] See Royal Commission into Misconduct in the Banking, Superannuation and Financial Services Industry, Financial Services Royal Commission, *Final Report*, Vol 1 (Financial Services Royal Commission, Canberra, ACT, 1 February 2019), 457: 'Co-ordination must go beyond the current memorandum of understanding and informal meetings between representatives of the agencies', https://parlinfo.aph.gov.au/parlInfo/download/publications/tabledpapers/bc83795c-b7fa-4b42-a93b-fa012cffffc2/upload_pdf/fsrc-volume-1-final-report.pdf;fileType=application%2Fpdf#search=%22publications/tabledpapers/bc83795c-b7fa-4b42-a93b-fa012cffffc2%22.

[51] RBA, Submission, Financial System Inquiry (March 2014), 66. For an outline of the views of the regulators and Treasury on the benefits of the existing 'soft law' framework, see Godwin and Ramsay (n 6) 265–7.

[52] See n 112.

[53] 2019 MoU, para 2.

[54] Ibid para 12.

- inform – where one agency is aware of information that is relevant to the other agency's responsibilities;
- consult – where one agency is considering or undertaking an activity that has an impact on the other agency's responsibilities;
- collaborate – where there are opportunities to maximise outcomes for both prudential and conduct regulation; and
- in limited circumstances, consent – where one agency's action may have a material impact on the other agency's responsibilities.[55]

Anticipating a proposed reform to impose a statutory duty on the agencies to cooperate, the 2019 MoU provides that '[e]ach agency agrees to inform the other where it identifies matters that are materially relevant to, or have material impact on, the other's responsibilities'.[56] This reform follows a recommendation by the Final Report of the Financial Services Royal Commission[57] that 'the law should be amended to oblige each of APRA and ASIC to co-operate with the other; to share information to the maximum extent practicable; and to notify the other whenever it forms the belief that a breach in respect of which the other has enforcement responsibility may have occurred'.[58] This was the third occasion on which information-sharing between ASIC and APRA was found lacking, combined with a further attempt to address this issue through the 2019 MoU. As at the date of writing, the government has proposed an amendment to the legislation governing APRA and ASIC which would provide that each regulator 'must, so far as is practicable, work in co-operation with' the other regulator.[59] Although this would place regulatory cooperation on a formal statutory basis by imposing a duty on the regulators to cooperate, the framework would still predominantly rely on informal, 'soft law' mechanisms for its implementation.

By contrast, the United Kingdom imposes a prescriptive statutory duty on the financial regulators to cooperate in discharging their functions. The duty is expressed as a duty of the market conduct regulator – the Financial Conduct Authority (FCA) – and the Prudential Regulation Authority (PRA) to ensure the coordinated exercise of their functions.[60] The FCA and PRA must coordinate by obtaining information from each other in matters of 'common regulatory interest'.[61] This only applies to the extent that it 'is compatible with the advancement of each regulator's objectives, and provided the burden of compliance is not unduly disproportionate to the benefit'.[62] For the purposes of the FCA, 'objectives' means 'operational objectives'.[63] The Memorandum of Understanding between the FCA, BoE and PRA echoes this duty by stating that 'the FCA, the Bank [of England] and the PRA, will share information related to

---

[55] Ibid para 13. The 2019 MoU further provides in para 14 for the establishment of 'a formal engagement structure by APRA Members and ASIC Commissioners (the APRA-ASIC Committee or AAC) and supported by standing committees'.

[56] Ibid para 18.

[57] For information on the Royal Commission and the Final Report, see n 50.

[58] See Final Report, Recommendation 6.9, 461.

[59] For details of the proposed amendments, see https://treasury.gov.au/consultation/c2019-40503.

[60] Financial Services Act 2012 (FS Act), Part 2 amendments to the Financial Services and Markets Act 2000 (FSM Act), s 3D.

[61] FS Act, Part 2 amendments to the FSM Act, s 3D(1)(b).

[62] Ibid s 3D(2)(a), (b).

[63] Ibid s 3D(4). The operation of this provision was explained in the Explanatory Note to the *Financial Services Act 2012*: Explanatory Note, FS Act, para 168.

markets and markets infrastructure where materially relevant to another of them both at their own initiative and upon each other's request, where legally permissible'.[64] A separate duty to cooperate exists between the Treasury, the Bank of England and the PRA to coordinate the discharge of their functions 'so far as they ... relate to the stability of the UK financial system ... and affect the public interest'.[65]

5.2.3 *Funding Arrangements*

The Basel Core Principles require the banking supervisor to have adequate resources.[66] A similar requirement applies to the insurance supervisor under the Insurance Core Principles.[67] The basis on which a regulator is funded is important in securing its operational independence. The Wallis Report in Australia recommended a funding structure that reflected the costs of the regulatory agencies, stating that '[a]s far as practicable, the regulatory agencies should charge each financial entity for direct services provided, and levy sectors of industry to meet the general costs of their regulation'.[68]

This ability to levy industry to meet the costs of regulation – namely, an industry-funding model – was adopted in respect of APRA. According to the Explanatory Memorandum for the APRA Act, APRA's independence from government was reflected in its ability 'to impose charges and receive levy funding from the institutions regulated'.[69] The Explanatory Memorandum went on to state that '[t]he levies are designed to raise funds to cover the cost of all regulation of prudentially regulated institutions'.[70]

Section 50 of the APRA Act provides that the minister will determine the levy payable to the Commonwealth for the cost of prudential supervision, and the amount to be paid to APRA and credited to the APRA Special Account, on an ongoing basis.[71] In its 2012 assessment against the Basel Core Principles, the IMF noted that APRA was self-funding and that government support for APRA appeared to be strong and adequate to date.[72]

APRA included a discussion on funding and budgetary independence in its submission to the FSI, noting that '[b]udgetary independence refers to the ability of the prudential regulator to determine the size of its own budget and the specific allocation of resources and setting of priorities'. APRA further submitted that 'financial arrangements [had] not to date materially affected its ability to conduct effective supervision' but it was 'likely to face increasing constraints on its funding and operating flexibility. . . an important issue for a risk-based prudential regulator like APRA, where the ability to attract and flexibly utilise highly skilled staff is critical to the delivery of its mission'.[73]

---

[64] Memorandum of Understanding between the Financial Conduct Authority and the Bank of England, including the Prudential Regulation Authority (March 2015) para 8.

[65] FS Act, s 64.

[66] Basel Committee, 'Core Principles' (n 30) Principle 2.

[67] International Association of Insurance Supervisors, 'Insurance Core Principles' (October 2011), Principle 2.

[68] Wallis Report, 'Overview' (n 6) 37.

[69] Explanatory Memorandum, Australian Prudential Regulation Authority Bill 1998 (Cth) para 4.13.

[70] Ibid para 4.41.

[71] See APRA Act, s 50(1) and s 50(1A).

[72] International Monetary Fund, 'Australia: Basel Core Principles for Effective Banking Supervision – Detailed Assessment of Observance' (IMF Country Report No 12/313, November 2012), 26.

[73] Australian Prudential Regulation Authority, Submission, *Financial System Inquiry* (31 March 2014), 29–30. Cf Australian Prudential Regulation Authority. *Capability Review* (June 2019), 85; 87; 91, https://treasury.gov.au/sites/default/files/2019-07/190715_APRA%20Capability%20Review.pdf: 'While some expertise will be required in-house, it

A different approach, however, had previously been adopted in respect of ASIC. Prior to reforms in 2017, ASIC was largely funded by government appropriation. In its submissions to the FSI, ASIC noted the 'limitations and inefficiencies in the way ASIC is currently funded' and submitted that consideration be given to 'moving to a user pays funding model that better reflects the costs associated with regulation'.[74] Pursuant to legislation that came into effect on 1 July 2017, ASIC has now moved to an industry funding model, under which regulated entities share the costs of ASIC's regulatory services.

5.3 SURVEYING THE TERRAIN IN AUSTRALIA

The years 2014 and 2019 were significant for Australia's financial system. In late 2013, the Financial System Inquiry was established to examine 'how the financial system could be positioned to best meet Australia's evolving needs and support Australia's economic growth'.[75] The FSI issued its final report on 7 December 2014 (FSI Final Report).[76] In late 2017, the Royal Commission into Misconduct in the Banking, Superannuation and Financial Services Industry (Financial Services Royal Commission) was established. Its terms of reference included identifying 'misconduct and conduct falling short of community standards and expectations', examining the 'adequacy of existing forms of self-regulation' and 'the effectiveness and ability of regulators to identify and address misconduct'.[77] The Financial Services Royal Commission issued its final report on 1 February 2019.[78]

The FSI was the first comprehensive review of developments in the Australian financial system since the Wallis Inquiry and the Global Financial Crisis. Included within the terms of the FSI was a review of Australia's regulatory architecture and 'the role, objectives, funding and performance of financial regulators, including an international comparison'.[79]

The consensus from the submissions to the FSI was that the system was sound and had served Australia well. The FSI Final Report made the following comments about the adequacy of Australia's regulatory architecture: 'Australia needs strong, independent and accountable regulators to help maintain confidence and trust in the financial system, thereby attracting investment and supporting growth. This requires proactive regulators with the right skills, culture, powers and funding.' So, while Australia's regulatory architecture was found not to need major change by the FSI, the inquiry did make recommendations to improve the current arrangements. For example, government currently lacks a regular process that allows it to assess the

---

will be difficult for APRA to retain all the required expertise internally. A partnering model using outside experts is more likely to deliver sustainable capability for APRA into the future' (at 85).

[74] ASIC, Submission (n 36) 18. In its 2012 assessment of Australia, the IMF stated that '[t]he independence and sufficiency of resources of ASIC [had been] hampered by the flattening of its overall operating funding over the last three years and a not insignificant dependence on non-core funding'. The IMF recommended that 'the authorities consider alternative possibilities to arrange the funding of ASIC in such a manner that it will be best equipped to respond to the current and emerging challenges in securities regulation both domestically and globally' and that the government 'ensure that ASIC's core funding will be sufficient to meet the future regulatory and supervisory challenges, also in light of the global regulatory commitments'. IMF, 'Australia: IOSCO Objectives and Principles of Securities Regulation – Detailed Assessment of Implementation' (IMF Country Report No 12/314, November 2012), 30, 47.

[75] The Hon Joe Hockey MP, Treasurer of the Commonwealth of Australia, 'Financial System Inquiry' (Media Release, 20 December 2013), https://ministers.treasury.gov.au/ministers/joe-hockey-2015 (FSI Media Release).

[76] FSI (n 42).

[77] See https://financialservices.royalcommission.gov.au/Documents/Signed-Letters-Patent-Financial-Services-Royal-Commission .pdf.

[78] See https://financialservices.royalcommission.gov.au/Pages/reports.aspx.

[79] FSI Media Release (n 75).

overall performance of financial regulators. Regulators' funding arrangements and enforcement tools have some significant weaknesses, particularly in the case of ASIC. In addition, it is not clear whether adequate consideration is currently given to competition and efficiency in designing and applying regulation.

The inquiry's recommendations to refine Australia's regulatory system and keep it fit for purpose aimed to:

- Improve the accountability framework governing Australia's financial sector regulators by establishing a new Financial Regulator Assessment Board to review their performance annually.
- Ensure Australia's regulators have the funding, skills and regulatory tools to deliver their mandates effectively.
- Rebalance the regulatory focus towards competition by including an explicit requirement to consider competition in ASIC's mandate and conduct three-yearly external reviews of the state of competition.
- Improve the process for implementing new financial regulations.

These recommendations seek to make Australia's financial regulators more effective, adaptable and accountable.[80]

The model was also endorsed by the Financial Services Royal Commission, which recommended that the model be retained. The FSI, however, recommended various areas of improvement, including better coordination between the regulators (particularly in relation to the supervision of superannuation funds), greater clarity in terms of their functions, stronger macroprudential regulation and the need for a process to assess the overall performance of the regulators. Crucially, eleven years after flaws in coordination were first identified in the HIH Report,[81] and despite further instances of the same criticism, the problem remained. In addition, the FSI Final Report identified the need to ensure that the financial regulators paid sufficient attention to competition concerns. For this purpose, the FSI recommended that ASIC be given an express competition mandate which, as outlined below, occurred in 2018.

The following discussion outlines the recommendations of the FSI Final Report in the following areas: (1) objectives; (2) independence; (3) accountability; (4) coordination; (5) periodic reviews of the regulators; (6) regulatory overlap; and (7) the need to strengthen the enforcement powers of ASIC. The analysis is supplemented by references to the findings and recommendations of the Financial Services Royal Commission, where relevant.

5.3.1 *Objectives*

Section 8(2) of the Australian Prudential Regulation Authority Act 1998 provides that '[i]n performing and exercising its functions and powers, APRA is to balance the objectives of financial safety and efficiency, competition, contestability and competitive neutrality and, in balancing these objectives, is to promote financial system stability in Australia'.

By contrast, prior to 2018, the objectives of ASIC as stated in section 1(2) of the ASIC Act did not make reference to competition. In its FSI submission, ASIC suggested that this was anomalous, and was supportive of a formal requirement 'to consider the effect of its decision making on competition' which, it said, 'would drive a greater focus on the long-term benefits for

---

[80] Financial System Inquiry, *Final Report* (November 2014) (n 42) xx–xxi.
[81] See n 26.

the end users of the financial system' and 'help ensure that ASIC's approach to regulation considered market-wide effects more explicitly'.[82] The effect of including a formal competition objective would be that ASIC would 'select the most "competition-friendly" option from a range of potential regulatory responses, provided that this option was also capable of achieving ASIC's other regulatory objectives'.[83]

This was accepted in the recommendations of the FSI in its Final Report, which recommended that ASIC 'be given an explicit competition mandate' and that 'periodic reviews of the state of competition should be conducted'.[84] The ASIC Act was subsequently amended in 2018 to provide that 'ASIC must consider the effects that the performance of its functions and the exercise of its powers will have on competition in the financial system.'[85]

5.3.2 *The Independence of the Regulators*

Independence is identified as a core principle under Principle 2 of the Basel *Core Principles for Effective Banking Supervision* (Core Principles):

> Principle 2 – Independence, accountability, resourcing and legal protection for supervisors: The supervisor possesses operational independence, transparent processes, sound governance, budgetary processes that do not undermine autonomy and adequate resources, and is accountable for the discharge of its duties and use of its resources. The legal framework for banking supervision includes legal protection for the supervisor.[86]

Independence – often expressed in terms of the operational independence of a regulator – may be measured by reference to a range of factors, including the nature of a regulator's relationship with the executive government, its governance structure, its funding arrangements, the protection its members and employees enjoy from liability,[87] its public accountability and the oversight to which it is subject in the performance of its functions and duties. Establishing the right balance, particularly in the area of funding and accountability, can be challenging – a point that was acknowledged by the Treasury in its FSI submission[88] and in the FSI Interim Report.[89]

The importance of operational independence was noted both by Parliament when establishing the regulators[90] and by subsequent reviews.[91] Both APRA and ASIC are subject to ministerial direction on their policies under section 12 of the APRA Act and section 12 of the ASIC Act respectively. By contrast, the RBA is not subject to ministerial direction. Instead, there is a consultation process that is triggered in the event of a difference of opinion between the

---

[82] ASIC (n 36) 13.

[83] Ibid 18–19. ASIC noted that the Australian Competition and Consumer Commission (ACCC) would remain the competition regulator.

[84] Financial System Inquiry (n 42) 237.

[85] See ASIC Act, s 1(2A). This is expressed to be 'without limiting subsection (2), which outlines the existing functions and powers of ASIC'.

[86] Basel Committee on Banking Supervision, *Core Principles for Effective Banking Supervision* (September 2012), 10.

[87] See, for example, APRA Act, s 58.

[88] Treasury, Submission, *Financial System Inquiry* (3 April 2014), 59.

[89] Financial System Inquiry, *Interim Report* (July 2014), 3–108, states that 'independence should be maximised to the greatest extent possible, together with clear and robust accountability mechanisms that provide appropriate checks and balances. Balancing these objectives is challenging'.

[90] See, for example, the APRA Act Second Reading Speech, which noted that 'APRA [would] be an independent regulator, but, like the Reserve Bank, [would] be subject to an overriding policy determination power of the Treasurer in the very rare event of unreconciled disagreement with the government of the day': Commonwealth, *Parliamentary Debates*, House of Representatives (26 March 1998), 1650 (Peter Costello MP).

[91] See the Palmer Report and the Uhrig Review, as referred to in Treasury (n 88) 27.

government and the RBA about whether a policy is 'directed to the greatest advantage of the people of Australia'.[92] If the treasurer and the RBA are unable to reach agreement, the treasurer may submit a recommendation to the Governor-General, who, 'acting with the advice of the Federal Executive Council, may, by order, determine the policy to be adopted by the Bank'.[93] A similar process applied to APRA before it was replaced by section 12 of the 2003 amendments, which came about as a result of the recommendations of the HIH Royal Commission.

In its FSI submission, APRA voiced concerns about amendments to the APRA Act that had eroded its independence since its establishment, asserting that 'Australia falls short of global standards in this area'.[94] In addition to the insertion of section 12 as noted above, APRA pointed to an amendment to its objectives in section 8(1)(c) of the APRA Act, which also occurred in 2003. This section originally provided that APRA's purposes included 'developing the policy to be applied in performing [its] regulatory role' and was amended by replacing the word 'policy' with 'administrative practices and procedures'. APRA noted that '[t]he accompanying Explanatory Memorandum stated that this amendment was intended to "remove some confusion that has arisen in the past and led to uncertainty about where responsibility resides for formulating the policy behind the prudential regulatory framework"' and that it 'was in response to Government concerns at the time about early APRA attempts to involve itself in broader policy issues without prior consultation with the Government'.[95]

The power of the minister to give a direction, which may not be given about a particular case, has not, to date, been used in relation to APRA, and has only been used once in relation to ASIC. However, in the Financial System Stability Assessment of Australia, conducted in November 2012, the IMF team expressed concern that the existence of such a power 'could potentially diminish the ability of APRA and ASIC to carry out their supervisory and regulatory functions effectively'.[96] This was noted by APRA in its FSI submission:

> APRA accepts that it is necessary and appropriate for the Government to decide matters of financial system policy, such as those affecting the structure of the financial industry and how it best serves the needs of the Australian community. Nonetheless, the original APRA Act recognised APRA's authority to develop and implement prudential policies that it has judged as necessary to meet its statutory objectives, and restoration of that authority would be consistent with the independence of a prudential regulator envisaged by the Wallis Inquiry. There are now sufficient accountability mechanisms in place, including consultation with the relevant Minister and through the Council of Financial Regulators, as well as the Parliamentary disallowance process, to address any concerns that APRA might act in a manner inconsistent with broader Government policy.[97]

---

[92] Reserve Bank Act 1959 (Cth) s 11(2).

[93] Ibid s 11(4).

[94] APRA, Submission, *Financial System Inquiry* (31 March 2014), 5.

[95] Ibid 28. For more on independence, see James R. Barth, Daniel E. Nolle, Triphon Phumiwasana and Glenn Yago, 'A Cross-Country Analysis of the Bank Supervisory Framework and Bank Performance' (2002) 2 *Economic and Policy Analysis Working Paper* (September 2002); Thorsten Beck, Asli Demirgüç-Kunt and Ross Levine, *Bank Supervision and Corporate Finance* (Policy Research Working Papers, published by the World Bank, 2003), https://doi.org/10.1596/1813-9450-3042.

[96] International Monetary Fund (IMF), 'Australia: Financial System Stability Assessment' (November 2012). See also IMF, 'Australia: Financial System Stability Assessment' (February 2019), para 26, 61–2.

[97] APRA (n 94) 30. The point was reiterated in APRA's second-round submission, in which APRA stated that it was 'preferable that the law clearly recognise APRA's ability to set prudential policy, within the bounds set out by the APRA Act and relevant Industry Acts. APRA's policy-making role could also be reflected clearly in the Government's Statement of Expectations (SOE) and APRA's Statement of Intent (SOI)'. APRA, Response to the Interim Report, *Financial System Inquiry* (26 August 2014), 66.

Similar concerns were expressed by the IMF team in its assessment of Australia against the Basel Core Principles for Effective Banking Supervision. In its report, the IMF noted the response of the Australian government to these concerns:

> The Australian authorities agree with the need for an independent supervisor and are of the view that APRA is already unambiguously independent. APRA is established as a statutory authority, at arm's length from Government and with substantial statutory and operational independence, including extensive powers to determine prudential standards. There is no evidence, past or present, of any Government or industry interference that compromises APRA's operational independence.[98]

The FSI Final Report did not make any specific recommendations in relation to strengthening the operational independence of the regulators, except to suggest that its recommendations on the financial system would make the regulators 'more effective, more adaptable and more accountable, with greater independence in some areas, such as funding'.[99]

5.3.3 *Accountability*

As noted, the Core Principles acknowledge the need for a supervisor to be 'accountable for the discharge of its duties and use of its resources'. The accountability of the regulators was a theme that figured prominently in the submissions to the FSI.

In Australia, APRA is required to produce annual reports to the minister and is also subject to a half-yearly review called the Financial Stability Review. Similarly, ASIC is required to provide an annual report to the minister. ASIC is also subject to the oversight of the Parliamentary Joint Committee on Corporations and Financial Services.

In its submission to the FSI, the Treasury suggested that 'the existing mechanisms for accountability should be further strengthened by defining measures of success that recognise the trade-offs inherent in the regulators' statutory mandates', and noted that the government was 'developing a framework for assessing regulator performance drawing on work by the Productivity Commission'.[100]

In its Final Report, the FSI recommended 'establishing a new Financial Regulator Assessment Board to undertake annual ex post reviews of overall regulator performance against their mandates'.[101] This was the first of three recommendations, handed down by formal inquiries, that regulator performance indicated a need for greater oversight and accountability. This board would replace the current Financial Sector Advisory Council and 'could be supported by a separate secretariat housed in Treasury'.[102] It would not direct the regulators or examine individual complaints against regulators, or the merits of specific regulatory or enforcement decisions. However, it would 'assess how regulators have used the powers and discretions available to them'.[103]

---

[98] International Monetary Fund, 'Australia: Basel Core Principles for Effective Banking Supervision – Detailed Assessment of Observance' (November 2012), 21 [47].

[99] FSI (n 42) 238.

[100] Treasury (n 88) 6 [11]. This involved issuing new statements of expectation and considering 'specific indicators for assessing agency performance, including explicit metrics of success that take account of policy objectives and compliance costs'. The need for regulators to be given key performance indicators was also suggested by KPMG in its submission: KPMG, Submission, *Financial System Inquiry* (31 March 2014), 47.

[101] FSI (n 42) 235.

[102] Ibid 239.

[103] Ibid 239.

The FSI made a further recommendation in relation to regulator accountability: that 'clearer guidance [be provided] to regulators in Statements of Expectation and [that] the use of performance indicators for regulator performance [be increased]'.[104]

The recommendation to establish a Financial Regulator Assessment Board was not accepted by the government following the FSI Final Report. In what some have argued[105] was a self-serving submission against greater accountability, APRA in its FSI submission suggested that there were challenges in assessing the performance and effectiveness of regulators. The challenges as outlined by APRA included 'demonstrating causality or an explicit link between the prudential regime or supervisory actions and the outcomes for individual financial institutions or the financial system as a whole';[106] the secrecy obligations that prevent a regulator from 'offering public commentary on its day-to-day activities';[107] and also the fact that 'performance assessment of a prudential regulator does not lend itself to straightforward cost–benefit analysis'.[108]

The government subsequently reversed its position and confirmed its intention to establish an oversight body following the Financial Services Royal Commission's recommendation in this regard and growing calls for an oversight body to be established.[109] The Financial Services Royal Commission recommended that '[a] new oversight authority for APRA and ASIC, independent of Government, should be established by legislation to assess the effectiveness of each regulator in discharging its functions and meeting its statutory objects'.[110] This was the second time such a recommendation was made by a formal inquiry. The third recommendation was by the APRA capability review, which supported the call for an oversight body.[111]

As at the date of writing, the government had released exposure draft legislation to implement this recommendation.[112] Under the proposed legislation, a statutorily independent Financial Regulator Assessment Authority would be established, and would consist of three appointed part-time members and an ex-officio member, being the Secretary of the Department of the Treasury or a nominated employee in the department. The explanatory materials provide that '[i]n order to not unreasonably impact regulators' independence … the new authority will not have the ability to direct, make, assess or comment on the regulators' specific enforcement actions, regulatory decisions, complaints and like matters'.[113] The Authority's key functions would be to assess and report on the effectiveness of APRA and ASIC; when requested by the minister, to 'undertake or cause someone else to undertake capability reviews of each of APRA and ASIC'; and 'on an ad hoc basis, either on its own initiative or when requested by the Minister, report to

---

[104] Ibid 239. As noted by Treasury on its website, 'Ministers issue Statements of Expectations to statutory agencies. Through issuing a Statement of Expectations, Ministers are able to provide greater clarity about government policies and objectives relevant to a statutory authority, including the policies and priorities it is expected to observe in conducting its operations': https://treasury.gov.au/the-department/accountability-reporting/statements-of-expectations.

[105] Andrew Schmulow, Karen Fairweather and John Tarrant, 'Restoring Confidence in Consumer Financial Protection Regulation in Australia: A Sisyphean Task? (2019) 47(1) *Federal Law Review* 91–120, 105.

[106] APRA (n 94) 62.

[107] Ibid 63.

[108] Ibid.

[109] For examples of these calls, see Andrew Schmulow, Karen Fairweather and John Tarrant 'Twin Peaks 2.0: Reforming Australia's Financial Regulatory Regime in Light of Failings Exposed by the Banking Royal Commission' (2018) 12(4) *Law and Financial Markets Review* 193; Schmulow et al (n 105).

[110] Financial Services Royal Commission, Recommendation 6.14. This recommendation provided also that the authority should be comprised of three part-time members and staffed by a permanent secretariat, and that it should be required to report to the minister in respect of each regulator at least biennially.

[111] The APRA Capability Review Report, xix. For the APRA Capability Review report, see https://treasury.gov.au/sites/default/files/2019-07/190715_APRA%20Capability%20Review.pdf.

[112] See https://treasury.gov.au/consultation/c2020-48919a.

[113] *Financial Regulator Assessment Authority Bill 2020*, Exposure Draft Explanatory Materials, para 1.8.

the Minister on any matter relating to either or both of APRA's effectiveness and ASIC's effectiveness'.[114] The explanatory materials make it clear that as the regulators are independent entities, the Authority would not have the power to direct the regulators to implement any recommendations it makes.[115]

5.3.4 *Council of Financial Regulators (CFR)*

As previously noted, effective coordination between the regulators is an essential element of the Twin Peaks model. According to the Basel Core Principles, one of the preconditions for effective banking supervision is a 'well established framework for financial stability policy formulation'. This in turn requires mechanisms for effective cooperation and coordination among the relevant agencies:

> In view of the impact and interplay between the real economy and banks and the financial system, it is important that there exists a clear framework for macroprudential surveillance and financial stability policy formulation. Such a framework should set out the authorities or those responsible for identifying systemic risk in the financial system, monitoring and analysing market and other financial and economic factors that may lead to accumulation of systemic risks, formulating and implementing appropriate policies, and assessing how such policies may affect the banks and the financial system. It should also include mechanisms for effective cooperation and coordination among the relevant agencies.[116]

As noted in Section 5.2.2, the legislative framework for regulatory coordination in Australia is informal in nature. Many submissions to the FSI called for a more formal approach to coordination, including the coordination of cross-agency regulatory changes, and the reporting processes between the regulators.[117] Some recommended that the CFR be given statutory recognition[118] and that the membership of the CFR be expanded.[119]

In its submissions to the FSI, the Reserve Bank of Australia cautioned against a move towards formalised arrangements, suggesting that 'it remains to be seen whether more formalised arrangements of co-operation between regulators are superior to informal mechanisms'. Further, according to the RBA co-operation without formal arrangements appears to be working well in Australia[120] and 'during the crisis in particular, it has proven to be an effective means of coordinating responses to potential threats to financial stability':[121]

> In Australia, high level coordination between agencies is achieved through informal (non-statutory) arrangements, through the Council of Financial Regulators (CFR). While this approach has worked well in Australia (Section 3.2.6.2), regulators can also coordinate through formal arrangements. Some other jurisdictions, including the United States, United Kingdom, the European Union (EU), Sweden and Norway have formalised arrangements in the last few

---

[114] Ibid para 1.26.
[115] Ibid para 1.34.
[116] Basel Committee on Banking Supervision (n 86) 15 [49].
[117] See ANZ, Submission, *Financial System Inquiry* (31 March 2014), 46–7; Commonwealth Bank of Australia, Submission, *Financial System Inquiry* (March 2014) 75; NAB, Submission, *Financial System Inquiry* (2014), 4.
[118] KPMG (n 100) 5.
[119] KPMG recommended that AUSTRAC and the ACCC be included in the council: KPMG (n 100) 5. CBA called for the membership of the CFR to be extended to include all financial sector regulators and agencies: CBA (n 117) 90.
[120] RBA, Submission, *Financial System Inquiry* (March 2014), 5, 53.
[121] Ibid 66.

years to delineate their respective financial stability mandates, powers and tools ... It is too early to judge the performance of these more formal structures for coordination between agencies.[122]

The Reserve Bank warned that 'adopting such an approach in Australia by formalising the CFR with explicit responsibilities and policy tools would involve transferring agency constituent powers to the CFR, with the risk of blurring lines of responsibility that to date have worked well'.[123] While the RBA's assertions may be correct, that to formalise the CFR would be problematic, its positive assertions about informal cooperation and collaboration generally are subject to question in light of the findings of two Royal Commissions, a financial system inquiry and a parliamentary standing committee's findings.

In its Final Report, the FSI stated that it did

> not see a need to expand the permanent membership of the CFR to include the Australian Competition and Consumer Commission (ACCC), the Australian Transaction Reports and Analysis Centre (AUSTRAC) or the Australian Taxation Office (ATO), as these agencies may already attend meetings as necessary. However, the Final Report stated that there would be benefit in increasing the transparency of the CFR's deliberations, including its assessment of financial stability risks and how these are being addressed.[124]

In addition, the FSI did not identify a need to give the CFR statutory recognition.

5.3.5 *Periodic Reviews*

The FSI recommended that the financial regulators undergo periodic capability reviews to ensure that they had the skills and culture to be effective in an environment of rapid change. In July 2015, ASIC became the first regulator to undergo a review. Following the capability review, which reported in 2016, the government agreed to commit additional funding and resources to enhance ASIC's data analytics and surveillance capabilities, and to strengthen its powers (including its product intervention power).

In addition to the capability review, a review of ASIC's enforcement powers was undertaken to ensure that the penalties were set at the right levels. The FSI Final Report had recommended stronger licensing powers and substantially higher criminal and civil penalties. The ASIC Enforcement Review Taskforce released a position paper entitled 'Strengthening Penalties for Corporate and Financial Sector Misconduct' on 23 October 2017,[125] and provided its recommendations to the Australian government in December 2017. Issues regarding the enforcement powers and activities of the regulators are considered further in Section 5.3.0.

In 2019, a capability review was conducted in respect of APRA. The government announced that the review 'was intended to provide a forward-looking assessment of APRA's ability to respond to an environment of growing complexity and emerging risks for APRA's regulated sectors'.[126] Issued in June 2019, the report made recommendations across a range of areas,

---

[122] Ibid 53.

[123] Ibid 67. The Reserve Bank noted that '[i]n a number of countries the approach has been to create separate macroprudential and microprudential regulatory bodies. The Bank, along with APRA, is not convinced of the merits of such a division between macroprudential and microprudential policy'.

[124] FSI (n 42) 234.

[125] Australian Government Treasury, 'ASIC Enforcement Review Taskforce consults on strengthening penalties' (media release, 23 October 2017).

[126] APRA Capability Review report (n 111).

including macroprudential policies;[127] APRA's supervision of governance, culture and accountability (GCA);[128] and APRA's enforcement strategy.[129] The report also endorsed the recommendations of the Financial Services Royal Commission, including the expansion of APRA's statutory powers;[130] the establishment of a new oversight authority for both APRA and ASIC;[131] and the completion of capability reviews of the regulators on a four-yearly basis. Although welcomed by APRA as '[recognising] APRA as a high quality prudential supervisor',[132] the report was considered by many to be highly critical of APRA's culture and regulatory approach.[133]

5.3.6 *Regulatory Overlap*

A functional or objectives-based approach to regulation means that there will be dual-regulated entities; namely, entities that will be subject to the regulation and supervision of both regulators. In relation to the question of overlap, the submission to the FSI by Treasury suggested that there was a need to draw clearer demarcations between the responsibilities of ASIC and APRA. One submission noted the possibility of reducing regulatory overlap by adopting a system where an institution would have a primary regulator depending on the sector to which it belonged. Although regulators would regulate in their respective areas of responsibility, the direct compliance and enforcement responsibilities would rest with the primary regulator. Such a model, it was suggested, 'would ensure a consistent and coordinated approach for regulated entities informed by a regulator who understands the business of their regulated entities and ... ensure that any regulation is enforced in a manner that promotes innovation, efficiency and competition in the particular sector'.[134]

Although a logical solution to regulatory overlap, the 'primary regulator' or 'lead supervisor' approach has been said to '[create] problems in terms of coordinating supervisory action, information flows and, ultimately, crisis intervention',[135] and was not recommended in the FSI Final Report. That said, it should be acknowledged that Australia's experience over the past fifteen years or so indicates continuing challenges for regulators in resolving issues concerning the nature and scope of functions of each. This has created challenges in terms of the tools that should be made available to the regulators to enable them to carry out their functions. For example, calls have been made for ASIC to impose capital adequacy requirements on its regulated entities, namely, the holders of Australian Financial Services Licences, and for the

---

[127] Recommendation 3.3 identified the need for APRA to 'take a more transparent and assertive role in articulating the objectives of its macro-prudential policies' and to 'continue to develop its public communication around the extent of systemic risks, conditions required for macro-prudential actions and assessments of any actions taken'.

[128] Recommendation 4.1 identified the need for APRA to 'ensure the policy framework is focussed on assessing appropriate outcomes around GCA risk in regulated entities, not just appropriate processes'.

[129] See further in Section 5.3.0.

[130] The recommendations of the Financial Services Royal Commission included joint information-sharing between APRA and ASIC, and the extension of BEAR (the Bank Executive Accountability Regime) across other prudentially regulated industries.

[131] See Section 5.3.0.

[132] APRA, 'APRA welcomes Capability Review report and outlines action plan' (media release, 17 July 2019).

[133] See, for example, Paul Karp, 'Apra to Be Given New Powers after Scathing Review of Financial Watchdog', *The Guardian* (Wednesday 17 July 2019), www.theguardian.com/australia-news/2019/jul/17/financial-watchdog-apra-to-be-given-new-powers-after-scathing-review.

[134] Minter Ellison, Submission, *Financial System Inquiry* (April 2014). Minter Ellison noted that it did not expect that the primary regulator regime would apply to all regimes (e.g. the investigation and enforcements powers of the Australian Taxation Office in relation to the taxation of financial institutions).

[135] Wymeersch (n 5) 262.

prudential perimeters to be expanded accordingly.[136] This has previously been resisted by ASIC on the basis that it is not within ASIC's regulatory mandate to ensure the solvency of entities that it regulates.[137] In addition, APRA has recently been granted expanded powers, including enforcement powers, in respect of bank executive remuneration, which appear to blur the lines between prudential regulation and market conduct regulation. This has raised questions about whether APRA can – and should – be both a prudential supervisor and a conduct regulator.[138]

Adding to the potential overlap challenges faced by the regulators in Australia, the Financial Services Royal Commission recommended that ASIC and APRA strengthen co-regulation in relation to superannuation and the Banking Executive Accountability Regime (BEAR).[139] The concept of co-regulation or joint administration would involve APRA overseeing the prudential aspects, and ASIC overseeing the market conduct and consumer protection aspects, of super-annuation and BEAR.[140]

5.3.7 *The Need to Strengthen the Enforcement Powers of the Regulators*

The effectiveness of the regulator's enforcement powers over corporate wrongdoing came under intense scrutiny by both the FSI and the Financial Services Royal Commission. A detailed review of ASIC's weaknesses in this regard had previously been undertaken by the Senate Economics References Committee in its report on ASIC's performance.[141] One of the recommendations in the report was that 'the penalties currently available for contraventions of the legislation ASIC administers should be reviewed to ensure they are set at appropriate levels'.[142]

In its FSI submission, ASIC suggested that '[a] review of penalties under ASIC-administered legislation would help establish whether such penalties currently provide the right incentives for better market behaviour'.[143] ASIC noted that the public would expect that it would 'take strong action against corporate wrongdoers' and that effective enforcement was critical in terms of 'promoting fair and efficient financial markets, and ensuring confident and informed investors and financial consumers'.[144]

The FSI Final Report acknowledged that ASIC's enforcement tools had significant weak-nesses[145] and that '[i]nstances of misconduct and consumer loss in the financial system [had] prompted questions about the effectiveness of consumer protection, as well as the adequacy of ASIC's resources and the design of the regulatory framework in which it operates'. Accordingly,

---

[136] See, for example, the recommendation that ASIC be authorised to impose capital adequacy requirements in the case of agribusiness managed investment schemes, in the Parliamentary Joint Committee on Corporations and Financial Services, Parliament of Australia, *Inquiry into Aspects of Agribusiness Managed Investment Schemes* (2009).

[137] For a discussion about regulatory overlap, see Godwin, Kourabas and Ramsay (n 36). In the United Kingdom, the Treasury has the power to establish the 'boundaries' between the two regulators. This effectively allows the Treasury to determine who should be the lead regulator in a regulatory investigation. In this way, the United Kingdom has deliberately built features into its Twin Peaks model to ensure that only one regulator will act where necessary.

[138] For related discussion about this issue in the context of consumer protection, see Chapter 18. The difficulties in delineating prudential regulation from conduct regulation has been noted in Pamela Hanrahan, 'Twin Peaks after Hayne: Tensions and Trade-offs in Regulatory Architecture' (2019) 13 *Law and Financial Markets Review* 124.

[139] See Recommendations 6.3–6.6.

[140] See, for example, Recommendation 6.6.

[141] Senate Economics References Committee, Parliament of Australia, Final Report on the Performance of the Australian Securities and Investments Commission (June 2014).

[142] Ibid xxi.

[143] ASIC (n 36) 14. The need 'to ensure that ASIC [had] the regulatory tools to achieve its mandate' was reiterated in ASIC's second-round submission: ASIC, *Interim Report Submission, Financial System Inquiry* (August 2014), 58.

[144] ASIC (n 36) 45.

[145] FSI (n 42) xx–xxi.

it recommended 'stronger licensing powers to address misconduct, and substantially higher criminal and civil penalties'.[146] Significant increases to many of the penalties in legislation administered by ASIC were introduced by the *Treasury Laws Amendment (Strengthening Corporate and Financial Sector Penalties) Act 2019* (Cth). The increases were based on recommendations in the 2017 report of the ASIC Enforcement Review Taskforce.

The Financial Services Royal Commission was even more blunt about the weaknesses of enforcement on the part of both ASIC and APRA:

> When misconduct was revealed, it either went unpunished or the consequences did not meet the seriousness of what had been done. The conduct regulator, ASIC, rarely went to court to seek public denunciation of and punishment for misconduct. The prudential regulator, APRA, never went to court. Much more often than not, when misconduct was revealed, little happened beyond apology from the entity, a drawn-out remediation program and protracted negotiation with ASIC of a media release, an infringement notice, or an enforceable undertaking that acknowledged no more than that ASIC had reasonable 'concerns' about the entity's conduct. Infringement notices imposed penalties that were immaterial for the large banks. Enforceable undertakings might require a 'community benefit payment', but the amount was far less than the penalty that ASIC could properly have asked a court to impose.[147]

In its Final Report, the Final Services Royal Commission stated that '[i]n the end, the critical question whenever ASIC is considering any contravention of the law must be the question ASIC now accepts must be asked: "Why not litigate?"'[148] Accordingly, it recommended that ASIC should adopt an approach to enforcement that 'takes, as its starting point, the question of whether a court should determine the consequences of a contravention'.[149] It also recommended that an approach that 'separates, as much as possible, enforcement staff from non-enforcement related contact with regulated entities'.

Although not itself the specific subject of a recommendation in respect of enforcement, APRA issued a report following a review of its own enforcement strategy on 29 March 2019. In the report, APRA indicated a move towards a 'constructively tough' approach.[150] The approach was endorsed by the report of the APRA Capability Review, which stated its belief that 'APRA's strong preference to do things "behind the scenes" with regulated entities [had been] limiting its effectiveness' and that this had '[limited] its scope to deter poor outcomes'.[151] ASIC conducted an Internal Enforcement Review in 2018 leading to the establishment of an Office of Enforcement, and has introduced what it describes as a 'why not litigate' enforcement stance to ensure a stronger focus on court-based enforcement outcomes.[152]

Two points arising out of this discussion are particularly relevant in the context of Australia's Twin Peaks model. First, the recommendations of the Financial Services Royal Commission

---

[146] Ibid 235.

[147] Financial Services Royal Commission, Interim Report, xix.

[148] Financial Services Royal Commission, Final Report, 424.

[149] Ibid Recommendation 6.2.

[150] APRA, Enforcement Strategy Review – Final Report (29 March 2019). Cf Andrew Schmulow, 'Why APRA's IOOF Attack Was an Epic Fail', *Australian Financial Review* (25 September 2019), www.afr.com/companies/financial-services/why-apra-s-ioof-attack-was-an-epic-fail-20190925-p52urt; Joyce Moullakis, 'APRA Faces Revolt over Crackdown', *The Australian* (24 July 2019), www.theaustralian.com.au/business/financial-services/apra-faces-revolt-over-crackdown/news-story/1f68904b2bcd2a04771a72fede15b5ae.

[151] APRA Capability Review Report (n 111).

[152] ASIC, 'ASIC Update on Implementation of Royal Commission Recommendations' (19-035MR, 19 February 2019), https://download.asic.gov.au/media/5011933/asic-update-on-implementation-of-royal-commission-recommendations.pdf.

Final Report and the APRA Capability Review were very much about changing the enforcement culture with ASIC and APRA. In the case of ASIC, which has traditionally been regarded as the enforcer in respect of market conduct compliance, this could be seen primarily as a matter of exercising its existing powers in a more effective manner. In the case of APRA, however, the cultural shift is more profound as it moves away from its 'behind the scenes' approach towards a more transparent approach to supervising regulated entities and enforcing compliance. Thus, the traditional cultural differences between the Twin Peaks regulators in Australia are starting to break down and, possibly, starting to intersect and converge.

Secondly, with the adoption of a statutory duty to cooperate and share information on the part of ASIC and APRA,[153] it is expected that cooperation between the two regulators in the area of enforcement will become stronger. This follows the recommendation of the Financial Services Royal Commission that each of APRA and ASIC should 'notify the other whenever it forms the belief that a breach in respect of which the other has enforcement responsibility may have occurred'.[154] Once again, it is possible that this stronger cooperation will blur the cultural, if not the functional, lines between the two regulators.

5.4 CONCLUSION

The analysis in this chapter reveals some key themes in relation to the evolution of Twin Peaks in Australia and its legal and regulatory framework. First, Twin Peaks in Australia has been as much about the journey, or trek, towards Twin Peaks as it has been about arriving at the destination. From the qualified endorsement of the model by Owen J following the collapse of HIH to the short recommendation by the Financial Services Royal Commission that '[t]he "twin peaks" model of financial regulation should be retained', the model has adapted to changing circumstances and challenges (to varying degrees of success) and has been tested, debated and adjusted (again to varying degrees of efficacy). Experience suggests that it is adaptable, and that its adaptability may be one of its key strengths over other regulatory models. That said, time will tell whether it reaches a point where it is adapted beyond recognition, at least beyond the model as it was traditionally conceived. Notably, few people – if any – have suggested that the model be abandoned.[155]

Secondly, Australia continues to be an outlier among Twin Peaks jurisdictions in at least two significant areas: the structure of the prudential regulator as a statutory body that is separate from the Reserve Bank of Australia, and the relatively informal, 'soft law' approach to regulatory coordination that has been adopted to date. Although regulatory coordination and information-sharing will soon be given a statutory basis, the high-level nature of the proposed statutory duty belies an innate reluctance to be prescriptive about how the regulators should work together, and a reluctance to surrender informality and flexibility in favour of transparency and certainty. In the years to come, comparisons between Australia's experience in this regard and the experience in jurisdictions that have adopted a more prescriptive approach, such as the United Kingdom and South Africa, will be instructive.

Finally, as the discussion about co-regulation and enforcement has revealed, the distinctions between each peak are increasingly being blurred. Time will tell whether this will increase the attractiveness of the integrated model and ultimately take us on a journey towards Mount Everest or whether we will explore different terrains altogether.

---

[153] See Section 5.2.
[154] Financial Services Royal Commission, Final Report, Recommendation 6.9.
[155] For a thought-provoking discussion about an alternative Three Peaks model, one involving a separate consumer protection agency as the third peak, see Hanrahan (n 138).

6

Twin Peaks Financial Regulation in New Zealand

Helen Dervan and Simon Jensen

6.1 INTRODUCTION

The Twin Peaks model of financial regulation was formally introduced in the aftermath of the Global Financial Crisis (GFC) in an attempt to remedy deep flaws exposed by the crisis in New Zealand's financial markets regulation. During the GFC, New Zealand experienced a partial regulatory failure. While the banking sector weathered the storm comparatively well, with banks only requiring liquidity assistance rather than bail-outs,[1] major sections of the finance company sector collapsed.[2] Between 2006 and 2012, over sixty companies failed.[3] Some 200,000 investors suffered losses in excess of NZD$3 billion[4] and payments to investors under an ad hoc government retail deposit guarantee scheme totalled approximately $2 billion.[5] These companies were not subject to prudential regulation or supervision before 2008,[6] and the market conduct legislation in place at the time failed to adequately control risky, negligent and, sometimes, fraudulent conduct. Insurance companies similarly fell outside the prudential regulatory perimeter.

The Twin Peaks model divides financial regulation into two broad regulatory functions: market conduct integrity and consumer protection on the one hand and prudential supervision and financial system stability on the other, regulating each separately and independently (hence 'Twin Peaks').[7] To take advantage of the model's benefits and achieve an effective regime, it is necessary to properly construct each peak regulator. This requires the consideration of complex issues such as who the regulator will be, how decisions will be made and what mandate and powers the regulator will have. In New Zealand, this process has proved problematic because of

---

[1] The Reserve Bank of New Zealand (RBNZ) provided emergency liquidity to banks. The government provided guarantees on wholesale debt (2008–10) and retail deposits covering banks and non-bank lenders (2008–11).

[2] Michel Prada and Neil Walter, 'Report on the Effectiveness of New Zealand's Securities Commission' (September 2009), 20.

[3] www.interest.co.nz/saving/deep-freeze-list. In 2008, the then RBNZ governor, Alan Bollard, said that there had been 'a "slow-burn" contagion of finance company failures', in 'News Releases' (2008) 71(4) *Reserve Bank of New Zealand Bulletin* 53.

[4] Commerce Committee (New Zealand), 'Inquiry into Finance Company Failures' (I.1A, October 2011), 7.

[5] Finance and Expenditure Committee, 'Report from the Controller and Auditor-General, The Treasury: Implementing and Managing the Crown Retail Deposit Guarantee Scheme' (31 May 2012), 2. Investor losses from 2006 to 2008 predated the introduction of this scheme.

[6] Commerce Committee (n 4) 7 and 10.

[7] Andrew Godwin, Guo Li and Ian Ramsay, 'Is "Twin Peaks" System of Financial Regulation a Model for China?' (2016) 46(2) *Hong Kong Law Journal* 621, 624.

the different approaches taken in constructing each peak regulator. While an entirely new regime was created for the market conduct peak which included the establishment of a new regulator, the Financial Markets Authority (FMA), construction of the prudential peak involved no change to the regulator – it remained the Reserve Bank of New Zealand (RBNZ), the country's central bank – and only piecemeal additions and adjustments to the regime already in place. This resulted in a prudential regulatory regime which, arguably, does not properly support the Twin Peaks model or contain all the critical components for a strong and coherent financial safety net.[8] Over the ensuing years, deficiencies in the *Reserve Bank of New Zealand Act 1989* (RBNZ Act), the principal statute governing prudential regulation, have become increasing apparent[9] and, in 2017, the International Monetary Fund (IMF) criticised various aspects of New Zealand's prudential regulatory regime.[10] As a result, New Zealand is currently conducting a fundamental overhaul of the RBNZ Act in a joint RBNZ/Treasury review (RBNZ Review).[11] In addition, market conduct regulation is being updated, in part because of a plan made when the new market conduct regime was first introduced to review its operation and in part because of a joint 2018 RBNZ/FMA review of retail bank conduct and culture.[12]

This chapter examines how Twin Peaks has been implemented in New Zealand, proposed changes to the prudential and market conduct regimes, whether regulatory vulnerabilities will remain and how matters such as regulatory overlap and coordination between regulators are dealt with. In addition, because New Zealand and Australia have a unique interdependence that impacts on regulation, this chapter considers mechanisms for cooperation between the two jurisdictions.

6.2 PRE-CRISIS REGULATION

Before the GFC, New Zealand's financial regulation was fragmented and irregular.[13] There was a separation of certain aspects of prudential and market regulation,[14] but the general approach lacked cohesion and had no overarching design. For prudential regulation, the RBNZ had responsibility for the prudential supervision of registered banks,[15] but not of other significant financial entities, such as finance companies (specifically, non-bank deposit takers [NBDTs])

---

[8] The term 'financial safety net' refers to regulatory features and tools such as prudential regulation and supervision, lender of last resort function, deposit insurance and bank resolution procedures that countries use to help maintain financial system stability.

[9] See Helen Dervan and Simon Jensen, 'Prudential Regulation in New Zealand: Time to Review the Reserve Bank of New Zealand Act 1989' (2017) 23 *New Zealand Business Law Quarterly* 165.

[10] International Monetary Fund, *New Zealand Financial Sector Assessment Program, Financial System Stability Assessment* (International Monetary Fund, Country Report No 17/110, 8 May 2017), 6–8.

[11] The Treasury and the Reserve Bank of New Zealand, 'Safeguarding the Future of Our Financial System, The Role of the Reserve Bank and How It Should Be Governed', Consultation 1 (November 2018); The Treasury and the Reserve Bank of New Zealand, 'Safeguarding the Future of Our Financial System, In-Principle Decisions and Follow-Up Questions On: The Role of the Reserve Bank and How It Should Be Governed', Consultation 2A (June 2019); The Treasury and the Reserve Bank of New Zealand, 'Safeguarding the Future of Our Financial System, The Reserve Bank's Role in Financial Policy: Tools, Powers, and Approach', Consultation 2B (June 2019); The Treasury and the Reserve Bank of New Zealand, 'Safeguarding the Future of Our Financial System, Update on the Reserve Bank Act Review' (December 2019); and The Treasury and the Reserve Bank of New Zealand, 'Safeguarding the Future of Our Financial System, Further Consultation on the Prudential Framework for Deposit Takers and Deposit Protection' (March 2020).

[12] Financial Markets Authority and Reserve Bank of New Zealand, 'Bank Conduct and Culture' (November 2018).

[13] Capital Market Development Taskforce, 'Capital Markets Matter Summary Report of the Capital Market Development Taskforce' (December 2009), 8.

[14] Prada and Walter (n 2) 12.

[15] Reserve Bank of New Zealand Act 1989, s 67 (NZ) ('RBNZA 1989').

and insurance companies. For market conduct regulation, responsibility was spread between the Securities Commission,[16] the then Ministry of Economic Development and the stock exchange, NZX Ltd.[17]

Concern was expressed at the state of New Zealand's financial regulation some years before the GFC. In 2004, the IMF undertook an independent review of New Zealand's financial system (2004 IMF Review).[18] It identified regulatory vulnerabilities, including the oversight of non-bank financial institutions,[19] such as NBDTs, and gaps in market regulation that hindered early detection of incompetent and fraudulent conduct.[20] In response, the government initiated reform projects,[21] and Cabinet determined 'in principle' that the RBNZ should act as single prudential regulator.[22] Unfortunately, by the time the finance companies started to fail in 2006 and the full force of the credit crunch hit in August 2007,[23] the regulatory framework remained largely unreformed. Post-crisis, inquiries were held into the finance company failures[24] and into the effectiveness of the Securities Commission.[25] These inquiries heavily criticised New Zealand's regulatory framework as being fragmented, inadequately rigorous and under-resourced. The inquiry into finance company failures reported the principal failings as including too many regulators with narrow mandates, overlapping responsibilities and limited enforcement powers, under-resourcing, as well as limited, slow and expensive avenues of redress.[26] The report on the Securities Commission found that the institution was in need of comprehensive overhaul.[27] In July 2008, the government formed the Capital Market Development Taskforce, appointing representatives from the business, finance, economic analysis and legal communities. The taskforce was mandated with producing a blueprint for the development of New Zealand's capital markets[28] and it recommended the adoption of Twin

---

[16] Established under the Securities Act 1978 (disestablished by the FMAA 2011, s 71).

[17] Office of the Minister of Commerce, 'Creating a Financial Markets Authority and Enhancing Kiwisaver Governance and Reporting' (Document No 991916), para 4.

[18] International Monetary Fund and Capital Markets Department *New Zealand Financial Sector Assessment Program, Financial System Stability Assessment* (International Monetary Fund Country Report No 04/126, April 2004), 8.

[19] IMF Report 04/126 (n 18) 6, 14–16, 20–21 and 32. See also M. Gordon, 'Outcomes of the Financial Sector Assessment Programme for New Zealand' (June 2004) 67(2) *Reserve Bank of New Zealand Bulletin* 51.

[20] IMF Report 04/126 (n 2)16 and 20–21.

[21] In 2004, a taskforce was appointed to look at regulation of financial intermediaries (www.beehive.govt.nz/release/government-looks-regulation-financial-advisers). In March 2005, a review of financial products and providers was commenced: Ministry of Economic Development, 'Review of Financial Products and Providers: Overview of the Review and Registration of Financial Institutions' (Discussion Document, September 2006), para 3.1. Treasury led a 'Domestic Institutional Arrangements' working group considering increasing the RBNZ's prudential role to include non-bank deposit takers (Chris Hunt, 'The 2016 New Zealand Financial Assessment Programme' (April 2016) 79(7) *Reserve Bank of New Zealand Bulletin* 4).

[22] Office of the Minister of Finance, Office of the Minister of Commerce and Cabinet Economic Development Committee, 'Institutional Arrangements for Prudential Regulation' (13 June 2007), para 2. See also Chris Hunt, 'A Short History of Prudential Regulation and Supervision at the Reserve Bank' (August 2016) 79(14) *Reserve Bank of New Zealand Bulletin* 15.

[23] In New Zealand, Bridgecorp Ltd failed in July 2007 owing about $490 million to 18,000 investors. Nathans Finance Ltd failed in August 2007 owing about $166 million to 6,000 investors.

[24] Commerce Committee (n 4) 7.

[25] Prada and Walter (n 2) 12.

[26] Commerce Committee (n 4) 11 and 31.

[27] Prada and Walter (n 2) para 2.1.

[28] Lianne Dalziel, 'Launch of Capital Markets Development Taskforce' (Media release, 22 July 2008), www.beehive.govt.nz/release/launch-capital-market-development-taskforce.

Peaks.[29] The implementation of this model is said to have 'spelt the end of the previously fragmented regime'.[30]

6.3 REFORM OF REGULATORY FRAMEWORK TO ADOPT THE TWIN PEAKS MODEL (2008–2013)

The principal legislative reforms to adopt the Twin Peaks model took place between 2008 and 2013. As mentioned earlier, the approaches taken to reform of market conduct regulation and prudential regulation were markedly different. While wholesale structural and legislative reform of market conduct regulation took place, reform of prudential regulation was far more circumscribed.

6.3.1 *Reform of Market Conduct Regulation*

Following extensive consultation, the Securities Commission was disestablished and, under the *Financial Markets Authority Act 2011* (FMA Act), the FMA was created as the single market conduct regulator.[31] It assumed the regulatory functions of the Securities Commission and Government Actuary, and certain functions of the then minister of commerce and the minister of economic development.

The Twin Peaks model relies on the creation of regulatory bodies with 'clear and precise remit[s]' and a regulatory process 'which is open, transparent and [publicly] accountable'.[32] The way in which the FMA was structured clearly seeks to fulfil this prerequisite. The FMA is an independent Crown entity under the *Crown Entities Act 2004* (CE Act)[33] and this Act creates clear lines of accountability between Crown entities, their board members, responsible ministers on behalf of the Crown and the House of Representatives.[34] As a Crown entity, the FMA is subject to the reporting obligations under Part 4 of the CE Act and must prepare a statement of intent, a statement of performance expectations and an annual report, which must all be published and presented to the House of Representatives.[35] As a body corporate, the FMA utilises a multi-member decision-making structure, and is governed by a board of between five and nine non-executive members, with the minister of commerce and consumer affairs having power to appoint up to five associate members.[36] The board members owe collective and individual duties to the minister.[37] All decisions relating to the FMA's operation must be made

---

[29] Capital Market Development Taskforce, 'Capital Markets Matter: Summary Report of the Capital Market Development Taskforce' (December 2009), 13.

[30] A. Godwin, T. Howse and I. Ramsay, 'A Jurisdictional Comparison of the Twin Peaks Model of Financial Regulation' (2017) 18 *Journal of Banking Regulation* 103 at 108.

[31] Financial Markets Authority Act 2011, ss 2 and 6 ('FMAA 2011'). The first new piece of legislation in the reform process was the Financial Advisers Act 2008 ('FAA 2008'). Section 97(1) Financial Services Legislation Amendment Act, which will be in force by 1 May 2021, repeals the FAA 2008.

[32] Michael Taylor, 'Twin Peaks: A Regulatory Structure for the New Century' (Centre for the Study of Financial Innovation, No 20, United Kingdom, December 1995), 1.

[33] CEA 2004, s 10 and sch 1, pt 3.

[34] CEA 2004, s 3. Pursuant to s 7 FMAA 2011, the CEA 2004 applies to the Financial Markets Authority (FMA) except to the extent that the FMAA 2011 provides otherwise.

[35] CEA 2004, ss 138–149A (statement of intent); ss 149B–149M (statement of performance expectations) and ss 150–56 (annual report).

[36] FMAA 2011, ss 7, 9 and 11. The minister must consult with the FMA chairperson on appointment of associate members.

[37] CEA 2011, s 26.

by or under the board's authority, with the board having power to delegate certain functions and powers to the chief executive officer of the FMA.[38]

Pursuant to section 8 of the FMA Act, the FMA's main objective is to promote and facilitate the development of fair, efficient and transparent financial markets, and its functions are broadly described in section 9 to include performing and exercising the functions, powers and duties set out under the financial markets legislation. This legislation includes a suite of statutes[39] which give the FMA overall responsibility for market regulation of issuers of securities (equity, debt, derivatives and managed investment schemes), supervisors, financial advisers, discretionary investment managers, market operators, crowdfunding and peer-to-peer lending platforms, and brokers. The *Financial Markets Conduct Act 2013* (FMC Act) is a central piece of legislation setting out the responsibilities of the FMA. It provides the regulatory framework for market conduct and regulates how financial products are to be offered and sold and the provision of other financial services. A licensing scheme was also created under the FMC Act for financial product providers. Further, financial markets legislation is generally administered by the Ministry of Business, Innovation and Employment (MBIE), rather than the FMA, and MBIE provides policy advice on the financial markets regulatory system to help keep legislation up to date.

6.3.2 *Reform of Prudential Regulation*

While there appears to have been some consideration of institutional arrangements for prudential regulation, it was determined that the RBNZ, which had undertaken a prudential role for over fifty years, should continue doing so. Importantly, the regulatory architecture by which the RBNZ undertook its functions was largely unchanged. Reform to prudential regulation, essentially, involved limited amendments to the RBNZ Act, the extension of the regulatory perimeter to include NBDTs and licensed insurers, the introduction of certain new policy initiatives, and the formation of memoranda of understanding (MoU) and cooperation.[40]

6.3.2.1 RBNZ Act Amendments

A new mandate was introduced in section 1A of the RBNZ Act which gave the RBNZ responsibility for 'promoting the maintenance of a sound and efficient financial system'.[41] This mandate is very broad and operates at a high level so that, arguably, prudential regulation had to be directed predominantly towards systemic matters which impact on the financial system as a whole. The RBNZ has taken the position that the soundness mandate operates essentially as a financial stability mandate and that 'soundness' is the key objective. The 'efficiency' mandate occupies a lesser role and is interpreted 'chiefly in terms of minimising or avoiding excessive compliance costs for financial institutions'.[42] It has also interpreted this mandate as excluding

---

[38] FMAA 2011, s 14(5) and CEA 2004, ss 25 and 73. The current CEO is Robert Everett.

[39] FMAA 2011, sch 1.

[40] For example, adoption of Basel II (2008) and Basel III (2011) capital regimes and development of the Open Bank Resolution policy (2012). See Hunt (n 22) 16–19.

[41] RBNZA 1989, s 1A. These purposes were further amended by the Reserve Bank of New Zealand (Monetary Policy) Amendment Act 2018, s 4 ('RBNZAA 2018'), but the Reserve Bank of New Zealand's (RBNZ) responsibility for promoting the maintenance of a sound and efficient financial system remains unchanged.

[42] Chris Bloor and Chris Hunt, 'Understanding Financial System Efficiency in New Zealand' (2011) 74(2) *Reserve Bank of New Zealand Bulletin* 26 at 27. An 'in principle' decision has now been taken by Cabinet to introduce a new financial stability mandate. Consultation Paper (March 2020) (n 11) 4.

consumer protection, and thus one of the two recognised rationales for microprudential regulation and supervision.[43] No material legislative changes were, however, made to the core purposes for prudential supervision in section 68, which, similarly, include promoting the maintenance of a sound and efficient financial system, and also avoiding significant damage to the financial system that could result from the failure of a registered bank.[44] In addition, the minister of finance was given powers to direct the RBNZ to have regard to government policy relating, inter alia, to prudential supervision of banks,[45] and new provisions governing accountability documents were introduced, including a requirement for the RBNZ to produce regulatory impact reports and financial stability reports.[46]

6.3.2.2 Extension of Regulatory Perimeter

When the RBNZ Act was initially enacted, the RBNZ only had statutory responsibility for supervising registered banks, although under earlier legislation it had had a broader mandate.[47] To make the RBNZ the single prudential regulator, the statutory supervisory remit was extended to cover insurance companies and NBDTs. Under the *Insurance (Prudential Supervision) Act 2010* (IPS Act), the RBNZ licenses and undertakes prudential supervision of licensed insurers.[48] In relation to NBDTs, the RBNZ Act was initially amended to give the RBNZ a prudential role.[49] That role is now set out in the *Non-Bank Deposit Takers Act 2013* (NBDT Act). Under the NBDT Act, the RBNZ is the prudential regulator and licensing authority for NBDTs.[50] In this role, the Bank relies on the trustees of debt securities for frontline supervision of compliance with regulatory standards.[51] The trustees are obliged to report to the RBNZ if they have reasonable grounds to believe that an NBDT is failing or is likely to fail to comply in a material respect with the NBDT Act or regulations under it.[52]

6.3.2.3 New Policy Initiatives

The Basel II (2008) and Basel III (2013) capital adequacy frameworks, adapted to New Zealand conditions, were adopted, replacing earlier prudential standards. A new liquidity policy for registered banks (applied generally through banks' conditions of registration)[53] and new liquidity guidelines for NBDTs[54] were introduced. Previously, there had been no formal prudential

---

[43] 'Prudential Policy in a Deregulated Environment' (1987) 50(1) *Reserve Bank of New Zealand Bulletin* 9 at 10. In opposing the introduction of an explicit deposit insurance scheme, the RBNZ stated it considered that consumer protection was outside its s 1A objective in the RBNZA 1989. See International Monetary Fund and Capital Markets Department *New Zealand Financial Sector Assessment Program, Technical Note-Contingency Planning and Crisis Management Framework* (International Monetary Fund, Country Report 17/116, 10 May 2017), para 34.

[44] RBNZA 1989, s 68. Requirements for Trans-Tasman cooperation with Australian financial authorities were put in place in 2006, under the Reserve Bank of New Zealand Amendment Act 2006 (NZ), s 6.

[45] RBNZA 1989, s 68B.

[46] RBNZA 1989, ss 162AB and 165A.

[47] Reserve Bank Act of New Zealand Act 1964 (NZ), s 38L ('RBNZA 1964'), amended by the Reserve Bank Amendment Act 1986 (NZ).

[48] Insurance (Prudential Supervision) Act 2010 (NZ), ss 3, 4 and 12 ('IPSA 2010').

[49] RBNZA 1989, pt 5D.

[50] Non-Bank Deposit Takers Act 2013, ss 3 and 7 ('NBDTA 2013').

[51] NBDTA 2013, ss 28 and 44–6.

[52] NBDTA 2013, s 45.

[53] For banks see Kevin Hoskin, Ian Nieldland and Jeremy Richardson, 'The Reserve Bank's New Liquidity Policy for Banks' (2009) 72(4) *Reserve Bank of New Zealand Bulletin* 5 at 10.

[54] For non-bank deposit takers ('NBDTs'), see Felicity Barker and Noemi Javier, 'Regulating Non-bank Deposit Takers' (2010) 73(4) *Reserve Bank of New Zealand Bulletin* 5 at 14.

standards for liquidity. Banks' liquidity risks were addressed through a disclosure and director attestation regime where directors were required to publish information about their bank's approach to managing liquidity and other risk, and attest that systems were in place to monitor and adequately control such risk, and that those systems had been properly applied. However, the detail of the reporting was largely left to a bank's own discretion.[55] This approach was seen as enhancing market discipline.[56] NBDTs' liquidity risks were managed internally by individual companies.[57]

Further, an open bank resolution policy (OBR policy) was introduced.[58] The OBR policy is aimed at allowing distressed banks to remain open by requiring a percentage of mainly depositors' money to be 'haircut' (that is, repayment rights would be suspended) to carry the cost of bank failure. This policy has proved contentious because it makes New Zealand one of the only countries in the world which expressly intends to use retail depositors to recapitalise a bank. This is because the RBNZ does not have any statutory objective of protecting depositors; nor does New Zealand have depositor preference rules or any deposit insurance scheme, although the government has recently announced that it will introduce the latter.[59]

6.3.2.4 Memoranda of Understanding and Cooperation

MoUs and a memorandum of cooperation were also entered into, including a Memorandum of Cooperation on Trans-Tasman Bank Distress Management between members of the Australian Council of Financial Regulators, New Zealand Treasury and the RBNZ (2010); an MoU on Information Exchange and Collaboration between the Treasury and the RBNZ (2012); and an MoU between the minister of finance and the governor of the RBNZ on macroprudential policy (2013).

6.3.3 *Inadequacy of Reforms to Prudential Regulation*

That insufficient thought was given to the construction of the prudential peak regulator is clear from the following three initial regulatory features: the retention of the single decision-maker model (SDM) in the RBNZ Act; the retention of monetary policy as the RBNZ's primary duty; and the failure to reform New Zealand's light-handed approach to prudential supervision.

6.3.3.1 Single Decision-Maker Model

The RBNZ Act utilises an SDM which gives the RBNZ governor full responsibility and accountability for all RBNZ functions, other than monetary policy.[60] This model was introduced mainly to support the conferring of operational independence in monetary policy decision-making to the RBNZ in 1989,[61] although this decision-making has since (in 2019) been transferred to a statutory Monetary Policy Committee (MPC).[62] The RBNZ Act establishes a

---

[55] Hoskin (n 53) 8
[56] Ibid 8
[57] Ibid 8.
[58] Hunt (n 22) 16–19.
[59] Consultation (March 2020) (n 11) 6.
[60] RBNZA 1989, s 41.
[61] Donald T. Brash, 'New Zealand's Remarkable Reforms' (Speech delivered at the Fifth Annual Hayek Memorial Lecture, Institute of Economic Affairs, London, 4 June 1996). Under the RBNZA 1989, a Policy Targets Agreement was agreed by the RBNZ governor and the minister of finance, the core of which was an inflation target. If that target was missed, the governor could be reprimanded or dismissed.
[62] RBNZA 1989 (as amended by RBNZAA 2018, s 8).

board of directors but its powers are limited to review, advice and recommendations.[63] New Zealand also has a Council of Financial Regulators (CFR), an informal body comprising the RBNZ, FMA, Ministry of Business, Innovation and Employment, Treasury and the Commerce Commission,[64] but it is not a decision-making body.[65] Accordingly, at a statutory level, the RBNZ governor, an unelected official, holds extensive regulatory power and the governor's sole opinion on regulatory matters can determine policy. In practice, the RBNZ has used informal committees for decision-making since 2013. Prior to the appointment of the new governor, a four-person committee known as the Governing Committee was used, but it has been replaced by a Senior Leadership Team, which is responsible for all strategic, financial, legal, operational and reputational matters.[66] The SDM, even with the Senior Leadership Team, leaves the RBNZ susceptible to 'groupthink', a defective form of decision-making to which groups are especially vulnerable where members have similar backgrounds and are insulated from outside opinions. This is because the Senior Leadership Team's members are all RBNZ officials or employees[67] and the SDM does not provide any formal avenues for challenging institutional thinking, which can become rigid, deficient and outdated. Arguably, on some issues such as the RBNZ's longstanding opposition to deposit insurance[68] and its maintenance of a light-handed supervisory regime after the GFC, the RBNZ's thinking did become restricted in this way, although there has been recent movement on both issues.[69] Moreover, the risks of groupthink and rigid thinking have been exacerbated because the RBNZ is responsible for reviewing the RBNZ Act, the statute under which it is established and operates. Given the complexity of modern financial markets and the extension of the regulatory perimeter after the GFC, in the authors' view it was not an appropriate decision-making structure for the Twin Peaks model.[70]

By contrast, the United Kingdom, which also adopted Twin Peaks post-GFC, established multi-member statutory committees to undertake prudential regulation for its central bank, the Bank of England.[71] Like New Zealand, the United Kingdom houses both monetary policy and prudential regulation within its central bank and its functions as micro- and macroprudential regulator are exercised through the Prudential Regulation Committee (PRC)[72] and Financial Policy Committee (FPC),[73] respectively. These committees have idiosyncratic membership structures, which include requirements for independent members to ensure that 'thinking and expertise in

[63] RBNZA 1989, ss 52–3, 53A and 53B (as amended by the RBNZAA 2018, ss 20–22).
[64] Reserve Bank of New Zealand, 'Statement of Policy-Making Approach', (April 2017), paras 52–60.
[65] New Zealand Council of Financial Regulators, 'Regulatory Charter: Financial Markets Regulatory System', para 3.2.
[66] For the governing committee, see Graeme Wheeler, 'Decision-Making in the Reserve Bank of New Zealand' (Speech delivered at the University of Auckland Business School, 7 March 2013), 5. For the Senior Leadership Team, see email dated 6 April 2020 from RBNZ Communications to Helen Dervan 'RBNZ governing committee' (on file with the authors).
[67] This committee's members are the governor, the deputy governor/general manager financial Stability, the Assistant governor/general manager economics financial markets and banking, assistant governor/CFO finance, assistant governor/GM governance strategy and corporate relations and the assistant governor/general manager of business operations (www.rbnz.govt.nz/about-us/organisation-chart-and-senior-management).
[68] Helen Dervan and Simon Jensen, 'Prudential Regulation in 21st Century New Zealand: The Case for Deposit Insurance' (2018) 28 *New Zealand Universities Law Review* 211 at 213 and 231.
[69] Adrian Orr, 'The Evolving Reserve Bank – The View from Tāne Māhuta' (Speech delivered to the Financial Services Institute of Australasia, Auckland, 11 July 2019), 2 and Geoff Bascand, 'Renewing the RBNZ's Approach to Financial Stability' (Speech delivered to 15th Financial Markets Law Conference, Auckland, 26 June 2019), 2.
[70] Dervan and Jensen (n 9) 6.
[71] Bank of England Act 1998 (UK), pt 3A, s 30A and Financial Services and Markets Act 2000 (UK) ('FSMA 2000'), s 2A (as amended by s 12 Bank of England and Financial Services Act 2016 (UK)).
[72] FSMA 2000, s 2A.
[73] Bank of England Act 1998 (UK), Part 1A, s 9B (as amended by the Financial Services Act 2012 (UK)).

addition to that gained inside the Bank of England is considered',[74] to safeguard against group-think and to provide a forum where competing views regarding policy are considered.[75]

6.3.3.2 Prudential Regulation and Monetary Policy

Under the Twin Peaks model, where prudential regulation is housed within a central bank and the central bank is also responsible for monetary policy, as was the case with the RBNZ until 2019, consideration needs to be given to ensuring that priorities are not mismatched or contradictory, and monetary policy prioritised.[76] Each function should be given equal status. When Twin Peaks was introduced, the then sections 8 to 13 of the RBNZ Act required monetary policy to take precedence because, under section 8, monetary policy was described as the RBNZ's primary function.[77] These sections were subsequently replaced when monetary policy decision-making was transferred to the MPC.[78] However, in the authors' view, problems may still potentially arise. At a statutory level, the RBNZ and MPC's functions and purposes are dealt with separately but the RBNZ Act does not clearly state that financial stability and monetary policy are to have equal priority. Further, it would still be difficult to ascertain whether there was a mismatch or downplaying of prudential regulation because the majority of MPC members must be RBNZ officials or employees, and members must include the RBNZ governor and deputy governor, so the RBNZ remains in control of both prudential regulation and monetary policy.[79]

6.3.3.3 Light-Handed Supervision Retained

In line with its first supervisory mandate in section 68 of the RBNZ Act, which requires promoting the maintenance of a sound and efficient financial system, the RBNZ has tradition-ally adopted a light-handed approach to supervising the safety and soundness of individual institutions.[80] The RBNZ operates a 'three pillar' regulatory approach which comprises three disciplines: market discipline, which refers to the way in which market participants influence a financial institution's behaviour by monitoring their risk profiles and financial position; self-discipline, which refers to a financial institution's own processes and risk management frame-works, including board accountability; and regulatory discipline, which refers to the mandatory

---

[74] www.bankofengland.co.uk/-/media/boe/files/about/insidetheboe.pdf.

[75] Paul Fisher, 'Microprudential, Macroprudential and Monetary Policy: Conflict, Compromise or Coordination' (Speech delivered at Richmond University, 1 October 2014), 10. This comment was made about the governing body of the Prudential Regulation Authority when it undertook prudential supervision directly, but it applies equally to the Prudential Regulation Committee (PRC) given the similarity of composition between the governing body and the PRC. See FMSA 2000, sch 1ZB (as amended by the Financial Services Act 2012, sch 3).

[76] Parliament of the United Kingdom of Great Britain and Northern Island 'Evidence Presented to the Joint Committee on the draft Financial Services Bill' (16 December 2011), 435 (evidence of Dr Malcolm Eddy) and Dr Ben Broadbent, 'Monetary and Macro-prudential Policies: The Case for a Separation of Powers' (Speech delivered to the Reserve Bank of Australia, Sydney via videolink from Bank of England 12 April 2018), 2, at www.bankofengland.co.uk/-/media/boe/files/speech/2018/monetary-and-macro-prudential-policies-the-case-for-a-separation-of-powers-speech-by-ben-broadbent.

[77] RBNZA 1989, ss 8 and 13.

[78] RBNZAA 2018, s 8.

[79] RBNZA 1989, s 63C(2) and (3) (as inserted by RBNZAA 2018, s 29).

[80] Although, arguably, some RBNZ policies, which are typically imposed on banks through conditions of registration, go further than is necessary to meet these objectives. While consistent with international practice and important in ensuring the soundness of individual financial institutions, many such policies probably deliver only minor benefits to the soundness of the financial system, especially when applied to smaller banks.

rules and requirements set by the RBNZ.[81] The traditional balance applied by the RBNZ has been in favour of market and self-discipline rather than regulatory discipline. Since 1996, the RBNZ has relied heavily on the disclosure and director attestation regime referred to earlier, to support market and self-discipline. Under this regime, registered banks must publicly disclose financial information and bank directors must attest that their banks have systems in place to adequately monitor and control material risks.[82] The RBNZ has also taken a 'hands-off' supervisory approach by not conducting on-site inspections or detailed independent verification of disclosure documentation,[83] although it has recently stated it will intensify its supervisory practices.[84] This regime was unorthodox even before the GFC in comparison to those operating in jurisdictions such as Australia and the United Kingdom because it was more light-handed than was conventional at the time.[85] It focused on public disclosure at the expense of supervision, relied more heavily on market and self-discipline than other jurisdictions did and failed to provide deposit insurance or depositor protection.

While the precise causes of the GFC are debated, there is general acceptance that one of the contributors was poor, overly light regulation and supervision, which depended on substantial industry regulation through market discipline.[86] Indeed, the IMF has said that '[t]he general belief that light-handed regulation based on the assumption that financial market discipline would root out reckless behaviour' was wrong.[87] As a result, many jurisdictions have reformed and strengthened their regulatory and supervisory frameworks by placing greater emphasis on macroprudential regulation[88] and intensifying microprudential regulation and supervision.[89] Although market discipline remains one of the three pillars of prudential regulation under the Basel Framework,[90] the GFC highlighted its limitations and complexities as a market control mechanism.[91]

---

[81] Hunt (n 22) 4.

[82] RBNZA 1989, ss 81 and 81AA. The disclosure requirements have been modified to take account of the RBNZ's Bank Financial Strength Dashboard, which is an online resource prepared by the RBNZ. See www.rbnz.govt.nz/regulation-and-supervision/banks/consultations-and-policy-initiatives/completed-policy-development/the-dashboard-approach-to-quarterly-disclosure.

[83] IMF Report 17/110 (n 10) 59–60.

[84] Orr (n 69) 2 and Bascand (n 69) 2.

[85] The RBNZ was aware its approach was unconventional. When the 1996 reforms were introduced, RBNZ governor Dr Don Brash claimed that its reforms were 'at least as effective in promoting a sound banking system as more conventional approaches to banking supervision' in 'The review of bank supervision arrangements in New Zealand; the main elements of the debate' (1995) 58(3) *Reserve Bank of New Zealand Bulletin* 163 at 171.

[86] G20, 'London Summit – Leaders' Statement' (2 April 2009) and Michael Taylor, *Twin Peaks Revisited ... A Second Chance for Regulatory Reform* (Centre for the Study of Financial Innovation, No 89, United Kingdom, September 2009), 4. Heidi Mandanis Schooner and Michael W Taylor (eds), *Global Bank Regulation Principles and Policies* (Academic Press, 2010), 280.

[87] International Monetary Fund, *International Monetary Fund Annual Report 2009: Fighting the Global Crisis* (24 September 2009), 9. See also Sabine Lautenschläger, 'Regulation, Supervision and Market Discipline' (Speech delivered at Financial Stability Institute conference, Basel, 18 September 2017).

[88] This looks at the resilience of a financial system as a whole and tries to identify monitor and respond to system-wide risks.

[89] For example, see Financial Services Authority, 'The Turner Review: A Regulatory Response to the Global Banking Crisis' (March 2009), 6, 54, 68–9 and 88.

[90] Basel Committee on Banking Supervision, Basel Framework (15 December 2019), DIS standard at www.bis.org/basel_framework/index.htm.

[91] See generally David Min, 'Understanding the Failures of Market Discipline' (2015) 92(6) *Washington University Law Review* 1421 at 1423. Flannery and Bliss state that various factors complicate the effectiveness of market discipline and that, while enhancing market discipline is not impossible, it is more difficult than simply asserting that imposing loses on creditors will elicit the discipline in Mark J. Flannery and Robert R. Bliss, 'Market Discipline in Regulation: Pre- and Post-Crisis' (22 October 2018), 1–2 and 40.

By introducing the new section 1A mandate (which gave the RBNZ responsibility for 'promoting the maintenance of a sound and efficient financial system' mirroring section 68),[92] the RBNZ could strengthen its macroprudential regulation but continue using its unorthodox supervisory practices, even though a light-handed supervisory approach was increasingly discredited. By neglecting to reform section 68, New Zealand missed an opportunity to require the RBNZ to modernise and intensify its supervisory practices so that they were more compliant with international standards. Shortcomings in the RBNZ's bank supervision have been exposed in recent years when both Westpac New Zealand Limited and ANZ Bank New Zealand Limited, two of New Zealand's largest banks, breached their conditions of registration by failing for considerable periods of time to apply approved models for calculation of regulatory capital.[93]

6.4 IMF 2017 FINANCIAL SECTOR ASSESSMENT

In 2017, the IMF completed an independent review of New Zealand's financial markets regulation (IMF Review).[94] It recognised the 'major overhaul' of market conduct regulation and significant improvements to the regulatory framework.[95] It also identified areas where further 'enhancements' were required to conduct supervision.[96] There were also recommendations on oversight of the insurance industry and financial market infrastructures, some of which the FMA jointly regulates with the RBNZ.

Significant steps are being taken to further reform the market conduct regulatory framework. A new regulatory regime for financial advisers has been established with the aim of improving access to quality financial advice for retail clients.[97] Principal changes include a new licensing regime, the introduction of duties which require financial advisers to prioritise clients' interests, a new code of conduct and new disclosure provisions.[98] The recent FMA and RBNZ reviews of conduct and culture of banks[99] and life insurers[100] have led to the introduction of the Financial Markets (Conduct of Institutions) Amendment Bill 2019.[101] This Bill would establish a licensing regime, to be monitored by the FMA, for the conduct of registered banks, licensed insurers and NBDTs. The Bill's purpose is to improve institutional conduct regarding the provision of retail services and products, and reduce the risk of consumer harm. It would require regulated entities to comply with a fair conduct principle, operate a fair conduct programme and ensure that

---

[92] RBNZA 1989, s 1A as amended by Reserve Bank of New Zealand Amendment Act 2008, s 5.

[93] Angus Barclay, 'Westpac Capital Requirements Increased after Breaching Regulatory Obligations' (Media release, 15 November 2017), www.rbnz.govt.nz/news/2017/11/westpac-capital-requirements-increased-after-breaching-regula tory-obligations; Serene Ambler, 'Reserve Bank Censures ANZ' (Media release, 17 May 2019), www.rbnz.govt.nz/ news/2019/05/reserve-bank-censures-anz.

[94] IMF Report 17/110 (n 10).

[95] Ibid 7 and 33.

[96] Ibid 7.

[97] The reforms are contained in the Financial Markets Conduct Act 2013 (FMCA 2013) (as amended by the Financial Services Legislation Amendment Act 2019 (FSLAA 2019)). They were due to commence on 29 June 2020 but are being delayed to early 2021 because of the Covid-19 crisis. The Financial Service Providers (Registration and Dispute Resolution) Act 2008 has also been amended under the FSLAA 2019, particularly to deal with extra territoriality issues.

[98] FMCA 2013, ss 431K, 431M, 431X and 432Y (as amended by the FSLAA 2019, s 29).

[99] Financial Markets Authority and Reserve Bank of New Zealand, 'Bank Care and Conduct: Findings from an FMA and RBNZ Review of Conduct and Culture in New Zealand Retail Banks (5 November 2018).

[100] Financial Markets Authority and Reserve Bank of New Zealand, 'Life Insurer Conduct and Culture Findings from an FMA and RBNZ review of conduct and culture in New Zealand life insurers' (29 January 2019). See also Financial Markets Authority and Reserve Bank of New Zealand, 'FMA and RBNZ Disappointed with Insurers' Response to Conduct and Culture Review' (Press release, 17 September 2019).

[101] Financial Markets (Conduct of Financial Institutions) Amendment Bill, Government Bill 203-1.

intermediaries similarly comply. It would also require compliance with any regulations over incentives based on volume or value sales targets and provide protection for contravention reporting.

Further, also in response to recommendations in the 2017 IMF Review, the government has introduced the Financial Markets Infrastructures Bill 2019 (FMI Bill) which would create a new regulatory regime for financial market infrastructures (FMIs), replacing provisions in the RBNZ Act.[102] The FMA and RBNZ would be joint regulators except where FMIs are designated as a pure payment system, in which case the RBNZ would be sole regulator. While the IMF Review wanted New Zealand to achieve greater conformity with international standards, the extent to which the FMI Bill does so is debatable.[103] For example, its coverage is much more limited than the equivalent regimes in the United Kingdom and Australia.[104] Further, it requires the rules for systemically important FMIs to be designated by Order in Council rather than adopting a broader, more flexible oversight approach focused on the infrastructure itself. Nevertheless, for those FMIs covered, the FMI Bill does provide a legal basis for oversight and incorporates a wider range of enforcement powers, crisis management and regulatory powers. Much of the detail of FMI regulation will be in standards promulgated under the FMI Bill and it will be important that those standards address the IMF's recommendation that New Zealand comply more closely with the Principles for Financial Markets Infrastructure, which provides international standards for payment, clearing and settlement systems.[105]

In relation to the prudential regulation, the 2017 IMF Review placed New Zealand in an uncomfortable position because serious concerns were raised over the adequacy and depth of RBNZ supervision. The IMF evaluated the supervisory regime, partially against the 2012 Core Principles developed by the Basel Committee on Banking Supervision (BCPs).[106] While not mandatory, the BCPs represent international best practice. New Zealand was found to be materially non-compliant with thirteen of the twenty-nine BCPs.[107]

The IMF stated that the RBNZ had developed a 'hands-off supervisory philosophy that departed from conventional, more resource-intensive supervisory practices'.[108] This approach was seen as inhibiting effective supervision and leading to ambiguities (or uncertainties) at an operational level. Examples of uncertainty included the RBNZ's limited appetite for independent verification of disclosure documentation and first-hand knowledge of the soundness and risk management of individual banks. The IMF considered that the RBNZ placed too much emphasis on market discipline and too little on regulatory discipline.[109] This is evidenced by the absence of independent testing of prudential returns and risk management practices, and in particular no on-site inspections. It found that the RBNZ's approach made the development of

---

[102] Financial Markets Infrastructure Bill, Government Bill 212-1

[103] International Monetary Fund, *New Zealand Financial Sector Assessment, Technical Note – Regulation and Oversight of Financial Market Infrastructures* (International Monetary Fund Country Report No 17/115, May 2017), 5 and 15.

[104] For the United Kingdom, see www.bankofengland.co.uk/financial-stability/financial-market-infrastructure-supervision and for Australia, see www.rba.gov.au/payments-and-infrastructure/financial-market-infrastructure/about.html.

[105] Bank for International Settlements and International Organisation of Securities Commissions, Committee on Payment and Settlement Systems, 'Principles for Financial Market Infrastructures' (April 2012).

[106] Basel Committee on Banking Supervision *Core Principles for Effective Banking* Supervision (Bank for International Settlements, Switzerland, September 2012).

[107] Chris Hunt, 'Outcomes of the 2016 New Zealand Financial Sector Assessment Programme' (2017) 80(6) *Reserve Bank of New Zealand Bulletin* 10–13 See also International Monetary Fund, *New Zealand Financial Sector Assessment Program Detailed Assessment of Observance – Basel Core Principles for Effective Banking Supervision* (IMF Country Report No 17/120, May 2017) (IMF No 17/120).

[108] IMF Report 17/110 (n 10) 31 and 59–60.

[109] Ibid 6 and 58.

expertise on bank operations difficult, hampering the effectiveness of analysis and policy development.[110] In relation to the RBNZ's reliance on directors' attestations of adequate risk management systems, the IMF found that there was insufficient guidance provided by the RBNZ to banks on what constitutes adequate risk management.[111] The IMF also considered that the RBNZ needed to focus more on preventative action rather than formal breaches of regulatory requirements, delineate more clearly its role and responsibilities from those of the Treasury in order to maintain operational independence, and take a more proactive approach to trans-Tasman collaboration.

As a principal objective of prudential regulation and supervision is to identify and seek to control sources of risk, the IMF's criticisms were serious. It should be noted, however, that New Zealand's four largest banks, which dominate the banking sector, are New Zealand subsidiaries of Australian-owned banks, so are subject to supervision by the Australian Prudential Regulation Authority which utilises more intensive supervisory practices. The appointment of a new RBNZ governor in 2018 has resulted in a significant change in position.[112] The governor has acknowledged that New Zealand must meet international regulatory standards[113] and both the governor and deputy governor have stated that the RBNZ's approach to regulation and supervision will become more intensive, though details are yet to be provided.[114]

6.5 REVIEW OF THE RBNZ ACT

As a response to the 2017 IMF Review, the government initiated the RBNZ Review in late 2017. Phase one of the RBNZ Review, which is now complete, focused on monetary policy and has resulted in the transference of monetary policy decision-making to the MPC. The on-going phase two focuses on the legislative basis for prudential regulation and supervision, and the governance framework in the RBNZ Act. Wide terms of reference were issued[115] and the government has already made some key decisions on the RBNZ's governance and accountability framework and 'in-principle' decisions about the regulation of NBDTs and deposit insurance.[116]

Key decisions include that RBNZ decision-making, except for monetary policy, will be undertaken by a governance board; the RBNZ will have a new overarching financial stability objective in addition to economic objectives; the minister of finance will issue a financial policy remit providing matters to which the RBNZ must have regard when pursuing the financial stability objective; accountability will be enhanced through changes to reporting and monitoring requirements; and coordination and cooperation between regulatory agencies will be reinforced by mandating the role of the CFR. The in-principle decisions include that registered banks and NBDTs will be subject to a single 'licenced deposit taker' prudential regime; standards will be the primary tool for imposing regulatory requirements rather than conditions of registration imposed on individual banks; accountability requirements for directors of deposit

---

[110] Ibid 58.

[111] Ibid 58. See also Deloitte, *Section 95 – Review of ANZ Bank New Zealand Limited – Effectiveness of the Directors' Attestation and Assurance Framework* (2019), www.rbnz.govt.nz/-/media/ReserveBank/Files/News/2019/ANZ-NZ-Section-95-Director-Attestation-and-Assurance-Review-December-2019.pdf?revision=760ef7ff-3bc4-42a7-9c17-c3f63baf8bf8&la=en.

[112] Adrian Orr was appointed the RBNZ governor from 27 March 2018.

[113] Adrian Orr, 'Aiming for Great and Best for Te Pūtea Matua' (Speech delivered to the Canterbury Employers' Chamber of Commerce, 21 February 2020), 11.

[114] See Orr and Bascand speeches (n 69).

[115] The Treasury *Review of the Reserve Bank Act 1989 Phase 2 – Terms of Reference* (21 May 2018).

[116] The Treasury and the Reserve Bank of New Zealand, *Safeguarding the Future of Our Financial System: Update on the Reserve Bank Act Review, Phase 2 of the Reserve Bank Act Review* (December 2019).

takers will be strengthened; RBNZ supervision and enforcement tools will be enhanced: the crisis resolution framework will be improved; and a deposit insurance scheme will be established. These changes are to be made by replacing the RBNZ Act with two separate statutes, an Institutional Act which will set out the RBNZ's functions and framework and a Deposit Takers Act which will integrate regulation for banks and NBDTs, and establish the deposit insurance scheme. It is intended that a Bill for the Institutional Act and final policy decisions on the proposed Deposit Takers Act will be available by mid-2020,[117] but some delay is likely due to the worldwide Covid-19 crisis.

While much of the RBNZ Review panel's work is positive, there have been some impediments to comprehensive public debate. Initially, the RBNZ Review was to consider decision-making generally, including whether a new separate regulator should be established or whether the role should remain housed within the RBNZ.[118] In June 2019, the minister of finance made unilateral in-principle decisions that prudential regulation and supervision should remain with the RBNZ and that decision-making should be undertaken by a governance board.[119] The minister specifically rejected following the United Kingdom approach by establishing a statutory financial policy committee because this model was 'little used' and no other Crown entities have statutory committees.[120]

There is merit in the RBNZ remaining the prudential regulator because of the limited size of New Zealand's financial markets, the synergies between prudential regulation and monetary policy, and the fact that the APRA plays a significant role in the prudential supervision of New Zealand's four largest banks. The rejection of the SDM is also positive. However, it is arguable that the minister's decision to introduce a governance board does not properly recognise the RBNZ's unique position as a market participant and operator, and its responsibilities for monetary and prudential policy, and that a single board would not provide sufficient focus or expertise for prudential regulation.

The RBNZ operates almost as a full-service central bank.[121] In relation to monetary policy, it provides the majority of members for the MPC and is responsible for implementation of monetary policy.[122] In addition, it is responsible for prudential regulation and supervision, payment systems and settlement systems (jointly with the FMA), management of foreign reserves and issuing cash. It holds crisis management powers over banks and insurers[123] and acts as lender of last resort.[124] It also carries responsibilities in relation to anti-money laundering and countering financing of terrorism legislation (AML/CTF) in respect of the entities it regulates.[125] It is likely too that the RBNZ will have an oversight role for any deposit insurance scheme. The governance board would be responsible for all these varied facets of RBNZ operations.

As currently proposed, the governance board would have between five and nine non-executive members, the RBNZ governor would act as chief executive and functions would be delegated to the governor by the board, replicating the decision-making structure for the

---

[117] Ibid 5.
[118] Consultation (1 November 2018) (n 11) 60.
[119] Consultation 2A (June 2019) (n 11) 2 and 40–42.
[120] Consultation 2A (June 2019) (n 11) 4.
[121] Wheeler (n 66) 3. The RBNZ does not provide transactional banking services to the Crown or manage the Crown debt so is not a full-service central bank.
[122] RBNZA 1989, ss 8 and 63C (as amended by the RBNZAA 2018, ss 8 and 29.
[123] RBNZA 1989, pts 5, 5B and 5C.
[124] RBNZA 1989, s 31.
[125] Anti-Money Laundering and Countering Financing of Terrorism Act 2009 (NZ), s 130.

FMA.[126] Because of the extent of the RBNZ's commercial operations, the governance board will require directors with commensurate experience. Arguably, the skills required to run the commercial side of the RBNZ differ considerably from the skills required for effective prudential regulatory and supervisory oversight. Prudential regulation and supervision are highly complex and require considerable technical skills and insight given the intricacies of financial products, the unpredictability of financial markets, the pace of financial innovation and the need for market participants to have confidence in the decision-making process of the regulator. It is difficult to see how the requisite specialist skills required for such oversight would be contained within a governance board of that size. Moreover, comparability to the FMA's governance structure is questionable because of the differences in each peak regulators' statutory roles. The FMA is predominantly responsible for conduct regulation and for the institutions it licenses which are involved in the securities market, aspects of AML and designated security settlement systems and does not have any commercial roles.

The minister of finance has taken a curious approach in deciding on the governance structure because the minister has approved the institutional framework first, leaving the issue of marshalling the necessary expertise into that structure to be determined later: 'The Reserve Bank's governance board will need to be designed carefully to ensure it can manage its board mandate, particularly details such as its composition, appointment/removal and decision-making processes.'[127]

In management terms, it has decided the structure before the strategy. A better approach would have been to consider what technical, market and other expertise is required for prudential regulation and supervision, how best to challenge institutional thinking and address the risks of groupthink, and then design the decision-making body around those requirements, as it appears the United Kingdom has done.[128] In opting at an early stage for a governance board, New Zealand appears to be putting in place a 'half-way house' model, between the SDM and United Kingdom models. While a governance board will remove some of the immediate risks associated with the SDM, it is unlikely to adequately address the specialist nature of prudential regulation and supervision and the need for a specialist body to act as multi-member decision-maker. Sir Paul Tucker, former deputy governor of the Bank of England, has commented on the problems with boards that 'combine, in varying degrees, "oversight" with some "general policy"', stating:[129]

> If they are purely for oversight but are not expert, they probably cannot penetrate what is going on, and so cannot dilute their director general's CEO-like power. If, by contrast, as in some cases, they are formally responsible for signing off and issuing legally binding rules or other substantial policy measures, it is hard to see how they could decently be anything other than independent experts, with each and every one of them able to defend and explain the rules or measures they approve.

Given the broad remit of the governance board, there is a danger that it would act more like a corporate board and see its role as supporting the RBNZ governor/chief executive and that all members would not be sufficiently skilled or experienced to fully comprehend and analyse the

---

[126] FMAA 2011, ss 7, 9 and 11.
[127] Consultation 2A (June 2019) (n 11) 4.
[128] HM Treasury 'A New Approach to Financial Regulation: Building a Stronger System' (Cm 8o122, February 2011), para 1.29.
[129] Paul Tucker, *Unelected Power: The Quest for Legitimacy in Central Banking and the Regulatory State* (Princeton University Press, 2018), 350–51.

detail of prudential regulatory and supervisory policy in the same way as a specialist committee would. Without all members having specialist knowledge, the board may also not be able to rein in a powerful governor who has strong (or, as has happened in the past, irregular or unconventional) views on regulatory and supervisory detail, or recognise areas where the governor/RBNZ is weak or even wrong. As a consequence, some of concerns about the SDM may still exist, most importantly that there would be insufficient challenge to groupthink and institutional and defective thinking, and no forum for market participants to challenge RBNZ executives, except through legal proceedings such as judicial review.

New Zealand has experienced an unconventional regulatory and supervisory regime since at least the mid-1990s.[130] In an increasingly complex and rapidly evolving financial world, it would benefit from having a specialist decision-making body in place for prudential oversight which could independently evaluate the RBNZ's work or views and determine policy accordingly. It would also help to ensure equal treatment between prudential regulation and monetary policy, particularly if members independent of the RBNZ had a majority, as is the case with the United Kingdom's PRC.[131]

In the authors' view, a statutory committee model would better cater for New Zealand's needs and it could be readily implemented because the RBNZ already has an internal structure that could support the model. The RBNZ has organisational separation of prudential regulation and supervision at the departmental level.[132] These functions are also operationally separate from the RBNZ's other core activities such as monetary policy, managing foreign reserves and providing the core payments infrastructure and a securities settlement system. Following review at departmental level, the Financial Stability Committee (FSC), which is chaired by the deputy governor/general manager financial stability, may discuss regulatory issues and make recommendations to the governor.[133] It could as easily make recommendations to a statutory prudential regulatory and supervisory committee or committees, if there were separate bodies for macro- and microprudential regulation. Changes to regulatory frameworks occur infrequently, and often because inadequacies and flaws in regulation are exposed by a financial crisis. New Zealand has the rare opportunity to create a new model for prudential and regulatory decision-making and it is hoped that further thought will be given to how best and by whom that decision-making should be undertaken.

If, however, a RBNZ governance board is established, more thought will need to be given to ensuring that monetary policy and prudential regulation receive equal treatment. The creation of a governance board would mean that there are separate statutory bodies for each function. However, whether prudential regulation receives proper emphasis will depend to an extent on the expertise of board members, the degree of delegation of functions to the RBNZ governor/

---

[130] The disclosure and director attestation regime introduced in 1996 under Dr Don Brash's governorship was 'unconventional'. John Singleton states that most jurisdictions saw disclosure and supervision as complementary strategies, not alternatives, and records Dr Brian Quinn, then head of banking supervision at the Bank of England, as describing these reforms as 'an interesting experiment'. John Singleton et al (eds), *Innovation and Independence: The Reserve Bank of New Zealand 1973–2002* (Auckland University Press, 2006), 228.

[131] Bank of England Act 1998 (UK), s 30A (as amended by Bank of England and Financial Services Act 2016 (UK), s 13.

[132] The RBNZ has two prudential regulatory departments: the Prudential Supervision Department which is responsible for supervision of regulated firms across the banking and insurance sectors, oversight of non-bank deposit takers and financial market infrastructures, and supervision of regulated firms' compliance with AML/CFT legislation (see www .rbnz.govt.nz/about-us/senior-management/andy-wood), and the Financial System Policy and Analysis Department which is responsible for developing and implementing public policy for regulation of key players in the financial system, notably banks and insurers, and exploring and analysing risks across the financial system (see www.rbnz.govt .nz/about-us/senior-management/toby-fiennes).

[133] See www.rbnz.govt.nz/about-us/organisation-chart-and-senior-management.

chief executive and the governor's level of influence on board decision-making. One option to ensure equality (and specialist decision-making) would be to establish a statutory specialist board committee, of three to five persons, which would be responsible for the prudential regulatory and supervisory mandate. There would, however, need to be consideration of coordination and cooperation between the main board and any specialist committee to deal with potential conflicts, and accountability of the board as a whole.

6.6 FUNDING AND ENFORCEMENT POWERS

6.6.1 *RBNZ Funding*

Funding of the RBNZ's supervisory role is determined under a periodic five-year funding agreement with the minister of finance.[134] The agreement specifies how much of the RBNZ's revenues can be retained by the RBNZ to meet its operating costs, the remainder of which is transferred to the government. The current agreement (dated 26 May 2015) determines funding until 2020. One of the principal issues raised by the 2017 IMF Review was the inadequacy of resources to cover the RBNZ's supervisory responsibilities.[135] The IMF considered that increased resources were necessary to improve the effectiveness of supervisory process and strengthen the ability of the RBNZ to take early preventative action. It considered that the RBNZ should develop 'a supervision policy that reflects a balance between risk and the efficiency costs of supervision'.[136] As mentioned earlier, the RBNZ has announced that it will adopt a more rigorous form of supervision and boost its core supervisory capacity; it is intended that the RBNZ will be empowered to conduct on-site inspections.[137] To meet the need for increased funding, the government has determined that, while the funding agreement will continue, the RBNZ will be able to collect a portion of the costs of its regulatory functions through levies charged to regulated entities.[138]

6.6.2 *RBNZ Enforcement*

The RBNZ has a range of enforcement powers in relation to banks, financial institutions, payment systems and settlement systems under the RBNZ Act; NBDTs under the NBDT Act; insurance companies under the IPS Act; and against regulated entities in relation to anti-money laundering under the *Anti-Money Laundering and Countering the Financing of Terrorism Act 2013*.

For registered banks, enforcement powers include requiring the supply of information or documents,[139] appointing someone to supply a report on certain prescribed matters relating to that bank,[140] giving directions (including to remove directors) with the consent of the minister of finance[141] and placing a bank into statutory management.[142] The RBNZ can take enforcement measures against breaches of a registered bank's disclosure obligations[143] and breaches of a

---

[134] RBNZA 1989, s 159.
[135] IMF Report 17/110 (n 10) 7 and 70.
[136] Ibid 32.
[137] Consultation (March 2020) (n 11) 5.
[138] Consultation (December 2019) (n 11) 10.
[139] RBNZA 1989, pts 4–5, particularly ss 93–8.
[140] RBNZA 1989, s 95.
[141] RBNZA 1989, ss 113–113B.
[142] RBNZA 1989, ss 117–119.
[143] RBNZA 1989, ss 89–91.

registered bank's conditions of registration.[144] In practice, the primary powers that the RBNZ has used to date against banks have been the power to require the supply of information and the power to require a bank to provide a report relating to areas where the RBNZ has concerns (typically operational or prudential matters). The RBNZ has also taken a number of enforcement actions against banks in respect of their anti-money-laundering obligations.

The RBNZ has a range of enforcement options for NBDTs, insurers, financial institutions and others.[145] In particular, it can require information, issue directions or modify or cancel the licence of an insurance provider or NBDT.[146]

When deciding whether to take enforcement action, the RBNZ states that it exercises its enforcement powers for the purposes of promoting the maintenance of a sound and efficient financial system, encouraging sound management practices by directors and managers, maintaining clear minimum prudential standards and, if major problems occur, seeking to minimise the impact on the wider economy and financial system.[147] This accords generally with the RBNZ's mandates and supervisory purposes.[148] The IMF's criticism of New Zealand's 'non-intrusive' approach to regulatory discipline encompassed enforcement.[149] It considered that the RBNZ 'needs to move towards communicating supervisory expectations and requiring action'.[150] Further, it suggested that the RBNZ should issue enforceable statutory standards on key risks, providing transparency for market participants in areas where directors provide attestations, to assist preventative enforcement. Pursuant to these recommendations, compliance would serve as evidence of prudent banking and insurance. The RBNZ does not have an objective relating to specific prevention of bank failure or depositor protection in its statutory purposes, only the objective of avoiding significant damage if a registered bank does fail. As a result, its policies have often been aimed at ensuring a well-equipped ambulance at the bottom of the cliff as opposed to, for example, more active and preventative on-site supervision. These policies, at times, have been contentious.[151] The RBNZ intends to take a tougher and more intrusive approach to supervision and enforcement so that it is better placed to take preventative action. To support this new approach, the government intends to strengthen the RBNZ's powers in the proposed Deposit Takers Act by empowering the RBNZ to conduct on-site inspections and broadening the range of available sanctions, to potentially include statutory public notices, enforceable undertakings, infringement notices and civil penalties.[152]

6.6.3 *FMA Funding*

One of the main criticisms of New Zealand's market conduct regulation before the GFC was underfunding of the Securities Commission,[153] which was largely Crown-funded. When the

---

[144] RBNZA 1989, s 74.

[145] For example, RBNZA 1989, ss 36, 38 and 66B–66H.

[146] IPSA 2010, pts 2–3; NBDTA 2013, pt 3.

[147] RBNZ Statement of Enforcement Approach, www.rbnz.govt.nz/regulation-and-supervision/statements-of-approaches/statement-of-enforcement-approach.

[148] RBNZA, ss 1A and 68; NBDTA 2013 ss 3 and 7 and 8; and IPSA 2010, s. 3.

[149] IMF Report 17/110 (n 10) 32.

[150] Ibid 31.

[151] For example, RBNZ, 'Outsourcing Policy' (Financial Stability Department Doc No BS11, January 2006); and 'Open Bank Resolution (OBR) Pre-positioning Requirements Policy' (Financial Stability Department Doc No BS17, September 2013).

[152] Consultation (March 2020) (n 11) 89–107.

[153] Ministry of Business, Innovation and Employment and Financial Markets Authority, 'Reviews of the Financial Markets Authority Funding, the Financial Markets Authority Levy, the External Reporting Board Levy and Companies Office Fees' (Consultation paper, July 2016), 19.

FMA was established with a broader mandate than the Securities Commission, it was recognised that additional funding would be necessary. The Crown now contributes the same level of funding as that provided to the FMA's predecessors, and the remainder is provided by industry levies, which were increased in 2017.[154] Some costs are also recovered through fees charged for services such as licensing. Consultation is taking place on funding (and the mix of funding) for the new financial advice and conduct regimes, and the FMA is looking for potentially a 50 per cent or more funding increase.[155]

6.6.4 *FMA Enforcement*

The FMA is responsible for monitoring and enforcing compliance with a suite of statutes covering the financial markets either in whole or in part.[156] The most significant is the FMC Act which gives the FMA a wide range of enforcement powers. Owing to the nature of its role, the FMA is far more active in using its enforcement powers than the RBNZ. In doing so, it focuses on financial activities and conduct that are likely to pose a serious threat to fair, efficient and transparent markets, although much of its enforcement action is also generated from complaints or queries by the general public or other market participants. In addition to bringing court proceedings (both civil and criminal), the FMA can and does use its power to issue administrative orders and impose other sanctions. In recent years, it has taken enforcement action against directors of finance companies and in relation to false statements in financial documents, market manipulation, deregistering financial service providers (where that registration may have misled overseas consumers), substantial shareholder disclosure obligations and breaches of financial reporting. Its compliance strategy emphasises a 'top of the cliff' approach, focusing on lifting standards and fostering a relationship with market participants so that participants actively engage with compliance and share information with the FMA, including reporting breaches.[157] This approach appears to be reflected in its enforcement conduct statistics. About 70 per cent of its investigations between 1 July 2015 and 30 June 2016 resulted in the FMA imposing sanctions rather than instigating court proceedings.[158] It does, however, use a wide range of its powers, including pursing legal proceedings, issuing warnings and obtaining enforceable undertakings.[159]

6.7 RISK OF REGULATORY OVERLAP, COORDINATION AND COOPERATION

It is important for the effective operation of Twin Peaks that the responsibilities and objectives of each regulator are clearly established and their respective roles properly demarcated to minimise regulatory overlap.[160] In New Zealand, the RBNZ's supervisory objectives are, as mentioned earlier, maintaining a sound and efficient financial system and avoiding damage to that system from bank failures, but it is intended that this will be replaced with a financial stability mandate. The FMA's main objective is promoting and facilitating the development of fair, efficient and

---

[154] Ministry of Business, Innovation and Employment and Financial Markets Authority, 'Discussion Paper, Review of Financial Markets Authority Funding and Levy' (29 January 2020), 14.

[155] Ibid 20.

[156] FMAA 2011, s 9.

[157] Financial Markets Authority Compliance Policy, www.fma.govt.nz/compliance/.

[158] Financial Markets Authority, 'Conduct Outcomes Report 2016', 2.

[159] Financial Markets Authority, 'Annual Report 2018/19' (26 September 2019), 12.

[160] Basel Core Principles (n 106) Principle 1, p 21.

transparent financial markets. Entities such as banks, NBDTs and insurance companies are regulated by both agencies.

There is no statutory duty requiring coordination between these two agencies and New Zealand adopts a 'soft law' approach. Under section 9(1)(f) of the FMA Act, the FMA's functions include cooperation with regulatory agencies, but the requirements under sections 30 and 31 are permissive. Coordination between the RBNZ and FMA is principally achieved through the implementation of a Memorandum of Understanding, which is informal (voluntary and cooperative), there being no obligation for the agencies to have an MoU and compliance not being subject to parliamentary oversight.[161] The MoU contains no prescribed time limit, but under its terms senior officials from each agency must meet at least every six months to discuss its operation. The purpose of the MoU is to help each agency cooperate in areas of common interest, operate efficiently and effectively, identify market risk and avoid duplication. The MoU contains fairly extensive, broadly worded commitments: to keep each other advised or notified in a timely way on regulatory policy guidance or decisions that might impact on the objectives of the other and coordinate media statements; to mutually assist, cooperate and coordinate at all levels especially with the exchange of information and supervisory activities; to share information and cooperate in information gathering; and to actively assist and share costs. It also requires the two agencies to establish procedures to facilitate regular contact between them on routine operational matters and for each to appoint a contact person to facilitate cooperation. The system appears to be operating satisfactorily, at least from the FMA's perspective. The FMA's Annual Report 2018/19 records that it achieved the measures in its Statement of Intent 2017–20 to work with other regulatory and government agencies to reduce regulatory overlap, minimise gaps and increase efficiencies.[162]

The CFR also operates as a forum for discussion.[163] It seeks to foster high-level cooperation and information-sharing between its members, addressing any regulatory issues, risks or gaps that arise or are being monitored to ensure a 'whole of government approach'.[164] It was within this forum that agreement was reached to request the 2017 IMF Review.[165] To underscore the importance of this body and ensure its continuance, the government intends to provide it with a legislative mandate in the proposed Institutional Act.[166]

6.8 THE UNIQUE INTERDEPENDENCE OF NEW ZEALAND AND AUSTRALIA

The financial sector in New Zealand is somewhat unusual as it is dominated by four subsidiaries of the largest Australian banks, whose share in the banking sector's total assets total about 86 per cent.[167] These subsidiaries are of systemic importance in New Zealand and for their parent banks. The IMF describes the New Zealand–Australian interdependence as 'unique among other countries with high foreign bank presence'.[168] There are three principal mechanisms in

---

[161] Memorandum of Understanding, Financial Markets Authority and Reserve Bank of New Zealand (9 September 2011), www.rbnz.govt.nz/about-us/memoranda-of-understanding/memorandum-of-understanding-between-financial-markets-authority-and-rbnz.

[162] Financial Markets Authority, 'Annual Report 2018/19', 40 and 43.

[163] New Zealand Council of Financial Regulators, 'Regulatory Charter', paras 3.2 and 4.

[164] Regulatory Charter (n 163) 7.

[165] Hunt (n 107) 4.

[166] Consultation (March 2020) (n 11) 50.

[167] www.rbnz.govt.nz/financial-stability/overview-of-the-new-zealand-financial-system/the-banking-system, and IMF Report 17/110 (n 10) 9.

[168] IMF Report 17/110 (n 10) 9.

place to enhance cross-border cooperation. First, the RBNZ Act recognises the co-dependence between the two financial systems by requiring the RBNZ, in its supervisory role over registered banks and insurance companies, to support Australian financial authorities in meeting their statutory responsibilities and, to the extent reasonably practicable, avoid any action that is likely to have a detrimental effect on financial system stability in Australia.[169] Secondly, the Trans-Tasman Council on Banking Supervision was established in 2005 to promote coordination of the regulation and supervision of trans-Tasman banks and other financial institutions. The council is chaired jointly by the Secretaries of the Treasuries of Australia and New Zealand and members include senior officials from the Reserve Bank of Australia, the Australian Prudential Regulatory Authority (APRA), the Australian Securities and Investments Commission (ASIC), the RBNZ and the FMA. Thirdly, a Memorandum of Cooperation on Trans-Tasman Bank Distress Management was signed in 2010 to assist in achieving a coordinated response to the financial distress of any bank or banking group that has significant operations in Australia and New Zealand. The memorandum looks to promote appropriate responses and does not pledge the parties to any position or rule out any particular resolution. Nevertheless, the IMF has recommended more intensive cooperation within the trans-Tasman agreements to support 'cross-border synergies'[170] and improve standards of prudential supervision. It has suggested that the RBNZ could seek active engagement during the on-site visits conducted by APRA in its 'robust monitoring' of the Australian subsidiaries to enhance the RBNZ's institutional knowledge and experience of this type of supervision.

6.9 SUMMARY

There is no doubt that New Zealand's financial regulatory system has been improved since the GFC by the adoption of Twin Peaks, the creation of the FMA and associated legislation,[171] and the increased remit of the RBNZ to include prudential supervision of NBDTs and insurers. Moreover, the creation of organisations like the CFR, which appears to be operating actively, increase confidence that risks inherent in financial markets may be recognised and dealt with, and gaps and overlaps in regulation identified and resolved. Incremental changes have been made to existing conduct legislation, and improvement is continuing with the implementation of the conduct licensing regime for banks and NBDTs and a new regulatory regime for FMIs.

However, post-GFC reforms to the prudential regulatory regime were insufficient properly to implement the Twin Peaks model and clear regulatory vulnerabilities remain. The RBNZ Review has created a rare opportunity to fine-tune the prudential regulatory framework to achieve a more rigorous and effective system. The government's proposed legislative reforms would, in many respects, advance that goal considerably, but two important issues require further consideration: the RBNZ's decision-making structure and the management of conflicts between monetary policy and prudential regulation. The proposed governance board does not ensure that the necessary expertise will be present, that RBNZ thinking will be sufficiently challenged and that the risks of groupthink will be minimised. This is, arguably, the most important aspect of regulatory reform because the decision-making body will determine regulatory and supervisory policy, probably for some decades. In relation to managing conflicts, it is not

---

[169] RBNZA 1989, s 68A.
[170] IMF Report 17/110 (n 10) 58–60.
[171] Ibid 7.

clear that the MPC and proposed governance board will provide sufficient structural and practical division to address the risk of prudential regulation and supervision being downplayed or underemphasised. While the government will wish to progress proposed reforms as far as it can before the next election,[172] it is hoped that further thought will be given to these issues so that New Zealand is better equipped to meet unpredictable future risk.

---

[172] Scheduled for 19 September 2020, the election was delayed until 17 October due to the Covid-19 pandemic.

7

Identifying Lessons and Best Practices for the Twin Peaks Model

Marco van Hengel, Olaf Sleijpen and Femke de Vries

7.1 INTRODUCTION

At the beginning of this century, the Netherlands adopted the Twin Peaks model of financial supervision. Prudential supervision was integrated on a cross-sectoral basis within the central bank (De Nederlandsche Bank; DNB) and a separate conduct-of-business supervisor was created with the Authority for Financial Markets (AFM).

The introduction of the Twin Peaks model represented a shift in supervisory approach and in the governance of supervision in the Netherlands. It was a response to the trend of disappearing sectoral lines within the financial sector and the analytical conviction that different policy objectives require separate organisations.[1]

The consolidation of sectoral supervision and the greater involvement of central banks can also be observed in other countries.[2] At the same time, there continues to exist broad variation among countries regarding supervisory structures, which create their own challenges and trade-offs. Moreover, recent developments in financial markets and international regulation after the Global Financial Crisis continue to provide new input to the considerations and choices with regard to the appropriate supervisory model.

This chapter will describe the experiences with the Twin Peaks framework in the Netherlands, based on various examples from Dutch practice. Based on this analysis, it identifies lessons and best practices for the governance of financial supervision in a national context and from a European perspective.

7.2 BACKGROUND

The supervisory structure of Twin Peaks is based on a functional approach, where supervision is organised not on the basis of sectoral activities, but on the basis of the objectives of supervision.[3]

Within the Twin Peaks model, DNB is responsible for strong and sound financial institutions and the stability of the financial system, while AFM is responsible for maintaining orderly and transparent financial market processes and market integrity and ensuring the adequate

[1] J. Kremers and D. Schoenmaker, 'Twin Peaks: Experiences in the Netherlands' (2010) *LSE Financial Markets Group Paper Series*, Special Paper 196.

[2] M. Van Hengel, P. L. C. Hilbers and D. Schoenmaker, 'Experiences with the Dutch Twin Peaks Model: Lessons for Europe' in A. Joanne Kellermann, J. de Haan and F. de Vries (eds) *Financial Supervision in the 21st Century* (Springer, 2013), 185–99.

[3] J. Kremers, D. Schoenmaker and P. Wierts, 'Cross-Sector Supervision: Which Model?' (2003) *Brookings–Wharton Papers on Financial Services* 225–43.

behaviour of institutions in the interest of consumers. Based on this role, AFM supervises the capital and securities markets, including investment firms and collective investment schemes, financial services providers and accountants.

7.2.1 *Introducing the Twin Peaks Model*

The most important argument for financial reform was the dynamic and innovative developments in the financial system, which caused the boundaries of traditional sectors to disappear. This was reflected in the Netherlands by the emergence of financial conglomerates, which combine banking and insurance activities. Integrated, cross-sectoral prudential supervision facilitates a group-wide approach and ensures that no financial activity falls outside the scope of supervision. It also contributes to a more harmonised approach to supervision between different sectors and to containing regulatory arbitrage.

The integration of prudential supervision within the central bank was driven by the potential synergies that stem from the different tasks. There is a strong link between macroeconomic and market developments, financial stability and sound financial institutions. Bringing together all the expertise within a single institution promotes cooperation and information-sharing between the different disciplines. Integration also has the advantage that supervision benefits from the reputation and independent position of the central bank.

The creation of a separate conduct-of-business supervisor acknowledges that different perspectives can exist which may inherently contain possible conflicts of interest. For example, the traditional focus on profitability and soundness of financial institutions may undermine attention on the protection of consumer interests and proper functioning of markets. In addition, there may also be differences in culture and supervisory approach between the two supervisors. These differences can arise because promoting transparency and consumer interests may involve publicly challenging the behaviour of financial institutions in the market, which can conflict with the discretion and confidentiality that is needed in prudential supervision.

7.2.2 *Governing Elements in the Cooperation between DNB and AFM*

Within the Twin Peaks model, it is important that both supervisors can work together effectively. The Act on Financial Supervision, which provides the legal basis for the Twin Peaks framework, offers several building blocks for effective cooperation.

- *Coordination*: DNB and AFM are required to ensure that the regulations and policy rules that they impose are equivalent to the maximum extent possible.
- *Consultation*: DNB and AFM need to formally request and take into account the view of the other supervisor before taking specific legal measures (for example, withdrawing a licence or imposing a prohibition).
- *Request of opinion*: DNB and AFM are obliged to assess the opinion of the other supervisor when processing an application regarding market access or a declaration of non-objection, that institutions need to apply.
- *Notification*: DNB and AFM are required to notify the other supervisor if one of them determines that a (co-)policymaker of an institution licensed by the other supervisor is no longer considered to be fit and proper.
- *Information exchange*: Before making a data request to institutions that are under the supervision of the other supervisor, DNB and AFM need to verify with the other supervisor if the data requested is not already available.

These elements are laid down in law and in a supporting covenant between DNB and AFM. In addition, there are regular meetings between DNB and AFM at the Executive Board and senior management level as well as regular contacts between the different relevant experts to smooth the cooperation process.

7.3 THE TWIN PEAKS MODEL IN PRACTICE

The first years of the Twin Peaks model can be described as a transition period. The AFM needed to build up its position within the financial sector and took a proactive and vigorous approach with a strong chair to define its territory. Financial institutions were cautious at first, because they did not know what to expect from this new organisation with its strong mandate and wide range of instruments.

In the same vein, DNB needed to adapt to its new partner. Differences in focus and supervisory approach naturally caused some tension. The AFM initiated a more direct and explorative approach to supervision, while DNB relied on its long-standing reputation, larger capacity and analytical power. As a result, cooperation was initially limited to the necessary elements and on a need-to-know basis. In addition, there were also practical obstacles for information-sharing, due to legal restrictions based on confidentiality requirements.

Following this transition period, the relationship between DNB and AFM has evolved into a mature system, where different roles and responsibilities are more clearly defined. In general, DNB and AFM have developed a professional working relationship, with different coordination structures to ensure that both supervisors are adequately involved when needed. Most of the time, cooperation evolves naturally as a result of regular contact between DNB and AFM. However, the level of cooperation differs from case to case and is sometimes dependent on the initiative of relevant individual experts. Achieving an adequate level of involvement also depends on the specific circumstances and the importance of different perspectives. As a result, there have been more and less successful examples of cooperation in taking account of the input of the other supervisor in a timely and adequate manner.

7.3.1 *Experiences during the Global Financial Crisis*

The Netherlands was heavily affected by the Global Financial Crisis. To a great extent, this can be attributed to its large and internationally oriented financial sector, which made the system vulnerable to the global economic downturn and to turbulence in the financial markets. Prior to the Global Financial Crisis, total assets of the Dutch banking sector exceeded 600 per cent of GDP, with several systemically and international active institutions. In addition, different problem cases developed from a combination of general international developments during the Global Financial Crisis and specific individual circumstances.

The first relevant case concerns the nationalisation of Fortis/ABN AMRO (October 2008), which followed the takeover of ABN AMRO by a consortium of three banks (RBS, Fortis and Santander) just a few months before the crisis erupted. On approving the takeover, DNB had limited macroprudential powers to address the financial stability effects of the split-up of this domestic systemically relevant bank. After the advent of the subprime crisis, the financial situation and integration process of Fortis/ABN AMRO came under such pressure that nationalisation was required to maintain financial stability.

In another case, the collapse of the Icelandic banking system resulted in the failure of the relatively small branch of Icesave in the Netherlands (October 2008). It highlighted shortcomings in cross-border coordination and underlined the need to strengthen international supervision and cooperation.

The failure of DSB (October 2009) has also been an important, though relatively isolated case. Its problems were not directly related to the Global Financial Crisis. Its business model was unsustainable, because of an unsound management structure and a practice of over-lending and mis-selling of financial products. This case can be regarded as a strong argument for a separate and strong conduct-of-business supervisor. It was also concluded that the cooperation and information-sharing between DNB and AFM could be further intensified.

Finally, SNS REAAL became a late victim of the subprime crisis. SNS REAAL acquired a large real estate portfolio in 2006, just before the real estate markets collapsed. Increasing losses from this portfolio in subsequent years eventually led to the nationalisation of the conglomerate in February 2012. The intervention provided a first experience with the complexities and interconnectedness of a large complex organisation and the challenges for effective resolution.

These episodes have been important elements in subsequent discussions on strengthening the governance of supervision.

7.3.2 *Organisational Changes after the Global Financial Crisis*

Several refinements have been made to the governance structure of DNB, reflecting the experiences and lessons from the Global Financial Crisis.

First, supervision is now more formally recognised as a separate task within DNB, to give it greater prominence and to prevent negative spill-over effects towards the central bank. This is reflected by the fact that within the Executive Board of DNB, a single member is appointed Head of Supervision with prime responsibility for prudential supervision. The Head of Supervision chairs the Supervisory Council. This is an internal forum that prepares most supervisory decisions. Only material and bank-wide decisions require the involvement of the entire Executive Board, based on pre-defined criteria. In addition, internal governance and quality control within DNB have been strengthened. The supervisory approach has become more comprehensive and intrusive. To support these organisational changes and strengthen the supervisory culture, a separate department for early intervention and enforcement and a department for internal quality control have been created.

Secondly, macroprudential supervision has been acknowledged as an important field of expertise, which requires a separate authority with its own mandate and instruments.[4] The macroprudential authority has been integrated within DNB, because it constitutes the link between already existing activities within DNB of monitoring financial and macroeconomic developments and safeguarding the soundness of individual institutions. Moreover, available macroprudential instruments, such as systemic and countercyclical buffers, have a direct link with prudential supervision. The Financial Stability Committee (FSC) was created to exchange information about the stability of the financial system, identify possible risks to financial stability and make (public) warnings and recommendations to mitigate these risks.[5] The FSC is chaired by the governor of DNB and consists of representatives from DNB, AFM, the Ministry of Finance and the Bureau of Economic Policy Analysis (CPB).

---

[4] See J. De Haan, A. Houben and R. van der Molen, 'Governance of Macroprudential Policy' (2012) 67(2) *Zeitschrift für Öffentliches Recht* 283–302.
[5] See also www.financieelstabiliteitscomite.nl/en.

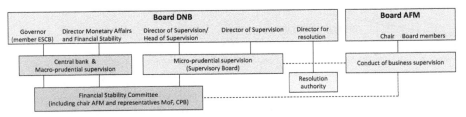

FIGURE 7.1. Governance Dutch Twin Peaks model after the Global Financial Crisis.

Finally, the orderly resolution of banks has emerged as a new and separate responsibility. This reflects the lesson that an independent authority should be able to resolve and safeguard viable functions of failing institutions in an orderly manner, while preventing the use of public funds as much as possible. This new resolution authority has also been integrated within DNB. The most important considerations for this inclusion were the synergies of knowledge and information-sharing and the interaction with prudential supervision. A Resolution Council was created to facilitate decision-making and a separate board member of DNB has been appointed as the responsible director of resolution. Decisions are ultimately taken by the Executive Board of DNB with the notable exception that the resolution director cannot be outvoted in the case of formal interventions in the banking sector. This reflects a requirement from European legislation that the ultimate decision-making power of the resolution authority should be placed independently of banking supervision to avoid regulatory forbearance.

As a result of these developments, DNB currently integrates a broad spectrum of four different tasks within a carefully designed governance structure, which combines the advantages and synergies of a collective management body while recognising separate lines of responsibility. The governance structure, as shown in Figure 7.1, reflects the different roles of the governor and members of the Executive Board, which is ultimately based on collective responsibility. Within that framework, tasks and responsibilities have been delegated to ensure the right balance between the individual responsibilities.

7.3.3 *Evaluating the Aspects of Effective Supervision*

The experiences of the last few years create an opportunity to evaluate the governance of the Twin Peaks model. To support the analysis, we use the concept of effective supervision as developed by the IMF.[6]

The IMF identifies the key elements that describe the way effective supervision should be carried out (see Figure 7.2). It is based on a governance structure that supports: (i) the ability to act and (ii) the will to act. These different aspects are discussed in the following paragraphs.

7.3.3.1 Ability to Act

LEGAL AUTHORITY Within the Twin Peaks model, both supervisors have a strong position and possess adequate powers to pursue their objectives. The integrated approach of a functional model provides opportunities for greater harmonisation and better monitoring of cross-sectoral risks, while identifying discrepancies and the possibility of regulatory arbitrage between sectors. For example, DNB and AFM have created several expert centres for specific supervisory tasks

---

[6] J. Vinãls and J. Fiechter, 'The Making of Good Supervision: Learning to Say "No"' (2010) IMF Staff Position Note 10/18 at 12–17.

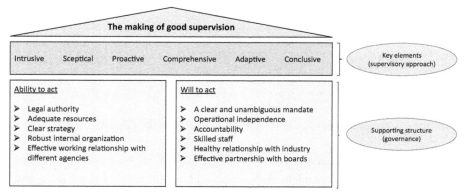

Based on: Viñals, J. and Fletcher, J.: 'The making of good supervision: learning to say no' (2010), IMF Staff Position Note 10/08

FIGURE 7.2. Elements of effective supervision (IMF).
Based on J. Viñals and J. Fletcher, 'The Making of Good Supervision: Learning to Say No'
(IMF Staff Position Note 10/08, 2008).

that operate sector-wide, based on their specialised knowledge and experience. This includes market access, fit-and-proper assessments and governance and culture supervision.

In addition, the AFM has been able to promote important initiatives such as the fair and efficient functioning of markets, the transparency of financial services and a robust product approval process. These elements may otherwise have attracted too little attention during the Global Financial Crisis when the most direct and primary focus of prudential supervision was on capital and liquidity and preventing the failure of individual institutions.

ADEQUATE RESOURCES DNB has separate budgets for prudential supervision and resolution, while macroprudential supervision is financed through the budget of the central bank. Within the yearly budget cycle, DNB and AFM have discretionary powers to request and shift budgetary resources. Because of the wide range of activities, there is flexibility for the supervisors to make choices between different sectors and supervisory themes. By the same token, the AFM needs to balance and combine its activities towards the market sector and investor protection on the one hand with its responsibilities in the retail market and consumer protection on the other. These activities are not necessarily closely connected.

CLEAR STRATEGY AND EFFECTIVE WORKING RELATIONSHIP DNB and AFM are professional organisations with a good reputation, mandated by clear objectives that are fully recognised within the sector. Moreover, there are low barriers for information-sharing and cooperation. This allows DNB and AFM to work closely on topics of shared interest.

Box 7.1 Fit and proper assessments

In response to the Global Financial Crisis, the responsibilities of DNB and AFM have been strengthened to assess whether management and supervisory board members are suitable for their position and whether their integrity is beyond doubt. Supervisory approval is a prerequisite for their final appointment.

DNB and AFM coordinate their activities when conducting a suitability screening. After differing views on the assessment of one high-profile case, which was highlighted in the public domain, agreements have been made to strengthen cooperation and clearly define responsibilities.

The assessments are led by whichever supervisor grants the authorisations for that particular sector. With regard to the banking and insurance sector, DNB is legally obliged to consult with AFM. During the assessment process, both supervisors separately assess the candidate and may conduct a joint or separate interview. DNB and AFM independently establish their views and conclusions. If either arrives at a negative conclusion, this legally prevails in the final decision.

A sound basis for cooperation does not preclude the risk of tension in the working relationship between DNB and AFM with regard to supervisory judgement and which approach is to be preferred. To a certain extent, this is the inherent choice of the organisational set-up. At the same time, it can also be traced back to differences in culture, people and organisation. It is important to maintain regular contacts between DNB and AFM to ensure good working relationships.

ROBUST INTERNAL ORGANISATION The integration of supervision creates room for synergies. For example, the integration of supervision within the central bank played an important role in managing the Global Financial Crisis. There have been some high-profile cases of (near) failure in the Netherlands that required immediate crisis management. Because the different tasks and responsibilities were under one roof, DNB was able to swiftly constitute joint teams combining different disciplines that could effectively work together without any impediments. From its role as the central bank, DNB had up-to-date information about the liquidity position of individual banks. Furthermore, DNB was able to take into account possible contagion effects within the sector. This promoted an efficient and well-informed decision-making process during these emergency situations.

However, without an imminent threat or a direct and specific situation, the synergy effects can sometimes be more difficult to achieve and the decision-making process can be more complicated, particularly when different interests are at stake. The need to balance the different interests can lead to prolonged coordination processes and turf battles.

Box 7.2 The housing market in the Netherlands (balancing different interests)

The Dutch housing market is characterised by high price levels due to scarcity in the market and a favourable tax treatment for house buyers. This has led to high mortgage debt levels within the economy and the increased indebtedness of households. From a microprudential perspective, this can present a risk because banks have large housing portfolios on their balance sheets. On the other hand, credit losses on mortgages have remained fairly low, indicating that current risk weights can be considered adequate.[7] Otherwise, from a macroprudential perspective, the characteristics of the housing market make the banking sector more vulnerable to financial shocks and may exacerbate the economic cycle. Furthermore, from a business conduct perspective, there are concerns with regard to over-lending to households. These different perspectives need to be considered in monitoring the housing market developing policy measures.

Finally, cost considerations should be taken into account. Both institutions currently have their own building and support functions (including Finance, HR and IT). This clearly reflects the view that DNB and AFM should be two separate and independent organisations. At the same

---

[7] 'Focus on Banking Mortgage Portfolios', DNBulletin, 22 November 2016, www.dnb.nl/en/news/news-and-archive/dnbulletin-2016/dnb349156.jsp.

time, it leaves room for operational efficiency if closer cooperation on specific activities is envisaged. In the extreme case where DNB and AFM were to operate from the same building and with shared support functions, there would be maximum cost efficiency. However, it would also beg the question as to whether the two different supervisors are clearly distinguishable and able to effectively fulfil the different roles that constitute the basis of the Twin Peaks model.

7.3.3.2 Will to Act

CLEAR AND UNAMBIGUOUS MANDATE The Twin Peaks model provides clarity on the role and responsibilities of DNB and AFM. Further, the framework has promoted communication of the different perspectives between DNB and AFM, and ensures that different views are adequately taken into account.

Box 7.3 Mis-selling in the insurance sector

The handling of the mis-selling of insurance products is a complicated case. In the past, investment products have been sold by insurers with high transaction costs, insufficient yield and high market risks that were not clearly communicated to non-professional consumers.

DNB and AFM have supported and strongly stimulated the efforts of insurers to provide reasonable compensation to these consumers for undue care in the past. At the same time, the impact of these agreements on the soundness and continuity of the institution have been taken into account because the compensation affects the financial position of the insurer and thereby affects the interests of all current policy holders for the future.

DNB and AFM have been working closely to bring both aspects into the discussion and to find a proper solution that strikes the right balance between these differing interests. The main advantage of the regular interactions and coordination structure between DNB and AFM is that the different interests are organised in a structural, professional manner, with each perspective given adequate attention.

At the same time, there continue to be grey areas. For example, in response to the Global Financial Crisis, the scope of prudential supervision has been widened. In a review of its supervisory strategy, DNB concluded that it not only needed to focus on traditional elements of capital and liquidity, but also on business models and strategy, culture and behaviour. These more qualitative elements of supervision determine the prospective profitability and financial position of a financial institution. However, these aspects are also directly linked to the responsibility of the AFM with regard to conduct of business and the fair and effective functioning of markets, thereby creating potential overlap.

In addition, some important elements could fall into the remit of both prudential supervision and conduct-of-business supervision. This is the case with regard to integrity. The supervision of anti-money laundering and combating of financial terrorism is a specialised part of supervision, which is currently placed within DNB because of its link with sound and solid financial institutions and as a condition for maintaining financial stability. At the same time, it can also be argued that the responsibility should be placed with the AFM, because of its greater investigative skills and supervisory approach. There is no predetermined requirement as to which supervisor should have responsibility for these areas, as long as the responsibility of governance and compliance with the relevant legislation is clearly assigned to a single supervisor and there are clear agreements on cooperation and information-sharing.

OPERATIONAL INDEPENDENCE AND ACCOUNTABILITY As indicated, there is a strong case for combining different responsibilities within DNB. At the same time, the different supervisory tasks are assigned to separate directors. An important lesson from the Global Financial Crisis is that macroprudential supervision is a separate field of expertise that requires its own dedicated capacity. In addition, there are legal requirements for resolution to be independent from daily supervision. This has evolved into a governance structure within DNB where the individual board members fulfil different roles as outlined above. This provides a clear and recognisable role for the different tasks. However, it also requires effort and discipline within the entire organisation to take all perspectives into account and to safeguard adequate involvement of other board members when needed.

Notwithstanding the separation of tasks, reputational effects in one domain may easily spread to other parts of DNB. This was the case, for example, when prudential supervision was criticised during the Global Financial Crisis, affecting the authority of DNB as a whole.

The current governance model of Twin Peaks also makes DNB a strong player because responsibilities are concentrated within one organisation. This could lead to DNB occupying too dominant a position under the supervisory framework. On the other side of the spectrum, creating different supervisors for different tasks creates more inefficiency and bureaucracy, such as when institutions need to apply to different supervisors to obtain approval for certain actions or provide comparable information. It is also important to create a system of accountability. DNB and AFM have taken steps to increase transparency, promote dialogue between supervised entities and other stakeholders and enhance their efforts to measure and demonstrate the effectiveness of their supervisory actions.

Table 7.1 provides a summary of the evaluation of the different aspects of effective supervision for the Twin Peaks model.

7.4 RECENT TRENDS

It follows from previous section that, to a large extent, the Twin Peaks model in the Netherlands has delivered on its main objectives. It also demonstrates that there is no unique single supervisory model. The governance structure of supervision depends on specific (national) circumstances and has to be tailored to relevant developments in the financial sector. In this respect, the following trends need to be considered.

1 The lines between the different sectors in the financial market continue to fade. However, a complicating factor in this respect is that international fora and European legislation are still predominantly organised along traditional sectoral lines, with the strengthening of banking rules such as Basel III and the European implementation within the Capital Requirement Directive (CRD IV) and Capital Requirement Regulation (CRR), the creation of a Single Supervisory Mechanism (SSM) for European banking supervision and the introduction of Solvency II for the insurance sector.

2 Within the context of further European integration along sectoral lines, it becomes more difficult for the Netherlands to maintain its cross-sectoral functional approach. Sectoral European directives have to be implemented in different segments of national legislation, which is structured along different goals and objectives of supervision. This makes legislation less accessible for a particular institution to have a direct overview of all its legal obligations within a European context. In addition, the requirements concerning

TABLE 7.1. *Good practices and challenges under the Twin Peaks model.*

Criterion	Evaluation	Description
Ability to act		
Legal authority	++	• DNB and AFM have clear responsibilities and adequate powers to promote harmonised and integrated supervision • Conduct of business is explicitly recognised as a separate objective
Adequate resources	++/–	• An integrated approach to resource planning • The wide range of tasks demand prioritisation between different activities
Clear strategy	++	• DNB and AFM are acknowledged as professional organisations, with clear and recognisable priorities following from their mandate
Robust internal organisation	+/–	• Integration of supervision creates room for potential synergies, which require efforts to achieve in practice
Effective working relationship with other agencies	+/–	• Low barriers for information-sharing and cooperation; some natural tensions remain • There can be room for savings on specific functions (e.g. building, Finance, HR and IT)
Will to act		
Clear and unambiguous mandate	++/–	• Clear objectives and structured approach of balancing different perspectives • Grey areas and potential overlap remain
Operational independence	++/–	• Different responsibilities assigned to an independent position • Potential negative spill-over effects • Relatively complex governance structure
Accountability	+/–	• Clear framework of responsibilities with structured process of planning and control • Possible dominant position
Skilled staff A healthy relationship with industry An effective partnership with boards		*These elements are not considered to be unique to the Twin Peaks model*

particular elements of legislation (such as good governance and the fit-and-proper criteria) continuously evolve within Europe, reflecting the latest developments and insights. As a result, there are no consistent definitions between European directives, which makes achieving uniform cross-sectoral implementation under national legislation more difficult.

3 At the same time, important developments within the financial sector are not necessarily captured within the lines of the functional model. The most notable examples are financial innovation and technological change. To accommodate this, DNB and AFM have set up joint initiatives to coordinate their activities. This works most effectively for clearly defined themes where interests are aligned.

> **Box 7.4 Common approaches in the Twin Peaks model**
>
> The InnovationHub is a joint initiative by DNB and AFM to create a single point of contact for the sector and provide information to relevant stakeholders about the supervision of new financial services and products. This creates room for innovation because it facilitates better access for new initiatives in the financial market and removes unnecessary barriers. It also deepens the supervisors' understanding of financial innovation and their knowledge about rapid developments in the financial sector. DNB and AFM work together in a single project. The challenge is to balance the positive impact of technological innovation, while managing potential risks for both financial stability and consumer protection.
>
> DNB and AFM also cooperate in monitoring technological developments in the financial sector (for example, big data and blockchain) because it changes the risks, market structure and nature of financial institutions. DNB and AFM carry out joint research, thematic reviews and organise dialogue sessions with financial sector participants to discuss relevant developments and review the consequences for effective financial supervision.

Another important aspect is that the distinction between prudential supervision and conduct-of-business supervision becomes less pronounced. As indicated before, the scope of prudential supervision has widened and qualitative elements, such as governance, behaviour, culture and sound business operations have gained greater prominence. As a result, prudential supervision shifts into the area where AFM also has a clear role. This is also the case for the supervision of pension funds. DNB, as the prudential supervisor, is the 'lead' supervisor. However, in addition to the traditional focus on the financial position and coverage ratio, much attention has recently been placed on qualitative aspects such as the prudent person, transparent communication towards beneficiaries and sound and balanced decision-making. These are also the main priorities of AFM. Relevant thematic reviews have therefore been carried out together with AFM. Currently, there is a fundamental debate in the Netherlands about the design of the pension system. Steps towards a new pension contract with a more defined contribution system reinforce the trend under which conduct-of-business elements become more important in pension fund supervision.

Overlapping activities are not necessarily an impediment for effective supervision within the Twin Peaks model but require continued coordination of competences and activities.

7.5 IDENTIFYING BEST PRACTICES

The previous paragraphs have indicated that the Twin Peaks model continues to provide a sound basis for supervision in the financial sector. At the same time, there needs to be an effective and efficient working relationship between the two supervisors with clear agreements for coordination and cooperation on specific issues.

Two aspects can be discerned that determine the adequate modus and extent of cooperation within the Twin Peaks model. First, the role and mandate of each supervisor determine whether the primary responsibility lies with a single supervisor or constitutes a common responsibility. Secondly, the nature of cooperation depends on whether the interests of both supervisors are fully aligned or whether different perspectives need to be considered. This leads to different structures between DNB and the AFM in the Twin Peaks model (Figure 7.3).

In the case of shared responsibilities where the interests of both supervisors are fully aligned (for example, market abuse, declarations of non-objection) it is most effective to form a single

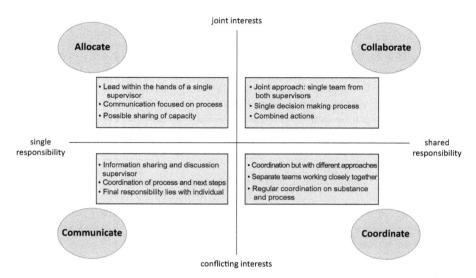

FIGURE 7.3. Cooperation within the Twin Peaks model of supervision.

team with members from each organisation acting together on a joint basis. They would operate, more or less, as a single organisation ('collaborate'). If interests are not aligned, because DNB and AFM have different perspectives, it is more useful to form different teams, which should frequently meet and discuss the next steps and their actions, respecting their different roles ('coordinate'). A key consideration in this quadrant is that both supervisors should inform each other in a timely manner in all steps of the process.

It may also be the case that the responsibility clearly lies with a single supervisor (for example, prospectus supervision on issuers of securities). The lead role should remain with the responsible supervisor with information-sharing on a need-to-know basis ('allocate'). In cases where actions or developments are relevant to the other supervisor (for example, reviews of governance, behaviour and culture) there should be a more regular and proactive exchange of information ('communicate').

This model gives guidance to the form and level of cooperation, respecting the role and mandate of both supervisors, while mitigating unnecessary overlap or bureaucracy.

Box 7.5 Examples of different forms of effective cooperation

SNS REAAL (allocate/communicate)

After 2008, the Dutch financial conglomerate SNS REAAL ran into prudential problems as a result of the Global Financial Crisis, having acquired a large real estate portfolio. This ultimately resulted in the nationalisation of the group in 2012. The lead role for the intervention lay with a single team within DNB. On those aspects that also touched the responsibility of AFM, like the investment of consumers in certain capital instruments of SNS REAAL, rules on public offerings or the assessment of the integrity of board members, DNB was in close contact with AFM. Relevant decisions on those aspects were made on a joint basis.

LIBOR (collaborate)

The manipulation of LIBOR quotes is a typical example of behaviour that is unacceptable from both a prudential and a conduct-of-business perspective. Responsibilities were shared. DNB focused on sound business practices and AFM was involved in assessing the benchmark rates in an orderly functioning of the market. DNB and AFM followed a joint approach because their interests were aligned. A single team coordinated the relevant mitigation actions and the formal measures that were taken.

Mortgage credit directive (coordinate)

The housing sector in the Netherlands is complex (see Box 7.2). The different supervisory perspectives have been discussed within FSC to come to a balanced approach to reforming the Dutch housing market. In addition, because of its unique position within Europe, DNB and AFM were in close contact to coordinate their input on a European level in the discussions concerning the European mortgage credit directive.

7.6 EUROPEAN INTEGRATION

The introduction of the SSM and the Single Resolution Mechanism (SRM) also has consequences for the Netherlands Twin Peaks model.

The shift of European banking supervision to the European Central Bank (ECB) reinforces the trend towards a more sectoral approach in prudential supervision. The internal organisation of DNB has been revised to mirror the structure of the SSM. Banking supervision within DNB now has its dedicated business unit with its own decision-making process and working methods in accordance with the governance and responsibilities of the SSM. Banking supervision is now part of a common European system. At the same time, there is no equivalent European supervisory mechanism for insurance and pension funds. This makes it more difficult to organise a cross-sectoral approach at the European level. Moreover, there is also no full European counterpart with regard to conduct-of-business supervision. Both aspects challenge the basic foundations of the Twin Peaks model in a European context.

Box 7.6 Towards a European Twin Peaks model?

In response to the Global Financial Crisis, the EU enhanced its supervisory system with a further strengthening of regulation towards a single rule book and the creation of three European supervisory agencies (ESAs). These agencies have been assigned regulatory powers to develop common rules within Europe and promote the harmonisation of supervisory practices between national competent authorities. The experiences in the first few years and the ongoing integration in the financial markets provide a good basis to identify the next steps.

The most important step forward would be enhancing the role of the European Securities and Markets Authority (ESMA) in the field of conduct-of-business supervision. The financial sector within the EU is becoming increasingly integrated, with the growing importance of financial services across national borders and the existence of markets of a pan-European nature – for example, Credit Rating Agencies (CRAs), central counterparties (CCPs), stock exchange and trading platforms. Moreover, conduct of business is becoming more important in promoting the sound business operations of financial institutions. Steps taken by the European Commission towards unifying capital markets further promotes integration and will ultimately require ESMA to become the single European capital markets supervisor.

On the prudential side, a shift towards a Twin Peaks model with a single supervisor at the European Central Bank is not warranted at this stage. The nature and level of European integration in different sectors varies too widely. Banking supervision is conducted under a single framework of the SSM, whereas insurance supervision remains a national responsibility under common European rules, while pension supervision primarily remains a national competence. Cross-sectoral integration within the ECB would bring no synergy effects. Moreover, it would create legal problems in respect of the current treaty. Further, the ECB might also become too powerful.

At the same time, there is room for strengthening cross-sectoral coordination. This could, for example, derive from greater consistency between European directives, further harmonisation and coordination of supervisory approaches between national authorities and a strengthening of the functioning of the Joint Committee. This is a committee that coordinates cross-sectoral elements in the work of the supervisory agencies.

These changes would allow Europe to benefit from the advantages of the Twin Peaks model within an integrating European market. It would also maintain flexibility towards the different national supervisory structures within Europe.

Recent developments have also put the ECB in a central and powerful position. In the current governance structure, the Governing Council not only has monetary authority, but also has ultimate responsibility for supervisory decisions. This increases the risk of potential conflicts of interests between these two activities. Before the creation of the SSM, these considerations were less relevant, because prudential banking supervision was a national competence, while the ECB conducted the monetary activities within the Eurozone. The roles of supervision and central banking have come closer again in the hands of the ECB. In addition, the ECB chairs the European macroprudential authority known as the European Systemic Risk Board (ESRB), which issues warnings and recommendations that may interact with other activities and responsibilities of the ECB.

The introduction of the SSM also leads to a supervisory structure where the Twin Peaks model basically has three supervisors. The ECB is responsible for prudential banking supervision, but the national competent authorities, like DNB, remain responsible for specific national tasks that do not fall under the mandate of the ECB. This includes, among others, supervision on integrity. It is important that these elements remain an integral part of the SSM because it is crucial for maintaining trust in the financial sector, and can have a direct impact on the financial health of institutions and consumer interests and protection.

The developments in Europe also affect the position of the AFM. Because of its sectoral nature, the scope of the SSM does not fully correspond with the activities of DNB. Some responsibilities of the SSM overlap with the role and mandate of the AFM.[8] As discussed earlier, there are several agreements and safeguards on a national level to guide the cooperation between DNB and AFM (see Section 7.2.2). However, there is no such formal structure between the SSM and AFM. DNB is the sole national competent authority for the Netherlands within the SSM and there is no detailed Memorandum of Understanding between the ECB and AFM. This may lead to unintended outcomes. Fit-and-proper assessments is a case in point. On a national level, both DNB and AFM have a formal final say if either supervisor comes to a negative decision (the so-called system of dual approval). However, this has changed under the SSM. DNB and AFM still work together to prepare a draft ECB decision and DNB will propose a negative draft decision when either supervisor comes to that conclusion. However, ultimately,

---

[8] See A. Van Gelder and P. Teule, 'Gedragstoezicht en Het SSM: Op Zoek Naar een Nieuwe Balans' (2014) 11 *Tijdschrift voor Financieel Recht* 462–8.

the ECB takes the final decision and could in principle deviate from the view of AFM, thereby undermining the current national arrangement of joint responsibility.

7.7 LESSONS LEARNED

The Twin Peaks model remains an effective governance framework for supervision. At the same time, authorities and supervisors need to continue to take account of relevant developments within the financial sector and in international regulation. This may result in changes to existing governance structures. This section describes governing principles that can provide guidance in this process and contain the most important elements in the design of any supervisory model.

- *Attribution and delegation of powers*: the responsibilities of the different supervisory roles (macroprudential, microprudential, resolution and conduct of business) should be clearly assigned to an individual organisational part with adequate powers and resources.
- *Creating synergies*: supervisors should develop policies and regulatory coordination structures between the different organisational units to fully exploit the benefits of taking different perspectives into account.
- *Balance of power*: an organisation should not become too powerful or complex. Checks and balances can be strengthened by promoting transparency and introducing policies to measure effectiveness.
- *Adaptive*: The supervisory model should also be able to respond to new relevant developments within the financial sector and the institutional environment.
- *Efficient*: the governance structure of supervision should not be overly complex or costly and needs to contain bureaucracy.

ATTRIBUTION AND DELEGATION OF POWERS Supervision has become more diverse, with many different dimensions that need to be taken into account. There is no longer solely a distinction between prudential and conduct-of-business supervision. Other functions, such as macroprudential supervision and resolution, have also emerged. These different roles interact and overlap. To consider all relevant aspects, each role should be clearly recognised and have its own mandate and responsibilities.

The key question is how to adequately balance the different interests. To this end, a distinction can be made for different categories. Those issues that predominantly fall within one supervisory domain should be delegated to a single authority, which is then also fully authorised to make ultimate decisions. This delegation of power leads to a clearer and stronger decision-making process. On more strategic issues, where joint interests need to be considered, the primary responsibility can be appointed to a lead supervisor, which maintains the initiative and coordinates the decision-making process.

In the case of inherent conflicts of interests or a natural tendency that one aspect may receive inadequate attention; joint decision-making rules should be developed. This can be organised in different institutional settings. A possible way forward is to create a separate organisation, such as a body responsible for supervising conduct of business in the Twin Peaks model. This provides a direct guarantee for a separate, independent approach. However, it also comes at a cost. A separation of tasks can also be realised within a single organisation. For example, the resolution authority is created within DNB through a separate position within the board and formal voting procedures. An intermediate approach – applied in the United Kingdom and

France – is to create a separate subsidiary for supervision as part of the central bank. This creates clear separate roles, while maintaining the proximity that is relevant in the decision-making process.

In addition, any responsible authority should also have the ability to act on the basis of sufficient and adequate instruments that it can effectively apply in those cases that are essential to achieving its objectives.

PROMOTING SYNERGIES An important driving force behind the current organisational structure in the Netherlands is the potential for creating synergies among the different supervisory tasks (and the central bank). These synergies are not always easy to achieve and need to be explicitly embedded within the organisation and its culture.

For instance, cooperation structures can be developed that reflect joint responsibilities and potential synergies. For example, within DNB senior management officials have been selected to coordinate important, overarching issues that contain different perspectives. Recent relevant examples are the Dutch housing market, the pension system reform and financial crisis management. The responsible managers do not necessarily operate along hierarchical lines but coordinate their work on specific issues across the organisation and consider the interests of DNB as a whole in achieving the ultimate objective of financial stability. This structure contains elements of a matrix organisation and helps to prevent turf battles.

Another important element in promoting synergy is to stimulate the exchange of knowledge and information within and between the different supervisory agencies. This prevents a silo approach, which undermines the benefits of integrated supervision. Where relevant and applicable, there should be no unnecessary practical or legal impediments to cooperation and information-sharing. In the Netherlands, DNB and AFM can basically share all information that is required for the fulfilment of their duties. Different approaches can be used to stimulate cooperation and may include the creation of knowledge networks, organising seminars or developing joint training.

Finally, it is also important to promote and actively stimulate the mobility of employees between the different supervisory domains. It broadens experience and stimulates a natural dissemination of different perspectives within the organisation. It also lowers barriers of contact between different departments necessary for good cooperation.

BALANCE OF POWER The different supervisory responsibilities need to be clearly assigned but should not necessarily be concentrated within a single entity as this would burden the system and undermine the added value of explicitly balancing the different perspectives. In its own supervisory approach, DNB stresses the need for a balanced and consistent decision-making process as essential building blocks of an institution's effectiveness.[9] This also holds for a supervisory model. An adequate organisation needs checks and balances.

An important aspect is transparency. Supervisors need to be able to explain their actions to the financial sector and the public at large. This is especially important because the different supervisory roles can lead to different positions. It should be clear how relevant interests are weighed and the intended outcomes of supervisory action.

---

[9] See Wijnand Nuijts, 'Chapter 5: Decision Making' in De Nederlandche Bank (ed) *Supervision of Behaviour and Culture* (DNB, 2015), 102–37.

As an organisation within the public domain, supervisors also need to be accountable. Their actions have a direct impact on the financial sector and other relevant stakeholders. It should be clear how the overall mandate and strategic objectives translate into supervisory priorities and actions.[10] Supervisory activities should be challenged internally and verified by external reviews.

In this respect, much attention has also been paid to measuring the impact of supervision.[11] Assessing and monitoring a range of qualitative and quantitative indicators provides insight to the activities and objectives of supervision. It can also give guidance to a consistent planning process and contribute to a further improvement of public reporting on supervisory effectiveness.

ADAPTIVE The governance structure needs to adhere to the applicable legal requirements. This particularly relates to the independence of monetary tasks and the responsibility of resolution. In addition, supervisors should be able to comply with developments in regulation and relevant international standards and best practices, such as the core principles for effective supervision by the Basel Committee of Banking Supervision (BCBS) and the International Association of Insurance Supervisors (IAIS).

In addition, supervision needs to operate within the existing international environment. Consequently, national and international governance structures need to be aligned. On a national level, supervisors need to respond to the trend of sectoral supervision. At the European Commission level, further steps can be made to strengthen the existing institutional structure. This would involve the evolution of a more cross-sectoral approach within Europe across banking and insurance supervision, as well as taking further steps towards strengthening conduct-of-business supervision. This would make an important contribution in Europe to meeting the challenges of future changes in the financial sector.

New trends within the financial sector will continue to emerge. The origination of new players and activities (for example, shadow banking) and the changing nature of the financial industry make it necessary for to continue to adjust their organisations. This could also mean that more hybrid forms of cooperation can evolve within DNB as well as between DNB and AFM. This could, for example, consist of more project structures on selected issues or even include shared service centres for specialised joint activities, such as market access, declaration of non-objection and conducting fit-and-proper assessments.

EFFICIENT Efficiency can be realised in the planning of daily activities. Supervisors should, for example, continue to improve the coordination and harmonisation of their forms and data requests, which are resource-intensive for the financial sector. Also, the planning of supervisory visits, thematic reviews and on-site inspections should be organised in such a manner that compliance costs are minimised as much as possible.

In addition, supervisors should continue to look for initiatives that contain the costs of supervision. Room for improvement can primarily be found in the supporting functions. This could particularly be the case for IT where big investments are required, following the trend of more structural and intensified use of data in the supervisory process.

---

[10] See Basel Committee on Banking Supervision, *Report on the Impact and Accountability of Banking Supervision* (July 2015).
[11] See P. L. C. Hilbers, K. Raaijmakers, D. R. Rijsbergen and F. de Vries, 'Measuring the Effects of Financial Sector Supervision' (DNB Working Paper No 388, 2013).

7.8 CONCLUSION

In the two decades since its introduction, the Twin Peaks model in the Netherlands has fully developed. Based on the experiences in recent years, it can be concluded that the model functions relatively well. DNB and AFM have developed a professional relationship and both have a strong and well-respected position within the financial sector, with each supervisor clearly having its own focus and priorities.

At the same time, the Twin Peaks model is not a panacea. Supervision has become more complex with more overlap and interaction between prudential and conduct-of-business supervision. In addition, the emergence of new supervisory dimensions, like macroprudential supervision and resolution, poses challenges to the existing governance structure. Moreover, international developments are directed towards more of a sectoral approach to supervision.

In the future, changes to the supervisory model will remain necessary in response to developments in the regulatory environment and trends in the financial sector. To this end, this chapter has introduced some lessons learned that should be taken into account in the design of any supervisory model. These principles can be used to perform regular evaluations of the governance structure and review the cooperation within the organisation as well as between the different supervisors. Particularly on a European level, further steps can be taken with the introduction of a single conduct-of-business supervisor, further harmonisation of supervisory practices and cross-sectoral supervision.

8

Twin Peaks in South Africa

Roy Havemann

8.1 SOUTH AFRICA'S JOURNEY TOWARDS TWIN PEAKS

In 2011 the South African National Treasury published a policy paper[1] called 'A Safer Financial Sector to Serve South Africa Better'.[2] This policy document, the 'Red Book', was the culmination of a review of the financial regulatory system started by the Treasury in 2007 and expanded in scope after the 2008 financial crisis. The Red Book assessed the structure and characteristics of South Africa's financial sector for gaps and weaknesses, took account of the lessons from the Global Financial Crisis, and set out proposals to reform the regulatory system for the financial sector.

Based on recommendations in the Red Book, the Cabinet approved the shift to a Twin Peaks system in July 2011.

The strategy was designed around three broad questions:

- What is regulated?
- Who regulates?
- How do they regulate?

While the Red Book is most closely associated with the decision to move to Twin Peaks, it made it very clear that it would be only one part of a more holistic reform programme. This programme was staggered to ensure that reforms were carefully sequenced, so as to cause minimal disruption to the financial system (Figure 8.1). Urgent regulatory reforms agreed by the G20 were prioritised. These included:

- The introduction of the legal framework for the implementation of Basel III in 2012, particularly the implementation of new regulatory requirements, by way of amendments to the *Banks Act*.[3]
- The introduction of a regulatory system for previously unregulated 'over-the-counter' derivatives in the *Financial Markets Act 2012*.[4]

---

[1] Most of the documents referenced in this chapter can be found at www.treasury.gov.za/twinpeaks. All submissions made to the Standing Committee on Finance and the Select Committee on Finance, and summaries of the hearings, can be found at https://pmg.org.za/bill/608/.

[2] National Treasury, *A Safer Financial Sector to Serve South Africa Better* (Pretoria, 2011).

[3] Act No 94 of 1990.

[4] Act No 19 of 2012.

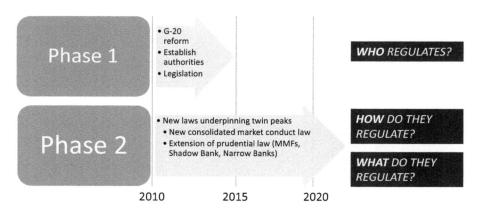

FIGURE 8.1. The phased approach to Twin Peaks.

- Bringing credit ratings agencies and credit ratings services into the regulatory net, through the *Credit Ratings Services Act 2012*.[5]
- The implementation of G20 proposals in respect of a number of investment, pension and insurance products, as part of the *Financial Services Laws General Amendment Act 2013*.[6]
- Beginning a process of phasing in Solvency Assessment and Management (SAM) criteria for insurance companies. SAM is a prudential regulatory regime, similar to that of Solvency II under the European Union Solvency II Directive.

Following these reforms, and from 2013 onwards, a process was set in motion to restructure the regulators. A Financial Regulatory Reform Committee (FRRSC) was established[7] to execute the reform process, co-chaired by the head of financial sector policy at the Treasury, the then deputy governor of the South African Reserve Bank, and the Executive Officer of the Financial Services Board. The *Financial Sector Regulation Bill* was tabled in Parliament in October 2015, and ultimately passed by both Houses of Parliament in August 2017. Transitional regulations to facilitate the creation of the two authorities have been published. The Prudential Authority began work on **1 April 2018**, and the Financial Sector Conduct Authority began work **on the same day**.

This chapter outlines the Twin Peaks system as it has been adapted to South Africa, the first emerging market to adopt the model. The next section outlines why Twin Peaks was judged to be the best system for South Africa. It shows that it is by no means the 'perfect' system, but it offers a number of advantages which align with long-term developments in the South African financial system. Section 8.3 outlines the institutions that make up the South African version of Twin Peaks, best described by one member of Parliament as 'A mountain, two peaks and some molehills'. Thereafter, in Section 8.4, certain aspects of the system and its challenges are highlighted. Section 8.5 concludes, noting again that the journey to Twin Peaks in South Africa has been a long one, and is not yet quite over.

---

[5] Act No 24 of 2012.
[6] Act No 45 of 2013.
[7] See Financial Regulatory Reform Steering Committee, *Implementing the Twin Peaks Model of Financial Regulation* (2013).

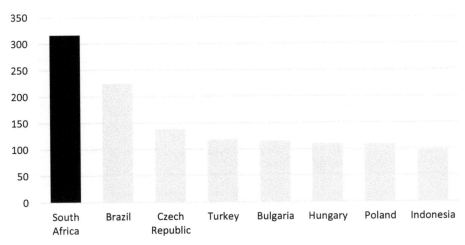

FIGURE 8.2. Financial sector assets (bank and non-bank), percentage of GDP, selected emerging markets (2016).
Sources: EDSS, WEO, IMF FSI Annex, and WB FinStats

8.2 WHY TWIN PEAKS?

The decision to move to Twin Peaks was informed by South Africa's particular economic and financial sector circumstances, particularly its status as an emerging market, with a deep and liquid financial centre, closely linked to the rest of the world.

South Africa has long been regarded as having a well-regulated financial system. South Africa weathered the 2007/08 Global Financial Crisis well, with limited direct impact. That said, the crisis also exposed some weaknesses and, of course, lessons were learned from the experiences of other countries. Against this background, the regulatory authorities were of the view that in order to maintain these strong rankings, on-going reforms would be required.

8.2.1 *South Africa's Relatively Large and Concentrated Financial System*

South Africa's financial system is large compared to its emerging economy peers (Figure 8.2). When the Twin Peaks process was initiated (2016), the broad financial services, insurance and real estate sectors contributed 20.2 per cent of gross value added, and 17 per cent of employment. It also plays an outsize role in tax revenue, contributing 38.5 per cent of corporate tax. Due to relatively high wages as compared with other sectors, and strong services, the sector accounted for 46 per cent of personal income tax and 34 per cent of value-added tax. Financial services, particularly banking, insurance and financial intermediation, comprise a large proportion of this subsector.

The South African financial sector is highly interconnected, and dominated by large financial groups, with each group typically comprising at least a bank and an insurance company, and often a medical aid and investment company (Table 8.1). This small number of large financial groups has also led to reduced competition. They sell complex products with opaque fee structures, charging for services at rates much higher than they would if the system were more competitive. Furthermore, financial institutions do not necessarily provide services to all South Africans – wealthier, urban customers tend to enjoy a wider range of more suitable products, while poorer and rural customers may suffer inappropriate or expensive financial services, or have access to none at all.

TABLE 8.1. *The four largest financial conglomerates (2016).*

Financial services conglomerate	Business activities in group	Market capitalisation	Market cap as % GDP
FirstRand Group	Retail banking, investment banking, insurance	R305.51 billion	7.0
Standard Bank Group Ltd	Banking, investment, insurance	R255.72 billion	5.9
Old Mutual Limited and Nedbank Group	Insurance, pension, banking, investment management	R172.54 billion[8]	4.0
Sanlam Limited	Insurance, Investment management, credit and banking	R135.79 billion	3.1

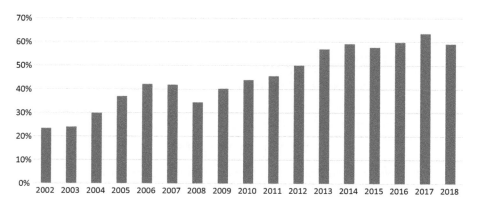

FIGURE 8.3. The ratio of other financial institutions assets to bank assets has risen.
This figure shows the increase in the ratio of other financial assets to bank assets, highlighting that the former has risen from just over 20 per cent in 2002 to nearly 60 per cent in 2013.

8.2.1.1 Risks Posed by 'Other Financial Institutions'

South Africa has a large and growing non-bank financial sector. The connection between other financial institutions and banks is particularly close in South Africa – in 2018 approximately 13 per cent of bank liabilities were owed to other financial intermediaries; in contrast, the advanced economy average was 4.3 per cent in the same year and the emerging market average was 2.6 per cent.[9] By March 2016, the South African mutual fund industry had approximately R1.7 trillion of assets under management, or 68 per cent of gross domestic product (GDP). As a comparator, retail bank deposits were approximately R912.5 billion, or 36 per cent of GDP. 'Shadow banks', defined as 'other financial institutions', have grown rapidly relative to banks (Figures 8.3 and 8.4).

The regulatory framework for these institutions is quite different from banks – arguably creating regulatory arbitrage and introducing risks. The Twin Peaks framework will shift the prudential supervision of prudentially relevant 'shadow banks' to the Prudential Authority, to create a framework for a consistent approach to supervising the risks arising from non-traditional financial intermediaries.

---

[8] Old Mutual Ltd and Nedbank Ltd have a market capitalisation of R167.43 billion and R5.11 billion respectively, combined to R172.54 billion.

[9] Financial Stability Board, *Global Monitoring Report on Non-bank Financial Intermediation 2019* (2020), www .financialstabilityboard.org.

FIGURE 8.4. South African banks are particularly exposed to other financial institutions. *This figure presents the share of bank liabilities from 'other financial institutions' (OFIs) such as money-market funds and mutual funds. The global average is for banks to have approximately 4 per cent of their liabilities to OFIs, whereas in South Africa the ratio is closer to 13 per cent. Argentina (AR), Australia (AU), Belgium (BE), Brazil (BR), Canada (CA), Cayman Islands (KY), Chile (CL), China (CN), Euro area (EA), France (FR), Germany (DE), Hong Kong (HK), India (IN), Indonesia (ID), Ireland (IE), Italy (IT), Japan (JP), Korea (KR), Luxembourg (LU), Mexico (MX), Netherlands (NL), Russia (RU), Saudi Arabia (SA), Singapore (SG), South Africa (ZA), Spain (ES), Switzerland (CH), Turkey (TR), United Kingdom (UK), United States (US).*

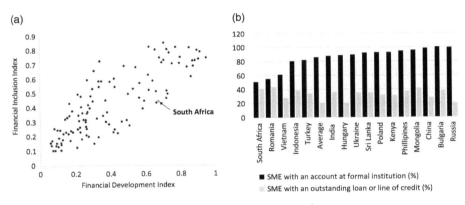

FIGURE 8.5. Financial inclusion indicators.
Source: International Monetary Fund, Article IV Consultation Final Report (2017)

8.2.2 *The Financial Inclusion Challenge*

While South Africa has a well-developed and sophisticated financial system, it has a mixed record in financial inclusion. Measured by access to bank accounts, South Africa performs relatively similarly to its emerging market peers. However, access to credit for small and micro-enterprises (SMEs) is a persistent challenge given its level of financial sector development. South Africa has a relatively low-level of financial inclusion (see Figure 8.5). Notably, access to credit for small- and micro-enterprises is relatively weak.

8.2.3 *The Legacy of Regulatory Fragmentation*

8.2.3.1 Multiple Regulators

During the 1980s, there were a number of Commissions of Inquiry into the banking and financial system in South Africa. Two of these, the De Kock Commission and the Melamet

Commission, recommended substantial regulatory reform. The government acted on these recommendations, shifting regulation to a sector-based institutional structure.[10] Ostensibly, it divided financial institutions into two types: banks and non-banks. The supervision of banks was moved from a unit in the Finance Ministry to a part of the Reserve Bank in 1987, and the supervision of non-banks was given to the Financial Services Board, which began its work in 1990.

It was a structure more honoured in the breach than in the observance. In the original arrangement, the banking regulator was only given prudential supervisory powers. The Financial Services Board was given a mix of prudential and conduct responsibilities over non-banks. Most importantly, conduct supervision of banks was not included in the arrangement.

Over time, three additional regulators were created. In 1998, a Competition Commission was created, with wide-ranging powers to deal with anticompetitive behaviour in financial services and other industries. Also in 1998 a Council of Medical Schemes was formed, to supervise medical schemes[11] for both prudential and market-conduct purposes. In 2005, a National Credit Regulator was established to supervise the market conduct of all credit providers, including banks.

From a coordination perspective, unfortunately, the five resulting regulators and five pieces of legislation were placed under three ministers – two under the minister of finance (*Banks Act*[12] and the *Financial Services Board Act*[13]), two under the minister of trade and industry (*National Credit Act*[14] and the *Competition Act*[15]) and one under the minister of health (*Council for Medical Schemes Act*[16]). To complicate matters, the Bank Supervision Department was placed inside the Reserve Bank, a constitutionally independent entity, but reported on many issues to the minister of finance (Figure 8.6).

But these were not the only regulators with a direct interest in the supervision of financial institutions. The supervision of foreign exchange dealers (large and small), in terms of the *Currency and Exchanges Act*,[17] remained the responsibility of the Reserve Bank, as did the oversight of the payments systems, in terms of the *Payment Systems Act*.[18]

8.2.3.2 Legal Fragmentation

The system was further fragmented from a legal perspective. Although the Financial Services Board was created as a single non-bank regulator, the legislative arrangements meant that, in law, it was a collection of multiple regulators. The intention was that the Executive Officer of the Financial Services Board would function, legally, as the Registrar of Insurance (prudential and conduct remits), the Registrar of Securities Services, the Registrar of Collective Investment

---

[10] The Melamet Commission proposed a single regulator, but the decision was taken to move banking supervision to the central bank. During the tenure of Trevor Manuel, a single regulator was again proposed. However, there was such strong opposition from the then governor of the Reserve Bank, Tito Mboweni, that the idea was subsequently abandoned. A full discussion on this proposal can be found in Jeffrey Carmichael, Alexander Fleming and David T. Llewellyn (eds), *Aligning Financial Supervisory Structures with Country Needs* (World Bank Publications, 2004).

[11] In South Africa, medical schemes (also known as medical aid) are run as not-for-profits, under the Medical Schemes Act, No 131 of 1998. Medical schemes reimburse medical expenses under certain conditions. Medical scheme administrators, on the other hand, are run as for-profit companies.

[12] Act No 94 of 1990.

[13] Act No 97 of 1990.

[14] Act No 34 of 2005.

[15] Act No 89 of 1998.

[16] Act No 131 of 1998.

[17] *Currency and Exchanges Act* 1933 (Act No 9 of 1933).

[18] *National Payments System Act* 1998 (Act No 78 of 1998).

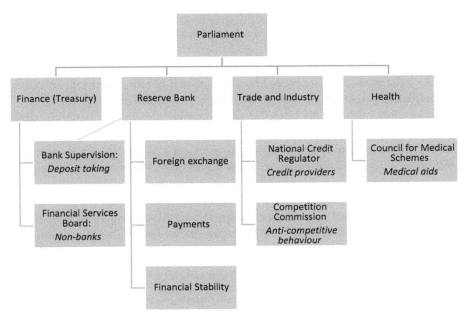

FIGURE 8.6. Financial regulatory system before Twin Peaks.

Schemes, the Registrar of Pensions and the Registrar of Financial Advisory and Intermediary Services. The Financial Services Board was created following the recommendations of the Melamet Commission. A key part of its recommendations was that a more holistic and consistent approach should be followed. However, this reform did not follow. Moreover, because each Registrar was created by a different statute, the Executive Officer had different powers, depending on the particular financial institution involved.

The multitude of regulators created a fragmented regulatory response. Within a large diversified financial services group, deposit-taking activities were regulated by the Banking Supervision Department; credit extension by the National Credit Regulator; and insurance business by the Financial Services Board.

The International Monetary Fund 2015 Financial Sector Assessment Programme Report noted that this fragmentation created substantial prudential risks. This fragmented approach also created significant risks for consumers. Most tellingly, a report commissioned by the National Treasury on consumer-credit insurance[19] highlighted the fragmented approach to regulating this particular product. Consumer protection for credit is regulated by the National Credit Regulator. For insurance products, the regulator is the Financial Services Board. Consumer credit insurance spans both regulators. While each regulator was making significant strides, the 'underlap' created a number of concerns, including a lack of transparency for the total costs of credit; high premiums; lack of competition between providers (often consumer credit is sold by a company within the same group as the credit provider, and customers are not afforded a choice). While consumer credit insurance is an isolated example, a more general finding is that large financial services conglomerates cross-sell different products, under different licences, leaving the customer not fully aware of the implications of each.

[19] National Treasury, *Technical Report on the Consumer Credit Insurance Market in South Africa* (2014), www.treasury.gov.za/public%20comments/CCI/.

Given South Africa's high levels of inequality, a large portion of the population does not have access to appropriate and adequate financial products or services. Often, these products are mis-sold. In 2016, for example, Lewis Stores, a large retailer, was found in contravention of the law by the National Consumer Tribunal for selling retrenchment insurance to pensioners[20]. Market conduct for credit products is supervised by the National Credit Regulator, but there is no market-conduct supervision for deposit taking or transactional banking.

A similar example relates to the selling of money-market investments. Money-market funds are regulated from a prudential and market-conduct perspective under the *Collective Investments Schemes Control Act*.[21] Bank deposits are regulated prudentially (under the *Banks Act*)[22] but are not regulated for conduct. Many banks offer 'money-market accounts' which compete directly with money-market funds.

A final example is the distinction between 'medical aid' and 'medical insurance'. Medical aid is a financial product, provided by a financial institution, regulated under the *Medical Schemes Act*.[23] Medical insurance is a very similar product, provided under the *Short-Term Insurance Act*.[24]

8.2.3.3 Trends in Credit and the Rise of Over-Indebtedness

South Africa is a highly unequal society, with one of the highest Gini coefficients in the world. Unemployment is also particularly high. Despite this, a large proportion of the population has access to credit. Over the past decade, unsecured credit to this particularly vulnerable group of consumers has risen rapidly. The effect has been an increase in household indebtedness and a deterioration of household balance sheets.[25]

The increase was most notable between 2009 and 2010 (see Figure 8.7). This necessitated both a prudential response, in order to guard against the financial stability risks of a potential unsecured lending bubble, and a market-conduct response, to guard against unscrupulous lenders. Coordination, however, was weak between the multitude of regulators.

Ultimately, African Bank, a monoline unsecured lender, failed in August 2014. The report into the failure noted a number of areas of weakness.[26] Firstly, the bank had grown due to a particularly risky business model. The holding company had three main subsidiaries – the bank, a furniture retailer (Ellerines) and a consumer credit insurer (Stangen). The business model entailed the bank providing unsecured loans to support customers purchasing furniture, with credit insurance. In addition, personal unsecured loans were provided directly. When the bank experienced financial difficulty, it became clear that its resolution would be complicated by the presence of three regulators: the banking supervisor for the bank, the insurance supervisor for the insurance arm and the Registrar of Companies and the stock exchange for the listed holding company.

---

[20] *National Credit Regulator v Lewis Stores (Pty) Ltd and Another* [2016] ZANCT 33, www.saflii.org/za/cases/ZANCT/2016/33.html. For a discussion of efforts to combat predatory lending, see Andrew D. Schmulow, 'Curbing Reckless and Predatory Lending: A Statutory Analysis of South Africa's National Credit Act' (2016) 24(3) *Competition and Consumer Law Journal* 220–47.

[21] Act No 45 of 2002.

[22] Act No 94 of 1990.

[23] Act No 131 of 1998.

[24] Act No 53 of 1998; Medical insurance and medical aid differ in one important respect – medical insurers are allowed to individually risk-rate customers, whereas medical aids are not (they may group risk-rate). This has compromised one of the intentions of medical aids, which is to create a medical safety net with a degree of risk pooling.

[25] See Schmulow (n 20).

[26] See South African Reserve Bank, *Ex Parte: African Bank Limited, in re: Investigation in Terms of s69A of the Banks Act, 94 of 1990* (2016), www.resbank.co.za/Lists/News%20and%20Publications/Attachments/7288/Report%20-%20Investigation%20in%20terms%20of%20s69A%20of%20the%20Banks%20Act,%2094%20of%201990.pdf.

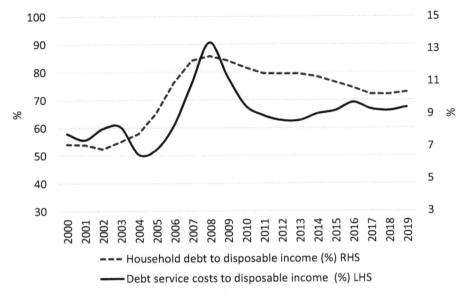

FIGURE 8.7. Household indebtedness and debt service costs.

In addition, the failure of African Bank highlighted the lack of effective group supervision powers and substantial systemic risk from its overreliance on funding from money-market funds.[27] The bank regulator had limited powers to force the group to improve its inter-group risks. The resolution of the bank was also complicated by different resolution powers. The bank went into curatorship under section 29 of the *Banks Act*.[28] The holding company and the furniture subsidiary went into separate business rescue proceedings under Chapter 6 of the *Companies Act*,[29] while the insurance subsidiary was resolved through powers in both the *Insurance Act* and the *Companies Act*.[30] Each subsidiary had a different administrator, tasked with deriving the most benefit for creditors. Inevitably, the coordination amongst administrators was complex.

Despite these challenges, the resolution of African Bank went well. Unfortunately, the failure of the bank delayed the implementation of Twin Peaks because much time was taken up by the authorities to manage the resolution process. However, the gaps in regulatory coordination, the lack of regulatory powers and the weakness in resolution powers only underscored the need to enhance and improve the regulatory system.

8.2.4 *Twin Peaks as a Response*

The South African authorities considered a number of aspects, including:

- whether prudential supervision would be best undertaken by separate agencies, for separate types of entities, or if prudential supervision was best undertaken by a single supervisor;

---

[27] For a discussion of the systemic consequences see Roy Havemann, 'Can Creditor Bail-in Trigger Contagion? The Experience of an Emerging Market' (2019) *Review of Finance* 23(6) 1155–80.

[28] Ibid.

[29] *Companies Act 2008* (Act No 71 of 2008).

[30] Ibid.

- whether conduct supervision would be best undertaken by the same agency as the prudential agency; or if it would be best to separate the two; and
- the role of the central bank.

Given the concentrated nature of the financial system and multiple financial conglomerates, the answer to the first question seemed without doubt to be that all prudential supervision should be undertaken by one agency. This was underscored by the decision to introduce the Solvency Assessment and Management (SAM) regime for insurance companies – an insurance regulatory approach closely modelled on Solvency II. While Solvency II and Basel III have differences, a common set of regulatory skills is required. Moreover, in the absence of a holistic prudential approach, at a group level, large financial conglomerates may be able to arbitrage the capital requirements for their insurance and banking subsidiaries.

The second question was less clear-cut. There are a number of arguments for having conduct and prudential supervision in the same agency. Most importantly, an in-depth understanding of a particular type of industry is important. However, in reviewing the nature of market conduct, the Financial Regulatory Reform Steering Committee noted that market-conduct requirements were inconsistent and fragmented across different industries. There was a notable lack of alignment between the requirements for financial intermediaries and service providers across multiple pieces of legislation, such as the *Financial Advisory and Intermediaries Services Act*, the *Financial Markets Act* and the *Collective Investment Schemes Control Act*.[31] For example, a financial institution selling a mutual fund would need to comply with sometimes contradictory or at least different requirements in each of these pieces of legislation.

Moreover, a mixed mandate can bring with it substantial risks. It has been argued that the combination of prudential and market-conduct functions at the Financial Services Authority, for example, may have led to an overconcentration on market-conduct issues at the expense of prudential supervision.[32] Indeed, the South African regulatory structure had long placed a strong emphasis on prudential safety and soundness – possibly too much emphasis. There were, for instance, no market-conduct requirements for transactional banking. The concern was that in a new structure of single supervision, staffed by experienced prudential supervisors, market conduct might be neglected.

For this reason, it was clear that two separate regulators, each tasked with a specific mandate, would make better sense.

8.3 THE SOUTH AFRICAN REGULATORS

8.3.1 'A Mountain, Two Peaks and Some Molehills'

In the South African context, the Twin Peaks system, as proposed, is similar in many ways to other systems around the world. However, it has some particular complexities.

As one of the members of Parliament wryly remarked, it is a system of 'a mountain, two peaks and some molehills'. The system is not a pure 'Twin Peaks' system, as there are more than two peaks. There are in the order of six authorities. These include:

---

[31] Respectively Act No 37 of 2002; Act No 19 of 2012; Act No 45 of 2002.
[32] See, for example, Financial Services Authority, *The Turner Review: A Regulatory Response to the Global Banking Crisis* (2009), www.fsa.gov.uk/pubs/other/turner_review.pdf.

- the Reserve Bank, 'the mountain', which is given new financial stability powers, and which retains responsibility for payments system oversight, and the supervision of foreign exchange transactions;
- the Prudential Authority and Financial Sector Conduct Authority, the 'two peaks';
- the National Credit Regulator;
- the Financial Intelligence Centre; and
- the Ombuds, which the relevant parliamentarian somewhat unkindly called the 'molehills'.

The next sub-section will look first at common aspects across all the regulators, and then look at each one individually.

8.3.2 *Underlying Principles*

The governance of regulators is a key component of any reform.[33] Regulators are given significant powers – they can set rules, take enforcement actions and licence. Their internal governance arrangements and the relationship between their stakeholders are critical components.

8.3.2.1 Pre-emptive, Intrusive and Effective Regulators

An important part of the Twin Peaks process has been to create regulators that have forward-looking, pre-emptive and risk-based approaches to supervision. This is partly achieved by requiring each of them to publish, and consult widely on, a 'regulatory strategy' which sets out key regulatory and supervisory priorities, for the Authority for the next three years.[34] The strategy sets out guiding principles for each Authority on how it should perform its regulatory and supervisory functions; what it should consider in performing those functions; how it should approach administrative actions; and how it will achieve transparency, openness to consultation and accountability.

8.3.2.2 Operational Independence

During the South African reforms there was a vibrant debate about operational independence. What does it mean? How can it be implemented effectively? How does one balance operational independence with effective oversight, particularly by Parliament? In particular, in South Africa, the central bank is constitutionally independent, a status it guards carefully.

In the South African system, the approach is that Parliament sets the mandate of the agency by way of statute; the Finance Ministry provides broad oversight of the implementation of the mandate; and then the agency is left to implement its mandate as effectively as it can. One key change was to take away a board – previously a board of directors exercised oversight over the Financial Services Board (FSB). This model proved to be ineffective, in that the role of the board was unclear, particularly vis-à-vis Parliament and the government. In the new arrangement, the Financial Sector Conduct Authority (FSCA) more closely resembles a commission.

The appointment of commissioners is, however, not at the sole discretion of the relevant line ministry. An appointment committee has been established, consisting of a range of government

---

[33] A comparison of the governance of the South African system with that in Australia can be found in Andrew Schmulow, 'Financial Regulatory Governance in South Africa: The Move towards Twin Peaks' (2017) 25 *African Journal of International and Comparative Law* 393–417.

[34] See ss 47 and 70 of the Financial Sector Regulation Act, No 9 of 2017 for the regulatory strategy requirements for the PA and FSCA respectively.

and non-government stakeholders, including the governor of the Reserve Bank, the head of the Department of Trade and Industry (DTI) and Parliament.

8.3.2.3 Accountability

Closely linked to the operational independence question is the accountability question. If an overly independent regulator is unable to do its work properly, it is very difficult to exercise adequate accountability and oversight. In the South African system, accountability is achieved by ensuring that the top officials in the regulators enter into binding performance agreements that flow directly from their statutory mandates. Annual reports to Parliament are required. Finally, the regulators can be removed for not performing their responsibilities, through a public process, designed to ensure that they are not removed for other reasons.

8.3.2.4 Transparency (and Accountability?)

Transparency is critical to ensuring that regulated entities know what is expected of them, and how they will go about achieving those ends. This is achieved, in part, through the regulatory strategy. But also decisions are often required to be made by administrative action committees[35] – committees set up to ensure that due process is followed when regulators exercise their powers. Extensive reporting in annual reports, on activities of the regulator, combined with presentations and interventions by Parliament, are also an important component of a transparent regulator.

8.3.2.5 Funding

International guidance on funding of the regulators generally requires both independent funding and the ability to independently set the amount of funding.[36] Both of these requirements can be difficult to implement.[37] Funding either comes from government (in the form of a budget transfer) or from industry (in the form of a levy). Some countries have a hybrid system.

Money from government can create significant questions in terms of regulator independence, and often government fiscal objectives can compromise the operation of the regulator. Most notably, during periods of financial system distress, tax revenues frequently decline. This is precisely the time that more capacity is needed at the prudential regulator, but government cost-cutting can cause funding cuts to the regulator.

Similarly, money from industry brings the possibility of industry lobbying to reduce the costs they incur and, of course, to reduce capacity at the regulator. In South Africa, there are some financial subsectors with only a few regulated entities, and they can exercise significant power over the regulator on the basis of funding they provide (for example, for decades there was only one licensed exchange). The contrary can also occur – the regulator may require a substantial fee for regulation from only a handful of companies.

In South Africa, the Constitution does not allow entities to raise their own money. This must be done through an Act of Parliament (a Money Bill). This, to some extent, allows for a public process, with an independent arbiter (the Parliamentary Committee). For simplicity reasons, the proposed levies are set as a percentage of assets, liabilities or turnover (depending on the type of financial institution). This will ensure that funding grows as the particular sector grows.

---

[35] See Ch 6 of the *Financial Sector Regulation Act* for details of the Administrative Action Committees.

[36] See Basel Committee on Banking Supervision, International Association of Insurance Supervisors and International Organization of Securities Commissioners guidance.

[37] See, for example, Michael W. Taylor, Marc Quintyn and Silvia Ramirez, 'The Fear of Freedom: Politicians and the Independence and Accountability of Financial Sector Supervisors' (IMF Working Paper No 7-25, 2007).

8.3.3 *The Central Bank*

One of the key choices to make in a Twin Peaks framework is the role of the central bank and its relationship with the prudential regulator. As detailed in other chapters, Australia chose to separate the central bank from the prudential regulator, whereas in the United Kingdom the Prudential Regulatory Authority is located within the Bank of England.

In the South African system, although the Prudential Authority is part of the central bank, the central bank has its own regulatory powers, separate from the Prudential Authority's powers. These relate to financial stability; systemically important financial institutions; macroprudential supervision; resolution; payments system oversight; and foreign exchange regulation. These are considered in turn.

8.3.3.1 Financial Stability

One of the key lessons from the Global Financial Crisis was the need for a clear and unambiguous financial stability mandate for the central bank. In 2010, the minister of finance wrote to the governor of the Reserve Bank to clarify that the Reserve Bank would henceforth also be responsible for financial stability. However, there were still some potential gaps.

The constitutional mandate of the South African Reserve Bank, provided for in section 224,[38] provides as follows: 'to protect the value of the currency in the interest of balanced and sustainable growth in the Republic'. Read together with the mandate on financial stability in the *Financial Sector Regulation Act* (FSRA), it could be argued that the Reserve Bank has sufficient power to fulfil its financial stability mandate.

To clarify this issue, it was the view of the Financial Regulatory Reform Committee that a clear statutory financial stability mandate for the central bank should be provided for, in the *Reserve Bank Act*, together with details of how the power should be exercised, provided for in the *Financial Sector Regulation Act* (chapter 2). Subsequent amendments to the *Reserve Bank Act* inserted an explicit financial stability mandate.

This also included relatively sweeping powers for systemic events, including a procedure for designating an event as 'systemic'; how these powers should be exercised during such an event was also included.[39]

8.3.3.2 Systemically Important Financial Institutions

Oversight of the financial system as a whole is a noble objective. But financial stability is likely to be compromised by the failure of a systemically important financial institution, which in turn would lead to financial system instability. Such a systemically important institution may be a large, interconnected bank; or an institution responsible for a critical aspect of the payments system or of the cross-border transactions system; or the failure of an institution responsible for the securities settlement system; or a large default by a member of a central counterparty.

To guard against these risks, the FSRA provides for the Reserve Bank to designate financial institutions as systemically important.[40] Institutions will be assessed on the basis of size, complexity, interconnectedness and the substitutability of products and services.

---

[38] Constitution of the Republic of South Africa, Act No 108 of 1996.
[39] See Pt 2 of Ch 2 of the *Financial Sector Regulation Act*, No 9 of 2017.
[40] See Pt 6 of Ch 2, of the *Financial Sector Regulation Act*, No 9 of 2017.

8.3.3.3 Macroprudential Policy

Once an institution is designated as systemically important, the Reserve Bank may direct the Prudential Authority to introduce additional requirements for these institutions. This provides a legal framework for 'macroprudential' tools.[41] The Reserve Bank has published a discussion document on the role of macroprudential policy frameworks and its proposed approach.[42] In brief, it is envisaged that the Reserve Bank will be able to use any one of the following measures:

- solvency measures and capital requirements, which may include requirements in relation to counter-cyclical capital buffers;
- leverage ratios;
- liquidity;
- organisational structures;
- risk-management arrangements, including guarantee arrangements;
- sectoral and geographical exposures;
- required statistical returns;
- recovery and resolution planning; and
- any other matter in respect of which a prudential standard or regulator's directive may be made, prescribed by regulations made for this section on the recommendation of the governor.

8.3.3.4 Interaction between the Reserve Bank and the Prudential Authority (PA)

In the South African system, the PA functions as a part of the Reserve Bank but has its own juristic personality. This was designed to give the PA some autonomy over its day-to-day supervisory functions, while maintaining the benefits of, and access to, resources from the central bank.

Essentially, the PA functions as an entity within the Reserve Bank. The main oversight body is the 'Prudential Committee', in terms of section 41 of the FSRA. This committee functions as the PA's 'board', modelled to some extent on the governance reforms introduced in the United Kingdom. The governor is chair of the Prudential Committee, with the deputy governors (including the head of the Prudential Authority) constituting the other members.

8.3.4 *The Two Peaks*

The FSCA is a stand-alone market-conduct authority, while the PA is an authority established within the Reserve Bank. Its two predecessors, the Financial Services Board (FSB) and the Bank Supervision Department, have ceased to exist. It is important to note that these existing regulatory institutions have not merely been 'renamed' under the Twin Peaks system.

The new authorities have clearly defined mandates, relating to market conduct and financial soundness respectively, and have broad jurisdiction over the financial sector. This is achieved through the definition of financial products and financial services.

---

[41] For further reading on the role of macroprudential policies under Twin Peaks, see Sandra Mollentze and Unathi Kamlana, 'Macroprudential Policy and the Twin Peaks' (2014) 19 *South African Financial Markets Journal* 5.

[42] Financial Stability Department of the South African Reserve Bank, *A New Macroprudential Policy Framework for South Africa* (2016), www.resbank.co.za/Lists/News%20and%20Publications/Attachments/7660/Macroprudential%20policy.pdf.

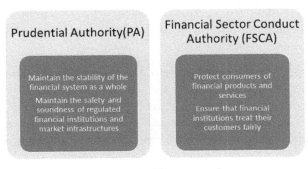

FIGURE 8.8. The two peaks.

8.3.4.1 Financial Products and Services

Financial products are essentially anything that financial customers 'purchase' from financial institutions and which they expect to function in a particular way. During the drafting process, it was considered whether to define products in terms of characteristics. However, a simpler approach was to define products in terms of a finite list of existing products: a bank deposit, an insurance policy, an interest in a collective investment scheme, a pension fund benefit and so forth.[43] In turn, a 'financial service' is a service in relation to such a product and these services include offering, promoting, marketing or distributing the product, or providing advice, recommendations or guidance in respect of the product.[44]

This distinction forms the basis for the remit of each of the 'two peaks'. The PA is responsible for the safety and soundness of financial institutions that provide products. It essentially ensures that the financial institution has sufficient resources (financial, operational and so on) to honour 'promises' made in respect of the institution's products. This is most obvious in the case of bank deposits or insurance policies – the promise is that the depositor will be reimbursed or that the policyholder's claims will be met.

The FSCA, on the other hand, is tasked with supervising financial services. Key questions it will ask in its supervisory ambit include the following: Is there sufficient disclosure at the point of sale? Is the advice in respect of the product appropriate? (Figure 8.8).

8.3.4.2 The Prudential Authority

One of the key innovations in the South African framework is that the PA is responsible, in law, for prudential supervision of *all* financial institutions. From this angle, South Africa might possibly have the purest 'Twin Peaks' model. All financial institutions are by default prudentially supervised. This, of course, is neither practical nor desirable.

To ensure that the PA only focuses on those financial institutions which are 'prudentially relevant', it may delegate prudential supervision to FSCA. The onus and responsibility of deciding what is 'prudentially relevant' is thus something for the PA and FSCA to negotiate.

The PA is tasked with four objectives (section 33 of the FSRA). These are to:

- promote and enhance the safety and soundness of financial institutions that provide financial products and securities services;
- promote and enhance the safety and soundness of market infrastructures;

---

[43] For a full list, see s 2(1) of the *Financial Sector Regulation Act*, No 9 of 2017.
[44] For a full explanation, see s 3 of the *Financial Sector Regulation Act*, No 9 of 2017.

- protect financial customers against the risk that those financial institutions may fail to meet their obligations; and
- assist in maintaining financial stability.

The first objective speaks to the primary role of the PA, which is to supervise the safety and soundness of all financial institutions. Safety and soundness of market infrastructure was added as a specific objective in order to ensure that the Prudential Authority has sufficient powers to supervise systemically important institutions such as central counterparties, settlements at the central securities depositories and, to some extent, the stock exchanges. The third objective explains the link between prudential supervision and the customer – for deposit takers, the key regulatory objective is protection of depositors' funds. For insurers, it is to protect the financial interests of policy holders. The final objective relates to the close relationship between the Reserve Bank's financial stability mandate (particularly macroprudential supervision as discussed in Section 8.3.3.3) and the PA's safety and soundness mandate (microprudential supervision).

In the first phase of Twin Peaks, the PA will supervise banks and insurance companies. New group supervision powers will provide for the supervision of financial groups (see discussion, below).

As part of the Twin Peaks process, significant amendments were made to the *Banks Act*[45] to facilitate the transfer of powers and functions to the PA. In particular, the PA will inherit powers and functions under the *Banks Act, Long-Term Insurance Act and Short-Term Insurance Act.*[46]

8.3.4.3 The Financial Sector Conduct Authority

The South African journey to Twin Peaks has been similar in some ways to that of the United Kingdom. The existing regulatory body (the Financial Services Board) will transition from being a mixed conduct/prudential regulator to a pure conduct authority. The difference being, of course, that prudential supervision of banks was already carved out of the FSB.

The key difference between South Africa and the United Kingdom, however, is the plethora of laws relating to market conduct. When the FSA was created, the United Kingdom largely took the opportunity to consolidate the law into a single *Financial Services and Markets Act.*[47] South Africa has not embarked on legislative consolidation and, as highlighted earlier, there are still, at the time of writing, multiple pieces of legislation. Each of these pieces of legislation has a different approach to market conduct. One of the key parts of the Twin Peaks reform is to shift to a single market-conduct framework. This will be contained in the forthcoming *Conduct of Financial Institutions Bill*, which will set out how a holistic conduct framework will operate.

The new legal framework will aim to ensure that complete, consistent and outcomes-focused conduct standards are applied across an increasingly converging and complex financial sector. In December 2014, National Treasury released a document outlining how the market-conduct framework would be implemented.[48] The document highlighted key areas of retail market-conduct problems, which would be addressed through the new conduct framework. This paper categorised these problems into areas of concern:

[45] Act No 94 of 1990.

[46] Ibid; Act No 52 of 1998; Act No 53 of 1998.

[47] *Financial Services and Markets Act 2000.*

[48] National Treasury, *Treating Customers Fairly in the Financial Sector: A Draft Market Conduct Policy Framework for South Africa* (2014), www.treasury.gov.za/public%20comments/FSR2014/Treating%20Customers%20Fairly%20in% 20the%20Financial%20Sector%20Draft%20MCP%20Framework%20Amended%20Jan2015%20WithAp6.pdf.

- *Non-credit transactional banking.* Here, key areas of focus include opaque and complex fee structures, incentives and inducements, unfair debit order practices and lack of competition for payments providers.
- *Savings and investment.* In this area, product design, commission-based structures and lack of adequate disclosure raise a number of market-conduct risks.
- *Credit.* This area includes poor practices that have led to over-indebtedness, abuse of attachment orders and exploitation of 'captive' customers, that is to say those that already have a relationship with a particular financial institution.
- *Risk and insurance.* Commission structures have often led to sub-optimal outcomes for customers, claims handling has been weak and there has been a relatively high number of unregulated providers (particularly funeral insurers).
- *Sales and distribution.* Here market structures may lead to conflicts of interest, especially around remuneration and outsourcing. Complicated relationships compromise account-ability between product provider and intermediary, often leaving the customer unclear as to the true costs of advice and who the intermediary represents. Intermediaries may structure themselves so as to avoid the law.

The FSCA was created on 1 April 2018.

8.3.5 *The National Credit Regulator*

In 2005, a market-conduct regulator for credit, the National Credit Regulator (NCR), was created with the passage of the *National Credit Act*.[49] The regulator is responsible for the market-conduct regulation of all credit extension, from large banks to '*mashonistas*' – small-time money-lenders. The broad remit of the NCR mandate creates a number of complexities for the Twin Peaks reforms.

Parliament held extensive engagement on the role of the NCR in the Twin Peaks reforms. A number of stakeholders raised concerns about keeping the NCR outside of Twin Peaks. In particular, a large proportion of retail market conduct would be focused on ensuring that customers had appropriate access to information on their credit products, particularly relating to interest costs and additional fees. However, a disjointed approach to these issues for non-credit products would create significant conduct risks. In particular, there has been a rise of bundled accounts, which combine transactional banking with a credit facility. If one regulator were responsible for the market-conduct standards relating to credit facilities and another for the market-conduct standards relating to transactional banking facilities there could be either overlap or underlap.

It was also noted that the UK market-conduct regulator for credit was shifted from the Office of Fair Trading to the Financial Conduct Authority after the FCA had been established. Many stakeholders highlighted that a 'true' Twin Peaks approach would consolidate all retail market conduct in one institution, much like had been done in the prudential peak.

The FSRA contains dedicated provisions to facilitate improved legislative alignment between the role of the NCR and the role of the FSCA. There are extensive references to both the *National Credit Act*[50] and the regulator, through the FSRA, referencing both and ensuring that there is broad alignment between them:

---

[49] Act No 34 of 2005.
[50] Ibid.

- the NCR is included explicitly as a financial sector regulator, on a par with the PA and the FSCA. However, only certain aspects of the law apply to the NCR;[51]
- clarity that a credit agreement is a financial product, except for the purposes of chapter 4 (the FSCA chapter) and section 106 (the power to make conduct standards) of the FSRA;
- included are frequent references to credit agreements and services relating to credit agreements, explaining the limits of the FSCA's powers.

8.3.6 *The Ombuds*

A fundamental component of an effective consumer protection framework is appropriate customer recourse channels. Customers should have access to affordable, effective and independent mechanisms to address complaints, resolve disputes and secure a fair outcome when broader customer protection frameworks have failed.

An Ombud scheme is an alternative to, rather than a substitute for, the courts. Such schemes are generally free for customers. Customers are not required to use the scheme; nor are they bound by a decision made by the Ombud and may at any time withdraw from the process and take their disputes to court. Ombuds may base decisions on what is considered fair and reasonable rather than the strict legal position. Financial institutions, unlike their customers, are generally bound by the decisions of an Ombud.

South Africa has multiple Ombuds, constituting a mix of voluntary and statutory Ombuds, generally organised on a sectoral basis. (Voluntary Ombuds are set up and funded by the relevant industry, whereas statutory Ombuds are set up by law.) The *Financial Services Ombud Schemes Act* (FSOS)[52] was introduced in 2004 and was intended to govern all Ombud schemes, both statutory and voluntary. Voluntary schemes are recognised by the Financial Services Ombud Schemes Council, in terms of the *FSOS Act*.[53]

To strengthen the Ombud system, the current *FSOS Act* provisions are brought into the overarching FSRA, and additional provisions create a much stronger, independent FSOS Council, intended to take over many of the functions currently assigned to the FSB.

Most importantly, under Twin Peaks, the journey towards a 'single Ombud' has begun. The FSRA establishes a 'Chief Ombud' in section 188. In the first phase of the transition, the Chief Ombud will function as a coordinator, to set broad standards for all Ombuds, so as to ensure consistency across the different systems. Over time, however, consideration will be given to implementing a true, single system of alternative dispute resolution that will cover all financial services.

8.4 KEY ASPECTS OF THE REFORM

This section outlines some of the key innovations that have been introduced as part of the Twin Peaks journey in South Africa. Twin Peaks has yet to be implemented, so these are the designs. It is expected that, during implementation, many of these issues will be improved upon and difficulties ironed out.

---

[51] But only in respect of Pts 2, 3 and 5 of Ch 2, and Pts 1, 2 and 3 of Ch 5 of the FSRA.
[52] Act No 37 of 2004.
[53] Ibid.

8.4.1 'Responsible Authority'

In a Twin Peaks system, the question of who is the 'lead regulator' inevitably arises. Theoretically, both authorities have equal say in licensing, supervision, enforcement and so forth. In practice, however, it would be expected that one authority would have more to do with a particular entity than the other.

In the South African system, one of the authorities is designated as the 'responsible authority'. This authority is responsible for the administration of the relevant sectoral law and acts as the primary interface with the regulated entity. For licence applications, for example, the applicant will approach the responsible authority, which manages the licence application and consults its fellow authority in terms of the standing memorandum of understanding (MoU) between them.

8.4.2 Achieving Inter-Agency Coordination

There are extensive requirements to create a collegial atmosphere between the authorities, and to encourage information-sharing and confidentiality, mutual respect, consultation and mutual cooperation in supervision and enforcement.[54]

8.4.3 Standard-Making Powers

Before Twin Peaks, South Africa's financial sector law had an inconsistent approach to 'regulatory instruments'. For example, subordinate legislation prescribed under the primary law is used to flesh out the requirements in the primary law. The type of subordinate legislation largely depends on when the law was passed – older laws tend to be substantially more prescriptive, with limited discretion to supervisors, while newer laws provide more discretion. In the *Pension Funds Act* (1956),[55] for example, most of the requirements that pension funds are required to meet are provided for in the Act itself,[56] which here is referred to as 'tier 1' legislation. While the *Banks Act*[57] has certain requirements, the majority of prudential, capital and liquidity requirements are contained in regulations ('tier 2' legislation) issued by the minister of finance as the relevant member of the executive, responsible for that particular piece of legislation. The regulations run to over 1,000 pages. Additional requirements are prescribed in 'directives' and 'guidance notes' – what could be termed 'tier 3' legislation. In the *Collective Investment Schemes Control Act*, however, the bulk of the requirements are contained in 'tier 3' legislation. This is issued by the Financial Services Board as a 'Board Notice', whereas the terminology in other laws is often 'Directive'.

The FSRA introduces a new, consistent type of regulatory instrument[58] – known as 'standards'. Standards are, essentially, additional legal requirements, specified by the regulator, to facilitate the achievement of the objectives of the Act.

---

54 Ch 5 of the FSRA sets out the cooperation and collaboration requirements in detail.
55 Act No 24 of 1956.
56 For a comprehensive discussion on the Act, see R. Hunter, J. Esterhuizen, T. Jithoo and S. Khumalo, *The Pension Funds Act, 1956: A Commentary on the Act and Selected Notices, Directives and Circulars* (Hunter Employee Benefits Law, 2010).
57 Ibid.
58 The legal and constitutional implications of standards issued by independent regulatory bodies is beyond the scope of this chapter. Interested readers are referred to the legal opinions submitted to the parliamentary hearings on Twin Peaks, www.pmg.org.za.

Two types of standards are contemplated: prudential standards and conduct standards.[59] Prudential standards must be aimed at ensuring the safety and soundness of financial institutions; reducing the risk that those financial institutions, and key persons, engage in conduct that amounts to, or contributes to, financial crime; and must assist in maintaining financial stability. In particular, the types of standards that can be made include financial soundness requirements, such as capital adequacy, minimum liquidity levels and minimum asset quality standards.

Conduct standards, on the other hand, are standards that safeguard the efficiency and integrity of financial markets: ensuring that financial institutions and representatives treat financial customers fairly; ensuring that financial education programmes or other activities promoting financial literacy are appropriate; reducing the risk that financial institutions, representatives, key persons and contractors engage in conduct that is, or contributes to, financial crime; and assisting in maintaining financial stability.

8.4.4 *The Role of Financial Sector Transformation*

South Africa's history of racial discrimination has left a legacy of wealth disparity. A key objective of the post-Apartheid government has been to create opportunities for previously marginalised groups and to secure an effective and sustainable redistribution of wealth. One aspect of this is the multi-pronged, broad-based black economic empowerment programme. In the financial sector, a Financial Sector Code has been developed between industry, government and civil society, setting out targets. These include access to financial services; representation of previously disadvantaged groups in management; and ownership. A key question that has arisen is what the role of the Twin Peaks authorities should be in transformation. On-going discussions will determine this – however, the need for regulators with clear mandates versus the need for appropriately enforced transformation objectives will underpin the final outcome.

8.5 PHASING IN OF TWIN PEAKS

As the newest adherent, South Africa is only at the beginning of its Twin Peaks journey. Many lessons will be learned, and the appropriateness, or otherwise, of a Twin Peaks system for an emerging market will become apparent. That said, to date Twin Peaks has proven to be an effective catalyst for a refreshed and updated approach to regulation, attuned to the challenges of a new era in financial services. It will be an era of rapid technological change, requiring regulators that are adept, resilient and adaptable. The intention of Twin Peaks is to firmly cement and improve South Africa's reputation for well-regulated, deep and liquid capital markets that can underpin a rise in living standards for all.

---

[59] See Pt 2 of Ch 7 of the *Financial Sector Regulation Act*, No 9 of 2017.

9

The Role of the SARB as Central Bank in the South African Twin Peaks Model

Corlia van Heerden and Gerda van Niekerk

9.1 INTRODUCTION

South Africa's journey to a Twin Peaks model of financial regulation, which eventually culminated in the adoption of the *Financial Sector Regulation Act 9* of 2017, has been comprehensively documented and commented on by Roy Havemann in Chapter 8 of this publication. As observed by Havemann, the South African model is not a 'pure' Twin Peaks model, as originally conceptualised by Michael Taylor – it actually comprises a 'mountain, two peaks and some molehills'.[1] The main role players in the South African model are the South African Reserve Bank (SARB), as central bank, tasked with an overall macroprudential financial stability mandate; the newly established Prudential Authority (PA), as systemwide prudential regulator of financial institutions; and the newly established Financial Sector Conduct Authority (FSCA), as systemwide market conduct regulator of financial institutions.[2] As part of their objectives, the PA and FSCA are tasked with assisting the SARB in maintaining financial stability.[3] Other financial sector regulators that function within the Twin Peaks model include the National Credit Regulator, tasked with regulation and supervision of the credit market, and the Financial Intelligence Centre, which oversees aspects related to money-laundering.

The purpose of this chapter is to take a closer look at the role of the SARB as central bank in the South African Twin Peaks model. The evolution of the SARB as central bank in the pre-Twin Peaks era and the changes to its objectives, functions and powers brought about by the adoption of a Twin Peaks model will be considered, as well as the expanded legislative and soft law basis for its interaction with other financial sector regulators and organs of state.

---

[1] See Chapter 8, Section 8.3.1. See further M. Taylor, 'Financial Regulation in the UK: A Structure for the 21st Century' (1996) *The Futures & Derivatives Law Review* 7–17; A. Schmulow 'Financial Regulatory Governance in South Africa: The Move towards Twin Peaks' (2017) 25 *African Journal of International & Comparative Law* 393. See also Chapter 8, Section 8.3.5.

[2] The PA and the FSCA were established in terms of s 32 and s 56 of the *Financial Sector Regulation Act* (FSRA) respectively. The objectives and functions of the PA are set out in ss 33 and 34 FSRA respectively, and that of the FSCA in ss 57 and 58 FSRA.

[3] See Chapter 8, Sections 8.3.4.2 and 8.3.4.3.

9.2 THE ROLE OF THE SOUTH AFRICAN CENTRAL BANK PRE-TWIN PEAKS

The SARB was established as central bank in 1921 in terms of the *Currency and Banking Act* 31 of 1920. It is the fourth oldest central bank outside Europe.[4] The SARB is currently regulated in terms of the *South African Reserve Bank Act* 90 of 1989, and its position as central bank is entrenched by section 223 of the *Constitution of the Republic of South Africa*, 1996. Over the years the SARB has gained recognition internationally as an independent and robust regulator, being a member of the Bank for International Settlements (BIS), with representation at the Basel Committee on Banking Supervision and the Basel Committee on Payments and Settlement Systems.[5]

In the pre-Twin Peaks era the SARB functioned within a sectoral (institutional) model of financial regulation, comprising various regulators that applied silo supervision to the specific financial institutions within their remit. This fragmented silo approach did not, however, enable a holistic view of the health of the financial system, and gave rise to significant regulatory gaps and arbitrage.[6] In this dispensation, the SARB's primary objective was stated in section 3 of the *Reserve Bank Act*, and later confirmed in section 224 of the Constitution, as 'the protection of the value of the currency of the Republic in the interest of balanced and sustainable economic growth in the Republic'.

The SARB fulfilled various traditional central bank roles in the pre-Twin Peaks landscape:[7] it was inter alia responsible for implementation of monetary policy by pursuing price stability through inflation targeting;[8] it was the prudential supervisor of banks; supervised the payments and settlement system; and acted as lender-of-last-resort and extender of emergency liquidity assistance (ELA). The SARB was also responsible for the maintenance of financial stability, a mandate that, in line with the general trend at the time,[9] was not captured in any express terms in the legislation and was exercised de facto, being implied in its position as central bank.[10]

---

[4] See further J. de Jager, 'The South African Reserve Bank: An Evaluation of the Origin, Evolution and Status of a Central Bank (Part 1)' (2006) 18 *SA Mercantile Law Journal* 159–74; and J. de Jager, 'The South African Reserve Bank: An Evaluation of the Origin, Evolution and Status of a Central Bank (Part 2)' (2006) 18 SA *Mercantile Law Journal* 274–90 for a historical overview.

[5] See South African Reserve Bank, 'International Memberships' (undated), 1, www.resbank.co.za/AboutUs/Pages/International-memberships.aspx. The SARB joined the BIS in June 1971.

[6] National Treasury, 'A Safer Financial Sector to Serve South Africa Better' (2011), (The Red Book), 28, www.treasury .gov.za/twinpeaks/20131211%20%20Item%202%20A%20safer%20financial%20sector%20to%20serve%20South%20Africa %20better.pdf. The Financial Services Board (FSB) was responsible for insurance regulation and supervision and also supervised fund managers and exchanges, and shared the responsibility for supervision of market intermediaries with the Johannesburg Stock Exchange (JSE). The JSE supervised listed companies, while the Department of Trade and Industry supervised unlisted companies. The National Credit Regulator, established in terms of the *National Credit Act* 34 of 2005, oversaw lending and reported to the Department of Trade and Industry.

[7] Section 10 of the *South African Reserve Bank Act* 90 of 1989 inter alia stipulates that the SARB is the supervisor of the payments and settlements system (s 10(c)); the supervisor of banks (s 10(v)) and in terms of s 10(s) it may 'perform such other functions of bankers and financial agents as central banks may customarily perform'. The bank's functions in relation to financial stability and acting as lender of last resort were not expressly stated but are captured under s 10(s) as a catch-all provision. See also s 225 of the *Constitution of the Republic of South Africa* (1996) which states that the powers and functions of the SARB are those customarily exercised and performed by central banks.

[8] Section 3 of the *South African Reserve Bank Act* 90 of 1989.

[9] C. A. E. Goodhart, 'The Past Mirror: Notes, Surveys, Debates – The Changing Role of Central Banks' (2011) Financial History Review 135.

[10] See s 10(c) of the *South African Reserve Bank Act* 90 of 1989. See also de Jager (Part 1) (n 4). Since 2010, government policy reflected a financial stability and macroprudential responsibility for the SARB, but this responsibility was not underpinned in legislation pre-Twin Peaks. See IMF, *South Africa: Financial Sector Assessment Program: Technical Note: Financial Safety Net, Bank Resolution, and Crisis Management Framework* (February 2015), para 9, www.imf .org/en/Publications/CR/Issues/2016/12/31/South-Africa-Financial-Sector-Assessment-Program-Financial-Safety-Net-

In pursuit of its de facto financial stability mandate, a Financial Stability Department (FSD) was established in the SARB to help with the identification and evaluation of systemic risks, and to make recommendations and policy proposals to the governor of the SARB to mitigate systemic risks. An interim Financial Stability Oversight Committee (FSOC) co-chaired by the minister of finance and the governor of the SARB was established, and a voluntary coordinating body, the Financial Sector Contingency Forum (FSCF), was created to coordinate plans, mechanisms and structures for managing financial crises. The FSCF was chaired by a deputy governor of the SARB, and its membership was drawn from the National Treasury, SARB, FSB, Banking Association South Africa, South African Insurance Association, Johannesburg Stock Exchange, Payments Association of South Africa, SA Bankers Services Company, South Africa's Central Securities Depository (Strate Limited) and the Association for Savings and Investment South Africa. Its work was organised around two subcommittees, one on operational risk that focused on infrastructure failures and operational risks and the other responsible for contingency planning for financial crises and identification of systemic risks and possible mitigating actions.[11]

Given that bank supervision has been removed from the SARB's regulatory remit in the newly introduced South African Twin Peaks model, it is apposite to briefly refer to the scope of this mandate pre-Twin Peaks. The main powers and functions of the SARB as banking supervisor were set out in the *Banks Act*[12] together with the regulations relating to banks issued in terms of section 90 of the *Banks Act*.[13] Prior to Twin Peaks, the SARB exercised its authority to supervise and regulate banks through the Registrar of Banks and the Bank Supervision Department (BSD) in the Office for Banks, established in terms of section 3 of the *Banks Act*.[14] The SARB's pre-Twin Peaks role as supervisor of banks entailed mainly prudential regulation, and neither the SARB nor any other entity exercised dedicated oversight of the business conduct of banks.[15]

Section 4(3) of the *Banks Act* empowered the Registrar of Banks to enter into written cooperation arrangements such as Memoranda of Understanding (MoUs) regarding supervisory matters with any supervisor or other person or institution as the Registrar deemed fit. Section 89 of the *Banks Act* further permitted the sharing of information by the Registrar of Banks with fellow regulators where essential for the proper performance of a lawful function. The BSD of the SARB and the Financial Services Board (FSB) signed an MoU in 1998 for coordination and collaboration. The MoU provided, inter alia, for mutual assistance in supervision, exchange of information and guidelines for cooperative supervision of financial conglomerates involving banks, mutual banks and financial institutions under the FSB's supervision.[16]

Bank-Resolution-and-42755.pdf. As pointed out by de Jager (Part 2) (n 4) at 499, the implicit responsibility of the SARB for monitoring macroeconomic risks was confirmed in a letter by the minister of finance to the governor of the SARB on 16 February 2010.

[11] IMF (n 10)para 12.

[12] The *Banks Act*, Act 94 of 1990.

[13] Regulations relating to Banks issued in terms of s 90 of the *Banks Act* 1990, published in *Government Gazette* No 34838 of 15 December 2011, www.gov.za/sites/default/files/gcis_document/201409/35950rg9872gon1029.pdf.

[14] International Monetary Fund Country Report No 14/340 *South Africa Financial System Stability Assessment* (3 December 2014), at 55, www.imf.org/external/pubs/ft/scr/2014/cr14340.pdf.

[15] Chapter 8, Section 8.2.3.1.

[16] IMF (n 10) para 11.

9.3 THE SARB IN THE SOUTH AFRICAN TWIN PEAKS MODEL

9.3.1 *Introduction*

The role of the SARB in the Twin Peaks model should be considered against the backdrop of the objective of the *Financial Sector Regulation Act*, which is to:

> achieve a stable financial system that works in the interests of financial customers, and supports balanced and sustainable economic growth in the Republic, by establishing, in conjunction with the other financial sector laws, a regulatory and supervisory framework that promotes financial stability; the safety and soundness of financial institutions; the fair treatment and protection of financial customers; the efficiency and integrity of the financial system; the prevention of financial crime; financial inclusion and confidence in the financial system.[17]

Financial stability is a notoriously 'fuzzy' concept for which no uniform and generally accepted definition exists.[18] In order to give some context to the concept of 'financial stability' for the purposes of informing the objectives of the regulatory financial stability mandate, as captured in the *Financial Sector Regulation Act*, section 4 describes 'financial stability' to mean:

(a) financial institutions generally provide financial products and financial services, and market infrastructures generally perform their functions and duties in terms of financial sector laws, without interruption;

(b) financial institutions are capable of continuing to provide financial products and financial services, and market infrastructures are capable of continuing to perform their functions and duties in terms of financial sector laws, without interruption despite changes in economic circumstances and

(c) there is general confidence in the ability of financial institutions to continue to provide financial products and services, and the ability of market infrastructures to continue to perform their functions and duties in terms of financial sector laws, without interruption despite changes in economic circumstances.[19]

It is pertinent to note that the newly introduced Twin Peaks model has created an entirely different operating environment within which the SARB and the financial sector regulators have to execute their mandates. In this model, the SARB has, with the exception of bank supervision, retained all the functions that it attended to in the pre-Twin Peaks regime. In particular, the *Financial Sector Regulation Act* has expanded the SARB's financial stability role by conferring on the central bank a comprehensive and express financial stability mandate.[20] It has also illuminated the importance of this mandate by amending section 3 of the *South African Reserve Bank Act* to provide that, *in addition to* its primary mandate of protecting the value of

---

[17] Section 7 FSRA.

[18] C. Borio and M. Drehmann, 'Towards an Operational Framework for Financial Stability: "Fuzzy" Measurement and Its Consequences' (BIS Working Papers No 284, June 2009, www.bis.org/publ/work284.htm), point out the 'fuzziness' surrounding the measurement of financial stability and, absent an appropriate definition, conclude that '[F]inancial stability is the converse of financial instability'. See also William Allen and Geoffrey Wood, 'Defining and Achieving Financial Stability' (2006) 2(2) *Journal of Financial Stability* 152–72.

[19] Section 4(2) FSRA provides that a reference to 'maintaining' financial stability includes, where financial stability has been adversely affected, a reference to 'restoring' financial stability.

[20] Section 11–31 FSRA.

the currency, the SARB is responsible for 'protecting and maintaining' financial stability.[21] The SARB's mandate for financial stability is thus now for the first time expressly captured in a legislative framework that emphasises and structures the broad parameters of this mandate, and elevates it to be on a par with the SARB's monetary policy responsibility.

9.3.2 *Removing Bank Supervision from the SARB's Remit to the PA*

As pointed out by Llewellyn, one of the most vexing considerations in a financial regulatory model is whether to give the central bank the overall financial stability mandate as well as the function of bank supervision or whether to entrust prudential regulation and supervision to a separate entity.[22] In the South African model, bank supervision has been excised from the regulatory and supervisory remit of the SARB and entrusted to a separate juristic person, the PA, which is not only the prudential regulator for banks, but also for other non-bank financial institutions. The PA is housed within the administration of the SARB and they share the same building along with certain administrative resources.[23]

In respect of the question as to whether the prudential regulator should be housed within the central bank, Godwin and Schmulow observe that the weight of opinion is in favour of a stand-alone regulator that is independent of the central bank, provided that adequate coordination is achieved between the prudential regulator and other regulators, and between the prudential regulator and the central bank.[24] The opinion is that such an arrangement would serve to avoid conflicts of interest and strengthen operational independence when conflicts may arise if the objectives of monetary policy and prudential regulation conflict, such as where a decision has to be taken on whether to allow a systemically important bank to fail or whether to rescue it in the interests of consumer protection.[25] They point out, however, that there are also benefits to housing the prudential authority within the central bank, including the ability to achieve synergies in relation to resources and expertise, and to avoid difficulties relating to information-sharing that do not present where the prudential regulator and the central bank constitute one organisation. Also, if the central bank has a reputation for being a strong independent bank, the housing of the prudential authority within the central bank may ensure that the prudential authority also operates more independently of government interference.[26]

For South Africa, the choice to give the central bank the overall financial stability mandate was a natural one, given the SARB's deep knowledge of the macroeconomy spanning nearly a

---

[21] Authors' emphasis. See Schedule 4 of the *Financial Sector Regulation Act*, titled 'Amendment and Repeals' where it is provided that s 3 of the *Reserve Bank Act* 90 of 1989 is amended by the addition of the following subsection, the existing section becoming subsection (1): '(2) In addition, the Bank is responsible for protecting and maintaining financial stability as envisaged in the Financial Sector Regulation Act, 2017'. Section 224 of the Constitution has however not yet been amended. See further IMF (n 10) para 9, where it was suggested that this objective should be entrenched in the legislation.

[22] David T. Llewellyn, 'Institutional Structure of Financial Regulation and Supervision: The Basic Issues' (Paper presented at World Bank Seminar, Aligning Supervisory Structures with Country Needs, Washington DC, 6–7 June 2006), 7, http://citeseerx.ist.psu.edu/viewdoc/download?doi=10.1.1.503.2388&rep=rep1&type=pdf. See also C. A. E. Goodhart and D. Schoenmaker, 'Should the Functions of Monetary Policy and Banking Supervision Be Separated?' (1995) 18(2) *Oxford Economic Papers* 539; C. A. E. Goodhart, 'The Past Mirror: Notes, Surveys, Debates – The Changing Role of Central Banks' (2011) *Financial History Review* 135.

[23] Section 32 FSRA.

[24] A. Godwin and A. Schmulow, 'The Financial Sector Regulation Bill in South Africa, Second Draft: Lessons from Australia' (2015) 132(4) *South African Law Journal* 756 at 758.

[25] Ibid 759.

[26] Ibid 760.

century and the variety of systemic functions it executed in the pre-Twin Peaks regime.[27] The decision to excise bank supervision from the SARB's remit and entrust it to the PA as systemwide prudential supervisor was possibly partly triggered by Goodhart when he remarked at the SARB's 2010 Financial Stability Conference that 'it is not good that the central bank does everything'.[28] National Treasury indicated that housing the PA under the same roof as the SARB would enable the efficient, effective and continual information-sharing that is key to a financial stability mandate, and will facilitate coordination with other relevant entities in the event of a crisis.[29] Given South Africa's position as a resource-constrained developing country, the decision to house the PA within the administration of the SARB was likely also motivated by cost savings that could be garnered from shared resources and other economies of scale, as well as by benefits from synergies between the SARB and PA. The staff of the PA mainly comprise persons who were previously employed by the SARB and the erstwhile market conduct regulator, the FSB (which has been replaced with the FSCA in the Twin Peaks model). Notably, the Prudential Committee that is responsible for the management and administration of the PA comprises the governor of the SARB, the chief executive officer (CEO) of the PA (who is also a deputy governor of the SARB, other than the deputy governor tasked with financial stability) and the remaining deputy governors of the SARB. The PA is thus managed by a 'full house' of SARB governors who must 'ensure that it is efficient and effective'.[30] Section 37 of the *Financial Sector Regulation Act* provides that when attending to the day-to-day management of the PA, the CEO must implement the policies and strategies adopted by the Prudential Committee.

Godwin and Schmulow aptly remark that the regulatory design in any country has to accommodate the circumstances and needs of that country. They accordingly concede that there may be cogent reasons for housing the PA within the SARB. However, they caution that it will still be necessary to ensure that the PA advances an appropriate level of operational independence in practice, and that the risk of conflicts of interest and competing priorities are appropriately managed.[31]

This is salient advice. The fact that the SARB and the PA are two different juristic entities, each with their own set of objectives, albeit housed in the same building and within the same administration, is a clear attempt to create them as independent of one another and dedicated to the specific objectives they are tasked to pursue. As such, the PA is not merely the 'handmaiden' of the SARB, and in the event of conflict between the objectives of financial stability and prudential regulation the PA should, at least in theory, be able to stand its ground if there are sound reasons for its stance. However, it is concerning that the PA's main decision-making body, the Prudential Committee, solely comprises SARB governors, and that the CEO of the PA is also one of the SARB's deputy governors.[32] It is submitted that this new arrangement may be problematic either way: on the one hand the SARB may become too involved with prudential

---

[27] National Treasury (n 6) at 31. Martha Gertruida van Niekerk, 'A Comparative Analysis of the Role of the Central Bank in Promoting and Maintaining Financial Stability in South Africa' (unpublished LLD thesis, University of Pretoria, 2018), at 12.

[28] C. Goodhart, 'Monetary Policy and Financial Stability in the Post-Crisis Era' (South African Reserve Bank Conference Series, 2010), at 43, www.resbank.co.za/Lists/News%20and%20Publications/Attachments/4908/Confproceeding2010.pdf.

[29] National Treasury Policy Document, 'Implementing a Twin Peaks Model of Financial Regulation in South Africa', at 32, www.treasury.gov.za/twinpeaks/20131211%20-%203%20Roadmap.pdf.

[30] Sections 41 and 42 FSRA.

[31] Godwin and Schmulow (n 24) at 761.

[32] Notably the IMF in its Country Report No 14.340, para 26 recommended that the operational independence of the PA's CEO should be made clear in the legislation. This appears not to have been done – see s 37 FSRA.

matters, even though they fall outside its new regulatory remit. The SARB may, in the process, compromise its reputation as an independent systemic regulator if, for example, it inappropriately steps in to prevent prudential failures or the collapse of financial institutions 'in the interests of financial stability'. On the other hand, the PA may be compromising its regulatory objectives and succumbing to conflicting interests if it tailors its approach to prudential regulation to appease the SARB rather than ensure that it is properly pursuing its prudential regulatory mandate.

9.3.3 *Legislative Framework for the SARB's Financial Stability Mandate*

The SARB's mandate in respect of financial stability, and the framework for exercising this mandate, is set out in Part 1 of Chapter 2 of the *Financial Sector Regulation Act*. Two dedicated committees, the FSOC and the FSCF, both of which were informal committees lacking any legislative basis pre-Twin Peaks, are now formally established by the Act to facilitate decisions taken by the SARB in relation to financial stability. The FSOC is the apex committee that supports the SARB when it performs its functions in relation to financial stability. This committee is, inter alia, tasked with facilitating cooperation and collaboration between, and coordination of action among, the financial sector regulators and the SARB in respect of matters relating to financial stability.[33] In terms of section 21 of the Act, the functions of the FSOC are to serve as a forum for representatives of the SARB and the financial sector regulators to be informed, and to exchange views about their respective activities regarding financial stability; to make recommendations to the governor on the designation of systemically important financial institutions; to advise the minister of finance and the SARB on steps to be taken to promote, protect or maintain, or to manage or prevent risks to financial stability, and on matters relating to crisis management and prevention; to make recommendations to other organs of state regarding steps that are appropriate for them to take to assist in promoting, protecting or maintaining, or managing or preventing risks to financial stability; and any other function conferred on it in terms of applicable legislation. The FSOC comprises the top officials of the SARB and the relevant financial sector regulators, namely the governor of the SARB (as chairperson), the deputy governor responsible for financial stability matters, the chief executive officer of the PA, the commissioner of the FSCA, the chief executive officer of the NCR, the director-general of the National Treasury, the director of the FIC and a maximum of three additional persons appointed by the governor.[34]

In order to ensure that the FSOC is apprised of all the critical information it requires to effectively and efficiently execute its mandate, the FSOC is supported by the Financial Sector Contingency Forum.[35] The FSCF is comprised of a deputy governor of the SARB as chairperson, representatives of the financial sector regulators and other organs of state, and any other relevant persons as determined by the chairperson.[36] Its primary objective is to assist the FSOC with the identification of potential risks of systemic events and coordination of appropriate plans, mechanisms and structures to mitigate those risks.[37]

Section 11 of the *Financial Sector Regulation Act* captures the essence of the SARB's expanded financial stability mandate by providing that the SARB is responsible for *protecting*

---

[33] Section 20 FSRA.
[34] Section 22 FSRA.
[35] Section 25(1) FSRA.
[36] Sections 25(3) and (4) FSRA.
[37] Section 25(2) FSRA.

and enhancing financial stability; and, if a 'systemic event' has occurred or is imminent, for *restoring or maintaining* financial stability. This entails that the SARB must monitor and keep under review the strengths and weaknesses of the financial system and *any* risks to financial stability.[38] The SARB is required to have regard to the nature and extent of such risks, including risks that systemic events will occur, as well as any other risks raised by the FSOC, or reported to the SARB by a financial sector regulator.[39] The SARB is further tasked with mitigating risks to financial stability. This includes advising the financial sector regulators and any other organ of state of the steps that should be taken to mitigate risks. The SARB must also regularly assess the observance in the Republic of principles developed by international standard-setting bodies, such as the Basel Committee and the Financial Stability Board, and must report its findings to the minister of finance and the financial regulators.[40] Consequently, the SARB will be in a position to detect, at an early stage, whether non-compliance with any international standards may put the financial system at risk.

Although the SARB has been issuing financial stability reviews for several years, pre-Twin Peaks, the *Financial Sector Regulation Act* now explicitly details the main components of this obligation. In terms of section 13, the SARB is required to issue a financial stability review at least every six months. The review must set out the SARB's assessment of financial stability in the period under review, and its identification and assessment of risks to financial stability in at least the next twelve months. It must further provide an overview of the steps taken by the SARB and the financial sector regulators to identify and manage risks, weaknesses and disruptions in the financial system during the period under review, and also of steps that are to be taken during at least the next twelve months. It should also include an overview of recommendations made by the SARB and the FSOC during the period under review, and set out the progress made in implementing those recommendations.[41] The Act thus makes it clear that the financial stability review is not only fixated on the current health of the financial system, but also takes a forward-looking risk-based approach. Spelling out the main features of this review and requiring the review to be tabled in Parliament also keeps the SARB accountable for properly executing this crucial part of its mandate.[42]

9.3.4 *The SARB's Power in Relation to Systemic Events*

It is trite that systemic events are the nemesis of financial stability. In order to give content to the concept, a 'systemic event' is broadly defined in section 1 of the Act as:

> an event or circumstance, including one that occurs or arises outside the Republic, that may reasonably be expected to have a substantial adverse effect on the financial system or on economic activity in the Republic, including an event or circumstance that leads to a loss of confidence that operators of, or participants in, payment systems, settlement systems or financial markets, or financial institutions, are able to continue to provide financial products or financial services.

---

[38] Authors' emphasis.
[39] Section 12(a)(i) and (ii) FSRA.
[40] Sections 12(b) and (c) FSRA.
[41] Sections 13(2)(a) to (d) FSRA. The ability of the review to trigger instability through publication of certain sensitive information is addressed by providing, in s 13(3), that '[I]nformation which, if published may materially increase the possibility of a systemic event, only needs to be published in a financial stability review after the risk of such event has subsided or has been addressed'.
[42] Sections 13(4)(a) to (c) FSRA.

Given the potential of a systemic event to cause wide-scale financial collapse, the *Financial Sector Regulation Act* aptly affords the SARB a legislative basis for exercising specific crisis management powers in relation to systemic events. These powers are triggered by the provision that the governor of the SARB may, after consultation with the minister of finance, determine that a specified event or circumstance, or a specified combination of events or circumstances, is a systemic event.[43]

The functions of the SARB in relation to systemic events are, in the first instance, preventative and require that the SARB must take all reasonable steps to prevent systemic events from occurring. If a systemic event nevertheless occurs or is imminent, the SARB must swiftly mitigate the adverse effects of such an event on financial stability, and must further manage the event and its effects. When dealing with a systemic event, the SARB has to act within particular legislative constraints: it is obliged to have regard to the need to minimise the adverse effects of the systemic event on financial stability and economic activity; to appropriately protect financial consumers; and to contain the cost to the Republic of the systemic event and the steps taken to mitigate or manage it. The SARB's power to determine that certain events qualify as systemic events which have either occurred, or are imminent, thus serves as the legislative basis for ex ante prevention, intervention and mitigation, and also ex post mitigation and management of the event and its effects.

Notably, South Africa has only recently begun its journey towards the adoption of an explicit deposit insurance framework – one that will operate in tandem with an internationally aligned resolution regime – currently also in the process of being fleshed out. At present the country still operates on the basis of a discretionary implicit deposit guarantee.[44] Certain amendments have, however, already been effected pre-Twin Peaks, via the 2015 *Banks Amendment Act*, which was adopted to facilitate the curatorship of African Bank in 2014. These innovative amendments demonstrate that the country is keenly aware of, and is aligned with, the post-Global Financial Crisis (GFC) shift from a culture of bail-outs to a system of bail-ins. This shift is also reinforced by the provisions of the draft legislation that seek to import the new resolution regime.[45] The *Financial Sector Regulation Act* consequently also constrains the SARB's power to engage in discretionary bail-outs of failing financial institutions, by providing that the SARB must contain the costs of systemic events as mentioned above; and also that the SARB may not, without the approval of the minister of finance, take a step in relation to a systemic event that will, or is likely to, bind the National Revenue Fund to any expenditure; have a material impact on the cost of

---

[43] Section 14 FSRA.

[44] National Treasury, 'Strengthening South Africa's Resolution Framework for Financial Institutions' (13 August 2015), http://pmg-assets.s3-website-eu-west-1.amazonaws.com/150813Resolution_Framework_Policy.pdf; SARB, 'Designing a Deposit Insurance Scheme for South Africa – A Discussion Paper' (May 2017), www.resbank.co.za/Lists/News%20and %20Publications/Attachments/7818/DIS%20paper.pdf; Financial Sector Laws Amendment Bill B-2018 clause 39.

[45] *Banks Amendment Act* 3 of 2015, s 2 which inter alia effected amendments to s 69 (curatorship) of the *Banks Act* 94 of 1990 to allow for disposal of assets and transfer of liabilities during curatorship, to override the requirement of equitable treatment of creditors in the interest of financial stability and to allow the curator to take certain decisions without the consent of the shareholders of the failing bank; for a discussion of these amendments see C. van Heerden, 'The Rescue of African Bank: A Step Forward in Banking Regulation in South Africa' (2017) 32(8) *Journal of International Banking Law and Regulation* 350–57. See the *Draft Financial Sector Laws Amendment Bill* B15 of 2020, clause 9 (repeal of ss 68, 69 and 69A of the *Banks Act* 94 of 1990 which deals with liquidation of banks, curatorship and the inquiry into the reasons for bank failure respectively), clause 35 (amendment of definitions in s 1 FSRA to introduce definitions relating to bank resolution and deposit insurance) and clause 51 (inserting Ch 12 A in the FSRA to introduce the envisaged bank resolution and deposit insurance regime).

borrowing for the National Revenue Fund; or create a future contingent liability for the National Revenue Fund.[46]

It is also trite that crisis times are not times for regulatory stand-offs and turf wars. Accordingly, the Act also imposes particular responsibilities on the financial sector regulators in the event that the SARB determines that a systemic event has occurred or is imminent. The regulators are obliged (apparently on their own initiative) to provide the SARB with any information in their possession which may be relevant for the management of the systemic event, or its effects. The regulators are further required to consult the SARB before exercising any of their powers in a way that may compromise steps taken or proposed in terms of the Act, to manage the systemic event or its effects.[47] The governor of the SARB is given the discretion to direct a financial sector regulator to provide the SARB with certain specified information that the bank or the governor needs for exercising their powers in respect of systemic events.[48] If it has been determined that a systemic event has occurred or is imminent, the governor may further specifically direct a financial sector regulator to assist the SARB in complying with its functions in relation to systemic events. This includes directing the regulator to support: the restructuring, resolution or winding up of any financial institution; the prevention or reduction of the spread of risk, weakness or disruption through the financial system; increase of the resilience of financial institutions to risk, weakness or disruption. The matters in respect of which directives relating to systemic events may be given by the SARB do not constitute a closed list. It is submitted that the SARB would, in principle, be able to direct a financial regulator to take any other step aimed at maintaining or restoring financial stability, for example suspension of the trading operations of a financial institution or banning the trade in certain high-risk financial products.[49]

The reach of the SARB's powers in relation to systemic events further extends to the activities of organs of state exercising powers in respect of a part of the financial system, given that they are responsible for the policy and legislation in accordance with which the regulators within their jurisdiction act. Consequently, in the event of a determination that a systemic event has occurred or is imminent, an organ of state may not without the approval of the minister of finance, acting in consultation with the Cabinet member responsible for that particular organ of state, exercise its powers in a way that is inconsistent with a decision or steps taken by the governor or the SARB to manage a systemic event or its effects. In order to avoid a stand-off between the SARB and the relevant organ of state and responsible Cabinet member, any unresolved issues in this regard must be referred to Cabinet.[50] So, for example, if a systemic event should relate to a build-up of risk in the credit market, the Department of Trade and Industry (DTI), being the organ of state responsible for the regulation of the credit market, will not be able to derail steps ordered by the SARB to mitigate credit risk, by giving instructions to the National Credit Regulator (which falls within the DTI's jurisdiction) that would be contrary to the steps indicated by the SARB.

---

[46] Sections 16(2)(a) to (c).

[47] Sections 17(a) and (b).

[48] Section 18(1). These directives must be in writing and relate to information in possession of the relevant regulator or obtainable by it.

[49] These matters would in principle be covered by the powers of the PA to issue directives as set out in s 143 FSRA. However, it is argued that in times where a systemic event has occurred or is imminent the SARB would be able to either directly or via the PA give directions of this nature to a financial institution.

[50] Sections 19(1) and (2) FSRA.

9.3.5 *SIFI Designation*

One of the main trends to emerge from the 2008 GFC was that systemically important financial institutions (SIFIs) that were labelled 'too big to fail' and the toxic cocktail of moral hazard and bail-outs they attracted had to end. In particular, the realisation emerged that SIFIs require more intensive and intrusive regulation and supervision in order, inter alia, to increase their loss absorbency and prevent their failure, and further that it was necessary to facilitate their orderly resolution in the event that they nevertheless failed.[51] This poignant lesson did not escape South Africa as a G20 member, and was reflected in the *Financial Sector Regulation Act* giving the SARB new and specific powers in relation to SIFIs. Accordingly, the SARB is now empowered to designate financial institutions as SIFIs and subject them to stringent prudential measures applied by the PA. Unlike the position in some other jurisdictions, SIFI designation in South Africa is not automatic, and the Act sets out a specific process to be followed.[52] In brief, it requires the governor of the SARB to give the FSOC notice of the intended designation in order to obtain its advice, and after considering such advice the governor then notifies the financial institution concerned of the proposed designation, inviting it to make submissions on the matter.[53] The Act follows an indicator-based approach (considering factors such as size, complexity, interconnectedness and substitutability) combined with a home jurisdiction discretion resembling the Basel D-SIB indicators.[54]

The Act further provides for emergency SIFI designation where a systemic event has occurred or is imminent and also allows the financial institution concerned to make ex post submissions in such instances.[55] In line with the regulatory sentiment set against 'too big to fail' and discretionary bail-outs, it is pertinently stipulated that the designation of a financial institution as a SIFI does not imply, or entitle, a SIFI to a 'guarantee or any form of credit or other support from an organ of state'.[56] The stringent prudential measures that SIFI designation attracts entail solvency matters and capital requirements, which may include requirements in relation to countercyclical capital buffers; leverage ratios; liquidity; organisational structures; risk management arrangements; sectoral and geographical exposures; required statistical returns; recovery and resolution planning; and any other matter in respect of which a prudential standard may be

---

[51] J. R. Barth, 'Too Big to Fail and Too Big to Save: Dilemmas for Banking Reform' (2016) 235 *National Institute Economic Review*; I. Moosa, 'The Myth of Too Big to Fail' (2010) 11 *Journal of Banking Regulation* 319–33. See further, Basel Committee on Banking Supervision G-SIB Framework entitled 'Globally Systemically Important Banks: Assessment Methodology and the Additional Loss Absorbency Requirement', www.bis.org/publ/bcbs201.pdf; and Basel Committee on Banking Supervision D-SIB Framework entitled 'A Framework for Dealing with Domestic Systemically Important Banks', www.bis.org/publ/bcbs233.pdf.

[52] See also SARB FSD, 'A Methodology to Determine Which Banks Are Systemically Important within the South African Context', www.resbank.co.za/en/home/publications/publication-detail-pages/media-releases/2019/9303. On 20 August 2019 the governor of the SARB designated the following banks as SIFIs: Absa Bank Ltd; The Standard Bank of South Africa Ltd; FirstRand Bank Ltd; Nedbank Ltd; Investec Bank Ltd and Capitec Bank Ltd – see the SARB Financial Stability Review 2019 (2nd ed), www.resbank.co.za/en/home/publications/publication-detail-pages/reviews/finstab-review/2019/9606.

[53] Sections 29(1) and (2) FSRA. SIFI designation is not necessarily permanent and can be revoked – see s 29(6).

[54] See ss 29(1) to (3) FSRA.

[55] In terms of s 29(4)(b), the financial institution must make a submission on its emergency designation as a SIFI to the governor within thirty days of such emergency designation. The governor is obliged to consider these submissions and must, by notice to the institution, either confirm or revoke the designation.

[56] Section 29(5) FSRA.

made (catch-all).[57] The Act also lists various steps relating to the licence cancellation or rescue or resolution of a SIFI that will be void if taken without the concurrence of the SARB.[58]

9.3.6 *Cooperation and Collaboration*

Effective and efficient cooperation and collaboration between the various role-players in the financial system is the bedrock of an effective and efficient Twin Peaks model, which in turn serves as an enabling regulatory environment for the promotion and maintenance of financial stability.[59] Without a proper network for cooperation and collaboration to support the exercise of the SARB's financial stability mandate, chances are slim that financial stability in South Africa will be promoted and maintained. Accordingly, unlike the limited approach taken to legislative entrenchment of measures for cooperation and collaboration pre-Twin Peaks, the *Financial Sector Regulation Act* contains extensive provisions aimed at achieving such cooperation and collaboration: first, specifically for the purposes of promoting and maintaining financial stability as a core pursuit and, secondly, more generally for the purposes of the broader effective and efficient operation of the South African Twin Peaks model.

The Act encourages a proactive approach to cooperation and collaboration, requiring financial sector regulators to take the initiative in various respects. All the financial sector regulators are required to provide such assistance and information to the SARB and the FSOC to maintain or restore financial stability as may reasonably be requested. They must also promptly report to the SARB any matter of which they become aware that poses or may pose a risk to financial stability.[60] They have to gather information from, or about, financial institutions that relate to financial stability, regarding aspects such as failure to comply with prudential requirements; protracted illiquidity; and toxic market conduct that may put the financial system at risk. As indicated above, each financial regulator must also provide the SARB with information for the purposes of crisis management when a systemic event has occurred or is imminent.[61] The SARB cannot, however, execute its financial stability mandate in a dictatorial fashion, as the Act obliges the SARB to take into account any views expressed, and any information reported by, the financial sector regulators, as well as any recommendations of the FSOC.[62]

In addition to cooperation and collaboration in support of the SARB's financial stability mandate, the Act further mandates general cooperation between the SARB and the financial sector regulators and between the regulators themselves. This includes supporting each other in the pursuit of their objectives; information-sharing; the adoption of consistent regulatory strategies; the coordination of actions; and the development of consistent policy positions.[63] In order to give practical effect to the requirement for cooperation and collaboration, the *Financial Sector Regulation Act* provides for the SARB and the regulators, as well as the regulators amongst

---

[57] Section 30(1) FSRA.
[58] Section 31 FSRA.
[59] M. W. Taylor, 'Twin Peaks: A Regulatory Structure for the 21st Century' (1996) 3 *The Futures & Derivatives Law Review* 7; M. W. Taylor, 'The Road from "Twin Peaks" – and the Way Back' (2009–10) 16 *Connecticut Insurance Law Journal* 64; Godwin and Schmulow (n 24) 758.
[60] Sections 26(1)(a)–(d) FSRA.
[61] Sections 17(a) and (b) FSRA.
[62] Section 26(2) FSRA.
[63] Section 76(1) FSRA. In accordance with s 76(2) the SARB and the financial sector regulators must, as part of their annual reports, or on request, report to the minister of finance, the Cabinet member responsible for administering the *National Credit Act* and the National Assembly on measures taken to cooperate and collaborate with each other.

themselves, to enter into memoranda of understanding.[64] The structure for collaboration and cooperation within the South African Twin Peaks model thus comprises several legislatively entrenched obligations, implemented practically by means of MoUs, as flexible soft law measures. MoUs were accordingly entered into towards the end of 2018 between the SARB and the PA; the SARB and the FSCA; the PA and the FSCA; the FSCA and the NCR; and the FSCA and the FIC.[65] Notably, the MoU between the SARB and the PA does not, however, address the handling of potential conflicts between financial stability and prudential objectives in any detail.[66]

9.4 CONCLUSION

The role of the SARB and its objectives, functions and powers have significantly changed in the Twin Peaks landscape: its mandate for financial stability is now captured in legislation in explicit terms, and put on a par with its price stability mandate. This mandate is made clearer by setting out the SARB's main functions in relation to financial stability, and by legislatively entrenching the broad powers necessary to achieve this expanded mandate. All these measures make the SARB more accountable for the proper execution of its mandate than was the case in the pre-Twin Peaks era, where its financial stability mandate was as fuzzy as the concept of financial stability itself. Importantly, the institutional context and regulatory milieu within which this mandate is to be exercised has been radically changed since Twin Peaks. South Africa has moved from a narrow-minded silo-regulation model to a macro-minded objectives-driven model – one that clearly sets out the objectives of regulation and the functions that have to be fulfilled to achieve those objectives, while operating within a multifaceted coordination structure.

The Twin Peaks model has further explicitly assigned responsibility for assistance with maintaining financial stability to the newly established PA and FSCA, which will provide such assistance through sound prudential regulation and supervision, and sound market conduct regulation and supervision, on a system-wide scale. The solid and extensive network for cooperation and collaboration created by the Act, and the accountability measures contingent upon the regulators for compliance with their obligations also strengthen the SARB's ability to execute its mandate: it makes it clear that cooperation and collaboration is a legislative imperative. Accordingly, the SARB is given various powers to ensure that it is kept abreast of any matters that may impact on and/or compromise financial stability, and that it has the mandated buy-in of not only the financial sector regulators, but also the organs of state that dictate their regulatory agendas.

In principle, the decision to remove bank supervision from the SARB's remit and entrust it to the PA appears to be strategically sound. Prudential regulation has over the years become more complex and burdensome and has, especially since the GFC, developed into a more exact science, with macro-dimensions. The establishment of a 'separate' prudential regulator ensures

---

[64] Section 77 FSRA. The obligation to enter into memoranda of understanding is stipulated in s 77 but the content of these memoranda is not dealt with or prescribed. Provision is also made in s 86 FSRA for independent evaluation of the effectiveness of the mechanisms employed for purposes of cooperation and collaboration.

[65] See further C. van Heerden and M. G. van Niekerk, 'The Importance of a Legislative Framework for Cooperation and Collaboration in the Twin Peaks Model of Financial Regulation' (2020) 1 *South African Law Journal* 110.

[66] SARB/PA MoU, 'Memorandum of Understanding between the South African Reserve Bank and the Prudential Authority' (26 September 2018), paras 2.1–2.4, www.resbank.co.za/Lists/News%20and%20Publications/Attachments/8792/PA-SARB%20Memorandum%20of%20Understanding.pdf.

that the SARB can focus more deeply on its expanded financial stability mandate, without being overburdened by the exigencies of prudential regulation that may in turn dilute its regulatory focus. It also ensures that the SARB is able, on the face of it, to avoid the conflicts between financial stability and prudential regulation that could inevitably arise if it had to execute both these functions. Notably, South Africa has heeded the caution to keep the prudential regulator close to the central bank – in fact, so close that for the person on the street there will probably be no perceived difference between the PA and the SARB. At first glance the many economies of scale and scope, and ease of information dissemination and collaboration, that this synergistic arrangement will yield makes this an optimal arrangement for a resource-constrained emerging market such as South Africa. However, although the PA is a separate juristic entity, and its composition and mandate differ distinctly from that of the former BSD of the SARB in the pre-Twin Peaks dispensation, its de facto independence is questionable. Given that the PA is housed under the same roof as the SARB, its steering committee comprises entirely top SARB officials, its CEO is a SARB deputy governor and a significant number of its staff will be persons previously employed by the SARB, it is difficult to conceive how any conflicts between financial stability and prudential regulation will be dealt with. This arrangement, although seemingly innocuous, should be reconsidered to avoid it becoming the Trojan horse that compromises the ability of the Twin Peaks model to deliver on its intended outcomes in relation to financial stability.

PART III

Different Topographies

10

Can the Twin Peaks Model of Financial Regulation Serve as a Model for Israel?

Ruth Plato-Shinar

10.1 INTRODUCTION

Financial supervision in Israel is predominantly sectoral, each financial sector having its own regulator. In addition, there are, in Israel, certain features of functional supervision where certain products or services are subject to a specific regulator, no matter which financial institution provides them.

In recent years, a number of proposals were put forward to change the financial regulatory model in Israel. One proposal called for the adoption of the single regulatory model, and for the establishment of one financial regulatory agency.[1] In contrast, in 2015, the Israel Securities Authority called for the adoption of the Twin Peaks model, under which the Securities Authority would serve as the conduct-of-business regulator and would oversee consumer protection issues for the entire financial system.[2] To date, these proposals have not materialised into practical initiatives.

This chapter will examine whether, and to what extent, the Twin Peaks model of financial regulation can serve as a model for Israel.

The chapter's structure is as follows. The next section (10.2) describes the financial sector in Israel, emphasising the clear borders that exist between the banking system and institutional investors. Section 10.3 describes the current structure of financial regulation in Israel. Section 10.4 examines the outstanding features of Twin Peaks against the backdrop of Israel's financial system and the

---

[1] Sharon Blei, Asher Balas and Avi Ben-Bassat, 'Summary and Recommendations for the Structure of Regulation of the Capital Market' in Avi Ben-Bassat (ed) *Regulation of the Capital Market*, Ch 5 (Israel Democracy Institute, 2007, in Hebrew).

[2] Israel Securities Authority: The Optimal Regulatory Structure of the Capital Market (January 2015), www.isa.gov.il/% D7%94%D7%95%D7%93%D7%A2%D7%95%D7%AA%20%D7%95%D7%A4%D7%A8%D7%A1%D7%95%D7%9E %D7%99%D7%9D/178/Documents/16022015_0.pdf. The Twin Peaks model is applied in several countries, such as Australia, The Netherlands, United Kingdom, Belgium, South Africa and New Zealand. See Andrew Godwin, Timothy Howse and Ian Ramsay, 'A Jurisdictional Comparison of the Twin Peaks Model of Financial Regulation' (2017) 18 *Journal of Banking Regulation* 103, 109–12; Dirk Schoenmaker, 'Financial Supervision in the EU' in G. Caprio (ed) *Safeguarding Global Financial Stability: Political, Social, Cultural, and Economic Theories and Models* (Elsevier, 2013), 355. For a proposal to apply the Twin Peaks model in Hong Kong, see Bryane Michael, Say Hak Goo and Dariusz Wojcik, 'Does Objectives-Based Financial Regulation Imply a Rethink of Legislatively Mandated Economic Regulation? The Case of Hong-Kong and Twin Peaks Financial Regulation' (2014), http://papers.ssrn .com/sol3/papers.cfm?abstract_id=2523346. For a proposal to apply the full Twin Peaks model in Canada, see Eric J. Pan, 'Structural Reform of Financial Regulation' (2011) 19 *Transnational Law & Contemporary Problems* 796. For the applicability of the Twin Peaks model to China, see Andrew Godwin, Guo Li and Ian Ramsay, 'Is Australia's "Twin Peaks" System of Financial Regulation a Model for China?' (CIFR Working Paper No 102/2016/ Project E018, April 2016), at 29.

possible repercussions from changing the current architecture of financial regulation. Section 10.5 deals with cooperation between the financial regulators. Regulatory models that are characterised by fragmented agencies, such as both Twin Peaks and the sectoral model, create a vital need for an effective mechanism of inter-agency cooperation. Section 10.5 examines the cooperation mechanisms that exist in various Twin Peaks jurisdictions, and their suitability for Israel. Section 10.6 concludes this chapter and recommends maintaining, for the present, the regulatory status quo. However, the chapter also suggests learning from the experiences of Twin Peaks countries, in particular in respect of inter-agency cooperation.

10.2 ISRAEL'S FINANCIAL SECTOR

The State of Israel has a liberal economy. It is included among the developed countries of the world and has been a member of the Organisation for Economic Co-operation and Development (OECD) since 2010. Israel successfully navigated the 2007–09 Global Financial Crisis without significant damage to its economy or financial system. Financial institutions – including banks – displayed resilience and maintained stability, while no institution collapsed.[3]

The financial system in Israel includes financial intermediaries, which satisfy various market needs, similar to financial systems in other developed countries. Among financial intermediaries, the dominant system is the commercial banking system, which is a key player in the financial sector and acts as one of the primary drivers of development in the Israeli economy.[4] Another dominant force is that of institutional investors: pension and provident fund managers, insurance companies and collective investment scheme managers.

10.2.1 *The Banking System*

The banking system in Israel consists of five large banking groups which control about 95 per cent of the market.[5] The rest of the system is occupied by three small independent banks and four international banks, whose activity in Israel is minimal.[6]

Banking corporations provide a wide range of financial services, including corporate, commercial and retail banking, as well as housing loans. In addition, they provide investment and pension counselling and brokerage services.[7] Other activities (which due to statutory restrictions are performed by subsidiaries) include underwriting and portfolio management.[8] Trust services are also provided by subsidiaries.

The banks are prohibited from engaging in insurance. The law not only forbids banks from engaging in insurance activities, but also prohibits control of insurance companies and insurance agencies[9] and limits holdings in an insurance company deemed 'a significant financial

---

[3] Bank of Israel: Israel and the Global Crisis 2007–09 (September 2011), www.boi.org.il/deptdata/mehkar/crisis/crisis_2007_2009_eng.pdf.

[4] For more on the Israeli banking system, its history and its main idiosyncrasies, see Ruth Plato-Shinar, *Banking Regulation in Israel: Prudential Regulation versus Consumer Protection* (Wolters Kluwer, 2016), 31–66.

[5] One of the characteristics of the Israeli banking system is its high level of concentration, and the existence of a duopoly. See Ruth Plato-Shinar, 'The Bank Fees Regime in Israel – A Political Economy Perspective' in E. Avgouleas and D. C. Donald (eds) *The Political Economy of Financial Regulation* (Cambridge University Press, 2019) 189.

[6] Supervisor of Banks: Israel Banking System – Annual Survey 2018 (September 2019), at 79, www.boi.org.il/en/NewsAndPublications/RegularPublications/Pages/Skira18.aspx.

[7] Activities permissible for banks are determined by the Banking (Licensing) Law 5741-1981, s 10.

[8] Banking (Licensing) Law 5741-1981, ss 10(7), 11(a)(3a) and 11(a)(3b); Securities (Underwriting) Regulations 5767-2007, s 2(b).

[9] Banking (Licensing) Law, s 11.

institution'.[10] There is only one limited exception to this prohibition: banks are permitted to provide, through special subsidiaries, property insurance and life insurance, as incidental services, for the provision of housing loans.[11]

As a result of the 2005 regulatory reforms to the capital market, banks are prohibited from managing provident and pension funds and from holding companies that manage such funds.[12] The same also applies to managing collective investment schemes.[13]

Three credit card companies operate in Israel. The credit card companies originally focused on issuing credit cards to customers, and on clearing and settling charges arising from credit card payments. However, in recent years they have expanded their activities and now also provide loans to households, a business that is expanding at an ever-growing rate.[14] Until 2019, the three credit card companies were owned by the major banks. However, legislation aimed at increasing competition in the credit market compelled the two major banks to sell their credit card companies, thereby leaving only one company which is still owned by banks.[15]

In summary, a clear demarcation exists between banking activities and the activities of other financial intermediaries, such as insurance companies, pension and provident fund managers and collective investment scheme managers. In addition, the legislation strictly limits the holding, directly or indirectly, of banks by other financial intermediaries, and vice versa, in order to achieve a clear separation between these entities.

10.2.2 *Institutional Investors*

In addition to the banking sector, institutional investors are a dominant force: pension and provident fund managers, insurance companies and managers of collective investment schemes, such as trust funds or exchange-traded funds (ETFs). Some of these institutions have grown rapidly in the Israeli capital market during the last decade. In particular, there has been a significant increase in the volume of assets managed by pension funds. One reason for this is the mandatory Pension Order introduced in 2008, requiring every employer to contribute to pensions for their employees.[16] The introduction of mandatory pensions for the self-employed, starting in 2017,[17] has further increased accumulated pensions savings.

---

[10] Banking (Licensing) Law, s 24A.

[11] Banking (Licensing) Law, s 11(b)(2).

[12] Banking (Licensing) Law, ss 10(7) and 11; and Ch C2.

[13] Ibid.

[14] Plato-Shinar (n 4) at 34–6; Knesset Research and Information Center: 'Description of the Credit Card Market and Analysis of the Interfaces between Credit Card Companies and Banks' (February 2014), 7, www.knesset.gov.il/MMM/ data/pdf/mo3356.pdf; Report of the Committee to Examine Reducing the Use of Cash in Israel's Economy, 45 (July 2014), www.boi.org.il/he/PaymentSystem/Documents/2017.7.14%-יפ-%20סוספ%20ן מזומ%20תדעו%20דוד.pdf. A translation of the report's main sections is available at www.boi.org.il/en/PaymentSystem/Documents/The%20Committee%20to% 20Examine%20Reducing%20the%20Use%20of%20Cash%20in%20Israel%E2%80%99s%20Economy.pdf; Israel Banking System (n 6) at 29–37.

[15] Law to Enhance Competition and Reduce Concentration in the Israeli Banking Market (Legislative Amendments) 5777-2017, s 1.

[16] Extension Order (Consolidated Version) for Comprehensive Pension Insurance in the Economy pursuant to the Collective Agreements Act, 5717-1957 (1 January 2008). This order was replaced by the Extension Order (Consolidated Version) for Mandatory Pension pursuant to the Collective Agreement Act, 5717-1957 (27 September 2011). The total amount of these deposits rose gradually each year, from 2.5 per cent in 2008 to 18.5 per cent in January 2017 – the completion of the implementation process. See Bank of Israel: Annual Report 2016 (March 2017), at 121, www.boi.org .il/en/NewsAndPublications/RegularPublications/Pages/DochBankIsrael2016.aspx.

[17] Economic Efficiency (Legislative Amendments to Implement the Economic Plan for the Fiscal Years 2017–2018) Law 5777-2016, s 16.

Against this backdrop of rapid and consistent growth in the volume of assets managed by institutions, institutional investors have expanded their activities into commercial lending in recent years, principally by granting loans to large commercial firms.[18] In recent years, total debt owed by these commercial firms to banks accounted for less than half of the business sector's total debt, compared with 55 per cent in 2008 and 74 per cent in 2002.[19] As a consequence, the traditional hegemony of banks is under threat in this market.

In addition, institutional investors have, lately, shown an interest in retail lending as well.[20] While their share of non-housing retail credit is still low,[21] housing credit has grown recently at a particularly high rate as a result of the purchase of mortgage portfolios from banks. Whereas in 2015 these mortgage portfolios amounted to NIS0.6 billion, in 2016 and the first months of 2017 their amount increased to NIS8 billion.[22]

Institutional investors are not permitted to engage in businesses which are considered core banking activities. The law provides banks with exclusivity in respect of two main activities: accepting deposits and simultaneously providing credit,[23] and managing current accounts.[24] In addition, institutional investors are not permitted to control banks or bank-related companies.[25] However, the legislation does not prohibit the creation of financial groups that include various financial firms other than banks. These groups may provide a variety of services in the fields of insurance and pensions, investments and finance. Accordingly, a few insurance companies and investment firms have developed into such groups.[26]

10.3 ISRAEL'S FINANCIAL REGULATORS

As mentioned previously, financial supervision in Israel is mainly sectoral, where each financial sector has its own regulator. The three financial regulators are: the Banking Supervision Department; the Capital Markets, Insurance and Savings Authority; and the Securities Authority.

10.3.1 *The Banking Supervision Department*

The Banking Supervision Department is responsible for the banking system: banks,[27] credit card companies[28] and credit card clearing companies.[29]

---

[18] Plato-Shinar (n 4) 27–9.
[19] Bank of Israel (n 16) 138–9. Bank of Israel: Annual Report 2018 (March 2019), at 112, www.boi.org.il/en/NewsAndPublications/RegularPublications/Pages/DochBankIsrael2018.aspx.
[20] Plato-Shinar (n 4) 29–30.
[21] Bank of Israel (n 19) at 123.
[22] Bank of Israel (n 16) at 133. For elaboration see Ruth Plato-Shinar, 'Sale of Bank Loan Portfolios to Non-bank Entities: The Implications of the Bank's Fiduciary Duty' (2019) 13 Mishpatim Online – *Hebrew University Law Review* 128 (in Hebrew).
[23] Banking (Licensing) Law, s 21(a)(1).
[24] Ibid, s 13.
[25] Ibid, Ch C1.
[26] Examples include Harel Insurance and Finance, the Phoenix Group, Meitav-Dash Investment House, Psagot Investment House.
[27] Banking (Licensing) Law, Ch B.
[28] Credit Card companies are defined as 'Auxiliary Corporations', as per s 1 of the Banking (Licensing) Law; and as 'Banking Corporations', as per s 1 of the Banking (Service to Customer) Law 5741-1981.
[29] Banking (Licensing) Law, Ch D2; Banking Ordinance, s 15C(b); Banking (Service to Customer) Law, as per the definition of 'Banking Corporation' in s 1.

The Banking Supervision Department is part of the Bank of Israel, which is Israel's central bank.[30] The department is headed by the supervisor of banks, who is appointed by the governor of the Bank of Israel.[31] Certain powers in respect of the banking system are conferred upon the governor, such as supervision of bank fees.[32]

The regulatory goals of the Banking Supervision Department are not determined by law. The *Bank of Israel Law* states that one of the bank's objectives is to maintain stability and normal economic functioning (prudential regulation), but this is stated in respect of the entire financial system.[33]

The objectives of the Banking Supervision Department are defined by the department itself, according to its own definitions of its role, as is reflected in its annual reports. In 2019, the objectives were maintaining the stability of banks; maintaining fairness in relations between banks and their customers; promoting competition; and ensuring that the banking system supports the activities of companies and individuals in the economy. To achieve these objectives, the Banking Supervision Department defined two supporting objectives: promoting innovation in the banking system and improving its efficiency.[34] In addition, several statutes impose a duty on the supervisor to promote consumer protection, or at least to take into account considerations for the welfare of consumers.[35]

Supervision over payments and clearing systems is conferred upon the Bank of Israel and is executed through a separate department – the Payment Systems Supervision Department.[36]

10.3.2 *The Capital Markets, Insurance and Savings Authority*

The Capital Markets, Insurance and Savings Authority is an independent statutory authority, which is in charge of insurance, non-bank long-term savings, such as pensions, and non-bank financial services. It supervises insurance companies,[37] insurance agents,[38] provident and pension fund managers,[39] pension advisors, pension marketing agents and operators of pensions clearing systems.[40] The authority is headed by the commissioner of capital markets, insurance and savings.[41]

Legislation introduced in 2016 (and expanded in 2017) imposed for the first time supervision over additional financial firms: non-bank lenders; peer-to-peer (P2P) platform operators; providers of services in respect of financial assets; credit and deposit unions; non-bank credit card issuers; and providers of cost-comparison services.[42] All these financial firms are subject to the

---

[30] For more on the Bank of Israel see Daniel Maman and Zeev Rosenhek, *The Israel Central Bank: Political Economy, Global Logics and Local Actors* (Routledge, 2011).

[31] The Banking Ordinance 1941, s 5.

[32] Banking (Service to Customer) Law, Ch B2.

[33] Bank of Israel Law 5770-2010, s 3.

[34] Bank of Israel, The Banking System in Israel – Annual Survey 2019, at 133 (13 May 2020), www.boi.org.il/en/ NewsAndPublications/RegularPublications/Banking%20Supervision/BankingSystemAnnualReport/Skira2019/FULL %20REPORT%20COMBINED%202019.pdf. See also Plato-Shinar (n 4) at 138–9.

[35] For example: Banking Ordinance, s 5(C1); Banking (Licensing) Law, ss 6(3) and 6(5).

[36] Bank of Israel Law, s 4(5); Payment Systems Law 5768-2008, Ch B.

[37] Control of Financial Services (Insurance) Law 5741-1981, s 15.

[38] Ibid, s 25.

[39] Control of Financial Services (Provident Funds) Law 5765-2005, s 4.

[40] Control of Financial Services (Pension Advice, Marketing and Clearing System) Law 5765-2005.

[41] Control of Financial Services (Insurance) Law, s 2.

[42] Control of Financial Services (Regulated Financial Services) Law 5766-2016.

supervision of the supervisor of financial services providers, a function fulfilled by the commissioner of capital markets, insurance and savings.[43]

The objectives of the Capital Markets, Insurance and Savings Authority are determined statutorily, and include the following: protecting and maintaining the interests of the insured, savers and customers of supervised entities; ensuring the stability and proper management of supervised entities; the promotion of competition in the financial system, especially in the capital market, insurance industry and savings industry; and encouraging technological and business innovation by supervised bodies.[44]

Despite being an autonomous authority, certain powers within its ambit are conferred upon the minister of finance,[45] including the power to promulgate subordinate legislation (regulations). In addition, the authority is obliged to take into account the fiscal policy of the government.[46] In respect of pensions, health insurance and nursing insurance it has to act according to the government's policies and decisions.[47]

10.3.3 *Israel Securities Authority*

The Securities Authority is an independent statutory authority whose goal is to protect the interests of the public when investing in securities.[48] The authority is in charge of securities issued by public corporations registered for trading on a stock exchange or which were offered to the public and held by the public. In addition, the Securities Authority supervises a long list of securities market entities, such as underwriters; trading platform managers; the Tel-Aviv Stock Exchange, securities clearing houses;[49] managers and trustees of mutual funds and ETFs (exchange-traded funds);[50] investment advisors; investment marketing agents and portfolio managers;[51] and credit rating agencies.[52]

The main focus of the Securities Authority is market conduct and investor protection. However, as regards several financial entities (managers of mutual funds and ETFs,[53] the Tel Aviv Stock Exchange,[54] trading platform managers[55] and securities clearing houses[56]) it has certain powers in respect of prudential regulation.

The authority is headed by the chairman of the Securities Authority, who is appointed by the minister of finance.[57] Although the Securities Authority is an autonomous authority, certain powers within its scope are conferred upon the minister of finance,[58] including the power to promulgate subordinate legislation (regulations) within its jurisdiction.

---

43 Ibid, s 2.
44 Control of Financial Services (Insurance) Law, s 1C.
45 Such as determining the minimum equity required in order to receive an insurance licence: Control of Financial Services (Insurance) Law, s 35.
46 Ibid, s 1C(b).
47 Ibid, s 1C(c).
48 Securities Law 5728-1968, s 2.
49 Securities Law, s 1, definition of 'supervised party'.
50 Joint Investments in Trust Law 5754-1994.
51 Regulation of Investment Advice, Investment Marketing and Portfolio Management Law 5755-1995.
52 Regulation of Credit Rating Companies Law 5774-2014.
53 Joint Investments in Trust Law, s 13(a)(2).
54 Securities Law, s 45A(a)(6).
55 Ibid, s 44M(b)(5).
56 Ibid, s 50C.
57 Ibid, s 3(b).
58 See, for example, Joint Investments in Trust Law, ss 9 and 13.

This survey is intended to demonstrate that Israel's financial regulation is primarily sectoral. However, it also includes certain aspects of the functional model, where regulatory oversight is divided according to the type of product or service offered. For example, investment services are subject to the Securities Authority, regardless of institution. Another example is that of pensions, which are subject to the Capital Markets, Insurance and Savings Authority, regardless of institution. Moreover, currently there is no separation between prudential regulation and consumer protection.

10.4 PRUDENTIAL REGULATION AND CONDUCT OF BUSINESS REGULATION

10.4.1 *Separation or Consolidation*

As mentioned in Section 10.3, financial regulatory supervision in Israel is primarily sectoral, with each of the three financial regulators responsible for both prudential regulation and conduct of business regulation. Therefore, in considering whether the Twin Peaks model could serve as a model for Israel, we must examine the salient features of the Twin Peaks model against the backdrop of the Israeli system and the possible repercussions of changing the current financial regulatory architecture.

The principal argument in support of Twin Peaks is the ability of each regulator to focus on a single objective. In this way, each regulator can develop expertise in one specific field and devote all of its resources to one single objective, and promote that effectively.[59] By contrast, when one regulator is concurrently responsible for several objectives, there is concern that it may be unable to devote the necessary attention to each one and to promote both of them simultaneously in an appropriate manner.

The rationale is strengthened due to the fact that prudential regulation and conduct of business regulation may contradict one another.[60] A regulator with consolidated powers may find it difficult to promote these contradictory objectives, and the outcome could be a sacrifice of one objective at the expense of the other.[61]

Conversely, there are strong considerations in favour of consolidating prudential regulation and conduct of business regulation in the hands of the same regulator. An argument in support of this approach is that the two fields are intertwined. There are many examples of failures in respect of conduct of business regulation, some of which ultimately led to financial crises. The most significant of these was the American subprime disaster, in which US mortgage providers

---

[59] Michael Taylor, '"Twin Peaks": A Regulatory Structure for the New Century' (1995) *Center for the Study of Financial Innovation* 1; Michael W. Taylor, 'Regulatory Reform after the Financial Crisis, Twin Peaks Revisited' in R. Hui Hang and D. Schoenmaker (eds) *Institutional Structure of Financial Regulation: Theories and International Experiences* (Routledge, 2015) 9.

[60] Taylor, 'Twin Peaks' (n 59), at 15 (noting that the two goals 'often conflict'); Richard K. Abrams and Michael W. Taylor, 'Issues in the Unification of Financial Sector Supervision' (IMF Working Paper 00/213, 2000), at 24 (noting that the skill-sets in each regulatory field are different); Joseph J. Norton, 'Global Financial Sector Reform: The Single Financial Regulator Model Based on the United Kingdom FSA Experience – A Critical Reevaluation' (2005) 39 *International Lawyer* 15, 42 (where he describes the 'inherent conflict' between the two objectives); E. J. Pan, 'Four Challenges to Financial Regulatory Reform' (2010) 55 *Villanova Law Review* 743, 759 (where he describes the 'fundamental differences' between the two regulatory objectives).

[61] Dirk Schoenmaker and Jeroen Kremers, 'Financial Stability and Proper Business Conduct: Can Supervisory Structure Help to Achieve These Objectives?' in R. Hui Hang and D. Schoenmaker (eds) *Institutional Structure of Financial Regulation: Theories and International Experiences* (Routledge, 2015), 29, 33. Political science scholars also support the separation of powers in such situations. See, for example, Eric Biber, 'Too Many Things to Do: How to Deal with the Dysfunctions of Multiple-Goal Agencies' (2009) 33 *Harvard Environmental Law Review* 1, 33–4, and the authorities included in fn 118.

engaged in predatory lending to unsophisticated borrowers and low-income families, many of whom lacked the ability to repay. This ultimately developed into the Global Financial Crisis, causing financial institutions to become insolvent worldwide.[62]

This connection between conduct of business and financial stability was also evident in the Israeli bank shares manipulation affair which erupted in 1983. It transpired that, for years, Israel's banks had provided biased investment advice to their customers and aggressively marketed their own shares. This scandal finally came to an end with the collapse of the four major banks, and their subsequent nationalisation by the state.[63] These, and other cases, demonstrate the difficulty in separating prudential regulation and consumer protection.

Unification of the two fields – prudential regulation and consumer protection – in the hands of the same regulator creates a number of important advantages:

- As a rule, an effective regulator cannot promote one specific interest without considering conflicting interests, or without seeing the broader picture. When a regulator is in charge of both fields it may be better equipped to perform its tasks thanks to a comprehensive view of the issues, and it may provide a more effective system of regulation.[64]
- A regulator in charge of several regulatory goals may be better equipped to resolve conflicts in regulatory objectives because of diminished frictions in deciding on resolutions and methods of implementation.[65]
- The integration of powers, including the use of an array of supervisory tools that accompany those powers, provides the regulator with effective mechanisms for resolving those conflicts between objectives and for achieving the best possible solution under the circumstances.[66] In addition, the fact that the regulator is able to resolve conflicts itself prevents interventions and rulings from the political echelon – a situation that could open the door to extraneous political considerations and pressures.
- The consolidated model increases the chances of regulatory coherence. The need to balance conflicting objectives and to adopt an intermediate solution naturally leads to a more moderate approach, easier to sustain over time. Needless to say, regulatory coherence is of the utmost importance for the financial system. Conversely, under Twin Peaks there are concerns regarding discrepancies and contradictions in the requirements laid down by the separate regulators.[67] With two strong, independent regulators, neither may agree to relinquish its position or stature. Thus, conflict between regulators may potentially exacerbate problems, spurred on by ego and power plays.
- The consolidated model reduces the chances for regulatory overlaps. Since many of the same supervisory issues would arise in both agencies and may require examination of very

---

[62] Pan (n 60) at 759–60; Andrew D. Schmulow, 'Twin Peaks: A Theoretical Analysis' (Center for International Finance and Regulation, Research Working Paper Series Project No E018, 2015), at 8.

[63] In the 1990s, Israel started a process of privatizing banks, a process that has not yet been completed. The state still holds 6 per cent of Bank Leumi. See Plato-Shinar (n 4) at 37–9.

[64] See, for example, in the field of retail lending: Onyeka K. Osuji, 'Responsible Lending: Consumer Protection and Prudential Regulation Perspectives' in K. Fairweather, P. O'Shea and R. Grantham (eds) *Credit, Consumer and the Law after the Global Storm* (Routledge, 2015), 62.

[65] Referring to a single regulator, compare James R. Barth, Daniel E. Nolle, Triphon Phumiwasana and Glenn Yago, 'A Cross-Country Analysis of the Bank Supervisory Framework and Bank Performance' (Office of the Comptroller of the Currency, US Department of the Treasury, Economic and Policy Analysis Working Paper 2002-2, 2002), at 7, www .occ.gov/publications-and-resources/publications/economics-working-papers/pub-econ-working-paper-2002-2.pdf.

[66] Compare Eilis Ferran, 'Examining the United Kingdom's Experience in Adopting the Single Financial Regulator Model' (2003) 28 *Brooklyn Journal of International Law* 257, 291 (referring to a single regulator).

[67] Pan (n 2) at 821.

similar issues, there seems little point in having two regulators making what are essentially duplicate decisions on broadly similar matters.[68]

Another possible argument for concentrating prudential regulation and conduct of business regulation in the hands of the same regulator is that of communication and cooperation at the operational level. Individual employees may find it easier to communicate and cooperate with one another on matters of common concern when they work for the same organisation as opposed to being scattered between different agencies. Moreover, they should all have a shared cultural approach to their tasks and operate consistently in accordance with the common policies set by management.[69]

By contrast, when it comes to a separation of powers between two different regulators a 'short circuit' may be caused by different cultures, institutional ethos and patterns of dialogue in each agency.[70] Thus, the interaction between a regulator that relies on a methodology of stability and financial parameters and bases its decisions on economic indicators on the one hand, and a regulator whose decisions are based upon conflicting objectives, such as consumer protection and social perceptions, on the other, may create a short-circuit in communication between the two.[71]

Finally, there is the issue of regulatory flexibility: a regulator in charge of both prudential and consumer protection issues may have more flexibility to respond to changes in the financial landscape. Flexibility would also enable the regulator to critically analyse existing rules and change them if need be. The result would be an ability to develop regulatory policies in light of changing conditions.

10.4.2 *Israel: Effective Regulation*

Israel's financial system survived the Global Financial Crisis of 2007–09 in a satisfactory manner, without any institutions suffering significant damage. One of the reasons for this was effective supervision, especially by the supervisor of banks, which compelled banks to adapt themselves to stringent requirements, designed to strengthen their stability.[72] This approach led to an improvement in the resilience and performance of the financial system, high profitability, high levels of capital adequacy and a reduction in credit risks.[73] The fact that the Israeli financial system survived the global crisis almost unscathed speaks for itself and indicates effective prudential regulation. Similarly, recent assessments by the International Monetary Fund (IMF) in the years after the crisis found that the Israeli financial system continued to be resilient and sound – a condition facilitated by strict and intrusive supervision.[74]

---

[68] Clive Briault, 'The Rationale for a Single National Financial Services Regulator' (Financial Services Authority, Occasional Paper No 2, May 1999), at 24, www.fsa.gov.uk/pubs/occpapers/OP02.Pdf.

[69] Compare Ferran (n 66) at 291; Briault (n 68) at 19 (where the author refers to a single regulator).

[70] Adi Ayal, Tzipi Iser-Itzik and Oren Perez, 'Regulation under Conditions of Decentralization: Collision or Synergy and a View to the Regulatory Reality in Israel' in Y. Blank, Roy Kreitner and D. Levi-Faur (eds) *The Governance of Regulation: Law and Policy* (Tel Aviv University, 2016), 213, 220–21 (in Hebrew).

[71] Compare Taylor, 'Twin Peaks' (n 59) at 12; Schmulow (n 62) at 28; Schoenmaker and Kremers (n 61) at 33 (noting that the prudential authority is dominated by the culture of economics, while the conduct of business authority is dominated by the culture of law).

[72] Bank of Israel (n 3) at 13, 15.

[73] Ibid.

[74] IMF Country Report No 12/69: Israel – Financial System Stability Assessment (April 2012), www.imf.org/external/pubs/ft/scr/2012/cr1269.pdf; IMF Country Report No 14/47: Israel 013 Article IV Consultation, 12–13 (February 2014), www.imf.org/external/pubs/ft/scr/2014/cr1447.pdf.

Although the IMF in 2006 praised the supervisor of banks' oversight of consumer protection,[75] the focus on prudential regulation at the expense of consumer protection provoked severe public criticism. The supervisor had been accused of prioritising the stability and profitability of banks over consumer protection.

However, careful examination of the supervisor's activities in the recent past, and especially since the social protests that erupted in the summer of 2011, reveal a greater level of attention given to consumer protection, and that the supervisor's focus on this area has been growing steadily. This new approach is reflected in, inter alia, the recent annual reports of the Banking Supervision Department. These reports expressly mention the objectives of consumer protection and the promotion of competition among the supervisor's regulatory goals, in the same breath as prudential regulation.[76]

In addition to such declaratory statements, the supervisor of banks instituted a variety of measures in order to implement these policies and to ensure a level of fairness in the relationships between banks and their customers. These include:

- issuing Proper Conduct of Banking Business directives, circulars and binding letters. This is in addition to preparing rules and orders to be promulgated by the governor of the Bank of Israel;
- handling thousands of customer complaints every year and requiring banks to refund large sums of money to aggrieved customers;
- identifying systemic problems in the conduct of banks, as a result of which banks were required to take corrective measures, such as determining or modifying work procedures, improving their service and issuing refunds to customers;
- dealing with Bills and legislative amendments addressing consumer protection;
- enforcement of consumer protection directives, by conducting regular compliance tests and audits;
- various activities aimed at financial education and the dissemination of information. For example, launching a user-friendly website, which includes a number of forms intended for use by customers as well as links to external websites for the purpose of expanding the information available to the public. In addition, various online calculators were launched which enable customers to calculate fees; convert nominal interest rates into effective interest rates; calculate the conversion rates of foreign currencies; linkages; and so forth;
- dealing with tens of thousands of enquiries in respect of restricted customers and accounts, so deemed because of cheques drawn without adequate funds;
- submitting applications to the Tribunal for Standard Contracts, with requests to abolish discriminatory conditions in bank contracts, where those arise;
- involvement in class-action lawsuits against banks: submitting opinions to the courts on professional matters; providing assessments on proposed settlement arrangements; and taking an active part in mediation proceedings between the bank and its customers;
- involvement in inter-ministerial committees, dealing with specific issues that have implications for consumers and so forth.[77]

---

[75] IMF Country Report No 06/121: Israel: Selected Issues (March 2006), at 110, www.imf.org/external/pubs/ft/scr/2006/cr06121.pdf.

[76] See the Annual Surveys of the Israeli Banking System for 2013 and following years, on the Banking Supervision Department website, at www.boi.org.il/en/NewsAndPublications/RegularPublications/Pages/Default.aspx.

[77] For more, see Plato-Shinar (n 4) at 198–200, 146–66.

These numerous activities, which require much knowledge and expertise in the field of consumer protection, attest to the capability of the Banking Supervision Department and its competence to oversee this area.

The considerable public criticism voiced against the supervisor of banks focused on two specific issues, which are interrelated: the lack of competition between banks and the high price of banking services.[78] The Bank of Israel was criticised for thwarting efforts to increase competition amongst banks, and between banks and non-bank institutions, due to fear that such reforms would damage the profitability and stability of the banking system.[79]

The public's dissatisfaction led to the involvement of Israel's Parliament (the Knesset), which responded by imposing supervision on bank fees[80] and amending existing laws to stimulate competition.[81]

Even if additional measures could be taken to further increase competition or reduce prices, it is doubtful that the significant reforms involved in adopting Twin Peaks would be justified. Furthermore, there is considerable doubt as to whether the Twin Peaks model and the relevant conduct-of-business regulator would succeed in solving these problems, as enhancing competition and reduction of prices are not the goals of the Twin Peaks regulators.

The fact that the sectoral regulators have broad authority, which includes both prudential and conduct of business regulation, has transformed the Israeli financial regulators into strong supervisory entities with significant power vis-à-vis the sectors they supervise.[82] The significant power of the regulators is an effective deterrent to financial institutions, resulting in a high level of compliance.[83] In addition, greater power for the regulator may strengthen their independence from supervised institutions: reducing the influence of interest groups (like banks) effectively guards against the phenomenon of regulatory capture.[84] This all contributes to the efficacy and success of regulations.

To the advantages that flow from consolidating prudential regulation and conduct of business regulation in the hands of the same regulatory agency, as is the case with the sectoral model, can be added the advantages that derive from sectoral separation. Keeping financial supervisory agencies separate permits them, as specialised agencies, to better recognise and address the

---

[78] Irit Avisar, 'Stability Is above Everything', *Globes* (16 July 2012), www.globes.co.il/news/article.aspx?did=1000766233. Sivan Aizescu, 'The Competition Committee Is a Display to the Public as if the Banking System Is Handled', *The Marker* (13 June 2012), www.themarker.com/markets/1.1730298.

[79] Thus, for example, when it was decided by the Finance Ministry to promote the establishment of a credit data-sharing system, and to use special expedited legislative proceedings to progress the matter, they were opposed by the governor of the Bank of Israel on the grounds that the issue was sensitive – invasion of privacy – which should be addressed as part of the normal legislative process. The bank also opposed the Finance Ministry's proposal to allow non-bank institutions to raise money by issuing bonds in order to provide loans to the public, on the grounds that such an initiative would require imposing supervision on these institutions first. While, on the merits, these reasons seem reasonable, it was argued by the media, as well as by the minister of finance, that the underlying motive was a fear of heightened competition for banks, and as a consequence, a threat to their profitability. See Plato-Shinar (n 4) at 203–4.

[80] Banking (Service to Customer) Law, Ch B2.

[81] See, for example, Law to Enhance Competition and Reduce Concentration in the Israeli Banking Market (Legislative Amendments) 5777-2017.

[82] For more on the powerful tools for enforcement of the Israeli financial regulators, see Ruth Plato-Shinar and Keren Borenstein-Nativ, 'Misconduct Costs of Banks: The Meaning behind the Figures' (2017) 32 *Banking and Finance Law Review* 495, 505–9.

[83] A good example is the Proper Conduct of Banking Business Directives that the Supervisor of Banks issues on a regular basis. It was only in 2005 that the Israeli Banking Ordinance formally empowered the supervisor to issue these directives. However, even prior to 2005, when it was not clear where the power to issue the directive derived from, no bank dared to oppose them and get involved in a dispute with the Supervisor. A similar phenomenon existed in respect of the supervisor's authority to handle public complaints. See Plato-Shinar (n 4) at 201.

[84] On regulatory capture in the Israeli banking sector, see Plato-Shinar (n 5) at 210–216.

unique characteristics of the specific sector that they supervise. Banking, securities and insurance firms possess certain distinctive features that require different supervision policies and segregated regulatory treatment. Each sector has its own idiosyncratic risks that necessitate adopting distinctive risk methodologies and modes of supervision. Diverse coverage of deposit insurance and lender-of-last-resort facilities leads to different kinds of moral hazard and requires sector-specific recovery and resolution plans. Thus the 'one size fits all' approach to regulation may be inappropriate and possibly counterproductive.[85]

This issue was well illustrated in Israel during the 2008 global financial crisis. As mentioned earlier, Israel survived the crisis relatively well. However, one sector seriously affected by the crisis was the institutional investors, who had invested large portions of public money (belonging to their clients) in bonds issued by commercial corporations that, because of the crisis and other reasons, suffered losses and could not repay their debts. Ultimately, debt arrangements were made, which included significant 'haircuts' in the sums repaid, generating material losses for these institutions' clients. The extent of this phenomenon created deep concern for policymakers and regulators and required a rapid response that was appropriate to the needs of a specific, distressed sector. Indeed, the sectoral measures that were undertaken immediately helped to achieve such a response.[86]

The impetus for Twin Peaks adoption has arisen in various countries with a high degree of interconnectedness between various segments of the financial sector due to a blurring of distinctions between various classes of products and services and the emergence of financial conglomerates that operate across multiple financial areas.[87] On the other hand, in countries where various segments of the financial sector (insurance and pensions, securities, banking) have little connection with one another, as is the situation in the Israeli market, arguments in favour of a two-regulator Twin Peaks' structure fall away.[88]

In Israel, as explained in Section 10.2, a clear separation is maintained between the banking system, the insurance and pension system, and other financial intermediaries. However, over the past few years a few insurance companies and investment firms have evolved into financial groups that provide a variety of services including pension savings, investment services and finance. The structure of regulation that exists in Israel, namely the combination of sectoral and functional regulation, answers this situation. Both investment services and pension savings are subject to functional supervision, that is, to a special regulator who oversees all the financial actors engaged in this field regardless of institution,[89] thereby achieving uniformity in supervision. The rest of the activities, such as provision of credit, are subject to sectoral regulation that, justifiably, addresses the distinctive features and risks of each separate sector. In other words, the current structure of regulation appears able to satisfy supervisory needs in respect of these developments, particularly when taking into consideration the advantages of keeping prudential regulation and conduct of business regulation united.

---

[85] Norton (n 60) at 40.

[86] Plato-Shinar (n 4) at 24–7, and the reports cited.

[87] Jose de Luna Martinez and Thomas A. Rose, 'International Survey of Integrated Financial Sector Supervision' (World Bank Policy Research Working Paper 3096, July 2003), at 9–11; Taylor (n 59) at 17.

[88] Abrams and Taylor (n 60) at 10.

[89] As explained in Section 10.2, investment services are subject to the Israel Securities Authority, while pension services are subject to the Capital Markets, Insurance and Savings Authority.

10.4.3 *The Ramifications of a Financial Regulatory Reform*

The implementation of regulatory reform is a complicated process. First, the extent of the fundamental legal change that would accompany such reform, requires considerable resources, efforts and time.[90] In addition, the legislative drafting stage, by its very nature, contains risks: issues that were previously thought to have been settled by existing legislation (such as the scope of regulated activities), may be thrown into flux. Depending upon the degree of influence of powerful parliamentary interest groups, legislation may emerge weaker than the original.[91] This issue is particularly relevant to Israel, where past experiences have demonstrated that banks, through their lobbying, have succeeded in watering down legislation prejudicial to their interests.[92]

The legislative drafting stage is only the beginning. The important part of executing reforms is the operational stage. Switching to the Twin Peaks model requires the unification of supervision over the entire financial system, establishing two new regulatory bodies, and transferring powers from the current sectoral agencies, to the two new peaks.[93] This process would involve significant challenges at all operational levels: person power, infrastructure and management.

Finally, with significant regulatory reforms comes unpredictability. When regulatory reforms start, we may not always know how they will end. This was well explained by Abrams and Taylor when they described the transition process as a 'Pandora's Box'.[94]

In light of all this, the logical conclusion would be that Twin Peaks reforms should only be embarked upon if absolutely essential.

10.5 REGULATORY COOPERATION

One of the important lessons learned from the global financial crisis was the value of effective cooperation between financial regulators, not only in times of crisis but also in times of stability. Effective cooperation requires not only information-sharing (within an appropriate confidentiality framework) and consultation but also active collaboration in areas of rule-making, supervision and enforcement, particularly in respect of issues where action by one regulator may have an impact on the regulatory responsibilities of the other.

Regulatory cooperation is a central issue, particularly under Twin Peaks, envisaging as it does two independent authorities. Therefore, in order to consider mechanisms of cooperation that could apply to Israel, the arrangements that exist in this regard in Twin Peaks countries will be examined. The examination will refer to three interrelated issues: first, is the jurisprudential approach to cooperation formal or informal? Put differently, is cooperation mandated by legislative or executive action, or performed voluntarily, based on soft law? Secondly, what forms of cooperation are used, and what is the role of Memoranda of Understanding (MoUs)?

---

[90] Martinez and Rose (n 87) at 27–8. For the legal aspects involved in the establishment of the FSA in the United Kingdom, see Ferran (n 66), in particular Ch III.

[91] Abrams and Taylor (n 60) at 16.

[92] For more on lobbyists that represented banks during debates about separating credit card companies from banks: Zvi Zrachya, 'The Banks Operate Lobbyists to Pressurize Members of Knesset to Change the Strum Committee's Recommendations', *The Marker* (6 September 2016), www.themarker.com/news/1.3059725.

[93] Even if the existing Securities Authority became the conduct of business regulator, as it has proposed (see n 2), and the prudential regulator fell under the Bank of Israel, the process would still require significant reforms.

[94] Abrams and Taylor (n 60) at 15–16, 27.

Thirdly, does an inter-agency collaborative body exist, and if so what substantive functions and powers does it have?[95]

10.5.1 *Australia*

At the one end of the spectrum, we find the Australian system, where coordination between agencies is mainly based on informal, voluntary arrangements.[96] The express reference to inter-agency cooperation can be found in only one isolated section of statute, which refers to one agency (the Australian Prudential Regulation Authority – APRA) and suggests, rather laconically, that 'APRA should, in performing and exercising its functions and powers, have regard to the desirability of APRA cooperating with other financial sector supervisory agencies'.[97] However, where they choose to coordinate, the law allows confidential information to be shared between the financial regulators in order to assist them to perform their functions.[98]

The Australian approach is that legislation, or formal arrangements, cannot be relied upon to promote cooperation. Instead, a culture of cooperation has been cultivated where regulators regard cooperation with other agencies as an important part of their job, acknowledging also that there is a strong expectation from the public and the government to do so.[99]

In Australia, this cooperative culture extends to notifying, discussing and jointly planning supervisory activities; discussing which regulator is the most appropriate to investigate certain matters or take a particular course of action; if necessary, modifying original timetables to accommodate other regulator's plans; and coordinating day-to-day operations, especially in an emergency.[100]

In Australia, a major part of cooperation between the two 'peaks', the Australian Securities and Investments Commission (ASIC) and APRA, is based upon a bilateral MoU.[101] Neither the form nor the content of the MoU is prescribed by statute and it is not legally binding. This MoU covers operational matters, such as information-sharing and prompt notification of any regulatory decisions likely to have an impact upon the other agency's area of responsibility. It also establishes regular bilateral coordination arrangements that aim, among other things, to ensure close consultation and avoid overlaps and gaps in regulatory coverage.[102]

Empirical evidence suggests that MoUs have limited practical effect or utility in terms of achieving desired outcomes, and that neither the Australian Securities and Investments Commission (ASIC) nor APRA rely upon them strictly. Instead, their main value is in signalling

---

[95] Andrew J. Godwin and Andrew D. Schmulow, 'The Financial Sector Regulation Bill in South Africa: Lessons from Australia' (CIFR Working Paper No 052/2015/Project No E018, January 2015), at 8–17.

[96] International Monetary Fund, 'Australia: Financial System Stability Assessment' (IMF Country Report No 12/308, November 2012), 28, www.apra.gov.au/AboutAPRA/Publications/Documents/cr12308%5B1%5D.pdf; Andrew Godwin and Ian Ramsay, 'Twin Peaks – The Legal and Regulatory Anatomy of Australia's System of Financial Regulation' (2015) 26 *Journal of Banking and Finance Law & Practice* 240, 260, 265.

[97] Australian Prudential Regulation Authority Act 1988, s 10.

[98] Ibid, s 56; Australian Securities and Investments Commission Act 2001, s 127(2A).

[99] Godwin and Ramsay (n 96) at 266; Godwin and Schmulow (n 95) at 9–10.

[100] Australian Securities and Investments Commission: Speech to Australian Prudential Regulation Authority Leadership Team, 6–7 (30 June 2011), http://web.archive.org/web/20140212234835/http://www.asic.gov.au/asic/pdflib .nsf/LookupByFileName/Speech-to-APRA-leadership-team-1.pdf/$file/Speech-to-APRA-leadership-team-1.pdf.

[101] Memorandum of Understanding between the Australian Prudential Regulation Authority and the Australian Securities and Investments Commission (28 November 2019), www.apra.gov.au/sites/default/files/APRA-ASIC% 20Memorandum%20of%20Understanding%202019.pdf.

[102] Ibid at ss 14–15.

to the public how the regulators intend to achieve effective co-ordination, and also in reviewing and confirming the arrangements from time to time.[103]

The process of cooperation is overseen by the Council of Financial Regulators (CFR). However, the CFR has neither a statutory basis nor legal functions or powers separate from those of its individual member agencies. Its members are the two financial regulators (APRA and ASIC), the RBA and the Treasury. Meetings are chaired by the governor of the RBA. They are typically held on a quarterly basis but can be convened more frequently if needed. The CFR members share information and views and advise the government on Australia's financial system regulation. The CFR also deals with prudential issues and coordinates responses to potential threats to financial stability.[104] As to transparency, the CFR has a webpage which contains information about the CFR, its media releases, publications and other resources.[105] Many of the issues discussed by the CFR are reported in the RBA's semi-annual Financial Stability Review, with input from the other CFR members.[106] To date, however, the minutes of the meetings of the CFR have not been published.[107] According to the RBA, the experience since its establishment, and especially during the last global financial crisis, highlighted the benefits of the existing, non-statutory basis for the CFR.[108]

In summary, the Australian experience shows the advantages of an informal framework: It is more facilitative, enabling, flexible and allows quicker responses.[109]

10.5.2 *The United Kingdom*

In contrast is the United Kingdom's model of Twin Peaks, where regulatory cooperation is enshrined in legislation. The legislation imposes a statutory duty on the two financial regulators, – the Prudential Regulation Authority (PRA) and the Financial Conduct Authority (FCA), to coordinate their activities and prescribes the nature of coordination between them as follows:

(1) The regulators must co-ordinate the exercise of their respective functions . . . with a view to ensuring

    (a) that each regulator consults the other regulator (where not otherwise required to do so) in connection with any proposed exercise of a function in a way that may have a material adverse effect on the advancement by the other regulator of any of its objectives;

    (b) that where appropriate each regulator obtains information and advice from the other regulator in connection with the exercise of its functions in relation to matters of common regulatory interest in cases where the other regulator may be expected to have relevant information or relevant expertise; . . .

(2) The duty in subsection (1) applies only to the extent that compliance with the duty –

    (a) is compatible with the advancement by each regulator of any of its objectives; and

    (b) does not impose a burden on the regulators that is disproportionate to the benefits of the compliance.

---

[103] Godwin and Ramsay (n 96) at 260; Godwin and Schmulow (n 95) at 12.
[104] The Council of Financial Regulators (n 102).
[105] www.cfr.gov.au.
[106] The Council of Financial Regulators (n 102).
[107] Godwin and Ramsay (n 96) at 264; Godwin and Schmulow (n 95) at 16–17.
[108] Reserve Bank of Australia: Submission to the Financial System Inquiry (March 2014), at 5, 53, www.rba.gov.au/publications/submissions/financial-sector/financial-system-inquiry-2014-03/pdf/financial-system-inquiry-2014-03.pdf.
[109] Godwin and Ramsay (n 96) at 266.

(3) A function conferred on either regulator by or under this Act relates to matters of common regulatory interest if –
    (a) the other regulator exercises similar or related functions in relation to the same persons,
    (b) the other regulator exercises functions which relate to different persons but relate to similar subject-matter, or
    (c) its exercise could affect the advancement by the other regulator of any of its objectives.[110]

In addition, the Act imposes a duty on the two financial regulators to enter into a binding MoU:
(1) The regulators must prepare and maintain a memorandum which describes in general terms –
    (a) the role of each regulator in relation to the exercise of functions conferred by or under this Act which relate to matters of common regulatory interest, and
    (b) how the regulators intend to comply with section 3D in relation to the exercise of such functions.[111]

The Act further details an extensive list of issues to which the MoU must refer. The regulators must review the MoU at least once in every calendar year. The MoU and its revisions are subject to parliamentary oversight, and the Bank of England relies upon them heavily. As for transparency, the regulators must ensure that the updated version of the MoU is publicly available.[112] Accordingly, the PRA and the FCA signed an MoU regulating the various aspects of cooperation between them.[113]

The British model satisfies itself by imposing a statutory duty of collaboration and of entering MoUs upon the regulators. Consequently, an inter-agency collaborative body, similar to that of the Australian CFR, does not exist. By way of comparison, South Africa, which recently adopted Twin Peaks,[114] has chosen a formal approach to inter-agency cooperation similar to the United Kingdom.[115] The South Africans have decided to establish a Financial System Council of Regulators, with a statutory basis and functions prescribed by law.[116] The objective of the council is 'to facilitate co-operation and collaboration and, where appropriate, consistency of action', between the institutions represented, by 'providing a forum for senior representatives . . . to discuss, and inform themselves about, matters of common interest'.[117] The Council is comprised of twelve members that represent various – not only financial – regulatory agencies, including the two 'peaks' (the Financial Sector Conduct Authority and the Prudential Authority), the Reserve Bank and the Treasury. The meetings of the council will be held twice a year, or more frequently if needed, and will be chaired by the director general of the Treasury.[118] A major part of the work is to be executed by working groups or subcommittees of the council, including one for financial stability.[119]

---

[110] Financial Services and Markets Act 2000, s 3D (as amended by the Financial Services Act 2012, s 6).
[111] Ibid, s 3E.
[112] Ibid. In addition, s. 3F imposes a duty on the two financial regulators to enter into a binding MoU in respect of with-profit insurance policies.
[113] Memorandum of Understanding between the Financial Conduct Authority (FCA) and the Bank of England (July 2019), www.bankofengland.co.uk/-/media/boe/files/memoranda-of-understanding/fca-and-bank-prudential-july-2019 .pdf. See also With-Profits, Memorandum of Understanding, www.fca.org.uk/publication/mou/mou-with-profits.pdf.
[114] Financial Sector Regulation Act, No 9 of 2017.
[115] Ibid, ss 76 and 77.
[116] Ibid, s 79.
[117] Ibid.
[118] Ibid, s 80.
[119] Ibid, s 81.

10.5.3 *Lessons for Israel*

In Israel, no statutory mechanism exists that requires cooperation between the financial regulators. A legislative amendment enacted in 2010 permits the regulators to share information between themselves despite the duty of confidentiality that is imposed on each of them.[120]

An Israeli team in the 1990s, which included the three financial regulators, recommended establishing a binding coordination mechanism between the financial regulators, one that would include a binding decision-making process and would be created by statute.[121] However, disagreements between the regulators surrounding the establishment of such a mechanism were so deep that not only could a consensual decision not be reached, but not even a consensual report could be released, leaving only a number of general recommendations to be made. Ultimately, even those recommendations were not implemented.[122]

Nevertheless, certain avenues of cooperation between the financial regulators have developed throughout the years and are described below.

10.5.3.1 MoU on Cooperation and Sharing of Information

In 2007, the three financial regulators signed an important MoU, which established a general framework for cooperation and information-sharing.[123]

This MoU is not created by statute, nor is it enforceable and therefore is considered as soft law. The MoU refers to four issues:

- First, it established a coordinating committee (described below).
- Secondly, it dealt with coordinating supervision policy over financial markets. In this regard, the MoU states that where a new regulation, albeit sectoral, may have an influence or impact upon other financial sectors or on the stability or competitiveness of the financial system, the acting regulator must inform the other regulators in advance and enable them to express their views. In addition, the regulators agree to establish additional joint mechanisms, if necessary, in respect of legislation, regulation and supervision of the financial system.
- Thirdly, the MoU refers to information-sharing and enforcement coordination, and sets rules in this regard.
- Finally, the MoU refers to mutual assistance and reciprocal relations. It obliges the regulators to assist each other in any matter related to the implementation of coordinated supervision over the financial system, including in gathering, processing and analysing information, and in compliance and enforcement.

10.5.3.2 The Coordinating Committee

One of the innovations of these MoUs was the establishment of a coordinating committee (known as the Forum of Financial Regulators). The committee was not created by statute and does not possess legal functions or powers. It serves as a voluntary meeting platform for the three

---

[120] Banking Ordinance, s 15A2. Securities Law, s 56E(b). Control of Financial Services (Insurance) Law, s 50B. See also Control of Financial Services (Regulated Financial Services) Law, s 98(a).

[121] The Report of the Committee to Examine Structural Changes in the Israeli Capital Market 74–6 (September 1996).

[122] Amiram Barkat, 'Prof. Avi Ben-Bassat Explains What Is the No 1 Challenge of Kachlon', *Globes* (27 March 2015), www .globes.co.il/news/article.aspx?did=1001022711.

[123] Ministry of Finance, Israel Securities Authority, Bank of Israel: Memorandum of Understanding on Cooperation and Sharing of Information between the Banking Supervision Department, the Securities Authority, and the Capital Markets Insurance and Savings Division (24 June 2007), www.isa.gov.il/Download/IsaFile_1956.pdf.

sectoral regulators, for the purposes of exchanging information, opinions and ideas. According to the MoU, the committee shall deal with trends and changes in the supervised sectors, propose legislative and regulatory amendments, and any other topic. The committee shall convene according to needs, and at least once a month. It is required to establish subcommittees, permanent and ad hoc, to deal with specific matters. It will determine its own procedures, and it may invite additional parties to its meetings. The discussions of the committee and its subcommittees are to be documented and published in a manner that the committee deems fit. In practice, no information of any kind has been made accessible to the public, stripping the committee of transparency.

10.5.3.3 Advisory Committees

Two sectoral regulators have advisory committees that include among their members representatives of the other two financial regulators.

The Advisory Committee of the Commissioner of Capital Markets, Insurance and Savings is a statutory committee, appointed by the minister of finance. The committee comprises seven members, who are civil servants or public representatives, including the supervisor of banks and the chair of the Securities Authority. The chair of the committee, who may not be a civil servant, is appointed by the minister. The committee occasionally convenes according to the decisions of its chair or the commissioner, who also determine meeting agendas. The law states that any member of the committee may refrain from participating in a discussion and from voting if they face a conflict of interest between their function as a committee member and their personal interest or another position that they hold.[124]

Another statutory advisory committee is the Advisory Committee of the Governor of the Bank of Israel on Matters Relating to Banking Businesses.[125] The Banking Ordinance grants the governor absolute discretion in appointing members to the committee, with no limitation on their number or qualifications. The sole restriction is that one member must be appointed by the minister of finance.[126] At present, the commissioner of capital markets, insurance and savings, and the chair of the Securities Authority serve on the committee. Meeting procedures are determined by the governor. The committee may establish subcommittees, determine their function and delegate to them some of its powers. As to transparency, the ordinance expressly states that the committee's deliberations are to be confidential.[127] The website of the Bank of Israel refers to the committee in a rather pithy fashion, describing it as an advisory committee of the supervisor of banks, and explaining that its function is to advise the supervisor in respect of new directives that the supervisor intends to promulgate. The list of the committee's members is not published or available to the public.

10.5.3.4 Committee to Examine Competition in the Credit Market

In 2016, the Committee to Enhance Competition in Common Banking and Financial Services published a report containing recommendations on various measures aimed at increasing competition in the area of credit to the retail sector.[128] The recommendations were adopted

---

[124] Supervision of Financial Services (Insurance) Law, s 4.
[125] Banking Ordinance, s 6(1).
[126] Ibid, s 6(1) and (3).
[127] Ibid, s 6(5).
[128] The Committee to Enhance Competition in Common Banking and Financial Services: Final Report (September 2016), www.gov.il/he/departments/PublicBodies/banks_sevices_competitiveness_committee.

by law.[129] In addition, the law established the Committee to Examine Competition in the Credit Market, which will operate for six years.[130] The committee chairpersons are the director general of the Ministry of Finance and a representative of the Bank of Israel. Other members are the director general of the Antitrust Authority, the supervisor of payment systems at the Bank of Israel, as well as the two financial regulators that are engaged in retail credit: the supervisor of banks and the commissioner of the capital market, insurance and savings. The functions of the committee are to monitor the implementation of the provisions of the law, to conduct periodic examinations of the state of competition in the sector and to identify barriers thereto, and to propose additional measures to increase competition in the retail credit sector. The law requires various authorities, including the financial regulatory authorities, to provide information to the committee at its request. The committee is required to submit to the government and the Knesset a report on its work once every six months. Although this committee is not a joint forum of the three financial regulators, nevertheless it enables two of them to collaborate in the increasingly developing field of retail credit.

10.5.3.5 Joint Initiatives

In respect of a few cardinal issues, the financial regulators have published joint documents, addressing cross-sectoral application. In 2010, for example, the three financial regulators published a document listing the criteria for examining compliance with the fit-and-proper requirements imposed upon controlling shareholders and officers of financial corporations.[131] Further examples include the guidelines for granting permits to control financial institutions, jointly issued by the supervisor of banks, and the commissioner of capital markets, insurance and savings, in 2013.[132] In 2017, the Banking Supervision Department and the Capital Markets, Insurance and Saving Authority entered into an MoU for the management of bank accounts for P2P platforms.[133]

10.5.3.6 The Financial Stability Committee

Following recommendations made by the IMF,[134] the Financial Stability Committee (FSC) was established in 2019.[135] Its members are the financial regulators (the supervisor of banks; the commissioner of capital markets, insurance and savings, who also serves as the supervisor of financial service providers; the director of payment systems at the Bank of Israel; and the chair of the Securities Authority); and representatives of the two financial stabilisers (the Bank of Israel,

---

[129] Law to Enhance Competition and Reduce Concentration in the Israeli Banking Market (Legislative Amendments), 5777-2017.

[130] Ibid, s 12.

[131] Capital Markets, Insurance and Savings Division, Israel Securities Authority, the Banking Supervision Department: 'Examination of Credibility by Supervising Authorities' (1 December 2010), http://mof.gov.il/hon/information-entities/controllicensingandtransferofgoods/documents/credibility2011.pdf.

[132] Banking Supervision Department, Capital Markets Insurance and Savings Division: 'Guiding Principles for Criteria and General Conditions for a Party Requesting Permit to Control and to Hold Means of Control in Supervised Bodies' (11 July 2013), www.google.co.il/url?sa=t&rct=j&q=&esrc=s&source=web&cd=1&cad=rja&uact=8&ved=0ahUKEwj8vO7Ww5PWAhULXBoKHTApAeYQFggkMAA&url=http%3A%2F%2Fwww.boi.org.il%2Fhe%2FBankingSupervision%2FSupervisorMethod%2FDocuments%2Fn310108.pdf&usg=AFQjCNGhSEtpKUE6zgFKBtbUMrfzv4FoIQ.

[133] Banking Supervision Department, Capital Markets, Insurance and Saving Authority, 'Memorandum of Understanding in respect of Managing an Account in a Banking Corporations for a Credit Intermediation System' (unpublished, Capital Markets, Insurance and Saving Authority, 25 July 2017).

[134] IMF Country Report No 12/69 (n 74) at 32; IMF Country Report No 14/47 (n 74) at 12, 15, 19.

[135] Bank of Israel Law, 5770-2010, ss 57A–57J.

and the Ministry of Finance). The chair of the FSC is the governor of the Bank of Israel, and the deputy chair is the director general of the Ministry of Finance.

The objectives of the FSC are to support the stability of the financial system and its normal functioning, through coordination, cooperation and sharing of information. This coordination is intended to focus on the identification, assessment and monitoring of systemic risks, as well as harmonising the rules of supervision that apply to various institutions and financial markets.

The FSC is empowered to warn the financial supervisory authorities when it identifies systemic risks, and to recommend measures to avoid or reduce it. The FSC is not authorised to instruct the financial supervisory authorities on how to act, and its power does not prejudice the independence and powers of the financial supervisory authorities. However, in order to encourage a regulator to implement whatever recommendation is directed to it, a mechanism of 'adoption or explanation' was determined.

From the foregoing survey it may be concluded that current cooperation between the financial regulators in Israel is non-statutory, informal, based upon soft law techniques and dependent upon the good-will of the regulators. In contrast, the Financial Stability Committee represents a formal approach to inter-agency cooperation, and not in vain: systemic stability is a sensitive issue that must be dealt with, and with the utmost diligence. However, the question of cooperation between the financial regulators in all other supervisory fields still remains: Should the informal status quo continue or should Israel adopt more formal arrangements?

In Israel, not only is there currently no compelling statutory requirement to cooperate as exists, for example, in the United Kingdom, there is not even a clause in the legislation that recommends it – as is the position in Australia. The Israeli legislation lacks any reference to inter-agency cooperation, and so the entire system of cooperation is founded in soft law. While soft law has important advantages, such as flexibility and speed, one of its major drawbacks is its dependence on the goodwill of the financial regulators involved.[136] Therefore, a prerequisite for using soft law techniques is an entrenched culture of cooperation, mutual trust and reciprocal support between regulators. We have observed that such factors exist, for example in Australia. There, the regulators regard cooperation with each other as an integral part of their job, implement it as part of their routine and strive to fulfil the high expectations the public and the government have that they will do so. The high level of transparency of inter-agency cooperation reflects this culture as well. Unfortunately, such a culture of cooperation, certainly to this extent, does not exist in Israel. Moreover, over the years struggles have arisen between the financial regulators when initiatives and proposals raised by one regulator are opposed by another regulator for fear that they might harm the bodies under its control or limit its regulatory power.[137] This phenomenon has recently intensified: a series of new legislative initiatives, which for the first time imposed supervision over financial entities and new financial services, have led to several power struggles between regulators when any of them seeks to subordinate these

---

[136] Chris Brummer, 'Why Soft Law Dominates International Finance – and Not Trade' (2010) 13 *Journal of International Economic Law* 623, 630–34; Rolf H. Weber, 'Overcoming the Hard Law/Soft Law Dichotomy in Times of (Financial) Crises' (2012) 1 *Journal of Governance and Regulation* 8, 10–13.

[137] Tomer Varon, 'Salinger Opposes Hedva Ber's Plan to Market Insurance by the Banks', *Calcalist* (7 September 2015), www.calcalist.co.il/local/articles/0,7340,L-3668897,00.html; Racheli Bindman, 'Kachlon's Initiative: An Explosive Idea with a Great Deal of Potential', *Calcalist* (13 June 2018), www.calcalist.co.il/money/articles/0,7340,L-3740132,00.html.

entities and services under its supervision.[138] When added to past experience – the failure to establish a voluntary mechanism of binding cooperation – it raises concerns that if a critical issue were to require a joint decision of the regulators, and consent could not be reached, reliance on soft law tools would prove inadequate.

It seems that Israel would benefit from adopting a more formal method of cooperation between its financial regulators, similar to that which applies in the United Kingdom. The desirable approach should include a general statutory duty that would oblige regulators to cooperate and would be complemented by a more specific duty that would detail the mechanisms of cooperation, such as a coordinating committee and MoUs, while still affording the regulators discretion in respect of the specifics of implementation.

Another issue that arises for Israel in respect of coordination more broadly is that of an inter-agency collaborative body. In Israel, as detailed above, a coordinating committee exists. However, it is informal, with no binding powers. If Israel were to prefer to adopt a more formal approach, and have a statutorily enabled collaborative body, the coordinating committee could be transformed into such a formal statutory forum. Alternatively, the FSC would be able to serve as a forum for broader cooperation, not limited only to stability matters.

The choice between these two options – soft law or hard – can only be made after taking various issues into consideration, such as:

- Who should be the members of such a collaborative body? While the coordinating committee is comprised of the three financial regulators, the FSC includes additional members, as detailed in Section 10.5.3.6.
- Should the collaborative body have substantive powers and functions that go beyond its consultative and coordinating role? Both the coordinating committee and the FSC do not have such powers. If, however, the collaborative body has the power to make binding decisions, the mechanism for the decision-making process should be expressly promulgated.
- What measures should be taken to ensure that the coordinating body will not serve as the only channel through which inter-agency coordination can be executed?
- How should this body be held accountable and remain transparent?

10.6 CONCLUSION

Financial supervision in Israel is mainly sectoral, where each financial sector has its own dedicated regulator. In addition, there exist some aspects of functional supervision where certain products or services are subject to a specific regulator, no matter which financial institution provides them.

Analysis of Israel's financial markets, the manner of their supervision and the minor impact of the global financial crisis on Israel's financial sector (attributed to effective regulation and the balance achieved between the interests of stability and consumer protection), all point in favour of consolidating prudential regulation and conduct of business regulation in the hands of the same regulator – an approach that is antithetical to Twin Peaks.

---

[138] See, for example, Meirav Arlozorov, 'Regulators Turning to Gladiators: Who Will Supervise over the Non-bank Credit?', *The Marker* (6 February 2018), www.themarker.com/markets/1.5790636; Racheli Bindman, 'The Battle between Ber and Salinger: Who Will Regulate Paypal?', *Calcalist* (2 May 2018), www.calcalist.co.il/local/articles/0,7340,L-3737210,00.html.

However, in respect of inter-agency cooperation and regulatory collaboration, it is suggested that Israel could benefit from the experiences of Twin Peaks countries, particularly the United Kingdom.

With either approach – Twin Peaks or sectoral – whether the regulatory environment is effective may depend more upon the culture of the regulators than on the specific mechanism through which they cooperate.

Towards a Twin Peak Regulatory Architecture for Hong Kong?

Douglas W. Arner, Evan Gibson and Janos Barberis

11.1 INTRODUCTION

This chapter comparatively analyses the effectiveness of Hong Kong's sectoral model of financial regulation against the Twin Peaks model, arguing for a transition to the latter. The proposed reforms are based on the identification of regulatory flaws and promoting Hong Kong as an international centre of finance and technological innovation.

Before beginning this analysis, it is important to highlight the nature of perpetual change that has historically characterised Hong Kong, from its transformation as a fishing village, entrepôt and manufacturing hub into an international financial centre and as a financial conduit for capital raising in China.[1] In the context of financial markets, Hong Kong continues to reinvent itself, for example by establishing the Stock and Bond Connect schemes with Mainland China and the ongoing development of its financial technology (FinTech) industry.

There is significant public and private sector support to maintain Hong Kong's competitiveness as an international financial centre. Technology company listings are increasingly becoming influential for financial centre competitiveness. In response, Hong Kong Exchanges and Clearing Limited (HKEx) has introduced regulatory changes to attract more technology companies, notably by allowing weighted voting rights.[2] With Mainland Chinese companies dominating initial public offerings (IPOs) and the listing of 'new economy' companies progressively displacing those of traditional companies in Hong Kong,[3] the effective regulation of new technology-driven participants, whether financial companies using technology to deliver services (FinTechs) or technology companies offering financial services (TechFins),[4] will be essential to maintain the integrity of capital markets and by extension Hong Kong's reputation as a leading international financial centre.

---

[1] We gratefully acknowledge the financial support of the Hong Kong Research Grants Council Impact Fund.
   This role has gathered impetus over the past few years as Hong Kong's capital markets have become integrated with Mainland China. The Shanghai (2014) and Shenzhen (2016) Stock Connect schemes and Bond Connect (2017) pose unique opportunities and regulatory challenges.
[2] The prohibition of weighted voting rights was a principal reason given by Alibaba in 2014 to explain why an HKEx listing was rejected in favour of a listing on the New York Stock Exchange and, following the relaxation of this prohibition, why a secondary listing on the HKEx was pursued.
[3] For example, Alibaba's secondary listing on the HKEx in November 2019. Potential FinTech IPOs on the HKEx include Dianrong.com (peer-to-peer lending) and Ant Financial (Alibaba's financial conglomerate).
[4] TechFin is a technology-based business model which uses FinTech to lever its services and products. In this chapter the term FinTech, when used generically, will encapsulate TechFin.

Likewise, the FinTech industry has received support from many policy initiatives to promote its development. All of Hong Kong's core sectoral financial regulators have dedicated FinTech contact points and regulatory sandboxes for innovation.[5] The FinTech community is organised around the FinTech Association of Hong Kong, which represents its interests and position on time-sensitive topics, while the financial services industry continues to lead engagement in accelerators, hackathons and educational events.

This chapter provides an analysis of regulation and technological developments. Ultimately the authors argue that in Hong Kong, the Twin Peaks model is more effective in regulating capital market integration with Mainland China and the ongoing technological evolution of finance than the current sectoral model. The need for coordination between regulators in Hong Kong and Mainland China necessitates comprehensive data gathering and exchange, which in turn requires the utilisation of, and advances in, regulatory technology (RegTech).

Section 11.2 discusses the history of regulatory functions, their purpose and the models of regulatory architecture. In particular, the application of the Twin Peaks model following the 2008 global financial crisis. Section 11.3 describes how Hong Kong's capital market integration with Mainland China has exposed the functional limitations of the sectoral model. A comparative analysis of the Stock and Bond Connect schemes assesses the effectiveness of the market conduct and financial stability regulatory functions. Section 11.4 outlines the emergence of 'new economy' companies in Hong Kong, noting that the rise of innovative companies is not a new phenomenon, nor are the policy challenges facing regulators. Section 11.5 emphasises the importance of smart regulation and data-gathering to regulate FinTechs and TechFins, RegTech options to supervise 'new economy' companies and, notably, the application of distributed ledger technology in this context. Section 11.6 discusses how an updated Twin Peaks regulatory architecture in a FinTech/RegTech era would function when applying new technological infrastructures and tools such as permissioned distributed ledger technology to the connect schemes and why the Twin Peaks model is more effective at mitigating regulatory gaps, underlap, inconsistencies and biases.

11.2 REGULATORY FUNCTIONS

11.2.1 *Background*

Historically, regulatory functions first evolved to mitigate financial instability and protect consumers. The earliest financial laws address market misconduct. Following multifarious economic and financial cycles, regulators concluded that market behaviour or conduct needed to be regulated to protect consumers and in extreme circumstances manage financial stability. The vulnerability of banks to contagious collapses en masse in financial crises ('systemic risk') compelled regulators to manage financial system stability to avert broader economic ramifications. Likewise, stock markets became a source of systemic risk as they developed and grew. The Black Thursday crash in 1929 elucidated how market booms could lead to crashes that can cause widespread financial and economic instability.[6]

---

[5] Hong Kong Monetary Authority, Securities and Futures Commission and the Insurance Authority.

[6] For a discussion on regulatory policy responses and mechanisms to manage extreme market volatility, see generally IOSCO, *Consultation Report on Mechanisms Used by Trading Venues to Manage Extreme Volatility and Preserve Orderly Trading* (March 2018).

Throughout the twentieth and early twenty-first century other regulatory functions were introduced, namely market development, financial inclusion, competition and market integrity (for example, anti-money laundering/counter-financing of terrorism).

11.2.2 *Financial Stability and Market Conduct*

The 2008 Global Financial Crisis (GFC) revealed that regulating financial institutions individually (that is, microprudentially) did not fully achieve the financial stability function. Transmissions of systemic risk caused severe financial instability across the financial system, adversely affecting institutions, products, services, markets and economies. Post-crisis a new consensus was reached whereby financial regulation necessitated a system-wide or macroprudential perspective.[7]

Macroprudential supervision is not a new concept, rather one that had become de-emphasised.[8] The GFC re-centred the debate around macroprudential supervision by addressing systemic risk, systemically important financial institutions and the interconnected nature of the global financial system.

The spread of systemic risk during the GFC drew comparative analogies, from nuclear meltdowns to biological epidemics.[9] These abstract and wide-reaching analyses are underpinned by an overarching theme – viewing the financial system 'systemically' as a globally interconnected network.[10] Macroprudential and microprudential financial stability regulation is essential for an effective regulatory model.

The initial regulatory reaction to the GFC centred on financial stability. In the following years, another design flaw emerged. Numerous scandals involving financial institutions (LIBOR[11]) and individuals (London whale[12]) exposed market misconduct as a key cause of the GFC. The response was to impose criminal liability on individuals[13] and impose hundreds of billions of dollars in fines on financial institutions for market misconduct offences.[14]

11.2.3 *Regulatory Models*

Regulatory functions alone do not mitigate market misconduct and financial instability; effective mitigation requires regulators with the requisite capacity and expertise to implement regulatory

---

[7] See generally Douglas W. Arner, 'Adaptation and Resilience in Global Financial Regulation' (2011) 89 *North Carolina Law Review* 101, 131–7.

[8] For a discussion, see generally Michael W. Taylor, Douglas W. Arner and Evan C. Gibson, 'Central Banks' New Macroprudential Consensus' in David G. Mayes, Pierre L. Siklos and Jan-Egbert Sturm (eds) *The Oxford Handbook of the Economics of Central Banking* (Oxford University Press, 2019).

[9] See generally Andy Haldane, 'Rethinking the Financial Network', *BIS Review* 53/2009 (28 April 2009); and Tim Hartford, 'What We Can Learn from Nuclear Reactors', *Financial Times* (14 January 2011).

[10] See generally Erland Nier, Jing Yang, Tanju Yorulmazer and Amadeo Alentorn, 'Network Models and Financial Stability' (Bank of England, Working Paper No 346, April 2008).

[11] London Interbank Offered Rate. See generally Financial Conduct Authority, *Internal Audit Report: A Review of the Extent of Awareness within the FSA of Inappropriate LIBOR Submissions – Management Response* (Financial Conduct Authority, March 2013); and Financial Stability Board, 'Reforming Major Interest Rate Benchmarks' (22 July 2014).

[12] See generally Financial Conduct Authority, 'Final Notice – JPMorgan Chase Bank, N.A.' (18 September 2013).

[13] Bernie Madoff, for example, will spend the rest of his life in prison for misleading investors and committing fraud (estimated at over US$60 billion).

[14] Market conduct regulation is not a new concept having its modern origins in the Great Depression. The market conduct function is critical for stable and efficient financial markets and an integral function of effective regulatory models.

tools effectively and efficiently.[15] Part of this involves clear delineations of responsibility and scope of authority. In financial regulation, five major regulatory models have evolved to fulfil this role, namely sectoral, institutional, functional, integrated and Twin Peaks.[16]

While the sectoral model regulates specific financial sectors (for example, banking, securities, insurance), both the functional and integrated models regulate across all financial sectors, with the former based around regulatory agencies assigned to specific functions (including financial stability, prudential regulation, competition and market conduct) and the latter having a single regulator. The United States, China and the European Union Lamfalussy structure are examples of the sectoral approach. Australia is the clearest example of a functional structure, while Singapore is a good example of an integrated structure. Institutional regulation is based on the regulation of activities for a given type of institution, regardless of sector. This is most typically seen in the context of banks, where the regulator often supervises all aspects of banking activities, for instance regulating authorised institutions in Hong Kong.

The Twin Peaks model is a combination of functional and integrated structures. Prudential and financial stability functions are integrated across all financial sectors and are regulated by one agency. Market conduct and integrity functions are regulated by a second integrated agency. Thus the model has two integrated regulatory agencies with functional mandates: the 'twin' peaks.

Since the GFC, the benefits of the Twin Peaks model in comparison with the sectoral model have been widely discussed, particularly as a result of the United Kingdom's decision to abandon its integrated model. This abandoned model comprised of two agencies – the Financial Services Authority and the Bank of England. The UK Twin Peaks model consists of the Bank of England, which is responsible for financial stability and prudential regulation, and the Financial Conduct Authority or FCA, which is responsible for market conduct and integrity.

A regulatory model requires the capacity to effectively discharge the core financial stability and market conduct functions across the financial system. The Twin Peaks model is designed with a regulator for each of these functions, while the integrated model discharges prudential regulation and the market conduct function within one agency and has been described as reflecting financial institutions that are sectorally integrated across banking, securities and insurance activities.[17] Discharging financial stability can involve the central bank, as in the United Kingdom from 1997 to 2009, or the function can be fully integrated within one agency, as in Singapore.

Theoretically, the Twin Peaks and integrated models have the requisite capacity to manage financial stability risks and market conduct risks that affect the entire financial system, not merely a single sector. These models are designed to overcome the generic design flaw inherent in the sectoral and institutional models when confronted with cross-sectoral entities and activities.

The Twin Peaks model is a relatively recent design that has emerged over the past twenty-five years. Two functions underpin the design: financial stability and market conduct, with a

---

[15] See generally Evan C. Gibson, *Managing Financial Stability and Liquidity Risks in Hong Kong's Banking System: What Is the Optimum Supervisory Model?* (University of Hong Kong, 2014).

[16] For a discussion of the models, see generally Douglas W. Arner and Evan C. Gibson, 'Financial Regulatory Structure in Hong Kong: Looking Forward' in Robin H. Huang and Dirk Schoenmaker (eds) *Institutional Structure of Financial Regulation: Theories and International Experiences* (Routledge, 2015).

[17] Clive Briault, 'The Rationale for a Single National Financial Services Regulator' (FSA Occasional Papers in Financial Regulation No 2, 1999), 17.

regulator tasked with each function.[18] The financial stability regulator is responsible for all financial institutions subject to an explicit systemic protection objective.[19] By contrast, the market conduct regulator is responsible for retail market consumer protection and market integrity.[20] Originally the functions for each 'peak' regulator were to ensure the stability and soundness of the financial system (systemic protection) and to protect depositors, investors and policyholders to the extent that they cannot protect their own interests (consumer protection).[21] Over time these design concepts have evolved with financial markets where financial distinctions have become blurred, regulators have been given clear statutory functions and regulatory structures have been designed to reflect a jurisdiction's financial system.

For example, in 2013 the United Kingdom launched its Twin Peaks model after following through on a plan first announced in 2009. Under the new Twin Peaks model, the Bank of England is responsible for the financial stability function, through its Financial Policy Committee and Prudential Regulation Committee, and the market conduct function is the responsibility of an independent regulator, the FCA. Both regulators are designed around explicit statutory functions or mandates.

This radical redesign was given much impetus by the widespread financial and economic ramifications of the GFC. A key reason for redesigning or completely changing regulatory models is to better address systemic risk. The GFC was instrumental in the creation of a series of new EU sectoral regulatory agencies and an institutional structure for banks in the context of the European Banking Union. For example, the European Central Bank is mandated as the single systemic supervisor for all EU banks. Other examples are the establishment of the Financial Stability Oversight Council and the Consumer Financial Protection Bureau in the United States and the Financial Stability and Development Committee in Mainland China. This was not the case for Hong Kong, which continues with a less formal system of committees, including a Financial Stability Committee created in 2003.[22]

More recently Hong Kong has instigated regulatory reforms because of two reasons. Firstly, Hong Kong and Mainland China's ongoing financial market integration, which has been steadily progressing for almost three decades. Hong Kong's recent capital market development and integration with Mainland China, namely the Shanghai (2014) and Shenzhen (2016) Stock Connect schemes and Bond Connect (2017), highlight the limitations and advantages of their regulatory models.

Secondly, the competitive importance of FinTech and TechFin companies to international financial centres is ample justification for reopening the topic of a new regulatory architecture for Hong Kong. Regulatory reforms which enhance FinTech/TechFin capital raising, innovation and growth can be viewed as a positive externality for the development and competitiveness of Hong Kong as an international financial centre.

---

[18] Michael Taylor, '"Twin Peaks": A Regulatory Structure for the New Century' (Centre for the Study of Financial Innovation 20, December 1995), 10.

[19] Ibid, 9–10.

[20] Ibid, 10.

[21] Ibid, 2.

[22] This is a cross-sectoral systemic regulatory body consisting of the banking, securities and insurance regulators. There is no evidence of a response by the Financial Stability Committee during the GFC or of whether the body is still operational.

11.3 HONG KONG CAPITAL MARKET INTEGRATION WITH MAINLAND CHINA

The Stock and Bond Connect schemes fall under the supervision of the Securities and Futures Commission (SFC) and the Hong Kong Monetary Authority (HKMA) respectively. If any material regulatory underlap exists, this is a possible point in favour of Hong Kong transitioning away from its sectoral model.

11.3.1 *Stock Connect*

11.3.1.1 Regulatory Cooperation

First launched in 2014, the Stock Connect schemes provide mutual access between stock exchanges in Hong Kong and Mainland China for eligible company stock. The stock exchanges involved are the Stock Exchange of Hong Kong (SEHK), the Shanghai Stock Exchange (SSE) and the Shenzhen Stock Exchange (SZSE).[23] There are two trading links for each scheme, Northbound and Southbound. The Northbound trading link enables Hong Kong investors to trade shares on the SSE or SZSE, and the Southbound trading link allows SSE or SZSE eligible investors to trade shares on the SEHK.

Regulatory oversight is the responsibility of the Hong Kong SFC and the China Securities Regulatory Commission (CSRC). A memorandum of understanding (MoU) was signed by the SFC and CSRC for the SSE Stock Connect scheme and updated with the subsequent introduction of the SZSE Stock Connect scheme. The purpose of the MoU is stated as follows: 'the Parties aim to further improve the mechanism for identification and notification of suspected misconduct and initiate effective investigatory cooperation to combat cross-boundary suspected misconduct including disclosure of misleading information, insider dealing, market manipulation, and other fraudulent activities, etc.'.[24] Moreover, the MoU cooperation arrangements provide for the exchange of investigatory information; notification of suspected misconduct and investigations; investigatory assistance; joint investigations; the use of information; cooperation in the execution of orders including administrative sanctions; the combating of cross-boundary suspected misconduct and the prevention of regulatory arbitrage; the circumvention of regulatory actions; and the obtaining of improper benefits. Market conduct is a core function of both the SFC and CSRC when regulating the Stock Connect schemes.

The cross-boundary nature of Stock Connect necessitates coordination between regulators as investors in both jurisdictions can trade stock. Prima facie, as Hong Kong and Mainland China operate under the sectoral model, the compatibility of each model's design should reduce frictions between regulators and ameliorate their supervisory mandates.

Regulatory flaws remain, however, as sectoral securities supervisors' regulatory purview is limited to the securities sector and to their statutory mandates. Any activities outside this regulatory purview (as defined by statute or determined by the sectoral approach) will fall outside of the regulators' legal capacity and expertise.[25]

---

[23] In 2014 the Shanghai–Hong Kong Stock Connect was launched, thereby enabling investors to trade shares on either market through local securities firms or brokers. The scheme provides access between the SEHK and the SSE. Similarly the Shenzhen–Hong Kong Stock Connect was launched in 2016, providing access between the SEHK and the SZSE.

[24] China Securities Regulatory Commission and Securities and Futures Commission, 'Memorandum of Understanding between the CSRC and the SFC on Strengthening of Regulatory and Enforcement Cooperation under Mutual Access between Mainland and Hong Kong Stock Markets' (16 August 2016), 1.

[25] For example, securities companies offering banking or insurance products.

11.3.1.2 Market Conduct

As sectoral securities regulators, the SFC and CSRC have similar statutory market conduct mandates and functional regulatory purviews.[26] A few examples of Stock Connect joint-enforcement actions demonstrate how the market conduct function operates in practice.

In March 2017, the first market manipulation case under a Stock Connect scheme (in this case the SSE) was successfully prosecuted. Investigations by the CSRC revealed that a connected stock in the Northbound trading link (Hong Kong to Mainland China), Zheijiang China Commodities City Group Co., Ltd, was subject to share price manipulation which realised an illegal gain of over RMB40 million.[27] The SFC cooperated with the CSRC in gathering evidence, under the MoU, which led to the successful prosecution pursuant to the *Securities Law of the People's Republic of China*. At trial, the defendant unsuccessfully argued that the evidence submitted by the SFC was inadmissible.

As another example, following the introduction of the Shenzhen–Hong Kong Stock Connect, the SFC and the HKEx rejected two rights issue applications which were viewed as unfair to minority shareholders. This signalled to the market that the regulators' position had become less lenient towards market abuse.

Both examples demonstrate that the SFC is effective when exercising the statutory market conduct function pursuant to the MoU, the *Securities and Futures Ordinance* (Hong Kong) and the Stock Connect schemes.

11.3.1.3 Financial Stability

While market conduct collaboration has been effective, there have been no instances of financial stability cooperation. One explanation is the absence of financial stability and systemic risk mitigation provisions in the MoU.

This does not imply that the SFC and CSRC will not act to manage financial stability in their respective jurisdictions – where in line with international financial regulatory standards both have systemic risk mandates. For example, the *Securities and Futures Ordinance* (Hong Kong) states that a regulatory objective of the SFC is to reduce systemic risks in the securities and futures industry and to assist the financial secretary in maintaining the financial stability of Hong Kong.[28] Instead, this can be explained by there being no obligation to assist the other jurisdiction for financial stability purposes. This is different, however, from the financial stability objective of the SFC within Hong Kong.

Traditionally securities regulators were not financial stability regulators – this was the remit of the central bank. Nonetheless, the trend towards giving securities regulators a financial stability mandate began to change following the 1987 Black Monday stock market crash and was formalised in the first set of international objectives and principles of securities regulation. These were drafted in 1998 by the International Organization of Securities Commissions (IOSCO) in the aftermath of the Asian financial crisis and were reinforced in the wake of the GFC. Financial history suggests that the pre-Asian financial crisis approach is indeed the modus operandi in Hong Kong, with the HKMA being the financial stability/systemic regulator, not the

---

[26] Section 5(1)(d), *Securities and Futures Ordinance (Cap 571)* (Hong Kong); Chapter X, *Securities Law of the People's Republic of China.*

[27] China Securities Regulatory Commission, 'CSRC Successful Crackdown on the First Cross-Border Manipulation Case under Shanghai–Hong Kong Stock Connect' (News Release, 21 November 2016).

[28] Sections 4(e) and (f), *Securities and Futures Ordinance (Cap 571).*

SFC.[29] At best the SFC acts in a supportive role to the HKMA's statutory financial stability mandate.[30]

11.3.2 *Bond Connect*

11.3.2.1 Regulatory Cooperation

Bond Connect was launched by the HKMA and the People's Bank of China (PBOC) in May 2017. The scheme enables mainland and overseas investors to trade bonds in Hong Kong and Mainland China through financial infrastructure institutions.[31] Currently, only Northbound trading is permitted, with Southbound trading to become operational in the future.[32]

Similar to the Stock Connect schemes, an MoU has been entered into between the HKMA and the PBOC for Bond Connect.[33] The purposes of the MoU are stated as follows:

> The Parties aim to enhance the information sharing and other cooperation arrangements between the Parties, to, as far as possible, ensure transparency of information and to prevent supervisory discord, regulatory arbitrage and other related cross-boundary illegal activities. The Parties will within their respective statutory functions and remit, use their best efforts to coordinate relevant institutions to ensure full compliance with and execution of the relevant laws and regulations of both places.

11.3.2.2 Financial Stability

In contrast to the purpose of the Stock Connect MoU, the purpose of Bond Connect MoU does not explicitly specify regulatory functions, except insofar as they are specified by statute. As Hong Kong's Bond Connect regulator, the HKMA's statutory functions are to promote the general stability and effective working of the banking system (in Hong Kong), which includes to promote and encourage proper standards of conduct and prudent business practices, suppress or aid in suppressing illegal, dishonourable or improper practices, cooperate and assist with recognised financial services supervisory authorities and take all reasonable steps to ensure that any banking business is carried out with integrity, prudence and a proper degree of professional competence.[34] The HKMA's financial stability function is also pursuant to the *Exchange Fund Ordinance*, which empowers the HKMA (that is, the financial secretary delegates this function to the HKMA) to maintain the financial stability and integrity of the monetary and financial systems of Hong Kong.[35]

---

[29] During the Asian financial crisis and the GFC, see Douglas W. Arner, Berry F. C. Hsu, Antonio M. da Roza, Franciso A. da Roza, Syren Johnstone and Paul Lejot, 'The Global Financial Crisis and the Future of Financial Regulation in Hong Kong' (Asian Institute of International Financial Law, AIIFL Working Paper No 4, 2009); and Andrew Sheng, *From Asian to Global Financial Crisis: An Asian Regulator's View of Unfettered Finance in the 1990's and 2000's* (Cambridge University Press, 2009).

[30] For a discussion of its role as a derivatives market regulator, see generally Gibson (n 15) 331–2.

[31] For details, see Securities and Futures Commission, 'Joint Announcement of China Securities Regulatory Commission and Securities and Futures Commission' (News and Announcements, 10 April 2014).

[32] Northbound – overseas investors via Hong Kong investing in the China Interbank bond market. Southbound – mainland investors investing in Hong Kong bonds.

[33] China Banking Regulatory Authority and Hong Kong Monetary Authority, 'Memorandum of Understanding between the People's Bank of China and Hong Kong Monetary Authority on Strengthening Supervisory Cooperation under Bond Connect' (Translation, 30 June2017).

[34] Section 7(2), *Banking Ordinance (Cap 155)*.

[35] Section 3(1A), *Exchange Fund Ordinance (Cap 66)*.

The statutory functions of the PBOC in relation to Bond Connect are to supervise and administer the interbank lending market and the interbank bond market, regulate and supervise the interbank foreign exchange market, take responsibility for statistics, undertake investigations, undertake analysis and forecasts concerning the banking industry and engage in international banking operations as the central bank.[36] More generally, the PBOC is to guard against and eliminate financial risks and maintain financial stability.[37] Thus the PBOC has the statutory functions of a central bank with limited banking supervisory powers that are limited to financial stability.

11.3.2.3 Market Conduct

The reference to illegal activities as contained in the 'purposes' of the MoU implies a market conduct function. In contrast to the HKMA having a market conduct function (limited to the banking sector), the PBOC does not have a statutory market conduct function. The absence of a PBOC market conduct function creates regulatory underlap – that is, the regulator has a mandate under the MoU despite the fact that it does not have the capacity or expertise to fulfil such a regulatory mandate.

Market conduct functions are not normally exercised by central banks, which are designed to manage financial stability and systemic risk. Central banks that are not banking or integrated financial sector regulators are designed to manage monetary policy. At a minimum, Bond Connect is supported by financial stability supervision pertaining to monetary policy and banking sector supervision. This creates another regulatory underlap for the PBOC, which is not a banking supervisor and therefore lacks the relevant banking sector financial stability capacity. By contrast, the HKMA has the requisite capacity as Hong Kong's de facto central bank and banking regulator to discharge the financial stability function pertaining to monetary policy and the banking sector.

These regulatory underlaps are compounded by the preamble to the MoU which refers to 'prudential risk management'. This implies a financial stability function and creates a friction with market conduct as to which function takes priority.

11.3.3 *The Necessity of Reform Following Stock and Bond Connect*

The preceding analysis illustrates some of the weaknesses pertaining to Hong Kong's sectoral model when regulating the Stock and Bond Connect schemes. It is argued that the Twin Peaks model is more effective than the sectoral and integrated models in overcoming this underlap when the financial stability regulator has both a microprudential and macroprudential regulatory purview. This is because the microprudential and macroprudential functions can be intertwined within one regulator.

For example, within the Bank of England the microprudential regulator is a member of the macroprudential regulator. This creates regulatory microprudential and macroprudential overlap within the Twin Peaks financial stability regulator. Applying this design to the PBOC, the market conduct underlap would be rectified by the Twin Peaks model because of the presence of an integrated market conduct regulator. This would require amendments to the Bond Connect MoU and statutory mandates to clearly define each regulator's role and function.

---

[36] Article 4, *Law of the People's Republic of China on the People's Bank of China.*
[37] Article 2, *Law of the People's Republic of China on the People's Bank of China.*

Certain eligible bonds that fall within each jurisdiction's securities sector regulations create regulatory underlap between: (i) HKMA and SFC; (ii) PBOC and CSRC; (iii) HKMA and CSRC; and (iv) PBOC and SFC. There are no MoUs between the HKMA and CSRC or between the PBOC and the SFC.

Current MoUs correspond with regulators within the same sector, for example, the SFC and CSRC. In this context, the market conduct function is the purview of the securities regulators, the SFC and CSRC. Discharging the market conduct function and therefore mitigating regulatory underlap when regulating Bond Connect is, however, contingent on cooperation between the HKMA and PBOC and, critically, the data-sharing arrangements between the regulators. The absence of the PBOC market conduct capacity limits the ability of the HKMA and PBOC to discharge this function regardless of cooperation and data-sharing arrangements.

This design flaw can be overcome if the Twin Peaks model is operational in both jurisdictions because each market conduct regulator can rely upon cooperation arrangements in the inter-agency and cross-boundary MoUs – similar to arrangements between the SFC and CSRC.[38] Sharing cross-boundary information between Twin Peaks' conduct regulators mitigates the incidence of underlap for bonds, which traditionally fall within the securities sector.

If the sectoral regulatory functions of the PBOC are subject to regulatory underlap, this will impede cooperation between the HKMA and PBOC, thereby compromising the discharge of the regulatory functions relating to cross-boundary issues.

These design flaws are not limited to the sectoral model. In the United Kingdom during the GFC, the integrated model also suffered from regulatory underlap. The Turner Review concluded that macroprudential underlap existed because the integrated regulator, the Financial Services Authority (FSA), was essentially a microprudential regulator and the Bank of England a monetary policy regulator. Macroprudential underlap existed because neither regulator had a mandate, or the capacity, to regulate systemic risk.

This design flaw is a characteristic of sectoral regulators, for example the PBOC with Mainland China's sectoral regulators.[39] One way to remedy this flaw is to merge the central bank and prudential regulator into a 'super' regulator[40] and redefine the character of the relationship, similar to the design of the Monetary Authority of Singapore.[41]

The macroprudential underlap between the PBOC and the China Banking and Insurance Regulatory Commission is analogous to the Bank of England and FSA, which needs to be addressed because monetary and banking sector financial stability are interrelated.[42] Adopting an integrated financial model will not overcome this flaw as the design can cause aspects of financial stability regulation to be neglected.[43]

---

[38] This is not the Stock Connect MoU. See China Securities Regulatory Commission and Securities and Futures Commission, 'Memorandum of Regulatory Cooperation' (1993).

[39] For example, China Banking Regulatory Commission, China Securities Regulatory Commission and China Insurance Regulatory Commission.

[40] To be analogous to the Monetary Authority of Singapore this would require merging the PBOC with the market conduct regulator – the CSRC – and the banking regulator – the China Banking and Insurance Regulatory Commission.

[41] Adair Turner, *The Turner Review: A Regulatory Response to the Global Banking Crisis* (Financial Services Authority, 2009), 84.

[42] See Gibson (n 15) 349; and Michael W. Taylor, 'The Road from "Twin Peaks" – and the Way Back' (2009) 16 *Connecticut Insurance Law Journal* 61, 83–4.

[43] Taylor (n 42) 94.

11.4 HONG KONG'S FINTECH FUTURE DRIVEN BY THE NEW ECONOMY

11.4.1 *Background*

FinTechs involves the use of technology in financial services.[44] It thus includes traditional participants, such as banks and insurers, and new economy companies (often called FinTechs). For example, the payment space is dominated by Visa, MasterCard and China Union Pay as well as new challenger FinTechs such as Stripe and Ripple, and 'BigTechs' such as e-commerce giants (like Alibaba and Amazon), social networks (like Tencent and Facebook) or sharing economy businesses (like Uber and Grab), which have varying levels of involvement in providing financial services (TechFin).

The rapid rise of FinTech start-ups and TechFin companies has led to debates on the most suitable regulatory architecture. Any legitimate solution needs to balance traditional regulatory mandates and functions while providing enough flexibility to foster innovation and develop the new economy.

In the context of Hong Kong being an international financial centre, establishing a Twin Peaks architecture is warranted as this can be levered as a competitive advantage to promote FinTech. There is plenty of scope for leverage because the FinTech market is proportionally small as compared with the rest of the financial sector.[45] Hong Kong's FinTech market size is nonetheless growing rapidly and attracting an outsized share of investment as compared with Japan and Singapore.[46] FinTech market growth, the Stock and Bond Connect schemes and the ongoing integration with Mainland China all have the potential to strengthen Hong Kong as an international financial centre for FinTech.

If implemented, it can be argued that the Twin Peaks architecture would improve Hong Kong's ranking among jurisdictions benefiting from a favourable regulatory regime for FinTech. In turn this would enrich Hong Kong as an IPO listing venue, given its pro-technology regulatory agenda and the liquidity brought by Hong Kong's capital market integration with Mainland China, while becoming an integral component of FinTech industry development.

This has already begun, with the HKEx moving forward with a range of listing reforms to enhance its reputation as a capital-raising market for innovative 'new economy' companies.[47]

11.4.2 *Comparative Regulatory Approaches to FinTech*

The regulation of FinTech poses challenges when balancing the policy considerations of innovation, inclusion and growth with the regulatory considerations of consumer protection, market behaviour, market integrity (including anti-money laundering and counter-financing of terrorism) and financial stability. To better understand the challenges faced by regulators, this section will examine some of the FinTech regulatory approaches in the United States, Mainland China and Hong Kong.

---

[44] Dirk A. Zetzsche, Ross P. Buckley, Douglas W. Arner and Janos N. Barberis, 'From FinTech to TechFin: The Regulatory Challenges of Data-Driven Finance' (EBI Working Paper Series No 6, 2017), 12.

[45] Accenture, 'The Win–Win Proposition – Why APAC's Fintech Momentum Is Driven by Partnerships' (2019), 3; and see generally HK Financial Services Development Council, 'Overview of Hong Kong Financial Services Industry' (May 2018).

[46] Ibid.

[47] HKEX, 'Hong Kong's Listing Regime Enters New Era, Featuring Emerging and Innovative Firms' (News Release, 24 April 2018).

The Office of the Comptroller of the Currency (OCC) is the US national banking regulator responsible for regulating FinTech banking service providers. In 2017 the OCC established the Office of Innovation, which stated from the onset that stringent regulations applying to banks will apply to newly chartered FinTech banks.[48] The OCC refers to the benefits of market growth in the context of 'responsible innovation' as follows: 'The use of new or improved financial products, services, and processes to meet the evolving needs of consumers, businesses, and communities in a manner consistent with sound risk management and aligned with the bank's overall business strategy.'[49]

Mainland China takes a similar approach to regulating FinTech and TechFin banking services. In 2015 Alipay, Tencent and Baidu, among others, obtained licences from the CBRC for their online banks. Tencent's WeBank specialises in personal micro-loans, having dispersed RMB800 million before obtaining a banking licence.[50] Alipay's MYbank, part of Ant Financial, provides loans from leveraging Alibaba's e-commerce business, limits loans to RMB5 million and has over 17 million micro and small business customers, with non-performing loans purportedly being 1 per cent, lower than the national average of 1.74 per cent.[51] These TechFin banking models offer innovative and inclusive finance that is not available from the traditional banking system.

Hong Kong has been rethinking its approach vis-à-vis regulation in the context of FinTech. A number of initiatives have been launched to assist regulators understand FinTechs better and for market participants to learn about their regulatory responsibilities. This is known as the 'ecosystem' approach.[52] For example, Hong Kong's 'FinTech Contact Point' was established by the SFC in 2016. Theoretically, the SFC's FinTech Contact Point is designed to enhance communications with businesses involved in the development and application of FinTech and RegTech, to facilitate an understanding of the current regulatory regime and to enable the SFC to stay abreast of developments.[53] In practice, the SFC's approach is policy-based.

The HKMA has established a FinTech Facilitation Office to support the development of the FinTech ecosystem.[54] Functions of the FinTech Facilitation Office are to act as a platform to exchange ideas among key stakeholders, be an interface between market participants and regulators, be an initiator of industry research and act as a facilitator to nurture talent to meet Hong Kong's FinTech needs.[55]

The approaches in the United States, Mainland China and Hong Kong all seek to balance regulatory objectives to support the evolution of FinTech to promote innovation, market growth and financial inclusion. It is when 'new economy' financial entities grow to a level to compete

---

[48] Thomas J. Curry, 'Remarks by Thomas J. Curry Comptroller of the Currency' (Lendlt USA 2017, New York, 6 March 2017), 6.

[49] Office of the Comptroller of the Currency, 'Recommendations and Decisions for Implementing a Responsible Innovation Framework' (October 2016), 3.

[50] Deng Yuanyuan, 'Alibaba, Baidu and Tencent and Their New Online Banks' (CKGSB Knowledge, 2 December 2015).

[51] Ibid; 'Jack Ma's Bank Expanding into Underservices Sector', *China Daily* (undated, 4 July 2017), 2, www.chinadaily .com.cn/business/2017-07/04/content_29982650.htm; and 'MYBank Teams Up with Chinese Policy Bank to Boost Financial Inclusion in Xiong'an', *China Banking News* (3 September 2019).

[52] Daniel Morgan et al, 'The Future of RegTech for Regulators – Adopting a Holistic Approach to a Digital Era Regulator' (Transatlantic Policy Working Group FinTech, June 2017), 8.

[53] Financial Conduct Authority and Securities and Futures Commission, 'Co-operation Agreement' (12 May 2017), 4 [2.1.2].

[54] Hong Kong Monetary Authority, 'FinTech Facilitation Office (FFO)', www.hkma.gov.hk/media/eng/doc/key-func tions/ifc/fintech/FCAS_2020_21_JD_HKMA_FFO.pdf.

[55] Ibid.

with traditional financial institutions (such as Mainland Chinese TechFins with state-owned banks) that financial stability regulators tend to enforce industry-standard regulations.

Notwithstanding this approach, when a non-traditional market grows to the extent where there is mainstream and mass-market adoption of services, regulators have also been known to implement lighter-touch regulatory standards than those applicable to traditional financial sectors (for example, stored-value facilities in Hong Kong).

Although relaxed or inadequate market conduct/consumer protection regulation can be perceived as an inept approach, subjecting small and medium-sized enterprise (SME) FinTechs to the reporting and regulatory requirements analogous to that of traditional finance companies (such as banks) is simply not feasible. Regulatory challenges abound when deciding on the means to gather the quality and quantity of data to achieve regulatory considerations while at the same time facilitating policy considerations which require a light-touch regulatory approach for innovation and the growth of FinTech markets.

11.4.3 *Recalibrating the Twin Peaks Model for FinTech*

To ascertain the most suitable FinTech regulatory architecture, this section compares Hong Kong's sectoral model with the Twin Peaks model. The integrated model is not considered on the basis of the preceding discussions, which highlighted design flaws (such as regulatory underlap).

11.4.3.1 Regulating InsurTechs

There is a convergence between the traditional financial sector and FinTech. FinTech has become an integral component of, if not a new driving force behind, traditional financial companies. For example, Goldman Sachs has been described by its former chief executive officer (CEO) as a technology company (FinTech), with the current CEO forecasting enormous technological change in the industry. This has led to distinctions between traditional finance and FinTech business models becoming 'blurred'. Blurring and overlapping business models are nothing new to the financial sector or its regulation. The rise of universal banking, the introduction of the integrated regulatory model and the repeal of delineating legislation such as the Glass–Steagall Act (United States) are testament to this fact. FinTech is redefining the financial services sector by enabling new types of business models.

For example, the first insurance technology (InsurTech) company to seek a listing in Hong Kong was Zhong An Online Property and Casualty Insurance, a subsidiary of the largest online insurer in Mainland China. InsurTechs fall under the regulatory purview of the Insurance Authority (IA), which is the lead supervisor of insurance companies and InsurTechs, including activities that fall within the purview of other sectoral regulators. Nonetheless, if wealth management products are offered by an InsurTech, SFC licences are required, deposit-taking activities require HKMA authorisation and Mandatory Providence Fund Authority registration would be required to sell pension products.[56]

This creates a number of cross-sectoral issues for Hong Kong's sectoral regulators, especially when issuing products that blur regulatory boundaries. An infamous example of a product that blurred sectoral boundaries is the Lehman Minibond. This product was subject to regulatory

---

[56] Douglas Arner, Evan Gibson and Janos Barberis, 'FinTech and Its Regulation in Hong Kong' in Douglas W. Arner, Wai Yee Wan, Andrew Godwin, Wei Shen and Evan Gibson (eds) *Research Handbook on Asian Financial Law* (Edward Elgar, 2020), 446.

underlap which theoretically should not have existed because both the HKMA and SFC were responsible regulators. Which regulator was responsible depended on which regulator was designated as the lead regulator of either the Minibond issuer or the Minibond intermediary.

In practice, non-insurance-based products issued by InsurTechs could also lead to regulatory underlap because of the complexities of Hong Kong's sectoral model. The emergence of cross-sectoral products, including those sourced from FinTechs and TechFins, has undermined the sectoral demarcations between regulators.[57] Regulating such products raises issues relating to the cross-sectoral market conduct function, which was the basis of subsequent investigations into the Minibond incident.

Hong Kong has several cross-sectoral coordinating mechanisms to overcome such issues. Notably, the Council of Financial Regulators (CFR) is responsible for, inter alia, information-sharing to contribute to the effectiveness of regulations and the supervision of financial institutions.[58] Responsibilities of the CFR theoretically encapsulate FinTech market conduct and prudential regulatory functions. In practice, the CFR can be exposed to sectoral flaws appertaining to the regulators. The fact that separate Minibond reports were issued by the HKMA and SFC undermines the effectiveness of the CFR and its ability to manage cross-sectoral regulation and information-sharing.[59]

The Twin Peaks model is designed to overcome cross-sectoral issues associated with the regulatory functions. Each regulator is 'integrated' across all traditional and non-traditional financial sectors, and the regulatory functions are isolated. The Twin Peaks model addresses the reality that regulations cover a wide range of financial institutions and products, which cannot be neatly compartmentalised into specific financial sectors or silos.[60] This applies to the market conduct function, in the case of the Minibond incident, and to financial stability (that is, systemic risks).

Being comprised of members that are predominantly sectoral regulators leaves the CFR highly susceptible to its members' regulatory underlap. In contrast, the design of the Twin Peaks model isolates the market conduct and financial stability functions among independent integrated regulators, with each regulator statutorily empowered to discharge their regulatory function. Cross-sectoral functional underlap is less likely to arise under the Twin Peaks architecture by comparison with the CFR.[61]

The key distinction of the Twin Peaks model, when compared with the sectoral model, is the 'integrated' design of each regulator having an independent regulatory function. For instance, financial stability is 'integrated' because it is concerned with detecting and preventing system-wide risks, regardless of the market or institution, with a focus on the interconnectedness of financial markets.[62] Market conduct is concerned, inter alia, with information asymmetries between management and consumers, regardless of the market or institution, with a primary focus on the honesty and transparency (disclosure) requirements arising from this relationship.[63]

---

[57] Richard K. Abrams and Michael W. Taylor, 'Issues in the Unification of Financial Sector Supervision' (IMF Working Paper, WP/00/213, 2000), 10; and Charles Goodhart, Philipp Hartmann, David Llewellyn, Liliana Rojas-Suárez and Steven Weisbrod, *Financial Regulation: Why, How and Where Now?* (Routledge, 1998), 143.

[58] Council of Financial Regulators, 'Terms of Reference' (2006), fso.gov.hk/pdf/CFR-TOR%20_Sep06_.pdf.

[59] See Gibson (n 15) 219.

[60] Michael W. Taylor, '"Twin Peaks Revisited"... A Second Chance for Regulatory Reform' (Centre for the Study of Financial Innovation 89, 2009), 8.

[61] Arner, Gibson and Barberis (n 56) 447–50.

[62] Taylor (n 60) 10.

[63] Ibid. This is an adaptation and reinterpretation.

11.4.3.2 Small and Medium FinTechs

Hong Kong is facing increasing competition from Mainland China and Singapore for FinTech companies. This competition has provided the impetus for policies that promote FinTech in Hong Kong. For instance, the Financial Leaders Forum held its first meeting in August 2017 to discuss the development and strengthening of Hong Kong as an international financial centre via listing platform reforms, notably to facilitate 'new economy' offerings.[64] Seeking a listing on the HKEx requires substantial resources. However, not all FinTechs have the backing of large parent companies; in fact, recent history suggests that most FinTechs will be private start-ups – SMEs – with limited resources.

When operating in an environment with high regulatory compliance and reporting burdens, the viability of FinTech SMEs is inhibited. Accordingly, a light-touch regulatory approach is required that promotes capital raising, innovation and market growth. For these reasons, private company SME FinTechs are the most difficult to regulate. Market conduct regulation is imperative to protect consumers and to support capital raising and market growth by reinforcing consumer confidence. Financial stability is also an important regulatory consideration when markets scale and become interconnected with the broader financial system.

It is important to appreciate that the innovative characteristic of SME FinTechs is not confined to stimulatory policy because history has shown that the regulatory functions will always be applicable to any form of innovative finance. For example, when Hong Kong eased banking restrictions in the late 1970s this stimulated the growth of innovative SME finance companies, deposit and loan companies, which at the time were unregulated because they were not considered banks. Despite the introduction of regulations and supervision in the early 1980s, this did not stave off a deposit and loan company crisis a few years later. The consequences of the deposit and loan crisis were catastrophic as contagion quickly spread to the banking system, triggering widespread financial instability.

In summary, after banking regulations were eased, this became the catalyst for the inception, innovation and growth in the deposit and loan company market. Conversely, the timing and scope of introducing a regulatory framework for deposit and loan companies proved ineffective. For regulators this dilemma is compounded because imposing current market regulations may impede the market growth of innovative products and services. The deposit and loan crisis emphasises that regulating innovative financial institutions/products based on traditional regulatory approaches may fail to discharge statutory and regulatory functions. In the context of FinTechs, the challenge for regulators is equally perplexing. How can SME FinTechs be efficiently and effectively regulated to discharge statutory and regulatory functions while promoting innovation and market growth? The answer lies in the use of smart regulation and data.

11.5 IMPLEMENTATION OF SMART REGULATION FOR A REGTECH ERA

11.5.1 *Smart Regulation and the Regulatory Functions*

Smart regulation and data are an effective and efficient means to achieve a light-touch regulatory approach. Permissioned distributed ledger technology (DLT) is infrastructure that enables

---

[64] The Financial Leaders Forum was established to deliberate on strategic and forward-looking proposals by government departments and other relevant organisations with a view to enhancing monetary stability, financial safety and market quality. See Legco, 'Legislative Council Panel on Financial Affairs – 2017 Policy Address: Policy Initiatives of the Financial Services and Treasury Bureau' (October 2017), [5].

smart regulation and data gathering to be synthesised on a single platform. This RegTech infrastructure enables the real-time monitoring of financial activity between regulators and regulated entities to strengthen market conduct surveillance. In comparison to traditional data-gathering techniques, digital data can be gathered far more expeditiously and with greater precision.[65] Potential fraud is reduced as a full transaction history can be established and transparency is increased because transactions can be verified.[66] Scalability is possible and is highly desirable for monitoring the financial stability of markets.[67]

To increase the efficiency of RegTech, supervision and auditing can be wholly or partially automated.[68] When supported by permissioned DLT infrastructure, this fundamentally shifts the traditional regulatory approach. When processes are automated, compliance costs can be reduced significantly.[69] Automation and permissioned DLT have the potential to overcome the limitations of traditional reporting and regulatory requirements, which are otherwise too oner-ous for SME FinTech markets to grow and innovate. FinTechs can lever technology to meet reporting requirements and, in turn, regulators can design supplementary light-touch RegTech infrastructure to better adapt to FinTechs' reporting capacities. With this approach, the regula-tory framework more closely mirrors the structure of the FinTech industry.[70]

RegTech can harvest deeper and more accurate data by automating standardised reporting requirements and verification in real time to become a seamless and resource-light process.[71] This is primarily achieved through supplementary infrastructures such as application program interfaces (APIs), smart contracts, artificial intelligence and automation designed by regulators (lawyers, economists, engineers and coders). APIs can collect data with the aid of artificial intelligence to detect anomalies, notably from permissioned DLT, or can be introduced to harvest and mine data directly from FinTechs on a real-time on-going basis.

One example of reporting RegTech infrastructure is the Austrian Reporting Services GmbH. This RegTech infrastructure has been developed in conjunction with the banking community to move away from static 'template-based' reporting to an 'input-based' approach.[72] Essentially the infrastructure standardises contracts (that is, smart contracts) to deliver micro-level data that is enriched with additional attributes that enable regulators to apply data analytical tools without

---

[65] Hong Kong Applied Science and Technology Research Institute, 'Whitepaper on Distributed Ledger Technology' (11 November 2016), 16; HK Financial Services Development Council, 'Hong Kong – Building Trust Using Distributed Ledger Technology' (FSDC Paper No 30, May 2017), 30; Bank for International Settlements, 'Distributed Ledger Technology in Payment, Clearing, and Settlement – An Analytical Framework' (February 2017), 18; World Economic Forum, *The Future of Financial Infrastructure – An Ambitious Look at How Blockchain Can Reshape Financial Services* (World Economic Forum, August 2016), 21; and David Mills et al, 'Distributed Ledger Technology in Payments, Clearing, and Settlement' (Federal Reserve Bank, Finance and Economics Discussion Series, 2016), 20.

[66] Hong Kong Applied Science and Technology Research Institute (n 65) 16; HK Financial Services Development Council (n 65) 30; Government Office for Science, *Distributed Ledger Technology: Beyond Block Chain – A Report by the UK Government Chief Scientific Adviser* (London, 2016), 65; Bank for International Settlements (n 65) 19; World Economic Forum (n 65) 19; and Mills et al (n 65) 20 and 26.

[67] Bank for International Settlements (n 65) 18; World Economic Forum (n 65) 23; and Hong Kong Applied Science and Technology Research Institute (n 65) 9.

[68] HK Financial Services Development Council (n 65) 33.

[69] World Economic Forum (n 65) 28.

[70] Taylor (n 60) 3.

[71] Hong Kong Applied Science and Technology Research Institute (n 65) 17; Mills et al (n 65) 28–9; and World Economic Forum (n 65) 28.

[72] Daniel Morgan et al, 'The Future of RegTech for Regulators – Adopting a Holistic Approach to a Digital Era Regulator' (Transatlantic Policy Working Group FinTech, June 2017), 12.

increasing administrative burdens on regulators and regulated entities.[73] Using smart contracts is an ideal way to replace traditional regulatory reports.

To support this regulatory process and RegTech infrastructure, the right regulatory model must be effective yet light touch. In this context, the Twin Peaks model which separates the regulatory functions of market conduct and financial stability, matches the regulatory requirements of the FinTech industry. Market conduct surveillance is essential to encourage market confidence, which in turn underpins market growth.[74] Prudential supervision – focusing on areas such as liquidity, capital and leverage requirements – is the foundation of financial stability. Both functions are critical for sustainable market development, which can be bolstered by ongoing monitoring on a real-time basis.

RegTech prudential supervision is capable of identifying microprudential financial stability risks from data gathered by permissioned DLT reporting, with the support of APIs and risk mapping.[75] The burdens on the FinTech entity and the financial stability regulator are negligible once the systems are established and operational.

A Twin Peaks market-conduct supervisor can lever data gathered from the permissioned DLT and APIs. Real-time compliance with conduct regulations could be assessed by applying network analysis tools that are analogous to existing applications. For example, the SFC conducts real-time market surveillance by using various software applications (data analytics) to identify misconduct.

In this context the macroprudential financial stability function plays a lesser role but should not be overlooked. Macroprudential financial stability data gathered by the permissioned DLT and smart contracts enable the monitoring of market developments. Smart contracts can be designed for annual reporting requirements that includes macroprudential data. Only in an impending crisis or in crisis situations is real-time prudential data and regulatory invention necessary. Nonetheless, on-going macroprudential data will be available to the Twin Peaks financial stability regulator because of the real-time data-gathering capabilities of the RegTech infrastructure. Purpose-designed crisis APIs and smart contracts deployed by the financial stability regulator should be designed to gather relevant data when systemic risk is volatile.

The incidence of data gaps and underlap are reduced when efficient RegTech infrastructure is deployed with the Twin Peaks model. Independent regulatory functions enable regulators to accurately target micro-data to better understand markets, products and entities. The regulators are capable of simultaneously addressing market conduct and financial stability risk, more precisely and in real time, by performing on-going calibration at the product, entity and market levels while maintaining a light-touch regulatory approach. Bespoke regulatory analysis is possible for real-time monitoring of market growth, product and service innovation, and market penetration. The Twin Peaks regulators have the capacity to calibrate their FinTech regulatory–functional purviews to better reflect the market while promoting capital raising, innovation and growth.

From a regulatory cooperation perspective, APIs are capable of coordinating the financial stability and market conduct regulators' data requirements and provide accountability protocols.

---

[73] Ibid.

[74] Jeffrey Carmichael, 'The Framework for Financial Supervision: Macro and Micro Issues' (Bank for International Settlements, Conference, Beijing China, 1–2 March 1999), 143.

[75] Risk mapping is essentially giant matrices of bilateral exposure data assembled from unified databases that track and record large sets of financial institution exposures, non-traditional financial institutions' exposures and interconnections between financial infrastructure and markets: see Stephen G Cecchetti, Ingo Fender and Patrick McGuire, 'Towards a Global Risk Map' (BIS Working Papers No 309, May 2010), 14.

RegTech algorithms can be written to overcome data conflicts-of-interest with regulated market participants.[76] Regulators will need to assess the financial viability of permissioned DLT RegTech, supporting infrastructures and the scope of their regulatory purview by conducting cost–benefit analyses.[77] New regulations and guidance will have to be drafted by each Twin Peaks regulator to direct SME FinTechs' compliance with automated and data-gathering requirements.[78]

11.5.2 *The Importance of Data*

FinTechs, especially those owned by technology companies, have the capacity to rival traditional financial institutions. Distinctions are becoming more prominent in respect of TechFin business model drivers (that is, monetising data).[79] Fundamentally, the financial aspect of traditional finance, FinTech and TechFin business models is based on data-driven transaction agglomeration, which should therefore form the basis of any regulatory approach. For example, the online insurance-based company, Zhong An Online Property and Casualty Insurance, levers artificial intelligence, machine learning and big data to bolster its services.[80] FinTechs and TechFins monetise data harvesting and mining because of the very nature of their business models.

Financial market regulation is facing mounting challenges to manage information and data-reporting requirements.[81] This is a burden for regulated entities and regulators which is causing market inefficiencies.[82] RegTech is playing an ever-increasing role in overcoming these reporting challenges.

Regulations and regulators tend to focus on data from one jurisdiction, financial institutions and financial infrastructures – such as the electronic trading platforms for the Stock and Bond Connect schemes. As the complexity of the financial system increases, especially with the rise of technology-driven entrants, fragmentation is taking place in terms of market participants, which strains regulators' limited resources including their monitoring capacity and the ability to gather, synthesise and analyse data.[83]

This undermines the market conduct function. For example, the regulation of market behaviour is undermined as regulators with partial data are not able to address all incidences of market misconduct, thereby eroding market transparency and efficiency. Moreover, market conduct regulatory practices outside the securities sector are archaic. To overcome these regulatory design flaws, jurisdictions need more effective and efficient RegTech data-gathering systems, that is, RegTech that enables the seamless transfer of essential regulatory data which is not overly burdensome on market participants and regulators.

---

[76] Bank for International Settlements (n 65) 4–5.
[77] Ibid, 20; and World Economic Forum (n 65) 30.
[78] Mills et al (n 65) 24; and Bank for International Settlements (n 65) 21.
[79] Zetzsche et al (n 44) 12.
[80] Steven Price, 'Insurance-Tech Typhoon Zhong An Is Coming, Western Fintech Are Bracing' (Good Audience, Medium, 23 September 2018).
[81] World Economic Forum (n 65) 28.
[82] Ibid.
[83] Prasanna Gai and Sujit Kapadia, 'Contagion in Financial Networks' (Bank of England, Working Paper No 383, 2010), 6.

11.5.3 *RegTech Options*

Data gathering on the scale required for financial markets requires the substantial development of infrastructure analogous to that of stock exchanges. There is, however, no consensus on a universal design for infrastructure to gather financial data.

Some of the prevalent types of data-gathering infrastructure are public company electronic filing systems, information repositories, APIs and DLTs.

- **Electronic filing systems** for publicly traded companies are essential for satisfying continuous disclosure requirements and are a condition of listing on public stock exchanges. This type of data gathering is the exception rather than the norm as data availability is contingent on highly regulated public exchanges.[84] The regulatory scope is limited to large publicly listed companies and is unsuitable for SMEs because of the onerous filing and compliance requirements. Electronic filing systems are nonetheless capable of being designed to accommodate the less onerous reporting and compliance requirements of SMEs.
- **Information repositories** have been created for specific markets. For example, the HKMA monitors OTC derivative markets by analysing information provided by entities to the OTC Derivatives Trade Repository – a entralized registry that maintains a database of records.[85] Information can be submitted digitally, which is essential for market surveillance and maintaining financial stability.[86] This type of RegTech infrastructure is a simpler version of the public company electronic filing system that is designed to enable regulated market participants to satisfy reporting and compliance requirements.
- **Application Programme Interfaces** are a set of commands (that is, functions and procedures) that allow access to data or a service in order to provide greater functionality to existing software.[87] APIs underpin FinTech as a means of gathering data to develop digital financial services. The use of APIs in the context of RegTech would most likely be relegated to a supportive role for RegTech data gathering infrastructure hubs, such as DLT.

11.5.4 *Distributed Ledger Technology*

11.5.4.1 Regulatory Applications

DLT, of which Blockchain (effectively a combination of DLT and cryptography, and the technological structure underlying BitCoin) is one form, can potentially enable vast quantities of data to be digitally transferred, updated and stored efficiently and securely, particularly when combined with automation and smart contracts.[88] The application of DLT as RegTech infrastructure, a type of electronic filing system, is relatively new but not unprecedented. DLT facilitates instantaneous transaction settlements, which is desirable for regulators seeking to increase efficiencies while reducing risk. For example, the Nasdaq stock exchange uses DLT (Linq) on a limited basis to record private securities transactions and the Australian Stock

---

[84] OTC derivative markets are also suitable for this type of data analytics.
[85] Hong Kong Monetary Authority, 'Principles for Financial Market Infrastructures: Disclosure for OTC Derivatives Trade Repository of HKMA' (9 September 2015), 2.
[86] Ibid.
[87] Payments UK, 'APIs – What Do They Mean for Payments? A Briefing from Payment UK' (April 2016), 5.
[88] Hong Kong Applied Science and Technology Research Institute (n 65) 5 and 17.

Exchange has announced that it will be replacing its Clearing House Electronic Subregister System (CHESS) securities settlement system with a Blockchain-based system in 2023. The HKEx has also announced that it is planning to develop a Blockchain settlement system.

DLT has been acknowledged by the public and private sector as having the potential to substantially increase regulatory efficiencies and the capacity of regulators to discharge the functions of mitigating systemic risk and market misconduct across the financial system.[89]

11.5.4.2 Permissionless Distributed Ledger Technology

In some cases, such as for BitCoin and Ethereum, DLT is designed around a public permissionless platform whereby information can be updated by market participants, each of whom has access to an identical ledger on a distributed database. The Bank for International Settlements (BIS) describes this type of DLT as 'the processes and related technologies that enable nodes in a network (or arrangement) to securely propose, validate and record state changes (or updates) to a synchronised ledger that is distributed across the network's nodes'.[90]

Risk management is essential for the effective operation of DLT. By contrast with payment and securities transaction DLT applications, when a DLT is designed to function as a data-gathering medium, the principal risks are operational and security. The sharing of data by market participants can nonetheless create RegTech challenges. How the distributed data is shared raises security issues. Protecting customer and proprietary data is critical yet difficult to achieve with permissionless DLTs.[91] Security is a paramount consideration, to protect consumers and guard against unscrupulous activity seeking to exploit financial data for illicit gains.[92]

Distributed validations and agreements for ledger updates may undermine regulatory functions as this determines what data will be added to the ledger.[93] In Blockchain systems, market participant consensus can be a requirement for the rules and procedures (protocols) that govern the ledger.[94] This may not be ideal for RegTech detecting market misconduct and discharging other regulatory functions. To achieve consensus in permissionless DLTs, a consensus mechanism known as 'proof-of-work' mining may be mandatory.[95] This mechanism is extremely computer intensive, time-consuming and lowers the capacity of the DLT, which may not be practical for optimal RegTech performance.[96]

11.5.4.3 Permissioned Distributed Ledger Technology

Despite the high-profile examples of BitCoin and Ethereum, the application of permissioned DLT systems are far more significant than permissionless DLT systems in the financial sector and elsewhere. The key distinction between permissionless and permissioned DLTs is that the former is a public network/database and the latter is private. Permissioned DLTs overcome the limitations of permissionless DLTs because they can be controlled and managed by a central party (or a group of parties),[97] for example a regulator. The regulator can apply protocols (rules)

---

[89] Government Office for Science (n 66) 65; World Economic Forum (n 65) 28.
[90] Bank for International Settlements (n 65) 2.
[91] Mills et al (n 65) 25.
[92] Ibid, 24; Bank for International Settlements (n 65) 21.
[93] Hong Kong Applied Science and Technology Research Institute (n 65) 10.
[94] Bank for International Settlements (n 65) 4.
[95] For example, in Bitcoin's blockchain. 'Proof of stake' is an alternative to proof of work that requires less computational power.
[96] Hong Kong Applied Science and Technology Research Institute (n 65) 11.
[97] Ibid.

and smart contracts to the permissioned DLT to restrict participants to regulated entities and licensed persons.[98]

Protocol and smart contract design can be verified and certified by the regulator to protect user confidentiality and proprietary data.[99] Reported data can be encrypted and identified by regulators with cryptographic signatures and timestamps.[100] Operating within a private or closed network reduces the risk of cyber-attacks and security breaches, lowering operational costs.[101]

With the validation process not contingent on 'proof-of-work mining' or other inefficient consensus mechanisms,[102] resources can be directed to lowering latency rates (that is, higher speeds) and increasing DLT capacity.[103]

11.6 REGTECH APPLICATION TO THE STOCK AND BOND CONNECT SCHEMES

11.6.1 *RegTech in Hong Kong*

The SFC has recently introduced new digital financial infrastructures (RegTech) and, in particular, a system to help analyse the growing number of paper and electronic documents generated by the increasing volume and complexity of enforcement actions.[104] In its 2016–17 Annual Report, the SFC stated that as the volume and types of information increase, the focus is on improving the processes for submitting information electronically to ensure timeliness, accuracy, efficiency and ease of use.[105] Further, the SFC acknowledges that RegTech infrastructure is essential in monitoring the Stock Connect schemes and is considering using DLT for an integrated northbound settlement system.[106] Similarly, RegTech infrastructure is essential for monitoring and settling transactions on Bond Connect. Permissioned DLT is ideal for these functions as administrative burdens such as reporting requirements can be drastically reduced while data can be gathered efficiently in real time.[107]

11.6.2 *Hardening the Soft Law of Cooperation Understandings*

Streamlining reporting requirements through the use of RegTech infrastructure is contingent on legal and regulatory frameworks.[108] Cross-border or cross-boundary regulatory cooperation is subject to soft law – MoUs between regulatory jurisdictions, namely the Connect schemes – which provides best guidance as to how regulators should act in certain circumstances.[109] These arrangements are not and cannot be rigidly enforced, and thus data dissemination between regulatory jurisdictions is based upon unwritten understandings, which are prone to regulatory

---

[98] HK Financial Services Development Council (n 65) 29 and 33.
[99] Bank for International Settlements (n 65) 18.
[100] HK Financial Services Development Council (n 65) 33; Bank for International Settlements (n 65) 18.
[101] Hong Kong Applied Science and Technology Research Institute (n 65) 11.
[102] Ibid.
[103] HK Financial Services Development Council (n 65) 33.
[104] Securities and Futures Commission, *Regulation for Quality Markets – Annual Report 2016–17* (Securities and Futures Commission, 2017), 94.
[105] Ibid.
[106] Ibid; HKEX, 'Request for Proposals – Distributed Ledger Technology (DLT) Implementation for Stock Connect' (March 2019).
[107] World Economic Forum (n 65) 29.
[108] Ibid.
[109] For a discussion, see generally Douglas W. Arner and Michael Taylor, 'The Global Financial Crisis and the Financial Stability Board: Hardening the Soft Law of International Financial Regulation' (2009) 32 *University of New South Wales Law Journal* 488.

bias. For example, in financial crises jurisdictions are predisposed to focus on local issues placing the financial stability concerns of other jurisdictions in a markedly subordinate position despite the contrary intention of an MoU.

One way to 'harden' cross-boundary or cross-border MoUs is to consider defining data gathering and analytics as a regulated activity.[110] In this way, soft arrangements concerning data sharing between jurisdictions are more transparent, and regulators can base cooperation arrangements on a recognised regulatory framework. This does not, however, ensure that data is readily open-source to regulators. Open-source data between cross-boundary regulators requires infrastructure to which regulators have unfettered access. Permissioned DLT has the capacity to become a shared data repository between regulators and regulated entities to transform reporting, compliance and transaction monitoring to on-demand and real-time monitoring.[111] Under these circumstances, MoU data-sharing arrangements pertaining to the Stock and Bond Connect schemes could effectively be hardened.

For example, the Connect schemes would comprise of at least two DLTs, one for each regulatory jurisdiction's Connect scheme, but more probably three – one for each exchange (SEHK, SSE and SZSE). RegTech interoperability is a prerequisite to ensure that legacy systems are compatible with non-local DLT and that data sharing is expeditious and seamless.[112]

11.6.3 *RegTech Gaps and Biases*

To effectively discharge cross-boundary or cross-border regulatory functions, data gathered by RegTech infrastructure must be harmonised and designed to mitigate regulatory underlap, gaps and biases.

In Section 11.3.2, the regulatory underlaps pertaining to Bond Connect were discussed. This analysis can also be applied to DLT – if the Bond Connect DLTs gather market conduct data, then the PBOC's systems will be incompatible in terms of effectively analysing data. This will create market conduct underlap with the DLT and therefore the HKMA. Similarly, if the Stock Connect DLTs are designed to gather financial stability-related data, then the systems of the CSRC, which is characterised as having only a market conduct mandate and function, will be incompatible in terms of effectively analysing this data. As a result, this will create a financial stability regulatory underlap with the DLT and therefore the SFC. The obvious remedy is to have regulators with mandates and regulatory functions that align with data gathered by the DLTs. However, aligning DLTs with a regulator's capacity can nonetheless cause regulatory gaps and biases.

With the HKMA's statutory mandates centring on the financial stability of the banking and financial system – the HKMA being the banking sector prudential regulator and empowered to deploy the exchange fund to manage financial stability – the financial stability function would most likely take precedence over the market conduct function of the banking sector.[113] Moreover, the PBOC would favour the financial stability function in the absence of a statutory market conduct function. This is inherent to the design of the HKMA and PBOC as central banks. Redesigning the PBOC as an integrated regulator would eliminate the regulatory gap but may not mitigate the incidence of bias. In the United Kingdom during the GFC, the

---

[110] Zetzsche et al (n 44) 36.
[111] World Economic Forum (n 65) 28.
[112] Mills et al (n 65) 23.
[113] Arner, Gibson and Barberis (n 56) 447.

FSA was found to give preference to market conduct supervision over financial stability.[114] If the Bond Connect DLTs focus on financial stability data at the expense of market conduct, this will create a regulatory gap for the HKMA and a bias towards financial stability for the HKMA and PBOC.

The design of the SFC and CSRC, being sectoral securities regulators, is best suited to market conduct supervision rather than financial stability. This characteristic is more pronounced in the CSRC, which lacks a financial stability mandate. The fundamental regulatory design of securities regulators favours the market conduct function. If the Stock Connect DLTs are designed to gather data based on the market conduct regulatory function of the SFC and CSRC, this will result in a financial stability data gap for the SFC, which will lead to SFC and CSRC market conduct bias.

To overcome these critical design flaws, there is a need to balance the regulatory functions, especially when the functions are merged within one regulator (that is, sectoral and integrated models).[115] The most prominent friction between regulatory functions is market conduct and financial stability.[116] This is where the Twin Peaks model has a decisive advantage over the sectoral and integrated models because the underlying design has a separate regulator discharging each regulatory function. For example, sectoral regulators such as the HKMA and PBOC are susceptible to financial stability bias, thereby subordinating market conduct supervision. Conversely, the susceptibility of the SFC and CSRC to prefer the market conduct function undermines financial stability supervision.[117] If separate regulators were designated to the market conduct function for Bond Connect (or financial stability for Stock Connect), then the susceptibility of the HKMA and PBOC (or SFC and CSRC) to suffer from functional bias can be mitigated. The Twin Peaks model is better suited to restore or establish a balance between regulatory functions, as opposed to bias because the design isolates and designates the function to each independent regulator. In these circumstances, the Connect MoUs would need to be redefined with the objective of mitigating potential bias. Clear statutory mandates for each Twin Peaks regulator are imperative for the design to effectively discharge the market conduct and financial stability functions.[118]

The philosophy of regulation can also create bias.[119] For example, conflicting regulatory functions in the preamble and the purposes of the Bond Connect MoU create confusion. When regulatory functions are blurred, this task becomes more demanding as bias may be inbuilt – a characteristic of the HKMA and FSA or the sectoral and integrated models respectively – and therefore beyond the best intentions of an MoU. The Twin Peaks model is designed to overcome any predisposition towards a particular regulatory function because, with each regulator focusing on one function, internal conflicts between functions do not arise. However, the Twin Peaks model will be challenged when a MoU is drafted with functional ambiguity because there will be confusion concerning the functional scope, which may undermine the effectiveness of discharging the regulatory functions.

---

[114] Turner (n 41) 87.
[115] Ibid; Taylor (n 42) 90–91; and David T. R. Carse, 'Review of the Hong Kong Monetary Authority's Work on Banking Stability' (2008), ii.
[116] For a discussion, see Taylor (n 42) 89–90.
[117] Arner, Gibson and Barberis (n 56) 447–8.
[118] Gibson (n 15) 196.
[119] Turner (n 41) 87.

11.7 CONCLUSION

The Twin Peaks model has gained impetus since the GFC. Prevailing regulatory models failed to fully discharge the financial stability and market conduct functions, which were exposed as suffering from regulatory gaps, underlap and biases.

With the continuing integration of Hong Kong's financial markets with Mainland China, coordination and information sharing between each jurisdiction's sectoral model is critical. Nonetheless, the Stock and Bond Connect schemes' sectoral regulatory architecture is subject to regulatory gaps, underlap and bias.

The Twin Peaks model overcomes this regulatory flaw because its design allocates the regulatory functions of financial stability and market conduct to independent regulators. A better balance can be achieved between regulatory functions than is the case under the sectoral and integrated models. Adopting the Twin Peaks model in conjunction with capital market reforms would solve a litany of current regulatory challenges created by the emergence of FinTech and TechFin companies.

As a starting point, the Twin Peaks model would benefit from being reformed with RegTech, by examining how its design can integrate permissioned DLT, APIs, smart contracts, automation, machine learning and artificial intelligence to facilitate ongoing monitoring while matching the regulatory requirements of the SME FinTech industry.

When deploying RegTech in conjunction with the Twin Peaks model, the separation of the regulatory functions can prioritise real-time monitoring more efficiently and support the policy considerations of innovation and market growth. The market conduct regulator can focus on market conduct and support market confidence, while the financial stability regulator can focus on liquidity, capital and leverage requirements.

Macroprudential financial stability data can be gathered from automated annual reports by the financial stability regulator. Data gaps, underlap and biases can be significantly reduced by RegTech infrastructure deployed within the Twin Peaks model. When compared to other regulatory models, each Twin Peaks' regulator is in the optimum position to calibrate their purviews to reflect the market while promoting capital raising, innovation and growth. This is critical for effectively and efficiently regulating the market conduct and financial stability functions pertaining to the Connect schemes and the FinTech ecosystem which underpin Hong Kong's future as an international centre for finance and technology.

Regulatory Structure and the Revolving Door Phenomenon in South Korea

Evidence from the 2011 Savings Bank Crisis

Youkyung Huh and Hongjoo Jung

12.1 INTRODUCTION

The focus of this book is on the 'optimal architecture' of financial system regulation. While the importance of the architecture cannot be overstated, however, it is argued here that optimal architecture can only bring us to a certain point, and that 'the *architecture* is only as good as the implementation and the enforcement'.[1] Using the South Korean savings bank crisis and subsequent reforms as a case in point, this chapter illustrates that both 'architecture' and 'plumbing' are equally important for a well-functioning system, and that poor implementation caused by the revolving door phenomenon can undermine any type of regulatory architecture.

For almost a decade, South Korea has failed in its quest to scale the 'Twin Peaks'. Every presidential election cycle and congressional term has produced numerous proposals to reform the Korean financial regulatory architecture along the lines of the Twin Peaks model. Many of the proposals renounced the current integrated supervisory architecture, to create and reassign a separate financial consumer protection agency.

In Korea, it was the 2011 savings bank crisis that shut down a fifth of the nation's savings bank sector, and which served as the critical impetus for structural reform. The crisis exposed a multifaceted problem – ranging from policy missteps by the regulators, to nepotism, a captured regulator, corruption and bribery facilitated by the revolving door phenomenon. The crisis also exposed potential flaws in the regulatory architecture. Damage done to savings banks' clientele – a group of particularly financially disadvantaged consumers – could have been mitigated had there been better coordination or conflict resolution within the financial regulatory system. Almost ten years after the crisis, and despite numerous proposals, structural reform aimed at a Twin Peaks approach, or otherwise, has not yet taken place.

In contrast, laws to eradicate the revolving door in the financial industry, which was exposed by the crisis, were almost immediately put in place. The revolving door – the movement of individuals between jobs in the public sector and the private sector, in either direction – which is one notable mechanism of capture, impairs good implementation regardless of the type of financial regulatory architecture in place.

---

[1] These ideas were presented in email correspondence with Dr Andy Schmulow, during development of this chapter. See also Jeff Carmichael, 'Implementing Twin Peaks: Lessons from Australia' in Robin Hui Huang and Dirk Schoenmaker (eds) *Institutional Structure of Financial Regulation: Theories and International Experiences* (Routledge, 2015), at 108: 'A good architecture does not guarantee good regulation; more than anything else that requires good quality regulators'.

This chapter first outlines the 2011 savings bank crisis, and the subsequent botched architectural reforms, with a focus on the proposed Twin Peaks approach in Korea. It then examines the risks of the revolving door phenomenon in general, and specifically in the context of the 2011 savings bank crisis. A brief description and analysis of Korea's anti-revolving door provisions, and revisions introduced in 2011, follows. Finally, the implications of the revolving door phenomenon for the Twin Peaks regulatory architecture are analysed.

12.2 THE 2011 SAVINGS BANK CRISIS

A savings bank in Korea is a specialised financial intermediary that takes deposits and provides small amounts of credit for underprivileged individuals and small businesses that have low credit ratings. They do so at interest rates that are typically higher than those charged by established lending institutions. Low- or middle-income consumers who find it difficult to borrow money from regular banks due to their low credit scores, or those who will tolerate higher interest rates in return for correspondingly higher risk, are the usual customers of savings banks.[2] Savings banks also have community reinvestment requirements (that is, to serve the credit needs of each savings bank's licensed regional district). As such, the main clientele of savings banks are financially vulnerable, and usually have lower levels of financial literacy skills. These characteristics aggravated client losses during the crisis, and increased its political consequences.[3]

According to statistics from the Korea Federation of Savings Banks,[4] as of 2019 there were 79 savings banks with 305 offices, and 9,210 employees, serving just over 5 million customers (as shown in Table 12.1). The total number of banks, as of 2019, was reduced drastically due to the 2011 savings bank crisis, although there had been a slow decline in their numbers since 2006. As indicated in the table, the sub-standard (non-performing) loan ratio, which was usually at 10 per cent before the crisis, increased to 25 per cent in 2011 and 2012. The ratio then began to decline over subsequent years, reaching 5 per cent in 2018.

As Table 12.1 implies, the 2011 savings bank crisis had the effect of suspending the operation of several savings banks which were saddled with high non-performing loans (NPLs). Between 2011 and September 2012, 20 of the country's 105 savings banks, comprising 38 per cent of the sector's assets, were closed.[5] Continued restructuring of the industry to restore financial soundness brought it to the current number of 79 banks, which has remained stable since 2015.

Savings banks, with their roots as private money lenders, were first legalised in the early 1970s. Over the decades, they faced more competition from mainstream commercial banks, which caused a gradual deterioration in their financial strength. Government policies aimed at boosting the economy, and propping up the savings bank industry, progressively peeled back prudential rules (that is, limits on loans to one borrower), and expanded the scope of permissible activities. This series of policy missteps, aggravated by a host of other conditions, such as worsened market conditions after the 2008 Global Financial Crisis, lax supervision, regulatory

---

[2] See Financial Services Commission, 'Current Report on the Savings Bank Corruption Investigation Submitted to the National Assembly Special Investigation Committee' [금융위원회, 저축은행비리 의혹 진상규명을 위한 국정조사 특별위원회 현황 보고] (3 August 2011), at 5–6.

[3] Ibid at 1.

[4] Found at www.fsb.or.kr.

[5] Financial Services Commission & Financial Supervisory Service, 'Additional Plans on Improving Prudential Regulation of Savings Banks' [금융위원회, 금융감독원 보도자료, '저축은행 건전□영을 위한 추가 제도개선 방안], 13 September 2012; National Assembly Research Service of Korea, 'Savings Bank Current Deterioration and Subject Report No 122 – Focus on Policies and Systems' [국회입법조사처, 현안보고서 제122호, 저축은행 부실 현황 및 과제 – 정책 및 제도를 중심으로], 7 July 2011, at 4.

TABLE 12.1. *Major management indicators of savings banks in Korea.*
(unit: number, person, %).

As of	General situation				Employees[2]	BIS Capital Adequacy Ratio	NPL ratio	(ROA)[3]	(ROE)[3]	Number of customers[4]	
	Number of banks[1]	Offices	Branch	Rep. offices						Deposits	Loans
Unit	Number				(Person)	(%)				(Person)	
2006.6	111	264	132	21	6,759	9.16	10.90	1.28	23.91	2,531,649	1,188,727
2007.6	110	293	155	28	7,455	9.09	10.21	1.24	17.85	2,769,036	916,333
2008.6	108	326	183	35	7,920	9.08	9.38	0.58	7.44	3,202,168	808,810
2009.6	106	344	199	39	7,828	9.43	10.34	△0.08	△1.18	3,811,891	822,752
2010.6	106	371	226	39	8,459	9.05	10.55	△1.39	△21.60	4,257,355	878,138
2011.6	104	378	230	44	8,955	0.84	26.93	△7.13	△104.79	4,350,578	1,203,899
2012.6	96	390	249	45	8,353	4.07	24.43	△4.40	△60.42	3,371,917	1,189,158
2013.6	91	343	219	33	7,510	9.88	21.31	△2.47	△30.44	3,383,039	1,190,533
2014.6	87	329	209	33	7,349	14.28	18.97	△1.31	△12.35	3,059,428	1,105,320
2015.6	79	328	216	33	8,362	14.24	12.47	1.23	10.99	3,130,227	1,403,497
2016.6	79	322	209	34	8,838	14.53	8.75	2.10	19.07	3,331,608	1,680,785
2017.6	79	321	207	35	9,051	14.26	6.01	1.84	17.43	3,507,124	1,794,132
2018.6	79	316	200	37	9,123	14.45	5.08	1.79	16.00	3,691,863	1,893,591
2019.6	79	305	194	32	9,210	14.89	5.04	1.69	14.95	3,798,167	2,038,295

[1] Based on the number of headquarters.

[2] Including part-time workers.

[3] Annualised performance, net profit, assets and capital before reserving allowance for bad debts.

[4] The number of transactions between 2006.6 and 2012.6 based upon records held at the Korea Federation of Savings Banks.

Source: Savings bank statistics, as of June 2019.

capture caused by the revolving door and at times outright corruption, gradually led to the 2011 crisis.

In 1972 Korea enacted the *Mutual Savings and Finance Company Act*[6] to legalise private moneylenders, and utilise their funds to serve underprivileged low- or middle-income consumers.[7] Until the 1990s, the mainstream commercial banks served as financial intermediaries for large enterprises, while avoiding savings banks' traditional clientele.[8] From 1997 to 1998, during the Asian Financial Crisis, major commercial banks were forced to change their business models by targeting the clientele of savings banks.[9] In response, savings banks, saddled with higher funding costs, were forced to extend loans to ever riskier borrowers.[10] Particularly after 2003, when Korea's first credit card crisis erupted, savings banks were squeezed out of their traditional niche market of low-income borrowers, and forced to extend their loans to real estate developments, mostly in the form of project finance (PF) loans.[11] This was enabled by a wide range of deregulatory polices, as discussed below.

Prompted by lobbying from the Korea Federation of Savings Banks – a trade association of savings banks – in 2006 the government eased prudential rules by raising lending limits for a select group of 'healthy savings banks' – the so-called 88 Club – to revitalise the troubled industry.[12] To enter the club, banks needed a capital adequacy ratio of more than 8 per cent, and a bad debt ratio of under 8 per cent.[13] The idea was that healthy savings banks were more capable in respect of risk management, so they were allowed to lend up to 20 per cent of equity capital to a single borrower.[14] The benefits afforded to the 88 Club proved to be a powerful incentive, but also an inaccurate benchmark of the financial health of these institutions.[15] This was evidenced by the fact that at one point up to 66 per cent of the nation's largest savings banks joined this group.[16] Ultimately, this system led to a number of undesirable and unintended consequences.

First, the higher lending limits to single borrowers resulted in heavy exposure to risky PF loans related to real estate.[17] The banks that were originally supposed to serve low- or middle-income customers, or businesses in a certain geographical area, took an easy and short-sighted expansion strategy by entering into high-risk, high return business beyond their legally permissible limits. As such, the volume of PF loans granted by savings banks doubled from 2005 to 2008.[18] Currently, and in the aftermath of the crisis and restructuring process, the savings bank industry has kept its business in real estate PF loans, but at a much lower level (Table 12.2).

---

[6] Sangho Shinyong Geumko Beop [상호신용금고법], Act No 2333, 2 August 1972 (S Kor). Later the term Sangho *Shinyong Geumko* (상호신용금고, mutual savings and finance company) was changed to *Sangho Jeochuk Eunhaeng* (상호저축은행, mutual savings bank). To reflect this change, the title of the statute was revised as *Sangho Jeochuk Eunhaeng Beop* [상호저축은행법], Act No 6429, 28 March 2001 (S Kor).

[7] FSC Report to the National Assembly (n 2) at 5.

[8] Ibid at 6.

[9] Ibid at 6.

[10] Ibid at 6, 27.

[11] Ibid at 7.

[12] Ibid at 23.

[13] Ibid at 23.

[14] Ibid at 24.

[15] Sang-jo Kim, 'Status, Causes and Remedies for the Savings Bank Crisis' (Korea Money and Finance Association, 2011) [김상조, 저축은행 부실의 현황, 원인, 대책, 한국금융학회], at 44, www.kmfa.or.kr/paper/annual/2011/2011_02_s .pdf.

[16] FSC Report to the National Assembly (n 2) at 24.

[17] Ibid at 28.

[18] Ibid at 28.

TABLE 12.2. *Outstanding PF loan amounts and delinquency rates.*

	2005	2006	2007	2008	2009	2010
Outstanding PF loan amount (unit trillion KRW)	6.3	11.6	12.1	11.5	11.8	12.2
Ratio of PF loans (%)	18.0	27.3	25.6	20.9	18.2	18.9
Delinquency ratio (%)	9.1	9.6	11.6	13.0	10.6	25.1

Source: Financial Services Commission, 'Current Report on the Savings Bank Corruption Investigation Submitted to the National Assembly Special Investigation Committee' [금융위원회, 저축은행비리 의혹 진상규명을 위한 국정조사특별위원회 현황 보고], 3 August 2011, 28.

Between the 2008–09 US financial crisis and the 2010–12 European financial crisis, and contrary to industry expectations, real estate prices in Korea did not recover.[19] Unsurprisingly, highly leveraged savings banks, which had narrower business models than their commercial bank competitors, and had heavily invested in real estate, suffered severely from these crises. Ultimately, the 88 Club's policies led to the demise of the over-leveraged savings banks, which were shut down by the authorities in 2011.

Second, perhaps more critically, the 88 Club's policies created perverse incentives for savings banks to maintain their 88 Club status, which they did by issuing subordinated debt.[20] The authorities permitted the issuance of subordinated debt to facilitate funding for savings banks, and to enable them to maintain their Bank for International Settlements (BIS) capital adequacy ratio.[21] Critically, between 2004 and June 2011 the most significant amount of subordinated debt was issued by savings banks during the period 2009 and 2010, in amounts of between five and ten times that of previous years (Table 12.3).[22] The consequences were especially troubling because sales of subordinated debt were targeted at traditional savings banks' underprivileged clientele – namely those who were financially challenged and had low levels of financial literacy.

Because subordinated debt is not covered by deposit insurance, subordinated debt holders are, in theory, more motivated to monitor the riskiness of financial institutions in which they are involved.[23] In reality, however, the legal nature of subordinated debt was not well understood, even by savings bank employees who were recruited to sell the debt.[24] As a result, subordinated debt was often mis-sold to investors who were, in most cases, the savings banks' existing clientele. Bank employees who sold the debt misrepresented subordinated debt in a number of ways. Some failed to explain the risks implicit in subordinated debt by emphasising its high interest rates, and by not disclosing the differences between deposits and subordinated debt.[25] In some cases, employees misrepresented the financial status of the savings bank, or even encouraged depositors to withdraw their savings to invest in subordinated debt.[26]

---

[19] Ibid at 28.
[20] Sang-jo Kim (n 15) at 44.
[21] FSC Report to the National Assembly (n 2) at 115.
[22] Ibid at 115.
[23] See William W. Lang and Douglas D. Robertson, 'Analysis of Proposals for a Minimum Subordinated Debt Requirement' (2002) 54(1) *Journal of Economics and Business* 115–36.
[24] Korean Financial Supervisory Service, 'Report by Financial Dispute Mediation Committee: Decision to Attribute Responsibility for Damages for Unfair Sales of Average 42% of Subordinated Debt of Busan Savings Bank etc.' [금융감독원 보도자료, '금융분쟁조정위원회, 부산저축은행 등에 대하여 후순위채 불완전판매를 인정하여 평균 42%의 손해배생책임을 결정'] (29 October 2011).
[25] Ibid.
[26] Ibid.

TABLE 12.3. *Annual issuance amount of subordinated debt.*
(*unit 100 million KRW*).

Year	2004	2005	2006	2007	2008	2009	2010	First half of 2011	Total	June 2011 outstanding amount
Amount	447	866	2,575	360	1,448	5,712	3,548	95	15,051	12,774
(Public offerings)	(200)	(300)	(1,850)	(300)	(500)	(5,039)	(3,218)	(40)	(11,477)	(10,472)
Number of Offerings	12	12	24	3	13	35	20	3	122	93
(Public offerings)	(3)	(3)	(11)	(2)	(3)	(25)	(17)	(1)	(65)	(54)

Source: Financial Services Commission, 'Current Report on the Savings Bank Corruption Investigation Submitted to the National Assembly Special Investigation Committee' [금융위원회, 저축은행비리 의혹 진상규명을 위한 국정조사특별위원회 현황 보고], 3 August 2011, 28.

To make matters worse, improper management at savings banks exploited the deregulatory policies that were in place to artificially support the struggling industry, even at the detriment of the public good. The controlling shareholders and CEOs of savings banks were mostly non-bankers of poor integrity, with neither experience in running a financial institution, nor copious amounts of capital at the disposal of their firms.[27] Unlike commercial banks in which stock ownership is dispersed or partially nationalised, most savings banks were closely owned by families and friends. Bank management and ownership were not separated, and so systems to ensure compliance with policies and the law were not properly implemented.[28]

Further investigations revealed that not only were there highly speculative PF loans made without adequate loan reviews based on the quality of the projects[29] but, even worse, many loans were fraudulent and in violation of legal loan ceilings.[30] Although the legal limit of PF loans was 20–30 per cent, banks created more than a hundred fraudulent special purpose companies (SPCs) under borrowed names, to evade loan limits.[31] Further, the loans granted to SPCs were eventually transferred to their owners for their private use.[32] Busan Savings Bank, for instance, issued PF loans to the value of US$4 billion, as well as loans to its CEO's related welfare foundation, without any of the collateral generally required by Korean banks.[33]

The casualties of the crisis were the underprivileged clientele of savings banks – the very people to whom policymakers intended to provide financial services through savings banks. As of June 2012, collectively approximately 88,000 customers, mostly comprised of individuals (as opposed to companies), had lost KRW1 trillion in the savings bank collapses.[34] Many of the victims were elderly, poor and financially illiterate; they had poured their life savings into subordinated debt, which they believed would deliver higher returns, while being as safe as bank deposits.

Just as many had wondered during the 2008 Global Financial Crisis, so too many in Korea wondered where the banking regulators were while all this misconduct took place.

One somewhat benign explanation was that for years before the crisis, the regulatory authorities had simply lacked the resources needed to effectively examine and supervise the savings banks.[35] On-site inspections were required to detect fraud committed by CEOs, or determine if management lacked integrity and/or experience and capability. The capacity of the banking supervisor (the Financial Supervisory Service, FSS) to examine savings banks was, however,

---

[27] FSC Report to the National Assembly (n 2) at 29.

[28] Prime Minister's Office of Korea, 'Plans on Innovating Financial Supervision' [국무총리실, 금융감독혁신방안] (2 September 2011), at 3. See also NARS Current Report (n 5) at 36.

[29] FSC Report to the National Assembly (n 2) at 30.

[30] Supreme Prosecutors' Office Republic of Korea Central Investigation Bureau, 'Explanatory Material for Prosecution of the Pusan Savings Bank Scandal' [대검찰청 중앙수사부, 부산저축은행그룹 비리사건 기소 관련 설명자료] (2 May 2011) at 16–17; Jeong-pil Kim, 'Busan Savings Executives Caught in $4.3B Fraud', *Hankyoreh* (3 May 2011), www.hani.co.kr/arti/english_edition/e_national/476101.html.

[31] SPO Investigation Report (n 32).

[32] FSC Report to the National Assembly (n 2) at 29, 30; SPO Investigation Report (n 32).

[33] SPO Investigation Report (n 32).

[34] Seon-jin Cha, 'Suicides, Arrests Show Trouble at Korean Savings Banks' (Bloomberg, 19 June 2012), www.bloomberg .com/news/2012-06-18/suicides-arrests-show-trouble-at-korean-savings-banks.html. The victims can be categorised into two groups: the first comprised those whose deposits exceeded the deposit insurance limit of KRW50 million. More than 90 per cent of the deposits that exceeded the coverage limit were held by individuals. The average individual depositor saw about KRW6 million (about US$5,507) of their uninsured deposits wiped out. For subordinated debt, 99 per cent were held by individuals, many of them elderly and/or with low income. This data is based on only the first seven savings banks that were shut down in 2011, but the ratio of individuals should be similar for other banks suspended thereafter. FSC Report to the National Assembly (n 2) at 77.

[35] FSC Report to the National Assembly (n 2) at 31–2; PMO Innovation Plan, at 8.

TABLE 12.4. *Number of executives at savings banks with backgrounds in financial authorities (Unit: number of persons).*

Year	2006	2007	2008	2009	2010
FSS	31 (69%)	36 (73%)	45 (78%)	53 (65%)	51 (72%)
KDIC	5 (11%)	4 (8%)	2 (3%)	2 (3%)	3 (4%)
KAMCO	2 (4%)	3 (6%)	3 (5%)	5 (7%)	5 (7%)
Others	7 (16%)	6 (12%)	8 (14%)	11 (15%)	12 (17%)
Total	45 (100%)	49 (100%)	58 (100%)	71 (100%)	71 (100%)

Source: Sun-ae Jun, 'Failures of Savings Banks and their Corporate Governance Structure' [전선애, 저축은행의 부실과 기업기배구조] (2011) 57 Corporate Governance Review 45–9 at 48. (Original data from the Korea Federation of Savings Banks.)

severely limited and deteriorated further over time, while the total assets held by savings banks steadily increased. In 2007, forty-five FSS employees were exclusively in charge of monitoring savings banks, but that number fell to thirty in 2010.[36] Over the same period, the combined assets of savings banks increased from KRW64 trillion to KRW86 trillion.[37] Even the Financial Services Commission (FSC), a government body in charge of financial policymaking and oversight of the operations of the FSS, had just one employee in charge of oversight of the savings bank industry.[38]

The lack of supervisory resources itself cannot explain the abject failure of supervision and moral hazard issues exposed by the crisis. But some of it can be attributed to regulators who were captured by industry due to the widespread occurrence of the revolving door phenomenon.

A survey shows that ex-FSS employees were the most numerous of the executive members of the savings banks who had career backgrounds in (quasi) government agencies related to bank supervision and resolution (see Table 12.4). Between 2006 and 2010, ex-FSS officials took up about 70 per cent of the executive members of the relevant banks who had worked at the FSS, Korea Deposit Insurance Corporation (KDIC), Korea Asset Management Corporation (KAMCO) or other government agencies.

Also, a position as a statutory auditor (*kamsa*) in a financial institution was a popular destination for retired financial regulators. The role of the statutory auditor was to independently observe and ensure proper management of the company by the board. For savings banks, auditors' roles were to ensure that the lending functions of the bank were in compliance with relevant laws. As of 2011, about half of the entire statutory auditor positions in financial institutions were filled by ex-regulators, of which 76 per cent were specifically ex-FSS officials.[39] In short, prior to the 2011 crisis, ex-FSS officials were the favourite choice for auditor appointments at savings banks.[40]

Investigations by law enforcement agencies and the financial regulators revealed that the financial conditions in troubled savings banks were much worse than initially portrayed by the industry. Egregious cases, such as collusion with illegal lending and accounting fraud – especially through the use of SPCs – perpetrated by senior ex-FSS employees, was exposed in the

[36] Prime Minister's Office of Korea (n 30) at 8.
[37] Ibid.
[38] Ibid at 9.
[39] Ibid at 22.
[40] Min-soo Kim, 'Only the FSS High-Level Staff that Retired before the Savings Bank Crisis Smiled' [저축은행 사태 이전 퇴직 금감원 간부들만 웃었다], Digital Times (13 September 2018), www.dt.co.kr/contents.html?article_no=2018091302109958033001.

aftermath of the crisis.[41] In some cases, there was a combination of the revolving door and corruption. For example, one ex-FSS employee received bribes to overlook illegal loans while in office as a bank supervisor, and in the following year was offered a position as an auditor in the same savings bank.[42] Reports noted that FSS employees' long-term employment in the same positions within the savings banks' divisions and their re-employment after retirement at related industry placements (in other words, the revolving door phenomenon) was one cause of lax supervision.[43] Through revolving door connections, savings banks lobbied politicians and supervisors heavily, with the aim of stalling regulatory actions that would eventually lead to the shutdown of the banks.[44]

Ethical issues regarding suspension of banks, and corresponding losses to investors and depositors caused by the scandal, presented the question of how to improve governance and the supervision system of the banks. Criticism of the powerful connection between the savings banks and supervisory agents led to reforms to stop the revolving door phenomenon.

The crisis sparked several different directions for reform. Here the focus is on two threads – first, the restructuring of the financial regulatory architecture (the Twin Peaks reforms) which has been unsuccessful to date; and second, the attempts to stem the revolving door, including the stringent employment restrictions for ex-financial regulators, which the government implemented almost immediately after the crisis.

12.3 THE UNSUCCESSFUL TWIN PEAKS REFORMS

Policy missteps and ineffective supervision led to a failure in the financial regulatory system – a failure that particularly resulted in harm to consumers of, and investors in, savings banks. This ignited public outrage that demanded a meaningful reform of the financial regulatory system, which, however, eventually failed. This section examines the current regulatory structure, the failure of the structure that the crisis exposed and the reform debates that followed.

12.3.1 *The Two-Tiered Integrated System Adopted after the 1997–1998 Asian Financial Crisis*

The current regulatory model for financial institutions in Korea is an integrated supervisory approach, through the two tiers of the Financial Services Commission and the Financial Supervisory Service. The FSC–FSS structure was implemented in 1999, after the Asian Financial Crisis, which ushered in sweeping financial regulatory reforms. The current structure, the two-tier integrated supervision system, was the product of regulatory innovation aimed at reducing government control of the private financial services sector, as well as bureaucratic resistance from government – initially as a result of serious discussions at the Financial Reform Committee (1996) – and then accelerated as a consequence of the Asian Financial Crisis (1997–98).[45]

---

[41] SPO Investigation Report (n 32) at 16–17.
[42] Supreme Prosecutors' Office Republic of Korea, 'Savings Bank Corruption Case 2nd Investigation Results' [대검찰청, 저축은행 비리사건 2차 수사결과] (7 February 2012).
[43] Prime Minister's Office of Korea (n 30) at 9.
[44] Supreme Prosecutors' Office Republic of Korea Central Investigation Bureau, 'Investigation Results of the Pusan Savings Bank Scandal' [대검찰청 중앙수사부, 부산저축은행그룹 비리사건 수사결과] (2 November 2011).
[45] See Kihwan Kim, 'The 1997–98 Korean Financial Crisis: Causes, Policy Response, and Lessons' (Presentation at the High Level Seminar on Crisis Prevention in Emerging Market, Singapore, 10–11 July 2006), www.imf.org/external/np/seminars/eng/2006/cpem/pdf/kihwan.pdf.

The Financial Services Commission is a government agency tasked with strategic policy-making, while implementation is effected by the Financial Supervisory Service, constituted as a semi-public institution.[46] The previous, sector-based approach was abolished, with consolidated oversight of all financial sectors (banking, insurance and securities) into the FSC–FSS system. As is often the case with bureaucracies, the FSC has expanded its profile and staff complement from a small secretariat into a significant and sizeable agency.

The structure of the FSC–FSS presents important points of interest and conflict, as distribution of power between the two agencies is often unclear and confusing. According to statute, the FSC is in charge of financial system regulatory policy, oversight of the financial system, the issuing of licences to financial institutions and the administration of the FSS's supervision and examination of financial institutions function.[47] The FSS oversees financial markets and conducts supervision and examination of institutions under the direction and supervision of the FSC.[48] As such, it is generally understood in Korea that the FSC is the more 'senior' agency.

Ambiguity and complexity in the law and practice surrounding the FSC–FSS, however, has encouraged frequent turf wars and criticism of the model. For example, the expansion of the FSC's mission and role to include industry development and supervisory policy in finance led to criticisms over its dual role, and to conflicts with the FSS. It appears that the successful survival of the FSC's powers is attributable to collective cohesion and an unwavering hunger for power and resources.[49] By comparison, reform initiatives emanating from academic or private sector interest groups have failed to effect transformation, despite years of discussion.

12.3.2 *The Implications of the Savings Banks Crisis for the Twin Peaks Reform Agenda*

Arguments favouring a Twin Peaks-style reform rest on a number of observations made from the crisis. First, the 2011 savings bank crisis was exacerbated because of conflicts in the regulatory objectives within the FSC–FSS integrated model – specifically, consumer protection was at odds with prudential regulation.[50] Resolving this conflict represents a foundational advantage in the Twin Peaks model.[51]

The financial regulators began to tackle the savings banks disaster from 2011, despite the fact that their financial viability began deteriorating well before that.[52] Instead of formally intervening earlier by imposing prompt corrective actions, regulators encouraged private solutions, such

---

[46] The FSC and the FSS share the common objective of promoting the advancement of the Korean financial industry, stability of financial markets, a sound credit market, fair practices in financial transactions and protection of financial consumers. *Act on the Establishment, etc. of the Financial Services Commission* [금융위원회의 설치 등에 관한 법률], Act No 11407, 21 March 2012, art 1 (S Kor).

[47] Ibid arts 17, 18, 19.

[48] Ibid arts 37, 51.

[49] This observation is consistent with public choice theories such as Niskanen's budget-maximising theory which predicts that rational bureaucrats seek to maximise their budgets, reputation, authority and the like in order to increase their own power. See William A. Niskanen, Jr, *Bureaucracy and Representative Government* (Transaction Publishers, 1971).

[50] Seok-heon Yoon et al, 'Financial Regulatory Architecture Reform, How Shall We Go about It?' [윤석헌, 금융감독체계 개편, 어떻게 할 것인가?] (Korea Money and Finance Association, 8 June 2012), at 8, www.kmfa.or.kr/paper/annual/2012/2012_06_08_special_symposium.pdf.

[51] Michael W. Taylor, 'Twin Peaks' Revisited... A Second Chance for Regulatory Reform' (Centre for the Study of Financial Innovation, 2009), at 5 (arguing that 'when prudential and consumer protection regulation are combined in a single agency, at least one of them is likely to be done badly').

[52] Prime Minister's Office of Korea (n 30) at 6; FSC Report to the National Assembly (n 2) at 25.

as raising equity capital or mergers and acquisitions among savings banks and, more problematically, by issuing subordinated debt.[53]

In their defence, the regulators claimed that the 2008 Global Financial Crisis had made the Korean economy extremely fragile.[54] The regulators' focus had been on sustaining the major *commercial* banks in order to secure their financial intermediary role.[55] Had they started to shut down savings banks earlier, the already weak financial sector might have suffered systemic collapse.[56]

In short, the regulators, in dealing with the ripples from the 2008 crisis, prioritised the safety, soundness and systemic stability of the banking sector as well as the prudential health of individual savings banks. Neither consumer nor investor protection were concerns in the early response to the crisis. This presents a classic situation where a conflict between regulatory wobjectives arises. Second, the 2011 savings bank crisis exemplified one of the most important criticisms of the integrated regulatory approach, namely that an integrated regulator has 'unclear objectives' and that 'it will be difficult for them to strike an appropriate balance between the different objectives of regulation'.[57] The FSC–FSS had to simultaneously prevent systemic risk in a weakened economy in the aftermath of the 2008 Global Financial Crisis, deal with an industry prone to fraud and bribery, and secure the financial health of deteriorating savings banks. But at the same time, individual consumers and investors needed protection from mis-selling and fraud. Korea's two-tiered model failed to balance these objectives due to its confused and conflicted foci. It was this lack of clarity in focus that made it challenging to hold the FSC–FSS accountable for the policy and supervisory failures that became evident. The two-tiered system, in which the FSS conducts day-to-day supervision but is overseen by the FSC, exacerbated this lack of accountability. Twin Peaks is a response to these observed shortcomings.[58]

The savings bank crisis also demonstrated a lack of transparency in the manner in which the FSC and FSS dealt with their conflicting goals. Although the regulators attributed their delayed intervention to a deliberate attempt to prevent a systemic failure, the consensus in policy and academic circles was that the crisis was exacerbated by the regulators' missteps in dealing with the weakened savings banks industry. The combined assets of Korea's savings banks was KRW74 trillion, accounting for only 2.4 per cent of the country's entire financial industry in 2011.[59] As such, one could argue that the impact of the savings bank failures was unlikely to present a systemic risk to the financial sector. It is unclear, therefore, how credible were the regulators' explanations of the systemic risks to the Korean financial system posed by savings banks from late 2008 to 2010.

Even if the regulators' systemic concerns were presumed correct at the time, the closed-door approach made it difficult to justify the regulators' action, or inaction, for forestalling such a

---

[53] Prime Minister's Office of Korea (n 30) at 6; FSC Report to the National Assembly(n 2) at 25.

[54] FSC Report to the National Assembly (n 2) at 25.

[55] Ibid.

[56] Ibid.

[57] Richard Abrams and Michael W. Taylor, 'Issues in the Unification of Financial Sector Supervision' (IMF Working Paper WP/00/213, 2000), at 17; David T. Llewellyn, 'Institutional Structure of Financial Regulation and Supervision: The Basic Issues' (Paper presented at the World Bank seminar 'Aligning Supervisory Structures with Country Needs', 2006), at 22.

[58] Abrams and Taylor (n 60) at 24; Michael W. Taylor, 'The Road from 'Twin Peaks' – And the Way Back' (2009) 16 *Connecticut Insurance Law Journal* 61, 88–9, 89–90.

[59] FSC Report to the National Assembly (n 2) at 1. The savings bank sector was insignificant, with total assets and deposits constituting only 1/17th of the total, as compared to the mainstream commercial banking sector, which represented the remainder. Data as at March 2011. FSC Report to the National Assembly (n 302) at 1–2.

systemic risk. In a consolidated agency, the resolution of conflicting objectives is internalised – described as 'internal conflict resolution' – in which lawmakers delegate the responsibility for several potentially conflicting objectives, without setting forth ex ante preferences.[60] Transparency is a prerequisite for which lawmakers hold the agency accountable.[61] To a certain extent, lack of transparency in the process for conflict resolution during the savings bank crisis invited malfeasance (fraud and bribery) in the regulatory system. Under the Twin Peaks approach, conflicts in the objectives that legislators assigned are able be resolved by an 'external conflict debate'.[62] The advantage is that by externalising the conflict, there is a higher likelihood that the legislature and the public can observe and scrutinise the regulatory policies. It is said that a public debate process – to the extent that it is public – can enable agencies to make more informed decisions based on empirical information generated by such process.[63]

Another problem commonly attributed to a unified agency model is that 'a single, integrated regulator has the potential to become a classic monopolistic bureaucracy, with all the related inefficiencies'.[64] This was evident in the regulatory monopoly in Korea, which was not about the size of the economy, but rather the scope of undivided authority and concentration of information within the FSC–FSS, to which agencies like the Bank of Korea (BOK) and Korea Deposit Insurance Corporation, had limited access.[65] The savings bank crisis had implications for financial stability as a whole, an outcome with which the central bank would be concerned. The crisis also affected the deposit insurance agency, because it would have had to make good on guarantees to any failed savings banks. Access to the true extent of the crisis in these institutions was limited, however, due to the monopoly power over information of the FSC–FSS.[66]

12.3.3 *The Rocky Road to Twin Peaks*

Reformation of the financial regulatory structure has been included in major policy agendas of every recent president. That is, every presidential candidate espoused transformation of the supervision of the financial system of Korea as an important economic issue. For example, former President Lee Myung-bak (in office from February 2008 to February 2013) of the Conservative Party focused on economic growth and changed the name and function of the Financial Supervisory Commission to the current Financial Services Commission to reflect support for the financial services industry. In the wake of the 2011 savings bank crisis, however, the Lee administration recognised that there was 'a conflict of interest between prudential regulation and consumer protection', and that the FSS was 'relatively negligent in consumer

---

[60] Larry D. Wall and Robert A. Eisenbeis, 'Financial Regulatory Structure and the Resolution of Conflicting Goals' (1999) 16 *Journal of Financial Services Research* 223, 232–3.

[61] Ibid at 224, 232.

[62] Ibid at 224, 232–4.

[63] Ibid. We note that the Twin Peaks model does not guarantee that external debate will be public. In Australia, for example, under the Twin Peaks model, conflicts are indeed resolved externally at the Council of Financial Regulators. However these debates are not conducted in public.

[64] Group of Thirty, *The Structure of Financial Supervision: Approaches and Challenges in a Global Marketplace* (2008), at 37, https://group30.org/images/uploads/publications/G30_StructureFinancialSupervision2008.pdf or https://group30.org/publications/detail/138.

[65] As a rule, the BOK and the KDIC both have joint examination authority with the FSS. But prior to the crisis, the FSS frequently denied joint examinations, asserting that in particular cases, joint examinations were unnecessary. Prime Minister's Office of Korea (n 30) at 10.

[66] Group of Thirty (n 67) at 37.

protection'.[67] Major studies, including one commissioned by the administration, recommended for adoption the Twin Peaks model, thus building momentum for reform.[68] President Park Geun-hye, from the same party, took office in 2013 and ordered the financial regulators to devise a plan to establish a strong and independent financial consumer protection regulator.[69] And the current president, Moon Jae-in, who assumed office in 2017, included the issue in his government's '100 Policy Tasks'[70] though, to date, without success.

Numerous legislative bills in South Korea have also ploughed a path to structural reform. Legislation to reform the financial regulatory system into some variation of the Twin Peaks model has been repeatedly introduced and discarded; since the first government-sponsored bill was introduced in 2012,[71] more than a dozen bills (including government-sponsored, as well as member-sponsored. bills) have been submitted and discarded over two congressional terms. Yet, as at the time of writing, there is no sign of reaching an agreement on the reforms.

The task of restructuring the financial supervisory system is complicated and challenging: the variety of policy options available, the political economy surrounding reform, the lack of consensus on which model to choose (that is, Twin Peaks or not), and finally, the organisational challenges to reform.

As mentioned, Korea has a unique FSC–FSS structure – integrated in the market but divided in hierarchy. Policymakers, as well as the financial industry, have long argued for the integration of the FSC and the FSS to remove redundancies, inconsistencies and lack of information sharing and coordination between the two.[72] The dual FSC–FSS structure has proven to be extremely inefficient, as financial firms must cross-check between two agencies for policy direction. Competition – even hostility – exists between the FSC and the FSS. As a result, there are times when they compete for hegemony in new policy spaces.[73] Consequently, any structural reforms, whether Twin Peaks or not, will first have to disentangle the complexities of the FSC–FSS structure, and the political economy surrounding the two agencies.

As political scientists have presciently recognised, structural choice concerns interest-group politics in which bureaucrats themselves are 'political actor[s] on their own'.[74] These political

---

[67] Prime Minister's Office of Korea (n 30) at 39.

[68] See, eg, Yoon et al (n 53) (advocating the establishment of a separate prudential supervisory agency and consumer protection agency); Seoul National University Center for Financial Law, 'Regulatory Architecture Reform Plans for Financial Supervision Modernization' [서울대학교 금융법센터, 금융감독 선진화를 위한 감독체계 개편 방안] (2012); Seung-yeon Won, 'Systemic Risk and Plan for Reform of Financial Supervision System' [원승연, 시스템 리스크와 금융감독체계의 개편 방향] (Korea Money and Finance Association. 2011); Sun-seop Jung, 'Financial Regulatory Reform and Consumer Financial Protection' [정순섭, 금융규제개혁과 금융소비자보호] (2009) 22 *Commercial Cases Review* 66 (discussing the deployment of the Twin Peaks model as potentially meaningful for consumer protection).

[69] Editorial from *Korea Herald*: Financial Reform Plans (12 November 2012) (outlining regulatory reform plans for presidential candidates in the 2013 presidential election in Korea), www.koreaherald.com/view.php?ud=20121111000160&ACE_SEARCH=1.

[70] Government of the Republic of Korea, '100 Policy Tasks: Five-Year Plan of the Moon Jae-in Administration' (Korean Culture and Information Service, 17 August 2017), https://english1.president.go.kr/dn/5afi07425ffod.

[71] A government-sponsored amendment bill for the *FSC Establishment Act*, the general statue governing the organisational structure of financial regulation, was submitted to the legislators on 2 February 2012. Along with this law, a bill for the enactment of the *Financial Consumer Protection Act*, which provided substantive reforms to enhance consumer protection, was submitted. Collectively, the two bills were to serve as a legislative response to the 2011 savings bank crisis, with the aim to enhance consumer protection, and to restructure the supervisory architecture. *Bill on Revision of the FSC Establishment Act* [금융위원회의 설치 등에 관한 법률 일부개정법률안], Bill No 14601, submitted by the government on 2 February 2012 (S Kor).

[72] SNU Plan (n 71) at 185.

[73] Dong-chan Jhoo, 'Feud between FSC, FSS Deepening', *Korea Times* (13 October 2019), www.koreatimes.co.kr/www/biz/2018/12/367_259956.html.

[74] Terry Moe, 'The Politics of Bureaucratic Structure' in John E. Chubb and Paul E. Peterson (eds) *Can the Government Govern* (Brookings Institution, 1989) at 282.

actors – the FSS, the FSC, the financial services industry and consumer interest groups – support, or are opposed to, the Twin Peaks model, based on their own political position or expected benefits. In general, the FSS supports the current integrated model because of the concentration of supervisory power and influence they enjoy. This has its roots in the Confucian culture, which pays respect to a larger authority. The FSC, however, prefers the Twin Peaks model, where the FSS would be split into two 'peaks', and where the FSC would maintain its role to oversee the two supervisory agencies.[75] In this way, the FSC would solidify its authority over the two smaller and more controllable watchdogs, to which the FSC would have more opportunities to second their personnel than in the case of the current integrated FSS system. The industry, concerned with increased compliance costs from two supervisory agents, has generally been opposed to the Twin Peaks model.[76] Consumer interest groups have generally favoured the Twin Peaks model because it promises enhanced consumer protection.[77] Academia and research institutes are spilt in their decisions.[78]

Bureaucratic turf grabbing has also hindered reform. Conscious of the increasing importance of financial consumer protection in the public policy domain, and imminent structural reform, both the FSC and the FSS have raised the organisational priority of consumer protection goals. Since 2011, The FSS has increased its rhetoric about consumer protection, announcing repeatedly that it would put consumer protection at the forefront of its policies.[79] The FSS also increased the staff available for consumer protection, established a separate division and increased the hierarchy of the head of the consumer protection division through a series of organisational restructurings.[80] Similarly, the FSC appointed staff exclusively to address consumer protection issues, set up a new division for that purpose and built it up into the Financial Consumer Bureau in order to lead the work, ahead of the FSS.[81]

Restructuring also presents an organisational challenge, which is complicated by the different legal status of the FSC, FSS and their employees. The FSC is a government agency, with civil servants as its employees, while the FSS is a private corporation in the form of a special-purpose entity, with non-civil servants as employees. With about 230 staff members at the FSC and 2,000 in the FSS it would be difficult to fold one agency into another, due to the differences in legal status, the way the two agencies are funded and employee salary levels.

The unsuccessful Twin Peaks-style reform in South Korea suggests that it is challenging to change the overall architecture of a financial supervisory system, as it impacts many

---

[75] Jeong-ju Na, 'Regulators in Discord over Reform' (22 July 2013), www.koreatimes.co.kr/www/biz/2019/04/488_139728.html.

[76] Prime Minister's Office of Korea (n 30) at 52.

[77] Ibid.

[78] Ibid. (noting the divided opinion of research institutes); supra note 71 (on the divided opinion of academia).

[79] See, eg, Ji-wan Cha, 'FSS Governor Hyuk-sae Kwon Says "Strengthened Examinations for Consumer Protection . . . End to the Light-Handed Approach"' [차지완, 권혁세 금감원장 '소비자 보호 위해 금융검사 강화... 더 이상 온정 ⊠다'] *The Dong-A Daily News* (29 March 2011), www.donga.com/news/article/all/20110328/35960372/1.

[80] The World Bank, Financial Sector Assessment Program Republic of Korea, Insurance Core Principles Detailed Assessment of Observance (May 2014), at 26, http://documents.worldbank.org/curated/en/986931468091183341/pdf/895010FSAP0P1400Box385284B00PUBLIC0.pdf.

[81] As of May 2019, the FSC has eight bureaus in the organisation – Financial Group Regulation; Planning and Coordination; Financial Consumer; Capital Markets; Financial Policy; Financial and Corporate Restructuring Policy; Financial Industry; and Financial Innovation. Financial Services Commission, Brochure, at 7, http://meng.fsc.go.kr/common/pdfjs/web/viewer.html?file=/upload/2019_ebook.pdf. On the other hand, the FSS holds nine divisions: Planning and Management; Strategic Supervision; Bank Supervision; Nonbank Supervision; Financial Investment Services Supervision; Disclosure and Investigation; Accounting Supervision; Insurance Supervision; and Financial Consumer Protection. Financial Supervisory Service, Organization Chart, http://english.fss.or.kr/fss/eng/wpge/eng115.jsp.

stakeholders, not the least of which are the regulators themselves. The next section examines the implementation aspect, or the 'plumbing' of, the regulatory structure, with a focus on the revolving door phenomenon.

12.4 THE REVOLVING DOOR AND LEGAL REFORMS

A better financial regulatory architecture can improve the quality of supervision. However, not all failures are caused, or can be resolved by, regulatory architecture. As seen in the 2011 savings bank crisis, one major defect was the pervasiveness of the revolving door phenomenon in the sector, which led to lax supervision and, worse, invited opportunities for corruption. This section examines the theoretical arguments regarding the revolving door phenomenon in general, then reviews it in the Korean context and examines the legislation intended to end it.

12.4.1 *Revolving Door Phenomenon and Hypothesis*

The phenomenon of the revolving door refers to the movement of people from industry into and out of key policymaking or enforcement posts in the executive and legislative branches, and in regulatory agencies.[82] Political scientists and economists have long argued that interest groups have significant influence over regulatory agencies, and that the revolving door can create undue influence – regulatory capture.[83] This risks an increase in the likelihood that those making policies are overly sympathetic, particularly to the needs of business – either because they come from that industry or because they plan to move to the private sector after working in government. Movement through the revolving door can be from industry to the public sector, public sector to industry, lobbyists to the public sector, or from the public sector to lobbyists.[84]

Evidence of the revolving door phenomenon is everlasting and everywhere. We see it in the United States, the United Kingdom, France, Germany, Japan, Korea and so on.[85] When US President Donald Trump took office, he addressed the issue and the potential for regulatory capture regarding his new staff members.[86] In Japan, *Amakudari* – meaning literally 'descent from heaven' and referring to post-retirement employment of elite government officials in high-ranking private sector jobs[87] – has presented an unresolved scandal in many government ministries, including Education, Defence and Finance.[88] Korea's largest conglomerates, Samsung, Lotte and SK group, appointed former government officials as independent directors

[82] Organisation for Economic Co-operation and Development, Revolving Doors, Accountability and Transparency – Emerging Regulatory Concerns and Policy Solutions in the Financial Crisis, GOV/PGC/ETH (2009) 2, OECD Conference Centre, Paris, 8.

[83] Daniel Carpenter and David Moss (eds), *Preventing Regulatory Capture: Special Interest Influence and How to Limit It* (Cambridge University Press, 2014), at 83–4.

[84] OECD (n 85) at 9.

[85] For examples of the revolving door around the world: ibid; High Pay Centre, 'The Revolving Door and the Corporate Colonisation of UK Politics', https://highpaycentre.org/wp-content/uploads/2020/09/FINAL_REVOLVING_DOOR .pdf.

[86] Brian Wallheimer, 'Should We Stop the Revolving Door', *Chicago Booth Review* (7 August 2017), http://review .chicagobooth.edu/public-policy/2017/article/should-we-stop-revolving-door.

[87] Tetsuro Mizoguchi and Nguyen Quyen, 'Amakudari: The Post-Retirement Employment of Elite Bureaucrats in Japan' (2012) 14(5) *Journal of Public Economic Theory* at 813.

[88] See, eg, Editorial, 'Get to the Bottom of "Amakudari"', *Japan Times* (25 January 2017), www.japantimes.co.jp/opinion/ 2017/01/25/editorials/get-bottom-amakudari/#.XjwJyy1L23U.

in executive-level positions, mostly recruited from the FSC and law enforcement authorities, including the Supreme Prosecutors' Office.[89]

Conceptually, the revolving door has both pros and cons.[90] The common concern – conflicts of interest – is that the revolving door may undermine the public interest, as well as promote particular benefits for industry. Conceptually, however, the revolving door can potentially facilitate the sharing of expertise and knowledge from one place to another. For example, the government can gain an understanding of fraudulent market conduct by hiring industry insiders, as illustrated by the phrase 'set a thief to catch a thief'.[91] Likewise, by hiring a person with experience at the regulator, a financial company can gain knowledge of complex regulation and minimise the cost of compliance.[92] Another benefit of the revolving door is that the very lure of lucrative private sector employment which follows a successful public service role may attract talent to low-paid public service in the first place.[93]

Some observers argue that the revolving door has had little impact in practice, as the 'revolving door is only open to a few' – a vast majority of government officials do not have private sector alternatives – and most never seek private employment because those alternatives are not always more attractive than public service;[94] the effects of the revolving door are overstated because regulators or law enforcers have much less discretion than once thought.[95] Other studies, however, show that the negative effects of the revolving door, from a public interest viewpoint, usually outweigh the bright side of private benefits.[96] For example, the positive effects of the revolving door stems from connections and special access rather than expertise or competence.[97] Some studies suggest that the phenomenon may have potentially impeded effective supervision and exacerbated the impact of the 2008 Global Financial Crisis.[98]

---

[89] Jin-ho Yoon, Yong-gun Lee and Yoon-gu Park, 'Revolving-Door Appointments up at Korean Top Chaebols after Bribery Charge', *The Pulse by Maeil Business News Korea* (29 March 2017), https://pulsenews.co.kr/view.php?year=2017&no=213007.

[90] The pros and cons can be exemplified by the *schooling hypothesis* and the *quid pro quo hypothesis*. The *schooling hypothesis* (or *expertise hypothesis*) sets forth that the expertise gained by an ex-regulator creates benefits such as improvements in risk management for the employing firm. The *quid pro quo hypothesis* (or *collusion hypothesis*) sets forth that financial firms recruit former regulators to seek undue gains, and 'future revolvers' create preferential treatment for the financial firms. In the United States, some studies have found that there is less evidence of quid pro quo behaviour, but more evidence supporting the schooling hypothesis. See, eg, Sophie A. Shive and Margaret M. Forster, 'The Revolving Door for Financial Regulators' (2017) 21(4) *Review of Finance* 1445–84, https://doi.org/10.1093/rof/rfw035. In Korea, studies found some evidence supporting the quid pro quo hypothesis. In that study, there was no improvement in risk management by hiring ex-regulators (rejecting the schooling hypothesis), while there was a short-term but significant decrease in regulatory penalties imposed upon the hiring firm after a revolving door employment. See, eg, Keeyoung Rhee and Sunjoo Hwang, 'Effects of Revolving Doors in the Financial Sector: Evidence from Korea', KDI Focus, No 94 (Korea Development Institute (KDI), 15 January 2019), https://doi.org/10.22740/kdi.focus.e.2019.94.

[91] Dieter Zinnbauer, 'The Vexing Issue of Revolving Door' (Edmond J. Safra Working Paper No 61, Edmond J. Safra Center for Ethics, Harvard University, 2015), at 9.

[92] See, eg, Ed de Haan, Kedia Simi, Kevin Koh and Shivaram Rajgopal, 'The Revolving Door and the SEC's Enforcement Outcomes: Initial Evidence from Civil Litigation' (2015) 60(2–3) *Journal of Accounting and Economics* 65–96 at 66.

[93] Zinnbauer (n 94) at 9.

[94] See, eg, David T. Zaring, 'Against Being against the Revolving Door' (2013) *University of Illinois Law Review* 507–49, https://illinoislawreview.org/print/volume-2013-issue-2/against-being-against-the-revolving-door/.

[95] 98 Ibid at 517–18; Zinnbauer (n 94) at 8.

[96] 99 Zinnbauer (n 94) at 12–17; Liz David Barrett, 'Cabs for Hire: Fixing the Revolving Door between Government and Business' (Transparency International UK, 2011), www.transparency.org.uk/publications/cabs-for-hire-fixing-the-revolving-door-between-government-and-business-2/.

[97] Zinnbauer (n 94) at 13.

[98] Ibid at 15.

Other studies show that private entities involved in the revolving door obtain private benefits at the expense of the public interest.[99]

Although the revolving door in the finance sector has existed for some time, the 2008 Global Financial Crisis brought the phenomenon to the attention of the public. Several countries have evidenced a common pattern of employing or appointing officials with close links with the banking or finance industries.[100] Not only does the revolving door move to and from the financial industry itself, but lobbyists for the financial industry, law firms and consulting firms with practices focused on finance also form the ecosystem of revolving personnel.[101] Prominent examples include Goldman Sachs alumni Robert Rubin, Henry Paulson and Steve Mnuchin, who served (or currently serve) as US Treasury Secretaries. But examples abound and are too numerous to list comprehensively.[102]

12.4.2 *The Revolving Door Phenomenon in Korea*

Korea was formerly a 'Platonic' country, which highly valued ethics, education and a contribution to society in daily life.[103] Steeped in two thousand years of history, dating back to ancient and medieval kingdoms (from Kochosun, Samkook, Shilla, Goryeo and Chosun), the Korean people long believed that educated individuals can and should lead society, as in Plato's 'the Republic', including at the level of the family, the village, corporations and the country. Confucianism, followed by Buddhism, traditionally taught that living ethically is more valuable than living opulently. As a result, humanism and generosity were regarded as indispensable elements of leadership, as well as guiding principles for daily life. Any conflicts of interest or conflicts of roles would, traditionally, have been controlled by an authoritarian or hierarchical order of importance in respect of self, the family, the village or the country.

Currently, however, Korea's traditional value system is not followed by many Koreans, unlike the position half a century ago. This is likely attributable to the period of military dictatorship, explosively rapid economic growth, an ageing society, the influence of modernity on Korean culture and widespread social values that emphasise outcomes over processes. While political power, economic wealth and social reputation were equally valued in the past, the first two have gained in relative importance as compared to the last – similar to what can be observed in the United States, whose influence has been underscored by the diplomatic and economic support it has provided to Korea since the end of the Second World War. Modernisation, the influence of the capitalistic economic system, globalisation and rapid economic development have all contributed to the prevalence of a more materialist outlook among Koreans.[104]

Put differently, 'the Kwan-jon-min-bee spirit' ('public officers are high, and civilians are low') has faded over time. This spirit, which used to involve a sense of pride in occupying public office (although it also encouraged authoritarianism), gave officers in the public service a sense of satisfaction with their social status, mitigated materialism and helped concentrate their attention on their jobs, as opposed to vying for lucrative public sector roles. As Korean society has

---

[99] Ibid at 13.
[100] OECD (n 85) at 23–36.
[101] For specific examples, see generally ibid.
[102] Ibid 23–36.
[103] Gizo Okura, *Korea Is a Philosophy* (originally in Japanese, translated into Korean by Sunghwan Cho (Moshineunsarandeul Publishing Company, 2018).
[104] Sang-seek Park, 'Why Are Koreans so Unhappy with Their Lot?', *Korea Herald* (25 January 2015), www.koreaherald .com/view.php?ud=20150125000326.

changed, with a growing preference for private sector over public vocations, and economic power over social reputation, the revolving door phenomenon has become ever more pronounced.

Longer life expectancy, coupled with low income from public sector roles and relatively low retirement ages, has also caused former Korean public officials to increasingly regard practical economic wealth as more desirable than platonic values or the romantic spirit of the past.[105] Post-retirement income in the form of a social security or a pension system available to former government officers or financial supervisors is generally not sufficient for sustenance.[106] At times, post-retirement employment, often resulting in a revolving door appointment, can be the only legitimate source of private income after retirement.

As demonstrated by the savings bank crisis, South Korea has had its share of revolving door woes. Being a highly regulated economy with traditions of strong state-led development,[107] relationships with the right government officials eased regulatory burdens and helped facilitate approvals and licences.[108] One important difference, however, is that unlike the phenomenon as discussed in Western literature, where the revolving door often completes its rotation, in Korea it tends only to complete a half-rotation – high-profile appointments from industry to the public service are extremely rare. Instead, government-to-industry appointments are common. As such, the revolving door phenomenon in Korea is often referred to as a 'parachute appointment' (*Nakasan Insa*) in Korean literature.[109]

The savings bank crisis exemplified several risks and conflicts of interest created by the revolving door. A multitude of former regulators were hired by the savings bank industry. Some abused their office by making industry-favourable supervisory decisions for savings banks, which in turn provided future employment. This type of influence represents a textbook example of capture, one that relies on 'crude incentives'.[110] Through revolving door connections, savings banks and their trade associations lobbied politicians and supervisors, and in some cases engaged in bribery. This points to another form of conflict that can arise when the social connections between former regulators and incumbent regulators create undue influence.[111] For example, former regulators can unduly influence the decisions of ex-colleagues who are 'inside' the revolving door. This type of influence can be particularly pervasive in the Korean context, where connections within the group are strong, and the

---

[105] See OECD, *OECD Economic Surveys: Korea 2018* (OECD Publishing, 2018), at 50, https://doi.org/10.1787/eco_ surveys-kor-2018-en. The rate by which Korea's population is ageing is the highest in the world. Between 2019 and 2050, it is predicted Korea will see a 23 per cent increase in the share of persons aged 65 years or over, www.un.org/en/ development/desa/population/publications/pdf/ageing/WorldPopulationAgeing2019-Highlights.pdf.

[106] According to OECD data, South Korea has the highest poverty rate for people aged 65 or older. OECD (n 109), Poverty rate (indicator), https://data.oecd.org/chart/5LTk.

[107] Sang-in Jun, 'The Origins of the Developmental State in South Korea' (1992) 16(2) *Asian Perspective* 181–204, www .jstor.org/stable/42704000.

[108] David S. Lee, 'South Korean Anti-Graft Law Misses Revolving Door', *Nikkei Asian Review* (16 November 2016), https://asia.nikkei.com/Politics/David-S.-Lee-South-Korean-anti-graft-law-misses-revolving-door. The revolving door phenomenon in Korea is not limited to the financial sector. The Sewol Ferry disaster, which claimed the lives of 304 people, most of whom were high school students on a school field trip, was caused in part because of the revolving door relationship between the government and industry. Jong-sung You and Youn-min Park, 'The Legacies of State Corporatism in Korea: Regulatory Capture in the Sewol Ferry Tragedy' (2017) 17(1) *Journal of East Asian Studies* 95–118.

[109] Seung-joo Lee and Sang-young Rhyu, 'The Political Dynamics of Informal Networks in South Korea: The Case of Parachute Appointment' (2008) 21(1) *The Pacific Review* 45–66.

[110] Carpenter and Moss (n 86) at 69.

[111] Ibid at 91; Transparency International UK (n 99) at 9.

former regulator is typically older and also senior in terms of the hierarchy of their previous agency positions.[112]

12.4.3 *Korean Revolving Door Laws before and after the 2011 Crisis*

South Korea has a number of laws and regulations in place to strengthen public service ethics and prevent conflicts of interest. Among them the *Public Service Ethics Act* (PSEA), enacted in 1981 and applicable to government and quasi-government officials, directly addresses of the revolving door phenomenon.[113] The PSEA imposes a cooling-off period – a restriction on private sector employment – after resignation from a government job. Several amendments – including one catalysed by the savings bank crisis – have strengthened the revolving door restriction over the years. As a result of the amendments, currently the law imposes a three-year cooling-off period on government officers, who may not accept employment with a private company[114] whose business is 'closely related to' the work that the government officer carried out in the five years before their resignation date. Adherence to these restrictions are mandatory – violators may face up to two years in prison, or up to KRW20 million in criminal fines.[115]

This post-public-employment restriction, while appearing to be strict in the letter of the law, in practice allows wide leeway in private sector employment. The law itself undermines employment restrictions by allowing special approval from the Ethics Committee for Government Officers (ECGO) for employment in certain cases.[116] Specifically, if the ECGO determines that the private sector firm's business is not 'closely related to' the applicant's previous work, the employment restrictions do not apply. Historically, the ECGO's approval rate has been extremely high: the approval rate for financial regulators between 2011 and 2017 was 94 per cent.[117] In fact, surveys show that more than half of all retired financial regulators secure employment at financial firms after they leave public sector employment.[118] Knowing that the cooling-off period applies only if the new job is 'closely related to' an officer's previous work, regulators typically reassign soon-to-retire staff to offices that are typically unrelated to potential post-public-employment opportunities. For example, in the case of the FSS, the

---

[112] In this case (former or incumbent) regulators may not deliberately create undue influence, but social dynamics or cultural norms, and at times simply personal trust may create influence. A new line of research focused on behavioural (as compared to materialistic) aspects of capture, seeks to explain this phenomenon as a type of 'in-group bias' or 'cultural capture'. Carpenter and Moss (n 86) at 91.

[113] *Public Service Ethics Act* [공직자윤리법], Act No 3250, 31 December 1981 (S Kor) (as amended). Enacted in 1981, the PSEA borrowed ideas from the US *Ethics in Government Act* of 1978. The PSEA contains several provisions aimed at reducing opportunities that may give rise to conflicts of interest, such as mandatory registration, or disclosure of assets and interests, and requirements in respect of Blind Trusts for stock and shareholdings during periods in office. Pan Suk Kim and Taebeom Yun, 'Strengthening Public Service Ethics in Government: The South Korean Experience' (2017) 19(6) *Public Integrity* 607–23.

[114] 'Private company' here is specified by size (ie, gross assets of KRW10 billion or more and gross revenues of KRW30 billion or more).

[115] PSEA (n 116) art 29.

[116] Ibid art 17 para 1.

[117] People's Solidarity for Participatory Democracy, Issue Report, 'Employment Status Report for Retired Officials of the Ministry of Strategy and Finance, the Financial Services Commission and the Financial Supervisory Service 2011–2017' [참여연대 이슈리포트, 기획재정부, 금융위원회, 금융감독원 퇴직공직자 취업실태 보고서 2011–2017], at 3.

[118] Congressman Ko Yong-jin, '106 High-Level FSS Officials Re-employed at Financial Firms over the Last 10 years' [고용진 의원 보도자료, 최근 10년, 금감원 고위공직자 106명 금융권 등 재취업] (Press Release, 13 September 2018).

consumer protection divisions, HR offices and general affairs offices are considered strategic choices for soon-to-retire staff.[119]

Although the PSEA had been in place for decades, critics deemed it ineffective.[120] As a result, in 2011 the PSEA was significantly amended, in terms of both scope and intensity, by imposing stricter employment restrictions after public service, some specifically targeting the FSS, whose poor performance was at the heart of the crisis.[121] First, the scope of government officials subject to a cooling-off period was broadened to include more junior FSS staff, as well as KDIC and BOK employees.[122] Second, the classification of a private company subject to a cooling-off period was widened to include law firms, accounting firms and tax-accounting firms.[123] Third, the government officer's previous work period reviewed to determine 'closely related to' was extended from three to five years.[124]

Contrary to expectations, however, the revolving door phenomenon has not diminished since the 2011 savings bank scandal. It has instead increased over time, as the law still provides great leeway to evade post-employment restrictions.[125] Lack of improvements in this area suggests that Korea should first tackle the more fundamental issue of post-retirement sustenance in order to resolve the revolving door problem. One option to alleviate the problem could be to introduce some form of legitimate compensation for the constraints imposed upon future employment – something akin to a paid 'gardening leave system' where employees remain on the payroll but are suspended from work.[126] This system is used to prevent an employee from gaining sensitive and up-to-date information before leaving the job. The fact that the revolving door often occurs in Korea at the staff level (compared to the political leadership or senior levels) also suggests that an effective revolving door restriction should be reasonably designed to take account of freedom of employment for the regulators and respect flexible career needs,[127] while also minimising the risks of conflicts of interest.

12.5 CONCLUSION: IMPLICATIONS OF THE REVOLVING DOOR ON REGULATORY ARCHITECTURE

This chapter has used the 2011 savings bank crisis as a case study to illustrate that for a system to function well, both regulatory architecture and good implementation matter, and that poor implementation caused by the revolving door phenomenon can undermine any type of regulatory architecture.

---

[119] Ibid.

[120] See, eg, Kim and Yun (n 116).

[121] PSEA Amendments on 29 July 2011, Law No 10982, Amendments Effective on 30 October 2011.

[122] PSEA Enforcement Decree, art 3, para 4 [공직자윤리법 시행령] (PSEA Enforcement Decree Amendments on 28 October 2011, Presidential Decree No 23271, Amendments Effective on 30 October 2011).

[123] PSEA (n 116) art 17, para 1.

[124] Ibid art 17, para 1. Before the 2011 amendment, the 'cooling off' period – the waiting period during which the officer was banned from working – was three years, whereas the 'review period' – the period which was reviewed in order to determine whether the new job is 'closely related to' the officer's previous work was five years. After the 2011 amendment, the 'cooling off' period was unchanged at three years, while the 'review period' was extended from three years to five years.

[125] PSPD Report (n 120) at 8.

[126] Transparency International UK (n 99) at 18; Julia Kagan, 'Gardening Leave', *Investopedia* (19 September 2019), www .investopedia.com/terms/g/gardening-leave.asp.

[127] See Transparency International UK (n 99) at 17–18 ('It is arguably unreasonable to prevent senior civil servants and Ministers from pursuing their careers freely. They are individuals with ambitions, interests, and families to support').

Assuming the Twin Peaks model can influence organisational activity, and that mechanisms for controlling the revolving door can affect the behaviour of individuals within the regulators, both devices may work independently to reduce collusive behaviour between the regulator and the regulated. Compared to the integrated model, Twin Peaks provides advantages in respect of specialisation of regulatory focus, and allows independent cross-checking between the two regulatory goals, without them compromising one another. Prudential supervision focuses primarily on the financial soundness of banks and insurers from an accounting or finance perspective, while market conduct supervision primarily oversees the legal and contractual aspects between consumers and financial firms. For instance, competitive pricing of any financial products can be considered differently from a prudential viewpoint and a market conduct one. Splitting the goals and tasks among each regulator may reduce each regulator's discretion in engaging in collusive behaviour because, in theory, each regulator draws from a narrower pool of information and uses different types of monitoring technologies.[128] Thus, the double screening process utilised by the Twin Peak system may be more effective and specialised than a single peak system, but at a larger economic cost and/or risk of omitting some points of supervision. In our 2011 savings bank case study, had there been a separate consumer protection regulator, that regulator could have questioned the FSC–FSS's ostensible systemic concerns and prevented the issuance of subordinated debt which caused great consumer harm.

Control of the revolving door, which in Korea comes in the form of employment restrictions, can, to some degree, prevent individual supervisory staff from being motivated to involve themselves in any conflicts of interest. Employment restrictions can minimise the collusive effect of social connections and illicit activities that might occur between individuals inside and outside the revolving door. In that sense, revolving door control can be analogous to the plumbing in the building structure of a financial supervisory system. Of course, without proper implementation, both architecture and plumbing may fail.

---

[128] Jean-Jacques Laffont and David Martimort, 'Separation of Regulators against Collusive Behavior' (1999) 30(2) *RAND Journal of Economics* 232–62, www.jstor.org/stable/2556079 (arguing 'separation of regulators may act as a device against the threat of regulatory capture' and providing economic models for that proposition).

13

China

Considering Elements of Twin Peaks to Upgrade Its Financial Regulation

Li Guo and Jessica Cheung

13.1 INTRODUCTION

As China's financial system becomes more complex and integrated, interest in and discussion of potential structural reform has intensified. In particular, many commentators advocate for a move towards the Twin Peaks model, along the lines of Australia's experience. In determining the suitability of the elements of Twin Peaks to upgrade China's financial regulation, this chapter provides a country-specific study of its financial system and the adequacy of its recent regulatory responses to its sources of risk.

This chapter finds that although China has made good progress in implementing regulatory measures to address the mounting risks in its financial system, its sectoral regulatory model is clearly under strain in dealing with its increasingly integrated financial sector. China, of course, is not asleep at the wheel but, to the dismay of some Twin Peaks advocates, the recent reform proposal of the government is to implement a Financial Stability and Development Committee, rather than moving towards Twin Peaks. In light of this recent policy, this chapter discusses one of the remaining risks – the lack of a general consumer protection agency – and explores the options for a strengthened consumer regulatory regime in China.

This chapter is structured as follows: Section 13.2 begins with an overview of China's financial sector and sources of risk to lay the foundation for a country-specific study. Section 13.3 proceeds with a brief discussion of China's current financial regulatory architecture and Section 13.4 examines how the authorities have responded to the sources of risk laid down in Section 13.2. The shortcomings of the regulatory responses to date have sparked a call for reform of the regulatory structure and these reform proposals are subject to scrutiny in Section 13.5. Section 13.6 concludes that Twin Peaks might serve as a model for China, which, as revealed, is not the latest reform trend announced by the Chinese government. In light of this, this section explores what can be done next to address the unresolved problems after the implementation of the latest reforms. Section 13.7 provides some concluding remarks.

13.2 OVERVIEW OF CHINA'S FINANCIAL SECTOR AND SOURCES OF RISK

China's financial system has been described as a highly repressive regime.[1] Rather than serving consumers' needs or pursuing economic returns, it has been functioning as a conduit for the

---

[1] Franklin Allen, Jun Qian, Chenying Zhang and Mengxin Zhao, 'China's Financial System: Opportunities and Challenges' in Joseph P. H. Fan and Randall Morck (eds) *Capitalizing China* (University of Chicago Press, 2012).

government to carry out the state's broader political, economic and monetary policy.[2] In comparison to both developed and emerging countries, China's financial system has been dominated by a large banking system,[3] and pervasive controls remain in areas such as interest rates, credit, market entry, and capital flows.[4] Other capital markets, such as the stock market and the bond market, are less significant than the banking sector in terms of both scale and importance.[5]

Notwithstanding the highly regulated banking system, unbalanced financial markets and even an ineffective legal system, China has continued to attain impressive economic growth in the past few decades, driven by a shadow banking system.[6] As estimated by Moody's Investor Service, assets held in China's shadow banking system reached 82 per cent of GDP by June 2016.[7]

13.2.1 *Traditional Banking Sector*

China's banking system is mainly controlled by the four largest state-owned banks (the Big 4), all of which have been publicly listed in recent years, with the government being the largest shareholder.[8]

Previously, the People's Bank of China (PBOC) had control over interest rates of state-owned banks by setting a ceiling on saving deposit rates and a floor on lending rates.[9] Through the suppression of interest rates, depositors' savings are effectively transferred through the banks to subsidise state-owned enterprises (SOEs) and policy-favoured projects.[10]

Meanwhile, the PBOC also imposes an administrative quota on the Big 4 banks, which, under political pressure from local governments, usually provide a quota to support local government-initiated projects.[11] Many of these projects are potentially unprofitable, with high

---

[2] Details and data can be found in International Monetary Fund Working Paper, 'Resolving China's Corporate Debt Problem', WP/16/203 (2016); International Monetary Fund Country Report, 'People's Republic of China – Selected Issues', No 16/271(2016).

[3] Franklin Allen, Jun Qian and Meijun Qian, 'China's Financial System: Past, Present, and Future' in Loren Brandt and Thomas G. Rawski (eds) *China's Great Economic Transformation* (Cambridge University Press, 2008), 507; and Allen et al (n 1).

[4] The World Bank, Development Research Center of the State Council, the People's Republic of China, China 2030 – Building a Modern, Harmonious, and Creative Society (2013).

[5] Allen, Qian and Qian (n 3).

[6] Franklin Allen and Jun Qian, 'How Can China's Financial System Help to Transform Its Economy?' in Shenggen Fan, Ravi Kanbur, Shang-Jin Wei and Xiaobo Zhang (eds) *The Oxford Companion to the Economics of China* (Oxford University Press, 2014); Allen et al (n 1).

[7] Laura He, 'China's Shadow Banking System Expands to 82pc of GDC: Moody's', *South China Morning Post* (13 December 2016; online).

[8] Michael Wines, 'China Bank I.P.P. Raises $19 Billion', *New York Times* (6 July 2010; online).

[9] The PBOC has taken steps towards allowing market forces to set the price of the RMB. While the deposit ceiling remains fixed by the government, the PBOC removed the floor on bank lending rates in 2013. Details about China's interest rate liberalisation can be found at Wei Shen, *Shadow Banking in China – Risk, Regulation and Policy* (Edward Elgar Publishing, 2016), 297–317.

[10] The problem of local government debts in China are outlined in Yiping Huang, 'Local Government Debts' in Shenggen Fan, Ravi Kanbur, Shang-Jin Wei and Xiaobo Zhang (eds) *The Oxford Companion to the Economics of China* (Oxford University Press, 2014); IMF Working Paper, 'Regulating Local Government Financing Vehicles and Public–Private Partnerships in China', WP/16/187 (2016); and Wei Shen (n 9) 149–86.

[11] Chinese banks have been accustomed to bad lending practices, due to the fact that more than 85 per cent of the profits of the banking sector come from the difference between government-set lending and deposit rates. This commercial reality has encouraged banks to lend as much as they can, in order to maximise profits. See IMF Working Paper, 'Financial Distortions in China: A General Equilibrium Approach', WP/15/274 (2015).

risk of default, and have facilitated a mounting number of non-performing loans.[12] Worse still, these local government debts soared after the 2008/09 Global Financial Crisis (GFC), as the Chinese government implemented a RMB4 trillion stimulus package. While, on the one hand, the package allowed China to transition to an investment-driven economy to boost GDP growth,[13] the International Monetary Fund (IMF), on the other hand, has suggested that, 'continued excessive investment and resource misallocation [in China] will ... expand debt to an unsustainable level with an elevated risk of a financial crisis'.[14]

As the quantum of outstanding credit had been rising faster than GDP, and lending was not pooled into the real economy, a credit crunch took place in June 2013, leaving the interbank lending market on the brink of collapse.[15] The unified national interbank market was established by the PBOC in 1996 to allow banks to borrow from one another in order to meet temporary shortfalls in funding. The market consists of a primary and a secondary network, connecting the largest PBOC branches, commercial banks and non-bank institutions.[16] Although the PBOC agreed to provide liquidity support to cash-strapped banks after the initial 'no-action' strategy to avoid a crisis,[17] it remains nonetheless important, in times of a credit collapse, to monitor financial contagion, embedded as it is in the interbank market.

13.2.2 *Shadow Banking Sector*

The market's response to distorted bank lending practices in China has included the proliferation of a shadow banking system, which is a network of 'credit intermediation involving entities and activities outside the regular banking system'[18] that purport to circumvent the regulations imposed on formal banking institutions.

One major aspect of China's shadow banking is banks' off-balance-sheet vehicles, such as wealth management products (WMPs).[19] In China, these WMPs consist of a pool of securities, including bonds and trust products.[20] Approximately 70 per cent of WMPs are non-capital protected products with floating earning rates unknown to investors, who assume that an implicit guarantee is provided by banks on a WMP's profitability.[21] In the past five years, WMPs have become increasingly popular in China. Depositors have shown a tendency to pile into WMPs because of their higher interest rates than the ceiling on deposit rates in formal banks,[22] whereas

---

[12] IMF World Economic and Financial Surveys, 'Global Financial Stability Report: Getting the Policy Mix Right' (Washington, DC, 2017).

[13] IMF Working Paper, 'Rebalancing in China – Progress and Prospects', WP/16/183 (2016).

[14] Ibid.

[15] By June 2013 credit had been growing at 20 per cent in China, more than double the rate of economic growth. The overall credit-to-gross domestic product ratio in China reached 200 per cent in mid-2013, indicating rising leverage throughout the economy. See Simon Rabinovitch, 'Echoes of Mao in China Cash Crunch', *Financial Times* (20 June 2013, online); Wei Shen (n 9).

[16] Allen et al (n 1).

[17] Wei Shen (n 9); Josh Noble and Simon Rabinovitch, 'PBOC Plays Hard Ball over Cash Crunch', *Financial Times* (24 June 2013, online).

[18] Financial Stability Board, 'Shadow Banking: Scoping the Issues – A Background Note of the Financial Stability Board' (2011).

[19] Detailed analysis of the regulation of WMPs in China is provided in: Wei Shen (n 9) 118–48; IMF Working Paper, 'China's Financial Interlinkages and Implications for Inter-Agency Coordination', WP/16/181 (2016).

[20] Li Guo and Daile Xia, 'In Search of a Place in the Sun: The Shadow Banking System with Chinese Characteristics' (2014) 15 *European Business Organization Law Review* 406–10.

[21] IMF Working Paper, 'Financial Distortions in China: A General Equilibrium Approach', WP/15/274 (2015).

[22] 'The Air Is Thinning – Are China's Banks Growing out of the Government's Strait-Jacket?', *The Economist* (19 May 2012).

banks in turn tap into the WMPs market in order to circumvent the official caps on interest rates, and to meet loan-to-deposit ratios for further lending.[23] However, the soaring number of WMPs issued has created heightened credit risks for banks that provided WMPs as they fail to make payment for the WMPs on maturity, and thus cause systemic risk in China's financial system.[24] This is illustrated by the scandals involving Huaxia Bank, China CITIC Bank and China Construction Bank (CCB).[25] WMPs and other off-balance-sheet vehicles are also highly interconnected with the stock market, generating a growing risk, as evidenced by the 2015 stock market turbulence.[26]

Another driving force in the growth of the shadow banking market is the aforementioned credit quota, and the state-owned banks' tendency to lend to SOEs. These lending irregularities have severely marginalised small and medium enterprises (SMEs) in China in the traditional banking system.[27] The 2012 Enterprise Survey conducted by the World Bank estimated that only 10 per cent of SMEs had access to formal banking loans.[28] This structural constraint leaves SMEs with no choice but to resort to shadow banking for credit, driving the development of businesses towards P2P and other forms of underground lending in China.[29] Currently, the booming P2P lending industry is largely free from regulatory oversight, with major risks stemming from insufficient investor protection and the chance of fraudulent business activities.[30] The underground lending market poses additional and severe systemic and credit risks.[31] Credit woes in turn are interconnected through 'debt triangles' where late payment of a small firm can create cash-flow problems to suppliers up the supply chain and worsen their credit woes,[32] giving rise to a domino effect on the wider financial system in cases of major defaults of an underground loan.[33] The formal banking system is in turn not insulated because underground banks are a major conduit for the illegal flow of overseas capital into China.[34] Ultimately, a lack of a centralised pool of funding and the government's inability to bail out underground banks elevate the social instability risk.[35]

---

[23] Wei Shen (n 9) 118–48.

[24] Allen and Qian (n 6).

[25] Daniel Ren, 'Guarantor Repays Principal on Failed Huaxia Product', *South China Morning Post* (23 January 2013; online); Wei Shen (n 9) 127–9.

[26] IMF Working Paper, 'China's Financial Interlinkages and Implications for Inter-Agency Coordination', WP/16/181 (2016), 12.

[27] The underpinning reasons include, but are not limited to SMEs' inability to meet the lending criteria set out by banks, and their weaker connections with the government, as compared with the SOEs.

[28] The World Bank, Enterprise Surveys – China: Country Profile (2012).

[29] Bence Varga, 'Current Challenges Facing Chinese Financial Supervision and Methods of Handling These Challenges' (2017) 16 *Financial and Economic Review* 126–39.

[30] Wei Shen (n 9) 187–225.

[31] The lack of regulatory oversight and uncertainty in the macroeconomic environment makes the underground lending market the most vulnerable sector in China's shadow banking sector; ibid.

[32] Zhao Hongmei and Koh Gui Qing, 'China's Runaway Bosses Spotlight Underground Loan Market', *Reuters* (29 September 2011; online).

[33] Jon Woo, 'China's Loan Sharks Circle in Murky Shadow Bank Water', *Reuters* (30 January 2014, online).

[34] Zhang Bing, Zheng Fei and Zhao Jingting, 'Cash Crash for Wenzhou's Private Loan Network', *Caixin* (11 October 2011).

[35] Emilios Avgouleas and Charles Goodhart, 'Critical Reflections on Bank Bail-ins' (2015) 1 *Journal of Financial Regulation* 3–29.

13.3 CHINA'S FINANCIAL REGULATORY ARCHITECTURE

Before a discussion of China's regulatory responses to various sources of risk, it is imperative to briefly introduce its financial regulatory architecture. China follows a predominantly sectoral, entity-based approach, with functional characteristics. The regulatory architecture in China comprises a central bank and two parallel supervisory agencies, often referred to as 'One Bank, Two Commissions'; that is to say, the People's Bank of China, the China Banking and Insurance Regulatory Commission (CBIRC) and the China Securities Regulatory Commission (CSRC).

13.3.1 *The People's Bank of China*

The PBOC is the central bank of China and, unlike the central banks of most economies which act as a lender-of-last-resort, the PBOC is a national financial administrative organ without any commercial lending responsibility.[36] The key function of the PBOC is to formulate and implement monetary policy. Article 3 of the PBOC Law 2003 states that the objective of monetary policy is to maintain monetary stability and, in this way, promote economic growth. The PBOC is also responsible for the control of inflation, defined as 'maintaining the stability of the value of the currency'.[37]

13.3.2 *The Two Commissions: CBIRC and CSRC*

The CBIRC and CSRC are the regulatory authorities for banking and insurance activities and the securities market respectively.[38]

The CBIRC is a product of a merger in April 2018 between the China Banking Regulatory Commission (CBRC) and the China Insurance Regulatory Commission (CIRC).[39] The CBRC was established in 2003 to oversee all banks and their activities.[40] It derives its supervisory powers from the *Law of the PRC on Banking Regulation and Supervision*. The CIRC was set up by the State Council in 1998 as the sole regulator of China's insurance market. The main legal instrument for authority comes from the *Insurance Law of the PRC*.

The CBIRC regulates a range of institutions, including banks, insurance companies, finance companies and trust companies. In a major expansion of the powers of the PBOC, it was announced in 2018 that the powers of the CBRC and the CIRC to make laws and regulations would be transferred to the PBOC.[41]

The CSRC was established by the State Council in 1992 to approve and supervise securities listing and trading. However, it was not until 1998, when the *Securities Law of the PRC* came into force, that the CSRC finally assumed regulatory powers. The CSRC is invested with broad powers under the *Securities Law*.[42]

---

[36] Wei Shen (n 9) 66–91.
[37] Art 3 of the Law of the People's Bank of China 2003.
[38] For a more detailed outline of the history and scope of responsibilities of each of the regulatory authorities, see Wei Shen (n 9) 66–91.
[39] See CBIRC, 'China Banking and Insurance Regulatory Commission Officially Unveiled' (CBIRC, 2019), www.cbirc .gov.cn/en/view/pages/ItemDetail.html?docId=176215&itemId=980.
[40] Wei Shen (n 9) 66–91.
[41] See Shu Zhang and Se Young Lee, 'China to Merge Regulators, Create New Ministries in Biggest Overhaul in Years', *Reuters* (13 March 2018), www.reuters.com/article/us-china-parliament/china-to-merge-regulators-create-new-minis tries-in-biggest-revamp-in-years-idUSKCN1GP003.
[42] Wei Shen (n 9) 66–91.

13.3.3 *Other Institutions: MOF and SAFE*

Of the other government agencies, the Ministry of Finance (MOF) and the State Administration of Foreign Exchange (SAFE) play an important role from a financial stability viewpoint. The MOF is the fiscal agent, with responsibilities covering debt issuance and the management of state-owned assets, whereas SAFE has custody of foreign exchange reserves. These two agencies, together, provide the government with a substantial 'financial backstop' for the financial system and the resources to intervene in times of crisis.[43]

13.4 REGULATORY RESPONSE TO CURRENT RISKS AND ISSUES

Section 13.2 outlined various sources of risk in China's financial markets, including the booming credit and local government debt markets and the interconnected regular and shadow banking systems, which potentially expose the market to higher systemic risks. A lesson from the GFC is that any build-up of risks should be identified and addressed by a macroprudential regulator well before they evolve into a systemic event.[44] Following on from the discussion in Section 13.2, the next question is whether the current institutional arrangements and recent improvements in China are able to control existing risks?

13.4.1 *Local Government Debt and Credit Expansion*

Since 2013, measures have been actively taken by the Chinese government and regulators to stop the growth of local government debts and credit expansion, including revision of the budget law in 2014[45] and the introduction of a debt swap programme to restructure local governments' liabilities.[46] That said, these measures can only mitigate the risk, not cure it.[47] Ultimately, the flaw lies in China's heavy reliance on an investment-driven model for economic growth.[48] Not only is this model unsustainable, it may also leave China in either the 'middle-income trap' or cause a crisis.[49] Having recognised this danger, China's reform intention has been clearly reflected in its 11th and 12th Five Year Plans, with a focus to move towards a consumption-based market economy.[50] At the heart of China's market economy reform is financial liberalisation, including liberalisation of interest rates, exchange rates and capital account.[51]

---

[43] IMF Working Paper, 'Strengthening China's Financial Stability Framework, China's Road to Greater Financial Stability – Some Policy Perspectives' (2013).

[44] IMF Working Paper, 'China's Financial Interlinkages and Implications for Inter-Agency Coordination', WP/16/181 (2016), 20.

[45] PRC Budget Law was first promulgated twenty years ago, and amendments were initiated a decade ago. The size of the newly amended Budget Law is double the size of the previous version, with changes in eighty-two areas, including its strengthened oversight by the legislatures, in line with the Third Plenum's call for a more transparent budgeting system.

[46] 'China to Continue Debt-Swap Program in 2016', *Wall Street Journal* (22 December 2015; online).

[47] Sara Hsu, 'China's Debt–Equity Swap Program Doesn't Address Its Debt Problem' (15 October 2016; online).

[48] Randall Peerenboom, 'Revamping the China Model for the Post-Global Financial Crisis Era: The Emerging Post-Washington, Post Beijing Consensus' in Lisa Toohey, Colin Picker and Jonathan Greenacre (eds) *China in the International Economic Order* (Cambridge University Press, 2015), 11–26.

[49] Ibid; The World Bank, Development Research Center of the State Council, the People's Republic of China, China 2030 – Building a Modern, Harmonious, and Creative Society (2013).

[50] The Central Committee of the Communist Party of China, The 13th Five-Year Plan for Economic and Social Development of the People's Republic of China.

[51] IMF Working Paper, 'China's Financial Interlinkages and Implications for Inter-Agency Coordination', WP/16/181 (2016), 20.

13.4.2 Regulatory Structure for Shadow Banking System

In 2013 the State Council took a preliminary step to tackle the shadow banking sector by issuing the Circular of the General Office of the State Council on Relevant Issues of Strengthening the Regulation of Shadow Banking (Circular No. 107). It outlines a regulatory framework, corresponding to the sectoral regulatory model, for regulating the financial markets. Each regulatory authority has its own jurisdiction over a specific sector, matching the regulatory architecture for traditional financial markets – brokerage firms and insurance companies are regulated by the CSRC and CBIRC respectively. Banks and trust companies are regulated by the CBIRC.[52]

While this regulatory framework maintains consistency with the one for formal financial markets, a clear defect of this institutional build-up is that the shadow banking sector is often cross-sectoral and a sectoral division may create regulatory arbitrage, overlap and inconsistency. Moreover, although Circular No. 107 may represent a sound regulatory approach to improving the regulation of shadow banking, it is merely a policy document, setting out broader legal, economic and policy considerations, in the absence of utility, clarity and details.[53]

The flaws of the sectoral regulatory approach for shadow banking can also be exemplified by the conduct-of-business regulation of WMPs. Unlike consumers in the formal banking system, where laws and regulations require the disclosure of credit terms and limit the activities of debt collectors, financial consumers in the shadow banking industry are less protected.[54] In response to this regulatory loophole, one measure employed by the CBRC was the issuance of new mandatory disclosure rules, which require banks to fully disclose information on WMPs and register WMPs with the CBRC.[55] These new disclosure rules aim to reduce information asymmetries and improve transparency of banks' off-balance-sheet activities. However, the new rules employed by the CBRC are only applicable to products issued by banks, leaving other financial institutions at large.

13.4.3 Strengthened Inter-agency Coordination

The ongoing financial liberalisation has driven intensive competition among banks, shadow banks and non-bank institutions.[56] With declining profit margins, resulting from the removal of lending floors in 2013, traditional banks have turned to the shadow banking industry for profit. The rise of banks' off-balance-sheet capital flows increases the linkages in the system, making the conventional microprudential regulatory approach – maintaining financial stability by monitoring the soundness of individual institutions – no longer effective.[57]

China has not been asleep on this issue. Following the recommendations by the Financial Stability Board (FSB) in its Financial Sector Assessment Programme (FSAP) in 2011, a macroprudential management framework has been developed in China to strengthen inter-agency cooperation and improve data collection.[58] The institutional arrangements for macroprudential

---

[52] Guo and Xia (n 20) 410–16.
[53] Wei Shen (n 9) 60–65.
[54] Ibid 119; Sara Hsu, 'China's Regulation of Wealth Management Products', *The Diplomat* (15 May 2014; online).
[55] CBRC's Interim Measures for the Administration of Commercial Banks' Personal Financial Management Services (effective as of 1 November 2005), arts 37 and 49.
[56] IMF Working Paper, 'China's Monetary Policy and Interest Rate Liberalization: Lessons from International Experiences', WP/14/75 (2014).
[57] IMF Working Paper, 'China's Financial Interlinkages and Implications for Inter-Agency Coordination', WP/16/181 (2016).
[58] Financial Stability Board, Peer Review of China – Review Report (2015).

management are set out in the laws of the National People's Congress (NPC) and its Standing Committee (NPCSC) – the highest-level organ involves the State Council, which chairs regular meetings held by the top leaders of the supervisory authorities and other related ministers. One tier below is the middle level, involving discussions at the ministerial level among the PBOC and regulatory agencies through an inter-agency committee.[59] Currently, the PBOC has developed the *Interim Rules on Information Sharing* to coordinate with the CBIRC and CSRC. The inter-agency cooperation and information-sharing between the two commissions consist of a series of Memoranda of Understanding.[60] Lastly, the lowest level comprises technical-level communications between the regulators and the regulated institutions.[61]

An important inter-agency body for coordination was formed in 2008 and named the Financial Crisis Response Group (FCRG). The FCRG is chaired by the State Council, and consists of representatives from the MOF, SAFE, CBRC, CSRC and CIRC. The group convenes meetings once or twice a month to discuss new financial system trends, major potential risks and coordination to solve cross-agency issues. To date, the meetings have covered various topics, including the regulation of shadow banking activities, the establishment of a deposit insurance system and the establishment of a Joint Ministerial Committee.[62]

In 2013, the Financial Regulatory Coordination Joint Ministerial Committee (JMC) was established by the State Council.[63] It is chaired by the governor of the PBOC, and comprises the chairs of CBIRC, CSRC and SAFE. The objective of the JMC is to enhance regular inter-agency regulatory coordination and information-sharing in respect of monetary policies and financial regulatory policies. The JMC is expected to meet quarterly, with the responsibility to prepare the agenda for the meetings residing with the PBOC.[64] Since its inception, the JMC has met eight times, as of 2016.

While the FSB may have described the JMC as 'a useful mechanism to facilitate discussion of cross-sectoral issues and to issue inter-agency regulations', it has exhibited some clear flaws, which render its effectiveness rather doubtful.[65] Of all the flaws, the lack of decision-making power by the JMC is one that is heavily criticised. The root of this flaw lies in the fact that the JMC was established by the State Council on an administrative basis, rather than a legal basis. In its approval of the establishment of the JMC, the State Council clearly stated that the JMC 'does not change the current mechanism of financial regulation, nor substitute or weaken the current division of responsibilities of relevant government agencies' and that it also 'does not act as a

---

[59] In the committee, the financial regulatory agencies regularly coordinate actions and communicate on major issues, such as financial stability, financial reform and risk mitigation.

[60] IMF Working Paper, 'China's Financial Interlinkages and Implications for Inter-Agency Coordination', WP/16/181 (2016).

[61] Financial Stability Board (n 58).

[62] Ibid.

[63] In fact, the 2013 JMC was not the first attempt by China to achieve regulatory coordination. China tried to hold joint conferences since 2000, but these remained largely inactive until 2003, when the CBRC replaced the PBOC in the supervision of banking institutions, and the members of the 2000 Joint Conference held the first meeting and signed an MoU. More details can be found in Andrew Godwin, Guo Li and Ian Ramsay, 'Is Australia's "Twin Peaks" System of Financial Regulation a Model for China?' (2016) 46 *Hong Kong Law Journal* 621.

[64] On top of the responsibility for setting the agenda of JMC meetings, the PBOC is also responsible for drafting the annual work plan for financial regulatory coordination; organising background materials to facilitate discussion of the agenda items; coordinating the implementation of JMC decisions; conducting research on financial regulatory coordination; and submitting briefings on the work of the JMC to the State Council and member agencies; IMF Working Paper, 'China's Financial Interlinkages and Implications for Inter-Agency Coordination', WP/16/181 (2016).

[65] 吴晓灵, 金融监管协调机制不能有名无实 [Wu Xiaoling, Financial Regulatory Coordination System Cannot Remain in Name Only], *The Wall Street Journal* (29 May 2014; online).

substitute for the decisions of the State Council'.[66] Consequently, the JMC is unable to issue any formal documents. On an operational level, there are no standing agenda items of JMC discussions, and issues deliberated tend to vary across meetings.[67] Also, communication on financial stability issues emanates from the PBOC and the two commissions. The JMC and other inter-agency bodies do not have a separate communication policy and little information is publicly available on the issues discussed.[68]

13.4.4 *Enhanced Analytical Macroprudential Framework*

In its 2014 FSAB, the FSB also recommended that China build a macroprudential framework for management of systemic risks.[69] Under the FSB's peer review in the following year, it was revealed that good progress had been made by the PBOC and the regulatory authorities.[70]

Currently, the systemic risk monitoring framework in China consists of three layers.[71] First, the FCRG, inter alia, convenes regular meetings to discuss systemic risks and prevention policies by considering recent financial system developments and concerns.[72] Secondly, the PBOC and regulatory agencies undertake risk surveillance and analysis for their respective sectors on a regular and ad hoc basis, at the request of the State Council. The JMC may also be involved in the analysis of policies to address identified systemic financial risks. Thirdly, there is the relevant agencies' cooperation in order to obtain an overview of risks. For example, in preparing the Financial Stability Report the agencies have established a steering group to facilitate full exchange of individual agencies' risk judgements and views.

Furthermore, each agency has interpreted its mandate as including a macroprudential dimension and has developed its own analytical framework, including stress tests, early warning systems and systemic risk analysis. On the cross-agency level, the PBOC reports that it coordinates with related agencies to carry out system-wide risk surveillance on both a regular and ad hoc basis.[73]

However, despite this recent progress, the analytical framework for systemic risks implemented is far from perfect. Each regulatory agency's macroprudential orientation reflects its sectoral mandate, which can limit the analysis of cross-sectoral effects and therefore constrain an overall view of systemic risks. Despite the macroeconomic inputs to stress test exercises, it appears that early warning and stress test exercises are generally carried out separately by the different agencies. In other words, the stress tests are restricted to firms under the remit of each agency and do not capture any cross-sectoral linkages.[74]

The lack of information-collection power poses another stumbling block for China's inter-agency cooperation. The FSB's peer review reveals that while the sharing of offsite data seems

---

[66] Godwin, Guo and Ramsay (n 63); 国务院 《国务院关于同意建立金融监管协调部际联席会议制度的批复》 [State Council and Government of the People's Republic of China, State Council's Reply on Agreeing to Establish the Joint Ministerial Conference on Financial Regulatory Coordination Mechanism].

[67] Financial Stability Board (n 58).

[68] Ibid.

[69] Ibid.

[70] Ibid.

[71] Ibid.

[72] As for financial stability topics, the PBOC, together with CBRC, CSRC and CIRC, prepares and submits a report that analyses the current financial risks, taking into consideration the feedback from the Ministry of Finance and the National Development and Reform Commission.

[73] Financial Stability Board (n 58).

[74] Ibid; IMF Working Paper, 'China's Financial Interlinkages and Implications for Inter-Agency Coordination', WP/16/181 (2016).

quite robust, and will be further enhanced by ongoing work to develop a joint statistical platform, the sharing of other information, such as results of stress tests and on-site inspections, appears more restricted.[75] When it comes to the fluidity of information among authorities, the relevant agencies indicate that information could be shared if requested or if the information raised financial stability concerns for the PBOC, or bank safety issues for the CBRC, and this information-sharing does not appear to occur on a regular basis. On the issue of information-sharing, the IMF has also expressed concerns about China's lack of a national, credible data-collection system to gather cross-sectoral granular data,[76] stating that while it is understandable to safeguard confidential institutional information, a discretionary approach to information-sharing may lead to insufficient sharing and important gaps in understanding.

13.5 REFORM PROPOSALS IN CHINA AND TWIN PEAKS

Overall, good progress has been made by China's policymakers in addressing the existing problems in its financial system – the credit expansion has been a top issue on the policymakers' agenda; a shadow banking regulatory framework has been established; and a macroprudential management framework and an analytical framework for systemic risk has been built in recent years. However, these regulatory measures are not enough to keep pace with market developments. Clear flaws are present in regulating the interconnected financial sector in China.[77] As recommended by the IMF and FSB, additional work is necessitated to operationalise a comprehensive and coordinated policy framework, which involves greater inter-agency cooperation and a system of information-sharing in order to promptly identify related risks and to ensure an effective policy response.

Meanwhile, in academia, calls for structural reforms have intensified. In light of this, this section provides an overview of institutional structures and reform proposals. Among all the models available,[78] many commentators have advocated for a shift towards the Twin Peaks model of financial regulation.

13.5.1 *Overview of Institutional Structures and International Experiences*

In broad terms, institutional structures for financial services oversight that have been adopted worldwide are: the sectoral model; the functional model; the integrated model; and the Twin Peaks model.[79]

The sectoral model determines the regulator responsible for oversight according to a firm's legal status – banks, broker-dealers or insurance companies. Each authority regulates the firm

---

[75] Financial Stability Board (n 9).

[76] IMF Working Paper, 'China's Financial Interlinkages and Implications for Inter-Agency Coordination', WP/16/181 (2016).

[77] This form of financing leads to a growing interconnectedness and greater diversity of the system, which in turn expands systemic risks in China. Drafting regulations on the shadow banking system has been a priority for China's government recently, in the context of the twelfth year (2011–15) plan.

[78] See Andrew D. Schmulow, 'The Four Methods of Financial System Regulation: An International Comparative Survey' (2015) 26(3) *Journal of Banking and Finance Law and Practice* 151–72.

[79] It is important to note that no pure model may exist in practice and it is prevalent for a model to exhibit features of different approaches. Also, no model has been proven to be superior to all the others for the simple reason that context matters.

falling under its radar, from both a prudential and a conduct-of-business perspective.[80] Jurisdictions employing a sectoral model include the United States after the Great Depression, where the model was in line with the segregated business lines under the Glass–Steagall Act of 1933. However, these sectoral boundaries in advanced economies have been substantially blurred in the past three decades with the rise of sophisticated product innovation and complex organisational structures.[81] Sectoral regulations organised along traditional business lines, therefore, generate regulatory overlap and arbitrage when supervising financial products with multiple institutional labels.[82] A remark made by the Group of Thirty in 2008 was that 'the institutional approach is based on a business model that ... no longer exists'.[83]

A functional model regulates firms in terms of the lines of business transacted by the entity, namely banking, insurance and securities, irrespective of the firm's legal status. A firm whose licence permits it to engage in various lines of business will be under multiple supervisors. Countries like France and Italy before the GFC saw the design flaws of the institutional approach and decided to adopt a functional approach. In theory, a single, technically expert regulator will apply consistent rules and principles to the same financial activity regardless of its legal status and, therefore, reduce regulatory overlap and arbitrage. However, the experiences of these two countries indicate that, in practice, a functional approach usually gives rise to jurisdictional uncertainty. Regulators and the regulated have found it difficult to differentiate activities that fall within the scope of the jurisdiction of separate regulators.[84]

An integrated model involves a single, universal regulator with fully consolidated responsibility for both prudential and business conduct oversight in all sectors of business. A jurisdiction with all key features of an integrated model was the United Kingdom between 2001 and 2013,[85] with its Financial Services Authority (FSA).[86] However, the GFC provided compelling evidence that when prudential and consumer protection regulation are combined into one single agency, some objectives are likely to be prioritised at the expense of others.[87] In the case of the FSA, it chose to dedicate resources to high-frequency consumer complaints, but did not allocate sufficient resources for prudential regulation prior to the GFC.[88] The leading advocate for the Twin Peaks model, Michael W. Taylor, suggests that except in smaller countries where the gains from economies of scale may be significant, the fully integrated regulator is unsuitable because it generates large inefficiencies by 'asking too much of a single regulator'.[89] More importantly, the

---

[80] To the extent that the institution's licence permits it to take part in additional lines of business, ancillary to its main business, these additional activities will also fall under the remit of the supervisor regulating the main business, even though the additional activities fall outside the scope of the supervisor's expertise.

[81] Group of Thirty, 'The Structure of Financial Supervision: Approaches and Challenges in a Global Marketplace' (2008); See also Michael W. Taylor, 'The Road from "Twin Peaks" – And the Way Back' (2009) 16 *Connecticut Insurance Law Journal* 73.

[82] Group of Thirty (n 81).

[83] Ibid 34.

[84] Taylor (n 81) 35.

[85] The reform took place in the wake of a series of scandals which befell the regulatory bodies, and the failure of the Bank of England to prevent the collapse of Barings Bank.

[86] Eilis Ferran, 'The Breakup of the Financial Services of Authority' (2011) 31 *Oxford Journal of Legal Studies* 455–80.

[87] Ibid; HM Treasury, Review of Enforcement Decision-Making at the Financial Services Regulators: Final Report (2014); see also Eilis Ferran, 'Institutional Design: The Choices of National Systems' in Niamh Moloney, Eilis Ferran and Jennifer Payne (eds) *The Oxford Handbook of Financial Regulation* (Oxford University Press, 2015), 97–124.

[88] Financial Services Authority, The Turner Review – A Regulatory Response to the Global Banking Crisis (2009).

[89] Ibid; Michael Taylor, '"Twin Peaks" Revisited... A Second Chance for Regulatory Reform' (Centre for the Study of Financial Innovation, 2009).

objectives of macroprudential regulation and microprudential policies are simply different and do not mix.[90]

In response, and in order to address the differences between the two objectives of prudential oversight and consumer protection, the current ascendancy in policy circles is to move towards a Twin Peaks model. A Twin Peaks model is an objective-based regulatory approach, in which regulatory functions are separated between two regulators, one of which monitors the safety and soundness of financial institutions, while the other focuses on conduct-of-business regulation. Before the GFC, Australia and the Netherlands were the only countries with a Twin Peaks regulatory approach.[91] With Australia's remarkable performance in minimising the severe impact of the GFC, the Twin Peaks model has attracted the attention of policymakers from other jurisdictions in the post-crisis era,[92] a few of which have had a regulatory overhaul in order to implement a Twin Peaks regulatory model, such as the United Kingdom and South Africa.[93]

13.5.2 *Reform Proposals for China's Regulatory Structural Reform*

Reform towards a Twin Peaks approach to financial regulation is extensive in the academic literature discussing reforming China's financial regulatory model, alongside the proposal to move towards an integrated model, along similar lines to the pre-GFC model in the United Kingdom, and the proposal to move towards functional regulation, along similar lines to the United States.

Some commentators argue in favour of a move towards the integrated model, similar to the FSA in the United Kingdom. However, the United Kingdom's experience and the academic literature have already illustrated the inefficiency of an integrated model in a large economy.[94] This reform proposal is also rejected by scholars arguing for a move towards functional regulation with an expanded role for the PBOC as the lead coordinator. The main argument for the proposal is that China is not yet well-prepared for a move towards an integrated model because of its limited experience in financial market regulation.[95] In this regard, scholars of this view advocate that the central bank would act as the umbrella supervisor responsible for leading permanent coordination.[96] With the umbrella model, and a greater extent of government involvement, it is more likely that China will achieve more balanced market safety and efficiency.[97]

---

[90] Markus Brunnermeier et al, *The Fundamental Principles of Financial Regulation* (International Center for Monetary and Banking Studies, 2009); Rosa Lastra, 'Systemic Risk and Macro-prudential Supervision' in Niamh Moloney, Eilis Ferran and Jennifer Payne (eds) *The Oxford Handbook of Financial Regulation* (Oxford University Press, 2015), 309–29.

[91] Group of Thirty (n 81).

[92] Such as the United States and the United Kingdom.

[93] See Andromachi Georgosouli, 'The FCA–PRA Coordination Scheme and the Challenge of Policy Coherence' (2013) 8 *Capital Markets Law Journal* 62–76; Andrew Schmulow, 'Financial Regulatory Governance in South Africa: The Move towards Twin Peaks' (2017) 25 *African Journal of International and Comparative Law* 3; A. Godwin, T. Howse and I. Ramsay, 'Twin Peaks: South Africa's Proposed Financial Sector Regulatory Framework' (2017) 134 *South African Law Journal* 665–702.

[94] Taylor (n 89).

[95] See Fan Liao, 'Regulation of Financial Conglomerates in China: From De Facto to De Jure' (2011) 12 *European Business Organisation Law Review* 267–313; Ge Jianguo, Wang Xuesong and Zhang Xiaolei, 'China's Financial Regulatory Reform in the Post-WTO Period' (2008) 23 *Journal of International Banking Law and Regulation* 480–88.

[96] Fan Liao (n 95); Ge Jianguo et al (n 95).

[97] Fan Liao (n 95); Ge Jianguo et al (n 95).

Since the recent GFC, commentators in China have shown a discernible interest in a move towards the Twin Peaks approach of financial regulation[98] and advocated Twin Peaks as a mid- to long-term goal, complemented by a move towards the US approach of regulation along functional business lines in the short term.[99] In line with the United States' practice, an agency similar to the US Financial Stability Oversight Council should also be established on top of the current sectoral arrangement to strengthen coordination and information-sharing. In the medium to long term, as the financial market structure of China matures, China's regulators should pay more attention to the macroprudential supervision of systemic risk by referencing Australia's Twin Peaks model.[100] Notably, the 2017 China Financial Supervision and Regulation Report recommended a move towards a double-layer Twin Peaks approach.[101]

13.5.3 *Twin Peaks in Australia*

The Twin Peaks model was first advocated by Michael Taylor in his 1995 paper, in which he argued for reform in the United Kingdom. However, the United Kingdom was not the first country to implement Twin Peaks financial regulation. Instead that fell to Australia. In the aftermath of the GFC, the failure of under-regulation sparked an intensified interest in the study of regulatory and supervisory structures.[102] As Australia fared remarkably well in the GFC, its Twin Peaks regulatory structure has been placed under scrutiny by policymaking and academic circles in the post-GFC era.[103]

The institutional design of Twin Peaks was introduced in Australia in 1998 and was based on the recommendations made by the Wallis Committee's Financial System Inquiry in 1997 (Wallis Inquiry). The central themes of the Wallis Inquiry were financial stability and competitive neutrality between institutions.[104] While some jurisdictions adopted specialised regulatory agencies to deal with the increasing complexity of financial products, the Wallis Report did not favour this approach as it was inconsistent with the emerging market structure, and could lead to regulatory gaps and inefficiencies.[105] Rather, it recommended that prudential oversight should be combined in a single agency to enhance flexibility in the intensity of regulation.[106]

The end product was a variation of the theoretical Twin Peaks model. The Australian Twin Peaks regime essentially comprises three peaks. One peak is the Australian Prudential Regulation Authority (APRA), responsible for prudential regulation of financial institutions, supervising deposit-taking, general insurance and life insurance. Another peak is the Australian

[98] Godwin, Guo and Ramsay (n 63); 巴曙松、吴博、刘睿, 金融结构、风险结构与我国金融监管改革《新金融》2013年5月 [Ba Shusong, Wu Bo and Liu Rui, 'Financial Structure, Risk Structure and China's Financial Regulatory Reforms'] *New Finance* (May 2013)].

[99] Hui Huang, 'Institutional Structure of Financial Regulation in China: Lessons from the Global Financial Crisis' (2010) 10 *Journal of Corporate Law Studies* 219–54.

[100] Godwin, Guo, and Ramsay (n 63).

[101] 尹振涛 高哲理, 中国金融监管:2016年重大事件述评, 中国金融监管报告（2017）[China Financial Supervision and Regulation Report, Important Issues of China's Financial Regulation in 2016 (2017)].

[102] Eddy Wymeersch, 'The Structure of Financial Supervision in Europe: About Single Financial Supervisors, Twin Peaks and Multiple Financial Supervisors' (2007) 8 *European Business Organisation Law Review* 237–306.

[103] Jennifer G. Hill, 'Why Did Australia Fare so Well in the Global Financial Crisis?' in Eilís Ferran, Niamh Moloney, Jennifer Hill and John Coffee (eds) *The Regulatory Aftermath of the Global Financial Crisis* (Cambridge University Press, 2012), 203–300.

[104] Ibid 203–300; Damien White, 'Greater International Links in Banking – Challenges for Banking Regulation' (2006) 25 *Economic Papers – Economic Society of Australia* 111–20.

[105] Phil Hanratty, 'The Wallis Report on the Australian Financial System: Summary and Critique' (Department of the Parliamentary Library of Australia, Research Paper No 16, 1996–97).

[106] Ibid 21.

Securities and Investments Commission (ASIC), responsible for business conduct and consumer protection.[107] The third peak is the Reserve Bank of Australia, which controls monetary policy, systemic stability and the payment systems.

13.5.4 *Other Twin Peaks Approaches: The Netherlands and the United Kingdom*

The Netherlands is another country that adopted a Twin Peaks approach to financial regulation before the GFC.[108] Unlike Australia, the Netherlands' Twin Peaks regime truly consists of two peaks. The Dutch central bank, De Nederlandsche Bank, serves as the prudential and systemic risk supervisor of all financial services, namely banking, insurance, pension funds and securities; whereas the Netherlands Authority for the Financial Market (AFM) is responsible for all conduct-of-business supervision.

During the GFC, the Dutch Twin Peaks regime was 'less lucky' than Australia[109] and experienced challenges. While the conduct-of-business objectives in the Dutch Twin Peaks were well served, the Dutch Twin Peaks found it difficult to achieve a balanced synergy between microprudential stability of individual firms and the macroprudential stability of the system.[110]

Based on the experience of the Netherlands in the GFC and the prevailing academic literature, a few Dutch scholars, particularly Kremers and Schoenmaker, have written extensively to revisit the policy framework of financial regulation. Primarily, they have made three arguments.[111] First, among all four primary objectives – namely monetary stability, macroprudential stability, microprudential stability and consumer protection – consumer protection has a different focus from all the other objectives. As commented by Pauli, 'the different focus as between investor protection and systemic stability is however so pronounced that there are good arguments for having the primary responsibilities for these two functions divided between separate bodies'.[112] Secondly, a distinctive macroprudential policy should exist alongside a microprudential framework as the GFC provided compelling evidence that macro- and microprudential policies have distinctive objectives and require distinctive toolkits and regulatory styles.[113] That said, despite the conflicts, the two prudential objectives are also interdependent in the decision-making process; therefore, a combination of macro- and microprudential regulations are more effective in crisis management. Third, in line with a common thread among recent studies, monetary and macroprudential policies complement each other in terms of effectiveness.[114]

These arguments are also embedded in the United Kingdom's regulatory overhaul, following the liquidity crisis at Northern Rock in 2007. In 2013, the UK government introduced its own version of Twin Peaks regulation, which shares some aspects with the Dutch approach. Like the

---

[107] The responsibilities of APRA and ASIC are clearly defined but intersect to some extent in the financial services area.

[108] Group of Thirty (n 81).

[109] Hill (n 103).

[110] Jeroen Kremers and Dirk Schoenmaker, 'Twin Peaks: Experiences in the Netherlands' (LSE Financial Markets Group Paper Series Special Paper 196, 2010).

[111] Ibid; see also Dirk Schoenmaker and Jeroen Kremers, 'Financial Stability and Proper Business Conduct: Can Supervisory Structure Help to Achieve These Objectives?' in Robin Hui Huang and Dirk Schoenmaker (eds) *Institutional Structure of Financial Regulation: Theories and International Experiences* (Routledge, 2015).

[112] Kremers and Schoenmaker (n 110); Ralf Pauli, 'Payments Remain Fundamental for Banks and Central Banks' (Bank of Finland Discussion Papers, June 2000).

[113] Peter O. Mulbert, 'Managing Risk in the Financial System' in Niamh Moloney, Eilis Ferran and Jennifer Payne (eds) *The Oxford Handbook of Financial Regulation* (Oxford University Press, 2015), 364–401.

[114] European Parliament, 'Interaction between Monetary Policy and Bank Regulation' (Monetary Dialogue, 23 September 2015).

Dutch Twin Peaks, the Bank of England (BOE) occupies a pivotal position in the model but, unlike the Dutch Twin Peaks, responsibilities for macroprudential and microprudential regulation are separated between a Financial Policy Committee in the BOE and the Prudential Regulation Authority, a subsidiary of the BOE, respectively. Altogether, the FPC and the PRA form one peak. Another peak is the Financial Conduct Authority responsible for business conduct regulation.[115]

13.6 IS AUSTRALIA'S TWIN PEAKS A MODEL FOR CHINA?

In the past few decades financial stability has always been the policy priority for China,[116] with the central bank and the regulators exercising control over facets of the financial system. This financially repressive regime has created mounting local government debt and turned financial investors and consumers to the less regulated shadow banking sector. Not only does the shadow banking sector provide less protection for financial consumers but it is also closely connected to regular banks due to China's ongoing financial liberalisation reforms.[117]

With such an increasingly mature and integrated financial market, it may be time for China to consider a shift towards a more integrated and well-rounded financial regulatory structure.[118]

13.6.1 *Twin Peaks Provides Guides for China*

Among all existing models, the Twin Peaks approach appears to provide all the essential elements a financial regulatory structure would need – a prudential regulator can supervise the large banking sector and deal with its overly concentrated risks.[119] Despite the growing concern for consumer protection under Chinese laws, business conduct rules have not yet been introduced in China, creating regulatory arbitrage in protecting consumers of cross-sectoral products. Therefore, a consumer protection regulator should be introduced. Due to its distinctive nature among all policy objectives, it is recommended to separate authority for consumer protection from prudential regulation.[120]

13.6.2 *Latest Reform by the Chinese Government*

To the dismay of Twin Peaks advocates in China, during the fifth National Conference on Financial Work in July 2017, it was announced that a new Financial Stability and Development Committee will be set up at State Council level to coordinate financial regulation. The committee aims to fill the gap in the current sectoral financial regulatory framework, as well as unify regulations for cross-market financial products and financial holding companies. It will

---

[115] Georgosouli (n 93).

[116] Central Committee of the Communist Party of China (n 50).

[117] Wei Shen (n 9); IMF Working Paper, 'Financial Distortions in China: A General Equilibrium Approach', WP/15/274 (2015); IMF Working Paper, 'Rebalancing in China – Progress and Prospects', WP/16/183 (2016).

[118] The cost/benefit analysis may be a counter-argument, but it is not the focus of this chapter.

[119] Miao Han, 'Twin Peaks Regulation after the Global Financial Crisis: A Reform Model for China?' (2017) 8 *Asian Journal of Law and Economics* 1–30.

[120] Charles Goodhart, 'The Organisational Structure of Banking Supervision' (FSA Occasional Papers No 1, 2000).

also help set up comprehensive financial industry statistics and information-sharing among all financial regulators.[121]

13.6.3 *What Can Be Done Next?*

The establishment of a Financial Stability and Development Committee will address the shortcomings of the current macroprudential management framework and the analytical framework for systemic risk in China. However, a general consumer protection agency will still be lacking in terms of dealing with consumer complaints and inquiries.

Under the current structure of financial regulation in China, financial consumer protection is spread over several financial regulatory agencies. On the one hand, when banking or insurance companies engage in distributing WMPs, the CBIRC has corresponding regulatory authority, but no one financial authority has focused on the whole spectrum of financial consumer protection. On the other hand, the State Administration of Industry and Commerce (SAIC) has an overall consumer protection focus, yet lacks jurisdiction over banks or financial institutions, not to mention its lack of jurisdiction over non-bank entities that offer financial services.[122]

With the rising interconnectivity between the sub-markets of equity, debt, derivatives and banking, it may make more sense to consolidate some functions within the segmented regulatory regimes.[123] The first proposal is, of course, Twin Peaks, which consists of a separate agency focusing on consumer protection. Alternatively, China can draw reference from the United States' approach of creating a new agency, the Consumer Financial Protection Bureau, with consolidated laws pertinent to consumer protection.[124] However, overhauling China's financial structure, or adding a new specialised authority to deal with financial consumer protection, may increase transaction costs between financial institutions and consumers.[125] Some suggest that a less costly approach may be to craft function-based regulation for various off-balance-sheet and cross-sectoral products offered to the public.[126]

13.7 CONCLUDING REMARKS

The inspiration for Twin Peaks for China is obvious as a result of the rise of systemic risks in China's interconnected market and the growing concern for consumer protection. A Twin Peaks model with prudential and conduct-of-business regulators can fill the gaps for arbitrage that are created by the current sectoral model. The Twin Peaks model might also claim an advantage over other models as a result of the better synergies achieved between macroprudential, microprudential and conduct-of-business regulators.

The latest policy involving the establishment of a Financial Stability and Development Committee, to some extent, conforms to some Twin Peaks advocates' proposal – implementing

---

[121] '第五次全国金融工作会议：指明金融发展新方向', 《新金融》 [The Fifth National Conference on Financial Work: Pointing to New Direction of Financial Development (23 July 2017; online)]; China Financial Information, 'China Financial Daily: What Is Financial Stability Committee Responsible For?' (18 July 2017; online).

[122] Wei Shen (n 9).

[123] Jeffrey Carmichael and Michael Pomerleano, *The Development and Regulation of Non-bank Financial Institutions* (World Bank Publications, 2002).

[124] Richard A. Posner, *The Crisis of Capitalist Democracy* (Harvard University Press, 2010).

[125] Wei Shen (n 9).

[126] Ibid.

an agency similar to the Financial Stability Oversight Council in the short term with a switch to Twin Peaks when the economy becomes further integrated. Whether this proposal will be adopted will be determined in the future. At present, the latest reform policies for financial regulatory structures would leave the issue of establishing a consumer protection agency unaddressed. In the short term, China may want to consider crafting relevant legislation, which appears to be the most cost-effective solution.

14

Financial Regulatory Structure in China

Challenges and Transitioning to Twin Peaks

Robin Hui Huang

14.1 INTRODUCTION

This chapter examines the legal and institutional regulatory framework for China's financial markets and evaluates how China may need to restructure its regulatory regime in order to keep up with market developments.

The chapter first provides a detailed discussion of the current Chinese financial regulatory framework and then identifies its major structural problems. In search of an appropriate agenda for reform of China's financial regulatory structure, it conducts a comparative analysis of financial regulatory structures in overseas jurisdictions, as well as a contextual consideration of China's local conditions. Finally, it discusses the recent developments and their implications for the future prospects of China's transition to a Twin Peaks model of financial regulation.

14.2 THE CURRENT FINANCIAL REGULATORY STRUCTURE

The current financial regulatory structure in China has the defining feature of being sector-based. As the central bank, the People's Bank of China (PBOC) assumes responsibility for monetary policy and the stability of the financial system generally. The China Banking and Insurance Regulatory Commission (CBIRC) and the China Securities Regulatory Commission (CSRC) are the authorities responsible for regulating the banking and insurance sectors and the securities sector, respectively. These regulatory bodies will be examined in detail.

It should be noted, however, that certain other government agencies also perform important regulatory functions in the financial markets. For instance, the Ministry of Finance has the authority to make strategic and policy decisions on finance and taxation, set accounting standards and issue treasury bonds; the National Development and Reform Commission is empowered to approve the issuance of enterprise bonds and to be involved in making financial and monetary policy; and the National Audit Office has responsibility for the audit of financial accounts of state-owned banks, securities firms and insurance companies. It is worth noting that these government agencies, along with the PBOC, the CBIRC and the CSRC, are all ranked equally under the direct leadership of the State Council.[1]

---

[1] Guowuyuan Guanyu Jigou Shezhi de Tongzhi [Notice on the Institutional Structure of the State Council] (promulgated by the State Council on 21 March 2008).

Apart from governmental agencies, there exist a variety of self-regulatory organisations (SROs), which are subject to regulatory oversight by the relevant governmental regulatory agencies and which have varying levels of responsibility for their respective markets and the conduct of their members. These include the China Banking Association (CBA); Insurance Association of China (IAC); Securities Association of China (SAC); China Futures Association (CFA); and China Trustee Association (CTA). In addition, the market operators, including the two stock exchanges and the four futures exchanges, play an important self-regulatory role, subject to the oversight of the CSRC.

14.2.1 *Central Banking*

The PBOC is the central bank in China, a role legally confirmed by the Law of the PRC on the People's Bank of China (PBOC Law).[2] Pursuant to the PBOC Law, the PBOC must formulate and implement monetary policy, guard against financial risks and maintain financial stability under the leadership of the State Council.[3]

As with most central banks in the world, the PBOC has a threefold role: the currency-issuing bank; the bank of banks; and the government bank. More specifically, the PBOC performs the following functions: (1) promulgating and implementing orders and regulations in relation to its functions; (2) formulating and implementing monetary policy in accordance with the law; (3) issuing China's currency, the Renminbi (RMB), and controlling its circulation; (4) supervising the interbank borrowing and lending market and the interbank bond markets; (5) administering foreign exchange and supervising the interbank foreign exchange market; (6) supervising the gold market; (7) holding, controlling and managing the state foreign exchange reserves and gold reserves; (8) managing the state treasury; (9) maintaining the normal operation of the systems for payment and settlement of accounts; (10) directing and handling the anti-money-laundering work of the financial industry, undertaking responsibility for capital supervision and oversight of anti-money-laundering; (11) being responsible for the statistics, investigation, analysis and forecasting of the financial industry; (12) undertaking relevant international banking operations as the central bank of the state; and (13) other functions assigned to it by the State Council.[4]

In 2003, the PBOC was divested of its direct banking supervisory powers. These powers were transferred to the newly established China Banking Regulatory Commission (CBRC, as it was then known) in order to provide the PBOC with the necessary independence to implement the nation's monetary policy. Currently the PBOC engages in measures to stabilise the currency and the financial system by indirect, macroeconomic means, rather than through a direct, interventionist approach as it did in the planned economy era. It therefore exercises macroeconomic control over the financial markets primarily through a range of monetary tools such as deposit reserves, the rediscount rate, interest rates and open market operations.

---

[2] Zhonghua Renmin Gongheguo Zhongguo Renmin Yinhang Fa [The Law of PRC on the People's Bank of China] (adopted at the 3rd session of the Standing Committee of the 8th National People's Congress of the PRC on 18 March 1995, amended on 27 December 2003), art 2.

[3] Ibid art 2.

[4] Ibid art 4. It should be noted that the State Administration of Foreign Exchange is a government agency under the leadership of the PBOC, and it acts as the implementation branch of the PBOC in relation to foreign exchange administration and supervision.

14.2.2 *Banking Regulation*

In 2003, the CBRC came into existence as the banking 'watchdog', taking over the role previously performed by the PBOC. The legal and regulatory framework for banking regulation comprises the *Law of the PRC on Commercial Banks*[5] and the *Law of the PRC on Banking Regulation and Supervision*.[6]

In April 2018, the CBRC and the China Insurance Regulatory Commission (CIRC) were merged to form the CBIRC.[7] Like its peers in the securities and insurance markets, the CBIRC is a ministry rank unit under the direct leadership of the State Council. The main objectives of the CBIRC as banking regulator are to: (1) promote the lawful, smooth and sound operation of the banking industry and maintain the confidence of the general public in the industry and (2) ensure fair competition in the banking market and improve the banking industry's competitiveness.[8] It should be noted that the CBIRC regulates not only banks, but also a variety of specified non-bank financial institutions. The former group covers commercial banks, policy banks, urban/rural credit unions and other financial institutions engaged in taking deposits from the general public. The latter group includes financial asset-management companies; trust investment companies; financing companies; financial lease companies; and other financial institutions established with the approval of the CBIRC.[9] As trust investment companies are subject to the CBIRC's regulations, approval is needed for the establishment of private equity funds, which usually take the legal structure of a trust.

In its regulatory role under the relevant laws, the CBIRC is responsible for both market conduct regulation and prudential regulation. Under Article 16 of the *Law of the PRC on Banking Regulation and Supervision*, the CBIRC is responsible for the examination and approval of the establishment, modification, termination and operational scope of the financial institutions it regulates.[10] Article 18 provides that certain types of financial operations, as prescribed by the rules of the CBIRC, need to be examined and approved by the CBIRC before a financial institution can carry out those operations.[11] Under Article 21 the CBIRC has powers to make and enforce rules regarding prudential regulation.[12] In this way the CBIRC exercises its supervisory functions through prudential standards such as the asset/liability ratio requirement, the capital adequacy ratio and risk management, as opposed to the more interventionist methods like the imposition of loan quotas, as used under the planned economy.

14.2.3 *Insurance Regulation*

Against the backdrop of the fast-growing insurance market, over the years the regulatory regime has been reformed. The CIRC was set up in 1998 to assume regulatory responsibility for the

---

[5] Zhonghua Renmin Gongheguo Shangye Yinhang Fa [Law of the PRC on Commercial Banks] (adopted at the 13th session of the Standing Committee of the 8th National People's Congress of the PRC on 10 May 1995, amended on 27 December 2003).

[6] Zhonghua Renmin Gongheguo Yinhangye Jiandu Guanli Fa [Law of the PRC on Banking Regulation and Supervision] (adopted at the 6th session of the Standing Committee of the 10th National People's Congress of the PRC on 27 December 2003, amended on 31 October 2006).

[7] See CBIRC, 'China Banking and Insurance Regulatory Commission Officially Unveiled' (CBIRC, 2019).

[8] *Law of the PRC on Banking Regulation and Supervision* (n 6) art 3.

[9] Ibid art 2.

[10] Ibid art 16.

[11] Ibid art 18.

[12] Ibid art 21.

insurance industry in China, under the *Insurance Law of the PRC*.[13] The principal duties and responsibilities of the CIRC are to supervise and administer the insurance sector in accordance with the principles of legality, openness and fairness, with the aim of maintaining stability in the insurance market and protecting the legitimate rights and interests of insurance purchasers, insurants and beneficiaries. As noted in the previous section, the CIRC was merged with the CBRC to form the CBIRC in April 2018.

As the insurance regulator, the CBIRC is charged with both market conduct regulation and prudential regulation in relation to insurance companies. The *Insurance Law of the PRC* devotes a whole chapter to the promulgation and enforcement of insurance contracts.[14] In China, life insurance is separated from property insurance. Consequently, one insurance company cannot conduct both forms of insurance business concurrently.[15] The CBIRC is also tasked with licensing and regulating insurance agents and brokers to make sure that financial intermediaries operate in a fair and efficient manner.

In respect of prudential regulation of insurance companies, the CBIRC needs to ensure the compliance of insurance companies with various prudential requirements, including the requirements to maintain guarantee funds, liability reserve funds, capital reserve and insurance protection funds. In addition, the CBIRC is required to set up and improve a system to monitor the solvency of insurance companies. Particular regulatory attention is paid to those insurance companies whose ability to pay insurance cover is regarded as inadequate, and the CBIRC has the power to take a variety of measures to deal with the issue, such as ordering an increase in capital or reinsurance; limiting the scope of business; restricting the payment of dividends to shareholders; restricting the purchase of fixed assets or the scale of operational costs; and restricting the level of salaries of directors, supervisors and senior managers.[16]

14.2.4 *Securities Regulation*

The legal and regulatory framework for the securities market in China is largely based on the *Securities Law of the PRC* (Securities Law).[17] As noted, established in 1992 and upgraded in 1998, the CSRC is the oldest of the industry-specific regulatory bodies in the financial markets. Since then, the CSRC has assumed responsibility for securities regulation in China. The coverage of the *Securities Law*, and therefore the authority of the CSRC, is broad and includes the regulation of shares, corporate bonds, treasury bonds, securities investment funds and derivative products such as futures contracts, options and warrants.[18] Thus, in terms of its regulatory remit, the CSRC is roughly equivalent to the combination of the Securities and Exchange Commission (SEC) and the Commodity Futures Trading Commission (CFTC) in the United States. However, the CSRC's regulatory territory is narrower than that of its Australian counterpart, the Australian Securities and Investments Commission, which acts as both securities regulator and corporate regulator in Australia.

[13] Zhonghua Renmin Gongheguo Baoxian Fa [Insurance Law of the PRC] (adopted at the 14th session of the Standing Committee of the 8th National People's Congress of the People's Republic of China on 30 June 1995, amended 28 October 2002 and 28 February 2009), art 9.
[14] Ibid Ch 2.
[15] Ibid art 95.
[16] Ibid art 139.
[17] Zhonghua Renming Gongheguo Zhengquanfa [Securities Law of the PRC] (promulgated by the 6th session of the Standing Committee of the 9th National People's Congress of the PRC on 29 December 1998 and effective from 1 July 1999, amended in 2004, 2005, 2013, 2014 and 2019).
[18] Ibid art 2.

The principal function of the CSRC is to 'carry out supervision and administration of the securities market according to law so as to preserve the order of the securities market and ensure the legitimate operations thereof'.[19] In discharging its duties, the CSRC has a number of important, semi-legislative, investigative and adjudicative powers. First, it is empowered to make relevant rules and regulations. Secondly, it can take a range of investigative measures. For instance, it has power to undertake an on-the-spot examination of securities intermediaries; to enter into the place of occurrence of misconduct to investigate and collect evidence; to question the parties concerned or any entity or individual relating to a case requiring them to give explanations on relevant matters; to examine the capital account, security account or bank account of any relevant party concerned in or any entity or individual relating to a case under investigation; to freeze or seal up relevant assets and/or evidence that is in jeopardy of dissipation, waste or improper removal, with the approval of the responsible officer of the CSRC; and to restrict the securities transactions of the parties concerned in a case under investigation when investigating any major securities irregularity such as manipulation of the securities market or insider trading, with the approval of the responsible officer of the CSRC.

The CSRC, according to the results of investigations, can decide to impose administrative sanctions for relevant securities irregularities. The usual weapons in the CSRC's arsenal include warning, fine, suspension and cancellation of licences. Further, the CSRC can issue a banning order (*shichang jinru*), under which a person is prohibited from undertaking any securities practice or holding any post of director, supervisor or senior manager of a listed company within a prescribed term or for life. Finally, if the case is serious enough to warrant criminal sanction, the CSRC will refer the case to the procuratorate to bring criminal charges.

14.3 CHALLENGES TO THE CURRENT STRUCTURE

14.3.1 *Cross-Sector Financial Conglomerates and Products*

In recent years China's financial regulation has come under increasing pressure from the latest developments in its financial markets. China has followed the international trend of gradually removing structural restraints, which have segmented financial markets and confined institutions to specific business lines – a process sometimes dubbed 'financial modernisation'. As a result, the once bright-line boundaries between different types of financial institutions have become increasingly blurred.

To start with, the *Law of the PRC on Commercial Banks* was revised in 2003 to add the clause: 'unless the State Council provides otherwise' to the traditional prohibition on banks engaging in securities business activities.[20] Not long thereafter, the amendment to the *Securities Law of the PRC* of 2005 provided an exception to the traditional sectoral segregation through a similar clause: 'unless the State Council provides otherwise'.[21] Finally, the *Insurance Law of the PRC* has recently been amended with a number of significant changes, including dismantling the previous rule strictly segregating insurance companies from other financial businesses. Article 8 of the *Insurance Law of the PRC* now provides that insurance shall be segregated from banking, securities and trust sectors, 'unless it is otherwise provided for by the state'.[22] This leaves the door open for insurance companies to branch out into other kinds of financial

---

[19] Ibid art 178.
[20] *Law of the PRC on Commercial Banks* (n 5) art 43.
[21] *Securities Law of the PRC* (n 17) art 6.
[22] *Insurance Law of the PRC* (n 13) art 8.

services. Under Article 106, insurance companies now have a broader range of investment options. Apart from those previously permitted investment options such as bank deposits, treasury bonds and financial bonds, insurance companies can now also invest in shares, securities investment fund units, real estate and other forms prescribed by the State Council.[23] The memorandum to the legislative amendment states that the change is in line with international trends, and is also suited to China's local economic conditions.

These legislative amendments have formalised and encouraged the ongoing process of financial modernisation in China. As discussed, strict segregation was traditionally enforced between the major sectors of the financial markets: namely banking, securities and insurance. Since China's admission to the World Trade Organization (WTO), financial modernisation has been carried out on a trial basis and has made significant progress. This development is exemplified by the emergence of some large financial conglomerates, such as the China Everbright Group, the CITIC Group and the China PingAn Group, which involve a diversity of institutions operating in a range of different sectors, including banking, securities, insurance, trust business and asset management. This gives rise to what is called the business model of *Hunye Jingying* (combining the business activities of banking, securities and insurance), which represents a departure from the traditional model of *Fenye Jingying* (separating financial services and markets). Now, with the previously mentioned legislative backing, the process of financial modernisation is set to accelerate, and it is predicted that there will be progressively more large financial groups.

Further, financial innovation has created products such as sophisticated derivatives, which cannot be easily accommodated within the traditional contractual forms of debt, equity and insurance. This development has resulted in significant changes to the nature and distribution of risk in the financial system, with the risk profiles of different financial institutions progressively converging. A prime example comes in the form of securitisation where securities firms become exposed to banking-type risks by holding mortgage-backed securities or securitised bank loans. China has used this financial technique, with considerable success, to deal with the massive amount of non-performing loans in the banking sector. As discussed earlier, although securitisation has the potential to be abused, it remains an ingenious financial innovation, which is capable of performing important economic functions, provided it is regulated properly. This is particularly so for China, where the banks still have a relatively high level of bad loans and the home mortgage market is huge and rapidly growing. It would seem to follow that China will not, nor should it, abandon financial innovation in the face of the global financial crisis. Hence, there will likely be more financial products that straddle the traditional boundaries of the financial sector.

Therefore, the ongoing process of financial modernisation and innovation – as symbolised by the emergence of large multi-service financial conglomerates and complex cross-sectoral financial products – has significantly changed the way the financial markets operate in China. These market developments pose a serious challenge to China's traditional sectoral regulation, under which regulatory responsibility is divided along the traditional lines of banking, securities and insurance. Not surprisingly, China's current regulatory structure has shown significant inadequacies in response to the changing financial landscape. For instance, it is difficult to have the system-wide perspective necessary to obtain an adequate supervisory overview of large financial groups. Separate regulators are responsible for supervising different lines of business within multi-service financial groups: the CSRC for securities and the CBIRC for banking and

---

[23] Ibid art 106.

insurance. Furthermore, some innovative financial products do not fit neatly into traditional classifications of banking, securities and insurance businesses, all of which underpin China's current sector-based regulation.

In short, the mismatch between China's regulatory structure and the underlying market it regulates has increased regulatory costs and, more importantly, has led to overlaps and gaps in regulatory coverage. The following section will explore this issue in greater detail and seek to find an appropriate solution from a comparative perspective.

14.3.2 *Shadow Banking and Internet Finance*

The rise of shadow banking over the past few years is one of the most important developments in China's financial system. It has, however, posed significant challenges to the current sector-based financial regulatory architecture in China.[24] Although the term 'shadow banking' has become widely used, there is no international consensus as to a definition. The term is generally believed to have been coined by economist and investment manager Paul McCulley, who used it to refer to 'the whole alphabet soup of levered up non-bank investment conduits, vehicles, and structures'.[25]

In January 2014, China promulgated an important instrument for regulating shadow banking, entitled *Guowuyuan Bangongting Guanyu Jiaqiang Yingzi Yinhang Jianguan Youguan Wenti de Tongzhi* [Circular of the General Office of the State Council on Relevant Issues of Strengthening the Regulation of Shadow Banking] (Circular No. 107).[26] This instrument uses the term 'shadow banking' to mean 'credit intermediation entities and activities outside the traditional banking system', and classifies shadow banking into three categories. The first category is credit intermediation entities that do not have financial licences and that are completely unregulated, including the so-called internet financing companies – *hulianwang Jinrong* such as peer-to-peer (P2P) online lending platforms and equity crowdfunding platforms – and third-party wealth management entities. The second category includes credit intermediation entities that do not have financial licences and are subject to an inadequate level of regulation, such as finance guarantee companies and small-scale loan companies. Last but not least, the term encompasses entities that hold financial licences and undertake activities that are not adequately regulated, such as money market funds, securitisation and some types of wealth management business.[27]

Against the overall sector-based regulatory background in China, Circular No. 107 subjects various types of shadow banking businesses to the relevant sectoral regulators. In doing so, an entity-based approach is adopted to divide regulatory responsibilities among different regulatory bodies: whoever approves the establishment of the shadow banking entity shall be responsible for regulating it.[28]

An example of a major shadow banking activity in China are wealth management products (WMPs), which Moody's Investors Service estimated was valued at $9.5 trillion in China, or

[24] H. Huang, 'The Regulation of Shadow Banking in China: International and Comparative Perspectives' (2015) 30 *Banking and Finance Law Review* 481.

[25] P. McCulley, 'Teton Reflections: Pimco Global Central Bank Focus', *PIMCO* (September 2007), 2.

[26] Guowuyuan Bangongting Guanyu Jiaqiang Yingzi Yinhang Jianguan Youguan Wenti de Tongzhi, *Circular of the General Office of the State Council on Relevant Issues of Strengthening the Regulation of Shadow Banking* (State Council Circular No 107, 2013).

[27] Ibid at s 1.

[28] Ibid at s 2(1).

about 87 per cent of the nation's gross domestic product by the middle of 2017.[29] WMPs are usually offered under a bank-trust cooperation model, which was initiated by Minsheng Bank in 2006. Trust companies create WMPs and banks use their client networks to market those products in return for a commission. The proceeds raised from the sale of WMPs are then invested by trust companies in a wide range of assets, including money market and bond funds, small and medium-sized enterprise loans, real estate loans and local government loans.

As banks and trust companies are regulated by the CBIRC under the current sector-based regulatory framework, WMPs are subject to the regulation of the CBIRC. However, WMPs are also offered by other financial institutions, including securities firms and insurance companies. Accordingly, the CSRC and the CBIRC have power to regulate the WMPs offered by securities firms and insurance companies respectively.[30] In practice, the CBIRC and the CSRC have issued their own rules to regulate WMPs offered by their respective regulatees, and there are significant differences amongst them. Hence, the same or similar financial products are subject to the jurisdiction of different regulators, creating issues of regulatory inconsistency and, with that, the opportunity for regulatory arbitrage.

As noted earlier, internet finance, which is more commonly known as FinTech in other jurisdictions, is considered part of the shadow banking system in China. Circular No. 107 did not specify who regulates internet finance businesses, largely because in 2014 the Chinese government was unsure of the best way to organise this. Rather, it authorised the central bank, the PBOC, to coordinate with other relevant regulators how best to regulate internet finance businesses. One year later, in 2015, the PBOC led a group of ten government agencies, including the CBRC, CSRC and CIRC, in issuing a rule to divide the regulatory responsibilities for various types of internet finance businesses, again along the lines of the sector-based regulatory approach.[31]

However, it is not entirely clear how the various internet finance businesses have been assigned to each of the three financial sectors. For instance, the CSRC is tasked with regulating equity crowdfunding, while online lending is assigned to the CBIRC. Online lending, however, is also known as debt crowdfunding, and could be regarded as a securities offering.[32] The US federal securities regulator, the SEC, has claimed jurisdiction over online lending, stating that the loans/notes being offered by online lending platforms constitute 'investment contracts', as defined by *SEC v W. J. Howey Co*,[33] and also 'notes' as per *Reves v Ernst & Young*.[34] Indeed, as internet finance represents a disruptive innovation, it can be difficult to ascertain its true nature and risk profile, making the sector-based regulatory framework increasingly unwieldy in the face of fast-developing financial technologies.

14.4 THE WAY FORWARD FOR CHINA

As discussed in the preceding section, the new financial landscape, brought about by financial modernisation and innovation, demands suitably designed reforms to China's current financial

---

[29] www.moodys.com/researchandratings.

[30] Circular No 107 (n 26) at s 2(2).

[31] Guanyu Cujin Hulianwang Jinrong Jiankang Fazhan de Zhidao Yijian [Guiding Opinion on the Promotion of Healthy Development of Internet Finance Businesses] (issued by a group of ten government agencies led by the PBOC, on 18 July 2015).

[32] H. Huang, 'Online P2P Lending and Regulatory Responses in China: Opportunities and Challenges' (2018) 19(4) *European Business Organization Law Review* 63.

[33] *Securities and Exchange Commission v W. J. Howey Co*, 328 US ss 293, 301 (1946).

[34] *Reves v Ernst & Young*, 494 US 56 (1990).

regulatory structure, which is based on the traditional segmentation of financial services and markets. Added to this picture is the longstanding problem of structural imbalances within China's financial system, which requires a regulatory framework better able to take concerted action across the financial sectors. In the quest for a solution, a comparative analysis of the financial regulatory structure in various jurisdictions will be conducted. The United States, the United Kingdom and Australia are chosen for comparison due to the fact that they are all advanced economies and, more importantly, because each one is, or was at one stage, typical of one of the three major regulatory models currently in use around the world.[35]

14.4.1 *International Experiences*

14.4.1.1 'Sectoral Regulation' Model

The US financial regulation is typical of this model, under which different financial sectors – banking, securities and insurance – are subject to separate statutes and supervised by separate regulatory agencies. In brief, the US sectoral regulatory framework includes: (1) five federal deposit institution regulators in addition to state-based supervision and including the Federal Reserve, which also serves as the central bank in the United States; (2) one federal securities regulator, the Securities and Exchange Commission, and one federal futures regulator, the Commodity Futures Trading Commission (the United States has additional state-based supervision of securities firms as well as self-regulatory organisations with broad regulatory powers); and (3) insurance regulation, which is almost wholly state-based, with more than fifty regulators. As this regulatory structure consists of separate agencies responsible for different financial sectors, with the boundaries divided institutionally or functionally, it can be termed a 'sectoral regulation' model.

In response to the Global Financial Crisis of 2008, the United States adopted the *Dodd–Frank Wall Street Reform and Consumer Protection Act* (Dodd–Frank Act). Those reforms made some structural changes to the US financial regulatory framework: the elimination of one financial regulatory agency (the Office of Thrift Supervision) and the creation of two new agencies (the Financial Stability Oversight Council and the Office of Financial Research) in addition to the creation of several consumer protection agencies, including the Consumer Financial Protection Bureau (CFPB). However, those reforms did not fundamentally change the 'sectoral regulation' model.

14.4.1.2 'Integrated Regulation' Model

This model was best represented by the United Kingdom until its recent reform to the financial regulatory structure in 2013. The United Kingdom was the first jurisdiction in the world – soon followed by other countries including Germany, Japan and South Korea – to adopt this model by setting up a powerful and nearly universal regulator for its financial services industry, namely the Financial Services Authority (FSA). The FSA integrated regulatory and supervisory functions previously carried out by nine separate bodies in the United Kingdom.[36] The FSA was a super-regulator in terms of its unusually broad regulatory mandate: it was mandated not only to regulate a diversity of businesses, including banking, securities and insurance, but also to

---

[35] For a more detailed discussion, see H. Huang, 'Institutional Structure of Financial Regulation in China: Lessons from the Global Financial Crisis' (2010) 10(1) *Journal of Corporate Law Studies* 219.

[36] E. Ferran, 'Examining the UK's Experience in Adopting the Single Financial Regulator Model' (2003) 28 *Brooklyn Journal of International Law* 257.

undertake prudential and business conduct regulation. Thus, this regulatory structure was termed the 'integrated regulation' model.

14.4.1.3 'Twin Peaks' Model

Australia was the pioneer of this model, being the first to establish a financial regulatory framework comprised of two main regulators in 1998. The first regulator, the Australian Securities and Investment Commission (ASIC), has responsibility for business conduct regulation and consumer protection across banking, securities and insurance.[37] Unlike the SEC in the United States, whose responsibilities are limited to regulating the market for corporate securities, ASIC's power extends to a wide range of financial products. However, the authority of ASIC is not as extensive as was that of the FSA in the United Kingdom due to the existence of a second regulator in the Australian regime, namely the Australian Prudential Regulatory Authority (APRA). As the name suggests, APRA is responsible for prudential regulation; namely, ensuring the financial soundness of all prudentially regulated financial institutions.

As the Australian regulatory regime consists of two separate regulators with different mandates in relation to prudential regulation and business conduct regulation respectively, it is vividly named the 'Twin Peaks' model and is also known as the 'objective-based regulation' model. It is noteworthy that apart from ASIC and APRA, other agencies perform certain regulatory functions in the financial markets, most notably the Reserve Bank of Australia, the central bank in Australia. It is responsible for monetary policy and financial stability, but no longer has any direct banking regulatory responsibilities.[38]

14.4.1.4 A Comparison of the Structural Models

As discussed, there are three major structural models of financial regulation in the international arena: (1) the 'sectoral regulation' model, (2) the 'integrated regulation' model, and (3) the 'twin-regulators' model. While the first model has a multiplicity of financial regulators segregated on the basis of the type of financial institutions or activities, the second model sits at the other end of the spectrum with only one universal regulator for most of its financial markets. The third model lies somewhere in between, dividing responsibility for financial regulation between two agencies.

Naturally, each regulatory model has its own advantages and disadvantages. The merits of one model are always the demerits of another, and vice versa. As to the sectoral regulation model, it has significant problems. First, it is essentially a model designed for the traditional segmented financial markets, and thus is ill-suited to the new financial landscape brought about by the tide of financial modernisation, such as the emergence of large financial conglomerates and

---

[37] *Australian Securities and Investments Commission Act 2001.*

[38] In this sense, the Australian financial regulatory system is composed of three regulators, the ASIC, APRA and the Reserve Bank of Australia, and is therefore sometimes classified as not two but 'three peaked'. This is in contrast to the Netherlands, one of the other six countries with a 'Twin Peaks' regulatory model. In the Netherlands, prudential regulation is combined with financial stability regulation in a single agency (the Dutch central bank called 'De Nederlandsche Bank'), with conduct-of-business regulation being assigned to a separate agency called the 'Autoriteit Financiele Markten' (Financial Markets Authority). There were three major reasons behind the Australian decision to separate prudential responsibilities from the central bank. First, the central bank was regarded as ill-equipped to deal with institutions other than banks; second, it would avoid the expectation that the central bank would automatically provide liquidity support in the event of a crisis; and third, separation of the central banking and prudential functions would enable each institution to become more focused and efficient. In recognition of the view that there was some degree of connection between prudential regulation and systemic stability and that the information gathered through prudential regulation is important for effective systemic regulation, the Reserve Bank of Australia has power to request APRA to collect financial sector data for it.

innovative financial derivatives. As each regulator is focused on its designated part of the financial system, they often fail to see the wood for the trees. In other words, no single regulator possesses all of the information and authority necessary to monitor systemic risk. By contrast, a unified regulator is able to approach financial regulation from a macro perspective, dealing with regulatory hazards in a holistic fashion.

Secondly, the demarcation of responsibilities between various regulators is not always clear-cut or logical as a result of historical and political reasons, which gives rise to both regulatory gaps and overlaps. In circumstances involving thorny problems, regulators may rationally shirk their responsibilities as much as they can, leaving the markets regulated by nobody. In other cases, regulators may fight hard over turf, resulting in regulatory duplication, causing significant costs for both regulators and regulatees.

Although the integrated regulation model addresses the problems facing the sectoral regulation model, it does not come without its own shortcomings. First, while the integrated regulation model has the advantage of being an economy of scale, it remains a legitimate concern that the single universal regulator is far too powerful. This problem is somewhat mitigated under the Twin Peaks model. Second, the broad scope of regulatory responsibilities assigned to a single regulator may be such that the senior management of the regulator is overloaded and regulatory efficiency is reduced. In contrast, the division of regulatory tasks to a number of regulators allows regulatory diversity and specialisation. Thirdly, a unified agency may be susceptible to reputational contagion, as a mistake in one part of the agency may undermine their credibility over a broad range of their responsibilities.

Finally, and most importantly, one should be wary of the one-size-fits-all approach under the single-regulator model. Although the distinctions between financial industry participants may be increasingly blurred at the fringes, the core businesses of banking, insurance and securities remain separate. It would be dangerous if insufficient attention was paid to the differences between financial industries.

Moreover, it is very difficult for one single regulator to discharge all regulatory responsibilities and meet various, and at times competing, regulatory objectives. For example, prudential regulation is concerned with the financial soundness of regulated institutions, whereas business conduct regulation is concerned with the way in which financial products are marketed and sold. It is argued that the two types of regulation are so different that they are best carried out by two separate agencies, as is the case under the Twin Peaks model.

14.4.2 *China Transitioning to Twin Peaks?*

14.4.2.1 Short and Long-Term Reform Suggestions

The foregoing discussion reveals the respective strengths and weaknesses of each of the three regulatory models. However, an objective assessment of each approach, in isolation from their jurisdictional financial landscapes, is hardly meaningful. Thus, this section will put the assessment into the Chinese context with a view to finding an appropriate solution to the problems confronting China's financial regulation.

As shown earlier, the Chinese financial regulatory regime is broadly similar to the United States, both adopting the traditional sectoral structure with a multiplicity of regulators. One major difference is that, unlike the United States, China has removed the central bank, the PBOC, from responsibility for regulating individual banks. This is in line with the previous international trend of divesting the central bank of a direct role in banking supervision.

In response to the problems with China's sectoral financial regulation, some have suggested that China should make an immediate transfer towards the previous UK model by merging the existing two sector-specific regulatory agencies, namely the CSRC and the CBIRC, into a single financial regulator. While there is merit in this suggestion, it does not adequately consider other options and China's local conditions. It is also necessary to perform a cost–benefit analysis of transferring to another system. An immediate and wholesale shift for China across to the previous UK model will not be cost-effective as it would involve large costs which may well outweigh the corresponding benefits. China would be best advised to adopt a staged reform agenda for its financial regulation in line with the gradual growth of the underlying markets.

In the short term, China can learn from the US practice, by improving its financial regulation without radically changing the overarching structural model. In the United States, the Federal Reserve was given umbrella regulatory authority over bank holding companies. Under the *Dodd–Frank Act* the Federal Reserve was given new authority to supervise all firms that could pose a threat to financial stability, even those that did not own banks.[39] This effectively extended the Federal Reserve's consolidated supervision to all large, interconnected financial groups whose failure could have serious systemic effects. As a result, financial firms would not be able to escape regulatory oversight simply by manipulating their legal structure. Moreover, a new Financial Stability Oversight Council for financial regulators was created on 21 July 2010 to improve interagency cooperation and prevent issues falling through the cracks between various regulators.

The above reforms seem to be a pragmatic response to the problems with the US financial regulatory landscape, as highlighted by the 2008 global financial crisis. Indeed, the *Dodd–Frank Act* stops short of holistically addressing the structural inadequacies of the US financial regulatory model, and structurally its model remains sector-based, with separate regulators responsible for each financial sector. But the reforms had the advantage of being quick and measured to deal with pressing issues in practice.

The US approach merits consideration in the context of China. On the one hand, the PBOC can be authorised to supervise the consolidated operations of large financial groups; on the other hand, an interagency oversight council can be created to bring together regulators from across markets and other relevant agencies to coordinate and share information, and to identify gaps in regulation. In order to promote efficiency and continuity, the council may set up a standing committee composed of the PBOC and the sector-specific regulatory agencies, namely the CBIRC and the CSRC. As with the case of the *Dodd–Frank Act*, this solution can be practically expedient for China in the short term.[40]

More importantly, this short-term recommendation is based upon a realistic appraisal of the present needs of China's financial markets. While the current US regulatory regime may be said to be sub-optimal for its financial markets, it may well be a suitable model for the less developed Chinese markets. Despite the rapid progress in recent years, China's financial markets are still largely segmented along traditional banking, securities and insurance lines. Financial innovation and modernisation are relatively limited in extent, and cautiously carried out at an experimental stage. Thus, the US model may well be adequate to meet the challenges

---

[39] HR 4173 §§ 162(a), 163.

[40] The Chinese government appears to have proceeded in line with the short-term reform strategy discussed here. On 20 August 2013, the Chinese government made an announcement to establish a financial regulatory inter-agency coordination mechanism which will be led by the PBOC, and will include representatives from the CBRC, the CSRC and the CIRC, as well as the State Administration of Foreign Exchange. See B. Wassener and C. Buckley, 'New Chinese Agency to Increase Financial Coordination', *New York Times* (21 August 2013).

China's financial regulatory regime currently faces with the emergence of financial conglomerates and financial innovation.

After all, China's current financial regulatory regime was shaped just several years ago and should be given time to demonstrate its ability to adapt to recent market developments. More importantly, although the Chinese financial regulators are suffering teething problems associated with maintaining independence from the government, they have done a good job of managing financial risks, as shown during the Global Financial Crisis of 2008. It follows that the current Chinese financial regulatory system is functioning reasonably well and radical structural changes are not warranted at this stage.

In the intermediate or long term, however, China cannot rely on the US experience, but instead needs to consider the Twin Peaks model or, to a lesser extent, the integrated regulation model. The US reform under the *Dodd–Frank Act* does little more than just fine-tune regulatory authorities within the pre-existing regulatory framework, which has proved to be an antiquated system for a well-developed economy like the United States. By contrast, the Twin Peaks and integrated regulation models attempt to thoroughly overhaul the regulatory structure, taking a novel approach to financial regulation. They are better adapted to the realities of modern financial markets than the sectoral model, dispensing with traditional boundaries between banking, securities and insurance. Both represent genuine efforts to modernise financial regulation to deal with the issues created by the formation of financial conglomerates and the blurring of distinctions between financial products. In this sense, they point out the right direction for financial regulatory reforms in the future.

The key difference between the integrated regulation and the Twin Peaks models is that while the former assigns all regulatory responsibilities to a single regulator, the latter divides responsibilities and creates two separate regulators: one for prudential regulation and the other for business conduct regulation. Compared to the Twin Peaks model, the integrated regulation model has a number of disadvantages.

First, as noted above, prudential regulation and business conduct regulation deal with different forms of market failure and therefore require different approaches to be taken. Indeed, there are significant differences in the focus of their work, and the way it is carried out, between prudential regulators and business conduct regulators. The former is focused on the soundness of financial institutions while the focus of the latter is on protection of consumer interests. What this means is that prudential regulators need essentially different mindsets and training from those of conduct-of-business regulators. This is broadly mirrored in the fact that prudential regulators typically have an economics background while business conduct regulators are often lawyers.

Secondly, it is difficult to reconcile the competing demands of prudential and business conduct regulation. There is a risk that if both prudential regulation and business conduct regulation are housed in one entity, one of them may be prioritised at the expense of the other. Potential conflicts of interest may arise between prudential and conduct-of-business regulation because of the different nature of their objectives. A good example is that a business conduct regulator might argue for early and full disclosure of a firm's problems while a prudential regulator might place greater weight on the potential threat to the solvency of the institution. Finally, there are a number of other considerations in favour of a 'Twin Peaks' model, such as clear mandates and accountability and avoiding the problem of reputational contagion.

Due to its strengths, the Twin Peaks model has attracted increasing attention as a template for reform in many countries, particularly after the Global Financial Crisis of 2008. The US government carried out a thorough investigation into its financial regulatory regime in 2008, concluding that the ultimate reform goal for financial regulation in the United States is not the integrated regulation model, but rather the Twin Peaks model.[41] Most interestingly, the United Kingdom, the pioneer and symbol of the integrated regulation model, has itself carried out reform in line with the Twin Peaks model: From 1 April 2013, the FSA was abolished and its responsibilities split into two agencies: (1) the Financial Conduct Authority, which watches how financial institutions treat their customers and (2) the Prudential Regulatory Authority within the Bank of England, which conducts prudential regulation of financial institutions. Moreover, South Africa has also adopted the Twin Peaks model pursuant to the National Treasury Policy Document in February 2011, which set out proposals for strengthening its financial regulatory system by adopting the Twin Peaks model.[42] These latest international developments should shed light on the debate over the future development of China's financial regulation.

14.4.2.2 Recent Developments and Implications

How likely is it that the above suggestions for staged reform will become a reality in China? Some recent developments show that China has proceeded to implement short-term reforms, namely improving coordination and cooperation between various regulators under the existing sector-based regulatory architecture.

On 14–15 July 2017, China's 5th National Financial Work Conference (NFWC) was held in Beijing, with a particular focus on the reforms of the financial regulatory architecture in China. This five yearly conference has held a special place in China's economic and political calendar since it was introduced to encourage more sustainable economic growth following the Asian financial crisis. The first conference in 1997 saw the establishment of the insurance regulator, the CIRC, and a plan to bail out China's largest banks. The 2002 conference led to the creation of the CBRC and a drive to list major state-owned banks on overseas stock exchanges, mainly in Hong Kong. In 2007, the third conference oversaw the creation of the sovereign wealth fund, the China Investment Corporation. The conference in 2012 focused on the fallout from the Global Financial Crisis of 2008.

The recent fifth NFWC made a significant change to the existing financial regulatory framework in China by proposing the establishment of a Financial Stability and Development Committee (FSDC), under the State Council. About four months later, in November 2017, the FSDC was officially established as an inter-agency body responsible for integrated monitoring, and prevention of systemic risk in China's financial system, with the goal of ensuring overall financial stability in China.[43] In doing so, the FSDC is required to coordinate the regulatory work of various bodies, particularly 'one bank and two commissions', and improve information-sharing amongst them. Pushing for better coordination between regulators is nothing new, but this is the first time that China has set up a formal committee at the level of the State Council to take on the task. In fact, China already had a financial regulatory coordinating mechanism, known as the inter-agency financial regulatory meeting, which is held from time to time with attendance of high-level officials from the 'one bank and (then) three commissions'.[44]

---

[41] US Department of the Treasury, *Blue Print for a Modernized Financial Regulatory Structure* (2008), 137–8.

[42] South Africa Department of National Treasury, 'A Safer Financial Sector to Serve South Africa Better' (February 2011).

[43] 'State Council Financial Stability and Development Committee Is Officially Established with Mr Ma Kai as Its Director' (9 November 2017).

[44] 2013 Guowuyuan Guanyu Tongyi Jianli Jingrong Jianguan Xietiao Buji Lianxi Huiyi Zhidu de Pifu [2013 Approval of the State Council on the Establishment of Inter-Agency Meeting Mechanism for Financial Regulatory Coordination]; 2008 Memorandum on the Regulatory Division and Cooperation of the CBRC, the CSRC and the CIRC.

TABLE 14.1. *Hierarchy of leaders of 'one bank and three commissions' and major banks.*

Level	Administration ranking	Position
1	Minister	President of PBOC
2	Minister	Chairperson of CBIRC, CSRC
3	Vice-minister	Senior vice-president of PBOC; president of the largest four state-owned banks
4	Vice-minister	Junior vice-president of PBOC; vice-chairperson of CBIRC, CSRC

The FSDC represents a significant improvement on the previous regulatory coordination arrangement in several important ways. First and foremost, the FSDC is headed by one vice-premier, which means it will have a higher political ranking than the central bank and the sectoral regulators, which are all ministry-level agencies. Further, the FSDC is a formal committee with clear regulatory mandates while the inter-agency meeting is merely an ad hoc mechanism for the various regulators to communicate. Finally, the FSDC's powers are broad and include, among other things, the authority to coordinate the development and regulation of the financial system, the relationship between financial policy, currency policy, fiscal policy and industrial policy, and the power to deal with systemic financial risks and safeguard overall financial stability.

However, the FSDC may not conduct direct regulation of financial institutions but must instead seek to discharge its duties through existing regulators. Importantly, the office of the FSDC is located within the central bank, the PBOC, which suggests that the PBOC will assume a significantly more important role in China's new financial regulatory landscape. In fact, the fifth NFWC explicitly mentioned the need to strengthen the function of the PBOC to conduct macroprudential regulation and prevent systemic risks. On 17 July 2017, just one day after the fifth NFWC, Zhou Xiaochuan, the then president of the PBOC, stated that the PBOC would strive to perform its duty through the office of the FSDC and strengthen financial regulatory coordination.[45] Further, as noted, in April 2018 the former sectoral regulators for banking and insurance, the CBRC and the CIRC, were merged to form the CBIRC. It is important to note that this reform gives the PBOC the power to make major laws and regulations concerning the banking and insurance industries as well as basic rules on prudential regulation.

The heightened status of the PBOC does not come as a surprise. Generally speaking, the central bank is well-positioned to take on macroprudential regulation and systemic risk prevention. Further, it follows the international trend towards strengthening the role of the central bank in financial regulation after the 2008 GFC. Finally, it fits well with the local political economy situation in relation to financial regulators and institutions in China. Table 14.1 lists, by order of seniority in the administrative hierarchy, the leaders of 'one bank and two commissions' and major financial institutions.

As the table shows, although 'one bank and two commissions' are all ministry-level agencies under the State Council, the PBOC enjoys a higher status than the three commissions in practice. Further, the presidents of the largest four state-owned banks are actually above the vice-chairmen of the two commissions. Under current practice, the chairmen of the two commissions are usually not chosen from among their vice-chairmen but rather from the presidents of the largest four state-owned banks.

---

[45] Ibid.

What implications does the recent reform have for the prospect of China transitioning to the Twin Peaks model? On the one hand, the establishment of the FSDC is clearly consistent with the short-term reform proposal as discussed earlier; namely, to follow the US experience to improve regulatory coordination of various regulators. From a comparative perspective, the recent reform is broadly similar to what the United States did in the aftermath of the Global Financial Crisis of 2008. The *Dodd–Frank Act* establishes the Financial Stability Oversight Council (FSOC) to strengthen regulatory coordination and systemic risk regulation.[46] More specifically, the FSOC is empowered to, inter alia, facilitate inter-agency information-sharing and designate systemically significant non-bank financial institutions. The direct authority to regulate systemically significant non-bank financial institutions is, however, vested in the hands of the Federal Reserve. Like the FSOC in the United States, the newly established FSDC in China is essentially a coordinating and advisory body without the power to regulate the financial system directly. In this connection, the FSDC is certainly different from the 'integrated regulation' model, as represented by the United Kingdom's FSCA before its 2013 reform.

On the other hand, however, the recent reforms mean that China may not consider any further structural reform in the foreseeable future. As discussed before, China should adopt the Twin Peaks model in the long term, but when is the time for it to do so will depend ultimately on the extent to which the recent reinforcement of the current sector-based regulatory structure can effectively cope with the challenges of new developments and innovations in the marketplace. For instance, the FSDC has held its first plenary meeting to decide on its short-term work plan, which puts emphasis on strengthening regulatory coordination and improving the ability to handle financial risks. Zhou Xiaochuan, the then president of the PBOC, commented that the FSDC would focus on four work priorities, including shadow banking, wealth management products, internet finance and financial holding companies. Soon after the first meeting of the FSDC, on 17 November 2017, the PBOC, together with the CBRC, the CSRC, the CIRC and other relevant agencies, issued a consultation paper on the regulation of wealth management products for the main purpose of harmonising the regulatory standards for these products when offered by different financial institutions.[47]

Financial reform is always crisis-driven, and this is particularly so for fundamental reform of the regulatory structure, which usually entails significant costs. Indeed, it would be a daunting task for the Chinese government to reorganise all existing sectoral regulators in line with the Twin Peaks model given the sheer number of people the two commissions employ. In sum, a cost–benefit analysis will be conducted when the Chinese government considers transitioning to the Twin Peaks model in the future, and recent reforms may create more sunk costs while reducing the benefit of more fundamental structural reforms towards Twin Peaks.

14.5 CONCLUSION

This chapter has shown that the current Chinese regulatory regime adopts a traditional sectoral regulatory structure, consisting mainly of the PBOC as the central bank and two sector-specific

---

[46] Dodd–Frank Act, at s 113.
[47] Guanyu Guifan Jinrong Jigou Zichan Guanli Yewu de Zhidao Yijian (Zhengqiu Yijian Gao) [Guiding Opinions on the Regulation of Financial Institutions' Wealth Management Businesses] (consultation paper) (issued by the PBOC, the CBRC, the CSRC, the CIRC and State Administration of Foreign Exchange on 17 November 2017). On 27 April 2018, the final version of this instrument was issued. On 28 December 2019, the amendment to the Securities Law was passed with effect from 1 March 2020. Under art 2, the State Council is authorised to promulgate measures to regulate the issuance and trading of wealth management products in line with the principles of the Securities Law.

regulators, namely the CBIRC and the CSRC. This regulatory framework is faced with increasing challenges due to recent market developments, such as the emergence of financial conglomerates, hybrid financial products, shadow banking and internet finance.

Largely following the US experience, the Chinese government has recently established a new high-level regulator, the FSDC as a division of the State Council, to improve regulatory coordination under its existing sector-based regulatory architecture. This reform represents a realistic and measured response to the challenges to financial regulation in China and may pave the way for China's possible transition to the Twin Peaks model. However, as the reform seeks to solve many of the issues presently plaguing China's financial system, it becomes less likely that China will consider fundamental reforms of its financial regulatory structure any time soon. The efficacy of the recent reforms remains to be seen, which will, to a large extent, determine whether, and if so when, China may ultimately transition to the Twin Peaks model in the future.

15

US Financial Regulatory Structure

Beneath the Surface of Twin Peaks

Heidi Mandanis Schooner

15.1 INTRODUCTION

The US financial regulatory structure is notoriously complex and defies categorisation. The structure embodies some of the principles of the Twin Peaks model, and yet a foggy mountain range better describes the US regulatory architecture – multiple peaks with murky demarcation. Criticism of the US structure is, at the same time, too easy and too hard. The structure is easy to criticise because of blatant overlaps that scream inefficiency, yet criticism is difficult because the clunky and complex structure works reasonably well, or at least is not obviously the primary cause of recent regulatory failures. Certainly, the Global Financial Crisis exposed regulatory gaps, the under-regulated shadow banking system is the classic example. Yet the then existing regulatory architecture did not account for the failure of agencies to utilise their authority in the run-up to the crisis.[1] Structure may be important, but leadership is essential.

Recent conditions make this an important moment to reconsider regulatory structure. This chapter considers two such circumstances as they relate to the systemic risk peak in the Twin Peaks structure. First, more than ten years have elapsed since the Global Financial Crisis. The behaviour of regulators is procyclical. Agencies are more likely to loosen their supervision, regulation and enforcement when the markets are stable or on the upswing. They will be more aggressive in their supervision, regulation and enforcement when markets and the economy are volatile or in a downturn. As the memory of the crisis fades, so does the zeal of regulators to insist on stringent controls. Moreover, the Trump administration has shown significant interest in reducing regulatory burden, which imposes additional deregulatory pressure. Second, technology in the financial services industry evolves apace. FinTech has captured the imagination and attention of the financial services industry and its customers. Not surprisingly, the distinctive features of financial innovation often expose, and sometimes exploit, gaps in regulation. Like the development of securitisation, which allows lenders to offload assets from their balance sheets and gave rise to the under-regulated shadow banking sector, FinTech innovations will develop outside the regulated sphere. Therefore, undetected or underestimated risk may emerge. The question considered here is how current agency structure can withstand the demands for deregulation (or, at least, regulatory forbearance) in an era of galloping and pervasive technological innovation.

---

[1] After noting regulatory gaps, the Financial Crisis Inquiry Commission concluded that 'we do not accept the view that regulators lacked the power to protect the financial system. They had ample power in many arenas and they chose not to use it'. Financial Crisis Inquiry Report at xviii, www.gpo.gov/fdsys/pkg/GPO-FCIC/pdf/GPO-FCIC.pdf.

This chapter begins with an overview of the US financial regulatory structure followed by a closer examination of the financial stability architecture in the United States following the Global Financial Crisis and the very recent developments in that arena. Those recent developments are then evaluated alongside the Twin Peaks model. The US model is analysed further by considering the case of the growing reliance on technology as a potential threat to financial stability.

15.2 US FINANCIAL REGULATORY STRUCTURE: AN OVERVIEW

The reliable US response to financial crisis is to create a new federal agency. The first federal regulator, the Office of the Comptroller of the Currency (OCC), was created during the Civil War. The financial panics at the end of the nineteenth century and through the panic of 1907 led to the Federal Reserve System (Federal Reserve). Following the Great Depression, Congress established the Federal Deposit Insurance Corporation (FDIC) and the Securities and Exchange Commission (SEC). The Office of Thrift Supervision (OTS) was established in the wake of the Savings & Loan Crisis of the late 1980s (it was later abolished, its duties absorbed by the OCC). The Financial Stability Oversight Council (FSOC), Office of Financial Research (OFR) and Consumer Financial Protection Bureau (CFPB) were established in response to the Global Financial Crisis.

While this list accounts for the most well-known federal agencies, there are more. According to a Government Accountability Office (GAO) report, fifteen agencies comprise the US financial regulatory structure.[2] The Federal Reserve, FDIC, SEC and Commodities Futures Trading Commission (CFTC) are assigned consolidated supervision or systemic risk-related oversight. The safety and soundness of depository institutions is the responsibility of the Federal Reserve, FDIC, OCC, the National Credit Union Administration (NCUA), as well as state regulators. Along with state regulators, the Federal Reserve, FDIC, OCC, NCUA, FTC and CFPB are responsible for consumer financial protection. Securities and derivative markets oversight is shared by the states and the SEC, CFTC, Financial Industry Regulatory Authority (FINRA), Municipal Securities Rulemaking Board (MSRB) and National Futures Association (NFA). Insurance oversight is left to the states[3] and the Federal Housing Finance Agency (FHFA) is responsible for housing finance.

This decentralised structure means that firms are supervised by a number of regulators. A relatively uncomplicated depository institution can be supervised by four federal financial regulators (but can escape state supervision if it is federally chartered). A broker dealer can be supervised by five federal financial regulators as well as state regulators. Overlap is self-evident. Numerous reform proposals highlight the potential for improved efficiency and effectiveness. A 2006 FDIC study, focused primarily on banks, identified twenty-four major reform proposals since the 1930s when the fundamental structure was established.[4] In the midst of the Global Financial Crisis, the US Department of the Treasury released its *Blueprint for a Modernized Financial Regulatory Structure* (2008 Blueprint).[5] The 2008 Blueprint proposed some modest

---

[2] US Government Accountability Office, 'Financial Regulation: Complex and Fragmented Structure Could Be Streamlined to Improve Effectiveness', GAO-16-175 (February 2016).

[3] The Federal Insurance Office was established in 2010, but it has no regulatory authority.

[4] R. M. Kushmeider, 'The U.S. Federal Financial Regulatory System: Restructuring Federal Bank Regulation', *FDIC Banking Review* (January 2006), www.fdic.gov/bank/analytical/banking/br17n4full.pdf.

[5] *The Department of the Treasury Blueprint for a Modernized Financial Regulatory Structure* (March 2008).

and other radical changes to the structure of regulation for the entire financial services industry.[6] While the legislation that followed the 2008 Blueprint, Dodd–Frank Wall Street Reform and Consumer Protection Act (Dodd–Frank),[7] adopted the recommended elimination of the federal thrift regulator and established the CFPB and FSOC as single-objective agencies, Dodd–Frank did nothing to fundamentally alter the regulatory structure. While the CFPB and FSOC are single-objective regulators, consumer financial protection and systemic risk regulation respectively, those agencies have limits on their jurisdiction and other agencies perform many of the same functions. For example, while the CFPB is charged with consumer financial protection, other federal and state agencies also share that mandate. FSOC, as discussed in more detail in Section 15.3, is not actually a regulator but is designed to identify systemic risk to be addressed by other federal regulators.

Calls for structural reform continue. In 2017, the US Treasury recommended changes to the regulatory restructure as a piece of a larger picture of regulatory reform. The Treasury's *A Financial System that Creates Economic Opportunities: Banks and Credit Unions*[8] is light on details but, in general, recommends 'that Congress take action to reduce fragmentation, overlap, and duplication in financial regulation. This could include consolidating regulators with similar missions and more clearly defining regulatory mandates'. A second report in 2017, *A Financial System that Creates Economic Opportunities: Capital Markets*,[9] includes lengthy discussion of the merger of the SEC and CFTC but stops short of making a recommendation.[10]

Perhaps the most consistent source of reform proposals has been the GAO. For at least twenty years, the GAO has been urging Congress to reform the structure of financial regulation.[11] GAO reports on regulatory structure are full of detailed recommendations for structural improvement. The focus of such reports is often the inefficiencies of the current structure, but the GAO also identifies gaps that might impede effectiveness. In its most recent report, the GAO noted FSOC's lack of certain regulatory tools to address systemic risk.[12] The structure of FSOC and its limitations are discussed next.

15.3 US FINANCIAL STABILITY REGULATORY STRUCTURE

The Global Financial Crisis highlighted two general deficiencies in the traditional system of financial regulation. First, banks are not the only systemically important financial institutions. Other financial institutions, such as investment banks and insurance companies, can also

---

[6] The 2008 Blueprint included near-term reforms aimed at reducing duplication such as combining the work of the SEC and CFTC. It also recommended long-term changes that envisioned a three-peak structure consisting of a market stability regulator, a prudential regulator and a business conduct regulator.

[7] *Dodd–Frank Wall Street Reform and Consumer Protection Act*, Pub L No 113-203, 124 Stat 1376 (2010).

[8] US Department of Treasury, A *Financial System That Creates Economic Opportunities: Banks and Credit Unions* (June 2017).

[9] US Department of Treasury, A *Financial System That Creates Economic Opportunities: Capital Markets* (October 2017).

[10] Treasury issued other similarly styled reports on 'Non-banks and Financial Technology' and 'Asset Management and Insurance'. Both reports discuss regulatory architecture but offer no recommendations for reform. With regard to non-banks and FinTech, the report finds that 'the financial regulatory framework is not always optimally suited to address new business models and products that continue to evolve in financial services'. US Department of Treasury, A *Financial System That Creates Economic Opportunity: Nonbanks, Fintech and Innovation* (July 2018), at 10.

[11] The most recent comprehensive report is: *Financial Regulation: Complex and Fragmented Structure Could Be Streamlined to Improve Effectiveness*, GAO-16-175 (February 2016). Others include: GAO-09-216; GAO-08-32; GAO-05-61; and T-OCE/GGD-97-103.

[12] GAO-16-175 at 66.

contribute to a systemic financial crisis. Second, protecting the solvency of a financial institution does not always prevent systemic risk since a firm may take steps to protect its own solvency (for example, by selling assets), and that action, if repeated by other firms, may be what triggers the systemic crisis. Therefore, many post-crisis reform proposals highlight the importance of adding a macroprudential focus to the traditional microprudential regimes. Stated another way, the post-crisis approach focuses not only on the solvency of commercial banks (microprudential) but also considers the impact of the activities of all financial institutions on the financial system and real economy (macroprudential).

Dodd–Frank reflected this new macroprudential approach through the creation of FSOC. FSOC[13] was established with a three-fold statutory purpose: first, 'to identify risks to the financial stability of the United States that could arise from the material financial distress or failure, or ongoing activities, of large, interconnected bank holding companies or nonbank financial companies, or that could arise outside the financial services marketplace';[14] second, 'to promote market discipline, by eliminating expectations on the part of shareholders, creditors, and counterparties of such companies that the Government will shield them from losses in the event of failure';[15] and third, 'to respond to emerging threats to the stability of the United States financial system'.[16] While FSOC's duties include various forms of monitoring for threats to financial stability,[17] its most significant power is the authority to require the Federal Reserve to supervise non-bank financial institutions that present a risk to financial stability ('systemic non-bank financial companies')[18] and make recommendations to the Federal Reserve regarding the imposition of heightened prudential standards on systemic non-bank financial companies and large, interconnected bank holding companies. FSOC may determine that systemic non-bank financial institutions should be subjected to Federal Reserve heightened supervision if 'material financial distress at the U.S. nonbank financial company, or the nature, scope, size, scale, concentration, interconnectedness, or mix of activities of the U.S. nonbank financial company, could pose a threat to the financial stability of the United States'.[19] FSOC has designated four non-banks as systemic non-bank financial companies: American International Group (AIG), GE Capital Holdings, Prudential Financial and MetLife. Responding to the firms' reduced size and changes in activities, FSOC rescinded the designations of AIG (on 29 September 2017) and GE Capital (on 28 June 2016). MetLife challenged its designation and won in the federal court.[20]

---

[13] FSOC is comprised of the following voting members: Secretary of the Treasury (who serves as the chairperson of FSOC), the chairman of the Federal Reserve, the Comptroller of the Currency, the director of the Bureau of Consumer Financial Protection, the chairman of the Securities Exchange Commission, the chairperson of the FDIC, the chairperson of the Commodity Futures Trading Commission, the director of the Federal Housing Finance Agency, the chairman of the National Credit Union Administration Board and an independent member with insurance experience appointed by the President upon advice and consent of the Senate. Non-voting members of the Council include the director of the Office of Financial Research (a new office of the Treasury established under the Dodd–Frank Act), the director of the Federal Insurance Office (a new office of the Treasury created under the Dodd–Frank Act), a state insurance commissioner, a state banking supervisor and a state securities commissioner. 12 USC s 5321(b).

[14] 12 USC s 5322(a)(1)(A).

[15] 12 USC s 5322(a)(1)(B).

[16] 12 USC s 5322(a)(1)(C).

[17] 12 USC s 5322(a)(2) (enumerating FSOC's duties).

[18] Prior to the passage of the Dodd–Frank Act, the Federal Reserve supervised bank holding companies, but not non-bank financial companies. A bank holding company is a company that owns or controls a bank. 12 USC s 1841(a). For these purposes, a 'bank' is generally an FDIC-insured commercial bank, but (along with numerous other exceptions) not an insured thrift. 12 USC s 1843(c).

[19] 12 USC s 5323(a)(1). FSOC's determination is subject to judicial review. 12 USC s 5323(h).

[20] *MetLife v FSOC*, 177 F Supp 3d 219 (DDC 2016).

FSOC appealed but, after the change in administration, moved to dismiss its appeal on 18 January 2018. On 17 October 2018, FSOC de-designated Prudential. Thus, no non-banks are currently designated by FSOC for purposes of prudential supervision by the Federal Reserve.[21] Moreover, according to FSOC's 2019 Annual Report, FSOC has not voted to advance any firms to the final stages of the designation process, suggesting that additional non-bank designations are unlikely in the near future.[22]

On 21 April 2017, President Trump ordered the Department of Treasury to conduct a review of FSOC's non-bank designation process (Treasury Report). The Treasury Report includes a significant assessment of the non-bank designation process and recommendation for the future: 'The Council's authority to designate nonbank financial companies is a blunt instrument for addressing potential risks to financial stability. Treasury recommends that the Council prioritize its efforts to address risks to financial stability through a process that emphasizes an activities based or industry-wide approach.'[23]

The Treasury Report recommends a three-step process beginning with a review of activities or products that could affect financial stability. If such risks are found, then FSOC would work with the primary regulators to address such risks. The last step would be to consider designation of a non-bank financial company only after consultation with the primary regulators. The report also includes recommended revisions to FSOC's non-bank designation process including a cost–benefit analysis.

In December 2019, FSOC adopted Final Interpretative Guidance (2019 Interpretative Guidance)[24] that replaces its 2012 Interpretative Guidance regarding non-bank designations.[25] The recommendations of the Treasury Report are amply reflected in the 2019 Interpretative Guidance which prioritises an activities-based approach; resorts to entity designations only if an identified risk cannot be addressed through an activities-based approach; and requires a cost and benefit analysis with regard to both identifying activities and entities which may require enhanced supervision.

The 2019 Interpretative Guidance represents a significant change in priorities. It represents a move from an entity-focused approach to non-bank regulation to an activities-based approach.[26] From a statutory viewpoint, FSOC has the authority to impose Federal Reserve supervision on non-bank financial companies through its designation process. Specifically, that means that when MetLife, for example, was designated a non-bank SIFI, it was subject to prudential supervision by the Federal Reserve (including, capital, leverage and liquidity requirements, among other prudential tools).[27] FSOC, however, does not have similar statutory authority with regard to financial activities and practices.[28] Instead, FSOC may *recommend* that the primary financial regulators (Federal Reserve, SEC, CFPB and so on) apply new standards if FSOC

---

[21] For a full discussion of the de-designation process, see Jeremy C. Kress, *The Last SIFI: The Unwise and Illegal Deregulation of Prudential Financial* (December 2018) 71 *Stanford Law Review Online*.

[22] FSOC 2019 Annual Report at 112.

[23] Department of the Treasury, *Financial Stability Oversight Council Designations: Report to the President of the United States* (17 November 2017), at 10, www.treasury.gov/press-center/press-releases/documents/pm-fsoc-designations-memo-11-17.pdf.

[24] 84 Fed Reg 71740 (30 December 2019).

[25] 77 Fed Reg 21637 (11 April 2012).

[26] See J. Kress, P. McCoy and D. Schwarz, 'Regulating Entities and Activities: Complementary Approaches to Nonbank Systemic Risk' (2019) 92(6) *Southern California Law Review* 1455.

[27] 12 USC s 5325.

[28] FSOC's organisational structure reflects the statutory emphasis on entity designation as opposed to an activities-based approach. FSOC's operations depend on a committee structure designed to match its statutory responsibilities. Thus, FSOC maintains a Nonbank Financial Companies Designation Committee but has no similarly dedicated

determines that the activity or practice could create or increase significant risk to the financial system.[29] If the primary regulators decide not to follow FSOC's recommendation, they need only provide a written explanation of the reasons.[30]

Looking ahead, given that the Treasury Report labels the non-bank designation process a 'blunt instrument' for addressing financial stability, and the fact that the Treasury Secretary must vote in favour of any non-bank designations,[31] the odds seem stacked against a future entity designation meeting the cost–benefit standard. As to the identification of systemic activities, the effective date of the 2019 Interpretive Guidance was 29 January 2020, making predictions difficult. Not surprisingly, FSOC's 26 March 2020 open meeting was focused entirely on the response to Covid-19.

15.4 EVALUATION OF THE US FINANCIAL STABILITY STRUCTURE AGAINST THE TWIN PEAKS PARADIGM

The Twin Peaks paradigm envisions a regulatory structure quite different from the current US regime. The Twin Peaks structure is consolidated with only two regulators: one regulator with a financial stability mission and one regulator with a market conduct and consumer protection mandate. In contrast, as discussed, the US system relies on numerous regulators with overlapping responsibilities at both the federal and state level.

Dodd–Frank, the legislation enacted in response to the Global Financial Crisis, certainly did not adopt the Twin Peaks model. The US regulatory architecture remains both fragmented and overlapping. Yet Dodd–Frank achieved some consolidation through the establishment of FSOC and the creation of the CFPB. With regard to the focus of this chapter and as discussed above, FSOC has a financial stability mandate and its scope is macroprudential in that its mission is not limited to the safety and soundness of banks but rather to the stability of the financial system. Therefore, at least on its face, FSOC represents the prudential peak in the Twin Peak model. The discussion below examines whether FSOC's constitution embodies the important elements of the peak structure.

In the middle of the Global Financial Crisis, Michael Taylor, guru of the Twin Peaks model, observed that 'each regulatory agency should have a clear and unambiguous mandate and should have a specific objective for which it can be held accountable'.[32] This means that the ideal Twin Peaks financial stability regulator would have a clear mandate to promote financial stability and would be held accountable to that mandate. FSOC's mandate is clearly macroprudential; it is tasked with identifying, monitoring and responding to threats to the financial system. What is less clear is FSOC's responsibility if it fails to identify those threats, fails to monitor them, or, perhaps most importantly, fails to respond to them. This is the question of accountability. Accountability can be measured in many ways but certainly if a financial stability regulator lacks independence, funding or power, accountability will suffer.

---

committee focused on activities or products. See https://home.treasury.gov/system/files/261/The%20Council%26%23039%3Bs%20Committee%20Charters_1.pdf.

[29] 12 USC s 5330(a).

[30] 12 USC s 5330(c).

[31] 12 USC s 5323(a)(1).

[32] M. Taylor, 'Twin Peaks', *Financial World Online* (London, 9 September 2009).

While a full discussion of agency independence[33] is beyond the scope of this chapter, the question of FSOC's independence is particularly thorny. FSOC is made up of the heads of the federal financial regulators along with representatives of other financial regulatory constituents. Thus, in some ways FSOC's independence depends on the amalgamated independence of each of the agencies. To be sure, the fact that the Treasury Secretary serves as the chairperson of FSOC is a significant factor in evaluating FSOC's independence. A report by the Congressional Research Service observed that '[o]ne possible outcome of the creation of FSOC is to give the Treasury Secretary greater influence over the independent financial regulators'.[34] Significantly, as the report notes, non-bank designations cannot be made without the assent of the Treasury Secretary.

In terms of FSOC's funding, its expenses are paid out of the OFR's budget.[35] OFR, in turn, is funded through assessments on large bank holding companies and any non-bank financial institutions supervised by the Federal Reserve (of which, as discussed, there are none currently).[36] On the one hand, this freedom from the annual appropriations process is beneficial in maintaining independence. On the other hand, funding by assessment means that the agency is dependent on the industry for its own survival.

Most relevant to the evaluation of FSOC against the Twin Peaks paradigm is the question of FSOC's powers. FSOC has a clear purpose to identify, monitor and respond to threats.[37] The statute provides that FSOC 'shall' collect information, monitor the financial system and make recommendations to other regulators.[38] With regard to FSOC's most significant power, non-bank financial institution designations, the statute provides only that FSOC 'may' determine that such companies shall be supervised by the Federal Reserve. FSOC does, then, have the discretionary authority to impose supervision on designated non-banks. With regard to systemic activities, however, FSOC 'may' issue only 'recommendations to the primary financial regulatory agencies to apply new or heightened standards and safeguards'.[39] The primary regulatory agencies are not obliged to do so as long as they provide a written explanation as to 'why the agency has determined not to follow the recommendation'.[40] FSOC does not have the authority to set supervisory priorities or write new regulations.[41]

Recent FSOC decisions may be evidence of actual, as opposed to potential, weakness on the accountability scale. Observers identify FSOC's move from an entity to an activities focus as a deregulatory move,[42] evidenced by the fact that FSOC de-designated the last non-bank firm but has yet to identify any systemic activities. Unless and until FSOC identifies certain activities as systemic and uses what little power it has to see that such activities are regulated, FSOC will be open to the criticism that the change in policy is purely in satisfaction of the administration's deregulatory agenda and not calculated to prevent future systemic crises. And yet it would be a mistake to translate this criticism into an indictment of activities-based regulation and a

---

[33] Independence is used herein in the broad sense – to refer to the relative autonomy from the President's agenda and other partisan influences.

[34] Congressional Research Service, Independence of Federal Financial Regulators, 7-5700 (24 February 2014).

[35] 12 USC s 5328.

[36] 12 USC s 5345(d).

[37] 12 USC s 5322(a)(1).

[38] 12 USC s 5322(a)(2).

[39] 12 USC s 5330(a)

[40] 12 USC s 5330(c).

[41] For a discussion of FSOC's designation authority, see D. Schwarcz and D. Zaring, 'Regulation by Threat: Dodd Frank and the Nonbank Problem' (2017) 84 *University of Chicago Law Review* 1813.

[42] www.marketwatch.com/story/fsoc-promised-it-would-pair-deregulation-of-individual-non-banks-with-an-increased-focus-on-risky-activities-it-hasnt-2018-10-22.

vindication of the entity approach. While both approaches have strengths, they both suffer from similar line-drawing weaknesses which can ultimately be the source of industry pressure to deregulate or for regulatory arbitrage.

The strength of the entity approach is that it aligns well with consolidated prudential supervision. Fundamentally, prudential supervisors focus on the firm's risk management practices to ensure safe and sound operations. Regulating the consolidated entity makes this possible (although, obviously, not easy). The downside of the institutional approach is the line-drawing, that is, deciding which institutions should be subjected to supervision. Firms will and do object to the entity model, claiming that their operations are safer as compared to others and therefore do not justify intrusive and expensive supervision. This type of objection was on display in the debates that led to the passage of the *Economic Growth, Regulatory Relief, and Consumer Protection Act* (the Act).[43] Small community banks and even large regional banks complained that Dodd–Frank imposed needlessly costly regulation on them despite the fact that their operations did not cause or contribute significantly to the Global Financial Crisis.[44] The Act provides for regulatory relief for community banks and certain large banks based on the premise that regulation must be tailored to a firm's risk not simply its charter.

The strength of the activities approach is that it levels the playing field by treating all market participants that engage in the particular activity in the same way.[45] In this way, it avoids institutional line-drawing, but it suffers from its own definitional constraints. Defining the regulated activity can be difficult and can encourage arbitrage. Further, activities are often most risky when combined. Unless activities are considered in concert with one another, risk can go undetected.[46] Finally, as with the entity approach, firms will and do object to the activities approach, claiming that their participation in the activity is not as risky as others' or that they are already subject to other forms of regulation that account for any of the activities' risks.

Therefore, the distinction between entity versus activities regulation does not readily seem to determine regulatory effectiveness. If Congress had given FSOC authority to designate activities as systemic instead of the authority to designate non-bank firms, we might have seen a similar evolution since the early days of Dodd–Frank. FSOC, in the zeal that tends to follow a financial crisis, might have designated various activities as systemic. Perhaps money market mutual funds would have been first. Then, perhaps, asset management activities would have been next. Eventually, various market participants would have called for an exemption from any subsequent regulation of those activities. Banks, for example, would have claimed that the regulation was duplicative since they are already comprehensively regulated. Non-bank firms might claim that their participation in such activities is not significant enough to justify costly regulation. We might have ended up in roughly the same place – a false start at prudential regulation of the non-bank sector.

Ultimately, because FSOC's powers are not as broad as its mandate, the entity versus activities debate has important ramifications for the question of accountability. A positive view of FSOC's accountability might note that the name itself, Financial Stability Oversight Council, is a

---

[43] Pub L 115–70 (24 May 2018).

[44] See H. M. Schooner, 'Regulating Angels' (2015) 50 *Georgia Law Review* 143.

[45] In discussions that led up to the dismantling of the Glass–Steagall separation between commercial banking and securities businesses, the activities-based approach was labelled 'functional' regulation. For a full discussion, see H. M. Schooner, 'Regulating Risk Not Function' (1998) 66 *University of Cincinnati Law Review* 441.

[46] Even traditionally, however, activities are viewed in combination and that combination is what makes them systemic. If we view traditional bank regulation through an activities lens, deposit-taking (short-term borrowing) is a risky activity because it is paired with long-term assets (long-term lending). That mis-match is what makes banks vulnerable to runs and justifies prudential regulation.

significant source of accountability. The name establishes FSOC's mission and the public rightly expects it to use all its power to ensure financial stability. A more critical view, however, is that the current structure allows for weak accountability. Suppose that a non-bank financial institution fails and is at the centre of a future financial crisis. If FSOC has designated the firm, then it can blame the ineffectiveness of primary regulators in doing the job of supervising the firm. If FSOC has not designated the non-bank, the failure of that firm can almost always be seen as part of broader risks that built up in the system. FSOC could claim that it was risky activities throughout the system that caused the crisis and, after all, it had no authority to impose regulation on activities. In turn, none of the primary regulators can be blamed because each has only partial responsibility. Ultimately, the amalgamated nature of FSOC diffuses accountability and potentially masks the possibility that the enhanced influence of the Treasury undermines the ability of FSOC to achieve its mandated purpose.[47]

Recall that the GAO has repeatedly called on Congress to reform the US financial regulatory structure. Particularly relevant to this discussion, the GAO has questioned FSOC's 'ability to effectively respond to different kinds of systemic risks, particularly those whose origins are not entity-specific. These limitations also make it difficult to hold FSOC accountable for maintaining financial stability'.[48] While the creation of FSOC seemed to embrace the goal of consolidated financial stability regulation, beneath the surface FSOC suffers from the sort of lack of accountability that can undermine effectiveness.

15.5 FUTURE STRESS ON US REGULATORY STRUCTURE: FINANCIAL TECHNOLOGY

As discussed in the prior section, threats to financial stability are not necessarily bounded by the identity of a firm or by a market activity. The sources of potential threats to any financial system are myriad. Innovation is often a threat to financial stability and its inherent newness presents unique challenges. Technological innovation magnifies this effect since adoption can be quick and quickly spread. Moreover, technology can present contrasting threats. On the one hand, cybersecurity is often the first threat mentioned when commentators are asked to identify the potential source of the next crisis. This is a known threat, which all constituents have strong incentives to address. From the vantage point of regulatory design, cybersecurity represents the type of threat that demands significant inter-agency and international cooperation. On the other hand, the role that new financial technology products or systems could play in the next crisis is not as easily imagined. Commentators often hedge when asked whether FinTech constitutes a current threat.

In recent years, FinTech has eclipsed all other forms of financial innovation in the popular imagination. FinTech is often associated with flashy, potentially disruptive cryptocurrencies such as Bitcoin or with the firms associated with its development, FinTech start-up firms in particular.[49] Yet FinTech encompasses many more, and perhaps many more important, types of technology-driven innovations. Marketplace lending, for example, refers to financial services firms that use online platforms to lend, directly or indirectly, to consumers and small businesses.[50] Mobile payments is an important area in which the innovators are not all banks or start-

---

[47] The whole thing begins to take on the plot of Agatha Christie's *Murder on the Orient Express*.
[48] GAO-16-175 at 87.
[49] For a list of notable FinTech firms, see www.businessinsider.com/fintech-companies-startups.
[50] 'Marketplace lending' seems to have replaced the earlier 'peer-to-peer lending' label. See www.treasury.gov/connect/blog/Documents/Opportunities_and_Challenges_in_Online_Marketplace_Lending_white_paper.pdf, at 5.

up firms. Consumer goods giants such as Starbucks and Walmart offer mobile payment services, as do large technology firms (such as Apple) and large banks (for example, JPMorgan, Citibank).[51] The impact of FinTech is also not limited to traditional banking services such as lending and payments. Digital wealth management platforms use algorithms to provide customers with investment and financial advice.[52] With regard to banks' activities, a recent OCC report identifies three top innovation trends: (1) cloud computing, (2) artificial intelligence/machine learning, and (3) digitisation of existing processes and products.[53]

The most significant financial innovations may draw on distributed ledger technology (DLT). DLT enables a multi-located (that is, distributed) store of information (that is, ledger). Blockchain is a type of DLT that facilitates the transfer and recording of certain cryptocurrencies including Bitcoin. But DLT has numerous other potential significant applications in finance (particularly in payments, clearing and settlement), mainly because it can eliminate inefficiencies.[54] For example, DLT might be used to achieve faster and cheaper securities settlement.[55] Some predict that the settlement applications will represent the enduring value of blockchain (in contrast to the flashier cryptocurrency applications).[56] Of course, the ultimate success or failure of DLT is still uncertain. Network effects will be a key factor in the future of DLT since a critical mass of participants must adopt any new system for it to be successful. In the case of securities settlement, DLT can be useful only if all constituents agree to use the new platform. Also, to the extent that cost reductions come from the elimination of intermediaries, some incumbents will be resistant to change.

The Financial Stability Board (FSB)[57] released a white paper examining the financial stability implications of FinTech.[58] The FSB's interest in FinTech points to the perception that FinTech innovations will have a significant impact on the future of finance. The FSB noted important limitations to its study given that relatively little data is currently available. Still, the FSB concluded 'that there are currently no compelling financial stability risks from emerging FinTech innovations'.[59] Naturally, if cryptocurrencies were to become ubiquitous or if FinTech innovations were to fundamentally alter existing institutions and practices, this systemic risk evaluation could quickly change.

---

[51] For a comprehensive discussion of developments in mobile payments, see GAO, 'Financial Technology: Information on Subsectors and Regulatory Oversight', GAO-17-361 (April 2017), at 18–30.

[52] See, eg, www.sec.gov/investment/im-guidance-2017-02.pdf (SEC issued advice on roboadvisors).

[53] Office of the Comptroller of the Currency, *Semiannual Risk Perspective from the National Risk Committee* (Fall 2018), at 7. See www.occ.treas.gov/publications-and-resources/publications/semiannual-risk-perspective/files/pub-semiannual-risk-perspective-fall-2018.pdf.

[54] 'The driving force behind efforts to develop and deploy DLT in payments, clearing, and settlement is an expectation that the technology could reduce or even eliminate operational and financial inefficiencies, or other frictions, that exist for current methods of storing, recording and transferring digital assets throughout financial markets.' See www.federalreserve.gov/econresdata/feds/2016/files/2016095pap.pdf, at 3.

[55] Securities settlement could be faster and cheaper because, among other things, DLT could eliminate the need for trusted intermediaries.

[56] Tom Buerkle, 'Blockchain Will Finally Make Itself Useful', Reuters Breakingviews (31 December 2018), www.reuters.com/article/us-tech-blockchain-breakingviews/breakingviews-blockchain-will-finally-make-itself-useful-idUSKCN1OU0RZ.

[57] The FSB is an international organisation established to promote coordination and standard setting among national financial authorities. See www.fsb.org/about/.

[58] Financial Stability Board, 'Financial Stability Implications from FinTech: Supervisory and Regulatory Issues That Merit Authorities' Attention' (27 June 2017), www.fsb.org/wp-content/uploads/R270617.pdf.

[59] Ibid at 1.

While immediate systemic threats from FinTech products and services may be unlikely,[60] it is not too difficult to imagine a future world (which probably also involves highways dominated by self-driving cars) in which traditional banks are irrelevant, completely disintermediated and, therefore, not the source of systemic risk. As imagined in a recent Basel Committee report:

> Incumbent banks are no longer a significant player in the disintermediated bank scenario, because the need for balance sheet intermediation or for a trusted third party is removed. Banks are displaced from customer financial transactions by more agile platforms and technologies, which ensure a direct matching of final consumers depending on their financial needs (borrowing, making a payment, raising capital etc.).[61]

Such imagined elimination of traditional financial institutions may never come to pass. What appears certain, however, is that financial institutions today are forced to respond to the emergence of new technology and new competitors. Thus, the business of finance is changing rapidly and the question here is whether the current regulatory architecture provides a sound foundation for such change.

Consider DLT. In its most revolutionary form, it defies institutionally oriented regulatory architecture. If a salient feature of DLT is decentralisation – no one person or firm has control over the ledger – then a regulatory architecture that is dependent on identifying entities presents a mismatch. Suppose blockchain is widely adopted as a platform for significant financial transactions (via cryptocurrencies or otherwise). A permissioned blockchain may not present many challenges if all parties with permission to access the ledger were regulated entities. However, a permissionless blockchain would present a challenge for an entity-based regulatory architecture (Bitcoin, for example, is governed by consensus[62]). FSOC's authority to designate a non-bank financial institution as systemic has little application when governance is not defined by an entity structure.

Similar problems can emerge with an activities-based approach. FSOC does not have the authority to designate a technology as systemic. As to the products and activities that are supported by new technology, line-drawing problems may be salient. In fact, cryptocurrency provides an excellent example of the boundary limitations of the activities-based approach – is it a currency,[63] a commodity,[64] a security.[65]

By definition, a Twin Peaks architecture is better suited to technological innovations that defy institutional and activity norms as its design is based on regulatory functions or goals instead of on activities or entities. In practice, this may challenge the actual implementation of the Twin Peaks structure. After all, FSOC is inspired by Twin Peaks thinking. It was established for the sole purpose of addressing systemic threats. In reality, however, its powers are more limited and likely to be challenged by future threats. Market pressures may force the development of governance structures for cryptocurrencies and other DLT applications that will enable more effective regulation. DLT-supported securities settlement, for example, will likely develop as a permissioned system. But cryptocurrencies, for example, can support an argument in favour of

---

[60] The threat of cyberattacks, however, tops most lists of current and significant threats.

[61] See www.bis.org/bcbs/publ/d431.pdf, at 20. The report classifies such disintermediation as '[a]t the moment ... far fetched' but identifies P2P lending and cryptocurrencies as limited examples.

[62] See www.economist.com/sites/default/files/economist_case_comp_ivey.pdf, at 12.

[63] Cryptocurrencies implicate money transmission laws. See http://digitalcommons.law.yale.edu/cgi/viewcontent.cgi?article=1121&context=yjolt. See also Uniform Regulation of Virtual Currency Businesses Act, www.uniformlaws.org/committees/community-home?CommunityKey=e104aaa8-c10f-45a7-a34a-0423c2106778.

[64] See www.cftc.gov/idc/groups/public/@lrenforcementactions/documents/legalpleading/enfcoinfliprorder09172015.pdf.

[65] See www.sec.gov/litigation/investreport/34-81207.pdf (SEC concluded that the DOA tokens are securities).

the single regulator approach. Like so many financial products, cryptocurrencies implicate the whole range of regulatory risks – systemic risk, investor protection, anti-money laundering and more.[66]

Taken together, consideration of FinTech further illustrates the weaknesses of FSOC's design. Even in its original iteration, in which designation of non-banks was seen as its important contribution to preventing systemic crisis, the entity focus might prove ill-suited to many FinTech applications.

15.6 CONCLUSION

Congress made an important step forward in conceiving FSOC as a single-peak, prudential regulator with a clear mandate to identify, monitor and respond to threats to the financial system. At the same time, Congress left a diverse set of primary regulators in place and failed to grant FSOC much direct regulatory authority. In addition, FSOC's structure may undermine its independence by elevating the role of the Treasury Secretary in financial regulation. All these deficits move the FSOC away from the Twin Peaks ideal and could undermine its effectiveness. And yet, setting aside the complex structure, US financial regulators have abundant formal and informal power to react to potential threats to financial stability. Regulatory design is best seen as a countercyclical buffer on agency behaviour, which encourages agency leaders to use their power in the public interest even when the economy is strong and threats appear remote. The Twin Peaks model of consolidated, goals-oriented structure endures in the face of deregulatory pressures and rapidly advancing innovation because it avoids the line-drawing problems of entity- or activities-driven regimes and demands accountability. Better implementation of the model, even in a country like the United States with its complex existing structure, is possible. The ability of agency leaders to lead despite an imperfect architecture is equally possible.

---

[66] The Basel Committee observes that 'Fintech developments are expected to raise issues that go beyond the scope of prudential supervision, as other public policy objectives may also be at stake, such as safeguarding data privacy, cybersecurity, consumer protection, fostering competition and compliance with AML/CFT'. See www.bis.org/bcbs/publ/d431.pdf, at 7.

16

A 'Twin Peaks' Vision for Europe

Dirk Schoenmaker and Nicolas Véron

16.1 INTRODUCTION

The organisation of the European Supervisory Authorities (ESAs) is based on a sectoral approach with one ESA for each sector: the European Banking Authority for banking, the European Insurance and Occupational Pensions Authority for insurance and pension funds, and the European Securities and Markets Authority (ESMA) for the securities markets. But is this sectoral approach still suitable?[1] Some countries, such as the Netherlands, France and the United Kingdom, have moved to a supervisory model known as 'Twin Peaks', with one supervisor for prudential supervision and another for markets and conduct-of-business supervision.[2] Other countries, such as Germany, Sweden and Poland, have adopted the single supervisory model.

This chapter outlines a long-term vision for the supervisory architecture of the European Union. In the aftermath of the Global Financial Crisis, the euro-area crisis and the Brexit vote, it is now time to work on this long-term agenda. There is a global trend towards the Twin Peaks model, based upon positive experiences.[3] Examples are found in Australia, the Netherlands and, more recently, the United Kingdom and South Africa.

There are several arguments in favour of a Twin Peaks structure for the European Union. The Brexit vote of June 2016 has raised awareness of the need for a strong market and conduct-of-business supervisor to build an integrated capital market for the EU27 and for the European Economic Area (EEA).[4] With the move towards bail-in of bank bonds, cases of mis-selling of such bonds to retail consumers, who were not fully aware of the bonds' risk profile, have come to widespread public attention. Addressing such malpractices requires a strong and proactive conduct-of-business supervisor, separate from the prudential supervisor. Finally, there are

---

[1] The authors would like to thank Andre Sapir for useful comments and Inês Goncalves Raposo for excellent research assistance.

In a March 2017 public consultation on the operation of the ESAs, the European Commission raised important questions about the supervisory architecture of the European financial system: European Commission, 'Public Consultation on the Operation of the European Supervisory Authorities (ESAs)', DG FISMA, Brussels (2017).

[2] M. Taylor, 'Twin Peaks: A Regulatory Structure for the New Century' (Centre for the Study of Financial Innovation, No 20, December 1995); M. Taylor, 'Twin Peaks Revisited: A Second Chance for Regulatory Reform' (Centre for Study of Financial Innovation, No 89, September 2009).

[3] See R. Huang and D. Schoenmaker (eds), *Institutional Structure of Financial Regulation: Theories and International Experiences* (Routledge, 2015).

[4] At the time of writing, it is not yet known which form Brexit may take, especially whether the United Kingdom will remain in the European internal market.

interlinkages between banks and insurers within financial conglomerates. Integrated prudential supervision would make it possible to supervise these conglomerates on an integrated basis.

16.2 SUPERVISORY MODELS

The organisational structure of financial supervision has changed in most EU countries over the last twenty years (see Table 16.1). All member states used to have a sectoral model of financial supervision, with separate supervisors for banking, insurance and securities, reflecting the traditional dividing lines between financial sectors. But the sectors have been converging. The universal banking model allows banks to combine banking activities, such as lending and deposit-taking, with securities activities, such as offering investment funds and underwriting securities offerings. Meanwhile, banks and insurers are allowed to operate as part of financial conglomerates. Financial products are also converging. Banking and life-insurance products, for example, both serve the long-term savings market. Mortgages are no longer the sole province of

TABLE 16.1. *Organisational structure of financial supervision (as of mid-2017).*

Countries	(1) Sectoral	(2) Cross-sector: Functional (including Twin Peaks)	(3a) Cross-sector: Integrated without central bank role in banking supervision	(3b) Cross-sector: Integrated with central bank role in banking supervision
			Basic models	
European Union	Bulgaria	Belgium (2011)	Denmark (1988)	Austria (2002)
	Cyprus	Croatia (2005)	Estonia (2002)	Czech Republic (2006)
	Greece	France (2003)	Hungary (2000)	Finland (2009)
	Lithuania	Italy (1999)	Latvia (2001)	Germany (2002)
	Luxembourg	Netherlands (2002)	Malta (2002)	Ireland (2003)
	Romania	Portugal (2017)	Poland (2008)	Slovakia (2006)
	Slovenia	United Kingdom (2011)	Sweden (1991)	
	Spain			
Outside EU		Australia (1998)		Japan (2000)
		Canada (1987)		
		United States (2011)		

Note: The United States is categorised as a functional model, because the Dodd–Frank Act of 2010 gave strong cross-sectoral powers to the Federal Reserve as the main systemic supervisor, while conduct-of-business supervision is mostly entrusted to the Securities and Exchange Commission (SEC), The Commodities Futures Trading Commission (CFTC) and the Consumer Financial Protection Bureau (CFPB). Underlying this are the multiple sectoral supervisory agencies that still exist in the United States at federal and state levels. France has Twin Peaks features, but with some retail conduct of business supervision for banks and insurance under the Autorité de contrôle prudentiel et de résolution (ACPR, the prudential supervisor) instead of Autorité des marchés financiers (AMF, the markets supervisor). Italy also has Twin Peaks features, with conduct-of-business supervision of banks at the Companies and Exchange Commission (CONSOB). Portugal is considering changing its sectoral model to a twin peaks model. For a list and detailed analysis of various countries and the systems they use, including enabling legislation, see A. D. Schmulow, 'The Four Methods of Financial System Regulation: An International Comparative Survey' (2015) 26 *Journal of Banking and Finance Law and Practice* 151.
Source: Updated from J. De Haan, D. Schoenmaker and S. Oosterloo, *Financial Markets and Institutions: A European Perspective*, 2nd edition (Cambridge University Press, 2012), 378.

banks but are also offered by insurers and pension funds. Because of the blurring of the dividing lines between financial sectors, cross-sector models of supervision have emerged. There are two main cross-sector models of supervision: a functional (or Twin Peaks) model and an integrated model.

In the Twin Peaks model, there are separate supervisors for each of the supervisory objectives: prudential supervision and conduct of business. In some countries, especially in the euro area, where central banks have transferred their responsibility for monetary policy to the European Central Bank, the central bank is responsible for prudential supervision. In other countries – Australia is one example – a separate agency is responsible for prudential supervision.

In the integrated model, there is a single supervisor for banking, insurance and securities combined (or, put differently, one supervisor who oversees both prudential supervision and conduct-of-business supervision). There are two versions of the integrated model. Denmark and Sweden have adopted a fully integrated model without central bank involvement in financial supervision. In Germany and Austria, the central bank still has a role in banking supervision, alongside the integrated supervisor – respectively, BaFin in Germany and Finanzmarktaufsicht (FMA) in Austria. The Twin Peaks model combines the objectives of systemic supervision and prudential supervision, leaving conduct-of-business supervision as a separate function. The integrated model combines the objectives of prudential supervision and conduct-of-business supervision, leaving systemic supervision (financial stability) as a separate function that is usually performed by the central bank.

Kremers, Schoenmaker and Wierts developed a framework to analyse the trade-offs by listing the synergies and conflicts of supervisory interests for both models.[5] Figure 16.1 summarises these. The first synergy in the left panel results from combining systemic supervision with the prudential supervision of financial institutions. The synergy between stability issues on the micro level (at the level of the financial institution) and the macro level (economy-wide) refers to the ability to act decisively and swiftly in the event of a crisis. Crisis management usually requires key decisions to be taken within hours rather than days. Combining both micro- and macro-prudential supervision within a single institution ensures that relevant information is available at short notice and that a speedy decision to act can be taken if necessary. The Northern Rock crisis in the United Kingdom in 2007 indicated that crisis management by two institutions might not be very effective. Coordination between the Bank of England and the UK Financial Services Authority was insufficient. Goodhart argues that the working of what was then called the tripartite regulatory system – comprising the Treasury, the Bank of England and the Financial Services Authority – failed in the United Kingdom during the great financial crisis.[6]

The second synergy in Figure 16.1 is 'one-stop supervision', that is, the synergy between prudential supervision and conduct-of-business supervision. Furthermore, synergies in the execution of supervision are exploited by combining different supervisory activities within one institution.

The first potential conflict of interest between systemic supervision and prudential supervision relates to the possibility of lender-of-last-resort (LoLR) operations by the central bank. How can the pressure to extend the benefits of LoLR operations (avoiding systemic risk, such as a financial

[5] J. Kremers, D. Schoenmaker and P. Wierts, 'Cross-Sector Supervision: Which Model?' in R. Herring and R. Litan (eds) *Brookings–Wharton Papers on Financial Services* (Brookings Institution, 2003).

[6] C. Goodhart, 'The Bank of England, 1694–2017' in R. Edvinsson, T. Jacobson and D. Waldenström (eds) *Sveriges Riksbank and the History of Central Banking* (Cambridge University Press, 2018). See also A. D. Schmulow, 'The Four Methods of Financial System Regulation: An International Comparative Survey' (2015) 26 *Journal of Banking and Finance Law and Practice* 158, for a summary of some of the key findings on this point.

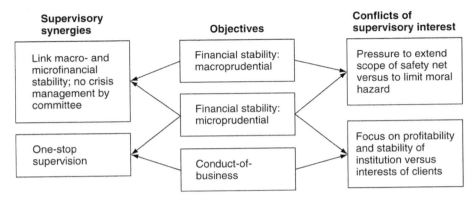

FIGURE 16.1. Supervisory synergies and conflicts.

Source: J. Kremers, D. Schoenmaker and P. Wierts, 'Cross-Sector Supervision: Which Model?' in R. Herring and R. Litan (eds) *Brookings–Wharton Papers on Financial Services* (Brookings Institution, 2003), 235

panic or bank runs) to all financial institutions be balanced against its costs (moral hazard)? The answer adopted by many central banks is to limit the possibility of LoLR operations to banks, because these are subject to systemic risk (and specifically panic runs) in a way that other financial firms are not. Thus LoLR operations are not available to insurance companies. However, when financial groups integrate, it might become more difficult to isolate only the banking part of financial institutions for potential LoLR operations. The financial panic of September–October 2008 in the United States provided an illustration of this. Hitherto non-bank financial groups such as Morgan Stanley and Goldman Sachs hastily converted to bank holding company status in order to access the federal banking safety net.

The second potential conflict of interest between prudential supervision and conduct-of-business supervision relates to the different nature of their objectives. The two types of supervision generally require different mind-sets and skills, and occasionally conflict with each other.[7] Especially in times of financial crisis, or to avert a crisis, the imperative of financial stability can be so overwhelming that authorities might neglect some conduct duties in order to help firms satisfy prudential requirements – for example, authorities might close their eyes to questionable commercial practices if these help a bank to increase its profitability and capital.[8] Conversely, in non-crisis times, conduct mandates might be so all-consuming that prudential considerations are neglected, as arguably happened in the run-up to 2007 with the UK Financial Services Authority in its supervision of several British banks (including Northern Rock and Royal Bank of Scotland), or with the US Securities and Exchange Commission in its supervision of large broker-dealers (including Bear Stearns and Lehman Brothers). Similar cases of mis-selling of securities have occurred in several European countries (including most prominently Italy in recent years, but also Finland, Slovenia, Spain and others in the past), where banks sold their own risky shares, subordinated debt and/or senior debt instruments to retail clients, including some with low levels of financial literacy. These experiences suggest that the enforcement of

---

[7] N. Véron 'Charting the Next Steps for the EU Financial Supervisory Architecture' (Bruegel Policy Contribution, 2017).

[8] For a discussion of some of the theoretical underpinnings for this argument, see A. D. Schmulow, 'Twin Peaks: A Theoretical Analysis' (Centre for International Finance and Regulation (CIFR) Research Working Paper Series, No 064/2015/Project No E018, 1 July 2015), 1–40, https://dx.doi.org/10.2139/ssrn.2625331.

consumer protection regulation in the financial sector should not be entrusted to prudential supervisors.

The prudential supervisor will be interested in the soundness of financial firms, including profitability, while the conduct-of-business supervisor will focus on the interests of those firms' clients. Mixing up the responsibilities of financial stability and conduct-of-business could create incentives for the supervisor to prioritise one objective over the other. By separating the supervisory functions, the conduct-of-business supervisor is ideally situated to supervise possible conflicts of interest between a financial institution and its clients, because it will focus only on the interests of the clients. Furthermore, the stability objective is consistent with preserving public confidence, and may require discretion and confidentiality, which could be counter-productive to the objective of transparency.

16.3 TWIN PEAKS FOR EUROPE

We argue that the European supervisory architecture should eventually move to a Twin Peaks model, for three main reasons. First, banks and insurers are often part of a financial conglomerate, which warrants integrated banking-insurance supervision. Secondly, the EU27 will need to upgrade the supervision of its capital markets after Brexit. A dedicated markets supervisor can adapt quickly to this new reality. Thirdly, prudential supervision and markets and conduct-of-business supervision require different skills and approaches. While the first deals more with technical capital adequacy issues, and requires staff trained in economics, finance and/or accountancy, the second is more behavioural and legalistic.[9] This behavioural and legalistic approach concerns policing the conduct of financial institutions in the markets (for example, insider trading, market abuse, disclosure) and towards clients (for example, adequate information provision, duty of care, know your customer).

We frame our recommendation for Twin Peaks supervision in the EU as a long-term aspirational goal. Defining a long-term goal is important for taking decisions on short-term issues, such as the necessary upgrading of ESMA.

16.4 PRUDENTIAL SUPERVISION

Close interaction between banking and insurance supervision is needed for the effective supervision of financial conglomerates that combine banking and insurance. Figure 16.2 shows that 31 per cent of banks in the EU and 36 per cent of insurers in the EU belong to a financial conglomerate. These percentages are for 2015 and are measured in assets (that is to say, bank conglomerate assets as a share of total banking assets and total insurance assets).

Why is such close interaction necessary? During the financial crisis, several financial institutions experienced solvency problems. These could emerge in any part of the financial institution (for example, subprime mortgages in the bank or on the insurance balance sheet). It appeared that several financial conglomerates made use of double counting and thus had insufficient capital. Double counting (also known as double gearing) is the practice whereby the same capital base at the holding level of a financial conglomerate is counted as regulatory capital for both the banking activities and the insurance activities.

---

[9] C. Goodhart, D. Schoenmaker and P. Dasgupta, 'The Skill Profile of Central Bankers and Supervisors' (2002) 6 *European Finance Review* 397–427.

Part of financial conglomerate

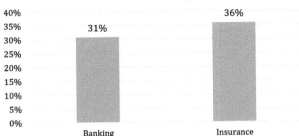

FIGURE 16.2. Share of financial conglomerates in banking and insurance at EU level (2015). Note: The graph shows the share of EU banks and insurance groups that are part of a financial conglomerate.

Source: Authors calculations based on Joint Committee of the European Supervisory Authorities, List of Financial Conglomerates (2016)

Such double counting was, and still is, allowed because of the fragmented financial architecture, both on the rule-making and supervisory sides. On the regulatory front, the so-called Danish compromise, agreed in the process of EU transposition of the Basel III capital accord, and enshrined in the EU Capital Requirements Regulation, allows double counting of capital.[10] On the supervisory front, the absence of an integrated focus (the supervisory focus is on the banking and insurance parts but not on the aggregate) leaves no one responsible for the overall capitalisation of financial conglomerates. The current weak form of supplementary supervision of financial conglomerates, in which either the banking or insurance supervisor has some responsibilities for the supervision of conglomerates, cannot replace proper integrated supervision.

Nevertheless, the industry and the supervisory authorities are keen to preserve the current sectoral structure and unwilling to adopt a Twin Peaks model.[11] From a political-economy point of view, this position is understandable. Financial institutions and their supervisors are keen to preserve the status quo, including any cosy relationships between them. In particular, the insurance sector is afraid that a merged banking/insurance prudential authority would be dominated by banking regulatory approaches. By contrast, some stakeholders, mainly from academia, are critical of the sectoral supervision model on the basis that it is outdated and ignores the reality of the retail financial markets in Europe.[12] Finally, consumer and public-interest advocacy organisations also support a Twin Peaks model of supervision that would separate market conduct from prudential supervision for the reasons mentioned above.[13]

On the political front, Table 16.2 shows that financial conglomerates have a substantial presence in the largest EU27 countries. In Germany, France and Italy, conglomerates make up between 20 and 90 per cent of the banking sector. For the same countries, the percentage of

[10] 'Editorial: Basel III – The Case for the Defence', *Financial Times* (23 January 2012).

[11] European Commission, 'Feedback Statement on the Public Consultation on the Operations of the European Supervisory Authorities Having Taken Place from 21 March to 16 May 2017', DG FISMA, Brussels.

[12] R. Huang and D. Schoenmaker (eds), *Institutional Structure of Financial Regulation: Theories and International Experiences* (Routledge, 2015); European Commission (n 11).

[13] See, for example, R. Lenz, 'Europäisches System der Finanzaufsicht effizient weiterentwickeln' (written statement for the German Bundestag Finance Committee hearing on 31 May 2017), www.bundestag.de/blob/508694/9d745061e6587efoe86c7aa42891d2c9/13-data.pdf.

TABLE 16.2. *Share of financial conglomerates in banking and insurance at country level (%, 2015).*

	Banking	Insurance
Austria	24	37
Belgium	40	22
Denmark	43	17
Finland	19	82
France	88	22
Germany	27	28
Italy	19	47
Malta	15	0
Netherlands	17	59
Spain	14	3
Sweden	45	27
United Kingdom	10	17
EU	31	36

Note: The table shows the share of EU banks and insurance groups that are part of a financial conglomerate. At the country level, only countries are shown where the head or parent company of a financial conglomerate is located. At the EU level, all financial conglomerates with their headquarters located in the EU are shown.
Source: Authors calculations based on Joint Committee of the European Supervisory Authorities, List of Financial Conglomerates (2016).

conglomerates in the insurance sector is between 20 and 50 per cent. So these large countries have an interest in appropriate supervisory arrangements for financial conglomerates.

How can close cooperation between banking and insurance supervision be implemented in order to enable a consolidated view of the capital adequacy of financial conglomerates? On the banking side, the Single Supervisory Mechanism (SSM) is responsible for the supervision of the banks in the euro area. The non-euro-area member states can join the EU banking union through the mechanism of close cooperation, set out in the SSM Regulation (EU/1024/2013). Given the cross-border banking links between EU member states, it is plausible that most, if not all, non-euro area countries might join the banking union at some future stage.[14] Bulgaria and Croatia have joined the banking union in 2020 through close cooperation, in the run-up to their adoption of the euro. Denmark and Sweden, in particular, have publicly debated that option.

The European insurance sector is highly integrated with a large and rising share of cross-border business. On average, insurance groups conduct 29 per cent of their business in other EU countries. For the large insurers, this increases to about 50 per cent.[15] While the global financial crisis led to a reversal in banking integration, there is no evidence for that in insurance. These large insurers run asset management and risk management functions from their head office in an integrated way. The Solvency II directive was implemented in 2016, allowing insurers to use their internal models for capital purposes. Given the strong cross-border nature of the large European insurers, the European Insurance and Occupational Pensions Authority (EIOPA) should become responsible for the approval and monitoring of these internal models.[16] EIOPA might thus be given responsibility for direct supervisory tasks in relation to large insurers in the European Union.

[14] P. Hüttl and D. Schoenmaker, 'Should the "Outs" Join the Banking Union?' (2015) 3 *European Economy* 89–112.
[15] D. Schoenmaker, 'European Insurance Union and How to Get There?' (2016) 4 *Bruegel Policy Brief* 3.
[16] Ibid; European Commission, 'Communication on Reinforcing Integrated Supervision to Strengthen Capital Markets Union and Financial Integration in a Changing Environment', COM (2017) 542, 20 September, Brussels.

A full merger of EIOPA and the ECB (as the SSM's central supervisor) is not possible without a treaty change. Article 127(6) of the Treaty on the Functioning of the European Union allows the ECB to conduct 'prudential supervision of credit institutions and other financial institutions with the exception of insurance undertakings'. This means that the ECB is not allowed to supervise insurance companies and is only allowed to conduct prudential supervision (that is to say, no conduct-of-business supervision) of banks. Nevertheless, close interaction between EIOPA and the ECB in the prudential supervision of financial conglomerates is possible. It is already facilitated by both institutions being located in Frankfurt and could be further improved by physical co-location.

A final question on the prudential side concerns the future of the European Banking Authority after Brexit. The European Banking Authority is required for technical rule-making and supervisory convergence for so long as the SSM does not cover all EU countries. In so doing, the European Banking Authority is able to balance the interests between the 'ins' and 'outs' of the banking union. In the long term, EIOPA could be responsible for the technical rules on insurance supervision, as well as the direct supervision of large insurers. If all 'outs' eventually join the banking union, the ECB could take over the European Banking Authority's current responsibilities, including the preparation of binding technical standards for the prudential supervision of banks.

16.5 MARKETS AND CONDUCT OF BUSINESS

In respect of the second peak, it is useful to make a distinction between the supervision of financial firms' conduct in wholesale markets and the supervision of financial firms' conduct in relation to their retail clients. London is currently the wholesale markets hub of Europe, providing corporate and investment banking services to the EU's twenty-seven countries and beyond. Since the United Kingdom left the EEA, and its single market for financial services, UK-based financial firms have, as a consequence, lost their passports to do business directly with EU27 clients. Brexit is therefore inevitably leading to a partial migration of wholesale market activity from London to the EU27.

A possible fragmentation of trading activity across several EU27 countries might result in increased costs and reduced access to capital for companies. A related risk is that of a regulatory race to the bottom among the EU27, leading to misconduct, loss of market integrity and possibly financial instability as a result of competing to attract migrating London wholesale banks. On the positive side, Brexit is also an opportunity to build more integrated and vibrant capital markets in the EU27, ones that would better serve all member economies, by improving risk-sharing to withstand local shocks and by making the EU27 an attractive place to conduct global financial transactions. This would speed up the rebalancing from a primarily bank-based to a relatively more market-based financial system, an objective implicit within the EU's Capital Markets Union (CMU) policy, which was launched in 2014.

To prevent intra-EU27 financial market fragmentation causing higher financing costs, Sapir, Schoenmaker and Véron argue that a single set of rules (or single rulebook) is necessary but not sufficient.[17] To achieve cross-border integration, consistent oversight of wholesale markets and enforcement of relevant regulation are critical. This requires integration of the institutional

---

[17] A. Sapir, D. Schoenmaker and N. Véron, 'Making the Best of Brexit in Finance: The EU27 Side' (2017) 1 *Bruegel Policy Brief* 6.

architecture, for which the tried-and-tested model in the EU is a hub-and-spoke design, which has long been used for competition policy and, more recently, for banking supervision. The straightforward way of implementing this approach, without the need for changes to the EU treaties, would be through broadening the scope of ESMA, which already has a direct EU-wide supervisory role, but only for limited market segments. The European Commission has proposed moving in that direction.[18]

A broadening of ESMA's scope would require reform of its governance and funding, which currently limit its independence and capacity, even after a limited legislative review concluded in early 2019. Such reform should not disrupt ESMA's operations, but should align them with better designed institutions, including the ECB's Supervisory Board and the Single Resolution Board. ESMA should be governed by an executive board of five or six full-time members vetted by the European Parliament, in place of the current supervisory board of national representatives (in which the chair cannot cast a vote). This would help to overcome distortions arising from influential local interests and reduce regulatory capture. In line with international practice, ESMA's funding should rely on a small levy on capital markets activity, under the scrutiny of the European Parliament, instead of relying upon the current political bargaining conducted as part of the general EU budget.

The new areas of responsibility for the reformed ESMA should focus on those market segments where EU activity is currently most concentrated in London:

1 Supervision of markets and infrastructure.
2 Wholesale market activities of investment banks.
3 Corporate accounting and auditing.
4 Non-EU firms.

While financial infrastructure (for example, clearing houses), accounting and auditing and non-EU (third-country) firms were mentioned in a March 2017 consultation document published by the European Commission,[19] Sapir, Schoenmaker and Véron argue that market oversight and, specifically, the conduct supervision of investment banks are also important tasks for ESMA – particularly in ensuring effective and efficient supervision of the newly emerging wholesale markets in the EU27 post-Brexit.[20]

Both the infrastructure and the markets are integrating in the EU27. An early example is Euronext, covering the stock exchanges of France, the Netherlands, Belgium and Portugal. Another example is Nasdaq Nordic (formerly known as OMX), covering the exchanges of the Nordic countries (Helsinki, Copenhagen, Stockholm, Iceland) and Baltic countries (Riga, Tallinn and Vilnius). It would be far more effective and efficient to make ESMA responsible for the direct supervision of these platforms (in a hub-and-spoke model, with relevant operational tasks duly delegated to national market supervisors) instead of four (in the case of Euronext) or seven (in the case of Nasdaq Nordic) separate local national market authorities. ESMA would thus become responsible for safeguarding the integrity of markets and avoiding insider trading and market abuse.

The wholesale market activities of the large players, comprising the large European universal banks and the US, UK, Swiss and Japanese investment banks, which will probably partly relocate

---

[18] European Commission, 'Communication on the Mid-Term Review of the Capital Markets Union Action Plan', COM (2017) 292, 8 June, Brussels; European Commission (n 16).
[19] European Commission (n 1).
[20] Sapir, Schoenmaker and Véron (n 17) 6–7.

to the EU27 as a consequence of Brexit, also need to be supervised. This supervision covers the wholesale banking aspects of the Markets in Financial Instruments Directive (MiFID).[21]

For other supervisory aspects, such as authorisations of initial public offerings and fund management registrations, ESMA's policy-setting role should be strengthened, but individual decisions could continue to be taken by national authorities for the foreseeable future. Similarly, conduct-of-business supervision of smaller investment and insurance intermediaries, to protect retail investors, can remain at the national level. These activities – IPOs, fund management and intermediaries – comprise the bulk of the current workload of the national markets authorities. This would remain at the national level and would be consistent with the subsidiarity principle, with ESMA given greater authority to ensure supervisory consistency in line with the European Commission's recent proposals.[22]

16.6 POLICY CONCLUSIONS

There are too many policy constraints for the European Union to adopt a Twin Peaks financial supervisory architecture in the short term, including the aftermath of Brexit, treaty provisions and possible changes to the geographical coverage of the banking union (initially the nineteen-country euro area, possibly expanded in the future through the close cooperation procedure). With this in mind, we suggest Twin Peaks as a long-term guiding vision for the EU, not a rapidly achievable target.

Even so, the vision could have practical consequences in the near term and in multiple areas, such as the reform of ESMA's governance and funding; the supervision of emerging (FinTech) financial markets segments; the future of the European Banking Authority; and the EU approach to consumer financial protection. The Twin Peaks model holds the promise of a financial system that is both safer, thanks to group-level, consolidated prudential oversight, and fairer, thanks to the better protection of savers, investors and more generally of users of financial services. It is desirable that the European Union should commit itself explicitly to that vision, even if the time needed for its fulfilment is likely to be measured in decades, rather than years.

---

[21] Directive 2004/39/EC, http://ec.europa.eu/finance/securities/isd/index_en.htm.
[22] European Commission (n 16).

17

A Complex European Financial Architecture

Ten Years On

Karel Lannoo

17.1 INTRODUCTION

A specific European supervisory structure is emerging, but post-crisis it is advancing more on an ad hoc basis than as a result of deliberate choices. The Review of the European System of Financial Supervision (ESFS), which commenced in 2017, got bogged down in arcane details, and too great a focus on the lack of adjustment of governance issues has so far prevented an in-depth assessment. The review almost failed as a result of an unbalanced Commission proposal, the unwillingness among member states to advance, and the desire of the European Parliament to go much further. The final outcome is a step towards more integrated supervision, but it is very haphazard, and makes it difficult to see the wood for the trees. The outcome also has to be seen in connection with other files, first the achievements of the Single Supervisory Mechanism (SSM), secondly Brexit and the supervision of central counterparties and, finally, the elusive fight against money laundering.

Making the new system work will primarily be an issue of consistent implementation, which will not be easy, given the reluctance of member states and the difficulty of the dossier. The functioning of the European Supervisory Authorities (ESAs) has become more complex as a result of the fine-tuning and of their additional tasks, all of which will have an impact on implementation. A contingent issue is the means available to the ESAs to effectively pursue their new tasks. The budget they will have at their disposal will, among other factors, depend on the increase in supervisory tasks, which differ now, importantly even among the ESAs.

The 2017 ESA Review was not an example of efficient and transparent rulemaking, but the additional requirements relating to money laundering and the progress on a parallel file relating to central counterparty (CCP) supervision by the European Securities Market Authority (ESMA) have made the review more important. The structure of the final outcome is difficult to unravel, and the following discusses the main changes brought about by the 2017 ESA Review and its implications. It evaluates the more generic changes, applicable to the three ESAs, followed by the requirements specific to each authority as a result of the 2017 ESA Review, or of separate pieces of legislation. This was the first review of the 2010 regulations, which were created by the EU in response to the financial crisis and further to the recommendations of the de Larosière Committee.[1] This chapter starts with a brief evaluation of the first ten years of the

---

[1] See Regulation (EU) No 1092/2010 of the European Parliament and of the Council of 24 November 2010 on European Union macroprudential oversight of the financial system and establishing a European Systemic Risk Board, https://eur-lex.europa.eu/LexUriServ/LexUriServ.do?uri=CELEX:32010R1092:EN:HTML.

ESAs but refers to the European Commission and other studies for a more in-depth assessment of the accomplishments of the ESFS. It concludes by noting that the evolution of the ESAs makes it difficult to argue that the EU has come closer to a Twin Peaks supervisory model, and that the focus has instead been on strengthening sectoral supervision.

17.2 THE EUROPEAN SYSTEM OF FINANCIAL SUPERVISION, TEN YEARS ON

The European System of Financial Supervision was established in 2011 and consists of the following: (1) three European Supervisory Authorities: the European Banking Authority (EBA), the European Insurance and Occupational Pensions Authority (EIOPA) and the European Securities and Markets Authority (ESMA)[2] and (2) the European Systemic Risk Board (ESRB).[3] Beyond any doubt, the ESFS has been a big step forward in European supervisory cooperation. Given the lessons of the 2007 and 2008 financial crisis, with its intense regulatory competition and lack of information exchange between supervisors in the EU, incompatible data templates and improper oversight, a strengthened structure for European regulatory and supervisory cooperation was long overdue. What has been achieved after only ten years with limited means and a relatively small structure is remarkable.[4]

The objectives at the start of the ESFS were to ensure more coherent and efficient financial supervision in the EU, at the micro as well as at the macro level. It established three different functional ESAs, as well as the ESRB. The role of the EBA was overtaken by the SSM, which was launched two years later, but both have managed to remain distinct and complementary.

Overall, the main focus of the ESAs in the first decade was regulatory convergence, with the single rulebook as the leitmotif. The effort spent on preparing level 2 measures, regulatory technical standards (RTS) and implementing technical standards (ITS), was enormous, as was the effort spent on guidelines (level 3). Related to the guidelines were the Q&As on legislative acts within the remit of the ESAs. They have become a widely used tool to ensure a common EU-wide interpretation, endorsed by the Board of Supervisors.

The ESAs have made an important contribution to establishing a European supervisory culture, mostly through peer pressure. A multi-layered structure has been established, from the Board of Supervisors and the management board of each ESA, to the Joint Committee of the ESAs, the various standing committees and the stakeholder groups. The ESRB is somewhat separate from that structure, and is fully integrated into the European Central Bank (ECB).

The ESAs initially had only a few unique supervisory tasks, and these were limited to the European Securities Markets Authority, which is the unique supervisor of credit rating agencies (CRAs) and trade reporting agencies. The expectation was that other unique supervisory tasks would follow, but this did not progress as rapidly as expected and, at the outset, the European Commission did not propose obvious supervisory tasks, such as IPOs, benchmarks and data providers. The initiative was only taken with the 2017 ESA Review, and is discussed in Section 17.3.

---

[2] EBA, EIOPA and ESMA 'supervise and provide regulatory guidance for individual sectors and institutions'. See Council of the European Union, 'Financial Supervision: Council Adopts a Review of the Supervisory Framework for Financial Institutions' (Press Release, 2 December 2019), www.consilium.europa.eu/en/press/press-releases/2019/12/02/financial-supervision-council-adopts-a-review-of-the-supervisory-framework-for-financial-institutions/.

[3] The ESRB 'oversees the financial system as a whole and coordinates EU policies for financial stability'. Ibid.

[4] See, for example, the assessment of ESMA in Niamh Moloney, *The Age of ESMA, Governing EU Financial Markets* (Hart Publishing, 2018).

TABLE 17.1. *Comparison of staffing and budget resources across five key agencies.*

2018	EBA	ESMA	EIOPA	ESRB	SRB
Total staff	182+12=194	217+14=231	140+18=158	62.8+49.9=113	315+19=334
Budget	38.9 million	41.9 million	25.2 million	9.2 million (only ECB staff)	103.1 million
Supervisory tasks	Participate in colleges of supervisors	Rating agencies (CRAs), trade repositories, CCP supervisory colleges	Participate in colleges of supervisors	Warnings, recommendations, opinions	Prepare resolution Plans and resolve banks
Review new tasks	AML coordination	Critical benchmarks, data providers, third-country CCPs	Pan-European personal pension product (PEPP) registration	–	–

Notes: The number of staff is divided between permanent staff and seconded national experts. In the case of the ESRB, seconded national experts refers to the input from national central banks expressed in full-time equivalents. Source: Latest annual reports of the respective agencies.

For the EBA, the supervisory tasks were overtaken by the creation of the SSM in 2012, although the EBA continues to be represented in the college of supervisors, and fulfils the non-eurozone dimension of coordination for EU-wide banking supervision matters. It needs to be added that the interaction between the EBA and the SSM has worked well since the start of the SSM. The EBA has focused on regulatory convergence in the context of the single market, with much attention on the implementation of capital requirement provisions and the resolution framework but also on the data collection and the stress-testing side; both entities are complementary. The best proof and guarantee of this fluid cooperation was the appointment of EBA Chairperson Andrea Enria as the successor to Danielle Nouy at the helm of the SSM in January 2019.

As can be seen from Table 17.1, the most important agency in terms of staff and budget is ESMA, followed by EBA and the European Insurance and Occupational Pensions Authority. The table gives the numbers for the Single Resolution Board (SRB) for comparison. The four different ESFS entities employed 696 persons at the end of 2018.

17.3 THE 2017 ESA REVIEW

In the review, published in September 2017, the European Commission proposed some changes in the decision-making structure of all the ESAs, and an important expansion of the competencies of the ESMA. In September 2018, the Commission added further roles for the ESAs relating to the fight against money laundering. The ESMA changes were not expected by most market participants, and faced strong opposition from some countries, industry associations and firms. They had to be watered down substantially to ensure agreement by the European Parliament and the EU Council of Ministers – reached provisionally before the end of the 8th legislature of the Parliament, and finally adopted by the EU Council of Ministers on 5 December 2019. Opinions are still divided on the end result, with some seeing it is a step forward, whereas others have argued the opposite. We will first discuss the so-called horizontal changes, followed by the additional competencies for the ESMA, including as they relate to the European Market Infrastructure Regulation (EMIR) Review for the EBA and the EIOPA.

Overall, the horizontal amendments refine the decision-making procedures of the ESAs, reinforce supervisory convergence, information exchange and the peer review of supervisors, facilitate consultation (including for Fintech) and emphasise the role the authorities have to play in protecting consumers and promoting sustainable finance. The principles of proportionality and transparency are now written into the legislation that creates these various authorities. The independence of the ESAs is further emphasised, and the role and composition of stakeholder groups of the different ESAs are further detailed.

The only change on the governance side is the strengthening of the powers of the chair, who will be able to propose decisions to the Board of Supervisors on issues relating to breach of Union law, binding mediation and inquiries into financial products or institutions. The chair sets the agenda of the Board of Supervisors. The decisions prepared by the chair should be adopted by the Board of Supervisors in a simplified 'no objection' procedure within eight days. The chair can now also vote as a member of the Board of Supervisors, subject to a few exceptions. All of this is an unexpected outcome of the proposed strengthening of the powers of the management board, which was rejected by the member states.

As regards external relations, an enhanced supervisory regime should ensure that third-country equivalence is more transparent, more predictable for the third countries concerned and more consistent across all sectors. Enforcement practices should be in place in third countries for matters for which equivalence decisions have been adopted and, where necessary, should include on-site inspections. The ESAs are required to inform EU institutions of the findings of their monitoring of all equivalent third countries. When a third-country competent authority refuses to conclude administrative arrangements, or when it refuses to effectively cooperate, the ESAs will inform the EU Commission.[5]

A new regulatory tool is the 'no action' letter. Unlike their US counterparts, EU financial watchdogs have no formal way to delay or suspend the enforcement of rules that would damage a market or particular firms. US regulators, such as the Securities and Exchange Commission (SEC) and the Commodities and Futures Trading Commission (CFTC), have the flexibility to suspend parts of regulations where they are poorly drafted, unworkable or need clarification. Article 9c now foresees the possibility for the ESAs to provide opinions when legislative or any delegated or implementing acts based on those legislative acts are liable to raise significant issues.[6] This was strongly requested by industry, but it remains up to the European Commission to decide.

Expansion of competencies also means an increase in the budget. But the Commission's proposal to make financial institutions pay more towards the budget of the ESAs was not maintained. In the end, the current system of a 40 per cent direct contribution from the EU budget and 60 per cent from the National Competent Authorities (NCAs) was kept, which

---

[5] See amendment to art 33 of Regulation (EU) 2019/2175 of the European Parliament and of the Council on 18 December 2019 amending Regulation (EU) No 1093/2010 establishing a European Supervisory Authority (European Banking Authority); Regulation (EU) No 1094/2010 establishing a European Supervisory Authority (European Insurance and Occupational Pensions Authority); Regulation (EU) No 1095/2010 establishing a European Supervisory Authority (European Securities and Markets Authority); Regulation (EU) No 600/2014 on markets in financial instruments; Regulation (EU) 2016/1011 on indices used as benchmarks in financial instruments and financial contracts or to measure the performance of investment funds; and Regulation (EU) 2015/847 on information accompanying transfers of funds (Regulation 2019/2175), available at https://eur-lex.europa.eu/legal-content/EN/TXT/PDF/?uri=CELEX:32019R2175&from=EN.

[6] Regulation 2019/2175 (n 5).

means some member states pay proportionally too much. The income raised through supervisory fees for the budget of a respective ESA is in addition, and is thus very important for the ESMA, which is expected to get 156 additional full-time employees as a result of the new competencies discussed in the next section.

17.4 THE ESMA'S NEW COMPETENCIES

The 2017 ESA Review was mostly about the ESMA, as the Commission initially proposed giving the ESMA more supervisory powers in four fields. This led to strong opposition from some countries, industry associations and firms and almost caused the demise of the proposal. Questions can be raised about the rationale of the sudden expansion of ESMA's powers in some of the fields mentioned, or why this was not done earlier. In the end, however, the expansion was limited to two fields, while CCP supervision was the subject of another proposal, EMIR 2.2.

The two new areas where the ESMA will obtain unique supervisory competencies relate to the licensing or recognition of administrators of critical benchmarks and data providers (under Market in Financial Instruments Directive, MiFID II). These concern benchmarks that underpin reference volumes of at least €500 billion (such as Euribor and Libor). The new rules enable the ESMA to authorise such administrators and monitor the equivalence of a third country's supervisory standards. It abolishes the College of Supervisors that were set up by the 2016 Benchmarks Regulations. The same applies for approved publication arrangements (APAs), consolidated tape providers (CTP) and approved reporting mechanisms (ARM), which are to be uniquely authorised by the ESMA. These data providers required a special licence under MiFID II (2018). The amendments allow the ESMA to set supervisory fees, to conduct on-site inspections and to impose fines and periodic penalty payments upon the entities concerned, as is already the case for rating agencies and trade repositories.

For certain public offerings and investment funds, the transfer of supervisory tasks to the ESMA was rejected. The rationale for these changes was insufficiently clarified and arrived unexpectedly. For public offerings, ESMA targeted offerings of bonds, asset-backed securities and offerings for specific types of companies, for instance property and shipping companies. For funds, it was concerned with venture capital (EUVeCa), and long-term investment funds (ELTIFs). Both were seen as limiting the room for manoeuvre for smaller financial centres, and more especially as a direct attack on Luxembourg's specialisations, particularly in relation to bonds. Yet the draft amendments had not addressed the most important issue: allowing for single EU-wide initial public equity offerings (or additional rights issues) of high-growth stocks or blue chips. EU equity offerings today have to happen in the home member state of a company, which is in most cases the state where the company has its registered office, thus maintaining a strong home bias. EU-wide acceptance of prospectuses or validity for a public offer in any member state should be possible after notification to each of the host member states, with ESMA maintaining a register.[7] This remains cumbersome, though, as it also requires the translation of prospectuses into the local language(s), and eventually additional investor protection measures.

Another proposal to give the ESMA more powers over delegation to third countries in asset management was also rejected. A new article, 31a, had aimed at strengthening the coordination

---

[7] This is foreseen in art 25 of the revised prospectus regulation (2017/1129), adopted in 2017, as one of the first initiatives under the Capital Markets Union (CMU) programme. ESMA manages a consolidated register of all nationally approved prospectuses.

function of the ESAs to ensure that the competent authorities effectively supervised outsourcing, delegation and risk transfer arrangements in third countries. This was, however, again seen as hampering the freedom of local financial centres to act as booking centres for funds, while leaving the effective management of the assets in other places, mostly London.

The supervision of third-country CCPs is the third and most important area of expansion in the ESMA's powers, which was not part of the 2017 ESA Review, but a consequence of Brexit and the EMIR 2.2 proposal. Likewise, this change did not come about in a fluid way, nor was its rationale entirely clear: the EU centralises the supervision of third-country CCPs that have important activities within the EU (Tier 2 CCPs), but not for its own CCPs, which remain mainly under national supervision. But the changes are important, as they create a new quasi-supervisory structure within the ESMA, the CCPs Supervisory Committee. The proposal was adopted on 15 October 2019, with Luxembourg abstaining and the United Kingdom voting against.

In its proposal, the Commission justified the streamlining of the supervisory framework for CCPs on the basis of their growing importance in the financial system and the associated concentration of credit risk in these infrastructures. While EMIR sets out common prudential rules for all EU CCPs, the Commission has been of the view that supervisory practices for applying these rules are too divergent and that the supervisory arrangements need to be more consistent. The ESMA had already raised concerns on several occasions about the divergence in the supervisory practices of CCPs in the EU. An ESMA report of December 2016 highlighted the variation in supervisory approaches adopted by the NCAs, as well as the variation in margin and collateral requirements. 'ESMA noted that NCAs supervising similar CCPs in terms of size, systemic importance, nature and complexity of the activities adopted different approaches with respect to the frequency and depth of their review, including whether to conduct on-site inspections.'[8]

EMIR 2.2[9] maintains the central role of the supervisory colleges for the effective supervision of Union CCPs, but it complements EU-level supervision by the CCP Supervisory Committee, which is under the responsibility of ESMA.[10] This committee will be appropriately staffed to monitor EU-based CCPs and supervise third-country CCPs, and will be funded by supervisory fees. The CCP Supervisory Committee will be composed of a chair and two independent members, the competent authorities of member states where a CCP is established and, where applicable, the respective EU central banks, in most cases the ECB, which must be consulted. The committee will be responsible for preparing draft opinions or decisions in relation to EU and third-country CCPs for adoption by the ESMA Board of Supervisors. The committee will participate in the supervisory colleges, but on a non-voting basis.

The CCP Supervisory Committee will prepare technical standards for the functioning of the supervisory colleges, conduct peer review analysis of the supervisory activities of all competent authorities in relation to the authorisation and supervision of CCPs, and conduct stress tests. Most decisions by national authorities regarding CCPs (Article 24a.8, Regulation (EU) 2019/

---

[8] ESMA, Peer Review under EMIR art 21, Supervisory activities on CCPs' Margin and Collateral requirements (December 2016), 41.

[9] EMIR 2.2 refers to Regulation (EU) 2019/2099 of the European Parliament and of the Council of 23 October 2019 amending Regulation (EU) No 648/2012 as regards the procedures and authorities involved for the authorisation of CCPs and requirements for the recognition of third-country CCPs.

[10] The European Commission initially proposed an entirely different structure for the supervision of CCPs, the 'CCP executive session', but the European Parliament (rapporteur Danuta Hubner) and the EU Council agreed on a committee within the ESMA.

2099), are subject to the ESMA's prior consent. Any third-country CCPs have to be recognised by ESMA, and for those that pose substantial exposure risk to the EU and the stability of its financial system – known as 'the Tier 2 CCPs' – establishment within the EU may eventually be required. This implements the controversial 'location policy', which the ECB previously failed to implement due to an EU Court ruling in favour of the United Kingdom, and against the ECB, in April 2015.

The requirements for these third-country CCPs to do business in the EU are very strict: (1) compliance with the relevant and necessary prudential requirements for EU CCPs; (2) compliance with the EU central banks' requirements on liquidity, payments or settlement arrangements; and (3) written consent allowing the ESMA to visit its premises (Article 25h, Regulation (EU) 2019/2099). The European Commission stated that these requirements would be applied in a proportionate manner, following standards specified by the FSB (Financial Stability Board), an international body created following the G20 gathering in 2009 to monitor and make recommendations about the global financial system. Reciprocal 'comparable compliance' will be established between the ESMA and any third country's competent authority (Article 25a, Regulation [EU] 2019/2099). In the event that the requirements are not met, the ESMA could recommend that the EC decline to recognise the third-country CCP in question. The ESMA can also impose fines or penalty payments on third-country CCPs. All these requirements generated much controversy with the United States, where even the chair of the Commodity Futures Trading Commission raised it with the US President in January 2018, it is said, and also in the United Kingdom, which voted against it in the EU Council of Ministers.

The EMIR-related amendments are only a halfway construction, however, and do not constitute another SSM, as the licensing of CCPs remains with national authorities and the ESMA's powers are mainly targeted at third-country CCPs, with the ESMA deciding to which tier a third-country CCP belongs. The ESMA's role here is to contribute merely to supervisory convergence, although it can request prior consent of national decisions regarding CCPs.

The ECB also wanted a direct extension of its powers in the domain of CCPs, but again without success. In June 2017, the ECB had proposed a change to its statute, and more especially Article 22, stating: 'The ECB and national central banks may provide facilities, and the ECB may make regulations, to ensure efficient and sound clearing and payments systems, and clearing systems for financial instruments, within the Union, and with other countries.' The ECB stated that this would give it an 'enhanced role for central banks of issue in the supervisory system of central counterparties (CCPs), in particular with regard to the recognition and supervision of systemically important third-country CCPs clearing significant amounts of euro-denominated transactions'. The European Parliament, however, saw this as an EU Treaty change, which led it to require additional safeguards, which the ECB saw as an infringement on its independence. Hence it withdrew the proposal on 20 March 2019. The ECB criticised the lack of ambition of the EMIR revisions, and the inadequacy of the supervisory structure, which involves the central bank as liquidity backstop and lender of last resort.[11]

17.5 THE EBA'S ENHANCED ROLE IN COMBATING MONEY LAUNDERING

The coordination of the fight against money laundering is the most important change regarding the EBA, but remains very limited in application, given the size of the problem. It was not part of

---

[11] See Benoit Coeuré, 'The Case for Cooperation: Cross-Border CCP Supervision and the Role of Central Banks' (2019), www.ecb.europa.eu/press/key/date/2019/html/ecb.sp190227~cf2acdb23d.en.html.

the original 2017 ESA Review, but came about as a result of a later amendment related to President Juncker's 2018 State of the Union speech. The amendments give the EBA an increased role, although the effective increase in budget and personnel for the task is limited. The question thus arises as to whether this will change much, and whether it might backfire, as happened in 2012 with the creation of the SSM.

The amendments give a central coordination and information-sharing role to the EBA, in cooperation with national authorities, the other ESAs and the ECB, in the fight against money laundering and terrorist financing (Article 9a). The EBA is required to develop common guidance and standards for the prevention of money laundering and to maintain a central database. It can, where appropriate, transmit information to the new European Public Prosecutor's office (EPPO).

The amendments foresee the creation of a new committee within the EBA, composed of member states' relevant authorities, the other ESAs and the ECB. They also allow the EBA to draft regulatory technical standards. The EBA can conduct peer reviews and perform risk assessments in respect of combating money laundering, and issue recommendations to national authorities on the performance of this task. In case there is a third-country dimension, the EBA will have a leading coordination role.

The EBA is authorised to request authorities to investigate breaches of EU law in relation to money laundering, and to consider imposing sanctions (Article 9b). Where a competent authority does not comply with the request, the EBA may adopt a decision addressed directly to a firm (Article 19e). In case a country is on the blacklist of money-laundering centres, the EBA shall not conclude equivalence agreements (Article 33). This may cause problems for the United Kingdom given its links with British Overseas Territories.

The EBA's additional responsibilities are onerous, and the question arises whether just ten extra staff will be sufficient, given the clear deficiencies in the efforts to combat money laundering to date. Money laundering is cross-border by nature and requires a solid and thorough approach. The finance ministers of six member states (the five largest by GDP and Latvia), in an open letter dated 8 November 2019, called for a European supervisory mechanism to tackle financial crime and money laundering.[12] This indicates that some member states believe much more needs to be done, just at the moment that the EBA is embarking upon its new tasks.

17.6 THE EIOPA, THE LEAST PRIVILEGED

The European Insurance and Occupational Pensions Authority's responsibilities have changed the least, apart from the generic changes discussed earlier. An attempt by the European Commission to give it a unique supervisory task failed in the context of Personal European Pension Products (PEPP). The EIOPA could have fulfilled an important role in stimulating the emergence of a large, long-term savings plan, but this will now be more difficult.

In its original proposal, the PEPP was intended to generate large-scale, portable, cost-efficient and simple long-term savings products that would be on offer alongside national pension product regimes throughout the EU. It would be uniquely authorised by the EIOPA for the whole of the EU, to facilitate portability, and be at scale. The final compromise text eliminated

---

[12] Towards a European Supervisory Mechanism for ML/FT (Joint position paper by the Ministers of Finance of France, Germany, Italy, Latvia, the Netherlands and Spain, 8 November 2019), www.rijksoverheid.nl/documenten/kamerstuk ken/2019/11/08/position-paper.

several of the key features of the original proposal. The EIOPA's function has been relegated to that of simply maintaining a registry of all the PEPPs available in the EU and their providers. The EIOPA could refuse to register a PEPP, but this would be perceived as a direct attack on a member state that had just authorised a PEPP. Moreover, the decision would have to pass through the Board of Supervisors of the EIOPA, where EIOPA management has a very limited say. The EIOPA also has some PEPP market monitoring and intervention powers, but again under the control of its board.[13]

A minor change allows the EIOPA 'upon request' to assist competent authorities in the decision relating to the approval of internal models in accordance with Directive 2009/138/EC of the European Parliament and of the Council (Article 32), but this seems a mere consolation prize.

17.7 THE ESRB CONFIRMED IN ITS ROLE

Almost ten years after its creation, the ESRB has undoubtedly done an important job in advancing the discussion about macroprudential policies and monitoring systemic risk. It has, however, been almost entirely absorbed in the ECB and its governance is fully part of the central bank's structure. It has produced a few warnings, several recommendations and plenty of opinions. It is composed of several committees, working groups and expert groups. Its main deficiency, as compared to other similar entities in other jurisdictions, is that it is purely advisory.

The amendments regarding ESRB are very limited and do not raise issues (Regulation 2019/2176). They essentially concern a few governance matters and adjustments to regulatory developments. The ECB president is confirmed as the chair of the ESRB, which was only provisional before, while the chair of the SSM Supervisory Board and the chair of the SRB are also confirmed as members of the General Board of the ESRB. An amendment specifies the procedure for adopting warnings and recommendations, which indicates that the ESRB has started to make a difference.

But the ESRB's role, and above all its authority, has gradually grown, of which its output is a testimony. It is also increasingly formally mandated to submit advice, such as on systemically importantly CCPs, as part of the EMIR 2.2 rules discussed earlier. In the amendments of the 2017 ESA Review, ESAs must take the recommendations of the ESRB into account: 'If the Authority does not act on a warning or recommendation, it shall explain to the ESRB its reasons for not doing so' (Article 36, Regulation 2019/2176). There are more than fifty references to the ESRB in the amendments, and the ESAs are also involved in the General Board of the ESRB.

17.8 CONCLUSION

Back in 2010, the ESFS was created almost from scratch, with important responsibilities given to four new entities. Ten years later, the ESAs and the ESRB have become essential elements in the EU's financial regulatory and advisory machinery, employing together about 700 people, and have coordinated a wealth of regulatory standards, reports and guidelines. They have also slowly stepped up their supervisory work, which is certainly the case for the ESMA, with its unique supervisory tasks, but also its growing action in the markets. This can be expected to

---

[13] See Karel Lannoo, 'Ceci n'est pas un PEPP' (European Capital Markets Institute, 2019), www.eurocapitalmarkets.org/publications/commentaries/ceci-n%E2%80%99est-pas-un-pepp.

expand further as a result of the amendments to Article 9,[14] regarding consumer and investor protection.

Decision-making in the ESAs remains very much oriented towards the member states, with the exception that the chair of an ESA now has a voting role on the Board of Supervisors, and has stronger control of the agenda of the board. But overall, member states' interests will prevail on sensitive issues and a more EU-wide approach may be precluded. This was also clear from the debate on the new supervisory tasks. The calls for a more integrated structure and more streamlined decision-making will thus remain.

For the most important new supervisory task, the supervision of CCPs, it is to be regretted that the structure has become byzantine between ESMA's CCPs Supervisory Committee, the ESMA Board and the national competent authorities. Such a structure is also maintained in the draft recovery and resolution procedures for CCPs, which is currently being discussed. This does not bode well if decisions have to be adopted rapidly, as will be the case when a CCP becomes distressed. It also makes little sense to leave so much power with member states for a financial market infrastructure that is so concentrated and interconnected, with about seventeen entities in the EU (or thirteen post-Brexit). But also in other areas, member states have stood up to protect their prerogatives, which is prejudicial to European market integration.

The ESA Review was a complex legislative exercise, which is also related to the fact that ten years after their creation, the different authorities and the ESRB have become fairly distinct entities. Bringing the review together in one legislative file is a confusing exercise, which confirms what we have previously called for, namely that in the future reviews should be carried out separately for the three different ESAs and for the ESRB. The organisations have evolved differently over the first ten years of their existence, and each of them requires a distinct treatment from further reviews. This also makes it difficult to argue that the EU has moved closer to a Twin Peaks supervisory model. The creation of the SSM in the ECB was a big step in that direction, but the ESAs have moved towards strengthening sectoral supervision in an incremental way and at different speeds, according to their sectors and not necessarily in a consistent way.

Any future review should start with a vision of what the EU wants to achieve in a particular financial sector and adapt the desirable European supervisory structure to that.

---

[14] Regulation 2019/2175 (n 5).

PART IV

Seismic Activity and Fault Lines

Twin Peaks and Boiling Frogs

Consumer Protection in One or Two Ponds?

Gail Pearson

18.1 THE PROMISE OF CONSUMER PROTECTION

Behavioural economics tells us that consumers are unlikely to perceive the risks in many decisions they take. Although risk, and risk management, is bread and butter for financial institutions, they are, on occasion, slow to perceive danger. Regulatory institutions, despite buying into risk regulation as an approach to regulatory decision-making, are also slow to perceive risks to themselves. The question is whether dividing financial regulation between two agencies, as in the Twin Peaks model, preserves consumers from harm or whether they are being boiled slowly.[1]

There are sets of opposites to describe and contrast the work of Australian Securities and Investments Commission (ASIC) and Australian Prudential Regulation Authority (APRA), the two Australian peaks: surveillance versus supervision; conduct versus safety for stability. There are also words in common such as culture and whether it can be regulated, cajoled or supervised, and risk, involving who or what is at risk. From a consumer protection perspective, the key issue is whether, taken together, ASIC and APRA ensure an open and fair market, in which there are suitable promises that do no harm and which are subsequently kept. There has been intense scrutiny of financial consumer protection in its various guises in recent years with parliamentary inquiries, industry inquiries, legislative reforms and proposals, and a Royal Commission into misconduct in the financial services sector (Financial Services Royal Commission).[2] This heightened level of activity suggests regulation may have failed, or it has successfully brought practices and ensuing harm to light. Consumer protection was a major focus of the Financial Services Royal Commission and has become a high priority. Commissioner Hayne did not recommend changes to the Twin Peaks model.[3]

---

[1] The title of this chapter is in part adapted from that of a speech given by Wayne Byres, Chair of APRA, 'Key Issues for the Year Ahead: Bank Capital and Boiling Frogs' (Remarks at Finsia's 'The Regulators' Event, November 2016).

[2] The Royal Commission into Misconduct in the Banking, Superannuation and Financial Services Industry released its Final Report on 1 February 2019. See also Senate Economics References Committee, Senate Inquiry into Consumer Protection in the Banking, Insurance and Financial Services Sector, Submission No 36 by the Australian Securities and Investments Commission, March 2017, Appendices 2 & 3.

[3] For an alternative view, see Pamela Hanrahan, 'Twin Peaks after Hayne: Tensions and Trade-Offs in Regulatory Architecture' (2019) 13 *Law and Financial Markets Review* 124.

The question of keeping a financial promise was a cornerstone of the Wallis Report, whose recommendations informed the Australian regulatory architecture.[4] Wallis focused on whether the promise could be subsequently made good, not on the nature or the quality of the promise. The subsequent Murray Report raised the issue of the quality of the promise for consumer protection through its discussion of product design and distribution obligations.[5] Whether a financial institution has the financial capacity to keep its promises and make payments is the province of APRA. How promises are made and the nature of those promises is the responsibility of ASIC. This is prudential regulation and conduct regulation respectively.

The law of consumer protection emerges from the law of the promise and encompasses both the nature of the promise and its performance. Regulation of the industrial economy gave primacy to the contract as the measure of the transaction. In nearly all jurisdictions, regulating the contract retains its central role in protecting consumers from the unscrupulous, unfair and careless. In the financial economy, the contract is the product. The quality of the contract and the quality of the product are interchangeable.

Neither the market for financial products nor the market for consumer goods exists without the consumer. The choices and decisions of retail clients flow through to commercial and institutional transactions. Nor do these markets exist as wholly national markets. Just as consumer goods are traded internationally, and there is a degree of international coherence regarding the standards for those goods, investments, credit and insurance exist within an international market. There is extensive international regulation of the financial services market, yet intense regulation remains national.

Both safety and conduct connect to consumer protection norms and the financial system as a whole. Conduct regulation is linked to two frames – how persons conduct themselves within the market, that is, market conduct, and how persons conduct themselves towards particular promisees such as individual consumers. Conduct can impact on the market as a whole and can result in questions such as: Is it a competitive market or is it a fair market? This sets the parameters within which individual transactions are made. Conduct also impacts the individual consumer and the questions are similar but different. Is this misleading or unconscionable conduct? Is the contract unfair? Is the contract suitable for the buyer? Is the contractual promise being properly met?

The idea of financial safety has gained currency and safety regulation has morphed from the market for goods to the market for credit. There are two interlocking notions of financial safety: that of the institution and that of the individual. For Wallis in 1997, safety was simply a synonym for prudent,[6] and financial safety did not require that all promises be kept.[7] It did require a greater intensity of regulation depending on the degree of adversity if promises were breached.[8] A conduct regulator will have zero tolerance for breaches of financial promises; the prudential regulator does not target a zero failure rate of institutions.[9] Safety is no longer confined to institutional soundness. Consumers are now exhorted to stay safe and safety is linked to the

---

[4] Stan Wallis, Bill Beerworth, Jeffrey Carmichael, Ian Harper and Linda Nicholls, 'Financial System Inquiry' (The Treasury, Australian Government, Canberra, ACT, 31 March 1997), 1–771, http://fsi.treasury.gov.au/content/FinalReport.asp (Wallis Report).

[5] Financial System Inquiry, 'Financial System Inquiry Final Report' (The Treasury, Australian Government, Canberra, ACT, November 2014), 1–320, http://fsi.gov.au/files/2014/11/FSI_Final_Report.pdf (Murray Report).

[6] Wallis Report (n 4) Ch 8.

[7] Ibid 299.

[8] Ibid.

[9] Australian Prudential Regulation Authority, '15/16 Annual Report' (Australian Prudential Regulation Authority, Sydney, NSW, 7 October 2016), 1–149, www.apra.gov.au/sites/default/files/AR-2015-16-WHOLE-FINAL-WEB.pdf.

quality of the contract. Lack of financial safety for individuals can pose another threat to the stability of the financial system. International regulators have said there are no doubts 'about the link between protecting consumers from abusive products and practices, and the safety and soundness of the financial system';[10] and have exhorted consumers to 'stay safe', listing dangers as 'dodgy salesmen, bad deals and outright fraud'.[11] Safety is no longer limited to whether an institution will fail because it cannot honour its financial promises; it is now also a question of the conduct towards persons in the market. It follows that both prudential regulation and conduct regulation are required to ensure institutions and individuals are safe.

When Australia put in place what has come to be called Twin Peaks regulatory architecture, the focus was more on market regulation per se. ASIC would be the market conduct and disclosure regulator and APRA would be the market safety or prudential regulator. The prudential regulator's task was to draw disparate regulatory bodies together and, in some cases, to integrate standards.[12] The conduct regulator's task was to assimilate responsibility for a wider array of products and services, including insurance and superannuation, but at that stage not lending. ASIC describes its fundamental objective as allowing 'markets to allocate capital efficiently to fund the real economy and, in turn, economic growth' thus contributing to 'improved living standards for all Australians'.[13] APRA refers to the 'financial well-being of the Australian community'.[14]

From the beginning, ASIC was concerned with consumer protection. The earlier Australian Securities Commission was charged with improving the performance of companies and securities and futures markets and with maintaining the confidence of investors by ensuring their adequate protection.[15] In 1998 the Act was amended to include reference to the confident and informed participation of investors and consumers.[16] Investors and consumers were distinct. At the same time the Act was further amended to incorporate specific consumer protection provisions for consumers or financial products and services.[17] These echoed those provisions of the then Trade Practices Act that no longer applied to financial services. The idea was that consumer financial protection required specialised regulation.[18] Since that time, and as the ASIC Act was re-enacted in 2001, it has been progressively amended to incorporate many, but not all, aspects of consumer protection applying to all other markets. In addition, in 2001 ASIC became responsible for new consumer protection legislation in chapter 7 of the Corporations Act for 'retail clients'.[19] In 2009 ASIC became responsible for the new national consumer credit laws.[20]

---

[10] Statement of Sheila C. Bair, Chairman of the Federal Deposit Insurance Corporation, on Modernizing Bank Supervision and Regulation before the US Senate Committee on Banking, Housing and Urban Affairs, 19 March 2009, in 'Safe, Fair and Competitive Markets in Financial Services: Recommendations for the G20 on the Enhancement of Consumer Protection in Financial Services', *Consumers International* (March 2011), 5.

[11] www.fsa.gov.uk/ consumerinformation/stay_safe.

[12] On regulatory harmonisation in 1998 see, for instance, Insurance and Superannuation Bulletin (December 1998).

[13] ASIC Statement of Intent (July 2014), https://asic.gov.au/about-asic/what-we-do/how-we-operate/accountability-and-reporting/statements-of-expectations-and-intent/statement-of-intent-july-2014/.

[14] APRA Annual Report 2015, www.apra.gov.au/AboutAPRA/Publications/Pages/ar2015-single.aspx.

[15] Australian Securities Commission Act 1989 (Cth) s 3(2).

[16] Ibid s 1(2). At the same time the name of the Act was changed to the Australian Securities and Investments Commission Act. See Financial Sector Reform (Amendments and Transitional Provisions) Act 1998 (Cth) Sched 1, ss 3, 268.

[17] Financial Sector Reform (Consequential Amendments) Act 1998 (Cth) Sched 2.

[18] Wallis Report (n 4) Ch 5, 175

[19] For the definition of a retail client see Corporations Act 2001 (Cth) ss 761A, 761G, 761GA.

[20] National Consumer Credit Protection Act 2009 (Cth).

APRA does not have a specific consumer protection mandate. There is no explicit statement about consumers or retail clients. However, the consumer protection comes in indirectly. Wallis,[21] and subsequently APRA, acknowledged inherent difficulties for a consumer to assess the creditworthiness of a financial institution and its ability to keep promises in the present and into the future: 'One of the reasons for prudential supervision is to protect the unsophisticated consumer with little understanding of balance sheets and esoteric notes to accounts.'[22] The withdrawal of implicit government guarantees in the financial services industry as governments withdrew from ownership of banks also underscored the importance of prudential regulation to consumers.[23]

When one looks at the position from a financial product or services perspective, ASIC and APRA have overlapping responsibilities. APRA is responsible for the prudential regulation of firms that are Authorised Deposit Taking Institutions (ADIs), hold superannuation monies (private pensions) in trust or offer insurance (general, life and medical). As the ADIs (banks) offer products that include financial advice, managed investments, credit and insurance, APRA has a broad mandate.[24] This is also the case for ASIC, which also has responsibilities for financial advice, wealth management, insurance, superannuation and consumer credit.[25]

18.2 THE PEAKS PERFORM FOR CONSUMER PROTECTION

From a consumer protection perspective, the critical difference between ASIC and APRA is the ability of ASIC to litigate for individual promisees.[26] The role each regulator plays in fostering a stable and fair market should minimise ASIC's necessity to do so. While APRA and ASIC take a different approach to the task of regulation, there is a Memorandum of Understanding (MoU) between the two agencies setting out the nature of their cooperation.[27] APRA is not directed towards specific promises to consumers but towards the viability of particular institutions and the system as a whole. The exception is the scheme administered by APRA to provide recourse for individuals in case a particular type of institution fails.[28] ASIC is concerned with both systemic issues and promises made to particular persons.

Supervision of financial institutions is an arcane art. It is not concerned with individual transactions. It involves in-depth and hands-on knowledge of aspects of the business. Prudential supervisors are proactive in ensuring that institutions meet the requirements set for them. Yet they, including APRA, take a risk-based approach to supervision.[29] Surveillance of conduct, on the other hand, is not traditionally pre-emptive. ASIC aims to detect wrongdoing once it has occurred and uses a risk-based approach to surveillance, along with other means of detection,

---

[21] Wallis Report (n 4) Ch 5, 181.

[22] G. Thompson, 'Institutional Self-Regulation: What Should Be the Role of the Regulator?' (Speech given to the National Institute for Governance/PricewaterhouseCoopers Legal Seminar, 8 November 2001).

[23] Wallis Report (n 4) Ch 3, 132.

[24] For a good overview see Productivity Commission, 'Competition in the Australian Financial System' (Submission by APRA, September 2017).

[25] For a succinct summary see Australian Government, 'Fit for the Future: A Capability Review of the Australian Securities and Investments Commission, A Report to Government' (December 2015), 34–5.

[26] As a result of the Royal Commission, ASIC has a adopted a more vigorous approach to litigation and new legislation gives both ASIC and APRA powers to enforce the statutory 'covenants' of superannuation trustees.

[27] The latest version of the MoU was signed on 28 November 2019 and is available at www.apra.gov.au/sites/default/files/APRA-ASIC%20Memorandum%20of%20Understanding%202019.pdf.

[28] This is the Financial Claims Scheme which is a bank deposit guarantee scheme and also applies to insurance.

[29] APRA Annual Report 2015 (n 14) 3.

including whistleblowing and reports of breaches.[30] ASIC is now moving to more proactive surveillance.[31] As well as policing who can be in the market to provide financial services to consumers through licensing and 'fit and proper' persons regimes, both APRA and ASIC monitor and supervise the ongoing provision of those services and both have powers to remove persons from the market. They have some regulatory tools in common, such as enforceable undertakings.

Both regulators provide extensive information to the regulated community as to how each regulator can meet its obligations. This differs between the regulators. Prudential standards are made under legislation and guide APRA's supervision. ASIC provides Regulatory Guides, which indicate ASIC's interpretation of legal compliance requirements and consequently its approach to non-compliance and enforcement. ASIC provides 'general information and advice to help educate, inform and protect the rights of consumers'.[32] Its MoneySmart site with calculator apps and guides for life events is renowned for its innovative methods of providing simple and sophisticated advice to approaching the financial world.[33] APRA does not give information directly to consumers. The APRA page directs people to ASIC's MoneySmart site.

Since the Twin Peaks system was established, the financial system has been challenged by the Global Financial Crisis, which did not impact on Australia as seriously as many jurisdictions but nevertheless resulted in consumer losses, particularly associated with financial planning and investment schemes. Overall, the system has been assessed as having the prerequisites for a strong financial system that meets the needs of the economy but at the same time facing challenges that require it to take steps to improve its 'resilience' and make it 'unquestionably strong' and by implication safe for consumers.[34] APRA has been given new tasks but its fundamental role and performance have been validated. ASIC has been subject to more criticism for failing to forestall 'bad' conduct particularly in the areas of financial advice and insurance. A scan of ASIC consumer-oriented litigation suggests it has concentrated on protecting the vulnerable.[35] Both regulators were examined in the course of the Financial Services Royal Commission.

Shortly after the introduction of the Twin Peaks architecture, APRA was scrutinised by a Royal Commission following the collapse of HIH Insurance, which had a devastating impact on insureds unable to claim and potential insureds unable to obtain cover. The Royal Commissioner commenting on the 'two agency' or Twin Peaks system of regulation at that time, was doubtful about it, but did not recommend a merger of the two agencies.[36] Justice Owen, the Royal Commissioner, characterised the corporate regulator as emphasising public enforcement of the law and the prudential regulator as privately detecting financial weakness

---

[30] ASIC's Corporate Plan 2016–10, 3, 15; ASIC, Chart showing surveillance of regulated populations, www.asic.gov.au/media/3339804/asic-surveillance-coverage-regulated-populations-chart-1-september-2015.pdf.

[31] ASIC Corporate Plan 2016–10, 3. Since the Royal Commission, ASIC has also engaged in activities akin to supervision by embedding regulators in some financial institutions.

[32] www.asic.gov.au/for-consumers/.

[33] www.moneysmart.gov.au/.

[34] Murray Report (n 5).

[35] Eg, payday borrowers in *Australian Securities and Investments Commission v Cash Store Pty Ltd (in liquidation)* [2014] FCA 926; remote indigenous borrowers in *Australian Securities and Investments Commission v Kobelt* [2019 HCA 18; *Australian Securities and Investments Commission v Channic Pty Ltd (No 4)* [2016] FCA 1174. It also published reports on micro lenders and payday lenders: ASIC Report 264, 'Review of Micro Lenders' Responsible Lending and Disclosure Obligations' (November 2011); ASIC Report 426, 'Payday Lenders and the New Small Amount Lending Provisions' (March 2015).

[36] HIH Royal Commission, *The Failure of HIH Insurance Volume 1* (Commonwealth of Australia, 2003), 203.

and taking remedial action.[37] His Honour noted that ASIC had raised concerns publicly, but the performance of APRA needed to improve.[38] Important recommendations were that APRA adopt a less consultative and more sceptical and questioning approach to prudential regulation and cooperate more effectively with ASIC.[39] Since that time there have been no major collapses of prudentially regulated firms, although there have been collapses of collective investment schemes.

Apart from the misconduct in the Financial Services Royal Commission, there has been no further sustained review of the performance of APRA as a regulator and its role for consumers in ensuring that institutions are able to keep their financial promises. Its Annual Reports are regularly scrutinised by the House of Representatives Standing Committee on Economics and it has been interrogated on the expansion of home lending[40] and on loan impairment.[41] APRA is clear that its role is with respect to the protection of depositors, systemic issues and stability: 'it is not in our statute right now to look at the bank's relationship with borrowers. APRA is, right now, not statutorily mandated to protect borrowers'.[42]

This contrasts with ASIC. Since the 2014 Senate Economics References Committee inquiry specifically into the performance of ASIC,[43] it has been subject to intensified oversight by the Joint Standing Committee on Corporations and Financial Services, particularly with respect to protection of retail investors and the prevention of fraud.[44] ASIC has a 'wide remit but limited powers and resources'.[45]

The 2014 inquiry into the financial system recommended that the existing regulatory architecture should be retained but made more capable and accountable.[46] The question of whether ASIC's consumer protection function should be part of the Australian Consumer Law administered by the Australian Competition and Consumer Commission had been raised earlier but not proceeded with.[47] The solution was a recommendation that ASIC gain competition powers.[48] A further result of the Financial System Inquiry (FSI) was an independent capability review of ASIC which found an expectations gap between ASIC and stakeholders regarding what ASIC could achieve.[49]

The Murray Inquiry made specific recommendations to improve 'resilience to institutional failure'[50] and that regulation be more efficient, competitive and accountable. As well as addressing capital requirements and risk weights for mortgage lending, the inquiry commented

---

[37] Ibid 203.
[38] Ibid 206.
[39] Ibid 221 (Recommendation 26), 224–5 (Recommendation 31).
[40] The Parliament of the Commonwealth of Australia, House of Representatives Standing Committee on Economics, 'Report on the Enquiry into Home Ownership' (December 2016).
[41] Parliamentary Joint Committee on Corporations and Financial Services, 'Impairment of Customer Loans' (May 2016).
[42] Ibid 91.
[43] Senate Economics References Committee, 'Performance of the Australian Securities and Investments Commission' (June 2014).
[44] Parliamentary Joint Committee on Corporations and Financial Services, 'Statutory Oversight of the Australian Securities and Investments Commission, the Takeovers Panel and the Corporations Legislation Report No 1 of the 44th Parliament' (November 2014), 12.
[45] Murray Report (n 5) 236.
[46] Ibid 29. On the accountability of APRA and ASIC see Joanna Bird, 'Regulating the Regulators: Accountability of Australian Regulators' (2011) 35 *Melbourne University Law Review* 739.
[47] Productivity Commission, 'Consumer Law Enforcement and Administration' (Research Report, March 2017), 32.
[48] Murray Report (n 5) 237. Australian Government, 'Fit for the Future: A Capability Review of the Australian Securities and Investments Commission, A Report to Government' (December 2015), 7.
[49] Australian Government (n 48) 174.
[50] Murray Report (n 5) 39.

on a specific consumer protection measure administered by APRA. It endorsed the Financial Claims Scheme which protects depositors and insureds in case of liquidation up to a specific amount.[51] The scheme, which has never been activated, is self-funded and depositors gain access to funds before the completion of a liquidation. The inquiry also recommended that APRA develop a framework for loss-absorbing and recapitalisation to combat the idea that government implicitly guarantees banks and that they cannot fail, despite the possibility that increased costs associated with this may be passed on to consumers.[52]

The Final FSI Report was released after the parliamentary inquiry into ASIC and made a number of very specific recommendations to increase consumer protection, including better consumer protection in payments services, a product design and distribution obligation, improving standards in financial advice and harnessing technology for better disclosure.[53] An important recommendation to increase ASIC's powers was a product intervention power, to be exercised in consultation with APRA.[54] The product intervention power, now in effect, enables the regulators to modify or ban products harmful to consumers and is an example of potential convergence, reinforced by the post-Financial Services Royal Commission approach by APRA to include responsibility for products as part of the Banking Executive Accountability Regime (BEAR).[55]

The recommendations and response to the Financial Services Royal Commission have hastened a tendency towards smudging distinct roles for ASIC and APRA. From early on, their roles were described as overlapping and the allocation of responsibilities and interaction between the two regulators was viewed as central to the overall system of financial regulation.[56] This was also a concern of a taskforce which investigated regulatory overlap between APRA and ASIC, and found very little in the way of duplicated or conflicting requirements.[57] More recently there seems to be permeability in the roles of ASIC and APRA so far as consumer protection is concerned. Each has taken up issues that at first glance may appear to be in the domain of the other. It is fair to ask if their roles remain complementary or are becoming blurred. If there is a trend towards convergence and there are few differences between conduct and prudential regulators from a consumer protection approach, what distinguishes them? There may be only one pond – even if it is not so calm.

18.3 CULTURE AND CONVERGENCE

The regulators have diverted their conversation about regulatory performance, its successes or failures and whether they are reactive or proactive, towards a conversation about culture – that is, the culture of the firm. This ascribes responsibility for consumer detriment to the internal workings of the firm and away from any failures to supervise or enforce. Culture has a wider frame than compliance, which sought to promote the internalisation of regulatory norms and values but became legalistic. The culture conversation is about unveiling modes of opposition and failures in that internalisation. There is an expectation that this will benefit consumers. There is a convergence in the approaches of APRA and ASIC in the conversation on culture.

---

[51] Ibid 82.
[52] Ibid 67, 70.
[53] Ibid xx, 28, 121, 194, 196.
[54] Ibid 206.
[55] See www.apra.gov.au/consultation-on-proposed-approach-to-product-responsibility-under-banking-executive-accountability.
[56] HIH Royal Commission (n 36) 201.
[57] APRA, 'Financial System Inquiry: Response to the Interim Report' (26 August 2014), 60.

Culture is about norms of behaviour. A former chair of ASIC described culture as a 'mindset', the 'unwritten rules' that guide attitudes and behaviour within an organisation and towards consumers.[58] This appears to be fully within the domain of conduct, something for which ASIC is responsible. Yet it has been APRA that has taken the lead on culture, twinning culture with risk and governance of prudentially regulated firms, matters for which APRA has responsibility. As early as 2005, in the wake of the collapse of the HIH insurance firm, APRA spoke of the 'cultural underpinnings' of 'personal behaviours' and of 'poor' culture.[59] This was set alongside 'the right attitude to create a culture of care and safety'.[60]

Risk culture has an impact on specific transactions. A bad culture may lead to transactions that are harmful to a particular consumer. APRA refers to risk culture as the way in which the culture of the organisation determines the ways in which risks within the organisation are managed.[61] It states that 'a culture that promotes good governance benefits all stakeholders of an institution and group and helps to maintain public confidence in the institution and group'.[62]

There is a debate as to whether culture can be regulated. APRA's view in 2016 was that it could not bring a sound risk culture into being through regulation but that it could intensify supervision of institutions 'unwilling or unable to address behaviours that are inconsistent with prudent risk management'.[63]

It is worth examining the evolution of APRA's recent approach to culture. It has linked supervision of the firm to fair outcomes for consumers. It recognises that internal conduct has an impact on individual consumers but focuses on this through the culture and subcultures of the firm.

In 2014 the Financial Stability Board (FSB) released a paper on risk culture, defining it as 'the norms of behaviour for individuals and groups within an institution that determine the collective ability to identify and understand, openly discuss and act on the organisation's current and future risk'.[64] Clearly this is about risk to the institution, its appetite for risk and the importance of these for systemically important institutions. The paper valued a risk culture that promoted integrity and a focus on consumers. In the light of subsequent issues regarding commission payments in Australia and the impact of these on consumer detriment, it is notable that the FSB paper commented that a positive culture should reward performance in the long-term interests of the firm and its clients rather than short-term revenue.[65]

After the release of this paper, APRA Chairman Byres commented that developments in the governance and culture of financial institutions could have as profound an impact on firms as changes to capital requirements. He commented on the lack of utility of aspirational statements of organisational culture and contrasted these with the question of incentives. He said that

---

[58] Greg Medcraft, Chairman, Australian Securities and Investments Commission, 'Why Culture Matters' (Speech at BNP Paribas Conduct Month, Sydney, Australia, 24 May 2016), www.asic.gov.au/about-asic/media-centre/speeches/why-culture-matters/.

[59] Steve Somogyi, 'APRA Stage II Reforms for the General Insurance Industry APRA Advocates a Prudent Culture', 2005 Prudential Regulatory Reform (Sydney, APRA, 17 June 2005), 2.

[60] Ibid.

[61] APRA Submission to the Parliamentary Joint Committee on Corporations and Financial Services' Inquiry into the Life Insurance Industry (November 2016), 20.

[62] APRA Prudential Standard CPS 510 Governance (July 2017), 1, www.apra.gov.au/sites/default/files/Prudential-Standard-CPS-510-Governance-%28July-2017%29.pdf.

[63] APRA, 'APRA Releases Snapshot of Industry Practice in Risk Culture' (Media Release, 16.40, 18 October 2016), www.apra.gov.au/media-centre/media-releases/apra-releases-snapshot-industry-practice-risk-culture.

[64] Financial Stability Board, 'Guidance on Supervisory Interaction with Financial Institutions on Risk Culture: A Framework for Assessing Risk Culture' (7 April 2014), 1.

[65] Ibid 9.

personal incentives signal what an organisation values and inform choices of right and wrong; that getting incentives aligned with the long-term interests of firms was so far under-developed.[66]

Prior to the FSB paper, APRA had already started work on consolidating and improving its guidance framework for 'behavioural' standards[67] and for risk management with the aim that boards and others focus on 'desirable values and behaviours'.[68] This led to two revised or new prudential standards: *Prudential Standard CPS 510 Governance* (CPS 510), which speaks of risk rather than culture and imposes obligations on the board, and *Prudential Standard CPS 220 Risk Management* (CPS 220), which requires institutions to have a risk management framework and make an annual risk management declaration to APRA. CPS 220 does speak of risk culture. It requires the Board to form a view of the institution's risk culture, whether this culture means it can operate within its declared risk appetite, identify if the risk culture should be changed and take steps to make those changes.[69]

In 2016, APRA published an important paper on risk culture.[70] This placed APRA's renewed focus on risk management in the context of left-over business from the Global Financial Crisis, the current long boom in the Australian economy, increased risk taking that it had detected and the excuse of 'bad apples' for poor behaviour. APRA was concerned that a downturn may reveal poor financial outcomes for firms, the implication being that this could impact on overall safety and stability. Consumer detriment was referred to as 'customer interests' that were neglected when short-term financial interests were pursued.[71]

This APRA paper scopes differences between risk culture and conduct risk, arguing that while both a prudential regulator and a conduct regulator have an interest in culture, the interest of each regulator comes from different perspectives and objectives. Basically this simply comes back to differences between the mandate of a conduct regulator to ensure fair outcomes for 'customers and investors' and that of a prudential regulator to ensure that undesirable behaviour does not threaten the viability of an institution and in turn its obligations to depositors, policy-holders and fund members and thus financial stability.[72] From a consumer protection perspective, there is a convergence of risky culture that threatens the ability to meet promises and conduct that could harm investors and others. There is also convergence in that conduct risk can be defined to include potential systemic risk[73] and risk culture may lead to financial instability

During 2016 ASIC also battled to conceptualise the challenges of culture and conduct risk. In a report on enforcement outcomes in the preceding year, ASIC said it was concerned with poor culture because culture drove conduct and poor culture and conduct diminished trust.[74] It referred specifically to financial advice and mis-selling of products and later added treating customers fairly, the need for products to perform in the way people have been led to believe and

---

[66] Wayne Byres, 'Perspectives on the Global Regulatory Agenda' (Speech given to the RMA Australia CRO Forum Sydney, 16 September 2014).

[67] See APRA, 'Harmonising Cross-Industry Risk Management Requirements' (Discussion Paper, 9 May 2013), 6, www.apra.gov.au/sites/default/files/Level-3-Discussion-Paper-Risk-Management-%28May-2013%29.pdf.

[68] APRA, 'APRA Releases Consultation on Harmonised and Enhanced Risk Management Requirements' (Media Release MR 13.13, 9 May 2013).

[69] APRA, Prudential Standard CPS 220, 'Risk Management', cl 9(b), www.apra.gov.au/sites/default/files/Prudential-Standard-CPS-220-Risk-Management-%28July-2017%29.pdf.

[70] APRA, 'Risk Culture' (Information Paper, October 2016), www.apra.gov.au/sites/default/files/161018-information-paper-risk-culture1.pdf.

[71] Ibid 7.

[72] Ibid 9.

[73] See International Organization of Securities Commissions (IOSCO) definition of harmful conduct at ibid 9 fn6.

[74] ASIC, 'ASIC Enforcement Outcomes: July to December 2015' (ASIC Report 476, March 2016), 8, www.asic.gov.au/media/4156870/rep476-published-17-february-2017.pdf.

the need for firms to consider information asymmetries and consumers' behavioural biases.[75] The commissioners went on to deliver several speeches incorporating comments on culture. ASIC appears to have drawn inspiration from the Financial System Inquiry (Murray) more than international organisations, and to some extent from conduct regulators in other jurisdictions, some of which intensified their discussion of culture around the same time as ASIC.[76] Referring to the view of the UK Financial Conduct Authority, ASIC stated: 'at the root of many conduct risks is the exploitation of conflicts of interest that have been built into financial sector structures, processes and management'.[77]

The Final Report of the Financial System Inquiry (Murray) has a brief section on the culture of financial firms. The Murray view was that consumers should be responsible for their decisions and that firms should act in the interests of 'their legal beneficiaries' and earn the trust of customers.[78] This requires a firm culture that supports 'appropriate risk-taking and the fair treatment of customers'; otherwise firms will not meet 'community expectations'.[79] The report rejected the idea of prescribing culture through rules as this would lead to over-regulation, high compliance costs and reduced competition. The Murray Report was firm that getting the culture right was the responsibility of the firm and its leadership. They are responsible for the behavioural norms of individuals within firms. ASIC endorsed the report's statement that firms should create a culture concerned with consumer interests if they wished to build trust and confidence.[80]

ASIC views risk management as management of conduct risk, which it defines as 'inappropriate, unethical or unlawful behaviour on the part of an organisation's management of employees'.[81] This is different from APRA, which in part sees risk management as the management of risk exposures in the market. Yet both are concerned with behaviour and ASIC also refers to 'risk culture'.[82] ASIC has developed seven indicators of culture within an organisation. These are: tone from the top (the attitude of leadership and how this drives decisions and risk management); spread (the way in which tone cascades through the firm); business practices (how tone impacts on practices); accountability; communication and challenge (of business practices); recruitment, training and remuneration (whether these support management of conflicts of interest); and governance.[83] ASIC's risk-based surveillance reviews now incorporate culture.[84]

One particular financial firm, the Commonwealth Bank of Australia (CBA), has been on notice of its poor culture for some time. This is exemplified by a financial planning scandal that resulted in a parliamentary inquiry[85] and an insurance scandal that resulted in a specific inquiry

---

[75] John Price, ASIC Commissioner, 'A Question of Risk' (Speech given to RMA Australia and PricewaterhouseCoopers Sydney, 22 November 2016).

[76] See www.fca.org.uk/news/speeches/getting-culture-and-conduct-right-role-regulator.

[77] ASIC, 'Culture, Conduct and Conflicts of Interest in Vertically Integrated Businesses in the Funds-Management Industry' (ASIC Report 474, March 2016), 9.

[78] Murray Report (n 5) 7.

[79] Ibid.

[80] Peter Kell, then ASIC deputy chairman, 'Why Are We Talking about Culture?' (Speech given at AFR Banking & Wealth Summit 2016, Sydney, Australia, 5 April 2016).

[81] ASIC Report 474 (n 77).

[82] John Price, ASIC Commissioner, 'Outline of ASIC's Approach to Corporate Culture' (speech given at AICD's Director's Forum: Regulators' Insights on Risk Culture, Sydney, Australia, 19 July 2017).

[83] ASIC Report 474 (n 77)10.

[84] Price (n 82).

[85] Commonwealth of Australia, Senate Economics References Committee, *Performance of the Australian Securities and Investments Commission* (June 2014); G. Pearson, 'Failure in Corporate Governance: Financial Planning and Greed' in C. Mallin (ed) *Handbook on Corporate Governance in Financial Institutions* (Edward Elgar, 2016).

by ASIC and consideration by another parliamentary inquiry, as well as litigation.[86] A markets scandal, rather than a consumer protection scandal, prompted an inquiry into the Commonwealth Bank.[87] It is APRA, not ASIC, which has conducted the inquiry into the governance, culture and accountability of the CBA.[88] Yet it is ASIC that has recently assessed the culture of the boards of large financial institutions.[89]

In earlier years, the Australian regulatory community spoke of a culture of compliance and expressed the belief that if firms complied with regulatory requirements then those firms and their consumers would be safe. In more recent years, the series of scandals in Australian financial services has revealed shortcomings in the search for compliance as it is evident that both compliance and lack of compliance may result in consumer detriment. The current emphasis on culture, seen not as the responsibility of the regulator but the responsibility of the board and management, seeks to allocate responsibility for poor culture squarely to the firm itself and is another way of attempting to challenge those who seek to evade their responsibilities to the consumer, their customers and clients. This may be little more than a shift in language as regulators seek the same results through slightly different language: that financial institutions should temper their short-term profit objectives in the interests of the longevity of the firm, the stability of the system, the confidence of the community and the interests of consumers. The change in language from compliance to culture may benefit consumers. A renewed emphasis on the responsibilities of leadership for treating consumers fairly and holding leadership to account may be more potent. This accords with community views that led to the Financial Services Royal Commission into the banks in Australia, which are vertically integrated financial services firms that also cover financial advice, wealth management and insurance.

18.4 HOME LENDING AND COMPLEMENTS

Mortgage lending has been a grave source of global financial instability, causing institutions to fail and consumer losses. It throws into stark relief the role of the prudential regulator and conduct regulator as each pursues the mandate to keep the system safe and stable and ensure the integrity and performance of promises. As APRA has said: 'Our ultimate goal is to protect bank depositors – it is, after all, ultimately their money that banks are lending.'[90] And, as ASIC said, home lending is of 'critical importance to the financial wellbeing of Australian consumers. Where we see poor lending practices in relation to home lending, we will take action'.[91]

---

[86] ASIC, 'ASIC Releases Findings of CommInsure Investigation' (Media Release MR 17-07, 23 March 2017) (an executive summary is attached to the media release and states that ASIC found no evidence to support the claim that doctors were pressured to alter their medical opinion; however, it did find outdated medical definitions; Commonwealth of Australia Joint Parliamentary Committee on Corporations and Financial Services, Report Life Insurance Industry (March 2018), www.aph.gov.au/Parliamentary_Business/Committees/Joint/Corporations_and_Financial_Services/LifeInsurance/Report; *Commonwealth Financial Planning Ltd v Couper* [2013] NSWCA 444.

[87] The catalyst was a money-laundering scandal. See www.austrac.gov.au/media/media-releases/austrac-seeks-civil-penalty-orders-against-cba.

[88] APRA, 'APRA to Establish Independent Prudential Inquiry into Governance, Culture and Accountability within CBA' (Media Release 17.34, 28 August 2017); J. Broadbent, J. Laker and G. Samuel, *Prudential Inquiry into the Commonwealth Bank of Australia (CBA) Final Report* (April 2018).

[89] ASIC, *Corporate Governance Taskforce Report* (October 2019), https://asic.gov.au/regulatory-resources/corporate-governance/directors-and-corporate-culture/; https://asic.gov.au/about-asic/news-centre/speeches/launch-of-asic-s-report-on-director-and-officer-oversight-of-non-financial-risk/.

[90] Wayne Byres, 'Prudential Perspectives on the Property Market' (Remarks at CEDA's 2017 NSW Property Market Outlook, Sydney, 28 April 2017).

[91] Peter Kell, ASIC Deputy Commissioner, 'Regulation and Innovation in Mortgage Lending' (Speech delivered at the Australian Mortgage Innovation Summit, Sydney, 18 February 2016).

However as the Financial Services Royal Commission observed: 'The conduct regulator, ASIC, rarely went to court to seek public denunciation of and punishment for misconduct. The prudential regulator, APRA, never went to court.'[92]

It is noteworthy that home lending was the first area of inquiry for the Financial Services Royal Commission. One of the issues ultimately raised was whether regulatory action affected the availability of credit, also a matter of concern for consumers. The Financial Services Royal Commission rejected the proposition that measures taken by the regulators and explored later in this section impacted on tightened credit as other factors were at play.[93] The availability of credit has again become controversial.

Does Twin Peaks regulation work for home lending? How are regulatory responsibilities distributed? Are the roles of the regulators complementary or blurred and are their approaches converging or distinct? APRA's view, conveyed to the Financial Services Royal Commission, is that its work of prudential supervision and ASIC's regulation of responsible lending are complementary.[94] The Financial Services Royal Commission examined (among other sectors) home lending and mortgage brokers. It concluded that Twin Peaks does work and that the two regulators should work together even more closely pursuant to a statutory obligation to do so and make this a 'reality'.[95]

The Financial Services Royal Commission has crystallised much of what follows, and was guided by the insights of both regulators. Commissioner Hayne commented on greed driving misconduct and recommended that responsible lending laws 'should not be amended to alter the obligation to assess unsuitability'.[96] The ambit of responsible lending laws was tested in court, in favour of the banks. ASIC took a decision not to appeal, due to the covid crisis and external pressure about access to credit. There is now a contested Bill before the Parliament to repeal responsible lending laws – something outside the remit of either regulator and their joint enterprise for consumer protection.[97]

The culture of mortgage lending has been scrutinised in the context of commissions paid by lenders to mortgage brokers and bank staff and resulting conflicts of interest and consumer detriment. This has been undertaken by ASIC,[98] an inquiry commissioned by the Australian Banking Association[99] and the Australian Parliament.[100] Commissions are paid to increase sales targets of loans. Brokers and aggregators are responsible for well over half of all loans, and are often paid solely by commissions from lenders. The consumer detriment is that brokered loans are for higher amounts, cost consumers more in interest and insurance, have higher

[92] Financial Services Royal Commission Interim Report, Vol 1 (September 2018), Executive Summary, xix.

[93] Royal Commission into Misconduct in the Banking, Superannuation and Financial Services Industry, 'Final Report', Vol 1 (Financial Services Royal Commission, Canberra, ACT, 1 February 2019), 58, https://parlinfo.aph.gov.au/parlInfo/download/publications/tabledpapers/bc83795c-b7fa-4b42-a93b-fao12cffffc2/upload_pdf/fsrc-volume-1-final-report.pdf;fileType=application%2Fpdf#search=%22publications/tabledpapers/bc83795c-b7fa-4b42-a93b-fao12cffffc2%22.

[94] Financial Services Royal Commission, written submissions of the Australian Prudential Regulation Authority (APRA) in response to the Interim Report 2018, 18, para 108.

[95] Financial Services Royal Commission Final Report, Vol 1, Recommendation 6.1, 423; Recommendation 6.2, 446; Recommendation 6.9, 458; Recommendation 6.10, 464. As at the time of writing, a bill has been prepared to impose a statutory obligation to cooperate. See https://treasury.gov.au/consultation/c2019-40503.

[96] Financial Services Royal Commission Interim Report, xix; Final Report Recommendation 1.1. The Final Report made a number of recommendations regarding mortgage brokers see Final Report, 20 f.

[97] *Australian Securities and Investments Commission v Westpac Banking Corporation* [2020] FCAFC 111. Gail Pearson, 'The HEM and Hayne's Normative Principles Credit Data and the Individual' (2019) 13 *Law and Financial Markets Review* 131.

[98] ASIC Report No 516, 'Review of Mortgage Broker Remuneration' (16 March 2017).

[99] Stephen Sedgwick, *Retail Banking Remuneration Review Issues Paper* (January 2017), 29.

[100] Senate Standing Committee on Economics, Inquiry into Consumer Protection in the Banking Insurance and Financial Sector, www.aph.gov.au/Parliamentary_Business/Committees/Senate/Economics/Consumerprotection.

loan-to-value ratios and fall into arrears more than non-brokered loans from lenders. There has been little appetite to ban or reduce such commissions.[101] While APRA has been concerned with executive remuneration, it has not entered the lists in the details of the home lending commission culture beyond commenting that remuneration frameworks and outcomes are an indicator of risk culture,[102] and advocating that commissions should not create 'adverse incentives' and that ADIs should have arrangements for clawbacks.[103] Its revision of guidance in 2019 addressed serviceability floors but not broker remuneration.[104]

Australia has had a potential mortgage lending problem that may threaten stability, and it is evident that incentives to increase this form of consumer lending have driven provision of credit that arguably does not meet either prudent lending or conduct for suitability requirements. In the past, residential mortgages were a safe asset class for lenders and borrowers. In the last ten years there have been widespread changes in home loan debt as ADIs have expanded their balance sheets accompanied by a relaxation in lending standards. In 2007 housing lending comprised little more than 50 per cent of all ADI domestic lending.[105] In 2015 it was over 60 per cent.[106] More significantly, the changes in debt to household income are spectacular. This was around 40 per cent in 1980, 140 per cent after 2012[107] and approaching 200 per cent towards the end of 2017.[108] Much of this is attributable to housing debt.[109] The growth in lending and debt was characterised by steep increases in investor loans and increases in interest-only loans.[110] In 2015, there was an increase in the ratio of non-performing ADI loans to gross loans.[111] Escalating house prices added to this heady mix of high debt, little household income growth and low interest rates.[112] Following the financial crisis, banks gained market share at the expense of non-bank lenders.[113] Not all home lending is undertaken by ADIs, as lenders that are not prudentially regulated but require credit licences are also in this market.[114]

Home ownership and housing affordability, is a potent political issue and there have been many Parliamentary inquiries.[115] Affordability is formally a consumer issue through the *National Consumer Credit Protection Act 2009* (Cth), whose remit includes residential mortgages for

---

[101] Gail Pearson, 'Commission Culture: A Critical Analysis of Commission Regulation in Financial Services (2017) 36 *University of Queensland Law Journal* 155, 166, 167, 174. The Financial Sector Reform (Hayne Royal Commission Response – Protecting Consumers (2019 Measures)) Act 2020 introduces a best interests duty for mortgage brokers and prohibits conflicted remuneration.

[102] APRA, 'Risk Culture' (Information Paper, October 2016), 25.

[103] APRA Prudential Practice Guide APG 223, Residential Mortgage Lending (February 2017), 10, cl 18, cl 19.

[104] APRA Prudential Practice Guide APG 223, Residential Mortgage Lending (July 2019); APRA, 'APRA Proposes Amending Guidance on Mortgage Lending' (APRA Media Release, 20 May 2019).

[105] John Laker, 'Credit Standards in Housing Lending – Some Further Insights' (Address to the Institute of Chartered Accountants in Australia, 20 June 2007).

[106] APRA Submission, House of Representatives Standing Committee on Economics, Inquiry into Home Ownership (26 June 2015); Chair of APRA Speech at COBA CEO & Director Forum, Sydney (13 May 2015); Wayne Byres, 'Housing: The Importance of Solid Foundations' (Keynote address at the Australian Securitisation Forum, Sydney, 21 November 2017).

[107] APRA (n 106) 2, chart 2.

[108] Byres (n 106) chart 1.

[109] Ibid.

[110] APRA Submission (n 106) 4, chart 4, chart 5.

[111] APRA Annual Report 2015–16, 22, fig 1d. This figure was not limited to housing loans.

[112] APRA Letter, 'Wayne Byres to all ADIs, Further Measures to Reinforce Sound Residential Mortgage Lending Practices' (31 March 2017).

[113] Productivity Commission, Competition in the Financial System, Reserve Bank of Australia (Submission 29, September 2017), www.pc.gov.au/__data/assets/pdf_file/0008/221876/sub029-financial-system.pdf.

[114] Non-APRA regulated lenders have lost market share. See Productivity Commission Competition in the Financial System, APRA Submission No 22 (September 2017), www.pc.gov.au/inquiries/current/financial-system/submissions.

[115] Senate Select Committee on Housing Affordability in Australia, A Good House is Hard to Find: Housing Affordability in Australia' (June 2008); Senate Economics References Committee, 'Out of Reach? The Australian Housing

homeownership or investment.[116] This legislation contains responsible lending obligations, which impose an obligation on the broker and the lender to assess the affordability and suitability of a loan.[117]

Lending calculations are standard for ADIs. That said, in the years prior to the introduction of the responsible lending laws there was a series of cases where lenders engaged in unjust or unconscionable conduct by making 'asset stripping' loans to individuals who were unlikely to repay.[118] Prior to the introduction of responsible lending, APRA undertook a study of 'debt serviceability' to understand ADI models to calculate capacity to repay debt. It identified two models, a debt service ratio and a net income surplus model.[119] The traditional approach was that debt could only be up to 30 per cent of gross income. This did not take into account living expenses, which were assumed to rise with income. By 2006, 90 per cent of ADIs took into account living and other expenses to calculate a minimum net surplus of after-tax income.[120] APRA found discrepancies between stated lending policies and actual debt servicing ratios. It concluded, in 2007, that lending for housing was now riskier, particularly if housing values fell.[121] At the beginning of 2008, APRA introduced a number of prudential standards based on Basel II.[122] It pointed out in response to a parliamentary inquiry that it could increase capital adequacy requirements for an ADI depending on its lending practices; that this may curtail lending or increase the cost of loans; that capital adequacy requirements are lower for housing finance than for other lending; that the method for calculating capital adequacy involves risk-weighting mortgages according to a ratio of outstanding loan to the secured property, taking into account the characteristics of the loan and whether it is covered by insurance.[123]

Following the introduction of the new credit laws in 2009, ASIC issued eleven regulatory guides and nine information sheets.[124] Chief among them for home lending standards and suitability is *Regulatory Guide 209 Credit Licensing: Responsible Lending Conduct*,[125] updated in turn in response to judicial decision-making. The legislative responsible lending or 'not unsuitable' test requires a broker and lender to make inquiries about a prospective borrower's requirements and objectives in relation to the proposed credit contract and about the financial situation of the prospective borrower.[126] Both must verify the borrower's financial situation.[127]

Affordability Challenge' (May 2015); House of Representatives Standing Committee on Economics, 'Report on the Inquiry into Home Ownership' (December 2016).

[116] National Consumer Credit Protection Act 2009 (Cth) s 6, sched 1 National Credit Code s 5(1).

[117] Ibid Ch 3.

[118] Jeannie Paterson, 'Knowledge and Neglect in Asset-Based Lending: When Is It Unconscionable or Unjust to Lend to a Borrower Who Cannot Repay' (2009) 20 *Journal of Banking and Finance Law and Practice* 1.

[119] Laker (n 105).

[120] Ibid 3, 4.

[121] Ibid 8, 9.

[122] APS 112 Capital Adequacy: Standardised Approach to Credit Risk, www.apra.gov.au/sites/default/files/prudential_standard_aps_112_capital_adequacy_-_standardised_approach_to_credit_risk_0_0.pdf; APS 113 Capital Adequacy: Internal Ratings-Based Approach to Credit Risk, www.apra.gov.au/sites/default/files/APS_113_January_2013.pdf; APS 220 Credit Quality, www.apra.gov.au/sites/default/files/draft_prudential_standard_aps_220_credit_risk_management_march_2019.pdf; APS 120 Securitisation, www.apra.gov.au/sites/default/files/aps_120_securitisation.pdf.

[123] Senate Economics References Committee, APRA's Prudential Framework for Housing Lending, Submission No 51 to the Senate Economics References Committee (1 April 2008), 2.

[124] Damon Kitney, 'ASIC to Get Tough on Credit Providers under New National Regime', *The Australian* (3 September 2010).

[125] ASIC Regulatory Guide 2009, 'Credit Licensing: Responsible Lending Conduct' (February 2010; revised June 2010, March 2011, February 2013, November 2014), http://asic.gov.au/regulatory-resources/find-a-document/regulatory-guides/rg-209-credit-licensing-responsible-lending-conduct/.

[126] National Consumer Credit Protection Act 2009 (Cth) ss 117 (1), 130(1).

[127] Ibid. Further inquiries and steps may be prescribed by regulation.

A proposed credit contract must be found unsuitable and cannot be entered into if the credit contract will not meet the objectives or requirements of the consumer or if the consumer could comply with the obligations under the contract (that is meet the repayments) only with 'substantial hardship'.[128]

Taken together, APRA supervision with the stick of higher capital adequacy requirements and new legislation administered by ASIC, along with the international demonstration of the consequences of lax lending standards, should have resulted in responsible lending. Instead there are problems in the way some lenders reach the statutory conclusion that credit is 'not unsuitable' and then proceed to lend. These include failing to take into account actual living expenses and relying instead on benchmark calculations;[129] failing to take into account the length of time to repay the principal on an interest-only home loan;[130] failure to take into account a borrower's insurance expenses required for a loan;[131] lenders relying on information from brokers rather than on the borrower;[132] relying on the Henderson Poverty Index or the Household Expenditure Measure (HEM) to assess living expenses for basic needs rather than inquiring about actual living expenses;[133] use of automated processes rather than making reasonable inquiries about a person's financial situation;[134] and completely inadequate forms to record expenses.[135]

APRA and ASIC have worked in tandem to regulate the home lending market, drawing on their special expertise. APRA has been credited with dealing with the potential housing bubble or at least 'taking the air out of what was looking like a pretty stretched balloon'.[136] The story of both regulators since 2013 shows APRA taking the first steps, which are then supported by ASIC, whose remit is to protect all borrowers, not just mortgagors.

In 2013 APRA began collecting more data on housing loan risks, including loan-to-value and loan-to-income ratios (LVRs and LIRs respectively).[137] A targeted review of loan serviceability standards showed most lenders used a net income surplus model; there was no standard method to assess interest rate and therefore loan serviceability buffers; lenders used either the Henderson Poverty Index or the Household Expenditure Measure to assess living expenses, which are limited to basic living and do not reflect actual expenses. There were policies to verify income but not debt commitments.[138]

In the next year, 2014, APRA was particularly active regarding residential mortgages. It sought assurances from the boards of large ADIs that they were actively monitoring housing loan portfolios and credit standards, and also did this in the subsequent year.[139] It stress-tested and

---

[128] National Consumer Credit Protection Act 2009 (Cth) ss 128, 118, 131.
[129] This was the case with 20 per cent of files from eleven lenders in 2015. ASIC Report 445, 'Interest-Only Home Loan Review' (2014).
[130] This applied to 40 per cent of files. Ibid.
[131] *Australian Securities and Investments Commission v Channic Pty Ltd (No 4)* [2016] FCA 1164.
[132] ASIC, 'ASIC Concerns Prompt Wide Bay to Review Lending Standards' (Media Release 15-013, 3 February 2015). This was primarily about the objectives and requirements of the borrower.
[133] ASIC, 'ASIC Concerns Prompt Bank of Queensland to Improve Lending Practices' (Media Release 15-125 MR, 25 May 2015); Royal Commission Final Report.
[134] ASIC, 'MR Westpac Pays $1 Million Following ASIC's Concerns about Credit Card Limit Practices' (Media Release 16-009, 20 January 2016).
[135] *Australian Securities and Investments Commission v Cash Store Pty Ltd* (in liquidation) [2014] FCA 926 [30]–[33].
[136] Alan Kohler, 'APRA Chief Can Take a Bow', *The Australian* (19 December 2017), 22.
[137] Standing Committee on Economics, Inquiry into Home Ownership (APRA Submission, June 2015), 3; APRA, *Insight* (Issue One, 2016).
[138] APRA, *Insight* (Issue Two, 2013), 41–54.
[139] Standing Committee on Economics (n 137) 3.

conducted a hypothetical borrower exercise with seventeen ADIs to benchmark different serviceability assessments, discovering that there was limited consistency in how loans were assessed for the maximum amount an ADI was willing to lend.[140] In November 2014 it issued Prudential Practice Guide APG 223 *Residential Mortgage Lending*.[141]

This activity culminated in a public December 2014 letter to all ADIs.[142] APRA stated that at this stage it did not intend to increase regulatory capital but would intensify supervision. The letter flagged higher risk lending indicated by LVRs and LIRs; growth in investor lending; and serviceability assessments and buffers. The letter suggested (but did not make a firm rule) that ADIs should not increase the number of investor loans by more than 10 per cent a year and that prudent serviceability would mean a 2 per cent buffer above the interest rate of the loan and the floor rate for this should be 7 per cent. This letter would lead to amendments to APG 223.[143] In November 2014, ASIC complemented APRA by issuing the replacement Regulatory Guide on Responsible Lending Conduct.[144]

APRA had said it would continue monitoring home lending risk in 2015.[145] In January, it issued Prudential Standard CPS 220 on the management of risk and in July 2015 increased capital adequacy for Australian residential mortgage exposures.[146] Again, ASIC complemented APRA. In August 2015 it issued a report on interest-only home loans and a year later another on mortgage brokers and interest-only home loans.[147] By the end of June 2016, investor loans slowed to a 5 per cent increase, but started to increase again. This compared with a rate of 11 per cent in 2015.[148] Interest-only loans were an international high of 40 per cent of all residential mortgage lending.[149] Both investors and owner-occupiers were taking out interest-only loans.[150]

The combined efforts of APRA and ASIC were not enough to address the build-up of risk. In March 2017, APRA issued another public letter to all ADIs,[151] and the revised APRA Practice Guide APG 223 was released.[152] The letter addressed interest-only loans, investor loans and serviceability metrics. APRA expected ADIs to take steps to comply with its expectations 'immediately'. It said that only 30 per cent of the total of newly originated residential mortgage loans could be interest-only; investor loans should be less than the earlier 10 per cent; there should be strict internal limits on interest-only lending at LVRs above 80 per cent; any interest-only lending at an LVR above 90 per cent should be scrutinised and justified and these should be no more than 10 per cent; serviceability metrics including interest rate and net income

---

[140] Ibid 3, 6. This was also conducted in 2015.
[141] APRA Prudential Practice Guide APG 223, Residential Mortgage Lending (5 November 2014). There have been ongoing revisions to this.
[142] Wayne Byres, Chairman APRA, 'Reinforcing Sound Residential Mortgage Lending Practices' (9 December 2014).
[143] The Final APG 223 was released in March 2017. On the consultation see Wayne Byres, 'Reinforcing Sound Residential Mortgage Lending Practices – Response to Consultation on Revised Prudential Practice Guide' (23 February 2017).
[144] ASIC, Regulatory Guide 209, Credit Licensing: Responsible Lending Conduct (November 2014).
[145] Byres (n 142).
[146] APRA, 'APRA Increases Capital Adequacy Requirements for Residential Mortgage Exposures under the Internal Ratings-Based Approach (Media Release MR 15-19, 20 July 2015); APRA Annual Report 15/16, 34.
[147] ASIC Report 445, Review of Interest-Only Home Loans (20 August 2015); ASIC Report 493, Review of Interest-Only Home Loans: Mortgage Brokers' Inquiries into Consumers' Requirements and Objectives (September 2016).
[148] APRA Annual Report 15/16, 35.
[149] Wayne Byres, Chairman APRA, 'Further Measures to Reinforce Sound Residential Mortgage Lending Practices', 31 March 2017.
[150] ASIC Report 445 Review of Interest-Only Home Loans, 20 August 2015, 23.
[151] Wayne Byres, Chairman APRA, 'Further Measures to Reinforce Sound Residential Mortgage Lending Practices' (31 March 2017).
[152] APRA Prudential Practice Guide APG 223, Residential Mortgage Lending (February 2017, released in March).

buffers, should be reviewed and set at 'appropriate levels for current conditions'.[153] The revised APG 223 reflected the requirements of the letter to ADIs in 2014 and 2017.[154] It set out serviceability parameters, stating that the use of a net income surplus model requires an income buffer; non-salary income such as rental income should be discounted by at least 20 per cent; there should be interest rate buffers and floors (a buffer of at least 2 per cent and a minimum floor interest rate of at least 7 per cent); estimation of living expenses should not rely solely on benchmarks; interest-only loans are not suitable for all; and a borrower's ability to repay principal and interest should be assessed over the actual repayment period.

Through its work on lending standards, APRA has come to consider the interests of individuals as well as the system. This is evident in speeches where the chairman indicated that in its work on home lending, APRA has also come to focus on actual lending practices and the conversations lenders have with borrowers.[155] This brings it closer to ASIC's remit to protect particular consumers. Concerns with serviceability dovetail with ASIC's concerns about suitability. ASIC's 2015 report on responsible lending and suitability of interest-only loans found potential breaches including affordability calculations that assumed the borrower had longer to repay the principal than they actually did, files with no evidence that the lender had considered if the interest-only loan met the borrower's requirements and reliance on benchmarks instead of the borrower's actual living expenses.[156] It also took regulatory steps to deal with mortgage fraud.[157] In 2017 ASIC began surveillance to identify brokers and lenders who recommended unsuitable, more expensive interest-only loans to borrowers.[158] It then moved to reviewing individual files.[159]

APRA and ASIC have cooperated to tackle the benchmark problem in calculating serviceability and suitability. In one of its hypothetical borrower exercises, APRA found out that the major difference in lenders was the use of the HEM benchmark to calculate living expenses, declared expenses or a more nuanced calculation. APRA said the basic HEM was too simplistic, yet half of ADIs were still using it.[160] ASIC has also targeted the use of benchmarks for living expenses in the 'not unsuitable' calculation.[161] Its unsuccessful litigation against Westpac alleging unsuitable interest-only home loans revolved around the use of HEM and an automated system to calculate the net monthly surplus and automatic loan approvals. The HEM was scaled by location, dependants and marital status but not by income. There was no use of declared living expenses which were higher than the benchmark.[162]

Together, ASIC and APRA have reported improvements in home lending for the system and for borrowers. In October 2017, ASIC announced that major banks had reduced interest-only

---

[153] Byres (n 151).

[154] APRA Prudential Practice Guide APG 223 (n 152) 12, cl 32, cl 33.

[155] Byres (n 108).

[156] ASIC Report 445 (n 150).

[157] Eg, ASIC, 'Former Aussie Home Loans Mortgage Broker Permanently Banned by ASIC' (Media Release 17-016 MR, 27 January 2017). At this point ASIC had investigated over a hundred instances of fraud, brought fourteen prosecutions and gained twelve convictions. It has also banned sixty individuals and firms from the market: Kell (n 91).

[158] ASIC, 'ASIC Announces Further Measures to Promote Responsible Lending in the Home Loan Sector' (Media Release 17-095, 3 April 2017).

[159] ASIC, 'ASIC Update on Interest-Only Home Loans' (Media Release 17-341, 11 October 2017).

[160] Heidi Richards, APRA, 'A Prudential Approach to Mortgage Lending' (Macquarie University Financial Risk Day, 18 March 2016), 7, 8.

[161] See *Australian Securities and Investments Commission v Channic Pty Ltd* (No 4) [2016] FCA 1174 in a different loan context.

[162] *Australian Securities and Investments Commission v Westpac Banking Corporation (Liability Trial)* [2019] FCA 1244.

lending by $4.5 billion; however, other lenders had increased such lending. There was also a significant reduction in interest-only lending to owner-occupiers.[163] Investor lending slowed from 2014, and strengthened serviceability tests have introduced a price difference for owner-occupiers repaying principal and interest and investors taking out interest-only loans.[164] Competition has abated and hunting market share, which put downward pressure on lending standards, has reduced.[165] Yet both high household indebtedness and non-performing loans are trending upwards.[166]

In 2018, the Financial Services Royal Commission, making front-page news day after day, held the attention of all those interested in financial sector regulation. It is worth summarising some of its recommendations for home lending and mortgage broking as these reflect on any deficits in the combined efforts of APRA and ASIC. First, it did not recommend any change to the suitability obligation that informs home lending.[167] It did note that using a benchmark such as the HEM as a proxy for household expenditure in assessing suitability did not amount to verification.[168] The Financial Services Royal Commission identified ' greed' and commissions as a source of consumer detriment and it recommended that in connection with home lending, the law should be amended to require mortgage brokers to act in the best interest of borrowers; and any fee to brokers should be paid by the borrower, not the lender.[169] Further, licensees should have an obligation to report misconduct by mortgage brokers,[170] and all the recommendations of the Sedgwick Review should be implemented.[171] Some of the Financial Services Royal Commission recommendations suggest convergence rather than a complementary role for ASIC and APRA. An instance is that APRA should include misconduct in its guidance on sound management of remuneration,[172] and assess the cultural drivers of misconduct as part of its supervision process.[173] ASIC, for its part, should adopt a stronger approach to enforcement.[174] Part of this recommendation rebuts the convergence argument as ASIC should keep its enforcement staff at a distance from regulated entities, thus becoming less like APRA.[175] However, in favour of the argument, ASIC announced it had embedded non-enforcement staff with regulated entities, in a 'close and continuing monitoring' programme of supervision not unlike APRA.[176]

18.5 CONCLUSION

The Financial Services Royal Commission identified significant areas of consumer detriment. We will not know how effective the Twin Peaks of APRA and ASIC have been in protecting all

---

[163] ASIC Media Release 17-341 (n 159).

[164] Wayne Byres, Chairman APRA, 'Prudential Perspectives on the Property Market' (Remarks at CEDA's 2017 NSW Property Market Outlook, Sydney, 28 April 2017).

[165] Ibid.

[166] Byres (n 108)2, chart 1; 5, chart 6. In 2020 ADIs responded to covid 19 with loan repayment deferrals. These have been decreasing with those still in deferral in a higher risk category. APRA Insight, No 4 Dec 2 2020.

[167] Financial Services Royal Commission Final Report, Vol 1 2019 Recommendation 1.1, at 20.

[168] Ibid 56.

[169] Ibid Recommendation 1.2, Recommendation 1.3, at 20.

[170] Sedgewick Review (n 99); Financial Services Royal Commission Final Report (n 167) Recommendation 1.6, at 21.

[171] Ibid Recommendation 5.5, at 36.

[172] Ibid Recommendations 5.1, 5.2, 5.3, at 35.

[173] Ibid Recommendation 5.7, at 37.

[174] Ibid Recommendation 6.2, at 37.

[175] Ibid Recommendation 6.2, at 38.

[176] This began in October 2018. James Shipton, 'A Speech by James Shipton, ASIC Chair, Conduct Regulator's Address' (AFR Banking and Wealth Summit, Sydney, Australia, 27 March 2019).

consumers until the next downturn and if the stretched balloon becomes a bubble and bursts. There has been a turn from a focus on keeping promises to a focus on making suitable promises for all financial products including credit. This is in part a response to perceptions of risk in the system and a move away from a culture that fostered competition for short-term gains, driven by incentive systems that could result in conflicts between individuals in institutions wanting commissions and individuals seeking financial products. This chapter has explored this in the context of home lending where the build-up of risk was identified some years ago and addressed first by APRA and complemented, especially in the areas of interest-only loans and understanding commission payments, by ASIC. This reached a crescendo in the Financial Services Royal Commission. Each regulator understands its own mandate and although, unlike ASIC, APRA does not have a specific consumer protection remit, it understands the link between systemic risk and instability and the impact on consumers. ASIC, slower to address the culture of financial services firms and bring home lenders to account for breaching the law on unsuitable loans, is now engaged in litigation. If the culture debate is more than a shift in regulatory language and does have potential to leverage change in financial institutions, the convergence on this question by ASIC and APRA, which both address institutional norms and behaviour that ultimately put consumers and institutions at risk, will be beneficial. So will the renewed attention to enforcement. The different regulatory perspectives of the peaks, even if brought together, do not provide perfect consumer protection, but may be trending in the right direction. Both regulators have recognised risks and may prevent the pond from boiling over.

19

Twin Peaks

How Should Macrocultures Be Regulated?

Patrick McConnell

19.1 INTRODUCTION

This chapter looks at 'Twin Peaks' not from the perspective of distinct supervisory entities with reasonably well-defined responsibilities, as that is covered elsewhere in this book, but from the perspective of the supervision of a concept that must be considered by both 'peaks' – that of 'culture' and, in particular, 'macroculture'.

While the need to regulate 'conduct risk' is recognised within the name of, for example, the Financial Conduct Authority (FCA) in the United Kingdom, the Financial Sector Conduct Authority (FSCA) in South Africa and within the mandate of the Australian Securities and Investments Commission (ASIC) in Australia, it remains an ill-defined concept. For example, the FCA does not define the concept ('you will know it when you see it') and ASIC provides a wide-ranging definition[1] that has proved difficult to apply and to use in practice.[2]

Conduct supervisors have concluded that, in order to fulfil their mandate to supervise conduct risk, it is necessary to understand the influence of 'culture' in general, and 'risk culture' in particular, within the institutions that they supervise. At the same time, on the other peak, prudential supervisors have also identified that 'risk culture' has an important influence on the taking and management of risks other than conduct risks, such as credit risks. However, there appears to be little agreement between conduct and prudential regulators as to what exactly 'culture' and 'risk culture' mean, never mind how these complex concepts should be measured and manipulated. This chapter will expand on some definitions of these concepts from various regulators and point out the difficulties of measuring how culture influences conduct and, importantly, misconduct by individual staff.

In addition to these concepts, the chapter focuses on another set of cultures that appear to influence conduct, and importantly misconduct, by staff in financial institutions – that of 'industry culture', one of a number of so-called macrocultures.

---

[1] ASIC, 'Market Supervision Update Issue 57' (2015), defines 'Conduct risk' as 'the risk of inappropriate, unethical or unlawful behaviour on the part of an organisation's management or employees. Such conduct can be caused by deliberate actions or may be inadvertent and caused by inadequacies in an organisation's practices, frameworks or education programmes. Conduct risk can have significant ramifications for an organisation, its shareholders, clients, customers, counterparties and the financial services industry'. http://asic.gov.au/about-asic/corporate-publications/newsletters/asic-market-supervision-update/asic-market-supervision-update-previous-issues/market-supervison-update-issue-57/.

[2] See ASIC, 'REP 474 – Culture, Conduct and Conflicts of Interest in Vertically Integrated Businesses in the Funds-Management Industry' (2016), http://asic.gov.au/regulatory-resources/find-a-document/reports/rep-474-culture-conduct-and-conflicts-of-interest-in-vertically-integrated-businesses-in-the-funds-management-industry/.

Regulation of financial institutions has tended to focus on supervision of the individual firm, on the assumption that staff within a firm make commercial decisions always, and only, according to the policies set by the firm's management. However, several high-profile financial scandals, such as financial benchmark manipulation,[3] have shown that staff, in different business lines and in different jurisdictions, have engaged in misconduct with like-minded individuals in other firms or have copied unethical or unlawful practices from individuals in other firms. The chapter will give examples of these so-called 'systemic operational risk' events.[4]

The assumption that staff will always operate within strict control policies and processes is a hangover from the assumption that 'self-regulation' will be sufficient to manage systemic risks in the financial system. Such a perspective assumes that the financial behemoths that were created during the last quarter of the twentieth century would, somehow overnight, be brought under the control of a small group of individuals – the board of the conglomerate. But the constituents of these global corporations originated in different countries, with unique national cultures, and from different financial sectors, with different operating models. It would be, and was, naïve to assume that absolute control could be mandated and enforced from a remote centre. It would be equally naïve to assume that an individual could move, or be headhunted, from one firm to another and then immediately conform to new controls, forgetting and cutting themselves off from contacts with their previous colleagues. But these naïve assumptions were made by institutions and by regulators, to the detriment of the financial system.

Before considering the concepts of 'culture', 'risk culture' and 'macroculture' it is worth pondering this question: Will a trader who is employed by a Swiss bank to trade interest rate products in Tokyo have less/more in common with their ex-colleagues trading in the same markets in London than, say, with a retail bank manager working for the same bank in Basel, Switzerland? Why would one believe that merely changing the logo on a person's business card would make them, almost overnight, forget their ex-colleagues and the business practices that they previously shared with them? More to the point in this instance, why would supervisors believe that individuals would *always* change the habits of a working lifetime and would automatically embrace a whole new set of controls when moving from one firm to another? Human nature is just not like that, as is shown by the scandals documented here.

The chapter concludes by pointing out that the 'Twin Peaks' are not independent but sit on shared foothills, beset by common problems, in this case the need to understand the various 'cultures' of the individual firms that both peaks supervise. It makes little sense for one regulator to measure and try to 'influence' cultures in one way in a firm if another supervisor uses different definitions, measures and influencing mechanisms for the same firm. At the very least, there is a need for regulators to come to a shared understanding of problems that they have in common, such as how to influence the cultures of firms that they supervise. The chapter proposes a novel approach to addressing this quite complex problem.

19.2 REGULATORS AND CULTURE

Regulators' interest in 'culture' is relatively recent, emerging as an important issue after the Global Financial Crisis (GFC). It became obvious that prior to the crisis some (in fact many)

---

[3] See, for example, P. J. McConnell, 'Standardised Measurement Approach – Is Comparability Attainable?' (2017) 12(1) *Journal of Operational Risk* 71–110.

[4] Ibid.

financial firms had behaved badly, to the dismay of regulators such as Federal Reserve Chairman Alan Greenspan:[5]

> I made a mistake in presuming that the self-interests of organisations, specifically banks and others, were such that they were best capable of protecting their own shareholders and their equity in the firms ... Those of us who have looked to the self-interest of lending institutions to protect shareholders' equity (myself especially) are in a state of shocked disbelief.

Until the crisis, Greenspan and other regulators had assumed that banking organisations, large and small, would, as coherent entities, behave rationally in their self-interest and that any deviations would be noticed and be policed by the market. Greenspan's disbelief was not so much that an individual firm could behave badly, since that had happened frequently in the past, but that market participants had not punished such aberrant behaviour. In fact, as pointed out in the official US enquiry into the GFC, when other firms saw that a particular bad behaviour was profitable, they often joined in.

> We conclude there was a systemic breakdown in accountability and ethics. In our economy, we expect businesses and individuals to pursue profits, at the same time that they produce products and services of quality and conduct themselves well. Unfortunately – as has been the case in past speculative booms and busts – we witnessed an erosion of standards of responsibility and ethics that exacerbated the financial crisis.[6]

Following the GFC, several financial regulators and industry bodies identified that banking practices had been disastrously deficient throughout the sector. In particular, the then head of the UK Financial Services Authority (FSA), Hector Sants, noted that the GFC 'exposed significant shortcomings in the governance and risk management of firms and the culture and ethics which underpin them. This is not principally a structural issue. It is a failure in behaviour, attitude and in some cases, competence'.[7]

In a 2009 report, the influential Institute of Finance[8] (IIF) identified that '[t]he global financial crisis of the last two years revealed various weaknesses in the practices of much of the financial services industry. These included inadequate risk and liquidity management, misaligned compensation policies, limited disclosure, and lax underwriting standards'.[9] The IIF highlighted the role played by 'culture' in such misbehaviour, and in particular 'risk culture': 'it became apparent that *risk culture played an extremely important role* in determining whether firms were more or less successful in managing their risks during the crisis. *Culture is therefore essential to the efficacy of any future risk management recommendations*'.[10]

---

[5] Chairman Greenspan in testimony to the Oversight Committee of the US House of Representatives, for example, www.washingtonpost.com/wp-dyn/content/article/2008/10/23/AR2008102300193.html.

[6] Financial Crisis Inquiry Commission, 'Final Report of the National Commission on the Causes of the Financial and Economic Crisis in the United States' (Washington, January 2011), www.govinfo.gov/content/pkg/GPO-FCIC/pdf/ GPO-FCIC.pdf.

[7] H. Sants, 'Can Culture Be Regulated?' (Speech at Mansion House Conference on Values and Trust, Financial Services Authority, London, 4 October 2010), www.fsa.gov.uk.

[8] The Institute of International Finance (IIF) is an organisation funded by the financial services industry and describes itself as 'the leading voice for the financial services industry on global regulatory issues'. See www.iif.com/about.

[9] Institute of International Finance, 'Reform in the Financial Services Industry: Strengthening Practices for a More Stable System' (IIF Steering Committee on Implementation (SCI), 2009), www.iif.com.

[10] Ibid. Emphasis added.

While it is obvious why conduct regulators should be interested in 'culture', it is not so obvious why prudential regulators would consider culture as part of their supervisory remits. The Australian Prudential Regulation Authority (APRA) puts the case thus:

> Therefore, while conduct and prudential regulators both have a legitimate interest in cultures within financial institutions, their interest stems from different underlying objectives. ASIC's focus on culture is from the perspective of its mandate as a conduct regulator, and ensuring fair outcomes for customers and investors. ASIC is primarily interested in culture because it is a driver of conduct in the firms that make up its regulated population. APRA's focus on risk culture reflects its prudential mandate – that as a result of undesirable behaviours and attitudes towards risk-taking and risk management, the viability of an APRA-regulated financial institution itself might be threatened, and this may in turn jeopardise both the institution's financial obligations to depositors, policyholders or fund members, and financial stability.[11]

In summary, a 'bad' culture can lead to bad decision-making, especially bad lending decisions, which may jeopardise first a bank and then, if the bank is systemically important, the banking system itself. As a consequence, APRA identifies that cooperation with the other 'peak' is necessary 'given this common area of interest, conduct and prudential regulators need to work collaboratively on risk culture-related matters'.[12]

Table 19.1 summarises some definitions of 'culture' and 'risk culture' in two 'Twin Peaks' jurisdictions, Australia and the United Kingdom. As the changes to the Twin Peaks model are still being finalised in South Africa, there are few definitive statements on these topics from the new regulators, other than a desire to harmonise with the Basel III definition, which is included in the table.[13]

As can be seen from Table 19.1, there is little unanimity on the definitions of these concepts within or across jurisdictions. Some are informal (hardly definitions at all), such as ASIC's 'mindset of the organisation',[14] while some are more formal, such as APRA's 'a system of shared values'.[15] Cause and effect, meanwhile, are viewed from polar opposite positions, such as FCA's 'Culture is an *outcome* of many elements of the behaviour of institutions',[16] as against ASIC's '[Culture] *directs* how an organisation and its staff think, make decisions and actually behave'.[17] The definitions all, however, appear to take a hierarchical and absolutist perspective, assuming that:

- Culture is a top-down activity, where a board is *the* pivotal influence on culture, and by extension, on staff behaviours, in particular conduct towards customers.
- The board (through their managerial actions) can actually influence the behaviour of all staff throughout an organisation.

---

[11] APRA, 'Risk Culture, Information Paper' (October 2016), www.apra.gov.au.

[12] Ibid.

[13] See Daniel Mminele, Deputy Governor of the South African Reserve Bank, 'Conduct and Culture in the Banking and Financial Sectors' (Opening Address at the G30 Forum on Banking Conduct and Culture, Pretoria, 18 February 2016), http://www.bis.org/review/r160229c.pdf.

[14] Cathie Armour, Commissioner, Australian Securities and Investments Commission, 'Keynote Address: Regulatory Perspective on Conduct Risk, Culture and Governance' (Speech at Risk Australia Conference, Sydney, Australia, 18 August 2016), www.asic.gov.au.

[15] APRA (n 11).

[16] Andrew Bailey, Chief Executive of the FCA, 'Culture in Financial Institutions: It's Everywhere and Nowhere' (Speech at the HKMA Annual Conference for Independent Non-Executive Directors 16 March 2017).

[17] Armour (n 14).

TABLE 19.1. *Definitions of culture and risk culture by some Twin Peaks regulators.*

Regulator	Definition(s) of culture and risk culture
Australia	
Conduct regulator – ASIC[1]	Culture: 'Culture reflects the underlying "mindset of an organisation". It directs how an organisation and its staff think, make decisions and actually behave. Poor culture can be a driver of poor conduct. In a financial services firm, culture is an important driver of outcomes for investors and financial consumers.'
Prudential regulator – APRA[2]	Culture: 'a system of shared values (that define what is important) and norms that define appropriate attitudes and behaviours for organisational members (how to feel and behave)'. Risk culture: 'the norms and traditions of behaviour of individuals and of groups within an organisation that determine the way in which they identify, understand, discuss, and act on the risks the organisation confronts and the risks it takes'.
United Kingdom	
Conduct regulator – FCA[3]	Culture: 'Culture in financial institutions: it's everywhere and nowhere … Culture is an outcome of many elements of the behaviour of institutions, but also has an important normative part, namely of what good looks like. Cultural outcomes are the product of a wide range of contributory forces: the structure and effectiveness of management and governance, including the well-used phrase "the tone from the top"; and the incentives they create; the quality and effectiveness of risk management; and the willingness of people throughout the organisation to enthusiastically adopt and adhere to the tone from the top.'
Prudential regulator – PRA[4]	Risk culture: 'The PRA expects firms to have a culture that supports prudent management. The PRA does not have any "right culture" in mind when making its assessment; rather it focuses on whether boards and management clearly understand the circumstances in which the firm's viability would be under question, whether accepted orthodoxies are challenged, and whether action is taken to address risks on a timely basis. In particular, the PRA wants to be satisfied that designated risk management and control functions carry real weight within firms.'
BASEL Committee	
Corporate governance principles[5]	Risk culture: 'A bank's norms, attitudes and behaviours related to risk awareness, risk-taking and risk management, and controls that shape decisions on risks. Risk culture influences the decisions of management and employees during the day-to-day activities and has an impact on the risks they assume.'

[1] Cathie Armour, Commissioner, Australian Securities and Investments Commission, 'Keynote Address: Regulatory Perspective on Conduct Risk, Culture and Governance' (Speech at Risk Australia Conference, Sydney, Australia, 18 August 2016), www.asic.gov.au.
[2] Ibid.
[3] Andrew Bailey, Chief Executive of the FCA, 'Culture in Financial Institutions: It's Everywhere and Nowhere' (Speech at the HKMA Annual Conference for Independent Non-Executive Directors, 16 March 2017).
[4] PRA does not define 'culture' or 'risk culture' but describes what a good culture might look like. See PRA, 'The Prudential Regulation Authority's Approach to Banking Supervision' (2016), www.bankofengland.co.uk.
[5] Basel Committee on Banking Supervision, 'Guidelines CORPORATE GOVERNANCE PRINCIPLES for Banks' (2015),.

- Staff throughout an organisation will behave as directed by the board because, as ASIC notes, culture reflects 'the willingness[18] of people throughout the organisation to enthusiastically adopt and adhere to the tone from the top'.[19]

[18] This ASIC perspective immediately attributes any transgressions to the lack of willingness and enthusiasm of staff, rather than on management, who may not communicate the 'tone' correctly, or may send conflicting signals.
[19] Armour (n 14).

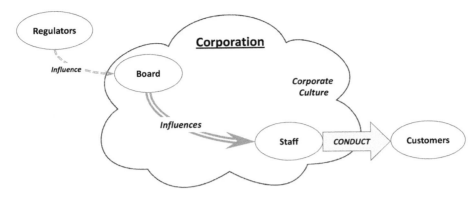

FIGURE 19.1. Corporate culture: influences.

- Because the board drives 'culture', the results will be homogenous throughout an organisation, or at least generally consistent.

Unfortunately, organisational theory and empirical research do not support such broad assumptions.[20] In some circumstances, the assumptions may hold but this one size, of regulatory view most definitely, does not fit all situations, as discussed later.

Figure 19.1 shows a model of culture and conduct, based on similar definitions of culture by the IIF and the Financial Stability Board (FSB), and widely accepted by regulators. In the diagram, there is a corporation led by a board that, through 'corporate culture', directly influences 'staff' as to their 'conduct' with 'customers'. In turn, a board is 'influenced' by its regulators.

In Figure 19.1, the influences exerted by a board are many, formal and informal, including:

1. remuneration: in particular, salaries and bonuses (performance and volume-based), recognition (such as corporate titles) and status (formal and informal acknowledgement of worth, such as office location and furnishings);
2. organisation: in particular, placement of staff within business units and business lines, with varying levels of status in the corporate hierarchy and the relative placement of business and support organisations within the corporate hierarchy;
3. processes and controls: in particular, the promulgation of formal corporate policies and operating procedures, and the controls put in place to ensure compliance with these policies (such as the role and status of audit, compliance and risk management functions);
4. recruitment: in particular, the types of personalities and individual competences who are hired as staff, the relative remuneration that they receive, and the training that they are given to do their jobs and their progress in the company;
5. leadership: in particular, the visibility of directors and senior executives in promoting certain aspects of corporate culture.

These influences are often referred to by regulators as 'tone from the top', indicating that it is the leadership at the 'top' that has an all-pervasive influence on staff throughout the entire firm.[21]

---

[20] P. J. McConnell, 'Risk Culture: A Framework for Systemically Important Banks' (2013) 3 *Journal of Risk and Governance* 23–68.

[21] See, for example, APRA (n 11), which uses definitions of 'risk culture' from Institute of International Finance (n 9).

And it is assumed that the 'tone', though not well defined, will influence all staff to behave in the way that the 'top' has determined, in particular as regards the conduct of staff towards customers. In this model, if a member of staff does not react as desired to the tone and the influences of the board, however opaque, then it is the staff member who is deficient, and a so-called 'bad apple' or a 'rogue trader'.

This is a hierarchical, almost feudal model, in which decrees from the top, however vague and self-contradictory, will be followed come what may, because those at the top are assumed to know best what is good for the firm and, by extension, individual staff members. It is a model promoted by business schools and in the 'cult of the CEO',[22] whose genius, heretofore disguised in a lower role, will lead the organisation to bigger and better things, provided that everyone else falls in line.[23] In fact, with this characterisation, regulators have traded one difficult concept, 'culture', with another imprecise idea, 'tone' – the difference being that there is a long history of research into 'culture' but not into 'tone'.

In the financial world, such a simplistic view of corporate culture might apply for founder-led firms in niche markets, such as hedge funds, and might also be applicable to a few larger firms, due to a particularly talented leader. However, the view is very unlikely to apply to *all* huge multinational corporations that are the consequences of multiple acquisitions in different markets and in different countries. For example, after a period of intense acquisition in the late twentieth century, and subsequent disposals following the GFC, the largest German bank, Deutsche Bank, employed almost 100,000 staff in seventy countries around the world in 2016.[24] It is a huge organisation and is designated as one of the most important (that is, riskiest) of the 'Systemically Important Financial Institutions' (SIFI) by the FSB.[25] As the history of the scandals that have had an impact on Deutsche indicate, particularly in its UK and US acquisitions,[26] it has proved impossible to impose a single culture on such diverse subcultures from the distance of its headquarters in Frankfurt.

Figure 19.1 also shows 'regulators' influencing the board, which is typically achieved through:

1 principles and rules: the formal articulation of high-level 'principles' of business conduct that firms are required to adhere to, and specific rules, particularly as regards regulatory reporting;
2 strictures: in particular fines and demands for remediation, or formal regulatory interventions, such as Deferred Prosecution Agreements (DPAs);
3 moral suasion: the informal, often behind-the-scenes, pressure by regulators on the boards and management of regulated firms. In some cases, pressure is exerted by a regulator publishing semi-formal communications, such as a 'Dear CEO letter',[27] using the public to help to pressure recalcitrant firms.

[22] See, among others, M. McArdle, 'The Cult of the CEO', *The Atlantic* (February 2008), www.theatlantic.com/business/archive/2008/02/the-cult-of-the-ceo/2849/.
[23] An example in banking is that of Richard Fuld, last CEO/chairman of Lehman Brothers, whose cult-like status in Lehman, based on his 'heroic' work in saving the bank following the destruction of its New York offices on 9/11, blinded his colleagues to the fatal flaws in his strategy, which resulted in the bankruptcy of the firm. See P. J. McConnell, 'Lehman – A Case of Strategic Risk' (2012) 34 *Journal of Financial Transformation* 51–62.
[24] See 2016 Deutsche Bank annual report at www.db.com.
[25] Financial Stability Board, '2016 List of Global Systemically Important Banks (G-SIBs)' (2016), www.fsb.org.
[26] P. J. McConnell, 'Behavioural Risks at the Systemic Level' (2017) 12(3) *Journal of Operational Risk* 31–63.
[27] See, for example, the 'Dear CEO' letter issued by the UK Prudential Regulation Authority (PRA) on contingency planning for Brexit, www.bankofengland.co.uk/pra/Documents/about/letter070417.pdf.

While it is obvious that regulatory rules, strictures and moral suasion will have some impact on a firm, and often its shareholders, it is not obvious how such influences will have an impact upon corporate culture, and how much they will directly have an impact on staff. Of course, a fine, particularly a large one, will cause a board and senior and mid-level managers and staff to pause and change some of their working practices, but will a fine have an impact on the corporate culture in the longer term? For example, the huge fines incurred in the London Interbank Offered Rate (LIBOR) scandal, described in Section 19.6, certainly caused interest rate traders across the industry to change their practices, but interestingly their foreign exchange (FX) trading colleagues, several desks along on the same trading floors, continued to manipulate markets until that misbehaviour too was discovered.

19.3 CULTURE

The cultural historian Raymond Williams noted that 'culture is one of the two or three most complicated words in the English language'.[28] 'Risk', too, is a complex concept that defies simple definition, and when the two terms are conjoined, as in 'risk culture', the concept becomes even more complex and difficult to come to terms with across a large organisation. Organisational theorists, such as Edgar Schein,[29] argue that because an organisation's culture is based on deep, often unconscious assumptions that are taken for granted in daily decision-making, it is difficult to identify, describe and change any culture.

As one would expect with an important topic that has been studied for many years, there are many definitions of 'culture'.[30] Schein, one of the pioneers of the study of 'organisational culture', noted that the concept had a 'fairly recent origin', when cross-cultural social psychology was applied to organisations. Building on insights from several social sciences, including anthropology, sociology, social psychology and organisational behaviour, Schein defined 'culture' as:

A pattern of basic assumptions, invented, discovered, or developed by a given group [organisation], as it learns to cope with its problems of external adaptation and internal integration, that has worked well enough to be considered valid and, therefore is to be taught to new members as the correct way to perceive, think, and feel in relation to those problems.[31]

In short, 'culture' is a 'learned response' to an organisation's environment. It is not something that can necessarily be dictated from above by a leader, but is an 'emergent phenomenon' which is continually adjusting to its changing environment.[32] Because it is partially a function of 'internal integration', management can, to some extent, manipulate organisational culture.

---

[28] See comment in Centre for Research on Socio-Cultural Change (CRSC), 'Written Evidence – Submission from Centre for Research on Socio-Cultural Change (S005)' (Parliamentary Commission on Banking Standards, London, September 2012), https://publications.parliament.uk/pa/jt201213/jtselect/jtpcbs/writev/banking/bs05.htm.

[29] See E. H. Schein, 'Organisational Culture' (1990) 45 *American Psychologist* 109–19, and E. H. Schein, *Organizational Culture and Leadership* (John Wiley, 2010).

[30] See, for example, M. Power, S. Ashby and T. Palermo, 'Risk Culture in Financial Organizations' (London School of Economics and Political Science, 2013), http://eprints.lse.ac.uk/67978/1/Palermo_Rsik%20culture%20research%20report_2016.pdf.

[31] Schein, *Organizational Culture* (n 29) at 17.

[32] K. A. Baker, 'Organisational Culture' in N. Taher (ed) *Organizational Culture: An Introduction* (ICFAI University Press, 2002).

However, how best to do so remains a matter of considerable debate,[33] since it means changing the 'basic assumptions' of all staff.

The approach of Schein and others, based as it is on observing humans in action in organisations, has been termed the 'anthropological' approach to organisational culture. This view has not gone unchallenged, most particularly from so-called scientific rationalists, such as the organisational theorist Geert Hofstede, who suggests that culture is just 'one aspect of the component parts of an organisation, a facet that can be measured, manipulated and changed'.[34] The scientific rationalist paradigm posits that organisational culture is primarily a set of values and beliefs articulated by leaders to guide the organisation, translated by managers and employees into appropriate behaviours and reinforced through rewards and sanctions. This top-down perspective is, of course, similar to that taken by the IIF, FSB and the Basel Committee and relies on *all* assumptions and actions being transparent, and always having the desired effect – that is, causes and effects are predictable.[35] For example, it assumes that there are no conflicts of interest between corporate directives (often articulated as 'strategic objectives'), such as 'profits should be maximised' and 'customers should be treated fairly', especially if the culture visibly rewards achievement of one measurable objective (such as profit) over another, which is difficult to measure (such as 'fairness').

However, what if the manipulation of culture is not mechanistic and predictable, but is, as the 'anthropological' school contends, situation specific – that is, contingent on the firm's business environment and structure – and will change as external and internal factors change?

Without an understanding of the often hidden assumptions underlying a particular culture, any changes to a prevailing culture (such as those at a large international bank) will be difficult to make stick. And because it is extremely difficult to influence 'culture' in any organisation, it will be even more difficult to regulate it from outside. As the FCA concluded: 'it needs to be recognised, however, that a supervisor's ability to assess true commitment to appropriate values (as against the ability to say the right words) is highly imperfect'.[36]

In a seminal book on organisational culture, Quinn and Cameron argued that there are four main 'organisational types' that are based on a set of core values on which judgments are made, and which are differentiated by having an 'internal' or an 'external' focus:[37]

1 *Hierarchy*: an 'internally focused' organisation that values stability and control, formalised structures and rules and internal efficiency, with a focus on the organisation itself, and is often characterised as a 'bureaucratic' culture.
2 *Clan*: an 'internally focused' organisation that values collaboration, participation and teamwork with a focus on individuals, and often characterised as a 'family' culture.
3 *Market*: an 'externally focused' organisation that values competition, market share and profitability, with a focus on transactions with customers, and often characterised as a 'results-oriented' culture.

---

[33] L. Willcoxson and B. Millett, 'The Management of Organisational Culture' (2000) 3 *Australian Journal of Management and Organisational Behaviour* 91–9.
[34] G. Hofstede, *Cultures and Organizations: Software of the Mind* (McGraw-Hill, 1991), 516.
[35] McConnell (n 20).
[36] Submission of the Financial Services Authority to the Parliamentary Commission on Banking Standards (6 December 2012), https://publications.parliament.uk/pa/jt201213/jtselect/jtpcbs/writev/banking/bs38.htm.
[37] R. E. Quinn and K. S. Cameron, *Diagnosing and Changing Organizational Culture: Based on the Competing Values Framework* (John Wiley, 2011).

4 *Adhocracy*: an 'externally focused' organisation that values innovation, risk taking and creativity, with a focus on creating new products for customers, and often characterised as an 'entrepreneurial' culture.

In these different organisational types, 'form follows function' in that each type is structured, or more often adapts its structure, to service the needs of a particular customer base. For example, in banking a 'hierarchal' type might be typified by retail banking credit card operations or a mortgage processing unit, with a focus on high-volume, efficient, cost-effective services aimed predominantly at a mass market. On the other hand, a 'clan' type might be typified by a research group or audit, compliance or risk management functions, where 'customers' are predominantly other internal groups. In banking, a 'market'-type organisation might be, as the name suggests, typified by market trading units and sales functions, driven by profitability. Lastly, an 'adhocracy' might be typified by a mergers and acquisitions (M&A) business unit with teams that come together to work on specific transactions.

It is not difficult to see that today's large financial institutions will normally consist of all of these types of organisations, from investment banking (for example, trading and corporate finance) to retail banking (from payments to mortgages), wealth management (pensions and investments) and support organisations (such as information technology). Each of these different types of organisation will coexist in the firms at the same time, and to operate effectively they will have to organise themselves internally to deliver their very different missions. In other words, there will be different 'cultures' that arise naturally from the interactions of these different subcultures with the outside world.

And even within a business unit, there may be different sub-organisations with different 'cultures'.[38] For example, a FX business line will obviously be dominated by 'market'-focused traders and sales staff but there will also be a 'back office' operations unit which is focused on efficient trade processing, thus tending towards the 'hierarchical' model. In addition, there will be market research units, with a 'clan'-like culture, and in larger banks there will be specialist groups focused on creating derivatives products, tailored to customers' needs ('adhocracy').

In large, international, 'universal banking' corporations, there will be multiple organisational units that have different foci, especially as regards the types of customers that they engage, and hence subcultures will emerge naturally to operate effectively in these different situations.[39] Even if a board wished to do so, it would make little economic sense to enforce one single overriding 'culture', which would have to be a mish-mash of the natural cultures, onto these very different businesses. It would be a sure way to hamstring staff, to lose money and, eventually, staff.

It should be noted that Trompenaars and Hampden-Turner also developed a model of organisational culture which identified four main organisational archetypes based on the two dimensions of 'management control' (centralised versus decentralised) and 'management style' (informal versus formal).[40] However, whether one prefers one organisational model over the other, the central point remains that organisational sub-units have very different ways of dealing with the outside world and hence will have different 'cultures'.

But the concept of 'culture' is not limited to the organisational context. Schein identified four levels of culture, which he described as:[41]

---

38 P. J. McConnell, *Systemic Operational Risk* (Risk Books, 2015).
39 Ibid.
40 F. Trompenaars and C. Hampden-Turner, *Riding the Waves of Culture: Understanding Diversity in Global Business* (Nicholas Brealey, 3rd ed, 2012).
41 Schein, *Organizational Culture and Leadership* (n 29).

1 *Macrocultures*: nations, ethnic and religious groups, and occupations that exist globally, such as 'bankers'.

2 *Organisational cultures*: private corporations such as banks, and public, non-profit, government organisations.

3 *Subcultures*: occupational groups within organisations, such as 'accountants'.

4 *Microcultures*: microsystems within or outside organisations, such as call centres.

Of course, staff are influenced by all of these various levels of culture, but the influences that dominate will be specific in time and location. For example, during working hours staff will be influenced by the 'microculture' in their office – that is, the people they work with day to day, all day. Obviously, staff will also be influenced by the management of their particular business units, the 'subculture' that determines their worth. And, of course, they will be influenced by the 'culture' of the organisation that pays their wages. The industry in which they work and the country in which they live will also have an influence. Outside of work, however, the influences will be very different, usually based on family, friends, community and ethnicity.

Humans are adept at handling different cultural influences at different times and in different places. Children learn how to adapt to different situations as they grow up, learning that what may be acceptable at home may (or may not) be acceptable at school or work. The relative importance of any one cultural influence over another therefore changes with the situation and people subconsciously adapt their behaviours to deal with changing circumstances.

19.4 RISK CULTURE

Regulators have argued that they should not attempt to regulate 'culture' within the institutions that they supervise as different firms will have different cultures because they operate in different markets and have different business models.[42] For example, some firms will be more entrepreneurial than others. There can be no one-size-fits-all model of culture in a market-driven economy.

But what, *if anything*, can regulators regulate? This question has given rise to the concept of 'risk culture', which focuses on the activities that regulators are primarily interested in, that is, the management of risks in a financial institution.

The concept of 'risk culture' emerged post-GFC as it became obvious that regulation had to come to grips with 'culture'. The IIF, which it must be remembered is an industry body, funded by the largest banks, was very quickly out of the traps in making recommendations as to how to fix the problems that it had a hand in creating[43] – a case of the horse shutting the stable door before bolting? In its influential 2009 report, the IIF proposed a definition of 'risk culture' as 'the norms and traditions of behavior of individuals and of groups within an organisation that determine the way in which they identify, understand, discuss, and act on the risks the organisation confronts and the risks it takes'.[44]

The FSB and the Basel Committee reference this IIF definition as illustrated by the Basel definition in Table 19.1, which is similar but not identical, namely a bank's norms, attitudes and

---

[42] PRA, 'The Prudential Regulation Authority's Approach to Banking Supervision' (2016), www.bankofengland.co.uk.

[43] Institute of International Finance (n 8).

[44] Ibid. It can be argued that this is a definition of a 'risk management culture' rather than a 'risk culture' per se, since there may be risks that 'individuals and groups' do not recognise or do not act upon although they should. But the difference is less important than recognising that the definition is about something that can, to a degree, be measured. In this case, conformance with an institution's risk management policies and frameworks, and regulators' expectations for such policies.

behaviours related to risk awareness, risk-taking and risk management, and controls that shape decisions on risks. Specifically, the Basel definition uses the term 'bank's' rather than 'individuals and of groups within an organisation', which assumes a homogenous view of culture across an organisation.

While the influence of the IIF on regulation has been somewhat muted in the aftermath of the GFC, with many of its leading members being fined by regulators, nonetheless its definitions of key concepts in this area have been adopted by important regulators, such as the FSB,[45] and subsequently by national regulators, such as APRA.

Two points about the original IIF definitions are important. First, the formulation of the term 'risk culture' followed a survey of the issues that some of the largest members of the industry body considered to be important and is, as a result, self-interested.[46] Secondly, the survey elicited what the senior executives of these organisations, not the bulk of staff, considered to be important to their firms. 'Leadership from the top is therefore essential for a firm to be able to mould and adhere to a robust risk culture. . . . The implementation of an effective and pervasive risk culture has been a top priority for IIF members after the crisis.'[47]

As might be expected from the seniority of those responding to the survey, the perspective is hierarchical (central and pervasive), self-assured (clear and effective) and predictable (top priority). Certainly 'leadership' is important, but is it *the* (or even *a*) key driver of culture? Although evidence has emerged that 'leadership' is significant, the reality of 'culture' is more complex than the IIF reports and the regulators that base their thinking on IIF constructs and definitions believe. There is evidence that regulators may have taken a wrong turn, or at least unnecessarily narrowed their thinking, from the outset when considering this complex concept.

Figure 19.2 shows the concept of 'risk culture' within 'corporate culture' in a corporation. The board, in addition to influencing staff through corporate culture, as in Figure 19.1, exerts influence over staff through an additional layer of 'risk culture'. As defined by the IIF and FSB, 'risk culture' is homogenous and subject to manipulation by direction of the board and management, as in the Basel Committee definition in Table 19.1: 'risk culture influences the decisions of management and employees during the day-to-day activities and has an impact on the risks they assume'. It should be noted that, although this definition implies the primacy of 'tone from the top', it does allow that other (unnamed) factors could also have an 'impact' on the risks assumed. But this definition does not identify the strength of any impact on staff, relative to other influences. The perspective of these regulators is firmly in the 'scientific rationalist' camp of top-down control that is assumed to be effective across the organisation.

Interestingly, a comprehensive study of 'risk culture' in banking, undertaken by researchers at the London School of Economics (LSE), did not select or promote a definition of 'risk culture', which gives a clue as to the complexity of the concept: 'There have been many efforts to define risk culture and this multiplicity tells us something, namely that it is conceptually rather fuzzy.'[48] The research, which catalogued many different approaches to the topic, did however identify 'risk culture' as the trade-off(s) between 'risk taking' and 'risk control', with any firm being, at any

---

[45] In particular, Financial Stability Board, 'Guidance on Supervisory Interaction with Financial Institutions on Risk Culture – A Framework for Assessing Risk Culture' (2014), www.fsb.org.

[46] The survey, which is reported in IIF (n 8), describes the methodology. The survey was conducted through interviews with CEOs, CROs and CFOs (the CEOs were not involved in all of the interviews). The survey covered thirty of the largest banks in over twenty countries, across all the major geographic regions.

[47] Institute of International Finance No 10, AIII.2, 22, www.yumpu.com/en/document/read/6768363/reform-in-the-financial-services-industry-institute-of-international-.

[48] See Power, Ashby and Palermo (n 30).

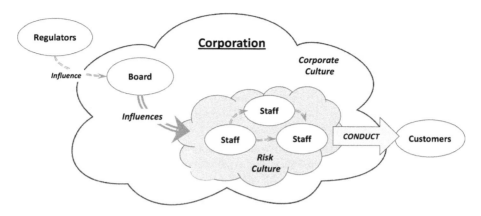

FIGURE 19.2. Risk culture: influences.

one time, somewhere on a continuum between the two. The researchers made three interesting prior assumptions (hypotheses) about risk culture, which were largely borne out by their literature research and the data collected:

- Risk culture is not a static thing but a continuous process, or processes, which repeat and renew themselves but may be subject to shocks.
- Risk culture will be a mixture of formal and informal processes. The former are easy to observe; the latter are harder to observe since they involve a myriad of small behaviours and habits which in aggregate constitute the state of risk culture at any one point in time.
- We do not assume either that an organisation has a single risk culture or that a risk culture may not be trans-organisational. Conceptually we would prefer to speak of 'risk cultures' which may be unevenly distributed within organisations (e.g. retail as compared with investment banking) or the financial industry as a whole (e.g. insurers as compared with banks).[49]

The LSE researchers are clearly not in the top-down 'rationalist' camp, but observe a 'bottom up' effect, describing 'a myriad of small behaviours and habits which, in aggregate, constitute the state of risk culture at any one point in time'. In line with their conclusion that risk culture is a continuum, the LSE researchers also concluded that it is hard to classify risk culture: 'In addition, both from our prior assumptions developed from desk research of practitioner and academic writings and from our data, it is clear that "good versus bad" risk culture is far too binary a view of what is at stake.'[50]

Researching risk culture in the field is extremely difficult, not least because it means attempting to observe the behaviours of individuals and groups in an organisation. It is a multidisciplinary activity that requires subject-matter experts in finance, psychology and organisational behaviour. One way to (begin to) study culture is to elicit the beliefs of the individuals involved here (bankers and insurers), always being aware that what people describe as their beliefs may not, in fact, be what they actually believe or, even if it is, may not result in the behaviours that they espouse. Schein notes that there is difference between values that are 'espoused' by an organisation (what they say they do, such as in advertising material) as against 'observed' values (what they actually do, such their behaviour to customers).[51]

---

[49] Ibid.
[50] Ibid.
[51] Schein, *Organizational Culture* (n 29) at 27.

To study such beliefs in the field, Sheedy and Griffin developed a survey questionnaire on the subject of risk culture, which was completed by over 30,000 staff in 270 business units in seven major commercial banks, headquartered in Australia and Canada.[52] The researchers defined 'risk culture' as the 'shared perceptions among employees of the relative priority given to risk management, including perceptions of the risk-related practices and behaviors that are expected, valued and supported'.[53] In other words, the research was considering the perceptions of staff and managers as to 'the actual practice of risk governance and how this might influence risk management behaviour' in their firms. While the overall perception of staff across the banks was that risk management was 'effective', the results of the study did not show a homogenous view of 'risk culture'. In particular, the research found that:

- there was 'variation both between and within banks' and 'statistically significant differences in risk culture at the firm level, business line level and [interestingly[54]] the country level';
- 'Contrary to the "tone at the top" hypothesis, there were significant differences in risk culture factor scores between different business units even within the same bank';
- 'risk structures are interpreted through the lens of culture' which means that 'reliance on risk structures, without also addressing risk culture, is likely to be less effective'; and importantly
- 'Senior leaders tended to have a rosier perception of risk culture than staff generally'.[55]

In short, the research found that 'culture exists at the local level as staff interact with one another and look to local management for guidance'. In other words, as suggested by Schein and others, culture is a bottom-up not a top-down concept and hence 'tone from the top' is less likely to be as influential as a 'nudge from a neighbour'. Worryingly, the research found that senior management believed that the 'tone' they were playing was being heard by staff on the front line and they (rosily) presumed that it was having a significant impact on staff behaviours. In a warning to regulators, the researchers cautioned that 'By focusing on externally observed governance mechanisms, researchers and regulators may neglect important factors influencing the behavior of staff and ultimately firm outcomes'.[56]

In short, with definitions, and importantly actions, which assume that the major influence on how staff conduct business with customers is from the board and senior management, regulators may be looking in the wrong place to regulate 'risk culture'.

19.5 MACROCULTURE

In their study of large Australian and Canadian banks, Sheedy and Griffin found that risk culture was identified at the business line or 'microcultures' level.[57] Interestingly, the study also found differences at the level of 'macrocultures', in particular differences between 'national cultures' with the findings highlighting 'the potential importance of national culture in risk management, implying that regulators and senior leaders in some countries need to work

---

[52] See E. A. Sheedy and B. Griffin, 'Risk Governance, Structures, Culture, and Behavior: A View from the Inside' (2018) 26 *Corporate Governance International Review* 4–22, https://doi.org/10.1111/corg.12200; and E. A. Sheedy, B. Griffin and J. P. Barbour, 'A Framework and Measure for Examining Risk Climate in Financial Institutions' (2017) 32(1) *Journal of Business and Psychology* 101–16.

[53] Sheedy and Griffin (n 52) 4.

[54] The study found 'Canadian banks enjoying more favorable risk culture than their Australian counterparts'. The reasons were not studied further in that survey.

[55] Sheedy and Griffin (n 49).

[56] Ibid 20.

[57] See ibid.

harder to achieve the same outcomes as others operating in a more favorable national environment'.[58]

That there is a difference between national cultures as regards risk management is not surprising, as research on the impact of culture on the decision-making behaviours, in particular that of Hofstede,[59] shows that there are considerable differences between cultures based on six so-called cultural dimensions.[60] However, here we are not considering 'national culture' but rather another 'macroculture', or, as identified by Schein, 'occupations that exist globally' – in this case, 'bankers' or the 'banking industry'.[61]

19.5.1 *But Can 'Banking' Be Considered a Culture?*

Obviously, regulators believe that there are considerable similarities between the corporate entities (banks and insurers) that they regulate, otherwise they would not be suggesting national and international standards, rules and regulations that cover banking activities. To answer the question, Schein's definition is decomposed, in bullet form:

- A pattern of basic assumptions, invented, discovered or developed by
  o a given group (organisation);
  o as it learns to cope with its problems of external adaptation and internal integration;
  o that has worked well enough to be considered valid and, therefore,
  o is to be taught to new members as the correct way to perceive, think, and feel in relation to those problems.

Certainly, international banks are considered to be a group, and identified as such by regulators, such as the Basel Committee, the FSB and within countries by regulators, usually in the form of a legal definition, such as Authorised Deposit Taker. Do these institutions ever operate as a 'group'? The many national and international industry associations, such as the Australian (or British) Bankers Association or the Financial Markets Association (FMA), attest to the belief that banks consider they have problems in common. They also adopt solutions in common, such as the SWIFT (Society for Worldwide Interbank Financial Telecommunication) global payments system and, in investment banking, they belong to ISDA,[62] the standard-setting body for developing legal contracts in the derivatives industry.

Basic assumptions in banking are embodied in the shared literature and models of international finance, such as fixed income and derivatives valuations and credit scoring. The assumptions are also embodied in so-called industry codes of conduct, such as the Global Foreign Exchange Code of Conduct.[63] Such basic assumptions emerge to cope with the problems of 'external adaptation', especially regulation.

---

[58] Ibid 20.

[59] Hofstede (n 34).

[60] Hofstede's cultural dimensions in a society are (in summary): Power distance (a measure of inequality as regards power); Individualism versus collectivism (attitudes to the group); Uncertainty avoidance (a measure of a tolerance for 'ambiguity'); Masculinity versus femininity (stereotypes of personal traits; Long-term orientation versus short-term orientation (attitude to the future); and Indulgence versus restraint (attitude to gratification).

[61] Obviously, another such 'macroculture' might be 'insurance' but here we will concentrate on banking, as the examples come from that industry.

[62] ISDA is the International Swaps and Derivatives Association, www.isda.org.

[63] J. O'Brien, 'The Global FX Code: Transcending Symbolism' (Australian Centre for Financial Studies, Sydney, 2017), https://australiancentre.com.au/wp-content/uploads/2017/06/4_The-Global-FX-Code.pdf.

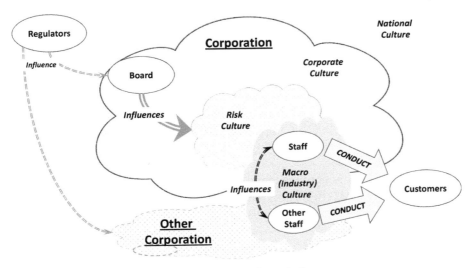

FIGURE 19.3. Macroculture: influences.

Likewise, 'internal integration' in the industry is expedited by common solutions such as, again, SWIFT and ISDA, which have worked well enough to be considered 'valid' and useful, and there are myriad similar standards in the banking industry that expedite internal business operations. Further, new bankers are 'taught' the correct way to address common problems, not only through the vast library of standard texts but also through national accreditation bodies, such as the Chartered Banker Institute in the United Kingdom,[64] and international education and training bodies, such as the Global Association of Risk Professionals (GARP).

More importantly, experienced bankers can move relatively easily between banks since the operating processes, *for the particular job that they do*, are similar across firms. However, unlike formal professions such as accounting or the law, the skills and experience gained from working in banking are only peripherally transferable to other industries. But banking is a large employer, so there are opportunities to move easily between firms, and many bankers do.

Figure 19.3 expands on the earlier figures by showing staff in different corporations that are part of a 'macroculture' that spans corporations and importantly hypothesises that staff can influence each other across organisational boundaries and, importantly, can influence each other's conduct towards customers.

An important question that arise from Figure 19.3 is: Can the influence between staff in different corporations be stronger than the influences exerted by boards (and regulators) through corporate and risk cultures?

Unfortunately, recent history shows that influences *between* staff in different financial institutions, particularly in the financial markets, can sometimes trump corporate loyalty and prudent risk-taking, as in the LIBOR manipulation scandal.[65]

---

[64] See www.charteredbanker.com/.
[65] McConnell (n 26).

19.6 EXAMPLES OF MACROCULTURES ACROSS THE BANKING SYSTEM

There are two types of cross-firm influences that have helped to create instances of serious misconduct that have been identified in recent banking scandals. One is the open communication of restricted information between staff in supposedly competing organisations. Sometimes of these have led to criminal collusion, such as in the scandals involving benchmark manipulation in the financial markets. The other type is where staff in many institutions independently commit the same illegal, unethical or imprudent activities, such as in the Payment Protection Insurance (PPI) scandal in the United Kingdom and the mis-selling of mortgages in the United States before the GFC.

Both types reflect a culture of misconduct across financial institutions that is not limited by geography or customer focus. Regulators have reacted by imposing record fines on financial institutions around the world, especially on banks that have been identified by the FSB as being 'systemically important'.[66]

The first type of malignant cross-firm influences is typified by the LIBOR scandal. To summarise, financial markets trading staff in several large banks around the world communicated sensitive information between each other concerning the setting of the widely used LIBOR benchmark.[67] By colluding with staff in other banks, and also market brokers,[68] bank staff were able to 'nudge' benchmarks in a direction that made money for their banks (and, at the same time, improved their bonuses). This illegal activity had been going on for years[69] before being detected by researchers considering market anomalies that had been detected during the GFC. To date, some US$10 billion in fines have been levied by multiple regulators on multiple banks around the world for misconduct concerning LIBOR and related benchmarks.[70]

But is there evidence of a 'culture' underlying this misconduct? Before addressing that question, it is worth discussing another scandal involving benchmark manipulation, that of the global foreign exchange benchmark World Markets Reuters (WMR) FIX.[71] In that scandal, multiple regulators fined multiple banks a total of over US$10 billion for collusion in manipulating the daily 'FIX'. Though the mechanics of the manipulation were different from LIBOR, the results were the same. A group of senior traders contacted each other each day before the time for the FIX in order to exchange sensitive information (itself illegal under competition law) and then, sometimes, to agree a strategy to 'nudge' the benchmark in a direction that would benefit their employers and themselves. Again, the manipulation appeared to be part of 'business-as-usual' in these banking giants and was only brought to light when trading was scrutinised during the LIBOR investigations. It should be noted that similar manipulation was detected in other non-currency traded markets, such as 'gold' and 'electricity'.

---

[66] Financial Stability Board (n 25).

[67] While the LIBOR (London Interbank Offered Rate) benchmark was by far the most important benchmark that was manipulated, other local benchmarks such as EURIBOR, TIBOR and the Australian BBSW were also manipulated. See, for example, https://theconversation.com/years-on-asic-still-grappling-with-swap-rate-fixing-scandal-35851?sg=9cae5790-74fc-4e42-90c8-50c249630ad2&sp=1&sr=4.

[68] P. J. McConnell, 'Analysing the LIBOR Manipulation Case: The Operational Risk Caused by Brokers Misbehaviour' (2014) 9(2) *Journal of Operational Risk* 59–100.

[69] See, for example, an attempt by a junior trader to do the right thing, but laughed at, in D. Keenan, 'My Thwarted Attempt to Tell of LIBOR Shenanigans', *Financial Times* (27 July 2012).

[70] McConnell (n 26).

[71] McConnell(n 38).

TABLE 19.2. *Cultural components in benchmark manipulation scandals.*

Components of Schein's definition of 'culture'	LIBOR benchmark manipulation	FX (WMR FIX) benchmark manipulation
'A pattern of basic assumptions, invented, discovered, or developed by	Industry policies and codes of conduct for submitting LIBOR rates *plus* well-known methods for nudging rate submissions	Industry policies and codes of conduct for conducting FX trading *plus* well-known methods for nudging market prices around benchmark
a given group [organisation];	Staff identified by the benchmark operator (BBA) as eligible to submit LIBOR rates, and the interest rate traders in their organisations	Staff identified by the benchmark operator (Reuters) as foreign exchange traders in their organisations
as it learns to cope with its problems of external adaptation and internal integration;	Interest rate trading units operated in a well-defined market (external) and within internal rules for submitting LIBOR rates, which were not well policed	FX trading units operated in a well-defined market (external) and within internal rules for trading with customers, which were not well policed
that has worked well enough to be considered valid and, therefore	The success of LIBOR manipulation in improving profits was, though not legal, evident over a considerable time	The success of FX manipulation in improving profits was, though not legal, evident over a considerable time
is to be taught to new members as the correct way to perceive, think, and feel in relation to those problems'	New traders (and brokers) were inculcated in 'how things are done around here'	New traders (and brokers) were inculcated in 'how things are done around here'

To answer the question of whether there was an identifiable 'culture' that helped to promote this cross-firm misconduct, Table 19.2 uses the decomposition of Schein's definition to identify traits common to these scandals.

Table 19.2 shows that the traders involved in both benchmark manipulation scandals, though not part of the same trading units in the firm, were part of groups that were well defined by external market bodies. These groups had evolved tried and tested methods for manipulating the respective benchmarks that were shared among themselves, though it was illegal to do so. And as new staff joined the groups they were quickly taught/induced to use the methods or were cautioned not to blow the whistle.

It is an indictment of the 'tone from the top' beliefs of senior management in the many banks involved that they were blissfully unaware of this toxic market behaviour until it was brought to their attention by regulators. But how could a culture that was so antithetical to beliefs of boards arise?

Though spread out around the world, the global financial market is, in fact, a 'small world'. Traders in the major markets all 'know' each other, not only from talking with one another every day by telephone, but they also attend the same conferences, read the same market commentaries and are wined and dined by the same brokers. For example, the world of FX trading comprises no more than a few hundred people who do the same high-pressure but lucrative job in the main trading cities around the world. Successful traders can, and often do, move between major bank employers, often for huge sign-on bonuses and, because market processes are so standardised, they can be effective almost immediately. Furthermore, traders do not lose contact with their ex-colleagues; in fact they retain these traders as close friends, and such contacts were used to manipulate the benchmarks.[72]

The opening question about the interest rate trader working for a Swiss bank in Tokyo is precisely the example of the Union Bank of Switzerland (UBS) trader in the LIBOR scandal, Tom Hayes, who colluded with colleagues at his previous employer(s) to manipulate the LIBOR benchmark. He was much closer to them, in terms of working methods, than to other UBS staff. After leaving UBS, the trader proceeded to do exactly the same benchmark manipulation, again colluding with his ex-colleagues, at his new employer, Citigroup. The logo on his business card meant much less to him than his relationships with ex-colleagues; his loyalty was to friends in the market rather than to fellow employees. Unfortunately, this trader was not unique; such camaraderie is commonplace in the testosterone- and money-fuelled financial markets.[73]

While scandals such as benchmark manipulation would naturally fall into the realm of conduct regulation, another type of cross-firm culture has importance for prudential regulation. The activities are not as obvious as the blatant benchmark manipulation described, but nonetheless provide some evidence of industry-wide macrocultures.

An example of this type is the collapse of the Irish housing market which led to the meltdown of the Irish banking system. A commission of inquiry into the collapse of the Irish housing market stated that 'frequently found behaviour exhibiting bandwagon effects both between institutions ("herding") and within them ("groupthink"), reinforced by a widespread international belief in the efficiency of financial markets'.[74] The official commission reported that problems in the Irish banks had been building for several years before the crisis. However, the problems were not operational but of:

> credit quality, sustainable lending practices and adequacy of internal procedures ... Bank loans seem to have expanded so rapidly because neither banks nor borrowers apparently really understood the risks they were taking ... Many banks were increasingly led and managed by people with less practical experience of credit and risk management than before ... Governance at these banks also fell short of best practice.[75]

In his testimony to the parliamentary inquiry into the UK banking crisis, the then head of the banking regulator, Lord Turner, echoed the perception that there appeared to be a system-wide consensus: 'The concept of market discipline in response to transparent information depends crucially on the idea that market prices will reflect all of the available information rather than reflect herd and momentum effects. I think that to a significant extent they reflect herd and momentum effects.'[76] In other words, bankers in different banks begin to think the same way and take the same, sometimes disastrous risks, until there is little diversification. This results in a situation where a particular type of large 'shock' will cause all banks to be impacted to a greater or lesser degree.[77]

Is there a 'culture' covering bankers, as regards lending into the market? Bankers are an identifiable 'group' and importantly are regulated as such. Their managements work on almost

---

[72] Ibid.

[73] See, for example, M. Fenton-O'Creevy, N. Nicholson, E. Soane and P. Willman, *Traders, Risks, Decisions and Management in Financial Markets* (Oxford University Press, 2005).

[74] P. Nyberg, *Misjudging Risk: Causes of the Systemic Banking Crisis in Ireland* (Ministry of Finance, 2011).

[75] P. Honahan, *The Irish Banking Crisis Regulatory and Financial Stability Policy 2003–2008: A Report to the Minister for Finance by the Governor of the Central Bank* (Ministry of Finance, 2010).

[76] Treasury Committee 2009, 'Banking Crisis: Regulation and Supervision – Fourteenth Report of Session 2008–09' (London, 2009).

[77] McConnell (n 38) likens particularly large shocks, such as the GFC, to 'earthquakes'.

identical assumptions about the economy, because economic commentaries are shared and, as in the Irish situation, they tend to share beliefs about the 'efficiency of the financial markets'.

Bankers move in the same circles and, at the top, inhabit the rarefied 'small world' of their local and international banking associations. Bankers adopt similar business models and, particularly in their local markets, battle for the same customer segments with the same set of financial products – which are essentially dictated by factors outside of their control, in particular the local and global economies. Differences between most banks tend to be at the edges rather than in their core businesses, and few bankers dare to be different, as that can be risky (to their personal status).

The risks in all banks behaving (misbehaving) in the same fashion are illustrated in the PPI scandal in the United Kingdom and by the mis-selling of mortgages before the GFC in the United States. Millions of words have been written on these topics,[78] and this chapter is not the place to repeat those words, other than describe evidence of 'macrocultures'.

The cost of remediation demanded by the FCA from most medium to large banks in the United Kingdom for mis-selling PPI contracts grows each year, and in 2017 stood at over £40 billion,[79] an enormous impost on banks' shareholders. A PPI contract, as the name suggests, protects a buyer from being unable to make regular payments on purchases as a result of, for example, serious illness and/or loss of income. PPI is a perfectly good insurance contract, *if sold properly*. However, in many cases contracts were sold to customers who did not need the insurance or, if they did, could never claim because of 'small print' exclusion clauses. After a decade of growing customer discontent (ignored by the banking community) UK competition and banking regulators were eventually forced to take action and after several high-profile studies demanded restitution and remediation.[80]

Why did so many banks do the same wrong thing at the same time? A study of the problems that beset the UK retail banking industry with the PPI scandal argued that there was an industry-wide 'sales culture' or cross-firm 'macroculture':

> The result is that bankers in a wide range of different organisations shared a set of routines, rituals, values and sets of assumptions about the world. The only thing which mattered to them was making a sale, irrespective of customer needs and longer term risk. This macro-culture gave bankers a shared way of looking at the problems they faced. At the same time, it enabled bankers to systematically overlook longer term risk and the genuine fulfilment of customer needs.[81]

In other words, bankers in many different firms, driven by the need to out-sell their competitors, migrated to the lowest common denominator of sales practices. This was obviously not intended by management nor was it coordinated through collusion but, nonetheless, the PPI product was successful and neither management nor insurance underwriters were prepared to 'kill the golden goose' by asking awkward questions as to why this particular product was so profitable.[82]

Another example of many banks doing the same wrong thing at the same time was the mortgage mis-selling scandal in the United States. By 2016, regulators had imposed on US and

[78] Financial Crisis Inquiry Commission (n 6).

[79] See, for example, www.theguardian.com/money/2017/mar/02/just-one-in-five-complaints-about-potential-mis-sold-ppi-made-so-far.

[80] P. J. McConnell and K. Blacker, 'Systemic Operational Risk: The UK Payment Protection Insurance Scandal' (2012) 7 *Journal of Operational Risk* 1–60.

[81] A. Spicer, J. P. Gond, K. Patel, D. Lindley, F. Fleming, S. Mosonyi, C. Benoit and S. Parker, 'A Report on the Culture of British Retail Banking' (New City Agenda and Cass Business School, London, 2014), 62, http://newcityagenda.co.uk/wp-content/uploads/2014/11/Online-version.pdf.

[82] McConnell and Blacker (n 80).

European banks over US$50 billion in fines, and requests for remediation and class action cases are still being considered, likely increasing the costs to bank shareholders.[83] Again, millions of words have been written on the topic but, in summary, the entry of private banks into the heretofore government-dominated mortgage-backed security (MBS) market led to a huge increase in demand for such securities and a consequential but largely unintended dilution of due-diligence standards.[84] In short, corners were cut across the industry to disastrous effect.

19.7 REGULATING MACROCULTURES

As shown in Table 19.1, Twin Peaks regulators agree on little concerning the concept of 'culture' other than it is important and is of interest to regulators. It is impractical to sustain such a situation in the long term, as financial institutions are faced with visits from (at least) two different regulators with very different perceptions of what culture is and how boards should attempt to influence it. Since the understanding of the problems are different, any prescriptions suggested to improve culture are also likely to be different and, possibly, contradictory. It cannot be long before exasperated boards will tell regulators to 'go away and get their acts together' – in the circumstances, not an unreasonable request.

In 2018, the current placeholder for regulators was that they will not explicitly mandate a definition of culture but leave it up to each individual firm that they supervise to define. Then those many definitions will be examined and tested by regulators as to their implementation – note, not to their coherence! Such an approach, of course, just kicks the can down the road, as it will become obvious when problems occur that it was not the implementation of a particular culture that was at fault but the culture itself. As a consequence, regulators will be forced to opine as to what types of 'culture' are likely, or not, to precipitate systemic problems. Back to square one – regulators must take a view on culture, either now or later, after the next crisis.

So, an obvious way forward is for regulators to come to some sort of agreement as to at least high-level definitions of 'culture' and, by extension, 'risk culture'. But that will not be easy, as the concepts, based as they are on theories of sociology, psychology and organisational behaviour, are outside the experience of most economics trained regulators, even those trained in the emerging discipline of 'behavioural economics'.[85] What is urgently needed is a programme of multidisciplinary research into these topics, adding financial regulation into the mix of disciplines that typically consider the thorny problem of culture. Who should undertake such a research programme (or more likely programmes) is beyond this chapter and is properly the responsibility of regulators themselves.

But there is a fundamental problem when considering such research: that of the paradigm (or set of fundamental assumptions) from which investigations start. As described here, there are two diametrically opposed paradigms of organisational culture:

1   **Scientific rationalist**: the belief that culture can be manipulated and managed, particularly by the board, through the 'tone from the top'.
2   **Anthropological**: the belief that culture is a phenomenon that 'emerges' at local levels to take account of the realities faced by staff.

---

[83] See detailed list until 2015 in McConnell (n 38).
[84] Ibid.
[85] For a summary of the field of behavioural economics see, D. Kahneman, *Thinking, Fast and Slow* (Allen Lane, 2011).

The reality facing regulators is that both of these paradigms describe actual cultures in different situations. Undoubtedly, culture can be strongly influenced by charismatic executives, especially in smaller, founder-led organisations. But for the largest financial institutions that operate in multiple markets, with multiple national cultures, staff are too remote to be solely influenced by distant board members. Research into such firms[86] has shown that 'risk culture' is 'local' and different business lines in the same firm can have different attitudes to risk management. Considering only management's perspectives will miss the realities that drive front-line conduct, and misconduct, as illustrated in the scandals described earlier.

It is highly unlikely that regulators, even with teams of expert researchers, will be able to develop a coherent theory on culture that will encompass both of these paradigms, if only because in excess of thirty years of research has failed, to date, to do so. So how to start?

Luckily, Twin Peaks provides a way to approach this 'two paradigms' problem. If one regulator was to embrace the top-down rationalist approach, and the other was to take the anthropological perspective, then the regulation problem becomes one of 'patrolling' the boundaries/fault lines between these two approaches, that is, understanding what is happening 'in the middle'. And the mandates of the two types of regulator lend themselves to such an approach.

Prudential regulation is not about supervising individual financial transactions but about understanding the aggregate, net risk of all transactions, such as overall credit risk to a sector. It is a natural top-down perspective with the objective of influencing boards to manage net risks rather than interfering in the details. Thus, it would be natural for prudential regulators to embrace the scientific rationalist approach to culture and consider what influences a particular board has on the risk-taking 'culture' of their institution.

On the other hand, conduct regulators are more concerned with how individual staff are conducting business with individual customers, observing whether there is any evidence of systematic misconduct in a firm and, by extension, any 'systemic' misconduct across firms. If conduct regulators were to start with the assumption that all frontline groups in an institution they were supervising had a somewhat unique culture, albeit with some similarities to other groups in the firm, then they would be taking an 'anthropological' perspective. They would be considering 'what is' not 'what should be', and importantly not making judgement calls on a particular situation, other than that there may be potential problems with a particular business group.

So, what happens when a particular group is not adhering to the culture desired by a board and the outcomes are likely to be serious? This problem is not for regulators to resolve, only for them to ensure that a firm is seriously addressing the problem. This is where the firm's Enterprise Risk Management (ERM) function could become involved, as illustrated in Figure 19.4.

In the proposed model shown in Figure 19.4, the two regulators would *both* require that it is the ERM function that patrols the regulatory 'boundary' between them, reacting to reports produced by either or both regulators. Regulators would monitor compliance of issues raised to ensure that boards and senior executives were informed of regulatory concerns; analyses by the ERM function, in particular the chief risk officer (CRO), were raised to the board; and, importantly, that appropriate actions were taken by the board.

In effect, for culture-related issues the first point of contact for prudential and conduct regulators with a firm, in this model, would be the ERM and CRO rather than the board, and only if not satisfied with the responses and/or actions taken would a board be addressed

---

[86] See Sheedy and Griffin (n 52).

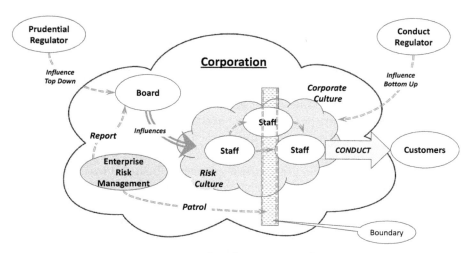

FIGURE 19.4. Regulating macrocultures.

directly. Coordination between Twin Peaks regulators would then be on two levels, directly between each other, as they would exchange information about a firm and the implications of any issues that they find. They would then engage with the ERM function, and only if not satisfied with the responses provided would they engage directly and jointly with directors. Beyond regulating individual banks, Twin Peaks regulators would also collate and compare the information that they had gathered, such that system-wide issues of 'macroculture' could be identified.

19.8 SUMMARY

If, as both prudential and conduct regulators claim, culture is important in the processes of regulating firms, then the current situation as regards the definition of 'culture' is grossly inadequate. Regulators have given different, ambiguous and incomplete definitions of 'culture' and the related concept of 'risk culture'. In addition, the definitions that they do provide make assumptions about the top-down nature of culture, in which the so-called tone from the top, plus remuneration and control policies, ensures homogeneity of conduct among staff. Research and case studies have shown that this characterisation is not universally correct and is likely to hold only in very specific conditions. Overwhelmingly, 'culture' is, as theorists have claimed, a 'local construct' that emerges in groups such as business units as they adapt to ever-changing external and internal pressures. As a result, subcultures in organisations are fluid, and not always amenable to the diktats of senior management.

In addition, staff, especially in frontline businesses, are also subject to explicit and tacit pressures from colleagues in the industry. There is evidence that in some circumstances the influence of such cross-firm 'macrocultures' is stronger than the internal 'microculture' and, as a consequence, misconduct by staff in multiple firms may arise simultaneously.

Finally, the chapter proposes a mechanism by which Twin Peaks regulators can approach the 'two-paradigms' problem from different perspectives and use the firm's Enterprise Risk Management to 'patrol' the boundaries between different cultural models.

Twin Peaks, Macroprudential Regulation and Systemic Financial Stability

Andrew Godwin, Steve Kourabas and Ian Ramsay

20.1 INTRODUCTION

The Global Financial Crisis of 2007–08 (GFC) led to a major rethink of the objectives underpinning many of the world's financial regulatory systems.[1] Primary among this has been the elevation of what we refer to as 'systemic financial stability'[2] to the top of the regulatory hierarchy, as well as the use of the once-neglected concept of macroprudential regulation, to achieve this goal. This post-GFC approach to financial regulation marks a shift in emphasis from the pre-GFC approach.[3] That approach had received broad support as a result of the implementation of policies that supported efficient market theories, and that had been identified as a major reason for a prolonged period of uninterrupted economic growth in much of the Western, industrialised world.[4] Public oversight was therefore limited to instances of market failure, where efficient market outcomes were ineffective, including, for instance, regulations that sought to

---

[1] Portions of this chapter are based on the following article: Andrew Godwin, Steve Kourabas and Ian Ramsay, 'Financial Stability Authorities and Macroprudential Regulation' (2017) 32 *Banking & Finance Law Review* 223–54.
   Daniel Tarullo has discussed how the GFC has shaken the intellectual foundations of finance including, importantly for the discussion in this chapter, the theory that financial stability should be an explicit economic policy goal: see Daniel K. Tarullo, 'Macroprudential Regulation' (2014) 31(3) *Yale Journal on Regulation* 505–21, http://digitalcommons.law.yale.edu/yjreg/vol31/iss3/2. Hall has described such a shift in public thinking as a 'third order change' in finance: see Peter Hall, 'Policy Paradigms, Social Learning and the State: The Case of Economic Policymaking in Britain' (1993) 25(3) *Comparative Politics* 275–96, www.jstor.org/stable/422246. Cf Eric Helleiner, 'A Bretton Woods Moment? The 2007–2008 Crisis and the Future of Global Finance' (2010) 86(3) *International Affairs* 622. Helleiner argues that the impact of the GFC was limited to generating a consensus at the level of transnational experts regarding the need to use macroprudential regulation to achieve financial stability.

[2] This term has been used by the IMF when discussing the problems that contributed to the GFC. See, eg, International Monetary Fund, 'Macroprudential Policy: An Organizing Framework' (14 March 2011), at 5, www.imf.org/external/np/pp/eng/2011/031411.pdf.

[3] Australia's Financial System Inquiry (Wallis Report) usefully sets out the predominant financial regulatory philosophy in chapter 5 of its review of the Australian financial system. See Commonwealth of Australia, *Financial System Inquiry (Wallis Report)* – 'Chapter 5: Philosophy of Financial Regulation' (1997).

[4] See generally Peter M. Summers, 'What Caused the Great Moderation? Some Cross-Country Evidence' (2005) 90(3) *Economic Review* 5. See also Craig S. Hakkio, 'The Great Moderation: 1982–2007', *Federal Reserve History* (22 November 2013). The efficient market hypothesis, put forward by the neoclassical economic school of thought, played an important role in this regulatory trend before the GFC. Eugene Fama, one of the most prominent proponents of this school of thought, argued that an economy is efficient when prices provide accurate signals for resource allocation: see Eugene F. Fama, 'Efficient Capital Markets: A Review of Theory and Empirical Work' (1970) 25(2) *Journal of Finance* 383–417, www.jstor.org/stable/2325486. See also Eugene F. Fama, 'Market Efficiency, Long-Term Returns, and Behavioral Finance' (1998) 49 *Journal of Financial Economics* 283–306. Under this theory, markets were not considered inherently unstable; it was government intervention in those markets that contributed to

maintain the integrity of the market and protect consumers from unscrupulous activity. Financial activity was, at least in theory, subject to more onerous prudential regulation for a limited number of financial actors, considered vital to the smooth operation of the economy.[5]

The regulatory framework in place to oversee financial activity varied according to jurisdiction.[6] However, there was some consistency in microprudential regulation, which had as its aim the safety and soundness of important financial institutions (so as to protect consumers), and monetary policy that sought to ensure price stability and foster economic growth.[7] While many of the world's financial regulators had a 'financial stability' mandate, it was unclear what significance was attached to the achievement of financial stability, relative to other financial and economic goals.

The GFC illustrated that this approach was not enough to ensure the stability of the financial system. It is now widely accepted that a key element missing in the lead-up to the GFC was an overarching policy framework that promoted systemic financial stability.[8] This resulted in calls for the development of policy and regulatory tools that focus on the minimisation of system-wide risks.[9] Macroprudential regulation, which has as its main goal the achievement of financial stability, has consequently come to form an important part of the financial regulatory framework of a number of key jurisdictions.[10] This chapter explores this shift in focus, and in particular its potential to affect the institutional framework adopted through the Twin Peaks model of financial regulation. This includes the modification of the Twin Peaks model to explicitly promote the goal of systemic financial stability above other regulatory goals, through the creation of financial stability regulatory authorities, backed by legal authority.

The chapter proceeds as follows. Section 21.2 provides a definition of systemic financial stability and sets out the increased (although still contested) rise to prominence of this regulatory goal since the GFC. Section 21.3 explores the concept of macroprudential regulation and its relevance in achieving systemic financial stability. Section 21.4 outlines some of the key features of the Twin Peaks model of financial regulation that were common before the GFC, and the justifications provided by some commentators and policymakers for the retention of the model after the GFC. Section 21.5 reviews the post-GFC UK regulatory model that attempts to

---

instability. For a useful discussion on efficient market theories, see, eg, Heidi Mandaris Schooner and Michael W. Taylor, *Global Bank Regulation: Principles and Policies* (Academic Press, 2010), 67.

[5] See, eg, Commonwealth of Australia, Wallis Report (n 3) at Chs 8 and 9 (discussing safety and soundness regulation and systemic stability).

[6] The different forms of institutional framework are explored in E. Wymeersch, 'The Structure of Financial Supervision in Europe: About Single Financial Supervisors, Twin Peaks and Multiple Financial Supervisors' (2007) 8 *European Business Organization Law Review* 237–306.

[7] See, eg, Dirk Schoenmaker and Peter Wierts, 'Macroprudential Policy: The Need for a Coherent Policy Framework' (Duisenberg School of Finance Policy Paper, No 13, July 2011), at 2; Luis I. Jacome and Erlend W. Nier, 'Protecting the Whole' (2012) 49(1) *Finance & Development* 30; Gianni de Nicolo, Giovanni Favara and Lev Ratnovski, 'Externalities and Macroprudential Policy' (IMF Staff Discussion Note SDN/12/05, 2012), at 4; Samuel G. Hanson, Anil K. Kashyap and Jeremy C. Stein, 'A Macroprudential Approach to Financial Regulation' (2011) 25(1) *Journal of Economic Perspectives* 3; Jacek Osinski, Katharine Seal and Lex Hoogduin, 'Macroprudential and Microprudential Policies: Toward Cohabitation' (IMF Staff Discussion Note SDN13/05, June 2013), at 5; Alastair Clark and Andrew Large, 'Macroprudential Policy: Addressing the Things We Don't Know' (Group of 30, Occasional Paper No 83, 2011), at 11.

[8] International Monetary Fund (n 2) at 5 (there were regulatory gaps in many existing financial regulatory frameworks).

[9] Ibid. See also Financial Services Authority, 'The Turner Review: A Regulatory Response to the Global Banking Crisis' (March 2009), at 86, www.fsa.gov.uk/pubs/other/turner_review.pdf. The Turner Review discussed the shift in the United Kingdom from a focus predominantly on regulating individual institutions to combining this with a systemic approach.

[10] International Monetary Fund (n 2) at 5. As with financial stability, there is no commonly accepted definition of macroprudential regulation. Ibid at 7.

reconcile the Twin Peaks model of regulation with the increased significance attributed to maintaining systemic financial stability as an underlying regulatory goal. Section 21.6 concludes.

20.2 'STABILITY' IN THE POST-GFC CONTEXT

Over the past decade there has been a general shift in public discourse that acknowledges the important role of regulation in ensuring financial stability. However, there is little agreement on what is meant by financial stability, largely because of ongoing disagreement regarding the role of public oversight of markets, and the ultimate goals of the financial system. This has meant that financial stability has often been described as a goal the purpose of which is to avoid 'instability', rather than as a prescriptive regulatory goal carried out by public authorities.[11] For instance, Paul Tucker, former deputy governor of the Bank of England (BoE) offered the following definition: 'financial stability prevails where the financial system is sufficiently resilient that worries about bad states of the world do not affect confidence in the ability of the system to deliver its core services to the rest of the economy'.[12] This definition says little about what is needed in a regulatory sense to avoid instability.

The difficulty in clearly setting out what is meant by financial stability has carried over to policy documents and legislation. In the United States, the *Dodd–Frank Act* creates a Financial Stability Oversight Committee (FSOC)[13] with responsibilities that include the identification of risks to the financial stability of the United States,[14] but does not provide a definition of financial stability. Instead, the legislation provides various indicators and parameters for the FSOC when undertaking its financial stability duties, including reference to risks to financial stability arising 'from the material financial distress or failure, or ongoing activities, of large, interconnected bank holding companies or nonbank financial companies, or that could arise outside the financial services marketplace'.[15] Therefore, while not defining financial stability, the United States has established some guidance for its financial stability regulator on what financial activities should be taken into account when attempting to avoid financial instability in the United States.

Commentators have also attempted to provide some further guidance on what is meant by financial stability. For instance, Allen provides the following more comprehensive definition of the term:

> a state of affairs wherein (i) financial institutions and markets are able to facilitate capital intermediation, risk management, and payment services in a way that enables sustainable economic growth; (ii) there is no disruption to the ability of financial institutions or markets to carry out such functions that might cause harm to persons (wherever they may be resident) who are not customers or counterparties of those financial institutions, nor participants in those financial markets; and (iii) financial institutions and markets are able to withstand economic shocks (such as the failure of other markets and institutions, or a chain of significant losses at

---

[11] Issing notes that most authors have attempted to define financial instability rather than financial stability. See Otmar Issing, 'Monetary and Financial Stability: Is There a Trade-Off?' (Speech given at the Conference on 'Monetary Stability, Financial Stability and the Business Cycle', Bank for International Settlements, Basel, 28–29 March 2003), at 1.

[12] Paul Tucker, 'Macroprudential Policy: Building Financial Stability Institutions' (Speech given at the 20th Annual Hyman P. Minsky Conference, New York, 14 April 2011), at 4.

[13] *Dodd–Frank Wall Street Reform and Consumer Protection Act*, Pub L No 111-203, 124 Stat 1376 (2010). The FSOC is made up of ten voting members and five non-voting members. *Dodd–Frank Act*, s 111(b) (codified at 12 USC s 5321).

[14] *Dodd–Frank Act*, s 112(a)(1)(A) (codified at 12 USC s 5322).

[15] Ibid.

financial institutions) so that (x) there will be no disruption to the performance of the functions set forth in (i) and (y) no harm will be caused to the persons set forth in (ii).[16]

While the debate concerning financial stability is ongoing, there appears to be broad acceptance on at least one aspect of financial stability: the use of the term, particularly after the GFC, to refer to stability at a systemic level rather than just at the institutional level.[17] An important question to consider when reviewing the suitability of financial regulatory infrastructure to achieve financial stability is whether the regulatory framework adopted by a jurisdiction is best suited to maintaining the stability of the system as a whole. This aim is reflected in the use of terms such as 'systemic stability' or 'systemic risk'.[18] The remainder of this chapter adopts the term 'systemic financial stability' to reflect the systemic approach to financial stability when considering regulatory reforms.

Having established the systemic goal of financial stability, it is necessary to consider what level of importance is attached to that goal relative to other financial regulatory goals, such as market integrity, consumer protection and fraud prevention.[19] This is particularly important when considering the Twin Peaks model of regulation, as this model does not expressly provide for the predominance of any one goal over others. Regulators under the Twin Peaks model are therefore offered little (if any) guidance as to how to prioritise the various goals within their own regulatory mandates, or the importance of their mandate relative to that of other regulators within the system.

The post-GFC environment provides an interesting challenge for the Twin Peaks model, as systemic financial stability has become a more prominent goal. Commentators such as Garicano and Lastra have argued that in constructing the architecture of a financial regulatory system, the ultimate goal should be to ensure financial stability.[20] Weber similarly identifies financial stability as a core financial regulatory principle. He argues that financial stability, along with trust and confidence in the system and relevant actors, as well as market integrity, now form a clear, multilayered system of financial governance at the global level.[21] However, Weber considers financial stability a sort of 'meta' norm within this framework, as trust and market integrity cannot be considered in isolation from the achievement of financial stability.[22] This

---

[16] Hilary J. Allen, 'What Is "Financial Stability"? The Need for Some Common Language in International Financial Regulation' (2014) 45 *Georgetown Journal of International Law* 929–52 at 932.

[17] There were some commentators that noted this distinction before the GFC. See, eg, Issing (n 11) at 1–2. Further, systemic matters were considered by policy-makers and regulators before the GFC, but were generally handled through monetary policy and microprudential regulation. See Wallis Report (n 3).

[18] The G10, in its report on the consolidation of the financial sector provided the following definition of systemic financial risk:

> Systemic financial risk is the risk that an event will trigger a loss of economic value or confidence in, and attendant increases in uncertainly about, a substantial portion of the financial system that is serious enough to quite probably have significant adverse effects on the real economy. Systemic risk events can be sudden and unexpected, or the likelihood of their occurrence can build up through time in the absence of appropriate policy responses. The adverse real economic effects from systemic problems are generally seen as arising from disruptions to the payment system, to credit flows, and from the destruction of asset values.

Group of Ten, 'Consolidation in the Financial Sector' (2001), 126, www.bis.org/publ/gten05.htm.

[19] Luis Garicano and Rosa Lastra, 'Towards a New Architecture for Financial Stability: Seven Principles' (2010) 13(3) *Journal of International Economic Law* 599, https://doi.org/10.1093/jiel/jgq041.

[20] Ibid.

[21] Rolf H. Weber, 'Multilayered Governance in International Financial Regulation and Supervision' (2010) 13(3) *Journal of International Economic Law* 693–4, https://doi.org/10.1093/jiel/jgq033.

[22] Ibid at 693–4.

approach has most prominently been adopted by the United Kingdom after the GFC and is discussed in detail in Section 21.5.[23]

Post-GFC studies that emphasise the importance of systemic financial stability and the role of regulators in its maintenance, predominantly through macroprudential regulation explored in Section 21.3, have thus forced defenders of the Twin Peaks model to justify its continued use. Regulators in Australia have, for instance, been reluctant to engage in reform of the Twin Peaks model, arguing instead that the model adequately deals with both systemic financial stability and caters for the effective use of macroprudential regulation.[24] The remainder of this chapter explores these debates in greater detail.

20.3 THE ROLE OF MACROPRUDENTIAL REGULATION IN ACHIEVING SYSTEMIC FINANCIAL STABILITY

In addition to reinforcing the importance of systemic financial stability, the GFC made it more acceptable to put forward interventionist regulatory approaches to achieve this goal. The once neglected concept of macroprudential regulation has consequently taken on added prominence since the GFC,[25] particularly as a means of overcoming problems identified with the micro-prudential approach to financial regulation.[26] Goodhart has usefully explained these problems as follows:

> the deeper problem is that controls and reactions that seem appropriate at the level of the individual financial institution may become seriously damaging at the level of the system as a whole. Thus, faced with adverse financial conditions, the reaction of the individual bank or other financial intermediary is to retrench, to hoard liquidity, to sell assets while the opportunity

---

[23] Haldane notes that the United Kingdom's new Financial Stability Committee, the FPC, has a macroprudential mandate that places financial resilience as the primary objective, with output and employment stabilisation as a secondary objective. Andy Haldane, 'Macroprudential Policies – When and How to Use Them' (Paper presented at Rethinking Macro Policy II: First Steps and Early Lessons Concepts, International Monetary Fund, Washington, DC, 16–17 April 2013), 1–2, www.imf.org/external/np/seminars/eng/2013/macro2/pdf/ah.pdf.

[24] Ibid. These views are considered further in Section 21.5.

[25] The term macroprudential regulation was first used in an international context in 1979 at the meeting of the Cooke Committee, the forerunner to the Basel Committee on Banking Supervision, and was then used sporadically throughout the next 20–30 years. Piet Clement, 'The Term "Macroprudential": Origins and Evolution' (2010) *BIS Quarterly Review* 59. Several commentators, in particular Claudio Borio, were early pioneers of use of the term macroprudential regulation. See, eg, Claudio Borio, 'Towards a Macroprudential Framework for Financial Supervision and Regulation?' (BIS Working Papers No 128, February 2003), at 1. Haldane notes that knowledge about macroprudential regimes today is roughly where monetary policy was in the 1940s, or even earlier, and this may account for the ongoing debate. Haldane (n 23). See also Eric J. Pan, 'Structural Reform of Financial Regulation' (2011) 19 *Transnational Law* 796 at 799.

[26] A number of commentators have discussed the differences between micro- and macroprudential regulation. See, eg, Markus Brunnermeier, Andrew Crockett, Charles Goodhart, Avinash D. Persaud and Hyun Song Shin, 'The Fundamental Principles of Financial Regulation' (Geneva Reports on the World Economy 11, International Center for Monetary and Banking Studies and Center for Economic Policy Research, June 2009), at 10, www.icmb.ch/ICMB/Publications_files/Geneva%2011.pdf (the objective of microprudential measures is to keep individual institutions behaving prudently, whereas macroprudential regulation seeks to safeguard the system as a whole); Borio (n 25) at 3 (those in favour of a microprudential approach would argue that for a financial system to be sound, it is enough that each individual institution is sound, while those in favour of a macroprudential approach would argue that a holistic approach to regulation needs to be adopted, and that this would in turn ensure the safety of individual institutions). For discussion regarding the problems with microprudential regulation, see, eg, José Viñals, 'Towards a Safer Global Financial System' (Speech presented at CFS Colloquium 2010 Series: 'Rebuilding Financial Markets', 9–11 November 2010); Ben Bernanke, 'Implementing a Macroprudential Approach to Supervision and Regulation' (Speech at the 47th Annual Conference on Bank Structure and Competition, Chicago, Illinois, 5 May 2011), www.federalreserve.gov/newsevents/speech/bernanke20110505a.htm.

to do so remains open, and to become far more restrictive in extending credit. Microstructural regulation often reinforces such tendencies, in part by encouraging all the regulated to act in the same way at the same time, as a herd.[27]

The G20 moved quickly after the GFC to emphasise the importance of reshaping the regulatory systems of member states so that regulatory authorities would be in a better position to take account of macroprudential risks.[28] To further this goal, in November 2010 the G20 tasked the Financial Stability Board (FSB), the International Monetary Fund (IMF) and the Bank for International Settlements (BIS) with formulating a macroprudential policy framework.[29] The three agencies produced a report on a macroprudential policy framework (Macroprudential Policy Report), that set out the following defining elements:

(i)   Its objective: to limit systemic risk – the risk of widespread disruptions to the provision of financial services that have serious negative consequences for the economy at large.
(ii) Its scope: the focus is on the financial system as a whole (including the interactions between the financial and real sectors) as opposed to individual components (that take the rest of the system as given).
(iii) Its instruments and associated governance: it uses primarily prudential tools calibrated to target the sources of systemic risk. Any non-prudential tools that are part of the framework need to clearly target systemic risk.[30]

Together, these elements call for the adoption of policies that reflect a significant change in the way that jurisdictions oversee financial activity. The instruments and associated governance arrangement referred to as the third element of the Macroprudential Policy Report are particularly important for the purposes of the discussion in the remainder of this chapter. The literature considering these issues has emphasised two key challenges, and the instruments needed to overcome these challenges.[31] These challenges and instruments help to analyse the effectiveness of a regulatory framework, including the Twin Peaks model, from a systemic perspective.

The first challenge relates to the build-up of financial imbalances over time, arising as a result of the economic cycle, characterised by upswings and downswings.[32] Tools of a macroprudential

---

[27] Charles A. E. Goodhart, 'The Macroprudential Authority: Powers, Scope and Accountability' (2011) 11(2) *OECD Journal: Financial Market Trends* at 101. Schoenmaker and Wierts provide a useful, practical example of the problem:
     Selling an asset when the price of risk increases may be a prudent response from the perspective of an individual bank. But if many banks act in this way, the asset price will collapse, forcing financial institutions to take yet further steps to rectify the situation. The responses of banks themselves to such pressures lead to generalised declines in asset prices, and enhanced correlations and volatility in asset markets. The micro policies can thus be destructive at the macro level.
     See Schoenmaker and Wierts (n 7) at 3. These examples point to problems associated with the 'fallacy of composition' (namely, the notion that what is right for an individual institution is right for the system as a whole) that was present in the pre-GFC financial regulatory ethos. For a detailed discussion of the fallacy of composition, see, eg, Osinski, Seal and Hoogduin (n 7) at 5.

[28] G20, 'London Summit Leaders' Statement' (London: 2 April 2009).

[29] G20, 'Seoul Summit Leaders Declaration' (Seoul: 11–12 November 2010).

[30] C. Lim, F. Columba, A. Costa, P. Kongsamut, A. Otani, M Saiyid, T. Wezel and X. Wu, 'Macroprudential Policy: What Instruments and How to Use Them? Lessons from Country Experiences' (IMF Working Paper WP/11/238, 2011), at 7 (discussing the different macroprudential tools that have been put in place at a national level since the GFC).

[31] See, eg, Daniel K. Tarullo, 'Macroprudential Regulation' (2014) 31 *Yale Journal on Regulation* at 506.

[32] Borio identifies this time dimension, and discusses how economic cycles necessitate the provision of cushions during upswings to rely on during downturns. The aim of macroprudential regulation is to ensure that institutions are able to weather deteriorating economic conditions when access to external financing becomes more costly and constrained: Borio (n 25) at 11. See also International Monetary Fund (n 2) at 8; Brunnermeier et al (n 26).

nature attempt to 'lean against' the build-up of risks during upswings, such as unsustainable credit expansion and asset price increases that could trigger, or exacerbate, downturns.[33] Countercyclical capital measures have proven a popular tool amongst regulators in protecting against such dangers, as they require financial institutions to add to their capital when there are signs of unusually strong credit growth, or signs of credit-driven asset booms.[34] Reliance on countercyclical buffers provides a clear indication of greater confidence in public intervention to forestall market failures so as to avoid systemic financial instability. The use of such tools supports the idea that tools need to be available to regulators to correct systemic failures that are beyond the failure of any one financial institution.

The second challenge relates to the danger to financial stability that arises through the risk of spill-overs (or negative externalities), namely, the risk that a financial crisis in one market or region spills over to other markets or regions. These may take place at any point in time due to interconnections in the financial system.[35] Macroprudential tools such as capital surcharges for systemically important banks, restrictions on asset composition and taxation seek to reduce the severity of these risks.[36] As with regulation addressing economic cycles, tools that aim to minimise negative externalities focus on the system as a whole. This means that, at times, regulations may be imposed on individual institutions to ensure stability at a systemic level, even if this may otherwise be considered inefficient for a particular institution.[37]

Having set out the challenges and the tools to address them, the Macroprudential Policy Report then sets out a number of factors that policymakers need to consider when constructing a regulatory framework, including institutional and governance matters.[38] The IMF expanded on this point by suggesting that institutional and governance arrangements would address the systemic nature of regulation by providing regulators with clear mandates, control over instruments that are commensurate with their mandates, and ensuring the operational independence of those regulators while at the same time providing for accountability mechanisms.[39] Of particular relevance to this chapter is whether, and if so how, the Twin Peaks model deals with systemic financial stability, and the role of macroprudential regulation in achieving that goal.

---

[33] Jacome and Nier (n 7) at 31–3; De Nicolo, Favara and Ratnovski (n 7) at 8 (providing an analysis of how time-varying capital requirements can alleviate externalities related to fire sales, as an example).

[34] See, eg, Brunnermeier et al (n 26) at 29–35 (recommending other measures); C. Goodhart and A. Persaud, 'A Party Pooper's Guide to Financial Stability', *Financial Times* (4 June 2008), www.ft.com/cms/s/0/94f92422-3238-11dd-9b87-0000779fd2ac.html (discussing countercyclical capital requirements). See also Bank for International Settlements, 'Basel III: A Global Regulatory Framework for More Resilient Banks and Banking Systems' (December 2010, revised June 2011), www.bis.org/publ/bcbs189.htm (providing details of global regulatory standards on bank capital adequacy and liquidity, including countercyclical buffers to be adopted by individual jurisdictions).

[35] Schoenmaker and Wierts (n 7) at 5; Nicolas Veron, 'Financial Reform after the Crisis: An Early Assessment, Peterson Institute for International Economics' (Working Paper Series WP 12-2, January 2012), at 13.

[36] Veron (n 35) at 13–14 (providing a comprehensive analysis of each of these instruments).

[37] International Monetary Fund (n 2) at 9.

[38] Lim et al (n 30) at 3.

[39] Erland W. Nier et al, 'Towards Effective Macroprudential Policy Frameworks: An Assessment of Stylized Institutional Models' (IMF Working Paper WP/11/250, November 2011), at 6, 16, 19–20, 38. The IMF notes that this must in turn be supported by policies promoting transparency and clear communication of decisions and decision-making processes. International Monetary Fund (n 2) at 38.

20.4 THE TWIN PEAKS MODEL OF FINANCIAL REGULATION: A REGULATORY MODEL FOR A PRE-GFC WORLD?

The Twin Peaks model of regulation was developed during a period when systemic financial stability, and the means to achieve it, including macroprudential regulation, were not necessarily considered central to financial regulation. This was because instability of the nature experienced during the GFC was not widely anticipated.[40] The main innovation of the Twin Peaks model was to divide financial regulation along functional lines between prudential regulation, market conduct and consumer protection regulation.[41] Two major variations of the model have since come to be adopted. Most jurisdictions have created a separate, independent regulatory authority to oversee market conduct and consumer protection regulation, while prudential regulation has resided within the central bank. By contrast, Australia similarly created an independent regulator, the Australian Securities and Investments Commission (ASIC) to oversee market conduct and consumer protection, but also created an independent prudential regulator, the Australian Prudential Regulatory Authority (APRA). Australia's central bank, the Reserve Bank of Australian (RBA) is also involved in oversight of the financial sector through its monetary policy mandate, and as a result of a broad (and unspecified) 'financial stability' mandate as lender of last resort.[42]

The Twin Peaks model appears to have evolved in response to shortcomings identified with two other commonly used financial regulatory models: the institutional model and the unified model.[43] The institutional model centres on the legal form of regulated institutions. Under this approach, regulators supervise all activities of institutions within a particular sector. As the financial sector has become more complex and integrated it has become increasingly difficult to divide regulatory authority along sectoral lines. The Twin Peaks model seeks to overcome this problem by dividing regulatory authority along functional lines rather than along sectoral lines as the latter approach no longer accurately reflects the financial activities undertaken by individual financial institutions. The unified regulator model also attempts to overcome the

---

[40] For instance, Alan Greenspan, Chairman of the US Federal Reserve during the longest period of US economic expansion, discussing the United States, noted his surprise that market processes had failed in the lead-up to the GFC:

> In the run-up to the crisis, the Federal Reserve Board's sophisticated forecasting system did not foresee the major risks to the global economy. Nor did the model developed by the International Monetary Fund, which concluded as late as the spring of 2007 that 'global economic risks [had] declined' since September 2006 and that 'the overall U.S. economy is holding up well ... [and] the signs elsewhere are very encouraging'. On 12 September 2008, just three days before the crisis began, J. P. Morgan, arguably the United States' premier financial institution, projected that the U.S. GDP growth rate would accelerate during the first half of 2009. The pre-crisis view of most professional analysts and forecasters was perhaps best summed up in December 2006 by The Economist: 'Market capitalism, the engine that runs most of the world economy, seems to be doing its job well.'

Alan Greenspan, 'Never Saw it Coming: Why the Financial Crisis Took Economists By Surprise', *Foreign Affairs* (November–December 2013), www.foreignaffairs.com/articles/united-states/2013-10-15/never-saw-it-coming. See also Alan Greenspan, *The Map and the Territory: Risk, Human Nature, and the Future of Forecasting* (Penguin, 2013), 7–8.

[41] The Twin Peaks model is explored in detail in a number of chapters in this book. This chapter explores only those aspects of the model that are relevant to considerations regarding systemic financial stability and macroprudential regulation.

[42] The different approaches to the Twin Peaks model are explored in detail in Andrew Godwin, Timothy Howse and Ian Ramsay, 'A Jurisdictional Comparison of the Twin Peaks Model of Financial Regulation' (2016) 18(2) *Journal of Banking Regulation* 103–31.

[43] The Twin Peaks model was first examined in Michael Taylor, '"Twin Peaks": A Regulatory Structure for the New Century' (Centre for the Study of Financial Innovation, London, 1995). See also, Michael W. Taylor, 'The Road from Twin Peaks – And the Way Back' (2000) 16 *Connecticut Insurance Law Journal* 61. For a comprehensive review of these models of financial regulation see Wymeersch (n 6).

problems of the institutional model by combining prudential and market conduct regulation within one super-regulator. However, some commentators and policymakers argue that prudential regulation and market conduct regulation are inherently incompatible, and their combination inevitably leads to the subjugation of one of these goals to the other.[44] The GFC has illustrated that this is particularly problematic when prudential regulation is sacrificed in preference to market conduct and consumer protection regulation in a way that underemphasises the potential for systemic financial stability.[45]

The Twin Peaks model as adopted in Australia was not devised in response to a serious financial collapse of the sort experienced during the GFC. It is therefore not surprising that systemic financial stability and macroprudential regulation were not commonly discussed as prominent features in the initial design of the model. Of course, this did not mean that the model ignores systemic financial stability completely. As noted in the introduction to this chapter, the stability of the financial system was generally thought to be addressed through microprudential regulation, and the monetary policy tools of central banks, which generally include a financial stability mandate. In light of the GFC, however, it is has become important to consider whether this approach is sufficient. It is necessary to ask whether the Twin Peaks model provides an adequate framework by which to ensure systemic financial stability and, if not, whether the model should be modified to address this goal.

These are questions with which jurisdictions that have already adopted the model or that are considering adopting the model have been grappling. Australia's response to the crisis provides a useful example of a jurisdiction justifying the continued use of the Twin Peaks model without any modifications to address systemic financial stability concerns, and to promote the use of macroprudential regulation as a means to achieve the goal. Luci Ellis, Head of the Financial Stability Department of the Reserve Bank of Australia, has for instance argued that the Australian Twin Peaks model does not need to be reformed to accommodate the increased importance attached to macroprudential regulation in maintaining systemic financial stability, on the following grounds:

- First, macroprudential policy is only a subset of the policies intended to enhance financial stability. For a start, it is not really designed for managing crises when they do occur. It does no good to muddy the waters by claiming things as macroprudential for the sake of it.
- Second, most supposedly macroprudential policy tools are in fact the usual prudential tools long used by ostensibly 'micro' prudential supervisors. What is 'new' is the motivation behind their use (although even that is not particularly new in many countries, including Australia).
- Third, the build-up to the recent crisis resulted more from a microprudential failure than a macroprudential one. The easing in US mortgage lending standards, the growing reliance on short-term wholesale funding and the low risk weights applied to complex and highly leveraged structured securities were all things that an avowedly microprudential supervisor could have – and arguably should have – noticed and responded to.[46]

---

[44] This was one of the criticisms of the United Kingdom's super-regulator model before the GFC, where it was argued that prudential regulation was sacrificed in favour of market conduct and consumer protection regulation. See, eg, Bank of England (n 44) at 198.

[45] See Tucker (n 12).

[46] See Luci Ellis, 'Macroprudential Policy: A Suite of Tools or a State of Mind?' (Speech delivered at Paul Woolley Centre for Capital Market Dysfunctionality Annual Conference, Sydney, 11 October 2012), www.rba.gov.au/speeches/2012/sp-so-111012.html. This view is reflected in Reserve Bank of Australia and Australian Prudential Regulation Authority, *Macroprudential Analysis and Policy in the Australian Financial Stability Framework* (September 2012).

Australia's Financial System Inquiry appears to have endorsed this approach, noting in its Final Report that the Twin Peaks model has generally worked well.[47] According to this assessment, the main elements that are needed to ensure systemic financial stability under the Twin Peaks model are that each regulator completes their mandate with systemic matters in mind, and that effective, often informal, coordination and cooperation mechanisms be in place to ensure that regulators can adopt this systemic approach.[48] A number of jurisdictions that have adopted the Twin Peaks model in the aftermath of the GFC have, however, concluded that something more is needed. Some of those jurisdictions have made minimal changes, most notably creating a regulatory authority that has as its aim the detection of financial risk.[49] While these authorities are meant to help detect the build-up of risk, they have little formal effect on the Twin Peaks model, other than to act as an additional coordination and information dissemination mechanism. Section 21.5 considers how the United Kingdom has adopted a modified Twin Peaks model that may serve as a useful example for other jurisdictions on how to retain the benefits of the Twin Peaks model while ensuring that concerns regarding systemic financial stability are appropriately taken into account.

20.5 FACING THE CHALLENGES OF A POST-GFC WORLD: REFORMING THE TWIN PEAKS MODEL TO INCORPORATE SYSTEMIC FINANCIAL STABILITY AND MACROPRUDENTIAL REGULATION

The generally positive assessment of the Twin Peaks model is not shared by everyone, particularly when it comes to ensuring systemic financial stability. Even Australia's market conduct and consumer protection regulator, ASIC, has expressed concern regarding the model's lack of 'flexible arrangements to respond to emerging systemic risk in the financial system'.[50] The United Kingdom has acted on these concerns in developing its Twin Peaks model in the aftermath of the GFC by adding a number of elements to reinforce the importance of systemic financial stability. This has altered the way in which the Twin Peaks model functions in a manner that may prove useful to other jurisdictions.

20.5.1 *The UK Twin Peaks Model*

The United Kingdom adopted a modified version of the Twin Peaks model in 2010 to replace its unified regulator model. That model combined prudential regulation and market conduct and

---

[47] Financial System Inquiry, *Final Report* (November 2014), xx–xxi. The Final Report identifies potential improvements to the framework but those do not relate to systemic financial stability.

[48] The RBA has argued for instance that there is no need to reform the Australian Twin Peaks model because, as evidenced during and after the GFC, the Australian framework contained effective, informal coordination mechanisms that ensured that financial stability was adequately taken into account. RBA Submission, Financial System Inquiry (March 2014), 5, 53. See Reserve Bank of Australia and Australian Prudential Regulation Authority (n 46).

[49] This approach has been adopted in South Africa. The Financial Stability Oversight Committee is a committee of the South African Reserve Bank. Its primary objectives are to help the reserve bank perform its financial stability mandate, and to facilitate cooperation and collaboration between the Reserve Bank and financial sector regulators in respect of matters that relate to financial stability. See Andrew Godwin, Timothy Howse and Ian Ramsay, 'Twin Peaks: South Africa's Financial Sector Regulatory Framework' (2017) 134 *South African Law Journal* 665–702 at 689.

[50] ASIC, *Financial System Inquiry* (April 2014), 107. ASIC ultimately endorsed the Twin Peaks model. Prominent law firm, Minter Ellison, similarly raised concerns regarding the financial regulatory framework, noting that 'business as usual' was not good enough and that a 'fundamental rethink of our regulatory structure and approach' was required: see Minter Ellison, *Submission, Financial System Inquiry* (April 2014), 6.

disclosure regulation within the Financial System Authority (FSA).[51] There were a number of reasons for the United Kingdom's financial regulatory reforms.[52] In its review of the GFC, the FSA noted the following systemic regulatory problems:

- The Bank of England tended to focus on monetary policy analysis as required by the inflation target, and while it did some excellent analytical work in preparation for the Financial Stability Review, that analysis did not result in policy responses (using either monetary or regulatory levers) designed to offset the risks identified.
- The FSA focused too much on the supervision of individual institutions and insufficiently on wider sectoral and system-wide risks.
- The vital activity of macroprudential analysis, and the definition and use of macroprudential tools, fell between two stools. In the words of Paul Tucker, now deputy governor of the Bank of England for financial stability, 'the problem was not overlap but underlap'.[53]

These observations affirm assessments that called for greater focus on ensuring the systemic nature of financial risks and the need to utilise macroprudential regulations to minimise those risks.[54] It is therefore not surprising that the regulatory model that the United Kingdom eventually adopted would inevitably place considerable emphasis on the maintenance of systemic financial stability as a primary goal of the model. In line with the observations of the FSA earlier in this section, the Bank of England noted that the United Kingdom's unified model was problematic because of an inherent cultural conflict between market conduct regulation and prudential regulation.[55] Tucker notes that in the United Kingdom this meant that systemic financial stability was underemphasised, while other more pressing and easily measurable regulatory objectives were pursued.[56]

The reform model in the United Kingdom therefore had two key concerns. First, it sought to ensure that each regulatory function received adequate attention by dividing authority along

---

[51] In 1997 the United Kingdom transferred responsibility for regulation of commercial banks from the Bank of England to the newly created, unified financial regulator, the FSA. Nergiz Dincer and Barry Eichengreen, 'Who Should Supervise? The Structure of Bank Supervision and the Performance of the Financial System' (NBER Working Paper Series, Paper No 17401, September 2011), at 1. However, this refers only to the combination of prudential and market conduct and consumer protection regulation. The model may therefore more accurately be referred to as a 'tripartite' system that provided financial oversight by the FSA, the BoE (in charge of monetary policy) and Treasury (responsible for financial policy).

[52] The perceived failures included the FSA's handling of the collapse of Northern Rock. See, eg, Financial Services Authority, 'The Supervision of Northern Rock: A Lessons Learned Review' (FSA International Audit Report, March 2008), at 19–20. Problems with the informal coordination mechanisms between the UK regulators also contributed to the GFC in the United Kingdom. UK Treasury Committee, *The Run on the Rock* (Fifth Report of Session 2007–08) HC 56-I at 104–6. See also Dincer and Eichengreen (n 51); Rt Hon George Osborne MP (Speech given at Lord Mayor's dinner for bankers and merchants of the City of London, Mansion House, June 2010), www.gov.uk/government/speeches/speech-by-the-chancellor-of-the-exchequer-rt-hon-george-osborne-mp-at-mansion-house. For a discussion of political motivations that may have contributed to the dismantling of the FSA see Eilis Ferran, 'The Break-up of the Financial Services Authority' (University of Cambridge, Faculty of Law, Legal Studies Research Paper Series, Paper No 10/04, 2010) (noting that the government may have been motivated to dismantle the FSA as it was a flagship initiative of its predecessor).

[53] Financial Services Authority, Turner Review (n 9) at 84.

[54] The analysis appears to contradict, to some extent, the theoretical views put forward by people such as Ellis, who tend to underemphasise the systemic nature of the GFC and therefore minimise the importance of regulatory reform. See Ellis (n 46).

[55] Bank of England (n 44) at 198.

[56] Tucker (n 12) at 9. Tucker provides his own experience to confirm this analysis as follows: 'Nearly all the bank supervisors I have known over the past three decades have invariably been drawn towards the parts of their inbox about individual firms, for the simple reason that that is where their individual accountability is starkest.'

functional lines, as is common in other Twin Peaks models.[57] Secondly, the United Kingdom's model sought to promote systemic financial stability as a primary regulatory objective. Other Twin Peaks models do not, however, explicitly give this goal any primacy.

The United Kingdom's new Twin Peaks model is explored in detail elsewhere in this book. For the purposes of this chapter, it is sufficient to note that the United Kingdom's Twin Peaks model divides regulatory authority between the BoE, which is responsible for prudential regulation (both microprudential and macroprudential)[58] and the Financial Conduct Authority (FCA), which is responsible for market conduct and consumer protection regulation, and has two high-level objectives: a 'strategic' objective of ensuring that 'the relevant markets function well' and an 'operational' objective of consumer protection, integrity and competition.[59] The United Kingdom has adopted two important innovations that distinguish it from other jurisdictions that similarly divide regulatory authority along functional lines. First, although the BoE houses prudential regulation and monetary policy, this is done through three discrete committees:

- The Financial Policy Committee (FPC): The FPC is a newly created committee of the BoE.[60] The main aim of the FPC is to assist the BoE in meeting its financial stability objective (FSO).[61] The FPC has responsibility for macroprudential regulation to meet this goal.
- The Monetary Policy Committee (MPC): The MPC existed as a committee of the Bank of England before implementation of the new structure, and continues to have responsibility for monetary stability in the United Kingdom.[62]
- The Prudential Regulatory Committee (PRC): The BoE exercises the United Kingdom's prudential regulatory authority through the PRC.[63] The PRC has responsibility for microprudential regulation over certain financial sectors in the United Kingdom.

The creation of the FPC is particularly relevant to our discussion as it was thought necessary to provide regulators with the capacity to identify and to address the big developments that could jeopardise stability.[64] While other jurisdictions have created similar authorities to help identify

---

[57] See, eg, KPMG, *Twin-Peaks Regulation: Key Changes and Challenges, Report* (2012), at 3; Taylor, 'Twin Peaks' (n 43) at 63; Tucker (n 12) at 3 (noting the division in Twin Peaks frameworks on the basis of objectives); International Monetary Fund, 'United Kingdom Financial System Stability Assessment' (IMF Country Report No 11/222, July 2011), 37 (noting that the proposed UK financial regulatory framework was a 'Three Peaks' system with authority divided between the then PRA, the FPC and the FCA).

[58] It has been suggested that providing the central bank with overarching responsibility in these areas seeks to leverage the BoE's knowledge and expertise in macroeconomic regulation, needed to make regulatory judgements at a systemic level. Osborne (n 52).

[59] *Financial Services Act 2012* [FS Act], Part 2 amendments to the *Financial Services and Markets Act 2000* [FSM Act], s 1B(2) and 1B(3).

[60] *Bank of England Act 1998* (UK), s 9B(1) [BoE Act]. The FPC was initially created as a subcommittee of the court of directors, but recent changes introduced by the Bank of England and *Financial Services Act 2016* [BoEFS Act] have elevated it to the status of a committee. BoEFS Act, s 6.

[61] BoE Act, s. 9C(1)(a).

[62] Part 2 of the BoE Act sets out the provisions regarding monetary policy.

[63] The FSM Act created the Prudential Regulatory Authority as a subsidiary of the BoE. From May 2016, s 12 of the BoEFS Act introduces amendments to both the FSMA and the BoE Act so as to bring the prudential regulatory authority of the United Kingdom directly within the BoE. References to the PRA in the FSMA are now considered references to the BoE as the PRA. S 12 of the BoEFS Act further provides that the BoE exercises its prudential regulatory authority through the newly created PRC.

[64] Tucker (n 12) at 9.

risks and coordinate relevant responses,[65] the second innovation that the United Kingdom introduced was to provide the FPC with a number of legal powers to emphasise the primacy of systemic financial stability as a regulatory goal. This means that the United Kingdom has explicitly established a hierarchy with systemic financial stability at the top. The hope is that systemic financial stability will not be sacrificed in pursuit of other more readily measurable and immediate financial regulatory goals. The remainder of Section 21.5 explores how the United Kingdom strikes this regulatory balance.

20.5.2 *Establishing a Clear, Predominant Stability Objective for the United Kingdom*

The BoE's objective is to protect and enhance the stability of the financial system for banking, including through the requirement to develop a FSO, and to put in place a financial stability strategy to meet that objective.[66] Although financial stability is not defined in the legislative regime, the FPC has a primary objective to help the BoE achieve its FSO.[67] The FPC then has *secondary* objectives that are subject to the financial stability goal and support the government's economic policy, including growth and employment.[68] The inclusion of this secondary object-ive was thought necessary because of the interactions between macroprudential policy and economic activity.[69]

The FPC's primary task is therefore to identify, monitor and take action to remove or reduce systemic risks so as to protect and enhance the resilience of the UK financial system.[70] Section 9 (C)(3) of the *BoE Act* sets out the following, non-exhaustive list of systemic risks:

(a) systemic risks attributable to structural features of financial markets, such as connections between financial institutions;

(b) systemic risks attributable to the distribution of risk within the financial sector; and

(c) unsustainable levels of leverage, debt or credit growth.

---

[65] See, eg, the European Systemic Risk Board in the EU and the Financial Stability Oversight Committee in the United States. South Africa, which recently adopted the Twin Peaks model, has established a Financial Stability Oversight Committee as a coordinating body.

[66] BoE Act, s 2A(1) defines the BoE's FSO as the objective of the BoE to protect and enhance the stability of the financial system of the United Kingdom. In pursuing this objective, s 2A(2) requires that the BoE aim to work with other relevant bodies including HM Treasury, the FCA and the PRC. The court of directors of the BoE must in turn determine the BoE's strategy in relation to the FSO (referred to as the financial stability strategy), and revise it from time to time. See BoE Act, s 9A(1). Before setting out its strategy in accordance with s 9A(1), the court of directors must first consult about a draft of the strategy, or any revision, with the FPC and Treasury. See s 9A(2) BoE Act. Further, the FPC may at any time make recommendations to the court of directors as to the provisions of the strategy. See s 9A(3) BoE Act.

[67] BoE Act, s 9C(1)(a).

[68] BoE Act, s 9C(1)(b).

[69] See HM Treasury, 'Financial Policy Committee Powers of Direction in the Buy-to-Let Market' (17 December 2015), www.gov.uk/government/consultations/consultation-on-financial-policy-committee-powers-of-direction-in-the-buy-to-let-market/financial-policy-committee-powers-of-direction-in-the-buy-to-let-market. For a discussion of other aspects of the UK legislation aimed at ensuring that other regulatory goals are adequately pursued, see Andrew Godwin, Steve Kourabas and Ian Ramsay, 'Financial Stability Authorities and Macroprudential Regulation' (2017) 32 *Banking and Finance Law Review* 223–54 at Part 3(a)(iv).

[70] BoE Act, s 9C(2). See also Paul Tucker, 'Macroprudential Policy at the Bank of England' (2013) Q3 *Quarterly Bulletin* at 192.

This alone does not really distinguish the UK model from other Twin Peaks models. However, section 9G(1) of the *BoE Act* also provides the FPC with the following specific functions and powers to help it achieve its financial stability goal:[71]

    (a) monitoring the stability of the UK financial system with a view to identifying and assessing systemic risks;

    (b) giving directions;

    (c) making recommendations;

    (d) preparing financial stability reports.

The power to give directions and to make recommendations alters the operation of the Twin Peaks model in the United Kingdom, and elevates the objective of systemic financial stability as a primary goal.

20.5.3 *Legislative Weight behind the Goal of Systemic Financial Stability*

The FPC has the power to make recommendations[72] to the PRC and the FCA about the exercise of their functions, and can issue these recommendations on a 'comply or explain' basis.[73] The FPC has used this power to make a recommendation to the BoE, the PRC and the FCA that they work with firms at the core of the financial system to ensure that they have completed cyber vulnerability testing and that they have adopted individual cyber resilience action plans.[74] The recommendation was made following the FPC's assessment that cyber-attacks were a serious and growing threat to the resilience of the UK financial system.[75] It is unclear how other jurisdictions that use the Twin Peaks model would deal with such a situation, particularly where there was disagreement among regulators regarding the significance of the threat, and the measures to adopt. It appears that Australia would seek to deal with such a situation through the various coordination mechanisms, including the Council of Financial Regulators (CFR).[76] This recommendation power ensures that in the United Kingdom, at the very least, a regulator would need to explain why they were not complying with the FPC's recommendations.

The FPC also has the power to make recommendations to the Treasury regarding macro-prudential tools that the FPC believes should be the subject of directions to the PRC and the FCA, as well as in relation to adjustments that the FPC deems necessary for the maintenance of

---

[71] The FPC makes available meeting reports that set out in detail the activities that it and its constituent members have been undertaking to achieve its functions. The meeting reports are available online: Bank of England, Financial Policy Committee Meetings, www.bankofengland.co.uk/financialstability/Pages/fpc/meetings/default.aspx. For an example of the substance of the meeting reports see Godwin, Kourabas and Ramsay (n 69).

[72] BoE Act, ss 9O to 9R.

[73] This means that if a regulator does not comply, then they need to explain their reasons for not doing so. BoE Act, s 9Q (3)(b).

[74] Recommendation 15/Q2/3 is noted in the FPC meeting notes of June 2015. For the meeting notes, see HM Treasury (n 69).

[75] Ibid.

[76] See Reserve Bank of Australia and Australian Prudential Regulation Authority (n 46) 3: 'In the few instances where members' responsibilities overlap, the CFR provides a venue to ensure that these are resolved.' See also the Memorandum of Understanding on Financial Distress Management between the Members of the Council of Financial Regulators dated 18 September 2008, para 5.3: 'The implementation of a response to resolve a distressed institution or broader financial system stress will be coordinated between the members of the Council, where more than one member has responsibility for responding to the situation.' For a detailed discussion about Australia's 'soft law' approach, see Godwin, Howse and Ramsay (n 49) at 124–5.

the boundary between regulated and unregulated activities in the United Kingdom.[77] This recommendation power ensures that the United Kingdom can extend the PRC's prudential boundary to counter risks associated with regulatory arbitrage that may undermine attempts to tighten bank regulation, and to deal with the evolution of the financial system in unexpected ways.[78] The recommendation power provides another contrast with other jurisdictions that have adopted the Twin Peaks model, and that have encountered difficulties in adjusting the prudential regulatory boundary to address new systemic risks.[79]

This recommendation power attempts to guide regulators toward decisions that ensure financial stability. However, there are other situations where the FPC may issue directions to the PRC and the FCA in respect of macroprudential matters.[80] Section 9H(1) of the *BoE Act* sets out this power as follows: 'The [FPC] may give a direction to the FCA or the PRA ("the regulator") requiring the regulator to exercise its functions so as to ensure the implementation, by or in relation to a specified class of regulated persons, of a macro-prudential measure described in the direction.' When directed to do so, the PRC and the FCA must exercise their functions so as to implement these macroprudential measures.[81] The FPC currently has direction power in two areas. First, the FPC may issue a direction in relation to two macroprudential tools: capital–countercyclical capital buffers[82] and sectoral capital requirements.[83] Secondly, in April 2015, the government provided the FPC with power to give directions in relation to the following housing tools: loan-to-value (LTV) ratios and debt-to-income (DTI) ratios, including

---

[77] BoE Act, s 9P.

[78] Tucker (n 12) at 10–11.

[79] See Andrew Godwin, Steve Kourabas and Ian Ramsay, 'Twin Peaks and Financial Regulation: The Challenges of Increasing Regulatory Overlap and Expanding Responsibilities' (2016) 49 *The International Lawyer* 273–97 (discussing the difficulties that Australian policymakers and regulators have had in defining the boundary between prudential and market conduct and consumer protection regulation, as the financial system has evolved over time). See also ASIC (n 50) (discussing ASIC's concern that the system is not able to evolve so as to address systemic risks).

[80] BoE Act, s 9L provides that macroprudential measures are those prescribed by the Treasury by order. Ss 9H to 9K detail the directions power. S 9I(1) requires that the regulator comply with a direction given to it under s 9H as soon as reasonably practicable.

[81] BoE Act, s 9H(1). The FPC website provides detail on all current directions orders. Bank of England, 'Policy Statements'.

[82] The order providing the FPC with directions powers over countercyclical buffers is the Capital Requirements (Capital Buffers and Macro-Prudential Measures Regulation) 2014. For the FPC's policy on setting countercyclical buffers, see Bank of England, 'The Financial Policy Committee's Approach to Setting the Countercyclical Capital Buffer: A Policy Statement' (April 2016). The power to impose countercyclical buffers is derived in the United Kingdom under EU directives: see European Union (EU) Directive 2013/36/EU on access to the activity of credit institutions and the prudential supervision of credit institutions and investment firms (CRD IV). The FPC set out its counter-cyclical policy in a January 2014 policy document, Bank of England, 'The Financial Policy Committee's Powers to Supplement Capital Requirements: A Policy Statement' (January 2014). In March 2016, the FPC set the UK countercyclical capital buffer at 0.5 per cent. See, Bank of England, 'Countercyclical Capital Buffer (CCyB) Rates'. The FPC has indicated that it may increase the rate to 1 per cent as the credit cycle moves into what it considers a more normal phase. Bank of England, 'Financial Policy Committee Statement from its Policy Meeting on 20 September 2017' (published 3 October 2017). See also Deloitte, 'FPC's Incoming Countercyclical Capital Buffer: A Wider Impact than First Thought' (2 December 2015); John Glover, 'Bank of England Sees Countercyclical Buffer Rising on Risk', *Bloomberg* (1 December 2015).

[83] *The Bank of England Act 1998 (Macro-Prudential Measures) Order, 2013 (Macro Order)*. The Macro Order relates to measures such as direction by the FPC to the PRC to impose on UK banks and investment firms the requirement to maintain capital requirements by reference to residential property exposures, and imposition of requirements by reference to a failure to maintain these capital requirements (such as restrictions on making certain discretionary payments). For the FPC's policy on setting sectoral capital requirements, see Bank of England, 'The Financial Policy Committee's Powers to Supplement Capital Requirements: A Policy Statement' (January 2014); HM Treasury, 'The Financial Policy Committee's Housing Market Tools' (October 2014), at 8.

interest coverage ratios (ICRs) in respect of buy-to-let lending,[84] as well as leverage ratio tools.[85] These directions powers highlight the prominence attributed to the maintenance of systemic financial stability and the use of macroprudential tools that is lacking in other jurisdictions that have adopted the Twin Peaks model.

For instance, the FPC recommended that it be granted power to direct the PRC and the FCA to require regulated lenders to place limits on buy-to-let mortgage lending, by reference to LTV and ICRs.[86] The FPC has recommended that it be given this directions power to address the potential clash between regulations that may advance systemic financial stability and those that take into account microprudential matters. This conflict could, for instance, involve the FPC seeking looser regulatory requirements to help protect and enhance the resilience of the financial system as a whole during a downturn, with the PRC placing more weight on maintaining standards to protect individual firms during such a downturn.[87] The resolution of such a conflict in other Twin Peaks jurisdictions is not clear. Although formal and informal coordination and collaboration mechanisms exist, and appear to have worked reasonably well in jurisdictions such as Australia, there is little certainty that regulation that promotes systemic financial stability will prevail in the case of a disagreement. Importantly, the directions power in the United Kingdom ensures that disagreement does not delay the imposition of regulations to protect financial stability when needed most.[88]

The directions authority, along with recommendation powers, and the explicit, legislative elevation of systemic financial stability as a predominant regulatory goal in the United Kingdom, provides mechanisms that Twin Peaks models that were adopted before the GFC currently lack. Section 21.6 offers some concluding observations regarding the different approaches to the Twin Peaks model, and the potential insights that the UK approach may provide to other Twin Peaks jurisdictions concerned about detecting and acting on risks of a systemic nature.

20.6 CONCLUSION: INSIGHTS FOR TWIN PEAKS FINANCIAL REGULATION

This chapter has highlighted the importance attributed to systemic financial stability and the role of macroprudential regulation in achieving this goal. These concepts, and the extent to which they should be relied on, continue to be debated. However, it is important that we review our existing models of financial regulation, including the Twin Peaks model, to see if they adequately address concerns that have been made manifest in the wake of the GFC and minimise the chances of similar financial collapse in the future.

Specifically, what insights to date does the experience of the Twin Peaks model offer from the perspective of macroprudential regulation? Does the Twin Peaks model enhance or detract from the goal of systemic financial stability or is it neutral in this regard?

One might argue that the Twin Peaks model is conducive to systemic financial stability concerns. This is because the functional approach to regulation represents a more holistic approach than the sectoral or institutional model and is more resilient than the integrated

---

[84] *Bank of England Act 1998 (Macro-prudential Measures) Order 2015.* See also Bank of England, 'The Financial Policy Committee's Powers over Housing Tools: A Policy Statement' (July 2015).

[85] *Bank of England Act 1998 (Macro-prudential Measures) (No 2) Order 2015.* The Bank of England, 'The Financial Policy Committee's Powers over Leverage Ratio Tools: A Policy Statement' (July 2015). For details of all current orders providing FPC with directions powers, see Bank of England (n 81).

[86] HM Treasury (n 69).

[87] Ibid.

[88] Ibid.

model, which may be susceptible to inherent tensions, as previously discussed.[89] In addition, it could be argued that its emphasis (and reliance) on effective coordination between the Twin Peaks regulators, the central bank and the government should augur well for inter-agency dialogue and coordinated action in response to systemic financial stability concerns.

However, as previously noted,[90] systemic financial stability and macroprudential regulation did not feature prominently in the design of the prototype Twin Peaks model as adopted in Australia. In this regard, the model is no different from any other regulatory model in terms of the central bank having a financial stability mandate and macroprudential regulation being the primary responsibility of the central bank and (if separate from the central bank) the prudential regulator.

In the wake of the GFC, and the subsequent global consensus that has formed around the importance of macroprudential regulation, a key question for any regulatory model is how to ensure that systemic financial stability is appropriately dealt with. The Twin Peaks model in the United Kingdom is noteworthy insofar as it creates the FPC as a macroprudential body within the Bank of England and expressly elevates systemic financial stability as a primary regulatory objective. As previously outlined, the model gives the FPC the power to give directions and make recommendations, thereby providing a mechanism for resolving any disagreements among regulators as to what the appropriate responses to macroprudential concerns should be.

The prescriptive, 'hard law' approach in the United Kingdom can be contrasted with the 'soft law' approach in Australia, where systemic financial stability is viewed 'as an essential part of effective prudential supervision, inextricable from the supervision of individual institutions',[91] and any disagreements among regulators are expected to be resolved through the various coordination mechanisms, including the Council of Financial Regulators.[92] A determination as to whether one approach is better is likely to turn on a number of questions. A threshold question is the nature and scope of macroprudential regulation, and whether it operates as a discrete objective, requiring a specific regulatory framework, or whether it follows naturally from microprudential regulation and prudential regulation generally.

Each approach has its pros and cons. The Australian approach is heavily dependent on having the right culture of coordination and, some might argue, has not yet been fully put to the test. By comparison, the UK approach is intuitively attractive in terms of providing an overarching framework for macroprudential regulation, under which systemic financial stability is elevated as a primary regulatory objective, and mechanisms are in place to ensure that this objective is achieved. That said, several questions remain to be answered. Is there a risk of regulatory creep on the part of bodies such as the FPC as the concept of macroprudential regulation becomes broader? Is there a risk that macroprudential regulation will intrude into, or interfere with, the functional separation and operational independence of the Twin Peaks regulators, particularly the market conduct regulator? More generally, is there a risk that undue emphasis will be given to macroprudential concerns over other concerns? Ultimately, the true test will be whether each approach proves resilient in the face of systemic financial stress.[93]

---

[89] See the text accompanying n 55: Bank of England (n 44) at 198.
[90] See the text following n 45: Tucker (n 12).
[91] Reserve Bank of Australia and Australian Prudential Regulation Authority (n 46) 4.
[92] Ibid 1, 3.
[93] For a discussion of financial crisis management under the Twin Peaks model, see Andrew Godwin, Steve Kourabas and Ian Ramsay, 'Financial crisis management under the Twin Peaks model of financial regulation: Australia and the UK compared' in D. Cash and R. Goddard (eds) Regulation and the Global Financial Crisis (Routledge, 2021).

For EU product safety concerns, contact us at Calle de José Abascal, 56–1°,
28003 Madrid, Spain or eugpsr@cambridge.org.

www.ingramcontent.com/pod-product-compliance
Ingram Content Group UK Ltd.
Pitfield, Milton Keynes, MK11 3LW, UK
UKHW030903150625
459647UK00022B/2840